G000271345

ChariTable Bookings
SIGNATURE♥DISH

The complete series includes

365 LEADING UK CHEFS'
FIRST COURSE RECIPES

365 LEADING UK CHEFS'
MAIN COURSE RECIPES

365 LEADING UK CHEFS'
PUDDING RECIPES

© ChariTable Bookings 2017
charitablebookings.org/recipe-book

Designed by Gravity Integrated Solutions.

Published in London by FH Publishing, a division of FH Global LLP.
fhpublishing.com
ISBN: 978-0-9957116-0-0

ChariTable Bookings

SIGNATURE♥DISH

FH PUBLISHING

Foreword

It is my pleasure to write the foreword to this wonderful recipe book that showcases some of the finest chefs working in the UK today while knowing that together we are all helping to support countless deserving causes.

We set up the restaurant booking platform, ChariTable Bookings, as a simple way to help charities generate additional unrestricted funds and awareness for themselves at no cost to them while continuing our ethos of encouraging individuals and organisations to support good causes as part of their daily life.

Diners can choose from thousands of UK registered charities who are supported by ChariTable Bookings every time they eat out. This costs the diner and the charity nothing and we hope that this will become an essential free tool to help charities boost their bottom line and to enable corporate organisations to increase the funds they generate for good causes. Of course, we are indebted to the support from our many thousands of restaurant partners who will help make a real difference to the lives of those in need both now and in the future.

With so many excellent restaurants on board we decided to showcase some of the chefs in what was planned as a small section on our website. The response was so overwhelming that we made the decision to publish our first ChariTable Bookings recipe book, featuring dishes from some of the finest chefs and restaurants in the UK. You are holding the result in your hands and we hope you will enjoy these masterful creations in the knowledge that every copy has generated funds for good causes.

Having encouraged you to cook at home with this book we are now going to encourage you to go out to eat. Use ChariTable Bookings for your personal and business restaurant bookings and help us support the restaurant industry and the causes dear to your heart in making a positive difference to those less fortunate. It's very easy to use and you can make a different charity benefit every time you go out – and it costs you absolutely nothing to do so!

I hope you enjoy the ChariTable Bookings Signature Dish recipe book and thank you again for supporting those wonderful organisations that do so much good for so many.

Kindest regards,

Lord Fink
Director
ChariTable Bookings

Editor's welcome

Welcome to the first ChariTable Bookings Signature Dish recipe book, an initiative which we set up as a way to support good causes.

Firstly, I would like to take this opportunity to dedicate this book to my late father, Michael, who continues to inspire and motivate me and taught me to appreciate great ingredients, the importance of tunnel vision and to always try to do good by others.

With his message as the springboard for this book I decided I wanted to do something different, something big, that hadn't been attempted before. I wanted to bring together a wide variety of leading UK chefs and restaurants in support of thousands of charities while creating the perfect gift for all foodies.

Compiling this has been a massive undertaking, but it has been an enjoyable journey allowing me to bring together 365 of the finest chefs in the UK with mouth-watering main course dishes for you to try at home. From simple hearty meals and exotic spicy creations, to Michelin star wonders and dinner party crowd pleasers, we have assembled a fantastic array of delicious restaurant quality recipes to give everyone the opportunity to cook like a professional chef.

This book is a perfect complement to the ChariTable Bookings restaurant booking platform that allows you to decide which charity to support every time you dine out and to do this at no cost to you or to the charity. With this book you are also supporting good causes by eating in! Each chef's dish will not only brighten up your table but will help brighten up the lives of people who need our help and support with £5 from every book purchase going straight to a charity. What a delicious way to support good causes.

We hope you'll find some exciting recipes here for you to try and hopefully buy this book as a gift to all your foodie friends and colleagues. Unusually for a recipe book, we heartily encourage you and your friends to eat out by booking through ChariTable Bookings which is free to use and help us to raise lots of money for causes who could really do with your support.

Enjoy!

David Johnstone
Editor-In-Chief

"Please select Best Beginnings when dining with ChariTable Bookings and help us make a difference for future generations." **Andy Serkis**

"Very proud to be an Ambassador for this exciting new app. Anybody who eats out should use ChariTable Bookings to support charities close to their hearts." **Sir Martyn Lewis CBE**

"Enjoy eating out? And want to support some of the world's bravest people? Make your restaurant reservations via ChariTable Bookings to sponsor Prisoners of Conscience while you wine and dine." **Zoë Wanamaker CBE**

"I love eating and I love St John's - a small but wonderful charity that supports some very vulnerable young people who have severe problems in finding their way through life. Now each time I book a restaurant through ChariTable Bookings I know I'll be helping St John's School and College in their work at the same time I do hope you'll consider doing the same." **Jane Asher**

"Now you can dine in style - whilst going the extra mile by booking your restaurant table through ChariTable Bookings you are automatically benefiting charities such as The House of St Barnabas. Simple as. Go on order seconds - you've earned it." **Jarvis Cocker**

"Please book your table through ChariTable Bookings and you will be helping to support Special Olympics GB which provides inspiring sporting and social opportunities for people with intellectual disabilities." **Jim Carter**

"As a proud supporter of Best Beginnings I encourage friends and family to book restaurants using ChariTable Bookings and to choose Best Beginnings as the charity that benefits, £1 for every person dining! ChariTable Bookings is so easy to use and helps Best Beginnings generate funds and awareness – do spread the word!" **Abbey Clancy**

"As a foodie expert and presenter I'm really excited to use ChariTable Bookings to book my many favourite eateries while guaranteeing that Rainbow Trust Children's Charity will be benefiting from every meal I enjoy." **Stephanie Brookes**

ChariTable Bookings

ChariTable Bookings has more table availability than any other UK restaurant booking platform. For every honoured booking we charge the restaurant an industry standard £2 per person from which ChariTable Bookings donates £1 to the users' chosen charity. It's free to use at no cost to the customer or the charity and with currently over 7,000 restaurants and 7,500 charities to choose from the potential gain for charities as well as the restaurants is significant.

Whether you want to reserve that special spot at your local pub, uncover a hidden gem around the corner from your office or discover a great little place when visiting friends and family; use ChariTable Bookings. Unlike any other online UK booking platform, we encourage you to use the restaurants phone number allowing you to contact them directly to secure your booking, giving you access to times and tables not available elsewhere online. Just simply call to book, nominate a charity and confirm your booking details – it's that simple.

Giving back to a cause close to you through ChariTable Bookings isn't only restricted to restaurant bookings. An additional feature of the booking platform is our Venue Finder service. Use it to book private dining rooms, private and corporate drinks parties and event spaces across the UK with £1 per guest going to your chosen charity. Find out more at charitablebookings.org/venue-finder.

There is absolutely no cost to use ChariTable Bookings so whenever you dine or entertain, nominate a charity close to your heart and enjoy giving back.

*"GIVING BACK FOR **FREE** HAS NEVER TASTED SO GOOD."*

charitablebookings.org

THE 365 CHEFS

TOM AIKENS

By supporting the efforts of the kids cancer unit at the Royal Marsden Hospital through ChariTable Bookings, the Tom's Kitchen team have managed to add an extra element to this recipe which now has what we call the 'tastes good – feels good' factor!"

7 HOUR-BRAISED SHOULDER OF LAMB with onions, thyme and balsamic

SERVES 4 | PREPARATION TIME 30 MINUTES | COOKING TIME 7–8 HOURS

For the Braised Shoulder of Lamb
- 2.5kg lamb shoulder
- 150ml olive oil
- 20g fresh thyme, chopped
- 2 bulbs of garlic, cloves peeled
- sea salt and black pepper to taste
- 8 medium onions, peeled
- 350ml balsamic vinegar

For the Mashed Potato
- 600g peeled potatoes, quartered
- 12g salt
- 200g butter
- 150ml milk, warmed
- 2g black pepper

To cook the lamb, place a large casserole pot onto a medium gas and add the oil. Season and place the shoulder into the pot once the oil is hot. Colour for 3–4 minutes on each side until nicely caramelised. Remove the lamb and put to one side. Colour the onions for 4–5 minutes, stirring now and again. After suitably cooked, add the garlic and thyme and place the lamb back on top.

Place the casserole dish into the oven at 110°C and cover with a lid. Leave to cook for 2–2.5 hours, remove the onions once they are soft. Carry on cooking the lamb for another 2.5–3 hours. Add the vinegar and carry on cooking without the lid so the vinegar reduces as the lamb cooks, basting the lamb every 30 minutes, being careful not to reduce it too much.

When the lamb is nice and tender, add the onions and garlic back and reduce the vinegar to a nice, thick consistency.

To make the mashed potato, place the potatoes into a pan of cold water with 10g salt and bring to boil. Turn the heat down and simmer for 30 minutes, then tip the potatoes into a colander to drain well. Place the cooked potatoes back into the pan and remove the moisture on a low heat for 1 minute, then add the butter, remaining salt, pepper and warm milk slowly while you mash.

To serve, slice or shred the meat from the bone and place the casserole dish in the centre of the table. Enjoy.

PAUL AINSWORTH

Philanthropy for foodies! What better way for a chef to support his favourite charity than donating a recipe to help raise money for them. From all of us at Number 6, thank you ChariTable Bookings for helping us help the RNLI."

CRISPY PORTHILLY OYSTERS

SERVES 4 | PREPARATION TIME 30 MINUTES | COOKING TIME 10 MINUTES

For the Oysters
12 large oysters
2 egg whites, let down with a splash of water
200g panko breadcrumbs
12 fine slices salami Milano

For the Apple and Fennel Salad
2 medium heads fennel
2 Granny Smith apples
fresh lime juice
4 stems bright green chervil

To Serve
sea shells and hay
pebbles
1 pinch of rock salt

To prepare the oysters, shuck and gently wash in cold water. Pass the oyster juices through a fine sieve to remove any grit. Pop the oysters into a container, cover with cling film and keep in the fridge until required. Scrub the shells clean and sterilise them in boiling water, ready to use later for serving.

To make the apple and fennel salad, trim the fennel tops off and peel the layers apart. Discarding the outer layer, trim off any chunky areas and slice into large, neat rectangles. Next, finely chop to 3mm slices and coat with a tablespoon of lime juice. Chop the apple in fine slices so it matches the fennel. Combine together with the fennel, ensuring the salad is well coated with fresh lime juice so it cannot discolour. Finely chop the chervil leaves and add a large pinch to the salad. Taste and add more lime juice if desired.

Dip the oysters in the egg white, then the panko breadcrumbs. Deep fry at 190°C until golden and crisp, taking care not to overcook them. The oyster should be just cooked in the centre.

To serve, decorate 4 plates with pebbles and hay. Divide the oyster shells onto the plates and fill each shell with the apple and fennel salad. Place the oysters, plump side up, on top of the salad, then sprinkle with a little rock sea salt. To finish, drape a slice of salami over each oyster at the last second and serve immediately.

ANGELO ALBERA

Really hope you enjoy my signature ravioli recipe from Cantina del Ponte. What a great initiative by ChariTable Bookings to share signature dishes and raise awareness for charities across the UK. I'm choosing Great Ormond Street Hospital for their fantastic work with sick children."

RAVIOLI DI PORCINI AL BURRO e salvia, purea di sedano rapa

SERVES 4 | PREPARATION TIME 1 HOUR 30 MINUTES | COOKING TIME 15 MINUTES

Equipment
  pasta machine

For the Pasta Dough
  2 eggs
  ½ tsp coffee powder
  100g flour
  100g semolina

For the Filling
  15g dried porcini mushrooms
  1 small onion, roughly chopped
  50ml olive oil
  200g porcini mushrooms, roughly chopped
  80g ricotta cheese
  60g Parmesan cheese, grated
  salt and pepper

For the Celeriac Purée
  1 small celeriac, peeled and diced
  300ml milk
  80g butter
  8 leaves of sage

To Serve
  freshly grated Parmesan

Make the pasta dough by combining the eggs, coffee powder, flour and semolina. Knead the mixture until a nice, smooth dough is achieved. Wrap in cling film and leave to rest in the fridge for 1 hour.

For the pasta filling, soak the dried porcini in warm water for 20 minutes, drain them and reserve the water, taking care to remove any grit or dirt. In a casserole dish, fry the onion in the olive oil until soft, without colour. Add the dried and fresh porcini, then stew the mixture in the porcini water, cooking until almost all the liquid has evaporated. In a food processor, blend the cooked mushrooms, adding a little olive oil to loosen if required. Allow the blended mixture to cool. Transfer to a mixing bowl, then fold in the ricotta and Parmesan cheese, seasoning to taste with a little salt and pepper.

Assemble the ravioli by rolling the dough with the pasta machine until thin enough to just about see through. Cut into 8cm discs with a round cookie cutter, then place a teaspoon of filling in the centre of each. Gently fold in half, ensuring all trapped air is removed. Dab a little water on the edges of the discs to help the dough stick.

Place the celeriac in a saucepan. Cover with milk and bring to a gentle boil. When soft, remove from the heat, strain the milk and purée with half of the butter until smooth. Season to taste and set to one side.

Melt the remaining butter in a pan and quickly fry the sage. Cook the ravioli in boiling, salted water for 4 minutes, drain, and toss in the buttered sage sauce.

Serve on a bed of celeriac purée and sprinkle with grated Parmesan.

JOSEPH ALBINA

7 million people live with heart disease in the UK which is why all of us at Blueprint Cafe have shared our signature dish with ChariTable Bookings to raise awareness for the great work of the British Heart Foundation."

PAN-FRIED PLAICE with capers, toasted hazelnuts, golden raisins and browned butter

SERVES 2 | PREPARATION TIME 15 MINUTES | COOKING TIME 20 MINUTES

For the Plaice
1 plaice, filleted and pin boned
150g butter
1 spritz of lemon juice
2 tbsp golden raisins
1 drizzle of olive oil
2 tbsp shallots, finely chopped
1 tbsp lilliput capers
1 bunch of parsley, chopped
1 tbsp hazelnuts, crushed

To prepare the dish, put the butter in a pan and cook until nut brown. Stop the cooking process by adding lemon juice and pass the liquid through a fine chinois.

Boil the raisins in water for 5 minutes then drain.

In another pan, heat the olive oil and add your plaice. If it is not a non-stick pan, dust with flour before frying. Depending on the size of the fish, it will take roughly 3 minutes on each side to reach a good colour and consistency. Add the finely chopped shallots, capers, parsley, hazelnuts and raisins. Fry the contents until they reach a good colour.

To serve, place the fish on the centre of the plate, cover generously with garnishes and drizzle with the browned butter.

DAVID ALEXANDER

" It gives me great pleasure to support the Ayrshire Hospice, a charity local to Glenapp Castle, that does such amazing work with terminally ill patients. I hope that you enjoy my beetroot risotto that I share with you here through ChariTable Bookings."

BEETROOT RISOTTO with feta, Parmesan and aged balsamic

SERVES 4 | PREPARATION TIME 25 MINUTES | COOKING TIME 1 HOUR

For the Juice and Baked Beetroot
2 large raw beetroots

For the Risotto
350g risotto rice
3 tbsp olive oil
100g unsalted butter
1 large white onion, chopped
2 cloves of garlic, crushed
1 sprig of fresh thyme
2 fresh bay leaves
1l vegetable or chicken stock
a little grated Parmesan
50g crème fraîche

For the Parmesan Tuile
150g Parmesan, grated

To Serve
100g crumbled feta cheese
3 tbsp rapeseed oil
3 tbsp good quality aged balsamic vinegar
wood sorrel or micro red veined sorrel

To prepare the dish, juice one of the large raw beetroots in a home juicer, reserving the liquid for the risotto. Take the second raw beetroot, wrap in tinfoil and bake for approximately 50 minutes at 160°C or until soft. Cool, peel and dice into approximately 5mm cubes.

To make the Parmesan tuile, scatter grated Parmesan on a baking sheet and bake in a high temperature oven at 180°C until crisp, which should take approximately 8–10 minutes. Cool and break into shards.

To make the risotto, add the olive oil and half of the butter to a pan on a medium heat. Add the onion and garlic, and cook until translucent and soft. Add the assorted herbs and rice, and stir until the rice is well coated in oil and butter. Spoon in the stock, a ladleful at a time, stirring until absorbed. Repeat this process until the rice is almost cooked. At this point, remove the bay leaves and thyme stalks and stir in the beetroot juice, crème fraîche and cooked beetroot. Finish with some Parmesan and the rest of the butter to make it glossy.

Check seasoning and serve in bowls with crumbled feta, Parmesan tuile, balsamic vinegar and rapeseed oil. Garnish with a little sorrel.

FRASER ALLAN

"All of us at Pompadour recognise the need to make a difference every day. ChariTable Bookings is helping us support Children with Cancer through this fantastic book. We hope you enjoy our signature dish too!"

LASAGNE OF CRAB with beurre nantais

SERVES 10 | PREPARATION TIME 1 HOUR 30 MINUTES | COOKING TIME 2 HOURS

Equipment
pasta machine

steamer

For the Mousse
400g fresh scallops, muscle removed

480ml double cream

1 pinch of sea salt

1 pinch of cayenne pepper

650g fresh white crab meat

For the Pasta Dough
280g strong plain white flour

1 pinch of sea salt

2 eggs

3 egg yolks

1 tbsp olive oil

For the Sauce
1 shallot, finely diced

200g unsalted butter, chilled and diced

50ml water

25ml white wine vinegar

50ml white wine

100ml chicken stock

25ml double cream

1 tbsp chives, finely chopped

sea salt

white pepper, freshly ground

To Garnish
4 sprigs of chervil

To prepare the pasta dough, sift together the flour and salt into a food processor. Add the remaining ingredients and blend for a few minutes until the mixture comes together to form small, pea-sized lumps. Lightly flour a workbench and place the dough mix on top. Lightly knead the dough for a few minutes, until it is completely smooth and quite springy. Firmly wrap the dough in cling film and place in the fridge to rest for a minimum of an hour before using; the dough will keep for up to 24 hours in the fridge. Once rested, remove from the fridge at least 30 minutes before using.

To make the lasagne sheets, lightly flour a workbench and roll the pasta out with a rolling pin until thin enough to pass through the widest setting on a pasta machine. Roll the dough through the pasta machine, decreasing the width of the setting each time you pass it through. Keep rolling until the pasta is thin enough to see your fingers through – about 8–10 rolls. Cut the rolled pasta into 30cm rectangular sheets, so they are easier to handle. Blanch each sheet, one at a time, in salted, boiling water for 1 minute, then immediately place each sheet into a bowl of ice water and allow to cool for another minute. Drain in a colander and lay the sheets out onto a clean workbench. Use a 6cm metal ring to punch out 30 pasta discs, transfer to a baking tray lined with cling film, cover and store in the fridge until needed.

For the mousse, place the bowl of a food processor in the freezer for an hour. Remove from the freezer and add the scallops. Blitz the scallops for 3–4 minutes until nicely puréed, using a spatula to scrape down the sides every minute to ensure the mix is evenly blended. While the machine is blending, gradually pour in half the double cream until incorporated. Season with salt and cayenne, add the remaining cream and increase the speed of the food processor. Continue to blend until the mixture is smooth. Scrape into a clean mixing bowl, fold in the crab meat, then poach a little of the mix until cooked. Taste and adjust the seasoning accordingly then transfer to a piping bag.

To finish the lasagnes, arrange the 6cm metal rings onto a baking tray lined with parchment paper. Delicately press a pasta disc into the base of each one, use the crab mousse mix to fill the rings halfway, then add another sheet of pasta. Divide the remaining crab mousse between the rings and add the final pasta discs to finish. There should be 3 layers of pasta and 2 layers of mousse in each ring. Place in the fridge.

To make the sauce, add a small knob of butter to a pan and place over a medium heat. When it foams, add the shallot and cook until soft but without colour. Pour in the water, vinegar and wine and cook at a simmer until reduced to a thick syrup. Add the chicken stock, bring to the boil and reduce by half. Add the double cream and return to the boil for a minute. Reduce the heat slightly and whisk in the cold butter a little at a time, maintaining the heat in the sauce as you go. Adjust the seasoning and keep warm.

To serve, place the lasagnes in a steamer or steam oven at 100% steam and cook for 12 minutes. Transfer each one to individual serving bowls. Run a small knife around the inside of each metal ring and carefully remove. Heat the sauce gently while stirring, then stir in the chopped chives. Pour some sauce over each lasagne to generously coat, and garnish with a chervil sprig.

CHRISTOPHER ARCHAMBAULT

Hospitality Action does amazing work for our industry and The Headland is proud to support it by being part of this new encyclopedia of recipes from ChariTable Bookings. I hope you enjoy our signature curried monkfish!"

CURRIED MONKFISH with soba noodle rolls, sprout tops and tempura nori

SERVES 2 | PREPARATION TIME 30 MINUTES | COOKING TIME 1 HOUR

For the Monkfish
2 x 170g monkfish tail portions

For the Soba Noodle Rolls
100g soba noodles
1 tsp soy sauce
1 tsp sesame oil
2 rice paper sheets

For the Sprout Tops
8 brussel sprout tops

For the Tempura Nori
1 nori sheet
100ml tempura batter

For the Curry Sauce
sunflower oil
1 tsp each fenugreek, fennel
and black mustard seeds
8 curry leaves
2 red chillies, roughly chopped
1 white onion, diced
20g each ginger and garlic, minced
1 tsp each cumin and turmeric powder
½ tsp chilli powder
30g tamarind concentrate
2 fresh tomatoes, chopped
500ml water
1 lime, juice and zest
palm sugar, to taste

To Serve
mango slices
coriander

To make the curry sauce, start by roasting the seed aromatics for 1 minute or so in a little sunflower oil in a medium saucepan. Then add the curry leaves and keep the heat up, stirring constantly to give all the spices a good blast of heat, releasing flavour. Add the chilli, onion, garlic and ginger and soften, reducing the heat somewhat, for about 15 minutes. Add the powders and incorporate well. Deglaze with the tamarind concentrate and fresh tomatoes, taking care to scrape the bottom with a spatula. Cook until the tomatoes are softened. Add the water and lime juice, and bring to boil, simmering for 15 minutes. Adjust seasoning with palm sugar, if required. Turn up the heat and reduce by half. Once reduced, blitz to a smooth and thick purée.

For the soba noodle rolls, place the noodles in boiling, salted water for around 3 minutes. Drain and let cool in a tray, mixing in the soy sauce and sesame oil. Dip the rice paper wraps in tepid water for 20 seconds, shake lightly to remove any excess water and lay flat on a board. Roll half the soba noodles in each sheet of rice paper and cover with a damp j-cloth until needed.

To make the tempura nori, cut the nori into triangles and dip them in a little tempura batter. Fry at 180°C.

Pan fry the monkfish until well coloured and just cooked. If cut thickly, finish them in a hot oven for 3 minutes. Rest well to remove unwanted juices. Cut each portion into three pieces and set aside.

For the sprout tops, rapidly boil for 1–2 minutes in boiling, salted water and then remove.

To serve, spoon the curry sauce onto the centre of the plates and arrange the thrice sliced monkfish. Cut the soba rolls in half and stand for decoration. Garnish with the nori, mango, sprout tops and fresh coriander as desired.

GUGLIELMO ARNULFO

"I'm very proud to be part of this new recipe book by ChariTable Bookings in support of the Alzheimer's Society, one of the sadly growing, incurable illnesses of our time. Enjoy my signature veal shank while raising awareness for this great cause."

SLOW COOKED VEAL SHANK

SERVES 4 | PREPARATION TIME 25 MINUTES | COOKING TIME 30 MINUTES (PLUS 36 HOURS SOUS VIDE)

Equipment
sous vide and vacuum pack bags

For the Veal
4 veal shanks, preferably osso buco
4 cloves of garlic
2 sticks celery, thinly sliced
2 carrots, thinly sliced
2 red onions, thinly sliced
1 potato
150g unsalted butter
750ml Chardonnay
50g brown sugar
5g iota carrageenan
50g salted butter
2 sprigs each of basil, sage and dill, chopped

For the Garnish
basil leaves
sage leaves
dill leaves
extra virgin olive oil

To prepare and cook the veal, separate the bones from the veal and place into a vacuum bag with 2 cloves of garlic, half a stick of celery, half a carrot and half an onion. Vacuum on full and cook in a water bath for at least 36 hours at 62°C.

Cut the remaining red onions into slices and, with the peeler, cut the remaining carrot and celery into long strips. Crush the garlic and dice the potato. Cook the potato in the microwave for 20 seconds and set to one side. In a medium saucepan, melt the unsalted butter and add all the vegetables, garlic included. Simmer with 100ml Chardonnay and reduce. As soon as it has evaporated, add the brown sugar and cook the vegetables for a further 5 minutes. If it gets too sticky, add a little water to loosen.

Cover a metal terrine with cling film. In a medium saucepan, bring the rest of the chardonnay to the boil and as soon as it's done, add the iota and stir well. Pour the mixture into the terrine and let it stand to one side to solidify. Melt the salted butter in a medium saucepan and cook the chopped basil, sage and dill. Allow to infuse, pass through a chinois and reserve.

Preheat the oven to 180°C and season the bone marrow with salt and pepper, place onto a baking tray and leave in the oven for about 10 minutes until cooked. Remove the jelly from the terrine, and cut into small cubes.

To serve, prepare a rectangular plate and place the bone marrow to one side with the fresh basil on top. Place the vegetables in the middle, with a little sage, and the veal shank on the other side, topped with the salted butter and fresh dill. Finish with 2 tablespoons of the diced jelly and a drizzle of extra virgin olive oil.

Editor's Note: Iota Carrageenan is a hydrocolloid taken from red seaweed, and is an exceptional thickening or gelling agent, available from specialist food shops.

SAM ASHTON-BOOTH

Some of the best dishes at Story start as a trial and error experiment so it seemed fitting for us to choose the hard work of Cancer Research UK, which is a cause very close to my heart, to promote through ChariTable Bookings."

DUCK with beetroot and gooseberry

SERVES 4 | PREPARATION TIME 30 MINUTES (PLUS 3 WEEKS TO HANG) | COOKING TIME 3 HOURS (PLUS OVERNIGHT TO DEHYDRATE)

For the Duck
1 large Challand duck
50g honey
10g each coriander seeds, lavender and Szechuan pepper
50g hay
10ml rapeseed oil

For the Beetroots
1 candy beetroot
1 golden beetroot
1 red beetroot
50g thyme
50ml Cabernet Sauvignon vinegar
salt, to taste
sugar, to taste
50ml rapeseed oil

For the Cauliflower Purée
1 large cauliflower
500ml single cream
250ml whole milk
salt, to taste

For the Duck Jus
1kg duck carcasses
2l water
2 cloves of garlic
1 onion
2 carrots

For the Gooseberry Vinegar
2 punnets of gooseberries
300ml Chardonnay vinegar

To make the duck, take the crown of the duck which we in the restaurant hang for minumum of 3 weeks, stuffed with hay to dry out and add flavour. Cover the whole crown in honey, season with salt, szechaun pepper, coriander seeds, lavender and then straight into the oven at 220°C. Bake it until it reaches 31°C in the centre which takes about 9–12 minutes, then take it out and let it rest for a good 10–12 minutes before carving the meat off of the bone. Each breast is cut down the middle lengthways to give two portions, then brushed with a little honey and rapeseed oil.

Preheat the oven to 180°C. Toss the beetroot with the thyme, vinegar, salt, sugar and oil, wrap in a tin foil parcel and bake them in the oven for 40–50 minutes until just cooked in the middle. Place them in a bowl covered with cling film to let the skins steam away. When cool enough to handle, peel off the skins, slice the beets and punch out discs.

To make the cauliflower purée, remove the florets from the cauliflower and place in a pan with the cream, milk and a good pinch of salt. Bring to the boil and simmer until soft. Pass through a chinois then blend until really smooth.

To make the duck jus, roast the duck carcasses with the vegetables at 200°C until golden. Place in a pot with the water and slowly bring to the boil. Simmer for 2–3 hours, then pass through a sieve. Reduce to a saucy consistency.

To make the gooseberry vinegar, bring the vinegar to the boil, then pour it straight over the gooseberries and cover the bowl with cling film. Leave to cool to room temperature. The longer you leave the vinegar, the more intense and beautiful the flavour profile is.

To make the confit duck tongue, lightly crush the salt and the peppercorns then mix with the thyme. Marinate the tongues in the rub on a flat tray for 2 hours. Wash off the rub, then pat dry. Place the tongues in the warm duck fat and confit at 60°C for 2–3 hours. Remove from the fat and whilst still warm, remove the bone and dice up the tongue. Add to the jus.

For the Confit Duck Tongue
200g duck tongue
50g sea salt
10g black peppercorn
10g thyme, chopped
300ml duck fat

For the Roasted Beetroot Juice
4 large red beetroots
10g thyme
10ml rapeseed oil

For the Watercress
1 bunch of English watercress
ice water

For the Gooseberry
1 punnet of gooseberries

To make the roasted beetroot juice, toss the ingredients together, wrap in tin foil and bake in the oven at 180°C for 45–50 minutes. Juice the cooked beetroot then reduce the liquid by half. Place some of the pulp in a dehydrator or a low oven to dry out. Blend in a Thermoix until fine and store in a container until needed.

To prepare the watercress, pick the best stems and leaves and store them in ice water to keep them fresh and crisp. Slice the gooseberries, allowing 3 or 4 slices per plate.

To serve, plate as pictured.

PAUL ASKEW

"The Adopt a School program run by the RACA is something that is very important to me. Sharing knowledge of food and nutrition with the younger generation and hopefully exciting them about it is hugely rewarding. I'm sharing my recipe from The Art School Restaurant through ChariTable Bookings to raise even more awareness."

PETERHEAD HALIBUT FILLET with saffron potato risotto, steamed oyster and charred leeks

SERVES 4 | PREPARATION TIME 30 MINUTES | COOKING TIME 1 HOUR 15 MINUTES

For the Halibut
4 x 150g halibut fillets, deskinned
and deboned, keep bones for stock
25ml vegetable oil
25g butter

For the Saffron Infused Fish Stock
1kg halibut bones
½ lemon
150g carrots, diced
150g celery, diced
1 tsp each whole black peppercorns
fennel seeds and fresh thyme
1 fresh bay leaf
1 large onion, diced
½ bulb of garlic
1 tbsp parsley
1.5l water
½ tsp saffron

For the Saffron Potato Risotto
4 large safari potatoes, cubed
2 banana shallots, finely diced
4 cloves of garlic, finely chopped
25ml extra virgin olive oil
50g butter
200g Parmesan, finely grated
50g each parsley, dill and chives,
finely chopped
10ml lemon juice
½ lemon, zest only
½ tsp each salt and pepper

For the fish stock, debone the halibut and set the flesh aside. Place all the ingredients, apart from the saffron, into a large pan of water. Bring to a boil, skim and simmer for no longer than 30 minutes. Add in the saffron to produce a golden yellow-coloured stock. Heat rapidly for 5 minutes, pass the contents through a fine sieve and reserve.

To prepare the halibut, skin, trim and portion the halibut fillet. Pat the fillets dry with a clean cloth or paper towel before pan frying. Preheat a pan until it reaches smoke point, season the halibut and place on the pan with vegetable oil for 1–2 minutes. Once seared, place under the grill for 3–4 minutes on a medium to high heat. Remove and keep warm.

For the saffron potato risotto, start by placing the cubed potato into boiling, salted water for approximately 3 minutes, then remove and allow to cool. Sweat the diced shallots, garlic and a little oil in a pan with half the butter. Add in the potatoes, then gradually add 1l of the saffron-infused fish stock, keeping 250ml for the sauce, incrementally feeding the dish, as you would with a rice risotto. Do so for 6–7 minutes. Once infused, add the remaining butter, Parmesan cheese and at the last moment, the finely chopped herbs. Finish with a splash of lemon juice and the zest. Season to taste and place the risotto into the base of a dish ready for the halibut.

To steam the oysters, begin by washing them thoroughly and checking for sand, grit and impurities. Place in a deep oven tray and steam in an oven at 240°C, for 3–4 minutes, until the shells open. Retain the juices and remove the meat. Set aside the juices for the sauce and wrap the oyster in a ribbon of courgette.

To make the sauce, combine the oyster juices and fish stock and reduce by half on a medium heat. Once thickened, whisk in the butter and cream and allow the mixture to thicken and reduce further. To season, add lemon juice to taste.

To serve, place the halibut on the saffron potato risotto, top with the courgette wrapped oyster and cover generously with sauce. Garnish with Bermuda cress and nasturtiums.

For the Oysters
- 4 rock oysters
- 1 large courgette, ribboned

For the Charred Leeks
- 8 baby leeks
- 25ml olive oil

For the Sauce
- 250ml oyster juices
- 250ml saffron infused fish stock
- 50g unsalted butter
- 100ml single cream
- 20ml lemon juice

To Serve
- Bermuda cress
- nasturtiums

CRAIG ATCHINSON

ChariTable Bookings is a great idea. I am very happy to have offered up my stone bass dish from the Grand Hotel and Spa, York. I absolutely support IDAS which is a North Yorkshire charity that does amazing work supporting people who have been affected by domestic abuse."

NORTH ATLANTIC STONE BASS with fennel, langoustines, coastal herbs and bisque

SERVES 4 | PREPARATION TIME 20 MINUTES | COOKING TIME 1 HOUR

For the Sauce
2 sticks of celery
2 shallots
2 tbsp tomato purée
20ml brandy
100ml white wine
200g langoustine shells, roasted until golden
1 bay leaf
2 star anise
175ml double cream
salt and lemon juice, to taste

For the Fennel Purée
100g butter
1 fennel bulb
250ml white chicken stock
175ml double cream
salt, to taste

For the Bass
4 live langoustines
oil, for cooking
4 x 140g stone bass fillets
1 knob of butter, for cooking
80g mixed coastal herbs

To make the sauce, sweat the celery and shallots until soft in a saucepan. Add the tomato purée and cook for 5 minutes. Add the brandy, burn the alcohol by lighting a match over the vapour or you can use the gas flame on your hob. Add the white wine and bring to the boil for a minute. Put in the langoustine shells and cover with cold water. Add the bay leaf and star anise, bring to the boil and simmer for 20 minutes. Don't simmer for more than that, otherwise the sauce will become bitter. Pass the stock through a fine sieve. Return to a clean pan and reduce by half, then add the double cream, reduce by half again and season with salt and lemon juice.

To make the purée, shred the fennel finely with a sharp knife. Melt the butter in a saucepan and warm until foaming. Add the fennel to the butter and sweat on a low heat until very soft, this can take around 1 hour before. Add the chicken stock to the fennel then reduce until all the liquid has evaporated. Pour in the double cream and again reduce until the pan is almost dry. Blend in a high powered food processor until the purée is smooth. Pass through a fine sieve ready to serve. Season with salt, if needed.

To prepare the langoustines, remove the intestinal tract and blanch the tails in boiling water for 1 minute. Dip the tails into ice water, then peel off the shells. To cook the fish, warm a non-stick pan with a touch of oil. Add the bass skin-side down and fry gently until the skin is golden and crisp. Flip the fish, add a knob of butter, and cook gently until the core temperature reaches 60°C. In the last 2 minutes of cooking, add the langoustines then serve immediately.

To serve, dip the coastal herbs in boiling water for 10 seconds. Dress a plate with the purée on the base, and build the other ingredients on the plate however you please.

JASON ATHERTON

Hospitality Action is a charity close to many chef's hearts, doing incredible work with people in our industry through its wide reaching programmes. I'm proud to support them and share Pollen Street Social's Roast Venison recipe through this fantastic initiative by ChariTable Bookings. Enjoy!"

ROAST VENISON AND BEETROOT with poached pears

SERVES 6 | PREPARATION TIME 1 HOUR | COOKING TIME 1 HOUR 30 MINUTES

For the Roast Venison
6 x 100g deboned loin of venison
25g unsalted butter
salt and pepper

For the Red Wine Sauce
1 tbsp olive oil
1 shallot, sliced
1 clove of garlic, chopped
1 sprig of thyme
¼ tsp white peppercorns
1 bay leaf
1 tbsp sherry vinegar
325ml red wine
400ml veal stock

For the Roast Beetroot
600g beetroot
4 tbsp caster sugar
4 sprigs of thyme
4 cloves of garlic, peeled
4 tsp sea salt
1 tbsp sherry vinegar

For the Spiced Honey Sauce
½ tsp lavender
½ tsp each coriander and cumin seeds
¼ tsp Szechuan peppercorns
60ml sherry vinegar
25g unsalted butter
½ tsp sea salt
200ml clear honey
1 squeeze of lemon juice

To prepare the beetroot, wash and trim off the stalks. Place in a saucepan and add the sugar, thyme, garlic, salt and vinegar. Simmer for about 45 minutes until the beetroot is tender. Drain and leave to cool. When cool enough to handle, peel the beetroot and cut each one into cubes.

To make the spiced honey sauce, toast the lavender for a few seconds in a dry hot pan. Tip in the coriander seeds, cumin and Szechuan peppercorns, and toast for a few more seconds to release oils and fragrance. Pour in the sherry vinegar and boil until reduced to a sticky glaze. Add the butter, salt and honey and bring back to a simmer. Continue to simmer until it has reduced by two-thirds to a syrupy consistency. Strain through a fine sieve and discard the spices. Season to taste with a squeeze of lemon juice. Set aside until ready to serve.

For the red wine sauce, heat the oil in a heavy-based pan until hot. If you have them, add the venison trimmings and fry them over a medium-high heat until golden brown on each side. Stir in the shallot and garlic and fry for a few minutes until lightly golden. Add the thyme, peppercorns and bay leaf. Deglaze the pan with the sherry vinegar and red wine, scraping the base to release sediment. Boil the liquid until reduced by three-quarters. Add the stock and bring to the boil. Reduce the heat and simmer for 20 minutes. Pass the sauce through a fine sieve into a clean pan and boil steadily until reduced to a syrup. Reheat before serving.

To poach the pears, put the water, sugar, lemon juice and spices into a wide pan. Stir to dissolve the sugar and bring the syrup to boil. Add the pears to the syrup. Cover with a dampened piece of baking parchment. Simmer for about 10 minutes until tender. Reheat before serving.

For the venison, heat the butter over a medium heat. Add the venison pieces and sear until golden brown all over, keeping the meat medium-rare. Remove and place in a warm tray to rest for a few minutes while you reheat the pears, sauces and beetroot. Place the beetroot pieces in a frying pan with 3 tablespoons of spiced honey sauce and toss to coat. Heat for 2 minutes, stirring frequently. Thickly slice the venison and divide between warmed plates. Cover with spiced beetroot, poached pears and red wine sauce and enjoy.

For the Spiced Poached Pears

1l water

375g caster sugar

1 tbsp lemon juice

5 star anise, lightly crushed

4 sticks of cinnamon

6 pears, peeled and cut into wedges

FRANCES ATKINS

Action Against Hunger must be a logical choice of charity for many chefs to support. They do an incredible job to fight hunger and malnutrition amongst children everywhere. Delighted to share the Yorke Arms' veal dish with ChariTable Bookings to help raise much needed funds for them."

LACQUERED ENGLISH VEAL with lobster, strawberry and cabbage cake

SERVES 4 | PREPARATION TIME 2 HOURS | COOKING TIME 2 HOURS

For the Veal

500g veal shin
½ onion
½ carrot
1 stick of celery
2 cloves of garlic
20g lemon thyme
1 sprig of rosemary
2 bay leaves
200ml white wine
200g chopped tomatoes
400ml veal stock
2 violet artichokes
lemon
acidulated water
thyme
salt
2 tbsp sweet sherry
4 tsp tamarind
50ml veal stock
50ml water

For the Cabbage and Strawberry Cake

500g Hispi pointed cabbage
olive oil
salt and pepper, to taste
120g sour dough
15g parsley
10g tarragon
4 large strawberries
50g goats curd

To prepare the veal, brown in a hot pan and place onto the chopped vegetables with herbs. Deglaze the pan with white wine and chopped tomatoes. Place in the oven at 175°C for 1 hour. When cool, remove the meat from the bone and strain off the stock. Refrigerate. Remove the top of the artichoke with a knife and pare down the side to the stalk with a peeler. Rub with lemon, cover with acidulated water, thyme, salt and cling film. Bring to boil, remove from heat and stand until cool. Then place the veal shin, sherry, tamarind, veal stock and water in a pan at 200°C for approx 8 minutes to glaze.

To prepare the cabbage and strawberry cake, season and oil the whole cabbage and place in an oven to roast for 45 minutes on 200°C. Remove from the oven and take off the outer burnt leaves. Chop up the centre of the cooked cabbage and season with black pepper, add goats curd and the green crumb. For the green crumb, mix together the sour dough crumb, parsley and tarragon. Mix in the beaten egg, sea salt, chilli powder to taste and nutmeg. Place in a lined ring measuring 12cm for 25 minutes at 160°C. Remove from the oven. Slice strawberries and place in honey and vinegar and arrange on top of cake. Place back in the oven for 4 minutes to soften and glaze strawberry top.

To prepare the lobster, place in boiling water with salt for 6 minutes. Once cooled, split and crack the shell, reserving the coral. Remove and refrigerate the meat, then make a stock with the shells, lemon thyme, onion, fennel, garlic and celery. Blitz the unsalted butter and reserved coral in a food processor, roll the mixture in cling film and refrigerate.

To prepare the fresh turmeric aioli to garnish the plate, blitz the ingredients together by feeding in oil to an emulsion and place in a piping bag.

To prepare the smoked tomato brandade, reduce the tomato water to 50ml. Finely chop the tomato petals and basil. Mix together with the smoked potato purée and oil.

To serve, melt the coral butter in a pan and toss the cooked lobster in it. Slice the cabbage and strawberry cake. Place the aioli on the plate. Place the brandade with the lobster on top. Place the veal on the plate with the artichoke on top and decorate with nasturtium.

For the Cabbage and Strawberry Cake *continued*

    30g beaten egg

    1 pinch of chilli powder

    1 pinch of sea salt

    0.5g nutmeg

    10g honey

    5ml cider vinegar

For the Lobster

    1½lb chix English lobster

    6l water

    60g sea salt

    250g unsalted butter

    60g coral

    15g lemon thyme

    1 onion

    1 bulb of fennel

    1 bulb of garlic

    1 stick of celery

For the Fresh Turmeric Aioli

    8g garlic

    50ml white wine

    3g sea salt

    20g mustard

    15g fresh turmeric

    2 egg yolks

    100ml vegetable oil

    50ml extra virgin oil or 150g

    pomace oil

For the Smoked Tomato Brandade

    160ml smoked potato purée

    5g salt

    65g tomato petals

    260ml tomato water

    5g basil

    30ml olive oil

PASCAL AUSSIGNAC

What a great way to promote Action Against Hunger who work the world over to prevent hunger and malnourishment for children. I hope you enjoy Club Gascon's roast scallops and that ChariTable Bookings raises awareness for all these fantastic charities."

ROAST SCALLOPS with polenta and squid ink sauce

SERVES 4 | PREPARATION TIME 30 MINUTES | COOKING TIME 1 HOUR

Equipment
   siphon with N₂O

For the Roast Scallops
   8 large scallops in shell
   50ml olive oil
   1g salt
   1g pepper
   250ml water
   1g espelette pepper
   25g butter

For the Polenta
   30g squid ink
   50g instant polenta
   500ml milk
   4 cloves of garlic, crushed
   50ml olive oil
   2g espelette pepper

To Serve
   1 handful of rocket leaves per serving
   8 sterilised scallop shells, boil in
   water for 5 minutes

Shuck the scallops from their shells, save the orange roes. Pull off the little nuggets of muscle from the sides. Wash the scallops well, pat dry and store in the fridge.

To make the sauce, heat half the olive oil in a small pan and sauté the scallop roes and muscle nuggets with a little salt and pepper, for 3–5 minutes. Cover with 250ml of water and simmer for about 10 minutes. Strain the liquid into a small bowl, pressing down with the back of a spoon to extract all the juices, and discard the trimmings. Add the remaining olive oil and the espelette pepper, and whisk together. At this stage, if you don't have a siphon to make the foam, spoon the squid ink into the strained liquid.

To cook the scallops, heat the butter in a small non-stick frying pan and fry the scallops for about a minute on each side, seasoning in the pan.

To make the squid ink polenta foam, begin by heating the milk in a large non-stick saucepan and add the garlic. Add the olive oil and espelette pepper. Then, when the milk is just on the boil, turn the heat to medium, pour in the polenta and squeeze in the squid ink in a steady stream, stirring briskly with a long-handled wooden spoon. The mixture will thicken and begin to plop and splutter, which is normal. Partly cover the pan and turn the heat to low. Cook for 10 minutes. Remove and let it stand.

To serve, place the squid ink polenta into the siphon and eject carefully into the bottom of the sterilised shells. Top with the scallops and the sauce. Garnish with a handful of rocket and serve hot.

HARVEY AYLIFFE

"Myself and the team at 34 Mayfair are thrilled to offer our signature Lobster Mac to raise awareness for Cancer Research in this ChariTable Bookings encyclopedia of recipes!"

34 MAYFAIR'S LOBSTER MAC

SERVES 4 | PREPARATION TIME 30 MINUTES | COOKING TIME 2 HOURS

For the Lobster
- 2 x 600g lobsters

For the Macaroni
- 300g macaroni
- 100g panko breadcrumbs
- 100g mature cheddar, grated
- 1 small bunch of flat leaf parsley
- salt and pepper

For the Lobster Sauce
- lobster shells
- 1 shallot, chopped
- ½ carrot, peeled and diced
- ½ stalk celery, peeled and diced
- 1 clove of garlic, crushed
- extra virgin olive oil
- ½ bunch of tarragon
- 1 tbsp tomato purée
- 20g unsalted butter
- 2 tbsp plain flour
- 100ml white wine
- 200ml fish stock (or a quality stock cube)
- 50ml double cream
- salt and pepper

For the Cheese Sauce
- 400g mascarpone
- 200ml double cream
- 100g Parmesan, grated
- salt and pepper

To Serve
- Périgord truffle shavings, optional

To make the lobster, bring a large saucepan of salted water to boil. Plunge the lobsters into the boiling water and cook for 10 minutes. Remove and leave to cool. Remove the lobster meat from its shells, retaining the shells, chop into portions and set aside.

To make the lobster sauce, fry the lobster shells, shallot, carrot, celery and garlic in the olive oil for 5 minutes. Add tarragon stalks and tomato purée and stir well. Add butter and allow to melt. Add the flour and stir well. Stir in the white wine and stock, and bring to the boil. Simmer for 20 minutes and reduce by half. Add the cream and stir well. Bring to boil and simmer for 15 minutes to allow the sauce to reduce and thicken. Strain through a fine sieve, pressing the shells with a spoon to ensure all sauce goes through.

To make the cheese sauce, bring the double cream and mascarpone to the boil. Add Parmesan and simmer for 5 minutes. Season to taste and liquidise until smooth.

To assemble the dish, begin by preheating an oven to 200°C. Place the macaroni in a large saucepan of salted, boiling water for 10 minutes. Mix the cooked pasta with the lobster pieces, finely chopped parsley, lobster and cheese sauces, and transfer to an ovenproof dish. Bake in the oven for 10 minutes. Remove and sprinkle the cheddar and breadcrumb mixture over the top. Put back in the oven to crisp for another 10 minutes.

Serve with green salad and, optionally, garnish with shaved truffle.

SRIRAM AYLUR

"Quilon is very happy to support the incredible work that Born Free does to keep wildlife in the wild by donating a recipe to ChariTable Bookings' new 365 recipes venture!"

MANGO CURRY

SERVES 2 | PREPARATION TIME 20 MINUTES | COOKING TIME 1 HOUR

For the Mango Curry

2 ripe mangoes
25g grated coconut
½ tsp cumin seeds
½ tsp chilli powder
¼ tsp turmeric powder
150ml yoghurt
30ml oil
¼ tsp mustard seeds
¼ tsp fenugreek seeds
2 whole red chillies
2 green chillies, thinly sliced
¼ tsp curry leaves
8 large Madras onions, finely chopped
salt to taste

For the curry, begin by dicing the mangoes and placing to one side. In a pestle and mortar, make a fine paste out of the grated coconut and cumin seeds and reserve. In a heated pan, toss the diced mangoes with the chilli powder, turmeric and a little salt. After 8–10 minutes, or once the mango is decently browned and slightly falling apart, add the coconut and cumin paste, making sure to stir continuously. After 5 minutes, lower the heat and slowly stir in the yoghurt. Leave to reduce.

Whilst the yoghurt and mango mixture cooks, heat the oil in a separate pan and add the mustard and fenugreek seeds, whole red chillies, green chillies, curry leaves and the finely chopped onions. Place a lid on the pan and allow the mixture to sweat and temper. After 8–10 minutes and once the onions are golden, pour the mango and yoghurt in with the onions and spices and allow to cook to desired consistency, seasoning to taste.

RICHARD BAINBRIDGE

"*Marie Curie's nurses do the most amazing work looking after terminally ill patients, giving them ease and comfort in their last few months. All of us at Benedicts wish ChariTable Bookings well in raising funds and awareness for them.*"

POT ROAST CHICKEN with fondant potatoes and watercress
SERVES 4 | PREPARATION TIME 15 MINUTES (PLUS OVERNIGHT SOAKING) | COOKING TIME 90 MINUTES

For the Pot Roasted Chicken
1 chicken crown
1 carrot, chopped
1 shallot, chopped
2 celery sticks, chopped
50ml white wine
10g garden herbs
1 tbsp rapeseed oil

For the Fondant Potatoes
12 red potatoes, cut into cylinders
150g salted butter
water, to cover
1 sprig of thyme
2 cloves of garlic
salt

For the Watercress Purée
1 egg yolk
150g watercress
25ml cider vinegar
100ml rapeseed oil
20g ice cubes

For the chicken, start by preheating an oven to 200°C. Place the vegetables, wine and herbs into a clay pot that has been soaked in water overnight. Season the chicken crown and colour in a large frying pan with the rapeseed oil. Place on top of the vegetables, close the lid and leave in the oven for 40 minutes. Remove the lid and bake for another 15 minutes. Take the pot out of the oven, cover with a tea towel and allow to rest for 15 minutes.

To make the fondant potatoes, place all the ingredients into a pot on a high heat and bring to the boil. Once boiling, turn the heat down to a rolling boil and take care to keep the potatoes from sticking. By the time they're cooked, all that should remain are the potato cylinders and a butter coating. Once coloured, leave in the butter until ready to serve.

For the watercress purée, blitz the egg yolk, watercress and vinegar into a smooth purée. Put in the ice cubes and slowly add the oil, continuing to blend on a medium speed. Once all the oil is in, a bright green watercress purée should remain. Season to taste and place in the fridge.

To serve, assemble the dish as pictured and top with an optional watercress salad, lemon juice, salt, pepper and a little rapeseed oil.

ED BAINES

I'm pleased that with this recipe ChariTable Bookings are helping me promote the great work that Starlight do in granting wishes to seriously ill children. The team and I at Randall and Aubin feel exceedingly fortunate to be able to do what we love every day and it is a privilege to be able to support deserving children and their families while doing so."

CRISPY DUCK SALAD

SERVES 4 | PREPARATION TIME 20 MINUTES | COOKING TIME 45 MINUTES

For the Dish

2 duck legs

3 star anise

½ head of garlic

1 thumb of ginger, roughly chopped

20g coriander stalks, roughly chopped

1 tsp Chinese five-spice powder

lime wedges, to serve

For the Duck Sauce

4 tbsp tomato ketchup

½ orange, juiced

1 tbsp each honey, soy sauce and sesame oil

For the Soy and Sesame Dressing

1 tsp soy sauce

1 tsp rice vinegar

1 clove of garlic, peeled and crushed

1 small piece of ginger, grated

1 tbsp sesame oil

3 tbsp vegetable or corn oil

For the Salad

1 packet of egg noodles

4 bunches of watercress, stalks removed

110g white radish, peeled and ribboned

50g bean shoots

1 bunch of spring onions, trimmed

20g coriander leaves

1 tbsp sesame seeds, lightly toasted

dry shrimps, optional

Asian sprouts or cresses, optional

Cover the duck with the water, add the herbs and spices and simmer gently for 45 minutes. Remove the duck from the stock and set it aside to cool. Skim the fat off the stock and use it as a base to make an Asian soup.

To make the duck sauce, whisk together all the ingredients in a bowl.

To make the soy and sesame dressing, whisk all of the ingredients together.

Remove the duck meat from the bone, then cut into 1cm thick slices. Toss the duck pieces in the sauce and grill for 2 minutes until hot.

To assemble the dish, arrange the watercress on the plates, take a good handful of salad ingredients per portion and a handful of noodles in a mixing bowl and drizzle with dressing. Place over the plated watercress, top with warm duck, sprinkle with sesame seeds, coriander leaves and finish with a wedge of lime.

SAT BAINS

We all know the great work that is done by Macmillan every year for cancer sufferers and their families. It was a no-brainer for me to support them by contributing Bains' recipe to this ChariTable Bookings publication for charity."

HAM EGGS PEAS

SERVES 4 | PREPARATION TIME 2 DAYS | COOKING TIME 3 HOURS

Equipment
  Pacojet

For the Poached Duck Eggs
  10 duck eggs

For the Pea Sorbet
  500ml water
  100g caster sugar
  500g frozen peas
  5 sprigs of mint
  salt, to taste

For the Chicken stock
  2 whole chickens
  2 shallots, chopped
  4 sprigs of thyme

For the Ham Butter
  200g beurre noisette
  200ml white chicken stock
  50g cured ham, chopped

For the Braised Peas
  300g peas, freshly shelled
  150ml white chicken stock
  30g ham butter
  salt, to taste

For the Sourdough Bread Starter
  150g wholemeal flour
  150g strong white flour
  450ml water
  50g live yoghurt
  10g caster sugar

To prepare the duck eggs, poach with the shell on for 2 hours at 62°C, making sure to keep the temperature constant.

For the pea sorbet, bring the water and sugar to boil. Allow to cool. Place the syrup into a blender, add the peas and mint and blitz for 30 seconds. Season to taste and blitz for another 30 seconds. Pass through a fine sieve straight into a Pacojet beaker and freeze. Churn at least 3 times before use. Alternatively, use an ice cream maker or freeze in a container and blend before serving.

To make the chicken stock, place the chickens, shallots and thyme into a pressure cooker and cover with cold water. Bring up to full pressure and cook for 25 minutes. Remove from the heat and allow to cool. Strain through a fine sieve and leave to cool overnight in the fridge. Skim any fat from the top, strain again and chill until needed.

For the ham butter, make a beurre noisette by melting and browning 200g butter, until a nutty aroma is detectable. Add the chopped ham, blend to a purée and pour in the white chicken stock. Season to taste and store in the fridge until needed.

To make the braised peas, blanch them in boiling, salted water for 30 seconds. Strain, then cool down in ice water. Warm the chicken stock and add the ham butter. Emulsify and add the peas. Warm gently and season to taste.

To prepare the sourdough, mix all the starter ingredients in a bowl, cover and keep at room temperature for 2 days, making sure to stir every few hours. Once it has trebled in size, begin making the sourdough. Dissolve the yeast and salt in water, add the 2 flours and mix. Blend with the starter dough and knead for 10 minutes until completely smooth and elastic. Transfer to a clean bowl, cover and leave to rise at room temperature for 2 hours. Knock the air out of the dough on a floured surface and place in a loaf tin. Leave at room temperature until it has doubled in size. Make a few slits along the bread and bake for 20 minutes at 250°C. Lower the temperature to 200°C and bake for a further 10 minutes. Remove from the oven and leave to rest for 10 minutes. Remove from the tin and allow to cool on a wire rack.

For the Sourdough Bread

100g starter dough

200g strong flour

50g wholemeal flour

120ml water

5g yeast

10g salt

For the Sourdough Croutons

10 slices wafer-thin sourdough bread

50ml olive oil

1¼ tsp fresh thyme

sea salt, to taste

For the Sherry Caramel

500ml sweet sherry

100g caster sugar

citric acid, to taste

For the Garnish

10 slices shonka ham (Hungarian Easter ham)

50g pea shoots

To make the sourdough croutons, cut wafer-thin slices of the now prepared sourdough and place onto a non-stick baking tray. Drizzle with olive oil and season to taste with sea salt and fresh thyme. Bake at 160°C until golden.

To make the sherry caramel, place the sherry and sugar into a pan and bring to the boil. Lower the heat a little and reduce the mixture by half. As it reduces, the sherry will sweeten and thicken. Use the citric acid to balance the flavour.

To serve, assemble the dish as pictured and garnish with pea shoots and a slice of shonka ham.

ANDREW BAIRD

Adopt A School is a fantastic charity that gets chefs across the UK teaching kids about the importance of nutrition. I'm very proud to be one of those chefs sharing my recipe with ChariTable Bookings to spread the word."

HALIBUT STEAK with new season peas à la Française
SERVES 4 | PREPARATION TIME 15 MINUTES | COOKING TIME 10 MINUTES

For the Dish
4 x 180g halibut steaks, or cod
10ml pomace oil
1 knob of Jersey butter
60ml fish stock

For the Peas
550g butter
10g flour
40g pancetta, cubed
200ml chicken stock, supermarket
stock or a cube is fine
20g carrot, diced
20g potato, diced
60g baby silverskin onions, peeled
300g new season peas, shelled,
frozen peas can be substituted
20g broad beans, peeled

To Serve
1 little gem lettuce
salt and freshly ground black pepper

Preheat the oven to 180°C.

To make the peas, mix 10g the butter with the flour to make a beurre meunière, a thickening agent. Put the remaining butter in a saucepan and heat. Add the pancetta and cook until it changes colour. Add the chicken stock and bring to a simmer, then add the carrots, potato and silverskin onions and cook until tender. Add the peas and broad beans. Bring back to a simmer. At this point break the beurre meunière into small pieces and gently whisk into the pea mixture. This will slightly thicken the stock and give it more body. Keep warm.

To cook the halibut, simply heat an ovenproof frying pan. Add a little pomace oil and when it starts to lightly smoke add the fish. Cook until golden brown on one side. Turn the fish over, add a knob of butter and the fish stock. Place in the oven for approximately 8 minutes.

To serve, at the last minute halve the little gem lengthways and shred. Add to the peas and beans. As soon as the lettuce has wilted, place in a bowl plate, remove the fish from the oven and place on top.

MACIEJ BANAS

"We are long time supporters of Leuka and are pleased that through ChariTable Bookings, Fisher's are able to find another way to battle leukaemia."

WIENER SCHNITZEL

SERVES 4 | PREPARATION TIME 4 HOURS | COOKING TIME 20 MINUTES

For the Veal Stock Reduction
- 1.5kg veal bones
- 750g chicken bones
- 500g chicken wings
- 150g carrots, chopped
- 300g onion, chopped
- 3 stalks of celery, with leaves
- 300g leek, chopped
- 7l water
- 2 banana shallots, roughly chopped
- 75g unsalted butter
- 600ml red wine
- 1 lemon, juiced

For the Wiener Schnitzel
- 40g soft flour
- 40g potato flour
- 4 x 170g veal escalope
- 2 eggs, whisked
- 60g breadcrumbs
- 4 free range eggs, fried
- vegetable oil, for frying

For the Garnish
- capers
- anchovies

To prepare the veal jus, chop the bones and wings and roast in the oven until golden brown, making sure to toss from time to time. Heat up a large saucepan and sweat the carrots, onion, celery and leek in a little oil until well coloured. Add the roasted bones, wings and water and allow to cook for 3 hours. Once suitably thick, strain through a fine sieve and place to one side. In another pan, melt the butter and sweat the shallots until soft. Add the wine and reduce by half, then add the reserved stock and allow to reduce for 40 minutes. Strain the sauce and reduce further until a syrupy consistency is reached. Season with a little salt and lemon juice to taste.

To make the wiener schnitzel, mix the flours together, beat the escalope down until about half a centimetre in thickness. Dip the flattened escalope in the flour, then the egg followed by the breadcrumbs. Pan fry in vegetable oil until golden brown. The veal should be served slightly pink.

To serve, line a warmed plate with veal jus, top with the wiener schnitzel, a fried egg and a few anchovies and capers as pictured.

MATT BARKER

Proud to be supporting the fantastic work of UNICEF by sharing the Westwood's signature ribeye recipe with ChariTable Bookings. Dig in and spread the word!"

WESTWOOD'S BONE-IN RIBEYE STEAK marinated in molasses, bourbon and thyme with Café de Paris grill butter

SERVES 2–4 | PREPARATION TIME 3 HOURS | COOKING TIME 1 HOUR

For the Steak

1kg aged bone-in rib, can be prepared by a good butcher, alternatively, 227g rib eye or fillet steak

olive oil

For the Molasses Marinade

a few sprigs of thyme

1 red chilli, halved and deseeded

3 cloves of garlic, finely chopped

1 thumb of fresh ginger, grated

1 drizzle of oil

50ml bourbon

50ml water

25ml balsamic vinegar

1 tbsp cracked black pepper

350g molasses syrup

1 tsp dried chilli flakes

For the Café de Paris Grill Butter

1 red onion, chopped

1 clove of garlic, chopped

250g butter, softened

10g each thyme, parsley and tarragon, chopped

1½ tsp each Dijon mustard, brown sauce and Gentleman's Relish

1 tbsp Worcestershire sauce

30ml port or sherry

½ lemon, juiced

salt and pepper to taste

To make the molasses marinade, gently cook the thyme, chilli, garlic cloves and ginger in a little oil, in a deep pan, for 5 minutes. Add the rest of the ingredients and bring to the boil, then simmer for 10 minutes. Set aside and leave to cool completely. Brush the raw steaks with the molasses marinade and leave for a minimum of 2–3 hours. For best results, make the marinade the day before.

To make the café de Paris grill butter, heat the onions, garlic, salt and pepper in a pan with 20g of butter and cook gently for 4 to 5 minutes. Transfer to a bowl, then add all of the other ingredients to make the butter. Shape into cylinders in cling film or parchment paper and refrigerate until needed.

To cook the steak, preheat the oven to 180°C. Place the rib in the oven for 20 minutes for medium rare. Because of the high sugar content in the marinade, the beef will blacken; don't worry as this adds to the flavour of the beef.

To serve, slice into individual portions. Melt the Café de Paris butter over the steaks and plate.

DAVID BARNETT

On behalf of the team at The Torridon, I'm pleased to be able to support Children with Cancer UK and the incredible work they do. I hope that our signature scallop recipe in this ChariTable Bookings collection helps to remind everyone of the need to support children suffering with this terrible disease."

BAKED SCALLOPS with citrus and fennel
SERVES 4 | PREPARATION TIME 30 MINUTES | COOKING TIME 15 MINUTES

For the Baked Scallops
8 large kings scallops in the shell, shuck and clean the shells
2 bulbs fennel, finely sliced
75g butter
100ml Noilly Prat
1 star anise
300ml fish stock
1 lemon, juiced
50ml double cream

For the Garnish
sweet cicely
fennel pollen
sea fennel
fennel oil
lemon verbena
borage flowers
seaweed powder
8 tsp smoked trout roe

To make the citrus and fennel, sweat off the fennel in the butter. Add the Noilly Prat, star anise and reduce rapidly until all the wine has gone. Pour in the fish stock, reduce by half and add the lemon juice. Strain the liquid into another saucepan and reserve the fennel. Bring the liquid back to the boil with the cream, then remove from the heat.

For the scallops, place a tablespoon of sliced, cooked fennel in the centre of the clean scallop shell and top with a scallop cut into 3 slices. Pour over 2 spoonsful of the sauce and season the scallops with a pinch of Maldon sea salt and some seaweed powder. Place the other half of the shell on top and seal around the edges with tinfoil. Place on the barbecue for 15 minutes, or alternatively in an oven at 190°C.

To serve, unwrap the shells from the foil and arrange on the plate. Garnish with fresh herbs, smoked trout roe and a few drops of fennel oil.

ALAN BARRINS

" The New Horizon Youth Centre has kept over 2000 young people off the streets. I'm sharing Corrigan's signature grouse pie to shout about their work and hope this ChariTable Bookings recipe book is successful in promoting charities all across the UK."

GROUSE PIE

SERVES 2 | PREPARATION TIME 1 HOUR 30 MINUTES | COOKING TIME 3 HOURS

For the Filling
- 2 grouse
- 50g butter
- 200g button mushrooms, washed
- 8 shallots, peeled and chopped
- 2 cloves of garlic, peeled and chopped
- 100ml Madeira
- 250ml veal stock
- 100ml olive oil
- 25g carrots, chopped
- 25g celery, chopped
- 25g shallots, chopped
- 25g leek, chopped
- 150g foie gras
- salt and pepper
- 6 savoy cabbage leaves, blanched and stalks removed
- 3 egg yolks, beaten

For the Pastry
- 250g strong flour
- 125g back fat, minced
- 20ml ice water
- 1 tsp cracked black pepper

To Serve
- pickled red cabbage

To prepare the filling, remove the legs and breast of the grouse from the bone, also reserve the livers and heart. Roast the bones and leave to one side. Seal the breast in a little butter for 1 minute on each side and place on a cooling tray to rest.

Caramelise the mushrooms in a large heavy pan, remove and chop until fine. Place the shallots and garlic in a pan and cook until soft. Combine with the chopped mushrooms and half the Madeira and cook until dry. Leave to cool. Chop the grouse bones, put in a pan with the chopped vegetables and a little oil, then caramelise. Add the remaining Madeira and cover with the stock. Cook for 1 hour, then pass through a fine sieve into a clean pan. Next, add the grouse legs and braise slowly for 1.5 hours, or until the leg meat is soft. Take the liver and heart from the grouse and chop; incorporate with the mushrooms. Heat a pan and cut the foie gras in half, colour on both sides. Season and remove from the pan; any fat left in the pan should be added to the mushrooms.

To make the pastry, combine everything together and wrap the pastry in cling film. Leave in the fridge for 1 hour.

Using a large square of cling film placed on a work surface, put a cabbage leaf in the middle, then the mushroom mixture on top, then the grouse breast, then a seasoned piece of foie gras. Add another grouse breast and a final layer of mushroom. Pull all 4 corners of the cling film together and tie. Leave in the fridge and repeat with the other grouse breasts. Roll out the pastry to 3mm thick and cover with egg yolk using a pastry brush, particularly the sides. Remove the cling film from one cabbage roll and place it in the centre, pull the pastry up and around to encase. Remove excess pastry. Do the same with the rest of the grouse.

To finish the dish and serve, reduce the braising liquid by half and add a knob of cold butter. Remove the thigh bone from the leg and warm in a little sauce. Place the pies in a hot oven at 230°C for 12 minutes. Put a spoonful of pickled red cabbage and place a leg on top. Cut the pies in half and place one on each plate. Spoon over the sauce and serve.

DANNI BARRY

Dementia is scarily becoming more and more prevalent. I'm pleased to be able to raise awareness of the Alzheimer's Society by donating Eipic's rack of lamb recipe to ChariTable Bookings' new recipe collection."

MOURNE BLACKFACE LAMB RACK with tender sprouting broccoli and lamb fat sauce

SERVES 4 | PREPARATION TIME 35 MINUTES | COOKING TIME 1 HOUR

Equipment
Thermomix
For the Lamb and Lamb Fat Sauce
1 x 8 bone lamb rack, untrimmed
150g lamb trim
1 onion, diced
1 carrot, diced
1 sprig of rosemary
4 cloves of garlic, finely diced
200ml white wine
500ml chicken stock
For the Broccoli Purée
4 dark green broccoli heads
75g butter, diced into even cubes
salt, to taste
To Serve
12 purple sprouting broccoli stems
rapeseed oil

Start by preheating an oven to 180°C. While it is coming up to temperature, remove most of the back fat from the lamb, cutting into even sized chunks. Place into a medium saucepan. Heat gently to render until it becomes liquid fat. French trim the rack by cutting between the bones and scraping them clean from any sinew or fat. Season and allow to sit at room temperature for 10 minutes. In a very hot, medium-sized frying pan, fry all the lamb trim until dark brown in colour. Pass off any excess fat and add the onion, carrot, rosemary and garlic, and cook until the vegetables begin to caramelise. Add the white wine and chicken stock and bring to the boil. Reduce the heat and simmer for 15 minutes. Pass through a sieve into another clean saucepan and reduce the liquid by two thirds over a high heat.

To make the broccoli purée, use a sharp knife to trim the florets from the stalk, and slice them as small as possible. Bring a large saucepan of salted water to the boil, add the chopped broccoli and cook for 2 minutes. Drain off the water and transfer the florets whilst hot into a food processor. Begin to blend on a low speed for 1–2 minutes, stopping to scrape down the sides if the food processor is struggling. Turn up to a higher speed and add the butter, 1–2 cubes at a time, at which point the mixture will begin to become smooth. When all the butter is added, leave to blitz for 1 minute, season and pass into a container.

To finish the dish, heat a medium frying pan and place your prepared lamb rack fat side down, cooking for 4 minutes until nice and golden. Turn over and cook for a further 4 minutes. Transfer to a roasting tray lined with tin foil and place into the preheated oven for 20 minutes. Remove from the oven, wrap in foil and allow to rest for 10 minutes. Pour any juices into your sauce for extra taste. While the meat rests, peel the sprouting broccoli stems and trim to a uniform size, cooking in a medium frying pan with rapeseed oil for 1 minute on each side. Season to taste. Carve the lamb rack and set aside while you plate the dish.

To serve, place 2 spoonfuls of broccoli purée onto each plate, then 2 cutlets of lamb onto the purée, laying one bone flat and the other sitting up. Place 3 pieces of the sprouting broccoli around the lamb and finish with the lamb fat sauce.

ALLISTER BARSBY

"Ty Hafan is a fantastic children's hospice in South Wales that looks after the needs of terminally ill children and their families. I'm proud to share The Grove's signature cod dish with ChariTable Bookings to raise awareness of the incredible work they do."

LINE-CAUGHT COD with black garlic, crosnes, samphire, brown shrimps, lemon verbena scented jus

SERVES 4 | PREPARATION TIME 30M (PLUS 5 HOURS TO MARINATE) | COOKING TIME 4 HOURS

For the Cod
650g cod loin, skinless
25g table salt
20ml olive oil
50g unsalted butter
lemon juice

For the Black Purée
200g black garlic
1 tsp balsamic vinegar
75ml Madeira
100ml water
10g butter

For the Verbena Jus
1 turkey leg, chopped into large dice
100ml vegetable oil
2 small onions, cut into rounds
1 head of garlic, halved
5 sprigs of thyme
5 sprigs of lemon verbena
500ml water
500ml chicken stock

For the Braised Crosnes
150g crosnes (Chinese/Japanese artichoke)
150ml water
150ml chicken stock
1 bay leaf
2 sprigs of thyme
25g butter
salt and pepper, to taste

To prepare the cod, sprinkle with salt, cover and refrigerate for 5 hours. Rinse well, pat dry and cut into 4 portions.

Preheat the oven to 185°C. Heat a non-stick pan until smoking. Add the oil, then the cod. Colour for 1 minute, add the butter and place into the oven for 3 minutes. Turn the fish and return for a further 2 minutes. Remove from the oven, squeeze over some lemon juice, baste and leave to rest for 2 minutes.

To make the black garlic purée, bring all of the ingredients to the boil, then simmer for 20 minutes. Blend until smooth, season and pass through a fine sieve.

For the lemon verbena jus, preheat the oven to 180°C. Roast the turkey leg in the oil for 40 minutes until golden. Remove from the oven and place in a pan, together with the onions and garlic. Add the thyme, three sprigs of lemon verbena and deglaze with the water and chicken stock. Bring to the boil and reduce to a simmer. Skim any scum and cook for 3 hours. Pass through a fine sieve and reduce. Add the remaining lemon verbena and set aside to infuse for 10 minutes.

To make the braised crosnes, bring all the ingredients to the boil, simmer for 20 minutes until tender, then allow to cool. To serve, drain the crosnes, then roast in a frying pan in a little butter.

To make the rosemary oil, heat the oil and rosemary to 80°C. Transfer to a blender and blend for 4 minutes. Pass through a muslin cloth and reserve.

To make the rosemary beurre noisette, melt the butter in a saucepan, then turn up the heat and cook to a nut brown colour. Add the rosemary and lemon juice. Set aside to infuse for 10 minutes. Pass through a fine sieve.

Warm the shrimps, hazelnuts and chives in a little of the beurre noisette and plate as pictured.

For the Rosemary Oil

100ml blended olive oil

10g rosemary

For the Rosemary Beurre Noisette

100g unsalted butter

20g rosemary

10ml lemon juice

For the Garnish

150g samphire

8 lemon segments

100g brown shrimps

50g hazelnuts, toasted and chopped

10g chives, chopped

8 sprigs of sea rosemary

RUSSELL BATEMAN

It means a lot to me to be able to support a charity like Hospitality Action that works so closely with people suffering in our industry. I hope you enjoy Colette's dish and thank you ChariTable Bookings for this great book supporting good food and great charities!"

JACOB'S LADDER OF BELTED GALLOWAY BEEF with foie gras, cabbage and mushroom raviolo

SERVES 4 | PREPARATION TIME 2 HOURS (PLUS 3 HOURS MARINATE) | COOKING TIME 10 HOURS

Equipment
sous vide and vacuum pack bags
dehydrator

For the Meat Brine
1l water
100g salt
10g pink salt
½ bunch of thyme
1 bay Leaf
1 Jacob's ladder

For the Red Wine Jus
1kg diced beef chuck steak
8 shallots, sliced
1 head of garlic
½ bunch of thyme
1 bay leaf
2 sprigs of rosemary
1 bottle port
2 bottles of red wine
2l chicken stock
2l veal stock

For the Foie Gras
1 lobe of foie gras
150ml apple vinegar

For the Hon Shimeji Mushrooms
100g Hon Shimeji mushrooms
beef fat
salt and pepper, to taste
splash of sherry vinegar
Savoy cabbage leaves

For the Mushroom Powder
1kg mixed wild mushrooms
shaved raw chestnut and raw Paris mushrooms

To prepare the brine, bring all of the ingredients to the boil and allow to cool before straining through a fine sieve. Pour onto your Jacob's ladder and leave to cure for 3 hours. Remove from the brine and dry on a cloth. Pan roast the Jacob's ladder to achieve good caramelisation all over. Blast chill and place in a vacuum pack bag with your red wine jus. Cook sous vide for 10 hours at 85°C. Once cooked, remove from the bag and remove the bones. Set aside somewhere warm until ready to serve.

To prepare the red wine jus, caramelise the beef chuck in a very hot pan until dark brown all over. Strain the fat and set the beef aside. Caramelise the shallots and garlic until well coloured, strain all fat and return to the pan with the beef. Add the herbs and port, reduce to a glaze. Add the red wine and bring to the boil, reduce by half. Add the stocks and simmer for 1 hour – until the beef chuck is completely tender. Strain through a fine sieve and reduce to 1 litre.

To prepare the foie gras, place the lobe into a vacuum packed bag with the apple vinegar. Leave to marinate in the fridge for 2 hours. After 2 hours, remove from the fridge and the bag. Drain off the vinegar and pat dry. Heat a long, sharp knife up and cut 4mm thick slices, set aside on parchment paper.

To prepare the mushrooms, pan fry them in the beef fat and season with salt and pepper. Once cooked, deglaze the pan with sherry vinegar.

To blanch the savoy cabbage leaves, remove them carefully one at a time being careful not to tear or damage them. Blanch the leaves in boiling, salted water and glaze with melted butter.

To make the mushroom powder, thinly slice the mixed wild mushrooms and place in a dehydrator at 57°C for 6 hours. Remove, cool to room temperature and blend in a food processor to a powder.

To serve, reduce the sauce to a glazing consistency and finish with a little sherry vinegar. Place the piece of Jacob's ladder on a small stainless tray, top with the mushrooms, chestnut and sliced Paris mushrooms. Cover with a slice of foie gras and lightly warm under the grill. Season with a little Maldon salt and pepper. Place onto a large bowl style plate and, in the middle, pour a little of the red wine beef sauce over the beef and foie gras. Cover with the hot cabbage leaf and dust with mushroom powder.

ROBERT BATES

The chef brigade at the The Belfry Hotel and Resort always goes the extra mile to look after their guests and provide a truly memorable dining experience. That is why we have chosen to support Cancer Research UK through ChariTable Bookings who work tirelessly to find cures for cancer."

CLASSIC CHATEAUBRIAND with chunky chips and sauce béarnaise

SERVES 4 | PREPARATION TIME 30 MINUTES | COOKING TIME 1 HOUR

For the Chateaubriand with Chips
2 x 650g beef Chateaubriand, 28-day aged
360g chunky chips
4 Portobello mushrooms
100g Chanterelle mushrooms, optional
100g vine cherry tomatoes

For the Herb Reduction
5g shallots
20g tarragon
5g chervil
60ml white wine vinegar
8 white peppercorns

For the Vegetables
100g broccoli
60g asparagus
120g carrots
20g unsalted butter
Maldon sea salt

For the Sauce Béarnaise
250g unsalted, clarified butter, warmed
4 egg yolks
10ml white wine vinegar
40ml white wine
¼ lemon, juiced
1 pinch of salt

To prepare the Chateaubriand, season the fillet and place in a hot pan with a splash of very hot oil. Turn every minute until fully sealed and golden brown on the outside. Place in the oven and cook on 190°C for 17 minutes. Remove from the oven and from the hot pan, allowing it to rest for at least 10 minutes.

Blanch and cook all vegetables and potatoes, ensuring all are well seasoned.

To make the herb reduction, put the peppercorns in a muslin to infuse only. Place all the chopped ingredients in a saucepan and reduce until all the moisture has evaporated.

To make the sauce béarnaise, place everything except the butter in a metal bowl over hot water. Whisk continuously until thick and creamy. Do not let it get too hot or the eggs will scramble. Add the warm clarified butter slowly, constantly whisking. Correct seasoning, add the herb reduction, keep warm and serve as pictured.

ALESSANDRO BAY

" Please help Diciannove support the important work of Cancer Research UK, one of the thousands of charities supported by ChariTable Bookings."

BEEF AND PORK RAGU TAGLIATELLE

SERVES 10 | PREPARATION TIME 15 MINUTES | COOKING TIME 3 HOURS 30 MINUTES

For the Dish

1kg beef mince
1kg pork mince
300g mixed cured meat
drizzle of olive oil
1 stick of celery, finely chopped
2 carrots, finely chopped
1 large white onion, finely chopped
red wine, to cover
2 tbsp tomato purée
1 tin tomato sauce
1 bouquet garni (rosemary, thyme, bay leaves)

To Serve

tagliatelle

To prepare the ragu, heat the olive oil in a large pan, add all the finely chopped vegetables and cook on a very low heat in order to sweat them. In another large sauté pan, heat the olive oil and start to cook the minced meat in small batches until golden brown, in order to eliminate all the water. Once the meat is ready, add to the vegetables until all the meat is done. Add the red wine to cover and let it evaporate completely. Once the wine is completely gone, add the tomato paste, and let it cook for a few minutes. Add the tomato sauce and some water, bring to the boil and once the sauce has reached boiling point, immediately turn down the heat to a very gentle simmer. Add a bouquet garni and let it cook for at least 2–3 hours making sure it doesn't stick to the bottom. After that time the ragu is ready.

Serve on fresh tagliatelle.

MARCUS BEAN

Teens Unite is a fantastic charity set up to support teenagers undergoing cancer treatment. I'm glad to be able to support them in this recipe collection by ChariTable Bookings and share The Brompton Cookery School's chicken supreme with you."

CHICKEN SUPREMES in lovage butter en papillote

SERVES 4 | PREPARATION TIME 20 MINUTES | COOKING TIME 30 MINUTES

For the Potatoes
20 baby new potatoes

For the Chicken Supremes
4 chicken supremes, skin on
3 tbsp olive oil

For the Herb Butter
125g salted butter, softened
3 tbsp chopped lovage or watercress
1 tsp chopped tarragon leaves
2 cloves of garlic, crushed

For the Papillote
120g samphire grass
60g podded peas
2 courgettes, roughly diced
2 large vine tomatoes, chopped,
including seeds

To Finish
55g chorizo, finely sliced
sea salt and freshly ground black
pepper, to taste

Preheat the oven to 180°C.

To cook the potatoes, place them in a saucepan of water, cover and bring to the boil over a high heat. Turn the heat down to medium and cook for 10 minutes until tender, then drain and leave to one side.

To prepare the chicken, season with salt and pepper. Heat 1 tablespoon of oil in a frying pan over a medium heat, add the chicken and fry for a few minutes until just coloured on all sides. Remove from the heat.

To make the herb butter, combine the lovage, tarragon and garlic with the butter and set aside.

To cook the chicken, put 4 large sheets of baking paper on the work surface. Divide the samphire, peas, courgettes and tomatoes between the papers. Top each pile with a tablespoon of the herb butter. Put a chicken supreme on top of the vegetables and a teaspoon of butter on top. Season with a little salt and pepper. Bring the edges of the baking paper up over the ingredients of the first parcel and fold and scrunch the edges together to seal. Repeat to form 3 more parcels and put them in a roasting tin. Bake the parcels for 15–20 minutes, then carefully open one to check that the juices run clear when the thickest part of the chicken is pierced with the tip of a sharp knife.

To finish, heat the remaining oil in a frying pan over a high heat. Add the chorizo and fry for a few minutes until browned, then add the potatoes and stir until heated through. Serve the chicken still in the paper so your guests can open their own parcel, with the potatoes and chorizo.

MATTHEW BEARDSHALL

" I am delighted to take part in this recipe book, and to share with you one of my favourite lamb dishes from Wild Garlic. What a fantastic way to support thousands of charities across the UK and to also replicate some of these great dishes."

RUMP OF COTSWOLD LAMB with marinated aubergine and persillade

SERVES 4 | PREPARATION TIME 20 MINUTES (PLUS OVERNIGHT TO MARINATE) | COOKING TIME 40 MINUTES

For the Lamb
4 x 250g lamb rumps
vegetable oil for frying

For the Marinated Aubergine
15g ginger, roughly chopped
3 cloves of garlic, roughly chopped
1 red chilli, roughly chopped
3 vine tomatoes, roughly chopped
60g honey
60ml red wine vinegar
1 sprig of rosemary
1 fresh bay leaf
1 sprig of thyme
1 aubergine
40ml extra virgin rapeseed oil, for frying

For the Persillade
½ bunch curly parsley
½ bunch wild garlic leaf
½ lemon, zested
1 shallot, finely diced
2 cloves of garlic, finely chopped

To Serve
purple sprouting broccoli
cavolo nero
kale
green beans

To make the marinated aubergine, place the ginger, garlic, chilli, tomatoes, honey, vinegar and herbs in a pan and bring to the boil, then pour into a deep metal dish. Cut the aubergine into wedges and colour the cut sides in a smoking hot pan with a good splash of oil. Transfer the charred aubergine into the warm marinade. Leave to cool and refrigerate overnight in a sealed container. This is best marinated overnight but can be used straight away.

To make the persillade, chop the parsley and wild garlic roughly, taking care not to bruise it; a sharp knife is a must. Simply mix all the ingredients together. It will keep for a few days in the fridge, but is best made and eaten fresh. Try mixing any leftovers with oil and utilise as a pesto.

To make the lamb rump, preheat the oven to 200°C. Seal the lamb rump in a hot pan with a touch of oil and colour all sides until golden brown. Transfer to the oven for 8 minutes, then leave to rest for a further 8 minutes.

To assemble the dish, roll each lamb rump in some of the persillade, then slice into 3. Gently warm the aubergine in the marinade over a low heat. Arrange on the plate as pictured. Finish with a spoonful of persillade and garnish with the chopped chilli, garlic and tomato from the marinade. Serve with seasonal vegetables.

ADAM BENNET

It's vitally important to recognise the achievements of local charities as well as large national giants. That's why The Cross has given a recipe in aid of St Catherine's Hospice and hope they raise a lot through the sale of ChariTable Bookings' fantastic recipe book."

COD with fresh white beans, chorizo, peppers and basil

SERVES 4 | PREPARATION TIME 30 MINUTES | COOKING TIME 1 HOUR 30 MINUTES

For the Cod
- 4 x 125g cod fillets
- 4 tsp Maldon salt

For the Beans
- 200g podded fresh coco beans
- 1l vegetable stock
- 2 sprigs of thyme
- 1 bay leaf
- 10 white peppercorns, cracked
- 2 cloves of garlic, cracked

For the Peppers
- 2 red bell peppers
- 2 yellow bell peppers
- 1 shallot, finely diced
- 1 clove garlic, finely diced
- 50ml olive oil

For the Garnish
- 50ml olive oil
- 50g chorizo, finely diced
- 125g unsalted butter
- 1 tsp lemon juice
- salt and espelette pepper, ground
- smoked paprika
- 1 pinch of saffron

To Serve
- basil oil
- 250g leaf spinach, washed
- 50g butter

To prepare the cod portions, coat each portion of cod lightly with Maldon salt. Refrigerate for 20 minutes and rinse in cold water; dry well and reserve in the fridge.

To cook the beans, bring to the boil in vegetable stock and reduce to a bare simmer. Skim the liquid, then add the other ingredients tied in a muslin bag. Cook until tender, which should take about 40 minutes. Remove from the heat, add a little salt and reserve.

For the peppers, brush with olive oil and grill to blister the skin; peel and dice the pepper flesh. Cook the shallot and garlic in the remaining olive oil until soft. Add the peppers and a pinch of salt, cook gently until they are soft and sweet. Reserve until needed.

To finish the beans, gently cook the chorizo in the olive oil for 3–4 minutes. Add 125ml of the reserved bean stock, the saffron, espelette and smoked paprika. Simmer for 3–4 more minutes. Whisk in the butter, then add the drained beans and heat through gently. Add salt if needed and a little lemon juice. Add the basil and the pepper mixture just before serving.

To cook the fish, brush with olive oil and cook in the oven at 80°C until the flakes separate when pressed but the fish is still moist. Next, brush with a little basil oil. Wilt the spinach in butter, season and drain.

To serve, place a little spinach at the centre of each plate. Spoon the beans around and place the fish on top.

ARNAUD BIGNON

The team at The Greenhouse are proud to be part of ChariTable Bookings modern way of giving back to good causes. We hope you enjoy our signature dish!"

VENISON with chestnut, quince, hispi cabbage and cranberry

SERVES 4 | PREPARATION TIME 48 HOURS | COOKING TIME 2 HOURS

For the Venison
- 4 x 130g venison saddle
- 1 pinch of salt
- 5g Malabar pepper, crushed
- 1 tbsp oil
- 25g butter

For the Hispi Cabbage
- 1 hispi cabbage
- 100ml chicken stock
- 25g butter
- orange zest

For the Venison Jus
- venison saddle bones and trimmings
- 1 tbsp oil
- 50g butter
- 1 shallot, chopped
- 1 sprig of thyme
- 500ml red wine
- 10g dark chocolate
- 1 tsp sherry vinegar

For the Cranberry Marmalade
- 100ml red wine
- 40g sugar
- 20g hibiscus flowers
- 3g Malabar pepper
- 200g fresh cranberries
- 10g butter

For the Chestnut Cromesqui
- 250g cooked chestnuts
- 20g butter

To make the cranberry marmalade, cook the wine with the sugar, hibiscus and the pepper for 2 minutes, leave it in the fridge for 1 night to infuse and pass it through a fine sieve. In a saucepan, melt the butter, add the cranberries and cook it quickly until the liquid has evaporated. Add the infused wine and finish cooking to obtain a marmalade, reserve and chill.

To make the venison jus, break all the bones from the saddle and chop the venison trimmings. Pan fry together in a large saucepan with some oil to colour. Add the butter, shallot and thyme and allow to sweat for 5 minutes. Remove the fat, deglaze with a little water and cook for an hour. To finish the jus, reduce 500ml of red wine until a thick syrup remains and add to the sauce along with the dark chocolate and sherry vinegar. Reduce until the mixture coats the back of a spoon.

To prepare the chestnut cromesqui, pan fry the chestnuts with butter and drain. Cook in a saucepan with the chicken stock, the cream and the wild anise for 5 minutes. Mix to obtain a paste and add the soft gelatine sheets. Pipe into half sphere, silicone moulds of 2.5cm and leave in the fridge until hardened. Remove from the mould, coat in flour, egg white and breadcrumbs twice and fry at 170°C. Rest and keep warm.

To prepare the quince, warm the water with the sugar, pepper and saffron. Add the peeled, quartered quince and cook until they become soft and tender. Allow to rest and chill. Pan fry the quarters once chilled with oil to colour and dust with smoked pimentón de la vera.

To prepare the hispi cabbage, remove all the green leaves and blanch for 2 minutes in salted boiling water. Allow to cool and dry. Fold each leaf one by one to obtain a nice rectangle. Warm in some chicken stock and butter. Grate some orange zest on top once plated.

To prepare the venison, season the fillets with salt and Malabar pepper and pan fry in oil and butter until cooked medium rare. Cut into 2 pieces and assemble the rest of the dish as pictured.

For the Chestnut Cromesqui *continued*
- 200ml chicken stock
- 50ml cream
- 5g wild anise
- 3 gelatine sheets, soaked in cold water
- flour, egg white and breadcrumbs, to pane

For the Quince
- 1 quince, peeled and quartered
- 1l water
- 100g sugar
- 1g saffron
- 2g Malabar pepper
- 1 tbsp olive oil
- 3g smoked pimentón de la vera

ANDREW BIRCH

" I thought a fish recipe from Fishmore Hall was appropriate! It is often underestimated how much suffering donkeys go through across the world and I'm pleased that ChariTable Bookings can help me raise awareness and hopefully funds for the Donkey Sanctuary's vital work."

GIGHA FARMED HALIBUT with bacon, onion, mushrooms and mustard sauce

SERVES 4 | PREPARATION TIME 15 MINUTES | COOKING TIME 1 HOUR 30 MINUTES

For the Halibut
4 x 175g halibut fillets
25g flour
salt and pepper
lemon juice

For the Mustard Sauce
100ml white wine
100ml chicken stock
100ml veal stock
500ml whipping cream
10g Dijon mustard
20g English mustard

For the Braised Onions
8 baby onions, peeled
1 sprig of thyme
50ml chicken stock
50ml veal stock

For the Chive Oil
100g chives
200ml rapeseed oil

To Serve
50g smoked belly bacon lardons
80g trompet mushrooms
100g spinach, picked
30g chives, chopped

To prepare the chive oil, blend the chives and the oil together, pass through a fine sieve and set aside ready for use.

To make the mustard sauce, reduce the white wine, chicken stock and veal stock to half. Add the cream and bring to the boil while whisking in the mustards.

To make the braised onions, place the onions and thyme in a pan and cover with the stocks and a cartouche. Place in a preheated oven at 180°C for 10 minutes, until the onions are tender and coated in the reduced stock.

To prepare the halibut, lightly flour and season the halibut and cook in a medium-hot frying pan and colour for 2–3 minutes until golden. Turn the fish and remove the pan from the heat to allow the residual heat from the pan to finish cooking the meat. When the halibut is cooked, season with fresh lemon juice and place on a clean tea towel to rest.

To prepare the garnishes, roast the bacon in a non-stick frying pan over a medium heat and colour, add the mushrooms followed by the spinach and allow to wilt. Season to taste.

To serve, put the garnish in the middle of the plate, and gently place the halibut on top. Sprinkle the chives onto the halibut, spoon over the mustard sauce and drizzle the chive oil around.

DANIEL BIRK

Social Eating House is proud to support the extensive work that Leuka puts into vital research by offering their signature dish recipe to ChariTable Bookings' latest initiative. Enjoy!"

LAMB NECK FILLETS

SERVES 6–8 | PREPARATION TIME 2 HOURS (PLUS 24 HOURS FOR HANGING) | COOKING TIME 1 HOUR 30 MINUTES (PLUS 6 HOURS SOUS VIDE FOR LAMB)

Equipment
sous vide
vacuum pack bags
muslin cloth
Josper
silpat

For the Cardamom Yoghurt
200g cardamom pods
5l natural yoghurt
½ bunch of mint, chopped

For the Lamb Sauce
10kg lamb bones, chopped and roasted
50g butter
1 onion, finely chopped
2 sticks celery, finely chopped
2 carrots, finely chopped
1 head garlic, peeled and roughly chopped
1 leek
2l each chicken stock
2l veal stock
4 bay leaves
2 sprigs of thyme
white peppercorns, crushed
1 bunch of rosemary
4 tbsp tomato paste
750ml white wine
rock salt, to taste

To make the cardamom yoghurt, toast the pods on a high heat in a little vegetable oil and blitz. Mix the powder with the yoghurt and a half bunch of chopped mint. Hang the mixture in muslin cloth and lightly press for 24 hours.

To make the lamb sauce, begin by roasting the lamb bones on a high heat until well coloured. Heat the butter in a large pan and sweat the vegetables until without colour. Add the bones and let the mixture sweat for 5–10 minutes. Add in the chicken and veal stock, along with the aromatics, and reduce by half. Add the tomato paste and simmer for 10 minutes, skimming regularly. Deglaze with the white wine and reduce the mixture by half again. Once the liquid has reached a nice consistency, strain the entire contents of the pan into another and reduce by a quarter until thickened. Season to taste and set aside.

While the lamb sauce reduces, trim the lamb and fry in foaming butter until well coloured. Remove, chill and allow to rest for 5 minutes. Place the lamb neck into a vacuum bag with infused duck fat and the rosemary. Seal tight and cook at 78°C for 5–6 hours until tender.

While the lamb cooks, prepare the falafel. Blitz the soaked lentils into a paste and gradually add all of the remaining ingredients. Blitz on a high speed, using a little of the soaking water for the lentils to loosen as needed. Remove from the blender and form into patties. Fry on a high heat in vegetable oil until browned and coloured. Set to one side.

To make the miso caramel glaze, start by making a light caramel with the water and sugar, then add in the miso paste and boil. Reduce a little lamb jus to a glaze and mix with the miso caramel. Set to one side until needed.

To make the miso butterscotch, spread the miso onto a silpat in an even layer. Roast in the oven at 180°C until golden brown and slightly burnt at the edges. Place the miso, sugar and vinegar into a blender and slowly add the butter whilst blending. Pass the liquid and chill.

For the Lamb Neck Fillets

6 lamb neck fillets
100g butter
infused duck fat
1 sprig of rosemary

For the Lentil Falafel

1kg lentils or split peas, covered in
cold water and soaked overnight
5 cloves of garlic, crushed
1 leek, finely chopped
2 onions, finely chopped
2 tsp bicarbonate of soda
6 tbsp coriander, chopped
6 tbsp parsley, chopped
5 tsp cumin seeds
5 tsp coriander seeds
2 pinches of cayenne pepper
salt and black pepper, to taste

For the Miso Caramel Glaze

200ml water
100g sugar
50g light miso paste
100ml reduced lamb jus

For the Miso Butterscotch

600g light miso paste
280g brown sugar
300g rice vinegar
350g melted butter

For the Roast Aubergine Purée

4 large aubergine, cut into strips
200g miso butterscotch

For the Garnish

peashoots

Roast the aubergines well in a high heat oven until nearly burnt. Leave to cool and drain all excess liquid. Then, once chilled, finish the aubergines in the Josper until well coloured. Blitz until smooth, season and pass. To finish, mix the aubergine purée with the miso butterscotch and allow to set in muffin tins.

To serve, heat all the ingredients. Drain the lamb neck fillets and pat dry with kitchen towel. Fry in foaming butter to colour and heat, and brush with a little reduced lamb jus to glaze. Plate the dish as pictured, starting with a reserved slice of roasted aubergine or courgette, a dollop of cardamom yoghurt, the miso butterscotch and lentil falafel. Finish with the lamb, brushing with lamb jus and miso caramel glaze and a handful of peashoots.

Editor's Note: The quantities for the lamb sauce and lentil falafel elements of the dish are for restaurant service. You can adjust them to suit the number of people you intend to serve.

RAYMOND BLANC

I cannot offer enough support to SeeSaw, a local Oxfordshire charity that offers grief support to children and young people. I very pleased to share Brasserie Blanc's signature pheasant dish with you through ChariTable Bookings and promote SeeSaw at the same time."

ROAST PHEASANT and winter vegetables

SERVES 4 | PREPARATION TIME 20 MINUTES | COOKING TIME 1 HOUR

For the Roast Pheasant
- 2 x 800g hen pheasants
- 50g butter
- 50ml vegetable oil
- 2 tsp game seasoning
- 100ml red wine
- 100ml port
- 2 sprigs of thyme

For the Game Seasoning
- 100g coarse sea salt
- ½ tbsp coarse ground black peppercorns
- 1 tsp juniper berries
- 2 star anise
- 5g stick of cinnamon
- 2 dried bay leafs
- 5g garlic, freshly peeled

To Serve
- roasted winter vegetables

To make the game seasoning, blend all the ingredients in a food processor for around 2 minutes. Transfer the blended mixture to a sterilised container with a lid, and allow to rest and infuse while preparing the pheasant.

To make the roast pheasants, begin by preheating an oven to 190°C. In a heavy-bottomed frying pan over a low heat, very gently brown the birds all over in foaming butter and oil, for approximately 5 minutes or until golden brown. Sprinkle the birds with game seasoning and place them in a roasting tin. Transfer to the oven and cook for 30 minutes, routinely checking and turning halfway through. Once cooked, cover and set aside in a warm place to rest. Meanwhile, strain the excess fat from the roasting tin and add the wine, port and fresh thyme. Reduce over a high heat, until you have two thirds of the original volume, making sure to scrape the flavour from the bottom of the pan. Season to taste if necessary and strain into a warmed jug.

To serve, carve the meat from the birds, pour over the jus and plate with roasted winter vegetables.

Editor's Note: At the Brasserie Blanc, this dish is often served with potato rosti, pumpkin and blackcurrant sauce, as pictured here.

JEFF BLAND

Every small act of kindness can lead to change... Number One at Balmoral Hotel are delighted to partner with ChariTable Bookings to support Children 1st, Scotland's national children's charity."

HAGGIS, NEEPS AND TATTIES

SERVES 4 | PREPARATION TIME 30 MINUTES | COOKING TIME 1 HOUR

For the Dish

400g haggis – purchased from a good quality butcher
4 red rooster baking potatoes
50ml double cream
50g butter
1 turnip
80ml port
200ml red wine
50g sugar
3 cloves of garlic
1 sprig of thyme
salt, to taste
8 shallots
500ml brown chicken stock
200ml cream
10ml whisky

To make the haggis, follow the butcher's instructions and boil for an appropriate length of time based on size.

Clean and scrub the potatoes and bake whole in the skins in the oven at 180°C until cooked through. Remove from the oven and scoop out the flesh. Pass the flesh through a fine sieve or potato ricer. Mix in the cream and butter until you achieve a creamy consistency.

For the turnip, peel, dice and boil in salted water until soft. Pass through a fine sieve or potato ricer.

Make a stock from the port, red wine, sugar, garlic, thyme and salt. Simmer in a pan together with the shallots until tender. Remove the tough outside layer of the shallot when cooked.

Make a whisky sauce with the brown chicken stock and cream before adding the whisky at the end to taste.

To build the final dish, use a stainless steel cooking ring. Layer the haggis, turnip and potatoes evenly in the ring. Serve or set aside and reheat in a medium oven until warm.

Serve the layered haggis dish with a dash of the stock, 2 shallots and the whisky sauce.

HESTON BLUMENTHAL OBE

Adopt a School is so important, without it, the next generation will really suffer. I'm very proud to support their work by sharing my recipe for Triple Cooked Chips and Steak with you."

TRIPLE COOKED CHIPS AND STEAK

SERVES 2 | PREPARATION TIME 20 MINUTES (PLUS 2 HOURS TO FREEZE THE CHIPS) | COOKING TIME 1 HOUR

For the Triple Cooked Chips

1kg Maris Piper potatoes, peeled and cut into chips

groundnut or grapeseed oil, for deep-frying

For the Steaks

olive oil, for frying

2 x 400g sirloin steaks

3 cloves of garlic, peeled and bashed with the flat part of a knife

4–6 sprigs of rosemary

2 strips of lemon zest, pared using a vegetable peeler

1 lemon, juiced

60g rocket leaves

40g Parmesan cheese, shaved

sea salt and freshly ground black pepper, to season

First make the chips, they need to be prepared a couple of hours in advance. Put them in a bowl under running water for 5 minutes to wash off the starch. Drain, then put 2l cold tap water in a saucepan and add the chips. Place over a medium heat and simmer until the chips are nearly falling apart, about 20–30 minutes, depending on the type of potato. Gently remove with a slotted spoon and place on a cooling rack to dry out. Once cool, place the rack in the freezer for at least 1 hour to remove even more moisture. Heat a deep-fat fryer, or a deep pan no more than half-filled with oil to a depth of around 10cm, to 130°C. Fry the chips in small batches until a light crust forms, which will take approximately 5 minutes, then remove from the oil and drain on kitchen paper. Put the chips on a cooling rack and place in the freezer for a minimum of 1 hour. If you don't want to cook and serve the chips immediately, they can now be kept in the fridge for 3 days.

Place a heavy-bottomed frying pan over a high heat. Add a thin layer of olive oil and heat until the oil is smoking hot. Season the steaks with a little salt and carefully place them in the hot pan for 15–20 seconds, then flip them over and fry for a further 15–20 seconds. Repeat this process, turning the steaks every 15–20 seconds, for 2–3 minutes. Remove the steaks from the pan and place on a wire rack, set over a plate to catch the juices, so they can rest for 5 minutes. Heat the oil in the deep-fat fryer or deep pan to 180°C and fry the chips for about 7 minutes, until golden. Drain and sprinkle with salt.

Meanwhile, take the pan off the heat and discard most of the oil but don't clean the pan. Let the pan cool for a few minutes, then pour in 120ml olive oil and add the garlic and rosemary sprigs. Rub the strips of lemon zest between your finger and thumb to release the oils, then put them in the pan as well. Let the mixture infuse for 5 minutes while the meat is resting, then squeeze in the lemon juice. Strain this dressing through a sieve and add whatever juices have come from the steak.

Slice the steaks into 5mm strips with a sharp knife. Season and lay on a serving dish. Spoon over half the dressing. Mix the rocket leaves with the rest of the dressing and place on top of the beef strips. Sprinkle with the Parmesan shavings and some sea salt.

TOMMY BOLAND

Contact the Elderly is the only charity tackling loneliness in older people by organising monthly tea parties across the country. As a chef, I'm fully aware of food bringing people together and donate my chop and cheek of pork recipe from Bird of Smithfield to ChariTable Bookings to raise further awareness of this great charity."

PORK CHOP AND CHEEK with creamed potato, glazed onion, roasted carrots, pancetta and roasting juices

SERVES 4 | PREPARATION TIME 30 MINUTES | COOKING TIME 2 HOURS

Equipment
Moulinex Mouli

For the Creamed Potato
300g Maris Piper potatoes, washed
coarse sea salt
70g butter
70ml milk
salt and pepper

For the Glazed Carrots
20 Chantenay carrots, topped
1 tbsp vegetable oil
25g butter
1 pinch of salt
250ml chicken stock

For the Button Onions
16 button onions, peeled
1 tbsp vegetable oil
25g butter
½ tsp salt
1 tsp sugar
250ml chicken stock

For the Brussel Sprouts
16 Brussel sprouts
½ tsp salt

For the Pancetta
100g pancetta, finely cubed

For the Pig Cheeks and Chops
4 large pigs cheeks, trimmed
4 pork chops
50g flour

To make the creamed potato, bake the washed potatoes on coarse salt in the oven until cooked. Remove from the oven and, whilst still hot, scoop out the flesh into a Mouli bowl. Pass through the Mouli with the butter. Lightly warm the milk on the stove and slowly beat it into the potato mix over a medium heat. Season to taste and pass through a sieve.

To make the glazed carrots, top and clean the Chantenays and, in a large pan, heat the vegetable oil and butter until it starts to foam. Add the carrots and gently sauté for a few minutes with salt. Add the chicken stock and cover with a cartouche. Gently simmer until the carrots are just cooked and the stock is a buttery, glazing consistency.

Sauté the button onions in vegetable oil and foamed butter. After a few minutes, add the salt and sugar, and allow the onions to caramelise. Add the chicken stock and cover with a cartouche, simmering until just cooked.

To prepare the brussel sprouts, break them into separate leaves. In a hot pan add the leaves, salt, splash of water and sauté with the lid on until soft.

To prepare the pig cheeks and chops, flour and season the cheeks and caramelise on all sides in a pan of vegetable oil. When the cheeks are done, pop them in the fridge to cool. Using the same pan, add the carrots and turnips, and cook until they start to soften and caramelise. Add the button mushrooms and crushed garlic cloves, making sure to colour everything well. Add the onion to the pan and the apple. Deglaze the pan with the vinegar and cook until it begins to glaze the vegetables. Add the cider and reduce to half. Add the stocks, bring to the boil and add the cheeks. Transfer to the oven, cook at 150°C for 2 hours. Allow to cool, remove cheeks, strain stock and reduce to sauce consistency. Just before the pork cheeks are done, season and grill the pork chops, ready for serving.

To serve, fry the pancetta cubes until golden and crispy. Pipe the mash onto the plate, place the pig cheek, the crispy pancetta cubes, Brussel sprout leaves, glazed carrots and button onions on top. Finish with a little veal and chicken stock.

For the Pig Cheeks and Chops *continued*

vegetable oil

2 carrots, chopped

2 turnips, chopped

1 handful of button mushrooms

2 cloves of garlic, crushed

1 onion, chopped

1 Granny Smith apple, quartered

100ml cider vinegar

100ml cider

250ml veal stock

250ml chicken stock

1 splash of apple vinegar and dry sherry

salt and pepper

SIMON BOLSOVER

I hope that you find this recipe one to remember as there are many out there who sadly cannot. I am glad to be able to support the work of the Alzheimer's Society by sharing Wedgewood's pork belly recipe with ChariTable Bookings."

SLOW COOKED PORK BELLY with Scottish langoustine and cider pressed apples

SERVES 4 | PREPARATION 15 MINUTES (PLUS 24 HOURS TO MARINATE) | COOKING TIME 8 HOURS

For the Pork Belly
2.5kg pork belly, skin off

For the Rub
500g sea salt
400g sugar
20g smoked paprika
20g ground coriander
20g garlic powder
10g chilli flakes

For the Sweet Onions
500g onions, sliced
250g butter
10g fresh thyme
800ml veal stock
salt and pepper, to taste

For the Langoustines
12 Scottish langoustines, blanched and peeled

For the Cider Soaked Apple
2 Granny Smith apples, peeled and diced
1l quality cider

To prepare the pork belly, mix the ingredients for the rub together well and massage into the meat. Leave for a minimum of 24 hours to allow the flavours to infuse.

To cook the sweet onions, fry in butter and thyme, cooking until the onions have colour. Add the stock and reduce until all the liquid has evaporated. Season to taste.

For the pork belly, lightly wash off the rub and roll it tightly with the sweet onions inside, securing with butchers string. Braise for 7 hours at 90°C. Once cooked, re-roll into cylinders with cling film and refrigerate. Make sure to set aside all excess cooking liquor so it can be passed through a fine chinois for the garnish.

To make the cider soaked apple, cut the apple into medium sized cubes and soak in the cider until fully infused.

To serve, quickly blanch and peel the langoustines until they're just cooked. Dress the plate as shown, with a slice of pork, the jellified cooking juices, seared langoustines and cider soaked apple.

FRANK BORDONI

"What a great idea to promote charity through this ChariTable Bookings recipe collection. Very happy to share my soft shell crab sliders with you for this worthy initiative!"

CRISPY SOFT SHELL CRAB SLIDERS

SERVES 4 | PREPARATION TIME 45 MINUTES | COOKING TIME 20 MINUTES

For the Crab
4 large fresh soft-shell crabs
½ tsp salt
½ tsp cracked black pepper
2 limes, juiced
100ml sriracha sauce
4 brioche burger buns, halved
4 leaves of baby gem lettuce, washed and picked

For the Guacamole
2 large avocados, peeled and stoned
1 green chilli, deseeded and finely chopped
1 small red onion, finely diced
50g coriander leaves, picked and finely chopped
20ml lime juice
salt and pepper to taste

For the Tempura Batter
125g all-purpose flour
8g baking powder
340ml sparkling water
1 tsp cayenne pepper
½ tsp salt

To prepare the crab, remove the lungs and tail, and arrange the crab on a large platter. If using frozen crab, this will have already been done for you. Sprinkle with seasoning, pour over the lime juice over and let marinate for at least 30 minutes, refrigerated. When ready to cook, season lightly with salt.

For the batter, sift together the flour and baking powder. Whisk in the water until the batter is smooth, then add the remaining ingredients, seasoning with cayenne and salt to taste.

Heat the fryer to 180°C. Dip each crab into the batter and coat well. Carefully place the crab into the hot oil and fry for about 2 minutes until golden brown. Remove with a slotted spoon and drain on paper or clean towelling.

For the guacamole, mash the avocado with a fork and mix in the chilli, onion, coriander, lime and seasoning.

To assemble, lightly toast the brioche buns. Place a lettuce leaf on the base of each bun and divide the guacamole evenly on top. Place a tempura crab on each and a dollop of hot sriracha sauce. Cover with the top of the bun and secure with a skewer, and serve immediately. Enjoy it on its own or with sweet potato fries, and an apple and fennel coleslaw.

NEIL BORTHWICK

Delighted to have the opportunity to support London's Air Ambulance by sharing Merchants Tavern's signature Quail dish with ChariTable Bookings."

ROAST QUAIL with hazelnut pesto, remoulade and foie gras

SERVES 4 | PREPARATION TIME 1 HOUR | COOKING TIME 1 HOUR

Equipment
mandoline

For the Dish
2 jumbo quail, legs removed
100g foie gras
200g duck fat
20g rock salt
1 clove of garlic, 2 sprigs of thyme
and 1 sprig of rosemary, chopped

For the Celeriac Remoulade
6 egg yolks
45g Dijon mustard
2 tsp wholegrain mustard
15ml white wine vinegar
½ lemon, juiced
12g salt
600ml grapeseed oil
¼ celeriac, peeled

For the Treviso Chutney
2 Treviso radicchio, cut into julienne,
reserve a few leaves to garnish
20g golden raisins
100ml port
200ml red wine
1 red onion, peeled and finely sliced
50ml red wine vinegar

For the Hazelnut Pesto
50g each hazelnut oil, Parmesan and
toasted hazelnuts
100g grapeseed oil
3g salt

To prepare the quail, mix the salt with the aromatics and cover the legs well with the mixture. Allow them to sit for 30 minutes. Towards the end of the half hour, heat the duck fat to 80°C in a pan. Once rested, remove the legs from the salt, knocking off any excess and drop into the duck fat. Allow to cook for another 30 minutes, checking the tenderness by popping out the thigh bone. If the bone is removed easily, they are done. Remove all the thigh bones from the quail and set aside on a tray to cool.

To make the celeriac remoulade, whisk the yolks with the mustard, vinegar, lemon juice and salt. Add the oil in a thin, steady stream, whisking vigorously to emulsify, and refrigerate until required. Pass the celeriac over a mandoline to create thin strips and cut into julienne. Lightly season and allow to rest for 10 minutes to soften. After rested, squeeze the strips to remove a little excess water. Add enough of the mayonnaise to bind the celeriac and add the wholegrain mustard to taste. Refrigerate for serving.

To make the Treviso chutney, place all of the ingredients in a pan and cook until completely soft and thick in consistency.

To prepare the hazelnut pesto, combine all of the ingredients in a food processor and blend to desired consistency.

To finish cooking and assemble the dish, colour the quail evenly in a non-stick pan until golden, and roast in an oven at 180°C until soft and springy to the touch at the fattest part. Allow to rest for 15 minutes. In the meantime, dress the treviso leaves in the pesto and divide between four plates with a spoonful of both the remoulade and the chutney. Remove the breasts from the crowns and season lightly. Pan fry the foie gras with the legs and finally, add the breasts skin-side down and cook until golden. Continually turn the breasts and cook until just pink.

Drain the meat carefully on a wire rack and divide between the 4 plates, serving immediately.

CLAUDE BOSI

"I'm very excited to be taking over the kitchen at the legendary Bibendum. Equally excited to be part of this ChariTable Bookings collection in aid of charities across the UK and worldwide."

CORNISH COD À LA GRENOBLOISE

SERVES 4 | PREPARATION TIME 15 MINUTES | COOKING TIME 30 MINUTES

Equipment
steamer

For the Grenobloise sauce
250 butter
½ lemon, juiced
750g milk
150g bread trims
salt, to taste

For the Dish
500g ratte potatoes, crushed
100g butter, to be browned for beurre noisette
1 tsp capers
1 tsp croutons
lemon zest, to garnish
1 dash of sherry vinegar
4 x 100g fillets of cod
salt, to season

First make the beurre noisette by browning the butter in a pan, whisking occasionally until the butter resembles a nut brown colour. Add the lemon juice and leave to cool slightly. Toast off your bread trim and gently warm the milk. Add the trims and infuse for 5 minutes. Pass through a sieve and add to the brown butter. Season and foam the sauce with a hand blender.

Cook the potatoes in salted water. Peel and lightly crush with a fork. Season with salt and sherry vinegar. Add the capers and croutons on top.

To finish, season the fish and steam. Place the potatoes in the centre of the plate, spoon the fish on top and sprinkle with the lemon zest and lemon segments. Pour over the foamed butter sauce and serve.

ALEXANDER BOYD

I'm proud to support the Chelsea Children's Hospital Charity by sharing St Ermin's Hotel recipe with you and ChariTable Bookings."

DUCK, CHARD AND STAR ANISE

SERVES 4 | PREPARATION TIME 30 MINUTES | COOKING TIME 20 MINUTES

For the Duck
4 duck breasts, fat trimmed
30g honey

For the Onion Squash Purée
20g butter
30g onion, finely diced
5g garlic, finely chopped
1 sprig of thyme
300g onion squash, peeled and diced
200ml whole milk

For the Chard
4 leaves of rainbow chard, stalks removed and reserved
10ml olive oil
5g butter

To Serve
6 baby heritage carrots, blanched and halved
4 star anise
100ml duck jus

To make the duck, season the duck breast and place in a dry frying pan over a medium heat skin-side down to crisp the skin. Turn over, and briefly sear the flesh side. Remove from the pan, brush with honey and place in an oven at 180°C for 5 minutes. Allow to rest before cutting.

To make the onion squash purée, melt the butter in a pot on a low heat, add the onion and cook gently until they become translucent. Add the garlic and cook gently for 3 minutes. Add the thyme and the onion squash and cook for a further 5 minutes, then add the milk. Bring to the boil and simmer gently until the squash is cooked, drain but keep the milk. Blend the squash until smooth, adding enough milk to get the right consistency. Season to taste.

To make the chard, cut the stalks into small pieces, then in a pan, heat the olive oil and quickly sauté the stalks with just a little salt until they are just cooked. Blanch the leaves in boiling, salted water for a few seconds, then add to the stalks and finish with butter.

To finish the dish and serve, warm the jus with the star anise inside so it can infuse. Spread the purée on the base of the plate, cut the duck into 3 pieces and arrange everything on the plate nicely. Finish with the jus over the duck.

MICHAEL BREMNER

" 64 Degrees is a local restaurant in Brighton and it's important to me to support local charities like the Rockinghorse Foundation. A great initiative of ChariTable Bookings to combine food and charity!"

BLACK BREAM CEVICHE

SERVES 5 | PREPARATION TIME 15 MINUTES

For the Ceviche
  250g fresh black bream fillets
  1 stick celery, keep celery leaves for garnish
  ½ red chilli
  ½cm piece of ginger
  100ml water
  1 lime, juiced
  salt to taste

For the Garnish
  celery, diced
  red chilli, diced
  celery leaves

Make a very fine dice with a small amount of the celery and chilli and set aside to use as garnish for the ceviche.

To make the ceviche, blitz the remaining celery, chilli and ginger with the water before passing through a fine sieve, then add the lime juice. Dice the bream into 1cm pieces and add to the ceviche mix. Season to taste with a little salt.

To serve, portion into 5 bowls. Garnish with the finely diced celery and chilli, as well as the celery leaves.

Editor's Note: *How long you leave your fish to 'cook'/cure in citrus juices is really something of a personal preference. Anything from 3 hours to a few minutes, or even just as long as it takes to combine the ingredients. It's said that in Peru it originally had a longer curing time but due to the influence of Japanese migrants and the development of Nikkei (Peruvian-Japanese) cuisine, the marinating time shortened considerably. You will see the flesh become more and more opaque the longer you leave it. Too long and the texture can become chalky. White fish with firm flesh tend to be favoured but the most important thing is that it is extremely fresh.*

HENRY BROSI

Children's Liver Disease Foundation is a unique national charity looking after children suffering from liver disease and supporting their families. It is such a specialist area that I am proud to support it through ChariTable Bookings and share The Dorchester's White Onion Risotto with you."

WHITE ONION RISOTTO with white chocolate, scallops and white truffle

SERVES 4 | PREPARATION TIME 5 MINUTES | COOKING TIME 30 MINUTES

For the Scallops
- 8 scallops, cleaned and trimmed
- sea salt and pepper
- 1 drizzle of olive oil
- 1 splash of lemon juice

For the Onion Confit
- 2 large onions
- goose fat
- salt and pepper

For the Risotto
- 150g Arborio risotto rice
- extra virgin olive oil
- 100ml white wine
- 1l chicken stock
- sea salt and white pepper
- 10g white truffle
- 2 tablespoons mascarpone
- 100g Parmesan
- 1 lemon, juiced
- 50g white chocolate
- 25g butter

To Serve
- 10g white truffle

To prepare the onion confit, cook very thinly sliced onions with goose fat over a very low heat until the onions are soft. Season and strain the onions. Keep aside for further use.

To prepare the risotto, heat up a pan and add some of the olive oil. Fry the rice quickly without colouring and cook for a further one minute. Add the white wine to the rice and cook whilst stirring continuously. Cook until the liquid is absorbed. Add the stock 100ml at a time and keep stirring until the rice has cooked and is slightly al dente. Season to taste. Add half of the sliced truffle and then add the mascarpone cheese, Parmesan cheese, white onions, juice from the lemon and finally the white chocolate and melted butter.

To prepare the scallops, season then heat a non-stick frying pan and add a little olive oil. Fry the scallops until golden brown. Turn over and cook for a further minute. Add a splash of lemon juice and then take the scallops out of the pan. Cut the scallops in half.

To serve, spoon the risotto onto the plates and place the scallops on top. Shave the remaining truffle and scatter over the top.

MICHAEL BROWN

Daphne's is very proud to support the amazing work that Cancer Research does in the UK in trying to find a cure for this horrible disease. We are delighted to contribute to ChariTable Bookings' new recipe book to help fund that continued research."

CHICKEN ALLA MILANESE with gremolata

SERVES 6 | PREPARATION TIME 30 MINUTES | COOKING TIME 30 MINUTES

For the Chicken

6 medium corn-fed chicken breasts, deskinned
50g Parmesan cheese, freshly grated
200g fresh breadcrumbs
salt and pepper, to taste
200g plain flour
6 free range eggs, beaten
100ml vegetable oil
100g unsalted butter

For the Gremolata

5 cloves of garlic, peeled and crushed
4 lemons, juiced and zested
200g parsley, washed, picked and finely chopped
200–250ml olive oil
salt and freshly ground black pepper

To make the gremolata, place all the ingredients in a bowl and mix well. Season to taste with salt and pepper.

To prepare the chicken, place one chicken breast between two layers of cling film and gently flatten with a meat tenderiser or rolling pin, turning after every 2 or 3 blows until just under a centimetre thick. Repeat with the other 5 pieces.

Take three even sized shallow bowls. Mix together the Parmesan, breadcrumbs, salt, pepper and place the mixture in a bowl. Pour the flour into the second bowl and the beaten eggs into the third. One at the time, coat each chicken breast in the flour, then eggs and finally the breadcrumbs. This can be done up to 6 hours in advance and the coated chicken breasts can be kept in the refrigerator.

When ready to cook, gently fry in vegetable oil until golden brown on each side, adding a few knobs of butter at the end.

Serve with generous amounts of gremolata.

RUSSELL BROWN

Alzheimer's is creeping up as one of the big diseases affecting more and more of us as we get older. Very proud to be supporting the work of the Alzheimer's Society by donating Sienna's signature dish to this great new book by ChariTable Bookings."

BUTTERNUT SQUASH AND OLD WINCHESTER AGNOLOTTI
with sage butter

SERVES 6 | PREPARATION TIME 1 HOUR 10 MINUTES | COOKING TIME 5 MINUTES (PLUS SQUASH ROASTING TIME)

For the Pasta Dough
200g 00 pasta flour
7g finely ground Maldon salt
1 whole Blackacre farm free range egg, plus yolks to make up to 115g
5g olive oil

For the Butternut Squash Filling
1kg butternut squash
olive oil
Maldon salt
freshly ground black pepper
2 cloves of garlic
50g Westcombe ricotta
40g finely grated Old Winchester
1 sprig of sage

To Serve
360g butternut squash brunoise
180g unsalted butter
6 tsp freshly chopped sage
Maldon salt
lemon juice, to taste

To Garnish
few small sprigs of rocket
Old Winchester shavings

To make the pasta dough, sift the flour and salt into the bowl of a food processor. Whisk together the eggs and oil. Start the motor running on the food processor and drizzle in the egg mix. Pulse until a breadcrumb texture is obtained. Tip onto the work surface and knead into a smooth dough. Rub with a little oil and then wrap in cling film. Rest in the fridge for at least 30 minutes before use.

To make the butternut squash filling, peel, de-seed and dice the squash. Place in a roasting tin and toss with olive oil, Maldon salt and coarse ground black pepper. Roast at 170°C for 10 minutes. Smash the garlic with the flat of a knife and peel, add garlic and sage to the roasting tin, turn the squash. Continue to roast until the edges of the squash are going dark, turning frequently. Cool the squash and blitz in a food processor with the roasted garlic cloves, Old Winchester and ricotta. Season to taste; the flavour needs to be robust to come through the pasta. Put the purée in a piping bag and chill.

To assemble the agnolotti, roll out the pasta dough until you can just see your fingers through it. Pipe squash purée along the long edge, 1.5cm inside. Egg wash lightly on the far side of the purée and fold the pasta over to encase the filling as if you were making a sausage roll. Press the joint down well and trim the excess pasta off with a fluted pastry wheel about a thumb's width beyond the filling. Pinch the pasta tube at 1.5cm intervals to separate the roll into individual pillows. The idea is to squeeze the filling out to leave a clean space to cut through. Cut into individual pieces with the fluted cutter. The parcels virtually self-seal but pinching the ends together gives a thinner join.

To finish the dish and serve, sauté 30g butternut squash brunoise per portion. Blanch 7 pieces of agnolotti per portion in boiling salted water, 3 minutes approx. Make a sage beurre noisette with 15g butter and half a teaspoon of chopped sage per portion. Season with Maldon salt, black pepper and lemon juice. In a sauté pan combine the squash brunoise, agnolotti and sage butter. Serve in deep bowls garnished with a few small sprigs of rocket and shavings of Old Winchester.

TOM BROWN

30,000 deaths occur in Africa each week due to dirty water supplies - Africa Water Enterprises works tirelessly to change this which is why I'm supporting them through ChariTable Bookings and donating Outlaw's signature bass recipe to this great initiative."

BASS with octopus, avocado and verjus
SERVES 4–6 | PREPARATION TIME 20 MINUTES | COOKING TIME 1 HOUR 30 MINUTES

For the Bass
4–6 x 180g bass fillets, deboned
1 drizzle of extra virgin olive oil
Cornish sea salt and freshly ground
black pepper

For the Octopus
1kg octopus, double sucker species
olive oil, for cooking
1 onion, peeled and chopped
5 cloves of garlic, peeled and crushed
100ml verjus
2 sprigs of thyme

For the Dressing
1 lime, finely grated zest and juiced
1 large handful of rocket leaves
1 clove of garlic, peeled and chopped
2 tbsp extra virgin olive oil
salt and pepper

To Serve
1 handful of small rocket leaves
1 lime, finely grated zest only
1 avocado, mashed with a fork
1 drizzle of extra virgin olive oil

To make the dressing, blend together the lime zest and juice, rocket leaves, garlic, extra virgin olive oil and some salt and pepper. Taste and adjust the seasoning, then put aside.

To braise the octopus in its own juices, heat a large pan and add a drizzle of oil. When the oil is hot, add the onion and garlic and cook for 2 minutes. Add the octopus, verjus and thyme sprigs. Put the lid on and cook gently for 1 hour until the octopus is tender. Remove the octopus from the pan. When cool enough to handle, slit the main body in half and remove the ink sac, stomach and eyes, then prise out the beak from the middle of the tentacles. Cut the tentacles and body into 4cm pieces and leave to cool.

To grill the bass, drizzle with vegetable oil, season with salt and pepper and place under a hot grill, skin-side up, for about 3–4 minutes until the fish is cooked through.

Once the octopus has cooled, heat a char-grill pan on high heat. When it is hot, toss the octopus in a little olive oil, season with salt and pepper and place in the hot pan. Cook for 2 minutes, turning once or twice to colour all over.

To serve, divide the dressing between warm plates and lay the octopus and bass pieces on top. Scatter over the lime zest and rocket leaves, and a spoonful of avocado. Add a drizzle of extra virgin olive oil and serve immediately.

WARREN BROWN

Perthshire Big Tree Country protects Scotland's spectacular woodlands, sometimes overlooked in favour of animals or humans when it comes to charity work. The team at Gleneagles and I are really happy to support them in this great recipe book by ChariTable Bookings."

PAN-SEARED SCOTTISH BEEF with capers and red pepper

SERVES 1 | PREPARATION TIME 30 MINUTES | COOKING TIME 1 HOUR

For the Beef
160g beef tenderloin
1 knob of butter
1 sprig of thyme
a little olive oil, for frying

For the Garnish
10g red pepper
10g celeriac
10g cucumber
10g pickled capers
50ml balsamic vinegar, reduced by half
100ml beef jus
20g butter, unsalted
10ml olive oil
2 sprigs of thyme
salt and pepper

For the Garnish
asparagus or seasonal vegetables

To prepare the beef, trim the beef tenderloin and wrap tightly in cling film. Shape as required and place in the fridge to firm up.

To prepare the garnishes, peel the red pepper, celeriac and cucumber, and dice into small squares. Remove the capers from their brine. Place the balsamic vinegar into a small saucepan and reduce to half: the more the liquid is reduced, the sweeter it will be. Place the beef jus into the mix and reduce until it can coat the back of a spoon. Place the butter and a little olive oil into a separate pan to sauté the diced celeriac until soft. Remove, and do the same for the red pepper.

To cook the beef, remove from the fridge and portion. Place in a frying pan with a knob of butter, a little olive oil and a sprig of thyme. Brown on all sides and place in the oven at 180°C for 7 minutes. Once cooked, rest for 10 minutes.

To serve, finish off the sauce with a little butter in order to give it a nice shine on the surface. Rewarm the sautéed vegetables. Season to taste and add the capers and cucumbers. Place the beef on top and garnish with the warm, finished sauce. Asparagus makes a great addition to the dish, but seasonal vegetables are preferred.

GRANT BRUNSDEN

" We're behind this great initiative of ChariTable Bookings to raise money for all charities across the UK and are happy to donate our famous Charred and Mixed Tomato recipe as one of our signature dishes in aid of Cancer Research UK."

CHARRED AND MIXED TOMATOES with tofu mayonnaise, basil and jalapeño dressing

SERVES 4 | PREPARATION TIME 20 MINUTES | COOKING TIME 30 MINUTES

Equipment
blowtorch

For the Mixed Tomatoes
500g mixed ripe tomatoes, yellow, red, black and cherry
½ small bunch of basil, with the leaves removed from the stalk
1 punnet of purple shiso leaves or 30g rocket if unavailable
Maldon salt flakes and freshly ground black pepper

For the Tofu Mayonnaise
400g tofu
1 tbsp extra virgin olive oil
2 tbsp fresh lime juice
1 tsp water
Maldon salt flakes and freshly ground black pepper

For the Jalapeño Dressing
80ml jalapeño juice, from the jar
150ml rice vinegar
100ml extra virgin olive oil

For the Cucumber Ribbons
1 small cucumber
50ml rice vinegar
2 heaped tsp caster sugar
1 lime, zested
1 pinch of Maldon salt flakes

To make the tofu mayonnaise, put all the ingredients into a blender and blitz until smooth, adding water if needed. This will make more than needed for the dish, but can be used for other dishes.

For the jalapeño dressing, mix the jalapeño juice, rice vinegar and extra virgin olive oil together in a small bowl.

For the cucumber ribbons, peel the cucumber and discard the skin. Slice long and even ribbons of cucumber using a mandoline or potato peeler. Discard the seeds from the centre. Put the rice vinegar, sugar and a pinch of salt into a saucepan. Bring to a boil and stir until the sugar dissolves. Let it cool, add the lime zest and cucumber ribbons. Transfer into a small bowl.

For the tomatoes, core and cut them into bite size pieces. Place under a very hot grill for a minute or blowtorch them to char lightly. Toss the tomatoes and cucumber in the jalapeño dressing.

To serve, spread the tofu mayonnaise on a serving dish. Place the tomatoes and cucumber on top of the mayonnaise, and finish with torn basil leaves, shiso cress, or rocket and freshly ground black pepper.

DARRON BUNN

"The restaurant team at Goodwood are happy to donate their signature dish to ChariTable Bookings in aid of Winston's Wish, the UK's leading childhood bereavement charity. I hope this book raises LOTS of funds for charities throughout the UK."

GOODWOOD ALE-BRAISED SUSSEX BEEF SHORT RIB with roasted and pickled onion

SERVES 4 | PREPARATION TIME 30 MINUTES | COOKING TIME 3 HOURS

For the Braised Section

4 beef short ribs on the bone, trimmed
salt and pepper
vegetable oil, splash
2 large carrots, peeled, roughly
chopped
1 medium leek, roughly chopped
1 onion peeled, roughly chopped
2 celery sticks, roughly chopped
1 head of garlic, split in half
4 tbsp tomato purée
500ml Goodwood ale
200ml sweet white wine
500ml brown beef stock
assorted sprigs of thyme, marjoram
and lovage

**For the Onion Purée, Roasted Onions
and Pickled Onion**

3 large white onions, 2 peeled and
thinly sliced
butter
salt and pepper
150ml milk
1 small red onion
200ml red wine, preferably rich
and dark
200ml red wine vinegar
100g sugar
50g redcurrant jelly

To Finish

English mustard, optional
300g pied de mouton mushrooms or
similar, cleaned and sliced
salty fingers, or other similar salty
marsh vegetable
butter

To prepare the beef, season with salt and pepper, place into a hot frying pan with a splash of vegetable oil and colour to a golden brown on all sides, this will give a nicely roasted flavour to the finished dish. Drain on a rack.

Lightly brown the roughly chopped vegetables and garlic in a casserole dish. Add the tomato purée, beer and wine. Bring to the boil and simmer for 2–3 minutes. Add the brown stock and bring to the boil; place in the browned ribs and the herbs. Cover with a lid or foil, and cook in a preheated oven at 120°C for around 2–3 hours. To ensure they are cooked, the meat should just start to feel soft to the touch and be moving slightly from the bone. Leave to cool in the liquid. Once cool, carefully remove the beef ribs with either surgical gloves or a slotted spoon, and place on a deep tray. Pour the remaining liquid and vegetables through a colander, keeping the liquid as this will form the sauce and glaze for the ribs.

Prepare the onion purée and roasted onions whilst the beef is cooking. Gently fry the 2 sliced onions in a knob of butter with some salt and pepper in a lidded pan until very soft, taking care to stir frequently. Once soft, turn up the heat and add a further knob of butter to colour the onions. Once a deep golden brown colour, cover with milk and cook for 10 minutes. Place the contents of the pan into a blender and blitz to a smooth purée. Take the third onion and cut into wedges, making sure to leave the root intact so that the onion stays together. Blowtorch the edges to blacken them, season with salt and place onto a small roasting dish. Add some butter and a splash of water and cook in a hot oven at 180°C for 15–20 minutes, until soft.

To make the pickled onions, cut the red onion into wedges and peel the layers, keeping to one side. In a saucepan, boil the red wine, red wine vinegar, sugar and redcurrant jelly down to a syrup. Remove from the heat, cool slightly and drop in the red onion pieces. Leave to completely cool. This can be done 1–2 weeks in advance and stored in a jar in the fridge.

To cook the beef and finish the dish, take the liquid from the ribs and sieve through a fine strainer or muslin cloth, place into a saucepan and bring to the boil. Ladle half over the ribs and place into an oven set at 150°C. Every 8 minutes, remove the ribs and baste with the juice until completely reduced and sticky, which should take about 30 minutes. Reduce the rest of the cooking liquor down to a smooth sauce consistency, whisking in a tiny knob of butter, taste for seasoning and add a pinch of salt or sugar as desired. For an extra kick, a nice third of a teaspoon of English mustard whisked into the sauce is also delicious. Reheat the purée in a saucepan, stirring constantly. Place the pre-roasted onions back into the oven to reheat for 5 minutes. In a frying pan, fry the mushrooms with a knob of butter and season with salt. Drain onto cloth or kitchen paper. Place a spoonful of purée onto each plate, add a sticky rib, scatter the fried mushrooms, some of the drained pickled onion pieces and finally the salty marsh vegetables.

SEAN BURBIDGE

The Ivy Market Grill and Ivy Chelsea Garden are proud to support Macmillan by donating their signature vegetarian dish to ChariTable Bookings' new project."

ROASTED BUTTERNUT SQUASH with buckwheat grains, chickpeas, pomegranate, and feta, harissa yoghurt and coriander dressing

SERVES 4 | PREPARATION TIME 15 MINUTES | COOKING TIME 45 MINUTES

For the Squash
2 medium sized butternut squash
30ml rapeseed oil
½ tsp Maldon salt flakes

**For the Buckwheat, Chickpea,
Pomegranate and Feta Grains**
200g buckwheat grains
1l cold water
1 pinch of Maldon salt flakes
150g tinned chickpeas, rinsed
30g pomegranate seeds
100g feta, roughly crumbled
2 tbsp toasted pumpkin seeds
1 tbsp toasted sunflower seeds

For the Harissa Yoghurt
250g natural yoghurt
1 tsp harissa paste
5 tsp ras el hanout paste
1 tbsp honey
1 pinch of Maldon salt flakes
1 pinch of ground cumin

For the Mint and Coriander Dressing
120ml extra virgin olive oil
35g baby spinach
1 small bunch of fresh mint leaves
1 handful of coriander leaves
1 clove of garlic, finely chopped
1 tbsp lemon juice
1 pinch of Maldon salt flakes

Peel the butternut squash and remove 1cm from both ends; cut the butternut squash lengthways into 1.5cm thick slices, then place into an oven tray and drizzle with rapeseed oil, seasoning with salt to taste. Cook in a preheated oven at 180°C for 30–35 minutes, until the butternut squash is cooked through and soft to the touch but still firm.

To make the buckwheat, chickpea, pomegranate and feta grains, place the water into a large pan, on a high heat, add salt and bring to the boil. Once the water is boiling, add the buckwheat and cook for 8 minutes. Drain and leave to cool. Next gently incorporate with the chickpeas, pomegranate and roughly crumbled feta. Mix well.

For the harissa yoghurt, place all the ingredients into a bowl and mix well with a whisk.

To make the mint and coriander dressing, place all the ingredients into a blender and blitz to form a smooth, green dressing.

To serve, reheat the mixed grains and the butternut squash in the oven at 180°C for 5 minutes until hot. Place the butternut squash on a plate and drizzle over 2 large tablespoons of harissa yoghurt. Divide the grains into 4 tablespoon portions and then carefully place over and around the butternut squash. Drizzle one tablespoon of mint and coriander dressing around the butternut squash and the grains and finish the dish with fresh coriander and mint leaves.

MARTIN BURGE

Being charitable is not a one off event, it's a lifestyle choice. Through ChariTable Bookings, the team at Whatley Manor are proud to support the catering industry through the humbling work of Hospitality Action."

ROASTED HARE LOIN with sausage, caramelised bacon and smoked shallot purée

SERVES 4 | PREPARATION TIME 48 HOURS | COOKING TIME 2 HOURS

Equipment
- sous vide and vacuum pack bags
- smoker
- Pacojet

For the Hare and Sausage
- 1 hare for roasting and 4 hares for sausage
- 100g pork and 700g pork fat
- 50g sausage skins
- 300ml each red wine and water
- 250g breadcrumbs
- 100g caster sugar
- 1 pinch each of thyme and juniper
- 1 shaving of orange peel
- 4g bay leaves and 1 clove of garlic

For the Smoked Bacon Bath
- 400g smoked streaky whole bacon
- 100g vegetable mirepoix
- 150ml each apple juice and white wine
- 15ml olive oil
- 30g garlic
- 1½ tsp each thyme and rosemary
- ¼ tsp five-spice and 1 tsp star anise
- 75g honey

For the Smoked Shallots and Purée
- 250g round shallots
- 12 banana shallots
- 75g smoking dust
- 160g double cream
- 8ml lemon juice
- salt and pepper, to taste

To prepare the hare loin, remove all skin and sinew. Make sure all sinew is removed from the loin and vacuum pack. Dice the leg and shoulders and set aside for the sausage.

To make the hare sausage, mix the red wine and sugar and reduce to a light syrup. Mix in juniper berries, orange peel, bay leaves and garlic and marinate the meat for 24 hours. Remove the bay leaves and thyme and finely mince the hare once, using a meat mincer. Add the pork, pork fat and then finely mince again. Combine the breadcrumbs, water and minced meat in a food mixer using a paddle attachment for 10 to 15 seconds. Season with salt and pepper. Allow another 24 hours for the meat to rest. Pipe into sausage skins using a piping bag fitted with a sausage nozzle.

Soak the bacon in ice water for 48 hours in advance. In a saucepan, add the mirepoix with the olive oil and lightly caramelise. Add the honey and continue to cook for another 2 minutes until the mirepoix is lightly glazed. In another pan, mix the white wine and apple juice and bring to the boil. Add the herbs, spices and garlic and reduce to a sticky consistency. Chill the mixture over ice and place in a vacuum pack bag with the streaky bacon. Cook in a water bath at 85°C for 12 hours until the bacon is soft to the touch. Cool in ice water. Discard the mirepoix, cut the bacon into cubes and set aside.

For the smoked shallot purée, remove the roots from the round shallots. Score the outside layer. Wrap in tin foil and bake in a pre-heated oven at 180°C for about 1 hour. Prepare the smoker with 50g smoking dust. Remove the shallots from the tin foil, scooping the flesh from the skins with a spoon. Place the flesh into the smoker and smoke for 30 minutes. Turn the smoker off, leaving the shallots inside for 30 minutes. Remove and place them into a blender. Mix the salt, pepper, lemon juice and double cream in a pan, bring to the boil, then leave to cool. Pour in the cream, blend until smooth, pass the mixture through a fine sieve and cool over ice. Transfer to a Pacojet container, freeze and blend 3 times.

For the baked smoked shallots, wrap the banana shallots in sea salt and tin foil and repeat the smoking process above with 35g of smoking dust. Halve the shallots carefully before returning them to the turned off smoker for the last 30 minutes.

For the Molleux Raisins

- 125g molleux raisins
- 100ml white wine
- 5ml sherry vinegar
- 18g caster sugar

For the Red Wine Sauce

- 75g sliced shallots
- 100ml olive oil
- 3.5l red wine
- 1.5l port
- 750g button mushrooms
- 10l chicken stock
- 2l water
- 200ml veal glace
- 20g garlic
- 12g thyme
- 1 bay leaf

For the White Balsamic Mayonnaise

- 300ml white balsamic vinegar
- 70ml water
- 1½ tsp caster sugar
- 3.3g gelespessa, xanthan gum

For the Confit of Red Cabbage

- 600g red cabbage, finely sliced
- 50g muscatel vinegar
- 2 juniper berries
- ½ clove of garlic
- 1 bay leaf
- 50g caster sugar
- 225g duck fat
- salt and pepper

For the molleux raisins, place all of the ingredients into a saucepan with a lid, bring to the boil and simmer for 20 minutes. Allow the mixture to cool down naturally and leave for 24 hours.

To prepare the red wine sauce, place the shallots and olive oil in a pan and sweat until translucent. Add the vinegar, garlic, thyme and bay leaf and reduce until there is no liquid remaining. Add the port and reduce again to a syrupy consistency. Add the red wine and mushrooms, and reduce further until only 20 percent of the liquid remains. Add the chicken stock and water to the pan and bring to the boil. Simmer for 2 hours, skimming regularly to remove impurities. Pass the stock through a fine sieve and chill on ice overnight. Remove the fat from the stock and return to the heat. Add the veal glace and reduce the stock until a sauce consistency is achieved. Pass once more through a fine sieve and set aside.

To make the white balsamic mayonnaise, whisk the ingredients together in a pan. Simmer for 10 minutes without reducing the liquid. Pass through a fine sieve and set aside to rest. To make the confit, place all the ingredients into a thick bottomed pan with a tight-fitting lid. Slowly braise in a preheated oven at 150°C for 2 hours and 15 minutes. Once cooked and tender, strain off the excess duck fat and chill over ice. Set aside until ready to use.

Place the vacuum packed hare loin in a water bath at 58°C for 16 minutes. Meanwhile, poach the sausages in chicken stock at 90°C. Remove the hare from the water bath and the sausages from the stock, then dry with a towel and season. Colour the sausages and bacon together in a pan until golden brown. Place the hare loin in another frying pan and quickly colour both sides.

To serve, cut the loin and each sausage in two and follow the image for presentation.

CHRIS BURT

ChariTable Bookings encourages us to think of others and The Peach Tree is pleased to do the same and support Children In Need."

CLAMS AND HAM

SERVES 4 | PREPARATION TIME 15 MINUTES | COOKING TIME 30 MINUTES

For the Razor Clams
8 razor clams
rapeseed oil

For the Clams and Ham
4 cloves of garlic
8 shallots, finely chopped
rapeseed oil
4 tomatoes, deskinned, cored and diced
1 knob of butter
200g chorizo, cut into 5mm dice
600g precooked black-eyed beans
24 normal clams
salt and pepper
4 tsp XO sauce
1 small bird's eye chilli, finely diced
12 leaves cavolo nero

To Serve
micro herbs

To make the clams and ham, spray them liberally with rapeseed oil, then pop them under the grill. The clams will start to open and when they do, take them out. They should take 1–2 minutes under a 160°C grill. Remove the gut sac and discard. Trim the clams, cut into thirds and place to one side.

Fry the garlic and shallots in a little rapeseed oil. Add the diced tomato. Now add a little butter and throw in your chorizo dice. Once they start to go brown, add the black-eyed beans. Don't be afraid to give it plenty of vigorous heat. Throw in the regular clams, turn down the heat and put a saucepan lid on top to keep in the steam. This will help to cook the clams and their shells will start to open. Discard any that don't. When the clams are open the dish is ready to be seasoned. Add the XO sauce and bird's eye chilli, then mix in the cavolo nero leaves. To finish, add the razor clam meat.

To serve, clean the razor clam shells, then gently spoon the mix into them. Add the remaining clams to the plate and spoon the black-eyed beans around. Garnish with micro herbs.

ADAM BYATT

"What better way to raise money for Action Against Hunger than by donating one of our favourite recipes here at Trinity? Very happy to support ChariTable Bookings in this exciting venture."

ROAST GROUSE with white polenta, cobnuts and blackberry

SERVES 4 | PREPARATION TIME 30 MINUTES | COOKING TIME 1 HOUR

For the Grouse
4 whole long legged grouse, hearts
and livers intact
salt and pepper
1 shallot, sliced
25ml port
¼ bunch of thyme

For the Polenta
800ml white chicken stock
180g white polenta
50g butter
5g truffle, grated
20g Parmesan
100ml milk
salt and pepper, to taste

For the Pastillas
2 sheets of filo pastry

For the Sauce
1 shallot, sliced
¼ bunch of thyme
25ml port
1l brown chicken stock

For the Garnish
200g cobnuts
200g blackberries

To prepare the grouse, preheat the oven to 190°C and season the bird well with salt and pepper. Sear on both sides in a heavy ovenproof frying pan, cooking for 2 minutes on each side. Place the grouse on its back and then into the oven for 8 minutes. Remove from the oven and allow to cool for 5 minutes.

To make the polenta, bring the white chicken stock to the boil and add the polenta, stirring regularly for 8–10 minutes. Season well with salt and pepper. Remove from the heat, add the butter, the grated truffle, Parmesan and milk. Work well with a wooden spoon until light and fluffy. Cover and reserve for later.

Remove the livers and hearts and return these to the frying pan. Add the shallot, port and a few leaves of thyme, then reduce until sticky. Once reduced, place onto a chopping board and chop well.

To make the pastillas, roll the chopped liver and heart up in the filo pastry like a cigar. Bake or pan fry.

To make the sauce, use the same pan again and fry the shallot and thyme. Add the rest of the port and reduce by half. Add the brown chicken stock and reduce by half again. Pass the sauce through a fine sieve into a pan with the cobnuts and blackberries ready to serve.

Remove the birds from the pan and serve as they are, or remove the legs and breasts. To dress the plate, add a large spoonful of the polenta, place the pastilla on top, and arrange the breasts and legs around, covering generously with the nuts and berry sauce.

AIDEN BYRNE

I'm choosing to support Brainwave in this great opportunity to combine recipes and charity awareness by ChariTable Bookings. I hope you enjoy my Obsiblue Prawn and Chicken Wing dish from Manchester House!"

OBSIBLUE PRAWN AND CHICKEN WING

SERVES 6 | PREPARATION TIME 2 HOURS | COOKING TIME 50 MINUTES

For the Poached Chicken Wings
    12 jumbo chicken wings
    1l white chicken stock

For the Obsiblue Prawns
    12 large obsiblue prawns
    250g fine sea salt
    250g sugar

For the Horseradish Juice
    200g fresh horseradish

To Serve
    60g Skyr yoghurt, in a piping bag
    12 oxalis leaves
    12 oxalis flowers
    18 oxalis flower buds
    Maldon salt, to taste
    freshly milled black peppercorns

To prepare the poached chicken wings, lay the wings out flat on the chopping board. Using a sharp, heavy knife cut through the elbow joint. Turn the wing around and cut through the bones nearest the shoulder. This should leave you with the biggest piece of meat from the wings. Roast all the trimmings until golden brown and dry. After, cover with cold water. Then place the trimmed chicken wings into a large pan and cover with cold water, then gently bring to the boil and refresh immediately under cold running water. Next, pour the white chicken stock into a large saucepan; add the blanched chicken wings and the roasted trimmings. Bring to a simmer for around 30 minutes or until the bones can easily be pulled from the poached wings. Remove the poached wings and, whilst still warm, pull the bones out. Place the deboned wings on a tray in the freezer for 30 minutes. Pass the stock through a fine chinois and discard any solids. Reduce the stock by around four fifths until it becomes like a thin jus. Pass again and place in the fridge to cool. After this, remove the poached wings from the freezer and square off on all sides. Be careful not to trim the outside edges, where the skin meets, too far. It is the skin that will hold it together when it's reheated. Reserve in the fridge.

To make the obsiblue prawns, remove the head from all of the prawns and retain 6 of them, set the heads aside. Peel all of the tails ensuring you leave the shell on the tail end of 6 of them for presentation purposes. Then, mix together the salt and sugar and completely immerse the prawn meat in for 30 minutes, brush the cure off and refrigerate until needed.

To make the horseradish juice, place the horseradish in the juicer. Collect the juice. Reserve in the fridge.

To finish the dish and serve, lay the 6 semi-shelled obsiblues on their backs. Make around 6 incisions, width ways, all the way up the tail. Warm 300ml chicken stock on the stove. Gently lower the 12 poached chicken wings in to warm. Then, warm the 120ml reduced chicken stock in a small saucepan, season with the horseradish juice and salt to taste. Slice 6 of the shelled obsiblues into 6 keeping all the pieces of the same prawn together. Season with salt and black pepper. Place the semi-shelled Obsiblues onto a wire rack and blowtorch, slightly, until the top just chars. Place the heads directly onto a coal BBQ and grill until you can smell them.

Transfer the tail and the head onto a hot plate and pipe 5 dots of Skyr yoghurt evenly down the prawns' backs and season with salt and black pepper. Place two chicken wings in each bowl and the 6 slices of prawn. Dress with the oxalis leaves, buds and flowers and pour 20ml of chicken and horseradish sauce into the centre.

Serve immediately.

DARIN CAMPBELL

Very proud to be able to support the British Dyslexia Foundation and share with you Cromlix House's delicious marsh lamb recipe. Great idea by ChariTable Bookings to raise awareness and share great food at the same time."

MARSH LAMB and seaweed consommé

SERVES 8 | PREPARATION TIME 2 HOURS (PLUS 12 HOURS TO MARINATE, OVERNIGHT REST FOR MEAT) | COOKING TIME 2 HOURS (16 HOURS FOR LAMB)

Equipment
sous vide and vacuum pack bags
Thermomix

For the Lamb and Seaweed Stock
5kg lamb bones
100ml pomace oil
325g celery, roughly chopped
750g carrots, roughly chopped
1.5kg roscoff onions, roughly chopped
150g garlic, crushed
150g tomato paste
15g cumin seeds, toasted
500ml white wine
500ml sweet white wine
20g rosemary
3l white chicken stock
3l pork stock, reduced by half
300ml light soy sauce
100g dried kelp
2 sheets of nori seaweed

For the Raft
1 small leek
1 carrot
½ stalk of celery
250g lean lamb mince
3 egg whites, plus shells

For the Lamb Neck
2kg lamb neck
200g duck fat
1¼ tsp juniper berries
1¼ tsp coriander seeds
120g smoked Maldon salt
120g caster sugar
¾ tsp each rosemary leaves, thyme
leaves and fennel pollen
¾ tsp fennel pollen
15g garlic
30ml pomace oil

To Serve
samphire, blanched
spring onions, fresh seaweed, parsley
leaves, carrot ribbons and micro herbs,
to decorate

To prepare the stock, roast the lamb bones at 200°C for 40–60 minutes until fully caramelised. In a pan, sweat all of the vegetables and garlic slowly in some oil and a little salt until soft and starting to caramelise. Add the tomato paste and cumin, then cook for 5 minutes, stirring regularly. Pour in the white wine and reduce until thick and sticky. Repeat this process with the sweet wine. Retaining the fat for further use, add the roasted bones to the pan, along with the rosemary, both stocks, soy sauce and kelp. Cook on a medium heat for 4–5 hours. After this time has passed, remove from the heat and add the nori, leaving the mixture to infuse for a further 30 minutes. Strain the entire contents of the pan and chill.

To assemble the raft, wash the vegetables and roughly chop into a food processor. Add the rest of the ingredients and blitz until the mixture starts to foam. Decant into a bowl and set to one side for serving.

To make the consommé, take 2l lamb and seaweed stock and bring to the boil in the saucepan. Ladle a third of the hot stock into the raft in the bowl and whisk quickly. Pour the mix into the pan of simmering stock and whisk for a few minutes. Simmer very gently, stirring occasionally to ensure it doesn't stick to the base of the pan and burn. The broth should start to become clear, at which point, rest the raft on the top. With a small ladle, break a hole in the centre of the raft, and every few minutes, ladle some stock out through the hole and filter it over the raft. After 45 minutes, remove the stock from the heat and leave to stand for 1 hour. Carefully remove the raft from the top and pass the consommé through a double muslin cloth.

For the lamb neck, put all the ingredients – except the necks and duck fat – in a Thermomix. Blitz for a few seconds and leave to sit. Trim the lamb necks and place in a large sous vide bag. Sprinkle half of the cure over the lamb necks, flip the bag over and repeat. Vacuum pack the necks and cure on a high vacuum, and leave for 12 hours. Next, remove the neck and wash off the cure. Place the neck into a fresh vacuum pack bag with the duck fat and seal on high vacuum. Drop into a 72°C water bath and cook for 16 hours. Remove from the bath and leave to cool in the bag for 30 minutes. Remove from the sous vide bag and roll in cling film very tightly, leaving to set in the fridge overnight.

To serve, dice the lamb neck into 1cm cubes, mix with some blanched samphire, spring onions and fresh seaweed, then place in a shallow bowl. Heat the consommé, then pour into a jug to be served at the table, alongside the parsley, micro herbs and carrot ribbon garnishes.

DAVID CAMPBELL

"I have chosen to support a local charity, *Julian House*, that offers direct support to some of the most marginalised people in society – the homeless. Great that I can champion a local charity simply by sharing one of **The Dower House** recipes with Chari**Table** Bookings."

SMOKED SALMON AND CAULIFLOWER

SERVES 6 | PREPARATION TIME 30 MINUTES | COOKING TIME 1 HOUR

Equipment
  sous vide
  vacuum pack bag

For the Salmon
  1 side of Loch Duart salmon,
  deskinned, trimmed and pin boned
  250g Maldon sea salt
  250g caster sugar
  1 lemon, zest
  1 handful of hay
  rock salt, to smoke

For the Cauliflower
  ½ cauliflower, trimmed to florets
  1 knob of butter, for cooking
  300ml milk
  100ml double cream
  ½ bay leaf
  salt and pepper, to taste

For the Lemon
  2 whole lemons
  reduced stock syrup, to blanch the
  lemon

For the Radish
  3 breakfast radishes

To prepare the salmon, skin the salmon, remove any brown fat from the skin-side, trim neatly and ensure all the pin bones are removed. Mix the sea salt and sugar together well and zest the lemon into this mixture. In a tray, pack this mixture onto both sides of the salmon evenly and allow to sit at room temperature for 30 minutes, which firms up the salmon, cures it and seasons it at the same time. Wash off the sugar and salt mix under cold water, pat dry on a cloth and transfer to a sous vide bag. Cook sous vide at 40°C for 24 minutes. Alternatively, steam the salmon. Chill in the bag in an ice bath.

To smoke the salmon, remove it from the bag and place on a steamer tray. Wrap the tray tightly in cling film, three layers should be enough. Place the hay and some rock salt in a separate tray. Blowtorch and then quickly drop the tray with the salmon on top, this extinguishes any flames and causes smoke to form. Leave the tray with the salmon on top for 10 minutes to take on smoke flavour.

To make the cauliflower purée, sweat the florets, reserving some for the blanched florets and slices, in a sauté pan with butter, add the bay leaf and season with salt and pepper. When the florets are just starting to cook add the milk and double cream with the bay leaf. Cook on a high heat for 15 minutes or until the florets are soft. Drain the cauliflower but keep the cooking liquid. Transfer to a food processor and blitz on high. Add the liquid slowly back in until the mixture is smooth and shiny, the consistency should be a similar thickness to custard. Adjust the seasoning, adding salt and pepper. Chill and reserve.

To make the cauliflower florets, pick some small florets, only one or two, and break them down in to mini florets the size of your small finger nail. Blanch in boiling water for 30 seconds, drain and refresh.

To prepare the raw cauliflower, cut two florets from the cauliflower and slice them down thinly with mandoline. Reserve for serving.

To prepare the lemon, peel 1 lemon carefully using a speed peeler, just remove the yellow outer skin. Blanch the lemon zest for 1 hour on a very low heat in the stock syrup with the juice of another lemon and set aside. Completely peel the first lemon to just leave the flesh. Segment this neatly, remove any pips, and place in a little stock syrup with lemon juice to balance. Place to one side for serving.

To serve, cut a piece of salmon approximately 4cm width and plate. Place 4–5 dots of the cauliflower purée carefully on top, add some mini florets, some of the lemon segments and then the raw cauliflower slices. Garnish with a few strands of the lemon zest and a few slivers of radish. Drizzle a tiny bit of smoked oil and rock salt on top. Place a generous blob of the purée next to the salmon.

GRAHAM CAMPBELL

Being able to support Blake Mcmillan and the fantastic work my mum Jenny does in this ChariTable Bookings new book is a great pleasure for me. I hope Castlehill's venison dish is a great pleasure for you as well!"

HIGHLAND VENISON with pear, chicory and chocolate

SERVES 4 | PREPARATION TIME 20 MINUTES | COOKING TIME 45 MINUTES

For the Dish
4 x 120g venison loin
oil, for searing
20g unsalted butter
1 head of chicory
rapeseed oil, for dressing
1 butternut squash, peeled
200ml each cream and milk
20g queen kale
500ml vegetable oil, for frying kale
salt

For the Poached Pear
1 pear, peeled and cut into 8
250ml cook's dessert wine
¼ cup sugar
30ml brandy
½ tsp salt
2 cloves

For the Chocolate Sauce
50g 70% chocolate
10ml sherry vinegar
10ml soy sauce
20ml rapeseed oil

For the Sauce
6 juniper berries
1 clove
4 whole spice berries
250ml red wine
200ml veal stock
200ml chicken stock

To prepare the venison, sear the loin in a pan until coloured all the way round. Add butter and place in a pre-heated oven at 180°C. Cook until temperatures reaches 55°C.

To prepare the chicory, pick the leaves and dress in rapeseed oil.

To prepare the butternut squash, cut the top half of the vegetable into batons measuring approximately 8x3cm. Cook in salted water. Put the rest in a pan and sweat slightly before adding milk and cream to cook out. Once soft, blend to a purée and pass. Keep to one side.

To prepare the poached pear, mix all ingredients together and bring to boil. Leave to cool.

To prepare the chocolate sauce, put all ingredients in a bowl and melt together. Mix and keep to one side.

To prepare the sauce, put the juniper, clove, whole spice and red wine into a pan. Reduce to almost nothing then add stock and reduce by half. Add the Dijon mustard, chocolate and lemon thyme, and pass through a fine strainer. Season with salt to taste.

To prepare the crispy kale, heat the oil in a fryer to 180°C. Add the kale and cook until crispy. Dry on a clean cloth and season.

To serve, assemble as pictured, covering the bottom of the plate with the sauces, dotting around the poached pear and spooning the venison on top. Garnish with the crispy kale.

For the Sauce *continued*
1 tsp Dijon mustard
10g 70% chocolate
2 sprigs of lemon thyme

CLAUDIO CARDOSO

Very pleased to donate SUSHISAMBA's Samba Salad recipe to raise funds for Cool Earth, a fantastic charity fighting to save the world's rainforests. Help ChariTable Bookings to support them by buying this great book."

SAMBA SALAD

SERVES 1 | PREPARATION TIME 20 MINUTES | COOKING TIME 3 MINUTES

For the Salad
50g kabocha squash
30g baby spinach
20g heritage carrot shavings
20g green and white asparagus, ribboned
10g heritage beet, finely sliced
10g radish shavings
25g red and yellow bell pepper batons
5g enoki mushrooms
10g caramelised macadamias
3g mixed micro cress
1 pinch of Maldon salt

For the Truffle Honey Ponzu Sauce
1 large drizzle of soy sauce
1 large drizzle of orange juice
1 large drizzle of truffle oil

For the Samba Dressing
200g mango
200g red apple
50ml rice vinegar
20g onion
50g tomato
1 pinch of salt

To make the salad, grill the kabocha for 3 minutes. Combine the soy, orange juice and truffle oil, mixing well, and marinate the squash in the mixture for 2 minutes. After this time, remove from the sauce and set to one side to rest.

Blend all the ingredients for the samba dressing together and season the spinach with it.

Take the vegetable shavings, ribbons and slices and assemble together with the grilled kabocha and enoki mushrooms. When arranging the dish, take care to place the heaviest items at the bottom and the lightest on top. Add a selection of cress and the caramelised macadamias. Sprinkle the final salad with the truffle honey ponzu and season with Maldon salt.

BRAD CARTER

The Stroke Association saves lives. Carter Moseley has chosen to support them via ChariTable Bookings, in order to help those at risk, those in recovery and to encourage prevention and early diagnosis."

TAMWORTH PORK with grains and seeds

SERVES 4 | PREPARATION TIME 45 MINUTES (PLUS OVERNIGHT DRYING) | COOKING TIME 4 HOURS

Equipment
blowtorch
dehydrator, optional

For the Tamworth Pork
500g Tamworth pork loin, deboned,
fat on but deskinned, skin reserved
sea salt
5ml grapeseed oil

For the Pig's Trotter Stock
4 pig's trotters
1 carrot, chopped
2 onions, chopped
1 white leek, sliced
1 sprig of thyme
2 bay leaves
6 black peppercorns
water, to cover

For the Crackling
1 skin Tamworth Pork, from the loin
300ml grapeseed oil
celery salt, to taste

For the Grains
100g pearl barley
100g spelt grain
2 shallots, finely chopped
1 clove of garlic, finely chopped
25ml grapeseed oil
1 bay leaf
1 sprig of thyme
800ml pig's trotter stock
10g Braeburn apple, peeled and
finely diced
10g sunflower seeds, toasted
10g linseeds, toasted
reduced white wine, any good white
wine reduced to ¾ volume

To prepare the loin, remove the skin from the outside of the loin, and put the loin to one side. Slice the skin into strips, add to a pan of salted, cold water and bring to the boil. Simmer the skin for 20 minutes, drain, discarding the water and leave to cool. When the skin is cool enough to handle, scrape any left over fat from the skin, and chop into smaller pieces, around 2mm in size. Lay the skin pieces onto a lined baking sheet and dry the skin completely in an oven set to 50°C overnight. If you have a dehydrator, place the skin in and repeat the same method, the skin has to be completely dry and brittle. Set the skin aside for later.

To make the trotter stock, singe all the hairs from the trotters using a cook's blowtorch on a high heat grill, then place into a roasting tray. Add the chopped vegetables, aromatics and pour on enough water to cover the trotters. Cover the trotter dish with foil and braise in an oven set at 150°C for 3 hours or until tender and falling from the bone. Allow the trotters to cool in the liquid. When cool enough to handle, pick all the meat from the bones, discarding the fat and skin. Don't be alarmed, pig's trotters don't have lots of meat but what they do have is delicious. When the meat is picked from the bone, set aside and attend to the stock. Pour the stock through a chinois or fine sieve, and discard the vegetables. Bring the stock to the boil, skimming constantly with a large spoon or ladle to remove fat and impurities, reduce the stock by three quarters of the original volume. When the stock has reduced, it should appear viscous. Add the picked meat back to the stock, pour into a container and set aside for service.

To cook the pork, oil the meat, season it all over with sea salt and place into an oven set to 185°C for 20–25 minutes, or until the core temperature reaches 63°C. Leave it to rest in a warm place for 15–20 minutes after cooking.

To make the crackling, heat the oil until it reaches 200°C on a temperature probe, and fry the pork skin in the oil until it puffs up, which should take around 10 seconds. Remove the crackling from the oil with a slotted spoon, working quickly, and drain on kitchen paper, season liberally with celery salt and set aside.

To make the grains, start by rinsing the barley and spelt under cold water to remove the excess starch. Then start sweating the shallots and garlic in the oil over a low heat, add the thyme and bay leaf, and cook for around 7–8 minutes until without colour. Add the barley and spelt, stir for 1 minute, then start adding the warmed trotter stock, ladle by ladle, until the grains are almost al dente. When the grains are almost cooked, add the diced apple, the toasted sunflower seeds and linseeds, and season with the reduced white wine and a little salt.

To finish the dish, carve the pork into 4 servings, season the flesh with sea salt and place onto the plates. Add the grains and seeds to the plate next to the loin and top the grains with the pork crackling.

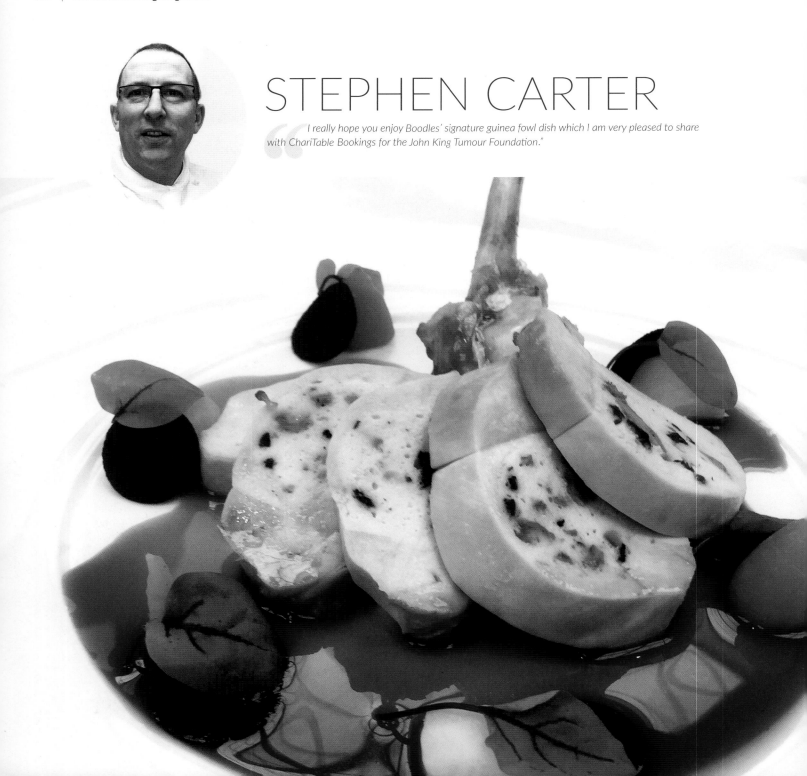

STEPHEN CARTER

"I really hope you enjoy Boodles' signature guinea fowl dish which I am very pleased to share with ChariTable Bookings for the John King Tumour Foundation."

GUINEA FOWL with fresh truffle and ceps
SERVES 2 | PREPARATION TIME 20 MINUTES | COOKING TIME 30 MINUTES

Equipment
deep freezer

For the Dish
1.2kg whole guinea fowl
75g fresh ceps, finely chopped
1 small shallot, peeled and finely
chopped
120ml double cream
2g truffle, plus 4 thin slices
2 slices of pancetta
6 chantenay carrots
6 baby turnips
50g butter
sugar, to season
200ml veal or brown chicken stock
salt and freshly ground pepper
50ml Madeira wine

For the Garnish
1 handful of red vein sorrel
thin fresh truffle slices

To prepare the guinea fowl, remove the legs and separate the thigh from the drumstick then debone and skin the thigh meat. Place in a bowl in a deep freezer to chill the meat rapidly as it needs to be very cold to make the mousse. The drumsticks can be chopped and added to the stock to enrich the sauce. Remove the breasts, leaving the skin on. Trim the wing bone until it is clean – we call this to French trim. You will have a clean wing bone with no meat on, still attached to the breast. From the thick meaty end, insert a knife to form a pocket. This is where we will pipe the mousse in, so it appears in the middle of the breast. Put it in the refrigerator for a few minutes while you prepare the next couple of tasks.

Sweat the finely chopped cep mushrooms gently with the shallot for about 5 minutes then chill until cold and reserve.

When the thigh meat is very cold, weigh it. There should be about 120g, you will need to match this with double cream. Purée the thigh meat with a pinch of salt in a food processor, slowly adding the cream until all is incorporated into the mix. At this point we would pass this through a fine sieve but at home, this is not necessary. Now add the chilled cep mixture and a couple of grams of finely chopped truffle and a little pepper, then place in a disposable piping bag and chill until needed.

Take 2 thin slices of truffle and place them between the skin and breast of the guinea fowl, then pipe the mousse mixture into the pocket you have formed in the breast. To finish, take the slice of pancetta and wrap around the guinea fowl breast, this will help keep it moist during cooking.

Peel and cook the small chantenay carrots and baby turnips separately in water, a little butter and a pinch of sugar, and reserve until service.

Reduce the veal stock or dark chicken stock with the Madeira until it thickens to a sauce consistency, and put to one side.

To cook the guinea fowl, place a little butter in a heavy-bottomed frying pan over a high heat until the butter begins to foam, then place the breasts skin-side down first and brown gently for 3–4 minutes. Turn them so they are now skin-side up, and place in a hot oven at 170°C for a further 10 minutes. Once cooked, rest somewhere warm for a further 10–15 minutes. This relaxes the meat, making it tender and juicy,

To finish the sauce, peel the skin off of the breasts and take the slices of truffle. Finely chop and add to the sauce. Next, whisk 10g cold butter in and taste for seasoning. Add more salt and pepper if you feel it needs it but it is important to taste. To assemble the plate, slice the guinea fowl and place in a ring in centre of the plate. Place the reheated vegetables in a larger circle around the meat and pour the sauce over though a tea strainer and finish with small slices of fresh truffle and red vein sorrel.

RHYS CATTERMOUL

Nobu are proud to be able to champion the MS Society and to know that this dish, promoted by ChariTable Bookings, will help in the fight against Multiple Sclerosis."

CHILEAN SEA BASS with truffle miso

SERVES 6 | PREPARATION TIME 10 MINUTES (PLUS 3 DAYS TO MARINATE) | COOKING TIME 20 MINUTES

For the Dish
6 x 100g Chilean sea bass fillets

For the Truffle Miso
10g mustard powder
230ml flamed sake
140ml flamed mirin
80g sugar
400g Yamajirishi miso
120g truffle peeling
40ml truffle oil

For the Garnish
black sesame
black truffle
shishito pepper
hajikami

To make the truffle miso, add the mustard powder into hot flamed sake and mirin. Mix well then add the rest of the ingredients in to the Vitamix. Use this sauce to marinate the sea bass for 3 days.

To prepare the sea bass, cook in the same way you would black cod. Caramelise the fish not the sauce.

To serve, after the fish is glazed and sauce has been applied, sprinkle some black sesame over the top. Cover with black truffle, garnish with shishito pepper and hajikami and serve a little miso on the side.

TOM CENCI

I'm pleased that ChariTable Bookings has given Duck and Waffle another opportunity to support the invaluable work of Action Against Hunger."

MISO GLAZED RABBIT with cauliflower purée and pie crust

SERVES 2 | PREPARATION TIME 30 MINUTES | COOKING TIME 8

For the Rabbit
2 rabbit legs
100g miso paste
100ml water

For the Cauliflower Purée
1 cauliflower
50g butter
100ml double cream
salt and pepper

For the Pie Crust
220g plain flour
110g suet
1 pinch of salt
12g baking powder
170ml water

For the Cabbage
2–3 cabbage leaves
oil, for frying

Place the rabbit legs into a sous vide bag with the miso paste and 100ml of water. Seal the bags and cook in a water bath for 7 hours at 74°C. If you don't have a water bath, you can braise the legs in the oven for about 2 hours but the amount of water will need to be doubled.

Slice the cauliflower into thin strips. Melt the butter in a large pan, then add the cauliflower. Gently cook until the butter foams and the cauliflower starts to brown. Pour in the double cream and blend in a food processor until smooth. Taste for seasoning.

For the pie crust, put the flour, suet, salt and baking powder into a mixing bowl. On a slow speed, gradually add the water until a dough has formed. The dough should be a bit sticky but dry enough to come away from the sides of the bowl. Roll out the dough onto a baking sheet with greaseproof paper and bake at 180°C for about 15 minutes until golden brown.

To make the cabbage garnish, take a small amount of cabbage leaf and deep fry for about 30 seconds until crispy; be careful as the oil will spit from the moisture so you may need a splash guard for this.

To assemble the dish, serve the rabbit legs with the sauce it was cooked in and finish with the cauliflower purée, pieces of pie crust and crispy cabbage.

SHRIMOYEE CHAKRABORTY

"The Hope Foundation is something very close to my heart as it rescues street and slum children from Kolkata, my home town. I bring the flavours of India to my restaurant Calcutta Street in London and now to you by sharing my curry recipe with ChariTable Bookings."

PRAWN MALAI CURRY

SERVES 1–2 | PREPARATION TIME 30 MINUTES | COOKING TIME 25 MINUTES

For the Prawns
- 200g king prawns
- ½ tsp turmeric powder
- salt
- 1 tbsp mustard oil

For the Curry Sauce
- 1 large clove of garlic, roughly chopped
- 4 small bay leaves
- whole garam masala
- 1 tsp ginger paste
- 1 onion, chopped
- 400ml coconut milk
- 130ml water
- ¼ tsp red chilli powder, adjust according to your tolerance level
- turmeric powder and salt, to taste
- 2–3 green chillies, halved lengthwise
- 1 pinch of sugar

Peel the prawns from the centre, leaving the head and tails on. Mix with turmeric and salt and keep aside to take on flavour for about 15 minutes.

Heat oil and shallow fry the prawns so they turn golden in colour. Reserve for later.

In the same oil, add the chopped garlic, bay leaves, garam masala, ginger paste and onion. Cook this for 5–7 minutes, then add the can of coconut milk.

Add a little water, about 130ml or a third of the coconut milk can, some red chilli powder, very little turmeric powder and salt. Add the green chillies, mix well and cook the gravy for 10 minutes. Adjust the balance using a little sugar to taste.

Lastly, add the fried prawns to the dish. Cook on a low heat for 5 minutes till the gravy thickens.

Editor's Note: You can buy the mixture of whole spices that make up a classic garam masala from any good Asian greengrocers or make the blend yourself.

SANDIA CHANG

"Bubbledogs is proud to help ChariTable Bookings support Action Against Hunger."

BUFFALO HOT DOG with Horny Devils

SERVES 2 | PREPARATION TIME 45 MINUTES | COOKING TIME 20 MINUTES

For the Celery
40g celery

For the Pickling Liquid
40ml white wine vinegar
40ml water
30g white caster sugar
5g juniper berries
5g coriander seeds
5g yellow mustard seeds
1 star anise

For the Buffalo Sauce (makes 150g)
80ml Frank's Hot Sauce
20ml white wine vinegar
8g honey
1 tsp Worcestershire sauce
1 pinch each of garlic powder, salt and cayenne pepper
40g unsalted butter

For the Horny Devils
60g flour
70g cornmeal
25g white caster sugar
5g baking powder
115ml buttermilk
1 pinch of salt
1 egg
100g sweetcorn kernels
50g cheddar cheese, grated
40g jalapeños, diced

To prepare the celery, peel to remove the strings and slice approximately 1mm in thickness at a 45° diagonal, reserving the leaves for garnishing.

To make the pickling liquid, mix the white wine vinegar, water and caster sugar together in a pan. Add in the juniper berries, coriander seeds, yellow mustard seeds and the star anise. Bring the mixture to the boil and allow the liquid to simmer for 5 minutes. Divide the chopped celery in half, place the first half into the simmering liquid and allow them to cool in the mixture. Place the other half of your celery in a container with a little water to keep fresh for serving.

To make the buffalo sauce, combine all of the ingredients apart from the butter in a large mixing bowl with a whisk, making sure everything is well mixed. Melt the butter and gradually add to the bowl, continuously mixing in order to emulsify the sauce. Any remaining sauce can be used for dipping at a later date if kept in the fridge.

To make the horny devils, combine the flour, cornmeal, white caster sugar, baking powder, buttermilk and the pinch of salt in a bowl and mix to form a batter. Add the egg, sweetcorn kernels, cheddar cheese and the jalapeños and mix well, allowing the mixture to rest for at least 30 minutes. Once rested, heat up the vegetable oil to 190°C and, using 2 tablespoons, fry the horny devils. Drain, place onto kitchen paper to soak up any excess oil and season with salt.

To assemble the dish, place each cooked frankfurter into a steamed bun and 25g buffalo sauce over each sausage, making sure to cover well. The frankfurter can be substituted for vegetarian alternatives. Divide the pickled and fresh celery between the 2 and crumble over some blue cheese. Place under a grill to allow the cheese to melt, adding a little more buffalo sauce and celery to garnish once the cheese has melted. Divide the horny devils equally between the 2 plates and serve.

For the Horny Devils *continued*
150ml vegetable oil
salt, to taste

For the Buffalo Hot Dog
2 frankfurters – beef, pork or vegetarian
2 steamed buns
50g buffalo sauce
20g pickled celery
20g fresh celery
30g stilton, crumbled

For the Garnish
celery leaves

NIK CHAPPELL

"Macmillan does so much good and it is a privilege for Lower Slaughter Manor to have chosen to support them through ChariTable Bookings."

SOY POACHED TURBOT with girolles and mushroom dashi

SERVES 4 | PREPARATION TIME 10 MINUTES (PLUS 1 HOUR 30 MINUTES TO MARINATE) | COOKING TIME 40 MINUTES

For the Turbot
4 x 170g turbot fillets
200ml soy sauce
20g coriander
olive oil, to drizzle

For the Celery Oil
100g celery leaves
50ml olive oil
2g celery salt

For the Dashi - First Half
1l water
150g dried shiitake mushrooms
100g mooli
50g fresh ginger
20g konbu

For the Dashi - Second Half
80ml mirin
8g salt
2g bonito
17ml rice wine vinegar

For the Garnish
100g radish
15ml extra virgin rapeseed oil
70g girolle mushrooms
100g rainbow chard
100g white beans, cooked
100g choi sum or pak choi

To prepare the fish, marinate the turbot in soy and coriander for 1.5 hours to take on colour and season the fish.

To make the celery oil, warm the celery leaves, oil and celery salt to around 80°C, blitz in a liquidiser and pass through a fine sieve.

To prepare the dashi, boil the first half of the dashi ingredients for 20 minutes, add the second half and let the mixture sit for 10 minutes. Pass the mixture through a fine sieve then strain through a j-cloth.

To prepare for service, slice half of the radish as finely as possible and place in salted, ice water. Quarter and poach the other half in simmering, salted water for 2 minutes, leave to cool in poaching water.

To cook the fish, pat the turbot dry, place on a tray, drizzle with olive oil and grill on a high heat for 3–5 minutes, or until cooked to your liking.

Meanwhile, in a medium hot sauté pan, add the extra virgin rapeseed oil and cook the mushrooms for 1 minute, then add the chard, white beans, choi sum or pak choi and 20g dashi. Cook for a further 3 minutes.

To serve, place the dashi cooked vegetables in the bottom of a shallow bowl, place the grilled fish on top. Scatter the raw and poached radish on and around the fish, finish with the dashi and celery leaf oil.

ÉRIC CHAVOT

Pleased to be able to promote the work of the Alzheimer's Society by donating my mackerel recipe to this fantastic initiative by ChariTable Bookings. Remember, fish oils are good for the brain!"

JOSPER GRILLED MACKEREL
SERVES 4 | PREPARATION TIME 15 MINUTES | COOKING TIME 45 MINUTES

For the Mackerel
4 mackerels, filleted and pin boned
fine sea salt and ground white
pepper, to season
1 tbsp herbs de Provence
½ tsp chilli flakes
espelette pepper to season
1 drizzle of olive oil

For the Lemon Yoghurt
200g Greek yoghurt
50g lemon confit
1 lemon, juiced and zested
12ml each lemon oil, white balsamic
vinegar and sparkling water
12 strands saffron

For the Coriander Pesto
⅓ bunch of basil, picked and blanched
⅓ bunch of coriander
1 clove of garlic
20g pine nuts, lightly toasted
1 tbsp Pecorino, grated
½ lemon, zested
150ml olive oil
fine sea salt and white ground pepper,
to taste

For the Green Bean Salad
6 Charlotte potatoes, quartered
1 shallot, diced
ground white pepper, to season
½ lemon, juiced

To make the coriander pesto, place all of the ingredients into a jug and blitz to a paste with a hand blender. Check seasoning and texture, keep refrigerated.

To prepare the lemon yoghurt, mix all the ingredients together well and keep refrigerated.

To prepare the green bean salad, cook the potatoes in salted water. When done, drain, add the shallot, pepper, half the lemon juice, 20ml lemon oil and the pitted olives. Cover with cling film and set to one side. Mix the Dijon mustard with the vinegar, remaining lemon juice and seasoning. Whisk in the crème fraîche, olive oil and remaining lemon oil.

To prepare the mackerel, remove the bones of the mackerel fillet by running the sharp blade of a knife on either side of the bloodline. Season with salt and pepper and cover with the lemon yoghurt. Dust with the dry herbs, chilli flakes and espelette pepper, drizzle with a little olive oil. Bake in a hot oven, 200°C, removing the mackerel after 3–4 minutes. Leave on the tray to gently finish cooking.

While the mackerel is cooking, fold the green beans into the crème fraîche dressing and add the chives and spring onions to the warm potatoes. Place the potatoes at the bottom of your serving dish, top with the green beans, semi dried tomatoes, croutons and celery cress.

To serve, brush a warm plate with the coriander pesto, sit the warm mackerel fillet on top, drizzling the lemon yoghurt cooking juices on top and dusting with a little coriander cress.

For the Green Bean Salad *continued*

    25ml lemon oil
    24 pitted Niçoise olives
    1 tsp Dijon mustard
    1 tsp white balsamic vinegar
    fine sea salt to season
    1 tbsp crème fraîche
    3 tbsp olive oil
    160g extra fine green beans, cooked
    1 tsp chives, snipped
    1 tsp spring onions, sliced
    16 petals semi dried tomatoes
    16 golden-baked potato sourdough
    croutons

To Garnish

    celery cress
    coriander cress

KARL CHEETHAM

Sadly I seem to hear more and more about Alzheimer's and the debilitating effect it has on both the sufferer and those close to them. I am proud to share Gliffaes recipe with you and hope you support the Alzheimer's Society through ChariTable Bookings."

SCALLOPS with crisp chicken wing and pea cream

SERVES 4 | PREPARATION TIME 15 MINUTES | COOKING TIME 4 HOURS

For the Pea Cream
1 onion, finely chopped
2 cloves of garlic, finely chopped
142ml double cream
300g fresh peas

For the Chicken Wings
4 chicken wings
1 chicken stock cube
plain flour, for coating
3 eggs, whisked
panko breadcrumbs

For the Pancetta
200g dry cured pancetta

To Serve
rapeseed oil
12 scallops, shelled and roe off
salt and pepper, to taste
pea shoots

To make the pea cream, sweat the onion and garlic in a medium saucepan, cooking until soft but without colour. After a couple of minutes add the cream and reduce by half. Blanch your peas for a few seconds in a small saucepan of boiling water, then plunge straight into cold water. Drain the peas, then blitz together with the cream using a hand blender or food processor. Pass the mixture through a fine sieve and set aside.

To make the chicken wings, in a medium saucepan, boil the chicken wings in water with 1 chicken stock cube for about 15 minutes. Remove the wings and allow to cool. Cut the cartilage part of the wing on each end then gently push the bones out one at the time. They should come out quite easily as the wing will be soft from cooking. Once deboned, have 3 bowls with plain flour, whisked egg and breadcrumbs ready. Place your wing in the flour first, then egg, then breadcrumbs. Keep in the fridge until needed.

To prepare the pancetta, preheat the oven to 65–70°C. Place 4–6 very thinly sliced strips of pancetta on a baking tray lined with parchment paper and cook in the oven for 4–5 hours until it dries out and becomes crispy. Dice up the rest of pancetta into 2cm cubes and gently fry in a medium frying pan until they turn golden brown.

To finish the dish, preheat the oven to 180°C. Place the pancetta strips and cubes onto an ovenproof tray. Deep fry the breaded chicken wings until light brown, then place on the tray with the pancetta. Pan fry the scallops by placing a medium frying pan on the heat until it starts to smoke a little. Add a drizzle of rapeseed oil and season the scallops with salt and pepper. Place in the frying pan for 1 minute on each side until golden brown. Add the scallops to the tray with the chicken wings and pancetta. Place the tray with all the elements into the hot oven for 2 minutes to heat everything through.

To serve, we like to use rectangular plates, but any plates will do. Add the pea cream, then the scallops, chicken wing and pancetta strips and cubes. Finish with a little garnish of pea shoots and serve immediately.

ALEX CHOW

" All of us at Kai Mayfair are thrilled to be able to support Cancer Research UK through this great ChariTable Bookings publication."

WASABI PRAWNS
SERVES 4 | PREPARATION TIME 45 MINUTES | COOKING TIME 3 MINUTES

For the Wasabi Dressing
   300g mayonnaise
   7.5g wasabi powder, dissolved in a
   small amount of water
   15ml lemon juice
   5g gelatine powder, mixed with a
   teaspoon of water

For the Prawns
   600g tiger prawns
   4g salt
   4g sugar
   ½ an egg white
   15g potato starch
   1 pinch of white pepper
   1 drop of sesame oil

To prepare the wasabi dressing, mix all of the ingredients together, stirring thoroughly, and leave to rest and infuse whilst you cook the prawns.

To make the prawns, peel, removing the thick black vein running down the back. Wash the prawns under running water and pat dry with a lint free cloth. Mix the remaining ingredients together thoroughly. Fully coat the prawns with the mix. Heat sufficient oil for deep frying to 180°C. Deep fry until golden brown. Remove and roll the prawns in the wasabi mayonnaise.

To serve, plate as pictured.

IAN CLARK

"St Mungo's provides a bed for more than 2,500 people every night... but there are still more that need one. I am giving my Gallimaufry recipe to ChariTable Bookings to raise awareness with all readers of this book of the amazing work St Mungo's does."

HAKE with curried cauliflower, almond and kohlrabi bhaji

SERVES 1 | PREPARATION TIME 20 MINUTES | COOKING TIME 20 MINUTES

For the Hake
- 200g hake fillet, pin boned
- 20g butter
- 1 splash of oil

For the Kohlrabi Bhaji
- 1 kohlrabi
- 1 shallot
- 15g curry powder
- 5g onion seeds
- 5g salt
- 100g flour
- 20g fresh coriander
- 100ml water

For the Curried Cauliflower Purée
- 1 heads of cauliflower, chopped
- 1 onions, sliced
- 1 tbsp vegetable oil
- 1 tbp mild curry powder
- 1 lime leaves
- 1 tbsp ground cumin
- 1 tbsp ground coriander
- 1 tins of coconut milk
- 50g ground almonds

For the Dressing
- 50g flaked almonds, toasted
- 50g fresh coriander
- 1 lemon, zest and juice
- 100ml rapeseed oil

To cook the hake, heat an ovenproof frying pan, then add oil. Place the fish skin-side down and fry for 1 minute. Finish in oven for 6 minutes at 200°C, then baste with butter. Rest for 2 minutes.

To make the kohlrabi bhaji, slice shallots and kohlrabi then add salt. Leave for 5 minutes to break down the vegetables, then rinse and dry. Add all other ingredients and mix. Deep fry until golden, then season with salt, pepper and chopped coriander.

To make the curried cauliflower purée, sweat down the onions and cauliflower with the almonds and spices, then add coconut milk and simmer for 10–12 minutes. Blitz in a blender until smooth and season to taste.

To make the dressing, blanch the coriander in boiling water then take out into ice water. Squeeze all water out of the coriander then add to a jug blender along with all other ingredients.

To serve, plate as pictured.

DERRY CLARKE

Charity and Food - logical idea by ChariTable Bookings! I'm including L'Ecrivain's crispy duck breast in support of Teenline Ireland, a much needed confidential helpline supporting young people no matter what background they are from."

CRISPY DUCK BREAST with sage and thyme glazed butternut squash, shallots, cured bacon and star anise jus

SERVES 4 | PREPARATION TIME 30 MINUTES | COOKING TIME 45 MINUTES

For the Duck
4 duck breasts
1 butternut squash, peeled and cubed
4 large shallots, peeled and halved
200g cured bacon, cut, blanched and cubed
1 orange, juiced
1 lime, juiced
1 tbsp olive oil
50g butter
50g fresh sage, chopped
50g fresh thyme, chopped
sea salt and freshly cracked black pepper
1 tbsp honey

For the Star Anise Jus
100g brown sugar
100ml red wine vinegar
2 oranges, juiced and zested
4 star anise, lightly crushed
250ml demi glaze or beef stock

To prepare the garnishes, put the butternut squash, shallots and bacon in a bowl. Add the orange, lime, olive oil, butter, sage and thyme; season with sea salt and cracked black pepper. Toss all the ingredients together and spread onto a roasting tray. Drizzle with honey and bake in the oven at 180°C until tender, about 15–20 minutes.

To prepare the duck, place skin-side down on a cold, heavy-bottomed frying pan. Place on a high heat until the skin is crisp, normally about 5 minutes. Turn the duck breast over and reduce the heat, cook for a further 3–5 minutes. This will cook the duck so it is still pink, cook longer for medium and well done.

To make the star anise jus, heat the sugar and vinegar in a saucepan over a medium heat until it forms a brown caramel, being careful not to overcook as it will become bitter. Add the orange juice, star anise and demi-glace or beef stock, then simmer for 5 minutes over a low heat. Strain, check the seasoning and add the orange zest.

To finish, allow the duck breast ample time to rest and carve lengthways. Spoon the vegetables onto serving plates, place the duck on top and serve with a little sauce on the side.

SALLY CLARKE

While many of us are lucky enough to work and eat in restaurants, many are going hungry while tonnes are going to waste every week. City Harvest works to prevent that waste and get that surplus to the hungry. It's so important to get the balance which is why I'm donating my recipe from Clarke's to ChariTable Bookings."

SEA BASS BAKED WITH POTATO AND FENNEL

SERVES 6 | PREPARATION TIME 35 MINUTES | COOKING TIME 1 HOUR 5 MINUTES (REDUCE TO 40 MINUTES IF USING FILLETS)

For the Dish

2.5–3kg whole sea bass, alternatively you can use fillets
60ml olive oil
100ml orange juice
1 orange, peel only
1 bunch of dill, stalks and leaves picked separately
1 tbsp fennel seeds
2 bulbs of fennel
3 large Desiree or other roasting potatoes
4 bay leaves
salt and pepper, to taste

To prepare, preheat the oven to 170°C. Rinse the fish in very cold water and dry inside and out with kitchen paper. Wash, peel and slice the potatoes thickly. Wash and cut across the fennel in medium-fine slices, keeping the leafy fronds for later. In a small pan toast the fennel seeds for a few seconds until fragrant, then crush using a mortar and pestle.

Place the vegetables in a roasting tray. Add the olive oil, salt, pepper, bay leaves, orange peel, half the picked dill leaves and half the crushed fennel seeds. Jumble together by hand until well incorporated and spread out flat.

Roast the vegetables for 15 minutes, remove from the oven and stir gently to prevent the pieces from sticking to the base. Meanwhile, fill the cavity of the fish with the fennel fronds, dill stalks and remaining dill, then season generously with salt and pepper.

Place the sea bass on top of the vegetables, drizzle with olive oil, sprinkle with the remaining fennel seeds and return to the oven for 45 minutes or until the fish flakes easily away from the bone.

If fillets are used, roast the vegetables first for 20–25 minutes until almost tender, then lay the fillets on top, skin-side up, sprinkle with fennel seeds, fennel fronds, the remaining dill leaves, salt, pepper and olive oil. Bake for a further 10–12 minutes or until the skin is crisp.

Five minutes before the end of cooking time, remove from the oven, pour the orange juice over the vegetables, taking care to avoid the fish skin, then bake until the vegetables have partially absorbed the juices and the skin of the fish is beautifully crisp.

Serve straight from the oven in the baking dish, or slightly cooled with a garlic and orange zest mayonnaise.

TOM CLARKE

I'm sharing L'Ortolan's signature quail dish in support of the amazing work that Brainstrust does with brain tumour sufferers across the UK. I hope this collection of recipes by ChariTable Bookings is a great success and raises awareness for the great work these charities do."

QUAIL

SERVES 2 | PREPARATION TIME 2 HOURS | COOKING TIME 2–3 HOURS

Equipment
sous vide and vacuum pack bags
smoker

For the Quail
1 quail
10g rock salt
hay and wood chippings
100g goose fat
5g mixed herbs

For the Quail Eggs
2 quail eggs
1l water
50ml white wine vinegar

For the Granola
25g light brown sugar
25ml pomace oil
25ml maple syrup
75g oats
25g flaked almonds
15g pumpkin seeds

For the Truffle Pomme Purée
300g potatoes
35g butter, melted
35ml milk
2ml truffle oil
fresh truffle, grated
salt, to taste

For the Sweetcorn Purée
2 banana shallots, finely sliced
10ml oil
2 tins Green Giant sweetcorn
200ml double cream

For the Sweetcorn Salsa
1 red chilli, seeds removed, brunoise
1 tin Green Giant sweetcorn
1 pinch of salt
beurre noisette, to bind

For the Garnish
1 corn on the cob (for charred sweetcorn)
1 tin Green Giant sweetcorn (for powder and ash)
50g kataifi pastry

To prepare the quail, begin by separating the legs, wings and crown. Cover and cure the legs with rock salt for 1 hour. While the legs cure, bring the sous vide machine to 62°C. Vacuum pack the crown and cook in the machine for 30 minutes. Once the crown is cooked, refresh it in ice water. Place a handful of hay and some wood chippings in a deep oven tray and light with a match until burnt and smoking. Place the cooked crowns in the tray and cover the pan with cling film, allowing them to smoke for 20–30 minutes. Wash the salt off of the legs and pat them down with a clean kitchen towel. Vacuum pack the legs with the goose fat and mixed herbs and cook in the sous vide machine 72°C for 2–4 hours or until well done. Once cooked, strain the jus and set to one side. Allow the legs to cool and trim as desired.

To make the granola, begin by warming the sugar, pomace oil and maple syrup over a low heat until thoroughly melted and mixed. Pour the mixture over the oats, flaked almonds and pumpkin seeds, making sure to stir continuously. Spread the mixture over a lined baking tray and cook at 160°C until golden, about 35–40 minutes.

To prepare the quail eggs, bring the water and vinegar to the boil in a large pan. Place the eggs in a spaghetti basket and boil rapidly for exactly 2 minutes and 5 seconds, immediately plunging them into ice water afterwards. Peel the eggs under a running tap. Set to one side.

To make the sweetcorn purée, sauté the shallots in the oil until translucent. In the same pan, add the 2 tins of sweetcorn and cover with the double cream. Cook until tender, then blitz the mixture until smooth. Finally, pass through a fine sieve and season as required.

To make the sweetcorn salsa, combine the chilli, sweetcorn, salt and butter to bind.

To make the truffle pomme purée, bake the potatoes on a tray of salt until the flesh is soft. Mash the potatoes until smooth. Mix the butter, milk, truffle oil, fresh truffle and salt together and slowly spoon into the mash, bit by bit. Store in a piping bag and set to one side.

To prepare the sweetcorn decoration, peel the husks from the corn on the cob and blanch in seasoned water for 10 minutes at a rolling boil, then refresh in ice water. Trim the sides into flat sections, making sure to keep them solid and attached. Blacken the top with either a blowtorch or in a hot pan, then place on the plate.

For the sweetcorn ash, roast the sweetcorn kernels on a roasting tray and bake at 200°C until blackened. Allow them to fully cool and blitz into a fine powder.

For the sweetcorn powder, allow the tin of sweetcorn contents to dry at room temperature until fully crisp then blend into a fine powder.

To serve, deep fry the kataifi pastry at 180°C until golden, drain on a paper towel, season with the sweetcorn powder, ash and salt. Decorate the plate as pictured, placing the quail egg on the kataifi pastry, the quail on top of the sweetcorn salsa, purée and granola. Cover everything generously with the reserved jus. Pipe the pomme purée around the plate and serve.

GARETH CLELLAND

It's a pleasure to create great dishes in The Wright Brothers' kitchen and to know that we are helping ChariTable Bookings support Cancer Research UK."

CRAB

SERVES 4 | PREPARATION TIME 15 MINUTES | COOKING TIME 10 MINUTES

For the Dish

1 x 800g–1kg brown crab, cooked
3 cloves of garlic, sliced
30g unsalted butter
2 tbsp fresh ginger, diced
1 red chilli, finely chopped
½ lemon, juiced
1 pinch of sea salt
35g coriander stalks and leaves, chopped

Remove the claws from the crab, and discard the dead man's fingers. Chop the body into 4 pieces, and crack the claws with a rolling pin.

Gently heat the garlic in the butter until soft. Add the ginger, chilli and crab.

Turn up to heat for 1 minute to start cooking the chilli and ginger, then transfer to the oven and cook at 200°C for 8 minutes.

Season with the lemon juice, salt and add the chopped coriander. Transfer to a bowl to serve.

DANIEL CLIFFORD

"The Poppy Factory is the country's leading employment charity for veterans with health conditions or impairments. Midsummer House and its team are delighted to support them by sharing our recipe with ChariTable Bookings and their new charity fundraising venture."

VENISON with chervil, elderberry and cavolo nero

SERVES 4 | PREPARATION TIME 2 HOURS | COOKING TIME 1 HOUR

Equipment
sous vide and vacuum pack bags

For the Venison
4 x 60g venison loins
salt

For the Chervil Root Purée
500g chervil root, peeled
25ml milk
salt

For the Chervil Fondants
1 kg chervil roots
40g unsalted butter

For the Pickled Elderberry and Jelly
200g elderberries
100ml each red wine, red wine vinegar and elderberry cordial
5g pickled spices
200ml elderberry liquor
2g agar agar

For the Venison Sausage Roll
1 small onion, diced
3 cloves of garlic, chopped
100ml whisky
500g venison neck, minced
500g lardons
100g venison liver
3 juniper berries
½ tsp smoked paprika
1¼ tsp salt
puff pastry

To prepare the venison loin, season the loin with salt then vacuum pack and cook at 62°C for 28 minutes. Take out of the bag and pan fry until coloured on all sides.

To make the chervil root purée, finely slice the chervil root and seal in a vacuum bag with the milk. Cook at 100°C for 30 minutes. Remove and blend until smooth, then season with lemon juice and salt.

To prepare the chervil root fondants, peel the chervil roots and halve lengthways. Melt the butter in a pan. Add the chervil root cut-side down. Bring the butter to a foam. Add a little water to control the temperature, cook until golden brown, then rest in the butter.

To prepare the pickled elderberry, bring the wine, cordial, vinegar and spices to the boil. When boiling, add the elderberries and remove from the heat. Allow to cool naturally. Prepare the elderberry jelly by bringing the elderberry liquor and agar agar to the boil. Remove from the heat and allow to set. Blend until smooth, then pass through a sieve.

To make the venison sausage roll, sweat the onion and garlic until soft. Add the spices and cook for 3 minutes, then add the whisky. Transfer to a bowl then mix with the rest of the ingredients. Roll the mixture into small sausages and wrap in puff pastry. Glaze with egg yolk and bake for 13 minutes at 210°C until the pastry goes crisp.

To prepare the venison sauce, roast the vegetables separately, then add the redcurrant jelly. Cook out until sticky. Deglaze with vinegar and reduce until sticky again. Add the stocks, bring to the boil and skim off any scum. Add the bones, garlic, parsley, thyme, tarragon, white peppercorns and juniper berries. Cook out for 25 minutes then sieve. Pass the liquid once through a single muslin and 7 times through a double muslin. Reduce to desired consistency.

Remove the stems of the cavolo nero, cut into 5cm pieces and cook in a light butter emulsion. When ready to serve, assemble the dish as pictured.

For the Venison Sauce

4 sticks of celery, sliced

6 shallots, sliced

2 tbsp redcurrant jelly

500ml merlot vinegar

4l veal stock

2l chicken stock

2 bulbs of garlic

1 sprig each parsley, thyme and tarragon

1 tsp white peppercorns

2 juniper berries, crushed

6 plum tomatoes

2kg venison bones, roasted

For the Cavolo Nero

cavolo nero

1 knob of butter

1 splash of water

LUKE COCKERILL

" The Rabbit In The Moon prides itself on its creativity and unique vision, qualities that ChariTable Bookings are able to use when supporting great causes like Beyond Food."

PAIN AU UNAGI

SERVES 5 | PREPARATION TIME 45 MINUTES (PLUS OVERNIGHT TO CHILL) | COOKING TIME 25 MINUTES

For the Unagi Eel Mousse
- 300ml cream
- 100ml milk
- 300ml unagi sauce
- 160g kuzu
- 600g smoked eel fillets, deskinned
- 20ml vinegar
- 20g salt
- 10 whole baby sand eels, frozen

For the Pastry
- 500g soft butter
- 920g P45 flour
- 14g osmo dried yeast
- 15g salt
- 95g sugar
- 370ml cold water

For the Glaze
- 1 egg yolk
- unagi sauce

To prepare the mousse, heat the cream, milk and unagi sauce to 40°C then blend with kuzu for 3 minutes on low speed. Add the smoked eel fillets, vinegar and salt and blend on high until smooth then pass through a chinois. Return the liquid to the pan and bring to a simmer stirring constantly. Decant while hot into a piping bag. Line the sand eels up on baking parchment and pipe the mousse over the sand eels so the head and tail are still seen. Cool in the fridge.

To prepare the pastry, roll the butter into squares between parchment to the thickness of 7mm and refrigerate. Weigh all the other ingredients into a dough mixer and knead for 5 minutes on a medium speed until fully incorporated. Leave the dough in the fridge overnight. Roll the dough to a thickness of 7mm and place the butter in the centre of the dough, folding the dough over the butter till covered. Roll to 7mm again but this time do a book fold with the dough. Repeat this step again then refrigerate for 30 minutes. Roll the dough to a 3mm thickness and cut into 4x10 cm rectangles.

To finish, place two frozen sand eels and mousse on the top and bottom of the rectangle then role into a pan au chocolate shape. Leave the pain au unagi in a warm place on a baking tray until it has doubled in size. Mix the egg yolk with unagi ($^{50}/_{50}$) until smooth and glaze the pain au unagi. Bake in the oven at 180°C for 25 minutes.

CLAUDE COMPTON

"
Everyone deserves somewhere to call home. Claude's Kitchen is supporting Shelter via ChariTable Bookings to help give everyone that chance."

LINE-CAUGHT COD with cabbage, lovage, buttermilk and new potatoes

SERVES 4 | PREPARATION TIME 3 HOURS | COOKING TIME 3 HOURS

For the Cod
1 fillet line-caught cod
1 dash of rapeseed oil
1 pinch of salt

For the Kale
1 big bunch of kale
oil, for frying

For the Lovage
1 bunch of lovage, the leaves on
organic celery will otherwise suffice
300ml buttermilk
2 lemons, juiced
1 pinch of sea salt

For the New Potatoes and Cabbage
500g new potatoes
1 dash of rapeseed oil
sea salt
1 clove of garlic, crushed
1 hispi cabbage

To prepare the kale, dry half the kale in a 50°C oven for about 3 hours. Whizz the dried kale at high speed in a blender and set aside. Preheat a deep pan half-filled with oil to 170°C. Add the remaining kale to the hot oil, take care as the oil will spit. Keep frying until the spitting just about stops, drain on kitchen paper and season with salt.

To prepare the lovage and buttermilk, set aside some nice lovage leaves for the garnish. Add the remaining lovage, buttermilk, lemon juice and a pinch of salt to a blender. Whizz at high speed and pour through a sieve. Keep in the fridge.

Place the potatoes in an oven tray, drizzle with oil and season with sea salt. Add a crushed garlic clove and roast covered with foil at 180°C for 15 minutes, then remove the foil and roast open for another 15 minutes.

To prepare the cabbage, remove and discard the outer leaves, wash and quarter into wedges. Add to salted, boiling water for 5 minutes and remove with a slotted spoon.

To prepare the cod, get the fishmonger to slice the cod into portion sizes, leaving the skin on but removing the scales. Season the cod skin with salt and drizzle with rapeseed oil. Place a heavy bottomed ovenproof pan over a medium-high heat and pour in a little oil. Once the oil is smoking, put the cod fillets in, skin-side down. Cook for 2 minutes until the skin is golden brown. Transfer to the oven for 5 minutes at 180°C until the fish is cooked. Bring the pan out of the oven and immediately turn the fish over.

To serve, place the hispi on the plate, scatter the new potatoes and rest the fish, skin-side up, on top. Add the lovage sauce, and sprinkle the kale dust and crisps.

STUART CONIBEAR

Colbert is proud to support Leuka and to join ChariTable Bookings in helping to raise funds and awareness to combat Leukaemia, support sufferers and help find a cure."

WHOLE PLAICE in brown butter with brown shrimps

SERVES 2 | PREPARATION TIME 15 MINUTES | COOKING TIME 30 MINUTES

For the Plaice

1 x 450g whole plaice, head and
back skin removed
20ml vegetable oil
50g unsalted butter, diced
½ lemon, juiced
10g brown shrimps
10g plum tomatoes, diced
2g flat leaf parsley, finely chopped
10ml veal jus
salt and pepper, to taste

To prepare the fish, season well on both sides and, in a non-stick pan, heat the vegetable oil and seal the plaice skin-side down until a nice caramelised brown colour is achieved.

Turn the fish and add the diced butter to the pan. As the fish cooks, repeatedly spoon the butter back over the meat allowing the colour to turn to a nut brown.

To finish the dish and serve, squeeze in the lemon juice, add the shrimp, diced tomatoes and finish with chopped parsley. Plate the dish as pictured, making a thin line on the plate with the veal jus to capture the butter. Generously pour over the pan juices and serve.

GENNARO CONTALDO

"What a wonderful way to support the work of The Jamie Oliver Foundation through this unique ChariTable Bookings recipe book and make such a vital difference to those most in need by simply buying this as the perfect gift for all foodies."

LA GENOVESE CON PENNETTE slow-cooked onion sauce with pasta, followed by veal
SERVES 4 | PREPARATION TIME 30 MINUTES | COOKING TIME 3 HOURS

For the Dish
- 800g veal joint
- 2 cloves of garlic, sliced
- 100ml extra virgin olive oil
- 2½kg large onions, sliced
- 1 celery stalk, finely chopped
- 1 large carrot, finely chopped
- 85g salami, finely chopped
- 3 sage leaves
- 1 sprig of rosemary
- 2 bay leaves
- 200ml dry white wine
- 350g pennette pasta
- 30g Pecorino Romano, grated
- salt
- freshly ground black pepper

To Serve
- green salad

To prepare the veal, rub it all over with salt and pepper, make some incisions in the meat and poke in the garlic slices.

Heat the olive oil in a large saucepan on a medium heat. Add the veal and brown well all over. Remove from the pan and set aside.

Add the onions, celery, carrot, salami and herbs. Season with salt and pepper and sweat for about 30 minutes on a low heat.

Put the meat back in the pan, add the wine and allow to evaporate. Reduce the heat to very low, cover with a lid and cook for 3 hours until the meat is very tender. Check from time to time to make sure it isn't sticking to the pan, turning the meat and stirring the onions. Remove the meat from the pan and set aside.

Using a potato masher, mash the onion mixture and season according to taste.

Cook the pennette in lightly salted, boiling water until al dente. Drain and toss with the onion mixture and any pieces of veal that have separated from the joint during cooking. Serve with grated Pecorino cheese and freshly ground black pepper.

Place the veal joint in a large dish, slice and serve as a main course with green salad.

SHAY COOPER

I'm delighted to be sharing The Goring's signature plaice dish in aid of Macmillan and the fantastic work they do supporting sufferers of cancer and their families. This is a great initiative by ChariTable Bookings."

PLAICE FILLET with gem lettuce, cucumber and potted shrimp butter

SERVES 4–6 | PREPARATION TIME 25 MINUTES (PLUS OVERNIGHT HANGING) | COOKING TIME 1 HOUR 30 MINUTES

For the Tomato Water

1kg ripe tomatoes

10g each basil, chervil, coriander and Maldon salt

10ml white wine vinegar

5g sugar

For the Potted Shrimp Butter Sauce

30g shallots, diced

1 star anise

1g each fennel seeds, cayenne pepper, mild curry powder, ground coriander and salt

200ml chicken stock

100ml tomato water

40g butter

lemon juice, to taste

For the Finished Sauce

50g hand peeled brown shrimps

30g fennel, brunoise

30g compressed cucumber, diced

5g each chives and dill, chopped

For the Baby Gem

assorted baby gem leaves

25ml vegetable oil

50ml chicken stock

salt, to taste

For the Plaice

1.5kg plaice

100ml olive oil

watercress, to garnish

To make the tomato water, blitz all of the ingredients together and hang in muslin cloth overnight.

To make the potted shrimp butter sauce, sweat the shallot with the star anise, fennel, cayenne, curry powder and coriander. Deglaze with chicken stock and reduce by half. Add the tomato water and monté in the butter. Add lemon juice and salt to taste. Strain into a clean pan and add the second set of sauce ingredients, warming the mixture gently and adjusting the seasoning to taste.

To prepare the baby gem, select a few choice leaves, heat a non-stick pan, add a little oil and sauté rapidly. Deglaze with chicken stock and allow the leaves to warm for serving.

To cook the plaice, fillet, remove the skin and lightly salt to firm the flesh, leaving to one side for 20 minutes. Once rested, wash under a running tap, pat dry, portion and grill in olive oil until just cooked.

To serve, assemble as pictured.

PHILIP CORRICK

This is one of my favourite winter recipes – it's a timeless classic. On behalf of the Royal Automobile Club, I'm thrilled to support the Dennis Wise and Frankham Group Charitable Trust, helping to improve the lives of children and adults with disabilities, and ChariTable Bookings."

ROSETTES OF VENISON with blueberries and spiced pear

SERVES 4 | PREPARATION TIME 1 DAY | COOKING TIME 1 HOUR 30 MINUTES

For the Venison
600g venison loin fillet, fully trimmed

For the Marinade
1 bottle of claret wine
100g carrot, diced
100g onion, diced
50g celery, diced
50g leek, diced
10g garlic
50ml olive oil
10ml red wine vinegar
1 sprig each of thyme and parsley

For the Spiced Pears
4 mini pears, de-cored
500ml water
100g granulated sugar
1 stick of cinnamon
1 lemon, juiced
1 vanilla pod

For the Sauce
1l game stock
100g carrot, diced
100g onion, diced
50g leek, diced
50g celery, diced
1 sprig of thyme
10g black peppercorns, crushed
50g redcurrant jelly
75g butter
100g blueberries
25g dark chocolate

To make the marinade, place all the ingredients in a pan, bring to the boil and cool. When cold, pour over the venison and place in the fridge for at least 24 hours.

For the spiced pears, place the water, cinnamon stick, vanilla pod, sugar and lemon juice in a pan, and bring to the boil. Place the pears in the syrup and cook until tender but still firm. Allow to cool in the syrup and set aside.

To prepare the sauce, put the carrot, onion, thyme, leek, celery, garlic and peppercorns with half the butter in a thick bottomed pan. Cook until the vegetables have slightly browned, add the marinade from the venison and reduce by three quarters. Add the game stock, boil and reduce to a sauce consistency. Finish with the redcurrant jelly, the chocolate and the remainder of the butter. Pass through a fine strainer into a clean pan.

To cook the venison, dry the meat on a clean cloth and season well with salt and pepper. Heat a pan, add a little oil and seal the meat over a fierce heat. Place in a hot oven for 10–15 minutes until cooked pink. Remove from the oven and leave to rest.

To serve, finish the sauce with the blueberries and a little Eau de Vie Myrtilles – optional. Remove the pears from the syrup, drain, sprinkle with ground cinnamon and place in the oven to warm through. Slice the venison and arrange on the plates. Pour sauce around and garnish with the pears. Serve with Dauphinoise potatoes and braised red cabbage.

Editor's Note: *Eau de Vie Myrtille is a spirit made with macerated blueberries.*

RICHARD CORRIGAN

I'm offering up my Royal Fish Pie from Bentley's in support of the fantastic work that the NH Youth Centre in King's Cross does to prevent young people ending up on the streets. A great concept by ChariTable Bookings to produce a cookbook for multiple charities, not just one."

ROYAL FISH PIE

SERVES 4 | PREPARATION TIME 45 MINUTES | COOKING TIME 1 HOUR 30 MINUTES

For the Dish

1kg fish fillets, including salmon, smoked haddock and white fish such as pollock and haddock (the smoked haddock trimmings will be used in the sauce)

1.5kg floury potatoes

2 egg yolks

For the Sauce

100g butter, plus a little extra for sweating vegetables

1 onion, diced

2 cloves of garlic, crushed

1 sprig of thyme

150ml white wine

smoked haddock trimmings

2l milk

100g plain flour

1 tbsp English mustard

1 handful of chives and parsley, chopped

salt and pepper

To Finish

a little lemon juice

a little green Tabasco sauce

1 handful of fresh breadcrumbs

a little grated Parmesan

lobster head, for optional decoration

To prepare the fish, remove the skin and cut into bite-sized pieces, reserving the skin of the smoked haddock for the sauce. Preheat the oven to 180°C.

To make the sauce, heat a little butter in a saucepan, add the onion, garlic and thyme and sweat until softened. Add the white wine and the smoked haddock trimmings and cook for a few minutes to burn off the alcohol. Add the milk and bring to just under the boil, then take the pan from the heat, pass the contents through a sieve into a bowl and keep hot. Melt the butter in a heavy-bottomed saucepan, add the flour and cook over a low heat, stirring well, for 5 minutes. Pour the hot, infused milk into the pan and whisk vigorously until the mixture is smooth and thick. Taste to make sure you can't taste the flour. If you can, cook gently for a little longer. Whisk in the mustard and add the chives and parsley. Check the seasoning and add salt and pepper and more mustard if you wish. Leave to cool down while you make the mash. It is best not to assemble the pie with hot sauce as it will cook the fish too quickly.

To make the mash, peel the potatoes and cook in boiling, salted water until tender. Drain in a colander and allow the potatoes to steam for a couple of minutes to rid them of excess moisture, then mash and season with salt and pepper. Add the egg yolks. Scoop the mash into a piping bag – it needs to be hot in order to pipe easily. If you prefer not to pipe, the mash can be spooned on carefully, then plough lines across it with the prongs of a fork.

To assemble, spoon a little of the sauce into the bottom of each of the pie dishes. Arrange a selection of fish on top of the sauce. Season with salt and pepper, a squeeze of lemon juice and a few drops of green Tabasco. Completely cover with sauce, then pipe or spoon on the mash. Mix together the breadcrumbs and Parmesan and sprinkle evenly over the pies.

Place the pie dishes on a baking sheet and cook in the oven for around 20 minutes until the top is golden brown and the centre of each pie is good and hot. Serve immediately.

JIM COWIE

Diabetes UK is the largest charity in the UK focused on research, assistance with and prevention of diabetes. The correlation with food makes it particularly close to our industry. Captain's Galley is pleased to donate our signature mussel dish to ChariTable Bookings fantastic new recipe book!"

MUSSELS STEAMED with lemongrass, basil chilli and coconut juice

SERVES 2 | PREPARATION TIME 15 MINUTES | COOKING TIME 20 MINUTES

For the Mussels

1 can of coconut milk
1 tbsp galangal
2 stalks of lemongrass
1 fresh green chilli
½ tbsp lemon zest, finely grated
60ml lemon juice, plus 1 tbsp to garnish
½ tsp salt
1 tbsp groundnut oil
1 tbsp garlic, sliced
3 tbsp shallots, sliced
3 tbsp red Thai chillies, sliced
mussels, debearded
½ cup Thai basil leaves, roughly chopped
¼ cup micro coriander leaves

To prepare the dish, place the coconut milk, galangal, lemon grass and green chilli in a saucepan, and bring to the boil over a high heat. Add the lemon zest and lower the heat, letting the mixture simmer for 10 minutes.

Remove the pan from the heat and strain, pressing down on the mixture. Cool to room temperature, uncover and add the lemon juice and salt. Stir well to combine and set aside.

To cook the mussels, heat some oil in a saucepan. Add the garlic and shallots and cook until lightly browned. Stir in the chillies, then the mussels and the lemongrass infusion. Shake the pan vigorously, then add the basil and season to taste. Cover and cook until the mussels open, which should take roughly 3 minutes.

To serve, transfer the mussels to a warmed serving bowl, top with the cooking liquid and garnish with the coriander leaves.

ALAN COXON

Prostate cancer is fast becoming the most common cancer in the UK, already killing 10,000 men per year. However, it can be cured if caught early. Prostate Cancer UK is fighting to achieve early diagnosis, prevent and cure the disease. I'm very pleased to help support them with ChariTable Bookings."

AUTUMNAL CHICKEN TAGINE with a casserole of pumpkin, chestnuts, apples and prunes

SERVES 4| PREPARATION TIME 45 MINUTES | COOKING TIME 30 MINUTES

For the Dish

2 x 250g skinless chicken breasts
250g minced pork meat
½ tsp smoked paprika
¼ tsp ground cumin
4 thin rashers rindless smoked bacon
1 tbsp olive oil
1 tbsp unsalted butter
2 small onions, thinly sliced
2 cloves of garlic, thinly sliced
1 Gala apple, sliced and core removed
100g chestnuts, roasted and quartered
250g pumpkin flesh, skin and seeds removed
¼ tsp each ground turmeric, ground cinnamon and fresh ginger, grated
1 star anise
175g prunes d'Agen, stoned
150ml chicken stock
1 tsp tomato purée
1 fresh bird's eye chilli, pricked all over with a cocktail stick
1 small sprig of fresh rosemary
sea salt and freshly ground black pepper

To Serve

couscous salad
a few sprigs of fresh garden mint

To prepare the chicken, using a sharp knife, carefully and evenly slice the chicken breasts lengthways. Place the breast in between 2 sheets of non-stick greaseproof paper. Gently and evenly tap out using a meat tenderiser or rolling pin. Lay on a tray and keep aside.

In a clean bowl mix the pork mince with the smoked paprika, cumin and a little salt and pepper. Divide into 4, rolling the meat into compact balls.

Place the pork balls into the centre of each chicken breast and roll the flesh around the pork forming a larger ball, set aside in a tray or plate. When ready, take the thin slices of smoked bacon and carefully wrap around the meatballs, using string to carefully tie each ball together so that it holds its shape.

To cook, heat the olive oil in a heavy-based casserole or flameproof tagine over medium-high heat. Put the meatballs in, followed by the butter, and fry for 6–8 minutes until evenly browned. Reduce the heat to medium, add the onion and garlic, and gently fry for 5 minutes until soft and slightly caramelised. Incorporate the apple, chestnuts and pumpkin and continue to colour lightly. Add the turmeric, ginger, cinnamon, star anise and prunes, stirring well for a couple of minutes. Mix in the stock, tomato purée, chilli pepper and rosemary. Season lightly with salt and pepper, cover with the tagine lid and cook for 18–20 minutes, stirring occasionally.

To serve, remove the string from the meatballs, arrange on 4 plates, scatter with a few lightly torn pieces of mint and serve with a couscous salad.

ALEX CRACIUN

"*Hospitality Action works hard within our industry helping those struggling with a wide range of issues. I'm sharing Sosharu's tonkatsu pork with this ChariTable Bookings project in support of them.*"

TONKATSU CRUMBED PORK with radish salad

SERVES 2 | PREPARATION TIME 30 MINUTES | COOKING TIME 5 MINUTES

For the Tonkatsu Sauce
- 80g ketchup
- 2 tbsp Worcestershire sauce
- 1 tbsp soy sauce
- 1 tbsp mirin
- 1 tbsp sugar
- 1 tsp Dijon mustard
- ¼ tsp garlic powder

For the Tonkatsu
- 2 x 150g pork loin steaks
- salt and pepper
- 50g flour
- 2 eggs, beaten
- 100g panko breadcrumbs
- 1l vegetable oil, for frying

For the Radish Salad
- 50g round radishes
- 50g kohlrabi
- 50g breakfast radishes

For the Salad Dressing
- 25ml white wine vinegar
- 150ml olive oil
- salt and pepper, to taste

First, make the Tonkatsu sauce by stirring together all the ingredients in a small bowl. Set aside to allow the flavours to develop.

Lay the pork loin fillets on a chopping board, fat-side up. Tap the fillet with the back edge of a knife to create some soft notches in the meat, before pounding them on both sides with the flat side of the knife to flatten them. Slice 1cm notches into the fat of each fillet, and season on both sides with salt and pepper. Fill a pan with the vegetable oil, and begin to heat to 180°C – if you don't have a thermometer, test the heat by sprinkling a few panko crumbs in – they should bubble and rise to the top.

Begin the bread-crumbing process while the oil is heating up. Line up 4 plates on your kitchen counter. Put the flour on the first plate, the beaten egg on the second, the panko breadcrumbs on the third, and layer some paper towels on the fourth plate.

Take a pork loin and dredge it in flour on both sides, shaking off the excess. Next, dip it in the egg, coating on both sides. Finally, lay the fillet on the panko breadcrumbs, piling the breadcrumbs on top of the pork with your fingers and gently pressing it into the meat. Repeat for the second pork loin. Once the oil is at temperature, carefully slide the pork loin fillets into the pan. Cook for about 4 minutes until golden, before removing from the pan with a slotted spoon and leaving on the paper-lined plate to drain.

Slice the radishes as thinly possible, preferably with a mandoline. To create the salad dressing, mix all the ingredients together, using a hand blender to emulsify, and season with salt and pepper. Dress the radishes with the dressing.

To serve, slice the Tonkatsu into 2.5cm strips, and place on the plate along with a heap of the radish salad and an extra dab of Dijon mustard, if you like. Top with around 2 tablespoons of the Tonkatsu sauce, or serve on the side in a small bowl.

RHIAN CRADDOCK

"Often it is circumstance that creates a need. The Feathers Inn is more than proud to champion the West End Refugee Service, and to introduce it to ChariTable Bookings, an excellent organisation with a long reach."

HEDLEY ROE DEER LOIN BAKED IN PASTRY with chicken liver pâté, field mushrooms
and spring vegetables

SERVES 4 | PREPARATION TIME 40 MINUTES | COOKING TIME 2 HOURS

For the Roe Deer Loin in Pastry

4 x 130g roe deer loin portions

200g field mushrooms

400g puff pastry, rolled 4mm
thick, divided into 4 squares of
approximately 15cm

200g chicken liver pâté, or any other
pâté of choice, cut into 4 x 25g slices

4 sprigs of thyme, picked and chopped

1 clove of garlic, very finely chopped

50ml olive oil

salt and pepper, to taste

1 egg yolk, whisked with 1 tsp water

**For the Red Wine, Port and Redcurrant
Jelly Sauce**

1 sprig each of rosemary and thyme

½ bay leaf

1 clove of garlic, peeled and bashed

½ leek, washed and chopped

1 carrot, cut into 2.5cm pieces

2 stalks of parsley

½ onion, diced into 2.5cm pieces

250ml red wine

100ml port

250g roe deer bones and trimmings,
roasted

500ml roasted chicken stock

water, to cover

25g redcurrant jelly

To Serve

a selection of seasonal vegetables

To make the roe deer loin in pastry, mix together the thyme, garlic and olive oil. Liberally drizzle over the mushrooms on a baking tray. Season and cook in a hot oven for 20 minutes. Remove when soft and cooked, with their juices leaking out. Chop finely, then dry the minced mushrooms in a pan on a low heat, until all the liquid has evaporated. Place onto a tray and leave to cool.

To cook the loin, season the loin portions and seal in a hot pan to caramelise the meat. Set aside and rest.

To assemble the pie, lay the rolled puff pastry out on baking parchment, so it won't stick to the bench. Spoon a layer of mushroom mixture onto the centre of each portion of the puff pastry. Place a slice of the pâté onto each pile of mushrooms, followed by the roe deer loin and finally, one more spoonful of the mushroom mixture. Lift the sides of pastry over the top of the filling before rolling each portion up into a parcel. Seal each parcel with the egg yolk wash and place on a tray lined with baking parchment. Finish by brushing with more egg yolk. Place in the fridge until ready to cook.

To make the red wine, port and redcurrant jelly sauce, caramelise the vegetables and herbs in a heavy-bottomed pan with a little oil. Deglaze with the red wine, then add the port. Reduce the liquor by half. Add the deer bones and cover with the stock. If there is not enough stock to cover the bones, top up with a little water. Bring the liquid to a boil and simmer for 1–2 hours. When the sauce is rich and has thickened slightly, pass the mixture through a sieve into another pan and whisk in the redcurrant jelly. Bring the sauce back to a boil and transfer to a container to cool.

To serve, preheat an oven to 220°C. Put the deer parcels into the oven. Bake for 15 minutes, or until golden brown and crispy. Remove from the oven and leave to rest for 5 minutes before serving. Reheat the sauce, slice the deer parcels into 2 halves and transfer to 4 warmed plates, with one side displaying the meat, the deer should be cooked rare to medium inside the pastry. Spoon the vegetables around the deer, then generously cover with the sauce.

ALISTAIR CRAIG

Oakhaven is a local hospice to us at Careys Manor providing palliative care to terminally ill patients. Please support them in their hard work and enjoy our dish through ChariTable Bookings as a thank you!"

HONEY ROAST PHEASANT with black pudding and celeriac

SERVES 2 | PREPARATION TIME 15 MINUTES | COOKING TIME 30 MINUTES

For the Pheasant
 2 pheasant crowns
 1 tbsp olive oil
 50g honey
 4 sprigs of thyme

For the Black Pudding and Celeriac
 1 large celeriac
 1 tsp olive oil
 1 clove of garlic
 1 sprig of thyme
 8 slices black pudding
 200g cavolo nero

To Serve
 roasting juices

For the pheasant, heat a tablespoon of oil in a pan and add the pheasant crown, making sure to brown all over. Transfer to an ovenproof tray, spreading honey over the skin and covering well in thyme leaves. Roast in the oven for 9 minutes or until the juices in the meat run clear. The time will depend on the plumpness of the pheasant. Rest for 10 minutes in a warm place before carving each breast from the bone. Remove the sinew from the fillet, then carve into 2 pieces.

Peel and chop the celeriac into 2cm dice. Toss in a little olive oil and thyme and a bashed garlic clove. Transfer to an oven proof dish and roast in the oven for 10 minutes whilst the birds rest.

To serve, steam the cavolo nero at the last minute and dress the plate as pictured, drizzling generously with roasting juices from the pan.

STEPHEN CRANE

"Always happy to support the great work of Macmillan where I can. This is a very novel idea by ChariTable Bookings to share 365 recipes and I'm very pleased that Ockenden Manor's pigeon recipe is part of it."

PIGEON with boudin blanc, croquette, red cabbage ketchup, white asparagus, flower sprouts and caramelised apple

SERVES 4 | PREPARATION TIME 3 HOURS (PLUS 24 HOURS TO REST) | COOKING TIME 8 HOURS

For the Pigeon and Pigeon Croquette

- 4 whole pigeons
- 2 bulbs of garlic, roughly chopped
- 2 handfuls of mixed herbs, chopped
- 4 handfuls of coarse sea salt
- 50g duck fat
- 100g foie gras
- 200g flour
- 200ml water
- 100g panko breadcrumbs
- 1 tbsp of honey

For the Boudin Blanc

- ½ slice of white bread, crust removed
- 1 tbsp milk
- 100g chicken fillet
- 15g foie gras
- 15ml brandy
- ½ egg
- 65ml double cream
- 1 tbsp truffle paste
- salt

For the Red Cabbage Ketchup

- 1 large red cabbage, shredded
- oil, for cooking
- 3 tbsp white wine vinegar
- 250g redcurrant jelly
- 1 bottle of red wine
- 1 cup of water
- 1 stick of cinnamon
- 2 bay leaves

To make the croquette, separate the legs and wings of the pigeon from the crowns. Reserve the crowns and keep the wings for stock. Line a container with half the garlic, herb and salt mixture. Lay the legs on top and cover with the remaining mixture. Lay a damp tea towel over it, place a container on top with something heavy inside to press the legs, then leave in the fridge for 24 hours. Remove the legs from the press and wash in a sink of running water for 20 minutes. Put them into a pan and cover with duck fat. Confit for 8 hours at 90°C. Remove the legs from the duck fat, remove the skin and discard any bones. Finely chop and mix with the foie gras and some of the duck fat until an easy to mould consistency is reached. Roll the mixture into a sausage shape, wrap in cling film, and leave to set in the fridge for a couple of hours. Once set, slice the sausage into 2cm thick slices, then remove the cling film. Make a rough mixture of flour and water and use to the correct consistency. Roll the slices into the mixture, then into panko breadcrumbs. Set aside for frying.

To make the boudin blanc, make a paste from the bread and milk, warming it slightly in a pan. Put in a container, cover with cling film and cool in the fridge. Once cooled, place in a blender with the other ingredients for the boudin blanc, except the cream and truffle paste. Blitz until smooth, then pass through a fine sieve. Gently fold in the cream, truffle paste and salt to taste. Fill a piping bag with the mixture, pipe a tube along a layer of cling film and roll in to a sausage shape, sealing completely. Bring a pan of water to a gentle simmer and add the tube, ensuring the boudin blanc is completely submerged. Cook for 20 minutes, remove from the heat and allow to cool in the water. Place in the fridge to set for a few hours. Once set, slice the tube on the diagonal, 1cm thick. Reserve the slices for frying.

Sweat the shredded cabbage in oil. Add the white wine vinegar and simmer until evaporated. Add redcurrant jelly, red wine and a cup of water. Once simmering, add the cinnamon and bay leaves, turn the heat to low and cover. When completely soft, remove the lid and reduce the liquid to a glaze. Remove the cinnamon and bay leaf, then place the cabbage in a blender. Meanwhile, bring the double cream to the boil. Pour the cream and sherry vinegar into the blender, along with salt to taste. Blitz until smooth and pass through a very fine sieve.

For the Red Cabbage Ketchup *continued*

    50ml double cream

    sherry vinegar and salt, to taste

For the Asparagus with Vegetable Nage, Flower Sprouts and Apple

    8 white asparagus

    1 carrot, finely sliced

    ¼ onion, finely sliced

    ¼ leek, finely sliced

    2 cloves of garlic, bashed

    3 star anise

    4 juniper berries

    1 handful of dill stalks

    chives, finely chopped, to finish

    1 knob of butter, for cooking

    6 flower sprouts

    oil, to cook

    salt, sugar and garlic butter, to finish

    16 x 1cm cubes of Granny Smith apple

    1 tsp caster sugar

    5g butter, to cook the apple

To make the white asparagus with vegetable nage, combine all the ingredients except for the asparagus in a pan and cover with water. Bring to the boil and reduce to a simmer for 20 minutes. Remove from the heat and allow to cool, leave to infuse for 3 hours. Then pass through a double layer of muslin cloth into a pan and reduce by half. Keep in the fridge. Finally, blanch the 8 asparagus for 2 minutes in a pan of salted water with a lid. Cool in ice water. Remove excess moisture and halve lengthways. Blanch the 6 flower sprouts in the same way.

In a hot pan, season and seal the pigeon crowns on all sides. Cook in a hot oven for 4 minutes. Rest before removing the breasts from the crown. Seal the boudin blanc slices on each side, then heat through in the oven for 2 minutes. Deep fry the pigeon croquettes at 190°C, until golden brown. Add 3 tablespoons of the vegetable nage to a saucepan, along with a large knob of butter and seasoning, to make an emulsion. Heat the white asparagus through and finish with finely chopped chives. Set aside on a cloth to absorb excess liquid. For the caramelised apple, add the sugar and butter to a hot pan. Once it starts to caramelise, toss the diced apple in the caramel. Put the halved flower sprouts, cut-side down, in a hot pan with oil and colour until golden. Remove, place on a tea towel and finish with salt, sugar and garlic butter. Warm the red cabbage ketchup in a saucepan. In a pan, caramelise some honey, drop the pigeon breasts skin-side down in the honey and coat. Remove and slice each breast down the middle, lengthways and then in half. Plate the dish and drizzle with jus.

REGIS CREPY

I love the concept of helping others through our joint love of food and this ChariTable Bookings recipe book. We at Lavenham Great House Restaurant are delighted to support and raise awareness of Lavenham Community Council."

PAN-FRIED WILD SEA BASS FILLET with Coco de Paimpol beans, bacon and butter sauce

SERVES 4 | PREPARATION TIME 10 MINUTES | COOKING TIME 25 MINUTES

For the Sea Bass

4 x 150g fillet of wild sea bass, skin on and pin boned

2 tsp olive oil

For the Sauce

100g fresh Coco de Paimpol beans, or black eye peas if unavailable

100g smoked streaky bacon, diced

60g shallots, peeled and finely sliced

50ml white wine vinegar

50ml white wine

200g unsalted butter, cut into small cubes

salt and pepper

For the Garnish

1 sprig of thyme

To prepare the Coco de Paimpol beans, place them in a deep pan of boiling water and cook them for 15 minutes. Remove from the heat, drain, and let them soak in cold water until cool. Drain and rinse the beans.

To prepare the sea bass, heat the oil in a non-stick frying pan over a medium heat and fry the sea bass skin-side down for 2 minutes, or until golden brown. Place the fish in a roasting tray with a little olive oil, skin-side up, and season. Roast uncovered for 20 minutes in a preheated oven at 62°C. The flesh should be white and very tender, the skin should be crisp.

For the sauce, heat 1 tablespoon of butter in a non stick pan over a medium heat. When the butter has melted, add the shallots and fry for 2–3 minutes until they have softened but not coloured. Add the white wine and wine vinegar and bring the mixture to the boil. Continue to boil until most of the liquid has evaporated and the shallots are plump with liquid. Remove from the heat and gradually whisk in the chilled butter cubes, one at a time, until all of the butter has been incorporated into the mixture, the sauce has thickened and is glossy. Season to taste.

Place the bacon under moderate heat in a non-stick pan, stirring occasionally and cook until most of the fat has rendered and the bacon is crisp around the edges. Transfer the bacon to a paper towel–lined plate and wipe out the pan. Add 1 tablespoon of unsalted butter to the pan, lower the heat and when the butter has melted, add the Coco de Paimpol beans. Stir gently until the beans have taken on a shiny golden colour. Raise the heat and add the bacon. Toss gently for 1 minute.

To serve, remove the fish from the oven and place the fillets onto warmed plates. Pour the sauce around the fish and add a few Coco beans, bacon and a sprig of thyme to garnish.

LESLEY CROSFIELD

"Delighted to be able to support the MS Society through this ChariTable Bookings initiative. The mousseline of Wild Turbot is one of The Albannach's most popular dishes and I hope you enjoy it too."

MOUSSELINE OF WILD TURBOT with lobster and langoustine

SERVES 4 | PREPARATION TIME 2 HOURS 15 MINUTES | COOKING TIME 1 HOUR 10 MINUTES

For the Mousseline

400g turbot fillet
1 pinch of sea salt
1 small free range egg, beaten
melted butter, for brushing
125ml, double cream
1 tbsp chopped dill
1 pinch of ground white pepper
1 pinch of cayenne

For Lobster and Langoustine.

1 x 750g live lobster
8 large live langoustines
1 star anise, optional
1 small onion, roughly chopped
½ stalk of celery, roughly chopped
1 small carrot, roughly chopped
1 bay leaf
6 white peppercorns
1 tbsp parsley, including stalks
1 tbsp thyme
1 tbsp brandy
150ml dry white wine
500ml fish stock
1 large tomato
75ml double cream
a few drops of olive oil
50g chilled unsalted butter

To make the mousseline, place the turbot and salt in a processor or blender and whizz. Add the egg while running, blend until smooth, and chill for at least 1.5 hours. Brush the dariole moulds with melted butter. Whisk the chilled fish and gradually add the double cream. Whisk until quite stiff, then pass through a fine sieve or moulis, and chill for 20 minutes. Fold in the dill, pepper, cayenne and salt. Spoon into moulds, two thirds full, tap bases to remove air bubbles, and chill for 20 minutes. Place in a roasting tray pour, half filled with boiling water, and cook in the oven at 180°C for 10 minutes until just springy to touch, then remove from the oven and rest in the tray for a couple of minutes.

To make the lobster and langoustines, cook the lobster in boiling salted water, with star anise for 12 minutes. Cook the langoustines in the same pan for 5–7 minutes depending on size. Cool, remove from shells, and reserve. Divide the lobster meat into 4 attractive portions. Sweat the onion, celery, carrot with the bay leaf and peppercorns for 5 minutes. Add lobster and langoustine heads and shells, and cook until hot. Add the brandy and cook for 1 minute. Next add the wine, cook for about 5 minutes, and then add the fish stock, herbs and tomato. Bring to boil, then simmer for 25–30 minutes. Strain through a fine sieve and reduce by about half. Add the double cream, and reduce until it has thickened sufficiently to coat a spoon. Just before serving add a few drops of olive oil, heat until just simmering, then whisk in the diced chilled butter. Keep warm.

To finish the dish and serve, run a thin knife around the mousselines to release them from the moulds. Upend carefully onto plates and, if necessary, shake gently to release. Arrange the langoustines and lobster around the mousseline, then spoon some of the sauce around them.

FABIO CUOFANO

"The Dog's Trust works relentlessly to prevent unnecessary destruction of dogs and give them a happy life. There are many worthwhile charities to choose from but the team and I at GOAT are particularly close to this one. I hope you enjoy our dish that we share with you through ChariTable Bookings."

SEA BASS with miso glaze, baby spinach, fennel and pomodori secchi
SERVES 1 | PREPARATION TIME 10 MINUTES | COOKING TIME 10 MINUTES

For the Dish

170g fillet of sea bass, halved

5g salt

5ml rapeseed oil

40g miso reduction

2g sesame or poppy seeds

20g pomodori secchi – mini sundried tomatoes

80g baby spinach

30g fennel

5g basil oil

1g micro basil leaves

2g extra virgin olive oil

To prepare the fish, season the sea bass with salt and sear the fish on the skin-side. Pour the rapeseed oil into a pan on a very high heat and fry the sea bass skin-side down for 1.5 minutes. Finish in the oven on 220°C in a baking tray for another 3 minutes.

Dress the plate by making a spiral of the miso glaze, then sprinkling the poppy or sesame seeds over the top. Place the pomodori secchi at intervals onto the glaze.

Cook the spinach on a low heat in a pan with virgin olive oil and place neatly in the middle of the plate.

Take the fennel and shave into slices, coating lightly in the basil oil and then place onto the spinach.

To serve, stack the sea bass on top and garnish with micro basil.

OLLIE DABBOUS

A no-brainer to support my favourite charity, the Global Fund for Children, by donating Dabbous' signature dish to ChariTable Bookings. I hope it raises lots of money for them and inspires budding chefs at the same time!"

CODDLED EGG with smoked butter and mushrooms

SERVES 8 | PREPARATION TIME 30 MINUTES | COOKING TIME 45 MINUTES

Equipment
egg topper

For the Eggshells
12 large free-range eggs

For the Nests
8 handfuls of hay

For the Fried Mushrooms
250g smoked butter
650g button mushrooms, thinly sliced

For the Egg Mix
600g whole eggs
65g fried mushrooms
1g salt
120ml whipping cream
150g smoked butter
1 tbsp chives, chopped

Remove the top of each eggshell using an egg topper. Empty out the egg and set aside to use in the egg mix. You will need 8 eggshells, but it's useful to have a few extra to allow for breakages. Place the shells in a large pan of salted water, of 3% salinity, and bring to the boil to sterilise the shells. Remove from the heat and leave to cool. Take out the inner membrane from the eggshells, clean them thoroughly and leave to dry.

To prepare the nests, mould the hay into 8 nest shapes using your hands and a pair of scissors. Place in earthenware bowls.

To make the fried mushrooms, heat the smoked butter until foaming, add the mushrooms and fry over a medium heat until golden, crisp and completely dehydrated. This process will take at least 20 minutes and the mushrooms will greatly reduce. Drain them thoroughly.

To make the egg mix, place the egg, fried mushrooms, salt, half the cream and half the butter in a bowl. Set it over a pan of simmering water and heat very gently until the mixture has thickened to the consistency of smooth porridge. Stir the whole time with a spatula, scraping the bottom of the bowl. The egg should be mousse-like and have very few lumps. Remove from the heat and whisk in the remaining butter and cream, along with the chives.

To serve, pour into the prepared eggshells and sit them in the nests, serving immediately.

YOGESH DATTA

"Great Ormond Street provides pioneering care and treatment for over 268,000 children a year. I couldn't be happier for The Painted Heron to donate this recipe to help raise awareness of this incredible hospital via ChariTable Bookings."

DUCK BIRYANI with onion, tomato and cucumber relish

SERVES 5–6 | PREPARATION TIME 40 MINUTES | COOKING TIME 2 HOURS

For the Duck Biryani

- 1 whole duck, cut into approximately
- 12 pieces on the bone
- 1kg basmati rice
- 1 bunch fresh mint, washed
- 1 bunch fresh coriander, washed
- 3 tbsp ginger/garlic paste
- 1 lemon, juiced
- 1 pinch of salt
- 200g butter, ghee or oil
- 2 tsp asafoetida, commercial variety, mixed with flour, optional
- 2 heaped tsp turmeric
- 2 onions, chopped
- 3 heaped tsp Kashmiri chilli powder
- 4 tomatoes, chopped
- 500ml low fat yoghurt
- bouquet garni – cinnamon sticks, cloves, green cardamom, bay leaves
- 1g saffron
- 120ml milk
- 50g special garam masala – black cardamom seeds, black cumin seeds (kala jeera), coriander seeds, cumin seeds, mace flowers (javitri) and grated nutmeg, powdered
- 100g prunes, pitted
- 150g cashew nuts, fried
- 10ml kewda water
- 100g brown onions, fried
- 100g paneer, grated

For the Onion, Tomato and Cucumber Relish

- 1 red onion, sliced
- 2 tomatoes, deseeded and julienned
- 1 cucumber, deseeded and julienned
- 100ml Greek yoghurt
- 3 cloves of garlic, chopped
- 50g fresh coriander, chopped
- salt and pepper, to taste

To prepare the biryani, wash and soak rice in cold water and set aside. Remove or leave the skin on the bird according to your preference. Wash the duck in running water. Chop the mint and coriander leaves and stems, keeping the leaves and stems separate. Pat dry the meat and marinate in a tablespoon of ginger/garlic paste, the lemon juice and salt and set aside for 30 minutes.

Heat a non-stick pan, drizzle with a little oil and add the duck pieces to brown on a high flame. Heat the ghee in a deep, heavy-bottomed pan and add the asafoetida and turmeric, followed immediately by the chopped onions. When the onions begin to colour, add the rest of the ginger/garlic paste and red chilli powder. Cook over a low flame until the mixture begins to stick to the bottom of the pan. Add the chopped stems of coriander and mint followed by the chopped tomatoes. Combine the duck with the yoghurt in the pan, cover and simmer gently until the duck is cooked.

For the rice, add plenty of water to another pan, along with salt and the bouquet garni, then bring to the boil. Add the rice and simmer until three quarters cooked. Drain off any excess water and allow the rice to cool to room temperature. Soak saffron in warm milk in a small bowl.

In a deep, heavy-bottomed pan, you need to layer the biryani. Start with a quarter of the rice. Next add half of the cooked duck, half the coriander and mint, half the special garam masala and half of the prunes and cashew nuts. Follow this with another layer of half of the remaining rice, followed by the rest of the duck, garam masala, prunes, cashew nuts and half of the remaining mint and coriander. Top this up with the remaining rice, mint and coriander. Drizzle the saffron milk around the pot, along with the kewda water. Finish with fried onions and grated paneer. Cover the pot with a tight lid and cook again over low flame for 10 minutes.

This is a sharing dish, so serve the biryani hot in the cooking pan, to trap all the flavours in and retain heat for longer. Accompany with the onion, tomato and cucumber relish on the side.

BERWYN DAVIES

Daisy's Dream's main aim is to help children who are dealing with bereavement or a serious illness in their family. The Glasshouse at Kew is very pleased to be able to support them further by donating their venison dish to ChariTable Bookings."

VENISON WITH SALSIFY PURÉE with roasted salsify and pine gnocchi

SERVES 4 | PREPARATION TIME 1 HOUR 30 MINUTES | COOKING TIME 20 MINUTES

For the Marinade
2g juniper berries
1 lemon, juiced
1 clove of garlic
1 small bunch of thyme
2g sugar
2g salt
100ml pomace oil

For the Venison
600g venison loin, cut into 4 x 150g steaks

For the Thyme Butter
100g butter
5g thyme, chopped
5g juniper berries, chopped

For the Salsify Purée
250g salsify, sliced
50g shallots, sliced
50g butter
1g salt
500ml water
100ml cream

For the Salsify Stick
2 sticks of salsify
1 pinch of salt

For the Pickled Shallots
100g shallots
100g sugar
100ml vinegar
50ml water

To make the marinade, blend all the ingredients in a blender. Pour over the venison and leave to marinate for as long as possible.

To prepare the thyme butter, toast the spices in a pan then leave to cool. Chop and mix with the butter and transfer to the fridge.

To make the salsify purée, roast the salsify and shallots in a pan with butter, until golden brown. Add salt and water. Continue to cook until there is no liquid left, then add the cream and bring to boil. Blend.

To cook the salsify sticks, peel and cut into 1.5cm pieces and poach in salted water.

To make the pickled shallots, thinly slice the shallots and leave to one side. Bring the vinegar, water and sugar to the boil, then pour over the shallots.

To prepare the pine gnocchi, peel the potatoes, then bring to the boil until cooked. Strain and dry in a pan. Pass through a chinois. Mix the mashed potatoes with salt, pine nuts, flour and egg yolk to create a dough. Roll into long cylinders with a diameter of 2cm. Cut into pillows. Transfer to simmering water until the gnocchi floats. Leave it on a tray to chill.

Preheat the oven to 200°C. Put a pan on the heat and wait until it gets very hot. Add a bit of oil, then put venison steaks in the pan; they should start sizzling straight away. Get them golden brown on all sides and transfer to a tray. Smother with thyme butter and bake for 5–7 minutes until medium rare. Rest the venison for 10 minutes. In the same pan, add juniper berries, peppercorns, port and red wine. Reduce to a glaze, then add the veal stock and chicken stock, bring to a simmer and reduce to the desired consistency. In a saucepan, roast the gnocchi and salsify until golden brown. Warm the salsify purée.

To plate, put the carved venison onto a plate, add 3 blobs of purée, roasted salsify, cabbage, pickled shallots, gnocchi, pine nuts and hot sauce. Enjoy.

For the Pine Gnocchi

250g potato

3g salt

3g pine nuts, chopped

40g flour

1 egg yolk

For the Red Cabbage

¼ red cabbage, thinly sliced and
mixed with lemon and salt

For the Venison sauce

1g juniper berries

1g peppercorns

50ml port

100ml red wine

50ml veal stock

250ml chicken stock

To Finish

50g pine nuts, toasted

MATT DAVIES

Shelter helps thousands of homeless people across the UK every day. All of us at The Moat House are pleased to be able to promote their great work by including our recipe for them in this ChariTable Bookings' recipe book."

FILLET OF STAFFORDSHIRE BEEF with slow cooked blade, haggis, cabbage confit, caramelised shallot purée, pied blue mushrooms and St. Emillion sauce

SERVES 6 | PREPARATION TIME 30 MINUTES | COOKING TIME 1 HOUR 30 MINUTES

For the Beef Fillet
1.5kg centre fillet of Staffordshire beef
salt and pepper

For the Braised Blade
1.5kg blade beef
3 stalks of celery, chopped
1 large leek, chopped
1 pinch of fresh thyme
1 bottle red wine, reduced by half
3 cloves of garlic, chopped
1 pinch of salt
beef stock to cover
1¼ tsp parsley, chopped
2 shallots, finely chopped
100ml beef glace, or a good beef stock

For the Cabbage Confit
200g green Savoy cabbage, finely shredded
80g shallots, finely diced
80g pancetta
1 pinch of thyme leaves
80ml duck fat
salt and pepper

For the Haggis Balls
150g haggis
25g shallots, finely diced
50ml red wine, reduced by half
25ml beef glace, or a good beef stock

To prepare the beef fillet, wrap in cling film to shape and chill for 1 hour. Remove cling film. Seal the fillet in a hot pan, then season and cook in an oven at 190°C for 12 minutes. For medium rare, cook the fillet to a core temperature of 58°C, then rest for 10 minutes.

To make the braised blade, seal the braising beef in a hot pan and place into a casserole dish. Pan-fry the vegetables with the thyme and add to the meat. Add the reduced wine, garlic, salt, and enough stock to cover the meat, then cook at 180°C for 3–4 hours. When cooked, shred the meat and add parsley, shallots and beef glace. Press the meat between 2 containers using silicone paper and a weight. Chill until set and cut into 3x4cm portions when needed. Reheat and glaze with beef jus before serving.

To make the haggis balls, break up the haggis and combine with the shallots, red wine and beef glace. Roll into balls a little bigger than a cherry tomato. Coat the balls using a double coating of flour, egg and panko crumbs. Deep fry until golden.

To make the cabbage confit, blanch the cabbage in boiling water. Sauté the shallots and diced pancetta then add the thyme leaves. Cook the blanched cabbage in duck fat until al dente. Mix the ingredients together, check the seasoning and keep warm.

For the shallot purée, use a heavy-based pan to melt the butter and caramelise the shallots by cooking over a gentle heat with the honey. Add water and cook until soft, then purée.

For the St. Emilion sauce, sauté the vegetables in 15g of butter. Add a pinch of thyme, then pour in the red wine and reduce by two thirds. Add the veal jus and reduce until it coats the back of a spoon. Season and whisk in the remainder of the butter. Pass through a fine sieve.

To make the pied blue mushrooms, melt the butter, add the mushrooms, sauté until just soft, season and add parsley.

To serve, assemble the dish as pictured.

For the Haggis Balls *continued*

    50g plain flour

    150g panko breadcrumbs

    1 egg

For the Shallot Purée

    200g shallots, peeled and diced

    20g butter

    20ml honey

    200ml water

For the St. Emillion Sauce

    1 carrot, chopped

    1 stick of celery, chopped

    1 small leek, finely diced

    1 pinch of thyme leaves

    1 bottle St. Emillion wine

    500ml veal jus

    50g hard unsalted butter

For the Pied Blue Mushrooms

    100g pied blue mushrooms, cleaned with

    a towel and small brush, then trimmed

    25g butter

    salt and pepper

    1 sprinkle of chopped parsley

SCOTT DAVIES

"I hope you enjoy this venison dish from The Three Chimneys. What a novel way to raise money for charity through the love of cooking delicious food."

LOIN OF HIGHLAND VENISON in onion ash with charred beetroot, salt-baked celeriac and reindeer moss

SERVES 2 | PREPARATION TIME 40 MINUTES (PLUS OVERNIGHT BAKING) | COOKING TIME 12 HOURS

For the Toasted Reindeer Moss
reindeer moss, purchasable from
specialist florists

For the Onion Ash
25ml Scottish rapeseed oil
½ small onion, cut into 8 wedges
½ small onion, thinly sliced
50g plain flour
5g smoked sea salt (sea salt smoked with oak or peat)
8 black peppercorns, toasted and crushed
8 juniper berries, dried

For the Salt-Baked Celeriac
225g plain flour
300g table salt
4 egg whites
150ml water
1 small whole celeriac

For the Charred Beetroot
500g charcoal
1 large beetroot

For the Sauce
fat trimmings from the venison loins
Scottish rapeseed oil, for cooking
1 carrot, finely diced
1 celery stick, finely diced
1 small onion, peeled and diced
1 clove of garlic, crushed

To make the toasted reindeer moss, preheat the oven to 60°C. Bake slowly overnight.

To make the onion ash, using a large thick-based pan, heat the rapeseed oil. Coat the onion wedges in the hot oil and cook over a medium heat until blackened on all sides. Drain the oil and place the onion wedges in the oven at 90°C for 12 hours until dried out and crispy. Coat the sliced onion in flour and deep fry until golden brown and crispy. Remove and drain well. Mix both forms of onion together with the salt, peppercorns and juniper. Thoroughly blitz in a food processor until smooth, then push the mixture through a sieve to create a fine powder. Reserve to one side until needed.

To make the salt-baked celeriac, put the flour, salt, egg whites and water into a bowl and make a smooth paste. Place 2 spoonfuls of the salt paste onto a greaseproof paper lined tray. Place the celeriac on top and then cover with the rest of the paste. Bake at 160°C for 2 hours. Remove from the oven and leave to cool. When cool enough, use a knife to scrape off the salt crust. Peel the celeriac and rip the flesh into small chunks. Set aside.

To make the charred beetroot, ignite the charcoal in a small barbecue. Let the charcoal burn for a while until there are no more flames, just glowing red embers. Place the beetroot on the barbecue and cook for 40 minutes, turning every 10 minutes. The beetroot should look black and be cooked all the way through. Leave to cool. Peel off the charred beetroot skin with a knife, then dice into 1cm cubes. Put to one side until needed.

To make the sauce, in a large saucepan, fry the venison fat trimmings in a little oil for 4–5 minutes over a medium heat until golden brown. Add the carrot, celery, onion and garlic and cook for 3–4 minutes. Add the mushrooms, thyme, juniper berries, peppercorns and bay leaf and cook for a further 2 minutes. Add the port, vinegar and brandy and reduce the sauce by two thirds. Add the stock and cook on a gentle simmer, skimming now and again, until the sauce is of a rich and smooth consistency. Finally, drop in the brambles for a few minutes then strain through a fine sieve. Reserve until needed but keep hot.

For the Sauce *continued*

- 50g button mushrooms, sliced
- 2 sprigs of thyme
- 6 juniper berries, crushed
- 6 black peppercorns, crushed
- 1 small bay leaf
- 100ml port
- 25ml bramble vinegar
- 50ml brandy
- 500ml good quality brown chicken stock
- 10 wild brambles, cut in half

For the Chestnut Purée

- 200ml double cream
- 100g cooked chestnuts
- ¼ lemon, juice only

For the Venison Loin

- 2 x 125g pieces of Scottish venison loin, fully trimmed of fat
- smoked salt
- Scottish rapeseed oil, for cooking

For the Garnish and to Serve

- 25g mix of autumn mushrooms, washed
- 3 whole chestnuts, cut in half
- 2 sticks of salsify, peeled
- 10g picked kale
- 50g butter, softened, plus a little more for sauté
- smoked salt
- dry powder of black pepper, fennel pollen and juniper

To make the chestnut purée, bring the cream, chestnuts and lemon juice to the boil. Blitz in a food processor until smooth. Taste the purée for acidity and check its consistency and seasoning. Adjust as required. Pass through a fine sieve and keep hot. Pour into a plastic saucing squeezy bottle when needed.

To cook the venison, season the venison on all sides with the sea salt and brush with the oil. Pan fry in a medium hot pan for 2 minutes on each side. Place in the oven at 140°C for 4 minutes depending on the thickness of the loin. The core temperature should be 45°C, which you can check using a temperature probe. Leave to rest for 4 minutes. Flash fry under a hot grill for 1 minute on each side. Then roll the loins in the prepared onion ash. Slice in half, season well and serve.

To make the garnish and serve, sauté the mushrooms, chestnuts, salsify sticks and kale in a little butter, water and seasoning. Brush the prepared charred beetroot cubes and salt-baked celeriac pieces with the butter and season the beetroot with the smoked salt. Place under a hot grill for 2–3 minutes until hot. Intersperse all the ingredients into colourful and decorative lines on the plates giving prominence to the sliced loins of venison. Finally, decorate with the delicate toasted reindeer moss on top.

NICK DEVERELL-SMITH

Variety is a charity very close to my heart, I grew up with my elder brother being disabled. I saw first hand the day to day struggles life threw at him, his outlook on life and his will to carry on was inspiring. Here at the Churchill Arms we try and support Variety where possible. Here is the locally shot venison main course from our last Variety dinner hosted at the Churchill Arms and shared with you in this ChariTable Bookings recipe collection. I dedicate this dish to Paul Deverell-Smith."

VENISON

SERVES 8 | PREPARATION TIME 30 MINUTES (PLUS OVERNIGHT MARINATE) | COOKING TIME 1 HOUR

Equipment
steam enabled oven

For the Venison
2 x 1kg venison loin
50g black peppercorns
50g juniper berries

For the Hispi Cabbage
1 hispi cabbage
120g salt, dissolved in 4l water

For the Butter Emulsion
5g salt
pepper
1 clove of garlic, crushed
200g wild garlic
4 sprigs of thyme
300ml water
500g butter
100ml UHT cream
1 tsp lemon juice

For the Blueberry Gastric
500g caster sugar
500ml distilled vinegar
1kg frozen blueberries

For the Honey Glaze
100g truffle honey
100ml water
100ml red wine vinegar

For the Vichy Carrots
4 orange carrots
4 purple carrots

To cook the venison, fry the juniper berries and black peppercorns on a high heat for 20 seconds and blend to a coarse powder. Trim the venison loin into 200g portions. Roll the portions in the mixture and sear in the same hot pan. Place the pan in a steam enabled oven for 3–4 minutes at 190°C and 20% steam.

To make the cabbage, cut into wedges and cook in salted, boiling water until tender. Strain and set aside for serving.

To make the butter emulsion, boil the seasoning, garlic and thyme in the water. With a hand blender, mix in the butter until the liquid thickens. Add the cream and lemon juice and season to taste. Simmer for 5 minutes and pass through a chinois.

To make the blueberries, reduce the sugar and vinegar until the mixture starts to caramelise. Add the blueberries and cook on a high heat for 1–2 minutes.

To make the honey glaze, reduce the honey, water and vinegar together in a pan until a thick, syrupy consistency is reached.

To make the vichy carrots, peel and add to a pan with thyme, garlic and sugar, and cover with water. Bring to the boil and simmer until the water is gone. Glaze the carrots with the honey glaze and a little melted butter.

To make the artichoke purée, clean and scrub the artichokes. Simmer in milk until soft. Remove from the milk and blend to a smooth purée, seasoning to taste.

To serve, assemble as pictured.

For the Vichy Carrots *continued*

    4 yellow carrots

    4 sprigs of thyme

    4 cloves of garlic

    2 tsp caster sugar

    40g butter

For the Artichoke Purée

    500g Jerusalem artichokes

    1l whole milk

JAMIE DOBBIN

Lesser known but equally important, Hearing Dogs for Deaf People provide trained dogs to deaf people to give them their independence. Great that ChariTable Bookings has given the team at The Groucho the opportunity to raise the awareness of this great charity."

CORNED BEEF HASH

SERVES 4 | PREPARATION TIME 30 MINUTES | COOKING TIME 15 MINUTES

For the Corned Beef Hash

450g potatoes, peeled and cut into chunks

6 tbsp vegetable oil

2 small onions

2 x 198g tins corned beef, chilled overnight in the fridge

1 large egg

25g butter

1 pinch of celery salt

worcestershire sauce, to taste

salt and freshly ground black pepper

To Serve

branston pickle

4 eggs, for frying

To make the corned beef hash, cook the potatoes in a pan of boiling salted water until tender. Drain well, then return the potatoes to the pan and place over a very low heat to evaporate any remaining moisture. Mash well using a potato masher and leave uncovered to cool. Heat 2 tablespoons of oil in a small pan and add the onions. Cook gently over a low heat until softened, but do not allow to colour. Using a sharp knife, cut the corned beef into 1cm cubes. The potato may stiffen up when cold, so re-mash slightly to break it down. Crack in one egg, add onions, corned beef and season well with the celery salt and Worcestershire sauce

To cook the corned beef hash, mould the mixture into 4 cakes and chill again in the fridge for about 30 minutes. Heat 2 tablespoons of oil and some butter in a frying pan. Cook the hash cakes on both sides over a medium heat until golden brown on the outside and heated through. Whilst the cakes are cooking, fry the remaining eggs in a separate frying pan.

To serve, place the hash cakes on plates, spoon on some pickle and top with a fried egg.

MARK DODSON

It costs £6.6m per year to run the Devon Air Ambulance so every penny counts. The Masons Arms is donating its signature dish recipe to ChariTable Bookings' recipe book to keep this vital service running in Devon. We hope you enjoy the dish at the same time!"

LOIN OF VENISON with poached pear and blue cheese gratin

SERVES 4 | PREPARATION TIME 1 HOUR | COOKING TIME 10 HOURS

For the Venison
4 x 150g venison loin, trimmed, keep the bones and trimmings for sauce

For the Venison Sauce
venison bones and trimmings
2 carrots, chopped
1 onion, chopped
1 stick celery, chopped
1 tbsp tomato purée
2 tbsp pear poaching liquid
water, to cover

For the Blue Cheese Gratin
4 medium potatoes, peeled
90ml full-fat milk
125ml double cream
3 cloves of garlic
200g blue cheese, preferably gorgonzola

For the Poached Pears
2 pears, peeled, halved and cored
200ml red wine
100g sugar
1 stick of cinnamon

To Serve
salsify
cavolo nero
baby carrots

To make the venison sauce, preheat the oven to 180°C. Roast the bones and trimmings for 45 minutes until golden brown before transferring into a smaller pan with the vegetables. Add a spoonful of tomato purée, sweat again, then cover with water. Leave the mixture to cook slowly for 8 hours. Once cooked, pass through a fine sieve and reduce until a good sauce consistency is achieved. Just before serving, reduce a couple of spoonfuls of the pear poaching liquid and add to the sauce to give a little depth and sweetness.

To make the blue cheese gratin, preheat the oven to 150°C. Boil the milk, cream, garlic and cheese together. Slice the potatoes and position in a suitable dish, pour the liquid over the slices. Cover the top of the dish with greaseproof paper and bake in the oven for 1–1.5 hours. Halfway through cooking, press down on the potatoes to ensure the gratin is compact, the potato should have a good colour but be soft all the way through.

To make the poached pears, poach in the red wine with sugar and the cinnamon stick until just cooked. Leave them to cool in the liquid.

To serve, cook the venison in a pan until pink and leave to rest before slicing. Cook the vegetables as desired. Arrange the meat on the plate with the vegetables and add a good piece of the gratin. Slice and fan the pear before finally pouring a little of the sauce around the dish.

DANIEL DOHERTY MCA

" Food is a right for everyone, not a luxury. Really happy to help raise money for Action Against Hunger, a humanitarian organization committed to ending child hunger and support ChariTable Bookings' great new book by donating Duck & Waffle's 'London Particular' dish."

LONDON PARTICULAR

SERVES 8 | PREPARATION TIME 30 MINUTES | COOKING TIME 4 HOURS

Equipment
sous vide

For the Dish
500g split peas, dried
1 ham hock, smoked
1 onion, peeled and left whole
2 celery sticks, chopped
1 bay leaf
1 sprig of thyme
8 slow-cooked eggs
plain flour, for dusting
2 handfuls of pea shoots
6 fresh mint leaves, finely sliced
sea salt
freshly ground black pepper
vegetable oil

To make the London particular, put the split peas, ham hock, onion, celery, bay leaf and thyme into a large saucepan and add water to cover. Bring to the boil, then lower the heat and cook for approximately 3.5 hours, skimming regularly, until the meat comes away from the bone. The peas may catch on the bottom, so stir frequently and top up with water as necessary. The final consistency should be that of a thick soup.

Remove the ham hock and allow to cool. In the meantime, remove the bay leaf and thyme and discard. Blitz the soup in a food processor until smooth. Taste and adjust the seasoning. When the ham hock is cool, take the meat off the bone and flake it into small strands. Pat dry with kitchen paper. Heat the oil to 180°C in a deep-fat fryer or in a heavy-based saucepan. Dust a handful of the ham flakes with flour and fry until crisp, this should only take 2 minutes, then drain and set aside for garnishing.

To make the slow cooked eggs, set a water bath to 63°C. When the temperature is reached, add the eggs in the shell and leave for 45 minutes. You can use them straight away, or chill in ice water and refrigerate for later.

Put some of the flaked ham in the bottom of each serving bowl, about a tablespoon per person. Fill the bowl with soup, put an egg on top and season with salt and pepper. Garnish with the pea shoots, finely sliced mint leaves and the crispy ham.

STEVEN DOHERTY MCA

CancerCare is a unique charity dedicated to helping families in the North Lancs area affected by cancer and other life limiting conditions. Great for The First Floor Café to be able to support a local charity through this ChariTable Bookings recipe collection."

CULLEN SKINK

SERVES 4 | PREPARATION TIME 20 MINUTES | COOKING TIME 1 HOUR

For the Cullen Skink

2 large potatoes, washed, peeled and cut into 6 even pieces

salt and ground white pepper

1l water

125ml milk

2 tbsp onion, finely diced

4 x 125g smoked haddock fillets, deskinned and pin boned

125g leeks, split lengthways, washed and finely sliced

125g savoy cabbage, quartered, washed and finely sliced

For the Garnish

parsley, chopped or picked

soft poached egg, optional

To make the cullen skink, put the potatoes into a pan of cold water with a teaspoon of salt. Bring to a simmer and allow to cook for 15 minutes. In a large pan, add the litre of cold water, the milk and onion and bring to a simmer. Add the fish and cook for 5 minutes. Remove the fish with a slotted spoon onto a clean plate, cover with cling film and keep warm. Add the leeks and cabbage to the cooking liquid and cook for a further 7 minutes. Drain the potatoes and mash until smooth. Stir enough mash into the leeks and cabbage to thicken the broth. Taste for seasoning, you may need to add a little pepper.

To serve, you can either flake the haddock and stir into the broth, or put the haddock into a deep soup plate and pour the broth over it. Either way, garnish with parsley and top with a soft-poached egg if desired.

JAVIER DOMINGUEZ SANTOS

"Maggie's Centres do great work and we at the Rocpool Reserve Hotel are pleased to support them with ChariTable Bookings."

HICKORY SMOKED SPRING CHICKEN JAMBONETTE with sweetcorn
purée, pickled girolle mushrooms and piquillo pepper dressing

SERVES 4 | PREPARATION TIME 1 HOUR 30 MINUTES | COOKING TIME 5 HOURS

Equipment
- bratt pan
- sous vide and vacuum pack bags

For the Brown Chicken Stock
- 10kg chicken bones
- 700g large carrots, diced
- 1.5kg large onions, diced
- 500g celery, diced
- 500g leek, diced
- 80g garlic, finely chopped
- 1 bouquet garni
- 20l water
- 5g black peppercorns, crushed

For the Chicken Jus
- 150g unsalted butter, diced
- 300g banana shallot, diced
- 500ml white wine
- 2l brown chicken stock
- 1 bouquet garni
- 20ml aged balsamic vinegar

For the Piquillo Pepper Dressing
- 90g banana shallots
- 50g piquillo pepper
- 50ml tomato ketchup
- 30ml sherry vinegar
- 15ml Worcestershire sauce
- 15g chives, chopped
- 3g chervil, chopped
- 7g tarragon, chopped

To make the chicken stock, chop the bones and roast in the oven until golden brown, stirring from time to time. Heat-up a bratt pan, and sweat the carrots and onions until golden. Add the water, the roasted bones and all the remaining ingredients. Cook for 3 hours on a high heat, allowing everything to reduce until relatively thick. Once done, strain the stock through a fine sieve.

To make the chicken jus, melt the butter and sweat the shallots until soft and golden. Add the wine and reduce by half, then add the stock and bouquet garni and cook for 40 minutes on a high heat. Strain the sauce into a clean pan and reduce to a syrupy consistancy. Add the vinegar and season to taste.

To make the piquillo pepper dressing, finely brunoise all the ingredients together. Mix and set aside for serving so the flavours can develop and the dressing is a little warm.

To make the piquillo pepper tuile, boil the tapioca in the water until thoroughly cooked. Blitz the piquillo pepper to a purée, stir in to the tapioca and mix well. Spread very thinly on a tray with greaseproof paper and leave to dry out in a warm place until crisp. Break into pieces and deep fry at 200°C until puffed up. Season to taste and place to one side for serving.

To make the jambonette, break down the poussin, keeping the breasts for the mousse, the wings and the carcasses for making the stock. Bone out the legs and lightly cold smoke with the hickory chips for an hour. Blitz the breasts in a food processor without skin or bone and a little egg white, and pass through a very fine sieve. Put back in the food processor and add all of the egg whites, blitzing for 2 minutes, then set over a bowl of ice and add the cream in 3 stages. Lastly, add the seasoning and cayenne pepper until it all comes together, making sure not to overwork. Score the inside of the legs and pipe the mousse into it. Wrap tightly in cling film and form a ballotine. Cook sous vide at 69°C for 90 minutes, then in a hot pan, colour the skin until golden brown. Trim the edges and set in a warm place.

150ml pomace oil

75ml extra virgin olive oil

2g salt and pepper, to taste

For the Piquillo Pepper Tuile

100g tapioca starch

25g piquillo pepper

500ml water

For the Jambonette

500g fresh poussin

200g fine hickory smoking chips

40ml pasteurised egg white

180ml double cream

6g cooking salt

5g fresh tarragon

1 pinch of cayenne pepper

For the Sweetcorn Purée

1 tin sweetcorn

1.2l white chicken stock

10g garlic

15g fresh thyme

500ml double cream

20g salt and pepper, to taste

2g cayenne pepper

For the Pickled Girolle Mushrooms

200g girolle mushrooms

50g banana shallot, cut into rings

200ml water

100ml white wine vinegar

100g caster sugar

1g saffron

5g coriander seeds

2g fresh thyme

For the Panko-Breaded Quail Egg

6 quail eggs

100g flour

2 eggs

panko breadcrumbs, to coat

To make the sweetcorn purée, place all of the ingredients apart from the cream in a deep pan and bring to a simmer, cover with greaseproof paper and cook until tender. Strain the leftover liquid and keep to one side. Reduce the cream by half and add the sweetcorn, blitz until smooth and pass through a fine chinois. Correct the consistency and seasoning, and place in a squeezy bottle.

To make the pickled girolle mushrooms, clean and wash the mushrooms really well, making sure there is no grit. Bring the liquid ingredients to the boil with the saffron and simmer for 5 minutes to intensify the saffron flavour. Add the mushrooms and simmer for another minute. Allow the girolles to cool in the liquid and set aside.

To make the panko-breaded quail egg, cook the quail egg in boiling water for exactly 1 minute and 45 seconds for a soft boil. Place in ice water and cool. Peel very gently, then pass through flour, egg and Japanese panko breadcrumbs. Deep fry at 180°C until golden.

To serve, lightly warm all of the ingredients and serve as pictured.

BRIAN DONALDSON

An honour to be among this group of peers in ChariTable Bookings' new publication supporting charities all over. I'm supporting the Alzheimer's Society and the great work they do with both sufferers and carers of sufferers."

RARE BEEF FILLET STEAK with egg and chips

SERVES 4 | PREPARATION TIME 3 HOURS | COOKING TIME 1 HOUR

Equipment
vegetable spiralizer

For the Beef
1 beef fillet tail
50g salt

For the Black Truffle Emulsion
40ml Clement hens egg whites
40ml lemon juice
200ml Broighter Gold black truffle infused rapeseed oil
salt and pepper

For the Confit Egg Yolk
4 Clements hens eggs
400ml Broighter gold rapeseed oil

For the Potatoes
4 small Comber potatoes, skin on
Maldon sea salt

To Serve
Broighter Gold rapeseed oil
Maldon sea salt

To prepare the beef, place 400ml of cold water in a large saucepan and add the salt, stir well to dissolve. Place the fillet of beef into the brine and soak for 2–3 hours.

To make the black truffle emulsion, in a mixing bowl add the egg whites and lemon juice together. Gently add the rapeseed oil, and blend with a hand blender until you have a consistency of mayonnaise. Season to taste with salt and pepper.

To make the confit egg yolk, preheat the oven to 65°C. Separate the egg yolks from the whites by cracking the eggs with your hands and allowing the white to run through your fingers. Gently place the egg yolks into an ovenproof dish with the rapeseed oil, ensuring the yolks are fully covered. Place the dish into your preheated oven for 45 minutes, be careful that none of the egg yolks are touching each other.

To make the potatoes, wash the potatoes and gently scrub the skins. Use a vegetable spiralizer to make potato ribbons. Season and deep fry at 180°C until they are golden brown and crispy. Season with a touch of Maldon sea salt and set aside to cool on greaseproof paper.

To finish the dish and serve, once the beef has brined, remove from the water and pat dry with kitchen roll. Heat a large frying pan and seal the steak all round, turning the steak on each side for about 2 minutes. Remove from the pan, cover with foil and allow to rest for 10 minutes. Start by slicing the beef into roughly 30–60g pieces and place on the centre of the plate. Brush with Broighter Gold rapeseed oil and sprinkle with a tiny pinch of Maldon sea salt. Lift the egg yolks carefully out of the oil with a spoon and allow the excess oil to drain off, then place on top of the beef. Dot the black truffle emulsion on the beef and off to the side, then place some of the potato crisps on the beef and serve.

CALLUM DOW

"CHAS is a charity that provides the only hospice services in Scotland for children and young people who have life-shortening conditions for which there is no known cure. All of us at Balbirnie are proud to support them in collaboration with ChariTable Bookings."

PAN-FRIED FILLET OF HAKE with roast garlic mash and peas served French style

SERVES 4 | PREPARATION TIME 20 MINUTES | COOKING TIME 1 HOUR

For the Hake
4 x 160g hake fillets, descaled and
pin boned
1 tbsp rapeseed oil
40g unsalted butter, diced
salt and pepper, to taste

For the Roast Garlic Mash
2 large baking potatoes
1 bulb of garlic, wrapped in tin foil
80ml double cream
40g unsalted butter

For the Sauce
3 tbsp rapeseed oil
100g roscoff onions, peeled with
root intact
85g pancetta, diced
125ml white wine
200ml chicken stock
80g fresh Scottish girolles
100g fresh peas
70g unsalted butter
1 bunch of fresh parsley, chopped
½ lemon, juiced
salt and pepper

For the Garnish
a selection of wild herbs

To prepare the roast garlic mash, preheat an oven to 180°C and cook the potatoes and garlic until soft, which should take approximately 40 minutes.

To prepare the sauce, in a large frying pan add 3 tablespoons of oil, onions and pancetta. Stir occasionally for an even colour. Add the wine, allow to almost evaporate, then add stock, turn the heat down and cover with a lid.

To make the mash, cut the cooked potatoes in half when warm, remove the flesh, and push through a ricer. Squeeze the garlic to remove the flesh and add to the mash. Bring the cream to a boil in a pan, add the mash, garlic and the butter and beat until smooth, season to taste.

To cook the hake, warm a frying pan on a medium-high heat, use a little silicone paper on the bottom of the pan to stop the fish from sticking if you don't own a non-stick pan. Add the oil and place fish skin-side down. Add the butter, season and put in the oven, cooking for 4–6 minutes.

To finish cooking the sauce, remove the lid from the pan and turn the heat up to full. Add the mushrooms, peas and butter. The sauce should coat the back of a spoon. Finish by adding the chopped parsley and lemon juice and a little seasoning to taste.

To serve, remove the fish from the oven, gently squeeze the piece of fish and it should spring back. Present the mash into the centre of the plate. Spoon the peas, onion and pancetta mix and a little of the sauce around the mash. Place the fillet of fish, skin-side up on top of the mash. Finally garnish with a few herbs of your choice.

WILLIAM DRABBLE

Springboard does amazing work in developing the skillset for young people to achieve their goals in the hospitality industry. I'm pleased to share Seven Park Place's griddled sea bass with ChariTable Bookings to raise more awareness of this great charity."

GRIDDLED SEA BASS with stuffed courgettes, tomatoes, olives and basil

SERVES 4 | PREPARATION TIME 30 MINUTES | COOKING TIME 3 HOURS

For the Sea Bass
4 sea bass fillets, skin scored
1 lemon
olive oil
salt and pepper, to taste

For the Aubergine and Courgette Farce
olive oil
1 shallot, finely chopped
1 clove of garlic, crushed
½ tsp herbs de Provence
1 small courgette, ½ small aubergine, and 1 flat mushroom, all 2mm diced
2 spinach leaves, chiffonade cut
2 tomatoes, diced
3 small handfuls breadcrumbs
salt, to taste
2 round courgettes, cut in half lengthways and centre scooped out

For the Basil Oil
20g basil, leaves picked
200ml olive oil
1 pinch of salt

For the Tomato Sauce
100ml olive oil
1 shallot, thinly sliced
1 clove of garlic, crushed
10 ripe tomatoes, peeled and chopped
1 pinch of cayenne pepper
salt, to taste
2 sprigs of basil

To make the basil oil, place the picked basil in a liquidiser with the olive oil and blitz into a purée with a pinch of salt. Set aside in the fridge until required.

Preheat the oven to 80°C. Blanch the heirloom tomatoes briefly in water and remove the skins, cut into wedges and place onto a non-stick baking tray. Season with salt, sprinkle over a little icing sugar and drizzle with some olive oil. Place a couple of sprigs of basil over the tomatoes and cook in the low oven for approximately 1–1.5 hours. Open the door at regular intervals to let any moisture out of the oven.

To make the tomato sauce, warm the olive oil in a wide, shallow, non-stick pan and add the shallot and garlic. Cook slowly until soft and sweet, but not coloured. Add the chopped tomatoes and season with a little salt and cayenne pepper. Cook slowly until the tomato sauce starts to thicken, you will need to stir it quite often to prevent it from burning. Once it has become thick, add the basil and leave to infuse for 10 minutes before passing through a sieve to remove the seeds. Set aside in a warm place.

To make the olive en croute, add the olives to a blender and blitz to make a paste, you may need to add a little olive oil to help the process. Slice the baguette very thinly to create a croute, then toast it slowly until nice and crispy. Set aside until ready to serve.

To make the aubergine and courgette farce, place some olive oil into a small pan and add the shallot, garlic, herbs de Provence and a pinch of salt. Cook until soft and sweet but not coloured. Add the diced courgette and aubergine and cook until soft, then add the chopped mushroom and cook until the moisture has evaporated. Add the spinach and cook until dry again. Add the diced tomatoes and cook for a minute, then add some breadcrumbs to stiffen the mix. Set aside and preheat an oven to 170°C. Blanch the round courgettes in boiling salted water until tender, but still firm and holding their shape. Refresh in ice water and drain. Stuff with some of the farce and sprinkle with a few more breadcrumbs. Place into the oven for 10–15 minutes, then remove and keep warm. Reduce the oven temperature to 150°C.

For the Slow-roasted Heirloom Tomatoes

8 heirloom tomatoes

2 sprigs of basil

1 dusting of icing sugar

1 drizzle of olive oil

salt, to taste

For the Black Olive Croute

1 small baguette

1 handful of black olives, pitted and marinated

1 drizzle of olive oil

For the Artichokes

4 baby artichokes, prepared, cooked and halved

olive oil

To prepare the fish, add some olive oil to a hot pan and season the fish. Place in the pan skin-side down and fry for 30 seconds, then transfer to the oven for 5–6 minutes to cook through. Meanwhile, quickly sauté the baby artichokes in a small pan with a dash of oil. Arrange the courgettes neatly onto plates, then spread on a little of the tomato sauce. Place the slow-cooked tomatoes and sautéed artichokes on top of the sauce.

Remove the sea bass from the oven and season with some salt and lemon. Place the fish on top of the vegetables and trickle some basil oil around the vegetables. Spread some black olive paste onto the croute and arrange on top of the fish. Serve immediately.

STEVE DRAKE

Disability Challengers work tirelessly to create inclusive play areas for disabled children and young people so that they can interact in complete safety. The team at Sorrel in Dorking are proud to share our Jerusalem Artichoke recipe with ChariTable Bookings in support of this fantastic charity."

JERUSALEM ARTICHOKE PANNA COTTA with veal sweetbreads, Wiltshire truffle and cep biscuit

SERVES 4 | PREPARATION TIME 1 DAY | COOKING TIME 1 HOUR 30 MINUTES

Equipment
Vitamix or similar food processor
Kenwood mixer with paddle
sous vide
vacuum pack bags

For the Jerusalem Panna Cotta
200g Jerusalem artichokes, finely sliced
375ml full fat milk
375ml double cream
5 leaves of gelatine
a few drops of black truffle oil
salt and pepper

For the Cep Biscuit
50ml double cream
200g butter
150g sugar
200g room temperature egg whites
100g cep powder, sieved
100g flour, sieved
100g Parmesan, grated
20 twists of pepper
1 tsp salt

For the Chicken Jus Gras
1 whole chicken
1 sprig of thyme
½ head of garlic
50ml grapeseed oil
250ml brown chicken stock

For the Veal Sweetbreads
1 small lobe of veal sweetbread
clarified butter

To Finish
small watercress leaves
black mushrooms
2–3 slices of truffle
veal tongue
watercress purée

To make the Jerusalem panna cotta, soak the gelatine in ice water. Meanwhile, place the artichokes, milk and cream in a pan with a little seasoning and bring to a simmer. Cook very gently for 8 minutes. Pour into the Vitamix and blend until silky smooth, adjust the seasoning and add a few drops of black truffle oil. Turn onto the lowest setting and add the gelatine squeezing out all the water. Pour into a bowl over ice to semi set and then into a rectangular mould, 18x28cm. Set and cut into 9x1.5 cm.

To prepare the cep biscuit, put the cream, butter and sugar in a Kenwood, using the paddle. Add a third of the egg whites and mix. Scrape the side of the bowl. Add another third of the egg whites, mix, scrape the side of the bowl, repeat. Add the cep powder, flour, salt and pepper and mix. Then add Parmesan and mix it all together.

Divide into 4 small yoghurt containers and freeze. Spread the biscuit mix over the stencil and cook at 140°C for 5 minutes. Turn the tray and cook for another 5 minutes.

To make the chicken jus gras, season the bird and place a sprig of thyme and half a head of garlic in the carcass. Put in a roasting tray and drizzle over the oil, then roast at 220°C for 50 minutes. Turn out into a colander and place a weight on top to squeeze out all the juice. Deglaze the tray with the brown stock and add that to the other chicken juice. Warm if necessary to pass through a muslin cloth. It should be an equal amount of fat and juice, so if there is more juice, separate it and reduce.

To prepare the veal sweetbreads, go through the lobes and remove the worst of the fat and veins. Soak in milk for 24 hours. Rinse in cold water thoroughly, pat dry and vacuum seal on full. Poach for 1 hour at 64°C, open the bag immediately and peel whilst hot. Then, press between 2 trays with a 5kg weight on top.

To finish the dish and serve, leave the panna cotta to get to room temperature and place on warm plates. Roast the sweetbread pieces in clarified butter and add to the plate, along with a few black mushrooms, truffle and watercress leaves. Finally finish with a spoonful of the chicken jus, not forgetting the lovely mushroom biscuits.

ANDREW DU BOURG

" *GOSH does incredible things for so many children every year that I couldn't be happier to put one of The Elderflower's signature dishes forward for this collection by ChariTable Bookings."*

BLACK SHEEP with caramelised cauliflower and roast root vegetables

SERVES 2 | PREPARATION TIME 1 HOUR (PLUS 12 HOURS TO MARINATE) | COOKING TIME 8 HOURS

For the Dish

1 rack of mutton, French trimmed

40ml veal glaze

50ml squid ink

20ml soy sauce

30g tomato ketchup

20g roast garlic purée

1 large sprig of mint, rosemary and thyme

10 black peppercorns

80g salted anchovies

2 cans Coca-Cola

1l chicken stock

For the Cauliflower Purée

1 cauliflower

double cream, to cover

salt and pepper

For the Root Vegetables

selection of root vegetables

rapeseed oil, drizzle of

2 sprigs of thyme, picked

2 cloves of garlic

rock salt

To prepare the mutton, put all the liquid ingredients together with the mint, rosemary, peppercorns, garlic purée and anchovies into a blender and blitz. Pour over the French trimmed racks of mutton and marinate for 12 hours.

Preheat the oven to 85°C and cook the mutton for 8 hours. Remove from the oven and allow the meat to cool in the sauce. Then remove the meat and reduce the sauce to a glazing consistency.

To prepare the caramelised cauliflower purée, remove the florets and place in a roasting tray. Drizzle with rapeseed oil and roast at 180°C until nice and golden brown. Place in a food processor, add seasoning and cover with double cream. Blitz until smooth and season with salt and pepper to taste.

To prepare the root vegetables, neatly cut them into nice cubes. Drizzle with rapeseed oil, picked thyme, cloves of garlic and rock salt. Roast at 180°C until caramelised and soft to touch.

JESSE DUNFORD WOOD

" *I thought Parlour's Reindeer Pie would be an appropriate recipe in support of the Children's Food Trust, a charity focusing on nutrition for children. The right diet is so important in formative years that I'm very happy to be able to support the trust through ChariTable Bookings' great new book.*"

VENISON AND ALE PIE – Reindeer pie

SERVES 6 | PREPARATION TIME 50 MINUTES | COOKING TIME 3 HOURS 30 MINUTES

For the Venison and Ale Stew

2kg venison, diced, lamb or beef
could be used as an alternative
1 drizzle of vegetable oil
10g cornflour
salt and pepper, to season

For the Onions

150g baby onions, peeled
1 tbsp sugar
1 drizzle of vegetable oil
3 tbsp balsamic vinegar, to deglaze
250g onions, sliced
250g button mushrooms, halved
25g thyme, chopped
125g butter
salt and pepper
150g flour
568ml of ale
1l chicken stock
Dijon mustard, to taste

For the Suet Pie Pastry

340g self-raising flour
15g salt
125g suet
90g butter, diced
175g ice water

To Serve

eggwash
deer horn, optional
mashed potatoes
green vegetables

To make the venison and ale stew, preheat an oven to 180°C, season the diced meat, drizzle with vegetable oil and place it in the oven for about 20 minutes.

In a wide pan, caramelise the baby onions with a little vegetable oil and sugar. Deglaze with balsamic vinegar, remove from the pan and set aside. In the same uncleaned pot, add the sliced onions and mushrooms and stew with half the chopped thyme and the butter, seasoning well until they are soft and start to release some of their natural juices. You can add the baby onions back at this stage if you like. Add the flour, and cook for 5 minutes, it should become thick and gloopy, then add the beer and chicken stock. Bring this mixture to the boil, making sure it is not sticking to the bottom of the pan. Re-season with salt, pepper and bit of Dijon mustard, keeping in mind that this will reduce, so the seasoning shouldn't be too strong. Add the beef and place in the oven for approximately 3 hours at 150°C.

When the beef is tender, remove from the pan. If the sauce is too thick, just add a little water, but more often than not it is not thick enough. Mix the cornflour with a tablespoon of water, to make a slurry, add it to the pot and bring back to the boil to thicken the sauce. Add the last of the thyme, salt and pepper to taste and perhaps a little more balsamic vinegar, for a little sweet and sour element. Add the reserved meat, and leave to cool down. This stew can also be frozen for later use.

To make the suet pie pastry, mix the flour, salt, suet and butter together and then pour the water gradually until you have a dough with little lumps of butter and flecks of suet running through it. Try not to over mix. Place the dough in the fridge until required, or it too can be frozen at this point.

To assemble the dish, select a dish approximately 4cm deep. If the dish is too deep, the pastry will brown and the filling will not be hot enough. You also want the horns to poke through. Egg wash the rim of the chosen dish, place the meat stew in, then place the pre-rolled pastry over the mixture, with a little hanging over the edge. Press the pastry down around the edge of the pie dish and tuck it under any rim too. Egg wash the top of the pie. At this stage you can keep the pie in the fridge for a couple of hours, even days, but you can also put it straight in the oven, but before you do you need to horn the pie. Ensuring the horn is washed well and thoroughly dried, make a little cross in the pastry and push in the horn, wrapping the pastry up against it. Cook in a hot oven at 180°C for 10–20 minutes until golden.

Take the pie out of the oven, and serve with some silky mashed potatoes, and some green vegetables.

SAM DUNLEAVY

This is a great way to spread the word about incredible charities like Dementia UK. I hope you enjoy cooking the duck recipe from Eastway Brasserie located in the Andaz Hotel, London, and that ChariTable Bookings raises awareness for charities across the UK."

ROAST GRESSINGHAM DUCK with caramelised carrot purée, roast carrots and fig jus

SERVES 4 | PREPARATION TIME 30 MINUTES | COOKING TIME 1 HOUR

For the Duck
    4 duck breasts
    salt and pepper

For the Caramelised Carrot Purée
    500g carrots
    1 pinch of salt
    150g butter

For the Fig Jus
    1l beef stock
    100g dried figs
    salt and pepper

For the Pan-fried Carrots
    12 baby carrots

For the Garnish
    coriander cress

To make the caramelised carrot purée, remove the tops and tails and peel the large carrots. Roughly chop them and place in a saucepan, covering with water and a pinch of salt. Cook the carrots until soft, approximately 30–40 minutes. Whilst the carrots are cooking, add the butter to a saucepan and place on the stove. Cook on a medium heat until the milk solids separate from the butter. Skim the foam off the surface and wait for the remaining butter to turn golden brown with a nutty aroma. Once cooked, drain, keeping some of the liquid for the purée. Place the cooked carrots in a blender with the brown butter and blend, adding a little bit of the carrot cooking liquid if the purée is too thick. Season to taste and set to one side.

To prepare the fig jus, reduce 1l of beef stock down to 300ml and add the dried figs, allowing them to rehydrate and flavour the sauce.

To cook the roast duck, remove the duck breast from the fridge 20 minutes before cooking. Trim any excess fat from the duck and season the breasts with salt and pepper. Cook on each side for 2 minutes in a hot pan, then place in an oven at 170°C for 5 minutes. Once cooked, let the meat rest for a further 5 minutes to achieve the perfect, pink duck.

To finish the dish and serve, quickly fry the baby carrots in the same pan as the duck, constantly turning them until they are nicely golden brown. Plate as pictured, covering the base of the plate with purée and topping with duck and baby carrots. Garnish with coriander cress and cover generously in fig jus.

JAMES DURRANT

This is a great new idea by ChariTable Bookings, mulitple chefs supporting multiple charities! Myself and the team at The Stafford are supporting Macmillan and the work they do to look after cancer sufferer's and their families."

DINGLEY DELL PORK BELLY with caramelised onions, cockle and white bean cassoulet

SERVES 4 | PREPARATION TIME 45 MINUTES (PLUS OVERNIGHT CHILLING AND SOAKING) | COOKING TIME 6 HOURS

For the Cockles
500g fresh cockles
100ml white wine
1 small bunch of parsley, chopped

For the Pork Belly
1.5kg pork belly
vegetable mirepoix, 2 onions and 2
carrots, chopped
6 cloves of garlic, smashed
30 cloves
1 star anise
2 sprigs of thyme
1 bay leaf
1 tbsp tomato purée
300ml honey
150ml red wine vinegar
3l veal stock
1l chicken stock

For the Bean Cassoulet
300g white beans, soaked overnight
2 sprigs of thyme
1 bay leaf
1 splash of cream
1 onion, finely chopped
2 cloves of garlic, finely chopped
100g chorizo, diced
4 rashers of smoked bacon, diced
4 sausage links, poached and
shredded
75g black pudding, diced

For the Garnish
10 baby onions, peeled and halved
1 large knob of butter
1 banana shallot
4 tbsp plain flour
100ml milk
oil, for frying

To Serve
1 handful of purslane
100g samphire, blanched

For the cockles, place a pan with a lid on a high heat. When the pan is hot add the cockles and wine and cover immediately. Steam for 1 minute then drain. Discard any unopened cockles and pick the meat from the shells, saving a few for garnish.

For the pork, preheat an oven to 150°C. Deskin, debone, roll and tie the pork belly. Heat a pan and seal the pork on all sides then place in a heavy ovenproof casserole. Using the same pan caramelise the mirepoix then add the garlic, cloves, star anise, thyme and bay leaf. Cook for another 3 minutes to allow the spices to open then add the tomato purée and honey. Add this mixture to the pork, deglaze the pan with the vinegar until reduced to virtually nothing then add to the pot and cover with the stocks. Seal the casserole with foil, cover with its lid and roast for 6 hours. Remove the belly from the casserole, cut away the strings and wrap tightly in cling film and refrigerate overnight. Next, pass the casserole liquor through a very fine sieve into a clean pan and reduce by half on medium heat. Set aside a small amount to use as a glaze later and use the rest in the bean cassoulet.

For the bean cassoulet, cook the soaked beans with the thyme and bay leaf for 30 minutes until soft through. Remove three quarters of them and continue to cook the rest until very mushy then drain, add a splash of cream and blitz with a hand blender. Spoon into a piping bag and keep warm until ready to serve. Next, in a casserole, sweat the onion and garlic without colour then add the chorizo, bacon and sausage. When cooked, add the black pudding and beans then stir in the pork sauce. Keep warm. Just before serving add the cockles and parsley.

For the garnish, fry the baby onions in butter until well caramelised to bring out the bitter onion flavour. Drain on kitchen paper. Slice the shallot into rings and soak them in milk for 2 minutes drain them and dust with flour. Deep fry until golden brown and crisp. Drain on kitchen paper.

To serve, reheat the pork belly in the sauce that has been set aside allowing the sauce to reduce to a glaze. Cut into medallions and present with dots of bean purée, caramelised baby onions, shallot rings, a few cockles, samphire and purslane. Serve the cassoulet on the side.

SANJAY DWIVEDI

Through this great new book from ChariTable Bookings, I want to support the work of Whizz Kids, helping kids to live their life to the full whatever their disability. I really hope you enjoy my Ceviche from Coya."

SEA BASS CEVICHE

SERVES 4 | PREPARATION TIME 30 MINUTES | COOKING TIME 15 MINUTES

For the Leche de Tigre
½ onion, peeled
½ head of celery
1 bulb of garlic
1 aji limo chilli
½ bunch of coriander, reserve a few
leaves for garnish
5g ginger
125ml fish stock
6 limes, juiced
1 pinch of salt

For the Vegetables
125g sweet potatoes
100g Peruvian white corn
1l water
1 star anise

For the Sea Bass
6 sea bass fillets, deskinned
1 pinch of salt
1 lime, juiced
coriander leaves
½ long red chilli, de-seeded and
finely chopped
½ red onion, finely sliced

To prepare the leche de tigre, in a blender, blitz the onion, celery, garlic, aji limo, coriander and the ginger with fish stock. Ensure you do not blend to a purée, you just want to break down the vegetables. The idea is to release the flavour into the fish stock. Pass the mixture through a sieve, add the lime juice and salt, and refrigerate.

Dice the sweet potatoes into 1cm cubes. In a pan, add 1 litre of water, the diced sweet potatoes and star anise, and gently bring to the boil. Cook the mixture for 5 minutes and refresh the sweet potatoes in ice water. Keep aside until ready to serve.

Blanch the Peruvian corn for 10 minutes in salted water, refresh in ice water and keep aside for serving.

To serve, dice the sea bass into 2cm cubes. Season with salt and the juice of one lime. Pour over the leche de tigre, and mix well. Season to taste. Add the sweet potatoes, Peruvian corn, chopped reserved coriander and the red chillies. Mix well and allow to marinate for no longer than a minute. Finish with finely sliced red onions and serve.

NICK EDGAR

" All of us at The Samling are proud to support the amazing work that Cancer Research does for thousands of sufferers every year by donating our signature dish recipe to ChariTable Bookings."

PORK with sage, onion and apple

SERVES 4 | PREPARATION TIME 1 HOUR | COOKING TIME 1 HOUR 30 MINUTES

For the Pork
1 pork tenderloin, trimmed and fat removed, ask your butcher to do this
20g butter

For the Onion Purée
10g butter
3 Spanish onions, peeled and sliced
50ml double cream
¾ tsp salt

For the Mustard Cabbage
2 spring cabbages
10g English mustard
50ml double cream

For the Apple Purée
3 Granny Smith apples
3 Pink Lady apples

For the Pickled Onion and Roasted Onion
1 Spanish onion, cut into wedges
1 red onion, cut into wedges
100g white wine vinegar
200ml water
50g sugar
2 tsp salt
10g butter

For the Sage and Onion Granola
20g honey
50g porridge oats
1¼ tsp black onion seeds
10g dried onion flakes
10g fresh sage, chopped
1¼ tsp sea salt

For the onion purée, melt the butter in a pan and add the sliced onion, stirring continually on medium heat until soft. After around 15 minutes, add the cream and bring to the boil. Strain off the liquid and blend the cooked onion until smooth.

Add the cabbage to a big pan of boiling water with a pinch of salt. Cook for 3 minutes, remove and transfer into ice water. In a pan, reduce the cream by half and whisk in mustard, then add the cabbage.

Peel all the apples and remove the cores. Place in a pan with a little water and cook until soft, then blend until smooth.

For the pickled onion, bring the water, vinegar, salt and sugar to a boil. Place the Spanish onion wedges in the liquid and boil for 3 minutes. Allow to cool.

To make the roasted onions, melt the butter in a non-stick pan and add the red onion wedges. Cook until golden brown and lightly season with salt.

To prepare the granola, start by melting honey in pan. Add all other ingredients and mix well. Place on greaseproof tray and bake at 180°C for 10 minutes until golden brown.

To cook the pork, melt the butter in a frying pan. Add the fillet and roll in butter until golden brown. Place pan in oven at 180°C for 4 minutes, season with salt and allow to rest for 3 minutes before carving.

To serve, put the cabbage in the middle of the plate and dot the apple and onion pureés around it. Arrange the roasted red onion and pickled onion pieces, place the sliced pork on top and spoon over the roasting juice. Finish the dish with a sprinkling of the sage and onion granola.

DEAN EDWARDS

Headway is the Uk-wide charity that works to improve life after brain injury, the losses through which can be terrible. Please support them with me and enjoy my recipe at the same time. Great to be able to enjoy great food and support many charities at the same time."

CHICKEN AND CHORIZO LASAGNE

SERVES 4 | PREPARATION TIME 15 MINUTES | COOKING TIME 1 HOUR

Equipment
food processor

For the Lasagne
4–5 chicken thighs, skinless and boneless
100g chorizo, cubed
1 tbsp olive oil
1 large onion, very finely diced
2 sticks of celery, very finely diced
1 tbsp thyme, chopped
3 cloves of garlic, crushed
150ml white wine
½ tsp smoked paprika
2 x 400g cans of chopped tomatoes
1 tsp sugar
sea salt and black pepper, to taste
8–9 fresh lasagne pasta sheets
70g cheddar cheese, grated

For the White Sauce
50g unsalted butter
50g plain flour
500ml milk

To prepare the filling, put the chicken thighs in a food processor and pulse until they are broken down. Don't over process though, as it's nice to have a few slightly larger pieces in the mixture. Add a dash of oil to a non-stick frying pan, tip in the chicken mince and brown over a medium to high heat. Remove the chicken from the pan and set aside.

Using the same pan with a little more oil if you need it, cook the chorizo, onion, celery, thyme and garlic for 5 minutes until softened. Add the wine and continue to cook until the liquid is reduced by half. Put the chicken back in the pan and add the paprika and tomatoes, then reduce the heat to a simmer and cook for 20 minutes. Season with the sugar, salt and pepper.

To make the white sauce, melt the butter over a medium heat. Whisk in the flour and cook for 2 minutes, stirring constantly. Pour in the milk and continue whisking until it comes to a boil, then reduce the heat and simmer the sauce for 5 minutes, stirring occasionally, then season.

Preheat the oven to 200°C. Grease an ovenproof dish measuring about 33x23cm. Spread a thin layer of chicken sauce in the bottom of the dish, then add a sheet of lasagne, then more chicken sauce. Add another sheet of pasta, followed by white sauce, then the chicken sauce. Continue until everything is used up, finishing with a layer of white sauce. Sprinkle with cheese and bake in the oven for 40 minutes.

JOSH EGGLETON

Skin diseases are much more common than you think. There are 8 million people living with a condition in the UK at this moment. The Pony and Trop team offer up their Brawn Fritters to this new book by ChariTable Bookings to support The British Skin Foundation's great work to prevent diseases from psoriasis to skin cancer."

BRAWN FRITTERS with pickled red cabbage and piccalilli garnishes

SERVES 6–8 | PREPARATION TIME 1 HOUR 30 MINUTES (PLUS OVERNIGHT PICKLING AND PRESS) | COOKING TIME 4 HOURS

For the Brawn

6–8l brine

1 pig head, halved and brain removed

5 white onions, peeled and halved

3 large carrots, peeled and split lengthways

3 sticks of celery, halved

1 bulb of garlic, halved

10 cloves

2 star anise

10 black peppercorns

3 bay leaves

½ bunch of thyme

1 bunch of flat leaf parsley, chiffonade

1 bunch of chives, chopped

150g cornichons, chopped

150g capers, chopped

150g shallots, finely diced

3½ sheets gelatine

For the Pickled Red Cabbage

300g red cabbage

50g sea salt

100ml red wine vinegar

100g sugar

1g pickling spices

2 star anise

For the Piccalilli

1 cauliflower, cut into small florets

100g small onions, peeled

2 shallots, finely diced

To make the brawn, place the pig head in a large non-metallic container, cover with the brine and leave in the refrigerator overnight. Remove from the brine, cut off the ears and discard the brine. Place all the ingredients except the shallots, cornichons, capers, parsley, chives and gelatine in a large pan. Gently pour over enough cold water to just cover the ingredients. Bring to the boil, then reduce the heat and simmer for 3 hours, or until the meat is tender. Set the pan aside, and cool until warm enough to handle the head. Skim any fat off from the top of the liquid in the pan, then remove the head and set aside. Pass the stock through a sieve into a clean pan and reduce it slowly. Strain through a fine sieve and set aside. Pick any meat out of the vegetables in the sieve and discard the vegetables. Place the head in a large dish and slowly pick off large chunks of meat and add them to a large mixing bowl. Be sure to discard any skin, bone, gristle or excess fat. Using a sharp knife, cut the meat into rough pieces and put back in the bowl. Thinly slice the ears if they're soft enough, and add them too. When the meat has cooled, gently fold in the parsley, chives, cornichons, capers and shallots. Soak the gelatine in cold water until soft then measure 600ml cooking liquor, and while still warm add the soft gelatine. Check the seasoning. When the stock has cooled to room temperature, gently pour it into the meat until covered, stirring all the while, until just covering. Line a terrine dish with a double layer of cling film and add the meat mix in layers, adding more stock as needed. Cover loosely with cling film. Place the terrine in a high-sided tray and place another terrine dish on top of the brawn. Weight it down and press overnight in the refrigerator. Gently turn the brawn out and place to one side.

To make the pickled red cabbage, quarter the cabbage and remove the core and any dirty outside leaves. Slice the cabbage as thinly as possible, preferably on a mandoline. Then toss the cabbage in the salt and leave overnight in the fridge. Meanwhile bring the vinegar, sugar, pickling spices and star anise to the boil, stirring regularly to prevent the sugar from catching on the bottom of the pan. Then take off the heat and cool to allow the spices to infuse further. The following day, wash the cabbage in cold water and pat dry with kitchen paper. Pass the pickling liquor through a fine sieve or preferably a chinois and pour over the cabbage to macerate for at least 1 hour. Drain the red cabbage and set aside.

For the Piccalilli *continued*

- salt, to taste
- 1 cucumber, deseeded and cut into large dice
- 310ml white wine vinegar
- 150ml malt vinegar
- 1 red chilli, deseeded and roughly chopped
- 50g caster sugar
- 1 pinch of turmeric
- 50g English mustard powder
- 2 tbsp xanthan gum

For the Brawn Fritters

- brawn, chilled and cut into large cubes or rectangles
- 2 eggs
- 300ml milk
- 1 handful of plain flour
- 1 handful of panko breadcrumbs
- salt and pepper, to taste
- cornichons
- watercress

To make the piccallili, combine the cauliflower, onions and shallots in a bowl, salt to taste, cover and leave in the refrigerator overnight. Rinse and pat dry. Sprinkle the cucumber with salt and leave for 20 minutes then rinse, pat dry, and mix with the vegetables. Place both the vinegars and the chilli in a medium-sized pan, bring to the boil and simmer for 10 minutes. Discard the chilli and sieve into a clean pan. Add the sugar, turmeric, mustard powder and a large pinch of salt, place back on the heat and simmer for 5 minutes. Whisk in the xanthan gum and simmer for a final 2 minutes, remove from the heat and cool. Combine the sauce and the vegetables in a large bowl and mix very well.

To make the brawn fritters, put the flour and breadcrumbs in 2 separate bows. In a third bowl, whisk together the eggs and milk. Dust the pieces of brawn in the flour, shaking off any excess, cover in the egg mix and finally in the breadcrumbs. Lay the breaded brawn on a tray and refrigerate for at least 30 minutes. Preheat a deep fat fryer to 180°C and fry the fritters until golden brown. If the fritters aren't cooked through, cook them in the oven at 180°C until done. If the fritters aren't cooked through or you don't have a deep fat fryer, cook them in the oven at 180°C until done.

To serve, rest on kitchen towel to drain excess oil and serve hot with the piccalilli, pickled red cabbage, cornichons and watercress.

MARK ELLIS

Hope you enjoy my firepit beetroot from The Peckforton Castle in support of the great work done by Macmillan. Wonderful new initiative by ChariTable Bookings to promote charity across the UK."

FIREPIT BEETROOT with ewe's curd

SERVES 6 | PREPARATION TIME 30 MINUTES | COOKING TIME 3 HOURS 20 MINUTES

For the Beetroots

6 medium sized, whole ruby beetroots

2 bay leaves

2 sprigs of lemon thyme

300ml organic beetroot juice

2g xanthan gum

To Finish

200g ewe's curd

baby beetroot leaves

100ml avocado oil

salt and pepper, to taste

To make the fire pit beetroot, dig a hole around 2 feet deep. Fill with wood and charcoal. Set alight and wait until the fire dies down and the charcoals are smouldering. Wash the beetroots well retaining the skin. Rub with rapeseed oil and season with salt and pepper. Add thyme leaves and wrap in foil. Then drop into the smouldering hole and cover with the charcoals. Cover with the earth and leave for 3 hours. Guard the area well from children and pets, the ground gets hot. Dig up the beetroots and remove the foil and any earth. Leave to cool until they can be handled. Carefully remove the tops and scoop out the flesh, leaving the exterior of the beetroot intact. After, put the extracted beetroot in a pan with the beetroot juice, thyme leaves and bay, and bring to the boil. Strain the beetroot and remove the herbs. Blend the beetroot with a little of the beetroot juice until smooth. Add the xanthan gum and blend for a further couple of minutes until smooth and thick.

To finish the dish and serve, season to taste and fill the hollow beetroots with the purée. Serve with the ewes curd, the baby beetroot leaves, and avocado oil.

STEVEN ELLIS

They weren't joking when they said children are our future! Save The Children is the most recognised children's charity in the world and for good reason. I'm very happy to share The Oxford Blue's partridge and truffle pie with ChariTable Bookings to support them."

PARTRIDGE AND TRUFFLE PIE

SERVES 2 | PREPARATION TIME 30 MINUTES | COOKING TIME 1 HOUR 45 MINUTES

For the Pie
- 1 whole partridge, deboned
- 20g black truffle
- 1 chicken breast, cleaned of any sinew
- 200ml double cream
- 50g parsley, finely chopped
- 3 baby carrots, peeled with tops
- 50g wild mushrooms
- 100g mash potato

For the pastry
- 250g flour
- 50g polenta flour
- ½ tsp Maldon salt
- ½ tsp bicarbonate of soda
- 75g beef dripping
- 80ml boiling water

For the sauce
- 2 chicken wings, chopped up in to 2 cm pieces
- 6 shallots, roughly chopped
- 3 cloves of garlic
- 4 sprigs of thyme
- 4 black peppercorns
- 1 block of butter, diced
- 500ml chicken stock
- 500ml veal stock

Firstly, begin by making the chicken mousse that will bind the truffle together to stuff in the middle of the partridge. Dice up the breast and place in a food blender along with a pinch of salt, blitz for 2 minuntes and pass through a drum sieve. Once passed, slowly fold in the cream until you reach a desired consistency. Mix in the black truffle, season to taste and put in a piping bag. Lay out the partridge on a sheet of cling film, season lightly with salt and pipe the truffle filling down the middle. Roll up tightly and poach in simmering water for 20 minutes. Once cooked, leave to the side to cool.

To make the pastry, place the water and beef dripping in a pan and bring to the boil to melt. Place all the dry ingredients into a mixer and slowly add the water. Once bound, turn it out onto a board and begin to roll out to about 5mm thickness. Using a tall cake ring, wrap the pastry around the outside to form a pie case. Using the same cutter, cut out a disk for your lid. If you would like to add a touch of class, cut out a smaller hole in the centre for where you will pour the sauce. Around the outside of the lid, I like to use a small leaf cutter to decorate it.

To make the sauce, roast the chicken wings in a large pan with a little vegetable oil. Once golden, add the butter and let it foam up around the wings, this will colour them further but help create a rich roast chicken flavour to your sauce. Once caramelised and crispy, add the shallots and thyme and cook for a further 5 minutes then add the stocks and leave to cook for about 40 minutes or until you reach a consistency you are happy with.

To assemble, fry the partridge until golden brown and place in the oven for 5 minutes before cutting into 3 equal pieces. Blanch the carrots, sauté the wild mushrooms and fry the spinach until wilted. To construct your pie, place the spinach in the bottom, followed by one piece of the partridge. Egg wash the rim and place the lid on top, place this back in the oven for 1 minute to seal. To dress the plate, place the pie slightly to the left, spoon the mash potato opposite and arrange 3 carrots nicely on top. Scatter the wild mushrooms around the outside and once served to your guests, pour the chicken sauce into the middle so it overflows down the sides.

STEPHEN ENGLEFIELD

"It's very important for us at the Jugged Hare, serving unique and interesting food all day, to recognise that there are others less fortunate in the world, malnourished, starving. Action Against Hunger tackles this head on which is why we support them through our signature recipe, The Jugged Hare, in this ChariTable Bookings publication."

JUGGED HARE

SERVES 8 | PREPARATION TIME 40 MINUTES (PLUS 24–48 HOURS TO MARINATE) | COOKING TIME 2 HOURS

For the Dish

8 hare hind legs
1l red wine
4 juniper berries, chopped
1 bay leaf
a few sprigs of thyme
1 tbsp flour, plus extra for dusting
vegetable oil, for frying
1 onion, finely chopped
50g butter
1 tbsp tomato purée
3l beef stock
300ml hare's blood, ask your butcher to reserve this for you when they butcher the hare
salt and freshly ground black pepper

Cut the hare legs in half at the joint, then cut them once more through the middle of the thigh, so you end up with 3 pieces from each leg. Put the pieces into a non-metal bowl or dish, together with the red wine, juniper, bay leaf and thyme. Cover with cling film and refrigerate for 24–48 hours.

Drain the hare in a colander over a bowl and pat the pieces dry with some kitchen paper. Season the pieces of hare and lightly flour them, dusting off any excess. Reserve the marinade for cooking.

Heat the vegetable oil in a heavy frying pan and fry the pieces, a few at a time, until well coloured, then put to one side on a plate.

Meanwhile, gently cook the onion in the butter for 3–4 minutes in a heavy-based saucepan, until soft. Add the tablespoon of flour and stir well over a medium heat until it begins to turn a sandy brown colour. Add the tomato purée, then slowly add the red wine and herbs from the marinade, stirring well to avoid lumps forming. Bring to the boil and simmer over a medium heat until the liquid has reduced to half the volume.

Add the beef stock and hare, bring back to the boil, cover and simmer gently for 1 hour Alternatively you can cook this in an oven that has been preheated to 160°C. Remove a piece of meat to check if it's tender. If not, continue cooking for another 30 minutes or so.

Once the meat is tender, remove from the sauce and set aside. Add the blood and continue to simmer the sauce until it has thickened to a gravy consistency. Return the pieces of meat to the pan to warm through until it's ready to serve. Adjust the seasoning if necessary.

DAVID EVERITT-MATTHIAS

" The NSPCC works tirelessly to not only counsel children post abuse but also to prevent it and give all children the childhood they deserve. Le Champignon Sauvage's fillet of huss is one of our favourites and I'm very happy to share this with ChariTable Bookings in aid of the wonderful NSPCC."

FILLET OF HUSS with cauliflower purée and pork mince

SERVES 6 | PREPARATION TIME 30 MINUTES | COOKING TIME 1 HOUR

For the Huss
6 x 200g huss fillets, membrane removed
salt and pepper, to taste
50ml olive oil
25g unsalted butter
½ tbsp Demerara sugar
50ml apple vinegar

For the Cauliflower purée
1 medium cauliflower
250ml milk
50g unsalted butter

For the Pork Mince
30ml olive oil
175g good lean pork mince
1 clove of garlic, finely chopped
200ml brown chicken stock
15g flat leaf parsley, roughly chopped

For the Garnish
3 medium cauliflower florets, thinly sliced
1 Granny Smith apple, cut into matchsticks
1 small bunch of chickweed
1 drizzle of olive oil
salt and pepper

Season the huss well and in a large heavy-bottomed frying pan, heat the olive oil. When hot, add the huss and cook until golden brown on one side. Flip over, add the butter, and cook until golden on the other side, which should take approximately 2–3 minutes depending on the thickness of the fish. Deglaze the pan with the sugar and the vinegar, making sure to swirl and glaze; continue cooking until the glaze has evaporated. Remove from the pan. Re-season and keep warm, allowing to rest.

To make the cauliflower, trim, discarding all the green and the major part of the stalk. Divide it into small florets and place in a saucepan with the milk. Bring to the boil, cover and simmer gently for 10–15 minutes, until the cauliflower is very tender. Drain, reserving the milk. Place in a blender, add 50g of butter and blend until smooth, adding a little of the reserved milk if the purée is too thick. If it is too thin, return it to a pan and cook gently until thick enough to hold its shape. Keep warm.

To make the pork mince, heat the olive oil in a large frying pan and when very hot, add the mince and cook quickly until golden. Just before it is finished, about 3–4 minutes in, add the garlic and stir, then tip out onto a warm tray. Pour the stock into the pan and stir to release any sediment. Bring to the boil, cook until syrupy and until approximately 6 tablespoons of liquid remains. Add the mince back in and coat well. Keep warm.

To serve, place a little of the cauliflower purée on the plate, then the huss to one side. Dress the cauliflower slices and the apple with the olive oil, season and arrange nicely around and on the fish. Stir the parsley through the pork mince then scatter over the plate and finish with the chickweed.

MICHAEL FACEY

"We hope you enjoy our glazed lamb shoulder recipe from The Laughing Gravy. It was a pleasure to offer up this recipe to ChariTable Bookings as well as raise awareness for The Prostate Cancer Charity."

MEAD AND MALT GLAZED LAMB SHOULDER with cheddar and parsnip hash

browns, salt-baked turnips, glazed carrots, turnip purée and lamb jam

SERVES 4 | PREPARATION TIME 1 DAY (PLUS OVERNIGHT TO MARINATE) | COOKING TIME 6 HOURS

For the Lamb

1.5kg lamb shoulder, on the bone

1l duck fat, or olive oil

2 sprigs each of rosemary, thyme
and mint, leave 1 sprig each of
whole, pick and chop the rest

2 bay leaves

3 cloves of garlic

25g sea salt

½ tsp each peppercorns, juniper, pimento
seeds, coriander seeds and cinnamon

15g garlic, chopped

For the Glaze

75g white onion, chopped

75g green apple, peeled and chopped

1 clove of garlic

1 pinch each of salt and black pepper

75g barley alt

35g light brown sugar

750ml mead

For the Lamb Jam

100g trimmings of the cooked lamb

40g mead glaze

40g caster sugar

100ml lamb or vegetable stock

For the Parsnip Hash

200g waxy potatoes

650g parsnips

50g butter

1 pinch each of salt and celery salt

100g white onion, chopped

50g cheddar cheese

25g potato starch or cornflour

1 egg, beaten

1 handful of Scottish rolled oats

For the Vegetables and Purée

500g turnips

rock salt, enough to cover the turnips

1 clove of garlic

150ml vegetable stock

50ml double cream

100g baby carrots

1 knob of butter

To prepare the lamb, warm the duck fat or olive oil in the oven with the whole herb sprigs, one bay leaf and garlic. Remove from the oven and leave to infuse. Place the rest of the dry ingredients except the lamb in a mixer and blitz to make a dry paste. Then, rub the paste all over the lamb, cover and refrigerate for 24 hours. Preheat the oven to 140°C, or 130°C fan. Fill a roasting tin with the fat and place in the oven for 5 minutes to warm through. Brush the marinade off the lamb and place the lamb into the warmed duck fat. Cover with foil and cook for approximately 1 hour 45 minutes. The lamb should feel tender and soft. Remove the lamb and leave to cool for 5 minutes on a flat tray. Pull the bone out of the lamb – if it does not come out easily, place back in the oven for a few more minutes. Once cool place in the fridge for 2 hours until set, remove and cut into 4 rectangles. Keep the trimmings for the lamb jam.

To make the glaze, fry the onions, apple and chopped garlic in a pan with salt and pepper for 3 minutes. Then, add the rest of the ingredients and simmer for 20 minutes. Put into a food processor and blitz until smooth. Return to the pan and simmer until the mixture becomes thick and syrupy – reduced by just under a half. Before serving, preheat the oven to 200°C. Place the lamb on greaseproof paper on a baking tray and brush with the glaze. Heat in the oven for 12 minutes. Every 3 minutes, brush more glaze over the lamb until it turns bronze and sticky.

To prepare the lamb jam, chop up the trimmings into small pieces. Place all the ingredients in a pan and bring to the boil. Leave to simmer until reduced to a jam-like consistency.

To make the parsnip hash, heat the oven to 200°C. Bake the potatoes whole in the oven for 20 minutes. Then leave to cool for 10 minutes and the place in the fridge for 15 minutes until cold. Peel the potatoes and grate and leave to one side. Peel and chop the parsnips. Smear with butter and season on a baking tray. Then, cover with foil and bake in the oven for 25 minutes. Remove the foil and cook for approximately 10–15 minutes until golden brown. Remove from the oven and mash. Next, fry the onions and add to the mashed parsnips with the grated potato, cheese and potato starch. Check for seasoning. Add more if needed. Roll into small cigar shapes and place into the fridge to set for an hour. Remove, dip into the egg, roll in oats and place on a tray. Pan fry until golden, or place in deep fat fryer if you have one.

To make the vegetables and turnip purée, wash the turnips, place on a baking tray and cover with rock salt. Bake in the oven with the lamb at 140°C for 1 hour. Then, rub the first skin off. Cut half of them into wedges and set to one side. When ready to serve, warm slightly in a frying pan. With the rest of the turnips, place them into a pan and fry with a clove of garlic. Add the stock and the cream and bring to a boil for 3 minutes. Place into a food processor and blitz until smooth.

For the carrots, place into a pan covered in water. Add a pinch of salt and the knob of butter and simmer for 7–8 minutes until soft. Drain to serve.

Serve with seasonal greens if desired.

SCOTT FAIRWEATHER

This ChariTable Bookings book provides a fantastic opportunity for established figures within the food industry to collaborate their work, as well as show support towards charities that may have had a direct impact on their lives. We, at The Black Swan, wholeheartedly dedicate this recipe to 'myelomaUK' and hope you can recreate it at home."

GUINEA HEN with sage and onion, bourguignon and roast parsnip sauce

SERVES 4 | PREPARATION TIME 20 MINUTES | COOKING TIME 1 HOUR

For the Dish
4 guinea hen breasts
salt
2 tbsp vegetable oil
creamed potato, for serving

For the Bourguignon
100g smoked Cumbrian pancetta lardons
3 tbsp vegetable oil
100g silverskin onions, peeled
200g button mushrooms, caps only
200ml red wine
4 sprigs of thyme, leaves picked
500ml each chicken and beef stock

For the Roast Parsnip Sauce
4 parsnips, peeled and thinly sliced, skins reserved
1 bay leaf, torn
2l semi-skimmed milk
2 small croissants, baked
1 pinch of table salt

For the Confit Onion
2 small white onions, halved
4 tbsp reserved pancetta fat
4 sprigs of thyme
50g unsalted butter, diced

For the Sage
40g sage, leaves picked
vegetable oil
1 pinch of table salt

Preheat the oven to 180°C. Season the guinea hen breasts with salt and roast skin-side down in a large frying pan with the vegetable oil until golden. Turn over then place in the oven for 6–8 minutes then remove onto a cooling rack and allow to rest for a further 8 minutes. Alternatively sous-vide the guinea hen on the crown then roast in a hot pan.

To make the bourguignon, fry the pancetta lardons in a hot frying pan with 1 tablespoon of oil until golden and crisp. Drain in a colander and reserve the cooking fat for the confit onions. Fry the onions and mushrooms in the same pan with the remaining oil until golden and softened then return the pancetta to the pan and deglaze with the red wine. Reduce by half then add the thyme and stocks. Simmer gently for 45 minutes over a low heat until the pancetta is tender and the stock has reduced to a glaze.

For the parsnips, preheat a deep fat fryer or small pan of vegetable oil to 150°C then fry the parsnip peelings in small batches until golden. Drain on paper towel and set aside. Place the parsnips and bay leaf into a large saucepan, cover with milk then boil until completely softened. Drain in a colander, discard the bay leaf but keeping the cooking milk, then place the parsnips, croissants and crispy parsnip into a food processor. Blend for 3 minutes, adding the reserved cooking milk to achieve a thick, smooth parsnip purée. Pass through a fine sieve and season with salt to taste.

For the confit onions, heat the reserved pancetta fat in a frying pan and add the onions, cut side down. Fry until golden, add the thyme and butter to the pan and roast at 180°C for 15–20 minutes until softened.

To make the crispy sage leaves, preheat a deep fat fryer or small pan of vegetable oil to 180°C. Fry the leaves in small batches until crisp then drain on paper towel and lightly season.

Serve as pictured on a bed of creamy mashed potatoes.

PHIL FANNING

Mia's Wood is a local charity, set up by one of our guests, that encourages local children to strengthen their interest in wildlife. Paris House at Woburn is happy to share one of our signature dishes with ChariTable Bookings to raise awareness of this great charity."

TROUT cured with Chase rhubarb vodka, rhubarb gazpacho and yoghurt

SERVES 4 | PREPARATION TIME 45 MINUTES (PLUS 12 HOURS TO MARINATE)

For the Cured Trout

½ tsp chopped tarragon

¼ orange zest

1 stick of rhubarb

½ small red beetroot

¼ tsp coriander seeds

35g coarse rock salt

35g demerara sugar

25ml Chase rhubarb vodka

500g sea trout or salmon

For the Rhubarb Gazpacho

100g rhubarb

20g shallots

30g red beetroot

20g carrot

20g cucumber, skin removed

20ml olive oil

¼ tsp salt

10g palm sugar

65ml water

½ tsp chopped oregano

½ tsp chopped mint

white balsamic vinegar, to taste

To Serve

2 tbsp Greek yoghurt

¼ cucumber, diced

2 spring onions, finely sliced

salmon or trout roe, if available

To prepare the trout, blitz the tarragon, orange zest, rhubarb, beetroot and coriander seeds into a coarse pulp then add the salt, sugar and vodka and mix well. Rub all the marinade around the outside of the fish and put it into a zip lock bag. Refrigerate for about 3–4 hours, then wipe off the marinade and reserve until it's ready to serve.

To prepare the gazpacho, finely slice the rhubarb, shallots, red beetroot, carrot and cucumber. Mix all the ingredients together and leave to marinate, covered in the fridge for 12 hours. Liquidise and then pass through a fine sieve, squeezing all the juice from the pulp. Season the juice to taste with salt and white balsamic vinegar. Chill and reserve until ready to serve.

To serve, thinly slice the trout and lay in the bottom of a bowl, top with a few small dollops of Greek yoghurt, the diced cucumber, spring onion and roe. Finally pour in a little of the gazpacho and serve immediately.

BRIAN FANTONI

A great idea to combine food and charity! On behalf of The Westbury, I'm honored to be able to contribute one of our signature dishes to ChariTable Bookings and highlight the wonderful work Macmillan does for so many every year."

PAPPARDELLE with wild boar ragu, herb breadcrumbs and Tuscan Pecorino

SERVES 4 | PREPARATION TIME 30 MINUTES (PLUS OVERNIGHT TO MARINATE AND REST) | COOKING TIME 2 HOURS

For the Ragu
450g wild boar, diced
½ bottle of red wine
1 tsp juniper berries
½ tsp black pepper
2 bay leaves
1 onion
1 large carrot
1 stick of celery
4 vine plum tomatoes
olive oil
500ml chicken stock
salt and pepper, to taste

For the Pasta
250g 00 flour
250g semolina
6 eggs
olive oil

For the Garnish
80g Pecorino di Pienza, flaked
80g herb breadcrumbs, blended
stale bread
parsley

For the ragu, dice the wild boar and marinate overnight in the red wine, juniper berries, black pepper and bay leaves. Wash, peel and dice the onion, carrot, celery and tomato. Strain the red wine from the marinade and reserve. Caramelise the boar in a heavy pan with a little olive oil, then add the vegetables and cook for a further 10 minutes. Pour in the reserved wine and reduce until almost no wine is left in the pan. Add the chicken stock, bring to the boil and cover with paper, and a tight fitting lid. Place in the oven at 160°C. Cook until tender, which should take approximately 1.5–2 hours. Remove from the oven and keep warm.

To make the pasta, sieve the flour and semolina. Make a well and add the eggs and oil, mix and work until smooth. Wrap the dough in cling film and leave in the fridge to rest overnight. Using a pasta machine, roll out the pastry twice every 2 numbers, until the desired thickness is achieved. Cut the pasta into 10 inch lengths, then fold in half and cut into 2.5cm wide pieces. Allow to dry and weigh 100g portions.

To finish the dish and serve, in a pan of boiling, salted water, cook the pappardelle until they rise to the surface. Add the pasta to the ragu and toss until creamy so the cooking juices stick to the pasta. Serve in a hot bowl and decorate with the Pecorino flakes and herb breadcrumbs.

FLORIAN FAVARIO

The team at Celeste at The Lanesborough are very pleased to be able to support the Children's Liver Disease Foundation through ChariTable Bookings' new recipe book."

ROASTED CAULIFLOWER with lemon curry infused oil and aged Parmesan

SERVES 4 | PREPARATION TIME 15 MINUTES | COOKING TIME 30 MINUTES

For the Cauliflower
1 cauliflower
100g onion
50g tempura mix
200ml milk
200ml single cream

For the Curry Dressing
1 tsp curry powder
150ml olive oil
30ml lemon juice
½ tsp salt

To Serve
coriander cress, for decoration
aged Parmesan, grated

To make the cauliflower, start by cutting all the florets off of the stem. Keep the four largest florets to the side for the garnish, utilising the rest for the purée. Add the four larger florets to a pot of salted, boiling water and cook for 8 minutes. Immediately chill in ice water. Once cold, remove and leave to drain.

To make the cauliflower purée, finely slice the smaller florets and place in a saucepan with a pinch of salt. Sweat them for 6 minutes on a low heat then add the milk and cream. Cook for 20 minutes on a medium heat, then mix in a Robot Coupe to make the purée. Pass through a fine chinois.

To make the curry dressing, mix all the ingredients together.

To prepare the tempura onion, make the tempura mix, whisking together the tempura and a little water until a creamy consistency is reached. Slice the onion into half centimetre thick slices, dip in the tempura mix and fry until crispy.

To serve, dress the plate with the cauliflower purée and a handful of chopped tempura onion. Fry the cauliflower florets until golden brown. Add the cauliflower on top of the purée and drizzle with curry oil. At the last moment, sprinkle with coriander cress, top with grated aged Parmesan and serve.

ANTONIO FAVUZZI

L'Anima is proud to share its Sardinian gnocchi recipe with ChariTable Bookings in support of Macmillan and the fantastic all-round care they give cancer sufferers. We hope you enjoy it too!"

HAND-MADE MALLOREDDUS with Mazara prawns and bottarga

SERVES 4 | PREPARATION TIME 45 MINUTES | COOKING TIME 30 MINUTES

For the Pasta Dough
50g black squid ink
190ml lukewarm water
500g semolina rimacinata

To Serve
1 head of Romanesco
ice water
24 Mazara prawns
1 pinch of salt
1 drizzle of oil
20g spring onions, finely chopped
20g garlic, finely chopped
20g chilli, finely chopped
80ml brandy
1 pinch of freshly ground white pepper
12g basil, finely chopped
8g parsley, finely chopped
60g Grana Padano cheese, grated
40ml extra virgin olive oil
4g baby basil leaves
12g bottarga, grated

To make the pasta dough, combine the ink and water. Make a big well in the centre of the flour and add the ink water. Using a fork, slowly pull the flour into the water, moving around in a circular motion. When the flour and the water are combined, test it with your fingers. Knead by hand until elastic, which should take around 5 minutes. The dough will be ready once it can be stretched and doesn't fragment. Wrap the ball in cling film and leave at room temperature for 30 minutes to relax.

To make the broccoli, blanch in salted boiling water for 2 minutes. Drain and place into ice water, before draining again.

To prepare the prawns, remove the intestinal tract and place to one side.

To make the pasta, divide the dough ball into four. Roll the first quarter between your palms or on a board dusted with a little extra flour, until it is 1cm in diameter. Using a knife, cut it into small portions, roughly 1cm long. Roll them on your gnocchi ridger in a single motion to obtain a rounded shape of pasta resembling a fat little bull. Dust with semolina and leave to the side until needed.

To serve, sprinkle the prawns with salt. Heat a pan with olive oil and add the spring onions, chilli and garlic. Sear the prawns and blanch with the brandy. Remove from the pan. In a big pot of salted, boiling water, cook the malloreddus for 2 to 3 minutes. Drain the pasta and add the Romanesco broccoli to the pan. Cook together for 2 to 3 minutes and finish with the prawns. Season with salt, white pepper, basil, parsley, Grana Padano and a touch of olive oil. Place the malloreddus and sauce in the middle of the plate. Lay some baby basil leaves and grated bottarga on top.

ROMUALD FEGER

The Brain Tumour Charity makes a difference everyday to the lives of people with brain tumours and their families. Both myself and Four Seasons Hotel London at Park Lane are proud to be able to support ChariTable Bookings in raising additional funds for such an inspiring cause."

ROASTED VENISON LOIN with celeriac mousseline and cranberry marmalade

SERVES 4 | PREPARATION TIME 30 MINUTES (PLUS OVERNIGHT TO MARINATE AND TO REST) | COOKING TIME 3 HOURS

For the Roasted Venison Loin and Cep

1 venison loin, trimmed of sinew
50ml olive oil
4 sprigs of thyme
2 sprigs of sage
½ clove garlic, crushed
6 juniper berries, crushed
2 tbsp vegetable oil
8 ceps, halved
25g unsalted butter, cubed

For the Marmalade

250g cranberries
75g of sugar
2 mandarins

For the Celeriac Mousseline

1 celeriac, half for purée, half for dice
1l skimmed milk
50g butter

For the Braised Venison Shoulder

500g venison shoulder
a little oil, for searing
½ large onion
1 carrot
2 cloves of garlic
1 stick of celery
½ bottle red wine
1l chicken stock
1 bay leaf
2 sprigs of thyme

A day ahead, combine the loin with the olive oil, herbs, garlic and juniper and leave overnight. Peel the mandarin and remove its segments, ensuring there is no white skin. Halve the cranberries and mix with the sugar. Mix all of the ingredients together and leave overnight to marinate.

To prepare the celeriac, peel one half and cook in milk with a pinch of salt. Once cooked, blend until smooth and season. Dice the other half of the celeriac and boil.

Season the loin and cook in a frying pan. Once browned, add the butter and baste. When cooked, remove from heat and set aside to rest. Using the same pan, add the ceps and the boiled, diced celeriac with butter and caramelise.

Preheat the oven at 160°C. Cut the venison shoulder into large chunks, sear in a pan with a little oil. Add the vegetables and caramelise on a medium heat. Add the spices with the wine and reduce by half. Add chicken stock to cover 3 quarters of the shoulder and bring to the boil. Cover with grease proof paper and seal with tin foil. Place in the oven for 2–2.5 hours, cooking will vary based on the venison. Leave to cool for 30 minutes. Sieve the remaining stock into a pan. Reduce to concentrate the flavour until you have a smooth consistency. Tear the venison into small pieces, add Parmesan, chopped parsley and 2 tablespoons of sauce.

To make the pasta, combine the semolina, flour and salt. Add egg yolks and knead the dough. Leave to rest for one hour. Roll out the dough, cut into small squares, fill with braised venison and fold to create a tortellini. Cook in boiling water for 4 minutes.

Boil the marmalade mix for 10 minutes, sieve the liquid and reduce by half. Chop the cooked cranberry into fine pieces and combine.

To serve, place the celeriac purée on the plate. Carve the loin into 4, placing one on each plate. Garnish the diced celeriac, ceps, tortellini and marmalade. Finish with fresh thyme sprigs and spoon over the venison sauce.

For the Braised Venison Shoulder *continued*

    3 juniper berries, crushed

    5 black peppercorns, cracked

    10 leaves of Italian parsley

    30g Parmesan, grated

For the Pasta

    200g semolina

    50g flour

    140g egg yolks

    1 pinch of salt

For the Garnish

    sprigs of fresh thyme

    cracked peppercorn

CHANAKA FERNANDO

Cheers for Cheer looks at supporting small projects in the UK, South America and Africa that might otherwise get overlooked. It's great that by donating a recipe to ChariTable Bookings, Buddha Bar can raise awareness of many fantastic works that are being fulfilled."

RED MONKFISH THAI CURRY with steamed rice, broccoli and daikon

SERVES 4 | PREPARATION TIME 15 MINUTES | COOKING TIME 30 MINUTES

For the Curry
4 x 200g monkfish fillets
800g lobster shells
2 tbsp coconut oil
150g Thai shallots, chopped
50g garlic, chopped
60g lemongrass, chopped
1 tbsp Thai tomato paste
100ml mirin
2 tbsp fennel seeds
1 tsp turmeric powder
150ml water
4 kaffir lime leaves
150ml fish stock
220ml coconut milk
2 tbsp lime juice
30g red chillies, chopped
1 handful of coriander, finely chopped
1 tsp palm sugar

To Serve
Thai steamed rice
broccoli, steamed
daikon, sliced
crispy lotus root

To prepare the curry, preheat your oven to 190°C and roast off your lobster shells for 8–10 minutes.

In a frying pan over medium heat, add the coconut oil, chopped shallots, garlic and lemongrass. After everything is sweated off, add the roasted lobster shells and finally the Thai tomato paste. Incorporate the mirin to finish binding all the ingredients and simmer to reduce the mixture. Add the fennel seeds, tumeric and a little water to form a curry paste.

Put the kaffir lime leaf in and continue the cooking process. Pour in the fish stock and leave to simmer on a medium heat for 20–25 minutes. Add the coconut milk, lime juice and red chillies, then blitz with a hand blender. Pass through a sieve. Continue to cook for about 2–3 minutes, stirring in the coriander and palm sugar until thoroughly combined.

Place the monkfish in a hot pan. Sear for 2–3 minutes on each side until cooked through, then carefully place into the sauce.

Serve with Thai steamed rice and steamed broccoli with daikon. Add crispy lotus root to garnish.

PETER FIORI

Honoured to be amongst so many great chefs in ChariTable Bookings' new book and donate a dish well-loved by our clients at Coutts in aid of Leuka, the UK's leading research body for fighting leukaemia."

PORK BELLY, CARROT AND APPLE

SERVES 2–4 | PREPARATION TIME 2 HOURS (PLUS OVERNIGHT TO MARINATE AND PRESS) | COOKING TIME 3 HOURS

For the Pork Belly
- 750g pork belly
- 30g black pepper corns
- 12 long peppers
- 1 whole nutmeg
- 5 bay leaves
- 10g fennel seeds
- 2 star anise
- 5 cloves of garlic
- 1¼ tsp thyme
- 10g sweet paprika
- 10g hot paprika
- 5 cloves
- 300g Maldon Salt
- 80g pink salt
- 450g demerara sugar
- 5 pimento peppers
- 15g juniper berries

For the Carrot Purée
- 1kg diced carrot
- 150g butter
- ½ tsp anise
- 100ml orange juice

For the Kaniwa
- 600ml vegetable stock
- 250g kaniwa
- olive oil, to finish

For the Baby Carrots
- 100g baby carrots
- 25g butter
- 1¼ tsp garlic and herb mixture
- 1¼ tsp honey

For the Red Onion Sauce
- 5 large red onions
- 100ml olive oil

For the Garnish
- dandelion leaf, sliced
- wood sorrel leaves
- 2 crab apples, or if unavailable, spheres cut from 1 Granny Smith apple, using a parisienne scoop
- 1 tsp butter
- 1 tsp demerara sugar
- 1 pinch of salt

To prepare the pork belly, remove the ribs and nipples from the belly and set to one side.

Blitz together all the herbs and spices, then blend the demerara sugar and the salts. Mix the 2 together by hand and massage into the meat. Leave overnight to infuse.

To cook the pork belly, quickly rinse the meat to remove the salt and herb crust and pat dry. Cook at 160°C for 3 hours. Once done, remove the skin and press the meat, keeping all the liquid for the sauce. Cut into desired number of rectangles and deeply score the fat. When ready to serve, fry in a hot pan on all sides until crispy.

To make the carrot purée, melt the butter with seasoning, anise and orange juice. Place the carrots into a bag, pour in the heated mixture and steam. Once the carrots are soft, set them to one side and pass the mixture through a fine sieve. Blitz the now steamed carrots, adding the sauce slowly to reach a creamy consistency.

Toast the kaniwa in a dry pan and slowly pour over the vegetable stock, stirring continuously. Once all the stock is used, cover the pan and cook for 50 minutes. Season to taste and add olive oil to finish.

Fry the baby carrots in a hot pan with oil and finish with butter, honey, garlic and herbs. Once the outsides are crisp, roast at 200°C for 30 minutes or until cooked.

To make the red onion sauce, start by peeling the onions and mixing well in a bowl with some salt, pepper and oil. Place on a rack within a tray and cover with foil, roasting at 200°C for 1 hour until tender. Remove and allow to rest for 30 minutes. Using a sieve in a muslin lined bowl, press overnight. Pour the onion juice into a pan and reduce by half, adding pork juice to taste.

To garnish and serve, slice the dandelion leaf into ice water to allow them to curl. Thoroughly wash the wood sorrel and set to one side. In a pan, add the butter, demerara sugar and a little salt, then stir until melted. Toss the crab apples or Granny Smith pearls in the mixture, assemble and serve immediately.

Editor's Note: *For the long peppers, the flavour profile of Marconi sweet peppers could work well here.*

The Kaniwa seed hails from the same region as quinoa, shares its nutty flavour and is also a complete protein. It differs in that it is slightly sweeter, with a crunchy texture. It has no saponins so does not have to be rinsed before use like quinoa. You can steam vegetables in a cook safe slide lock bag, either in a shallow pan of water or microwave.

NEIL FORBES

"I'm very happy to share Cafe St Honore's crisp oyster dish with ChariTable Bookings in support of DeafBlind Scotland, a fantastic charity supporting this community and their statutory rights."

CRISP LOCH CRERAN OYSTERS with sauce gribiche

SERVES 4 | PREPARATION TIME 20 MINUTES | COOKING TIME 5 MINUTES

For the Oysters
16–24 oysters, allow 4–6 oysters per person
1 tbsp plain flour, seasoned with salt and pepper
1 egg, beaten with a splash of milk
1 handful of breadcrumbs
2 tbsp cold-pressed rapeseed oil for shallow frying

For the Sauce Gribiche
1 hard-boiled egg, white and yolk chopped separately
4 tbsp mayonnaise
1 shallot, peeled and finely chopped
1 tbsp cornichons and capers, chopped
1 tbsp chopped parsley and tarragon
lemon juice, squeeze of
salt and pepper

To Serve
fennel fronds for garnish
coarse sea salt mixed with a little water, as a bed for the oyster shells

To prepare the oysters, be very careful not to puncture the oyster flesh when removing them from their shells. Ask your fishmonger to do this for you if you prefer, but make sure you keep the shells and clean thoroughly for serving. Roll each oyster through the flour, then the egg wash, then breadcrumbs and set to one side.

For the sauce gribiche, gently mix the chopped egg and mayonnaise, then add the shallot, cornichons, capers, parsley and tarragon, and a splash of lemon juice and season with salt and pepper. Mix together gently.

Place a frying pan on the hob and bring it to a medium heat before adding the oil. Once the oil is hot, gently cook the oysters, being careful not to burn them. Turn them often and cook for a minute or so either side. Remove the oysters from the pan and dab them with kitchen paper.

To serve, place the wet salt on a serving dish, arranging the oyster shells on top. Return the cooked oysters to the shells, placing a dot of sauce gribiche and a frond of fennel on top of each. Eat immediately.

FREDERICK FORSTER

London is fortunate to have a higher standard of living than most places in the world, highlighted by the fantastic restaurants featured in this ChariTable Bookings' project. Which is why the team at Le Pont de la Tour are supporting Street Child, a great charity that works with street children in West Africa and Nepal."

LOBSTER THERMIDOR

SERVES 10 | PREPARATION TIME 2 HOURS 30 MINUTES | COOKING TIME 45 MINUTES

For the Lobster

10 lobsters, 550–650g each
75g unsalted butter
100ml brandy or cognac
1 tbsp chervil, chopped
1 tsp tarragon, chopped
5 egg yolks
150ml softly whipped cream
salt and pepper, to taste
100g Parmesan cheese
lemon juice, to taste

For the Mustard Béchamel

2l full-fat milk
100g onion, peeled
1 clove
tarragon stalks
1 bay leaf
210g flour, sieved
210g unsalted butter
225g English mustard
150g Parmesan cheese, grated

For the béchamel, boil the milk with the onion, clove, tarragon stalks and bay leaf. Make a roux with the flour and butter. Use the milk to make a smooth sauce.

Once almost cooked, add the mustard and cook for 1 more minute. Pass the sauce through a fine sieve and keep warm.

To prepare the lobster, steam from frozen for 3 minutes. Chill and remove the meat from the body and claws. Dice the meat and quickly pan-fry the lobster in butter for a few seconds, then deglaze the plan with brandy or cognac. Remove from the pan and add the diced lobster to the mustard béchamel. Mix in the chopped herbs, egg yolks and whipped cream. Adjust the seasoning with salt, pepper and lemon juice if required, making sure the mixture is not too wet.

Place the shells in the oven for 1–2 minutes to remove any extra water. Fill them with the mixture, sprinkle with Parmesan, colour under the grill in a hot pan and serve.

GARY FOULKES

ChariTable Bookings has come up with this great idea of sharing recipes while shouting about charities close to our hearts. I'm delighted to share Angler's signature turbot recipe in support of Great Ormond Street Children's Hospital."

STEAMED CORNISH TURBOT with line-caught squid and dashi

SERVES 4 | PREPARATION TIME 20 MINUTES | COOKING TIME 5 MINUTES

For the Dish
100g nameko mushrooms
100g Golden enoki mushrooms
100g white shimeji mushrooms
100g brown shimeji mushooms
25g sliced, cleaned squid
4 x 120g portions of Cornish turbot
1 pinch of salt
100g rock samphire
80g monk's beard
1 spritz of lemon juice

For the Dashi
375ml water
35ml soy sauce
20ml mirin
9g bonito flakes
9g wakame flakes

Snip the caps off the mushrooms with a small pair of scissors and put to one side. Thinly slice the fresh squid and keep in the fridge. Place the turbot on a piece of greaseproof paper on a tray and lightly season with salt. Steam the turbot for 4 minutes or until cooked.

In the meantime, poach the mushrooms in a small amount of the dashi until they are just cooked. This should take around 3 minutes. Drop in the samphire and then the squid. Quickly blanch the monk's beard in some boiling, salted water and dress with lemon juice. Put to one side.

Place the mushrooms in a bowl and carefully set the steamed turbot fillet on the top. Place the monk's beard on top of the fish.

To make the dashi, bring the water to the boil and add in all the other ingredients and leave the mixture to infuse for 10 minutes.

Serve immediately with a little of the dashi on the side.

DAMIEN FREMONT

"ChariTable Bookings has enabled the Gastronhome to shout about Action For Orphans, please help us support their essential work."

ROASTED HALIBUT FILLET with Scottish mussels, white asparagus and Grenobloise sauce

SERVES 4 | PREPARATION TIME 5 MINUTES | COOKING TIME 30 MINUTES

For the White Asparagus
12 white asparagus
3 tsp plain flour
1 lemon

For the Mussels
500g Scottish mussels
1 shallot
1 tsp butter
250ml white wine
1 tsp parsley

For the Spinach Purée
250g baby spinach
mussel stock
½ lime, juiced

For the Fish
600g halibut fillet
100g flour
2 tsp olive oil
butter, for basting

For the Grenobloise Sauce
100g croutons
2 tsp capers
2 tsp parsley, chopped
1 lemon
2 tsp butter

To prepare the white asparagus, carefully peel the asparagus, poach them in a salted water with plain flour and half a lemon for 20 minutes. The asparagus must be soft.

To prepare the mussels, wash the mussels under cold water, discard the open ones. In a large pan, soften the shallots in butter, add the white wine, the mussels and the parsley. Cover and cook for 3–4 minutes. Reserve the stock and pass through a fine sieve.

To prepare the spinach purée, heat up the mussel stock, add the spinach leaves and cook it for 2 minutes. Poor everything in a blender and mix well with the lime juice.

To prepare the fish Grenobloise, cut 4 nice halibut steaks, about 150g each. Dredge them with plain flour. Cook the fish in a hot frying pan with olive oil for 2 minutes on each side. Add butter and reduce the heat, baste the fish with the melted butter for 1 minute. Add the croutons, capers, chopped parsley and lemon juice

To plate, draw a nice line of spinach purée with a tea spoon, put the asparagus, the fish and the mussels onto the plate harmoniously and lay out the Grenobloise sauce on the top.

NICK GALER

I'm passionate about UK produce and it's great to see such a collection of chefs in the UK taking part in this ChariTable Bookings recipe book. Alzheimers is an increasingly common disease here and so I'm pleased to be supporting the Alzheimer's Society and sharing my poached chicken recipe with you."

POACHED AND CONFIT BABY CHICKEN
SERVES 10 | PREPARATION TIME 2 HOURS (PLUS 4 HOURS TO SET) | COOKING TIME 4 HOURS

Equipment
sous vide and vacuum pack bags
mandoline

For the Herb Brine
1l water
100g salt
30 stalks of assorted herbs,
including sage
4 bay leaves
6g garlic

For the Chicken
5 baby corn fed chicken
1 sprig of thyme
duck fat, to cover chicken legs

For the Salsify Batons and Crisps
10 sticks of salsify, 5 for batons, 5
for crisps
10g vitamin C powder
20g butter
1 bay leaf
oil, to deep fry
salt and pepper, to season

For the Chanterelle Mushroom Sauce
150g unsalted butter
1.15kg whole button mushrooms,
brushed
150ml Madeira
2.25l cold tap water
11g thyme
4g black peppercorns

To make the herb brine, combine the salt and water, and bring to the boil. Remove from the heat, add the herbs and garlic and allow to cool.

To prepare the chicken, break down the legs and the breasts. Split the drumstick and thigh. Retain the breast on the crown. You won't need the wings and carcasses but you can reserve them for stocks. Add the chicken breasts in a large vacuum pack bag, add the herb brine and set aside for 2 hours. Allow to sit for 20–30 minutes in cold water. Place the chicken crowns in vacuum bags and seal on full. Water bath for 1 hour at 60°C. Refresh in ice water, then remove the breast from the carcass and reserve. French trim the drum stick, making sure the bone is nice and clean. Baste the meat end of the drum stick in duck fat and wrap in cling film with a stick of thyme. The cling film is to hold the shape when cooking. Place carefully into vacuum bags and cook for 3–4 hours at 85°C. Remove from the bath and allow to cool naturally. Reshape if needed while still warm. Prepare 10 vacuum pack bags each with 1 breast, 1 thigh and 1 drumstick.

To prepare the salsify, scrape the dirt from the edges with a green scourer. As the salsify are prepared they must go directly into vitamin C water and any further dirt can be washed off. To make the salsify batons, cut the thin salsify into 4cm batons. Vacuum the batons on full in a bag with one bay leaf, vitamin C powder and butter. Cook in an 80°C water bath for 15 minutes until just soft. Refresh into ice water and reserve. To make the salsify crisps, peel down the thick salsify to shavings of any length required. Drop into a 180°C fryer until golden brown. Dry on a paper towel.

To make the chanterelle mushroom sauce, melt the butter in a wide-bottomed saucepan over high heat. Once the butter begins to foam, add the mushrooms and cook until all the liquid comes out of the mushrooms and they begin to fry. Turn down the heat and cook until the mushrooms are evenly coloured, stirring occasionally so they don't catch on the bottom of the pan. Deglaze the pan with the Madeira and reduce to a syrup. Add the cold water, thyme and peppercorns and bring up to a simmer, skimming off any fat. Simmer for 1 hour, skimming if necessary. Strain the stock from the mushrooms. Chill the stock as

For the Pomme Anna Cake

10 medium chipping potatoes

250g unsalted butter, clarified

1 pinch of salt

For the Star Anise Salt

40g star anise, lightly toasted and ground

20g salt

20g sugar

½ tsp tarragon leaves

For the Garnish

small chaneterelles

quickly as possible. Pour the stock into a wide-bottomed pan and reduce by half over a steady heat. Weigh the stock and add the same amount of reduced chicken jus. Bring this to the boil and reduce to sauce consistency.

To make the Pomme Anna cake, peel and clean the potatoes. Do not wash as the starch helps to stick the cake together. Slice to 2mm think on the mandoline. Line a deep tray with greaseproof paper. Arrange the potato slices in circles overlapping by a third, pouring over some of the clarified butter, and at the same time seasoning lightly with fine salt. Place greaseproof paper on top and bake in the over at 190°C for 35 minutes, checking at 20 minutes. Press lightly and set in the fridge for a minimum of 4 hours. Turn out onto a chopping board and cut with a 65mm circle cutter.

To make the star anise salt, combine the ingredients in a blender before serving.

To finish the dish and serve, reheat each vacuum bag of chicken in a 60°C bath for 10 minutes. Remove the breast, thigh, and drum stick from the bag and colour the skins in a hot frying pan until golden brown. Season with the star anise salt. Fry salsify batons in a pan until golden brown. Season with salt and pepper and dry the fat on a cloth. Add four small chanterelle mushrooms to a small amount of warm mushroom sauce. Plate as pictured.

DANIEL GALMICHE

" I am so impressed by the work that Scotty's Little Soldiers does and very happy to share my signature halibut with ChariTable Bookings in support of this worthy cause."

PAN-ROASTED WILD HALIBUT with tomato confit, feta, rosemary crisps and aioli

SERVES 4 | PREPARATION TIME 45 MINUTES (PLUS 12 HOURS TO MARINATE) | COOKING TIME 20 MINUTES

Equipment
vacuum pack bag

For the Halibut
4 x 110g pieces of halibut

For the Tomato Confit
1-2 beef tomatoes
1 good pinch of salt and pepper
1-2 dashes of olive oil and Tabasco
micro Thai basil
1 spring onion, green only, chopped

For the Pickled Shallots
50ml sherry vinegar
50g brown sugar
20ml beetroot juice
1 banana shallot, peeled and cut into
segments, length ways

For the Rosemary Crisp
1 loaf of rosemary bread

For the Aioli
40g garlic, peeled
milk, to cover the garlic
1 large egg
1 pinch of saffron
200ml rape seed oil
1 lemon, juiced
2 dashes of Tabasco
1 dash of Pedro Ximenez
salt and pepper, to taste

For the Garnish
feta, for crumbling over halibut

To prepare the tomato confit, slice the large beef tomatoes 1cm thick. Place them flat into a vacuum bag, and mix together the salt, pepper, oil, Tabasco and a sprinkle of Thai basil and spring onion. Vacuum on full and marinate for 12 hours.

To prepare the pickled shallots, mix the sherry vinegar, brown sugar and beetroot juice together. Leave the shallot segments in the mixture for 45 minutes before serving.

To prepare the rosemary crisp, freeze the loaf. When needed, pre-heat the oven to 170°C. Take out the loaf from the freezer and cut into very thin slices. Place onto a silicon mat and drizzle with olive oil. Place into the oven for 7–8 minutes. Remove from the oven and allow to dry out completely. Keep to one side, ready for plating up.

To prepare the aioli, cook the garlic in milk until soft, remove and rinse briefly but keep warm. In another small saucepan cook the egg in boiling water for 5 minutes, then refresh in cold water. Combine the saffron, rapeseed oil, garlic and egg. Blitz in a food processor until smooth. Add the lemon juice, Tabasco and sherry, then continue to mix. Season to taste with salt and pepper. Keep to one side until your ready to plate up the dish.

To finish, get a frying pan nice and hot. Using a dash of rapeseed oil, pan fry the halibut on one side until golden brown. Remove the tomatoes from the vacuum pack, then place onto a baking tray. When your halibut is nicely golden on one side, flash grill, along with your sliced tomatoes. Put one slice of tomato in the centre of the plate. Spread some aioli on the bottom of the halibut fillet and sit on top of the tomato. Finish with the feta, pickled shallot, aioli and rosemary crisp, as pictured. Serve the remaining aioli in a dish on the side.

CHRIS GALVIN
JEFF GALVIN MCA

"We set up Galvin's Chance to work with young people and hopefully guide them into a safe career in the hospitality industry. So it's great that ChariTable Bookings is pairing chefs with charities in their latest book. I give you our signature John Dory dish to enjoy!"

FILLET OF JOHN DORY with orange glazed endive

SERVES 4 | PREPARATION TIME 40 MINUTES (PLUS 48 HOURS TO INFUSE CURRY OIL) | COOKING TIME 1 HOUR

For the John Dory
4 x 140g John Dory fillets, skin on
½ lemon, juiced
sea salt
white pepper

For the Curry Oil
50g curry powder, medium
300ml groundnut oil, or very light olive oil

For the Dressing
40g sultanas
20g pine nuts, lightly toasted
10g baby capers
40ml curry oil
10 coriander leaves

For the Cauliflower Purée
1 cauliflower
100g unsalted butter
100ml milk
50ml single cream

For the glazed endive
2 heads of Belgian endive
20g icing sugar
40g unsalted butter
2 oranges
1 lemon
2 tbsp red wine vinegar

Begin by making the curry oil. Place a large frying pan over a medium heat until warm, then add the curry powder directly to the pan. Cook the powder, stirring constantly to ensure it does not catch or burn, for 2 minutes until the spices are toasted. Add the oil and bring up to 60°C. Remove from the heat, leave to cool then store in a suitable air tight container for 2 days until required.

Place the sultanas in a bowl and pour over enough boiling water to cover. Wrap with cling film and leave the sultanas in the bowl overnight to soak.

To make the cauliflower purée, remove the outer leaves and slice the cauliflower into small florets, discarding any excess stalk. Melt the butter in a large pan over a medium heat, then add the cauliflower florets to the pan. Sweat the florets for 3–4 minutes until tender, then add the milk to the pan, cover with a lid and increase the heat slightly. Cook until very tender, then drain and transfer to a blender, discarding the liquid from the pan. Blend the cooked cauliflower in the food processor, gradually adding the cream until fully combined. Season the purée to taste, then strain the mixture through a fine sieve into a bowl. Cover the bowl in cling film and set aside, keeping warm until required.

To prepare the endives, remove any brown outer leaves, then slice the heads in half lengthways, dusting the cut sides thoroughly with icing sugar. In a large pan, melt the butter over a medium heat and cook until foaming. Add the endives to the pan, sugar side down, and cook until they begin to caramelise. Use a Microplane to finely grate the lemon and one of the oranges and add the grated zest to the pan. Continue to cook the endive, turning every couple of minutes, until they are well coloured and caramelised all over. Meanwhile, juice the lemon and both of the oranges and add to the pan along with the vinegar. Reduce the heat and allow to cook very slowly until the endive is tender and the liquid has become a sticky caramel. Season and set to one side, keeping warm until required.

To make the dressing, drain the soaked sultanas and place in a pan along with the pine nuts, baby capers and 40ml of the prepared curry oil. Heat very gently and stir to combine. Meanwhile, coat the John Dory fillets in the remaining curry oil and leave to marinate for 10 minutes. Place a large, non-stick pan over a high heat and allow it to get very hot. At this point, add the fish fillets to the pan, skin-side down. Using the curry oil marinade as cooking oil, leave the fish to cook for 2–3 minutes and allow the skin of the fish to crisp up. Once the fish skin has become crispy, reduce the heat to medium and turn the fish over to cook for a further minute. Remove the fish from the pan, season, and sprinkle with a little lemon juice. Leave to drain on the kitchen paper.

To serve, use a teaspoon to add a swipe of cauliflower purée around the top and bottom of each plate and place a piece of endive in the centre. Allow the endive to fan out slightly before topping with the John Dory. Add the coriander leaves to the warm dressing and drizzle over the fish. Serve immediately.

ANDRÉ GARRETT MCA

" *Hospitality Action does incredible work with anyone struggling in our industry and also their families should they be unable to work. On behalf of the team at Cliveden, I hope you enjoy our signature Dover Sole Veronique and the other recipes in this ChariTable Bookings collection."*

DOVER SOLE VERONIQUE

SERVES 2 | PREPARATION TIME 45 MINUTES | COOKING TIME 1 HOUR 30 MINUTES

Equipment
sous vide and vacuum pack bags
blowtorch
Japanese mandoline

For the Fish
2 x 800–900g Dover sole, deboned, keep the bones for the sauce
salted butter, melted
1 pinch of fleur de sel

For the Sauce
leftover sole bones
25g salted butter
50g button mushrooms, chopped
50g shallots, chopped
50ml dry white wine
200ml light poultry stock
2 stalks of parsley

For the Verjus Butter Sauce
30g finely chopped shallots
200g unsalted butter
100ml verjus
200ml sauce base
200ml reduced double cream
1 lemon, juiced

For the Braised Baby Fennel
2 baby fennel bulbs
20g shallots, sliced
20g carrot, chopped
5 fennel seeds
5 white peppercorns

To prepare the Dover sole, dress, fillet and deskin the sole, remove the thin membrane, brush with salted butter, and lightly season with the salt. Place the fillets head to tail. Roll tightly in cling film, into a sausage shape and tie the ends. Heat a water bath to 85°C, submerge the sole, cook for 3 minutes, then remove. Allow to rest for 3 more minutes before cutting.

For the sauce, cut the sole bones into small pieces. Sweat these in a pan with the salted butter, until the juices start to appear. Add the mushrooms and shallots, then cook for 4–5 minutes over a medium heat. Pour in the white wine and reduce by half. Add the stock and parsley stalks, then reduce by half again. Pass the sauce through a fine sieve.

To make the verjus sauce, sweat the shallots and heat the ingredients together.

Colour the baby fennel on each side, in a shallow pan. Add the shallot, carrot, fennel seeds, peppercorns, thyme and poultry stock. Bring to the boil, simmer gently, then cool. Take the baby fennel out of the liquor and cut in half lengthways.

Cut the baby gem lettuce in half, then vacuum pack with the butter and a pinch of salt. Cook at 85°C in a sous vide for 8 minutes. Remove the lettuce and trim the edges and drain. Toast with a blowtorch.

Peel and wash the potatoes. On a Japanese mandoline, slice the potatoes 2mm thick. Place the potato starch in a bowl, add a little water and mix to a thin paste consistency. Brush 20 of the potato slices with the paste and lay the other 20 slices on top. Cut into circles with a 3cm cutter and leave to dry for 30 minutes in a warm place. When ready to serve, fry the potatoes in the oil at 180°C. Work in small batches, 4 at a time. Keep moving them with a slotted spoon. Remove and drain when golden and puffed, and season lightly with sea salt.

To serve, spoon some sauce into the centre of each plate and place the sole on top. Place the baby gem and baby fennel on either side. Arrange the pommes souffles and garnishes on the fish. Finish by drizzling over the butter sauce.

For the Braised Baby Fennel *continued*
    2 sprigs of thyme
    poultry stock, to cover
    olive oil

For the Grilled Baby Gem
    1 baby gem, trimmed and washed
    10g butter
    1 pinch of fleur de sel

For the Pommes Souffles
    4 large Maris piper potatoes
    1 tbsp potato starch
    vegetable oil, for frying

To Garnish
    20 semi-dried green grapes
    30g pine nuts, toasted until crisp
    20ml reduced roast chicken juices
    10ml green chive oil
    12 small sprigs of parsley
    12 small pommes soufflés

LAURIE GEAR

The Artichoke have chosen St Catherine's Hospice, Crawley, Sussex as their charity of choice for ChariTable Bookings' new recipe book - St Catherine's holds a special place in our hearts as they took such dedicated care of my late mother with understanding and compassion."

SADDLE OF CHILTERN VENISON with caramelised shallots, salt-baked celeriac, hawthorn berry and rosehip emulsion, and venison sauce

SERVES 4 | PREPARATION TIME 45 MINUTES | COOKING TIME 1 HOUR 15 MINUTES

For the Venison
4 x 150g wild shot venison steaks, cut from the saddle
50g butter
salt

For the Salt-Baked Celeriac
1 celeriac
1 small handful of Douglas fir pine needles, or citrus peel if unavailable
4 egg whites
150g rock salt

For the Venison Jus
150g venison bones, roasted and browned
olive oil
2 carrots, roughly chopped
2 onions, roughly chopped
2 cloves of garlic, roughly chopped
1 celery stick, roughly chopped
80ml red wine
500ml brown chicken stock

For the Emulsion
100g hawthorn berries
100g rosehips, or 200g cranberries
50g caster sugar
200ml orange juice

To Serve
4 shallots, caramelised and peeled

To make the emulsion, place the berries, rosehips, orange juice and sugar in a small pan and set over a medium heat. Cook until tender. Once tender, blitz in a blender and pass through a fine strainer; it should have the consistency of a thin syrup and can be left at room temperature until serving.

To make the venison jus, sauté the vegetables in olive oil until lightly caramelised. Pour in the red wine and reduce. Add the roasted venison bones and top up with the chicken stock. Bring to the boil, then simmer for 30 minutes. Using a large slotted spoon or a pair of tongs, remove the bones. Pass the liquid through muslin cloth over a fine strainer to remove all of the solids. Return to a clean pan, bring to a rolling boil and reduce by three quarters.

To make the salt-baked celeriac, whisk the egg whites to medium peaks and incorporate the rock salt to form a paste. Chop the fir needles and add to the mixture. Preheat the oven to 180°C. Pat the salt mixture around the celeriac, place on a baking tray and bake for 40 minutes. Remove from the oven, crack open the salt crust, peel and cube the celeriac.

To cook the venison steaks, preheat an oven to 200°C. Place a pan over a medium heat, add the butter, and as soon as it begins to foam, pan-fry the venison steaks until caramelised all over. Season with salt and transfer to the oven for approximately 12 minutes. Remove and allow to rest for a further 10 minutes before slicing.

To prepare the garnish, blanch the cavolo nero in boiling salted water for 2 minutes and immediately plunge into ice water. Drain and squeeze out any excess. Reheat in a hot pan with some butter and season well.

To serve, brush a strip of emulsion across each plate. Place the buttered cavolo nero just off centre, and lay the slices of venison on top. Arrange the celeriac on each plate along with the shallots. Drizzle with the venison jus and serve.

To Serve *continued*
    2 heads cavolo nero, leaves
    picked and washed
    butter
    salt and pepper, to taste

HARI GHOTRA

SeeAbility fights to enrich the lives of those who have lost their sight, which is why I have chosen them as my charity on behalf of Tamarind Kitchen. I hope you enjoy my recipe and that I bring, through ChariTable Bookings, some further awareness of SeeAbility."

BAKED WHOLE HEAD OF CAULIFLOWER drenched in a creamy mughlai gravy

SERVES 2–4 | PREPARATION TIME 25 MINUTES (PLUS 2 HOURS TO SOAK CASHEWS) | COOKING TIME 1 HOUR 30 MINUTES

For the Cauliflower
1 head of cauliflower, outer leaves trimmed off
½ tsp salt
½ tsp turmeric
1 tbsp ghee or vegetable oil
1 tsp cumin seeds

For the Sauce
1 tbsp ghee or vegetable oil
1 red onion, roughly chopped
4 cloves of garlic, roughly chopped
2 tomatoes, chopped
3cm ginger, sliced into strips
1 green chilli, chopped
1 tsp coriander seeds, crushed
1 tsp salt
1 tsp Kashmiri red chilli powder
1 tbsp dried fenugreek leaves
1 tsp garam masala
3 tbsp raw cashew nuts
½ cup water

For the Garnish
1 handful of fresh coriander, chopped
naan bread

To start, soak the cashews for 2 hours and preheat an oven to 180°C.

To prepare the cauliflower, fill a tall pot with water and add salt and turmeric. Bring to the boil and gently submerge the cauliflower using a slotted spoon. Reduce the heat to medium and leave it to simmer for 5 minutes, then flip the cauliflower over and simmer for another 5 minutes. Keep the cauliflower submerged. Strain your cauliflower and set aside on some kitchen roll while you make the sauce.

To make the sauce, in a wide based pan, heat the oil or ghee and add the onions. Sauté the onions until they soften, this should take about 5 minutes. Stir in the garlic and cook until the onions start to brown. Add the chopped tomatoes, ginger, chilli, crushed coriander seeds, salt, Kashmiri chilli and dried fenugreek leaves. Cook this until it becomes wonderfully aromatic and the tomatoes break down, this should take about 7 minutes. When the tomatoes have melted into the sauce, add the garam masala and remove the sauce from the heat. Add the cashew nuts, some water and using a hand held blender, blitz the masala sauce until silky and smooth. Place it back on a gentle heat and cook through for a few minutes. The sauce should be the consistency of thick soup, add more water if the sauce gets too thick.

To cook the cauliflower, find an oven proof dish that it will sit in comfortably and add the ghee or oil. Heat this dish and add the cumin seeds. When they sizzle and become fragrant, remove the dish from the heat and place the blanched cauliflower into it. Pour the sauce over the cauliflower so it's completely covered. Some of the sauce will end up in the base, which is fine. You can also reserve a little sauce to be used as a garnish.

Place the cauliflower in the oven and leave to bake for 40–45 minutes until dry to the touch and starting to brown. The sauce will also have thickened.

To serve, garnish with fresh coriander, slice and serve with some naan bread.

STEPHEN GOMES

Velindre is a fantastic hospital, local to Moksh, that looks after cancer patients and the Welsh Blood Service. While all charities are worthwhile, it's important for us to support our local services through this ChariTable Bookings initiative. I hope you enjoy my signature lamb dish too!"

5000 MILES FROM ANDHRA

SERVES 2–3 | PREPARATION TIME 15 MINUTES | COOKING TIME 45 MINUTES

For the Lamb

600g Welsh leg of lamb, deboned and cubed
¼ tsp cumin seeds
2 tsp turmeric powder
1 pinch of salt
4 tbsp oil
2 onions, finely chopped
1½ tbsp ginger and garlic paste
3 tomatoes, finely chopped
1 seasonal chilli, finely chopped
6–7 curry leaves
250ml coconut milk

For the Masala

3 cloves
1 stick of cinnamon
1 bay leaf
3 cardamom seeds
1–2 whole red chillies
½ tsp whole black pepper
½ tsp cumin seeds
½ tsp fennel seeds
1 onion, finely chopped
1 tbsp coriander powder
25g fresh coriander leaves

Garnish

fresh coriander leaves
lemon wedges

Place the lamb in 250ml of water, together with the cumin seeds, salt and half the turmeric. Slow cook until tender, then remove the lamb, set aside and reserve the cooking liquid.

To prepare the masala, heat a pan and dry fry the cloves, cinnamon, bay leaves, cardamom, red chilli, whole black pepper, cumin and fennel seeds. Let the spices cool, grind them into a fine powder and keep to one side. In the same pan, fry 1 chopped onion until it becomes translucent. Combine with the powdered spices, ground coriander and fresh coriander leaves. Grind everything together into a coarse paste.

In a wide pan, add oil and the 2 chopped onions. Fry until they become golden brown. Incorporate the ginger and garlic paste, fry and then add the cooked lamb. Cook for a further 3–4 minutes. At this stage, add the chopped tomatoes, chilli, salt, remaining turmeric powder and the curry leaves. Leave to simmer for 3–4 minutes, then add the masala paste, a little of the reserved water used to cook the lamb and the coconut milk. Mix everything together and continue to cook for 5–10 minutes.

To serve, garnish with fresh coriander leaves and lemon wedges.

YAHIR GONZALEZ

The Make A Wish Foundation grants magical wishes to enrich the lives of children and young people fighting life-threatening conditions. Aqua Nueva is very proud to support them by being invited to include our recipe in this ChariTable Bookings collection."

COD, LARDO, FENNEL

SERVES 1 | PREPARATION TIME 30 MINUTES | COOKING TIME 20 MINUTES

Equipment
  sous vide
  vacuum pack bags

For the Cod
  1 cod fillet, salted
  ½ lime
  1 sprig of thyme
  2 thin slices of lardo

For the Fennel Purée
  300g fennel bulbs, thinly sliced,
  save the tops
  50g butter
  100ml double cream
  1 bunch of dill, chopped

For the Salsa
  1 red pepper
  10 padron peppers
  1 small bunch of spring onion,
  chopped
  1 lime, juiced
  extra virgin olive oil
  40g salt

For the Garnish
  fennel bulb tops
  1 tsp bottarga, grated

Place the cod in a bowl of salted cold water, enough to cover. Leave it to rest in the fridge for 20 minutes. Once this time has passed, briefly rinse under running water.

Set aside 50g sliced fennel, together with the tops, for presentation. Melt the butter in a pan on a medium heat. Add the rest of the fennel and cream, then cook until soft. Combine with the chopped dill, place into a blender and blitz until smooth.

For the salsa, peel the peppers, remove the seeds and cut them into 0.5cm cubes. Add in the chopped spring onions, lime juice, olive oil and salt, then mix together well.

To cook the cod, seal in a vacuum pack bag with a bit of olive oil, lime juice and the sprig of thyme. Submerge in a sous vide for 6 minutes at 67°C. Remove the cod from the bag and place under the grill very briefly to colour. Place the lardo on top.

To serve, spoon the fennel purée on the plate and add the salsa to the side. Place the cod on the purée. Sprinkle with the bottarga, then use the fennel tops and shavings to garnish as pictured.

PETER GORDON

"Leuka is more than charity, it is the specialist for leukaemia. It focuses not just on research but on getting new treatments to blood cancer sufferers as quickly and safely as possible. Both are important to beating this disease and so I am proud to contribute to this ChariTable Bookings compendium of fantastic recipes on behalf of The Providores."

LAMB NECK with baked pitta, figs, feta, tomato, cucumber, mint and Kalamata olives

SERVES 6 | PREPARATION TIME 10 MINUTES | COOKING TIME 30 MINUTES

For the Lamb and Pitta

900g lamb neck fillet, trimmed of excess fat and sinew

salt and pepper

1 tsp olive oil

3–4 pitta breads, torn into pieces

2 tbsp extra virgin olive oil

150g Kalamata olives

2 tbsp red wine vinegar

For the Salad

4 tomatoes

2 small cucumbers, peeled and sliced

30 mint leaves, torn

200g feta cheese, ideally 100% ewes' milk, roughly crumbled

½ tsp dried oregano

2 tbsp extra virgin olive oil

6 figs

For the Garnish

1 large lemon, cut into six wedges

Preheat the oven to 170°C. Place a roasting dish on the hob on a medium heat. Season the lamb with salt and pepper and brush with a teaspoon of oil. Put it in the heated roasting dish and cook until well browned on all sides. Remove the lamb and add the pitta bread, tossing it around to coat in the fats. Sit the lamb on the bread in the roasting dish and roast in the oven until the lamb is cooked. Because the lamb neck can be a little fatty, cooking it medium works best here. Neck fillets will take about 10 minutes. Remove the lamb to another dish and leave to rest in a warm place for 10 minutes. Slice, put it on a plate and reserving the cooking juices.

Drizzle the vinegar over the pitta, add the olives and 2 tablespoons of extra virgin olive oil and toss together. Bake until the bread is crisp, about 8–10 minutes, then remove from the oven.

While the bread is in the oven, cut the tomatoes in half, crossways. Gently squeeze out and discard the seeds. Cut the flesh into chunks and mix with the cucumber, mint, feta, oregano and extra virgin olive oil.

Remove the stems from the figs, peel if preferred, then thickly slice and add to the tomato salad. Toss everything together and season lightly with salt, the feta will already be salty, and a quarter of a teaspoon of coarsely ground black pepper.

To serve, pile the tomato salad on top of the crisp pitta. Lay the lamb on top and drizzle over the cooking juices. Serve with the lemon wedges.

IOANNIS GRAMMENOS

"I'm delighted to share the Heliot Steak House at the Hippodrome Casino's recipe of meatballs with mushroom sauce with this lovely book by ChariTable Bookings. Please join me in supporting The Royal Marsden who work so hard in the fight against cancer."

USDA PRIME MEATBALLS with mushroom sauce
SERVES 4 | PREPARATION TIME 45 MINUTES | COOKING TIME 1 HOUR

For the Meatballs
800g USDA prime beef, freshly minced
2 tbsp olive oil
50g shallots, finely chopped
10g garlic, freshly chopped
10g parsley, freshly chopped
6g fresh oregano, finely chopped
1 free range egg, beaten
10g salt and freshly ground pepper

For the Mushroom Sauce
150g wild forest mushrooms, sliced
1 tbsp olive oil or butter
1 small shallot, finely chopped
1 clove of garlic, crushed
10g dried porcini, soaked in 50ml water
200ml fresh double cream
salt and pepper
500ml olive oil to fry the meatballs

To prepare the meatballs, heat two tablespoons of the olive oil in a heavy saucepan over a medium heat and add the shallots and garlic. Sweat for a few minutes until soft and golden. Allow to cool. In a mixing bowl, add the USDA prime minced beef with the cold, sweated shallots and garlic. Add the chopped parsley, oregano, and the beaten egg. Season the mixture with salt and pepper. Fry a bit of the mixture to check the seasoning and adjust if necessary. Divide the mixture into 16 round balls, cover and refrigerate.

To make the mushroom sauce, heat the oil or butter in a medium saucepan over a medium heat and add the shallot and garlic until golden. Add the wild mushrooms and the porcini and cook until lightly browned. Add the 50ml of water from the porcini and cook until reduced. Add the cream, salt and pepper and bring to the boil. Cook for 6–8 minutes, stirring occasionally, making sure that the cream doesn't over boil. Once the sauce has reduced by half, remove it from the heat and blend in a food processer until creamy and smooth.

To cook the meatballs, heat a frying pan and cook the meatballs for about 8–10 minutes in 500ml of olive oil.

To serve, plate the meatballs and cover with mushroom sauce.

ADAM GRAY

Dine like a king 365 days a year and support your favourite charity? Great idea! I'm giving this recipe to help raise funds for the great work Macmillan does every day. Go and buy ChariTable Bookings' new recipe book and do the same!"

BRAISED SADDLEBACK PORK CHEEKS in porter beer with creamed carrots

SERVES 4 | PREPARATION TIME 30 MINUTES (PLUS OVERNIGHT TO MARINATE) | COOKING TIME 3 HOURS

For the Pork Cheek Marinade

12 saddleback pork cheeks

1 large onion, peeled and diced

3 carrots, peeled and diced

1 bulb of garlic, halved

2 Braeburn apples, quartered

1 bottle of porter style beer

For the Pork Cheeks

marinated pork cheeks

150ml rapeseed oil

2l chicken stock

1l brown veal stock

1 sprig of sage

2 fresh bay leaves

For the Creamed Carrots

65g unsalted butter

150g shallots, peeled and finely sliced

500g English carrots, peeled and finely sliced

1l chicken stock

salt and white pepper

To Serve

baby onions, halved and pan-fried

Put all the ingredients for the marinade in a large sealable container, cover with the Porter beer and place in the fridge overnight. Remove the ingredients from the beer, then drain off and reserve the liquid. Seal the marinated pork cheeks in rapeseed oil in a thick-bottomed, shallow saucepan until lightly coloured all over. Remove the pork cheeks and place in a colander over a bowl to drain any excess oil.

Place the pork cheeks into a large, thick-bottomed saucepan. Add the prepared cut vegetables to a shallow saucepan and colour until golden brown. Add the sprig of sage and the bay leaves. Add the reserved porter beer marinade to the coloured vegetables and reduce the beer by three quarters.

Add the deglazed vegetables to the pan with the pork cheeks. Cover them with the chicken and veal stock. Place the saucepan on a medium heat and bring it up to the boil, then simmer very gently for 2.5–3 hours. When the pork cheeks are tender to the touch, remove them from the stock and put to one side in a shallow tray. Pass the stock through a fine sieve into a saucepan, return to the stove and bring to the boil. Lower the heat and simmer gently until the stock thickens to a gravy consistency. Return the pork cheeks to the gravy and keep hot.

To make the creamed carrots, heat a saucepan to a medium heat and add the butter. When the butter starts to foam, add the sliced shallots and sweat for 2–3 minutes, then add the sliced carrots and continue to sweat for a further 4–5 minutes until the shallots become translucent. Add the chicken stock and bring to the boil. Simmer gently for 15–20 minutes until the carrots are fully cooked. Drain the carrots into a colander and keep the cooking liquor. Liquidise the carrots with a little of the cooking liquor and pass through a fine sieve. Season the creamed carrots with salt and white pepper to taste.

To serve, place the pork cheeks in a shallow serving bowl with the creamed carrots and pan-fried baby onion halves.

JOSE GRAZIOSI

"Working in the food industry, it's important to remember those that don't have it so easy. Action Against Hunger works with children the world over to tackle malnutrion and hunger. I'm proud to share Endsleigh Hotel's popular lobster dish with ChariTable Bookings to help raise awareness."

LOBSTER AND TURBOT with new potatoes, caviar, sea vegetables and beurre blanc

SERVES 2 | PREPARATION TIME 30 MINUTES | COOKING TIME 30 MINUTES

For the Court Bouillon
½ leek white and pale green parts only
1 small carrot
1 small stick of celery
3 cloves of garlic
1.5l water
350ml red wine vinegar
1 sprig of thyme
2 bay leaves
1½ tsp white peppercorns
1 tsp fine sea salt

For the Lobster
350g lobster

For the Beurre Blanc
140g unsalted butter, chilled and cubed
2 shallots, peeled and thinly sliced
½ clove of garlic, peeled and thinly sliced
1 sprig of thyme
1 bay leaf
3 black peppercorns, crushed
150ml dry white wine
1 tsp white wine vinegar
sea salt, to taste
1 tbsp lemon juice, freshly squeezed

For the New Potatoes
8 new potatoes
4g saffron
500ml water

To prepare the court bouillon and cook the lobster, dice the leek, carrot and celery, and in a large saucepan, bring to the boil with all of the remaining ingredients. Rapidly boil the mixture for 10 minutes and, once cooked, pour through a fine sieve into a clean pan. Poach the lobster in the court bouillon for 10 minutes and set to one side for serving.

To make the beurre blanc, heat one tablespoon of the butter in a non-reactive pan over a medium heat. When the butter has melted, add the shallots, garlic, thyme, bay leaf and peppercorns and fry for 2–3 minutes, or until the shallots have softened but not coloured. Add the white wine and wine vinegar and bring the mixture to the boil. Continue to boil until most of the liquid has evaporated, then gradually whisk in the chilled butter cubes, one at a time, until all of the butter has been incorporated into the mixture and the sauce has thickened and is glossy. Strain the beurre blanc through a fine sieve into a warmed bowl, then season to taste with salt and pour over the lemon juice. Keep warm, but not too warm or the sauce will separate and spoil.

To make the potatoes, cut the potatoes into barrel shapes and boil in saffron infused water until soft. Set aside for serving.

To make the turbot, heat a large frying pan over a high heat. Sprinkle the flour onto a plate and season to taste with salt and freshly ground black pepper. Pat the fish fillets dry with kitchen paper. Dredge the turbot fillets skin-side down in the seasoned flour and fry for 3–4 minutes, or until more than half of the turbot flesh has turned opaque and the skin is crisp and golden brown. The skin needs to be flat against the pan to crisp up all over, so press the turbot fillets down with a fish slice if the heat makes them arch up. Turn the turbot fillets over carefully and continue to fry for a further minute, or until the turbot fillets are almost cooked through, but are still slightly rare in the centre.

To prepare the sea vegetables, blanch in unsalted, boiling water for 2–3 minutes, or until tender. Drain well, then return to a pan with butter and lemon juice, and season with freshly ground black pepper.

For the Turbot

180g turbot fillet

flour, for dredging

salt and pepper, to season

For the Garnish

10g caviar

20g assorted sea vegetables

25g butter

½ lemon, juiced

To serve, divide the sea vegetables between four warmed plates, place the turbot on top, scatter the new potatoes around, and spoon over the beurre blanc. Finally, spoon some lobster on top and serve.

GERD GREAVES

"Centrepoint has been looking after the interests of homeless people in the UK for decades. The team at Sir Charles Napier are very happy to share their recipe with ChariTable Bookings to support such a great charity."

VENISON LOIN with pumpkin, cranberry, chestnut, maple and Douglas fir

SERVES 6 | PREPARATION TIME 1 HOUR (PLUS 24 HOURS TO MARINATE) | COOKING TIME 2 HOURS 30 MINUTES

Equipment
  sous vide and vacuum pack bags
  Vitamix Vita-Prep or similar

For the Venison
  120g venison loin fillet, trimmed
  olive oil and butter, for cooking

For the Venison Marinade
  2kg venison saddle, prepared
  2l red wine, reduced to 1l
  500ml ruby port, reduced for 2 min
  650g mirepoix
  15g black peppercorns, cracked
  2 bay leaves and 6 cloves
  4g thyme
  5g juniper berries, cracked

For the Venison Sauce
  1.2kg venison bones, in 2cm pieces
  100ml groundnut oil
  70g butter
  200g mirepoix, caramelised
  160ml Cabernet Sauvignon vinegar
  1.2l red wine
  2l brown chicken
  2l veal stock
  400g button mushrooms, sliced
  80ml whipping cream
  800g venison trimmings
  4g juniper berries
  40ml Cabernet Sauvignon, reduced by ½
  100ml cognac, rapidly boiled

To make the venison marinade, mix all the ingredients together, including the reduced wine and let cool to a tepid temperature. Marinate the venison saddle for 24 hours. Reserve the marinade for the sauce.

To make the venison sauce, separately sear the bones and trimmings in hot oil and then foaming butter until dark golden brown. Drain. Mix the bones and caramelised mirepoix together in a heavy based saucepan over a high heat and deglaze with the Cabernet Sauvignon vinegar and reduce completely. Add red wine and stocks, bring to the boil, skim and then simmer for 1 hour. Strain and pass through a fine chinois. Bring back to the boil, add the mushrooms and cream, then reduce quickly to sauce consistency. Add the venison trimmings and juniper berries, simmer for 5 minutes to refresh and then pass through a fine chinois. Finish the sauce by adding the cognac, redcurrant jelly and Cabernet Sauvignon vinegar to taste, lifting with a little seasoning. Garnish the sauce just before serving with a little grated chocolate.

To make the pumpkin batons, bring the duck fat to a simmer, with the thyme, bay leaf and garlic. Place the pumpkin batons, salt and fat into a large vacuum pack bag and seal. Place into a water bath and cook at 85°C for 15 minutes or until al dente. Remove, place into an ice bath and reserve until required.

To make the crushed pumpkin, place the pumpkin, maple syrup, diced butter and rosemary into a bowl and season with salt. Spread onto a flat tray, place in an oven at 210°C and cook until soft. Remove from the oven, drain any excess liquid and reserve. Crush the pumpkin with a potato masher and check the seasoning. If needed, add a little of the reserved pumpkin liquid to achieve the desired consistency. Reserve.

To make the poached cranberries, add the shallots, cinnamon, orange zest, thyme and rosemary to the red wine and reduce by half. Whisk in the honey, port and balsamic vinegar before adding the cranberries. Bring back to the boil, remove from the heat and allow to cool. Place in a sterilized jar and reserve in the fridge until required.

For the Venison Sauce *continued*
  80g redcurrant jelly
  30g bitter chocolate, grated
For the Pumpkin Confit
  40 pumpkin batons
  2% salt to weight of pumpkin
  200ml melted duck fat
  1 tsp thyme
  2 bay leaves
  10g garlic, peeled and crushed
For the Pumpkin and Maple Crush
  3kg iron bark pumpkin, chopped
  500g butter, diced
  300ml maple syrup
  2 sprigs of rosemary
  salt, to taste
For the Poached Cranberries
  30g shallot, thinly sliced, yield 20g
  10g Cassia cinnamon
  1¼ tsp orange zest
  2 sprigs of thyme
  1 sprig of rosemary
  200ml red wine
  50g Manuka honey
  100ml ruby port
  400g cranberries
  10ml 8 year old Balsamic vinegar
For the Braised Chestnuts
  1kg chestnuts, yield 500g shelled
  and peeled
  180g celery
  100g Granny Smith apple, peeled
  and sliced
  1 bay leaf
  20g butter
  100ml lemon juice
  600ml white chicken stock
  30g sugar
  1 tsp salt
  ½ tsp white pepper, freshly ground
For the Douglas Fir Oil
  70g Douglas fir needles
  30g flat leaf parsley, blanched
  300ml Grapeseed oil
  1¼ tsp salt
To Serve
  1 bunch of cavolo nero

To make the chestnuts, shell the chestnuts by making a circular incision into the chestnut shells and deep fry in batches of 10 for 1 minute. Drain and whilst hot, use a small knife to remove the shells, which will now peel away quite easily. Reserve in lemon water. Sweat the celery, apple and bay leaf in the butter for 3 minutes. Add the chestnuts, lemon juice, white chicken stock and seasoning. Bring to the boil, cover with greaseproof paper and simmer gently for 15–20 minutes. Taste, check the chestnuts are soft but still holding their shape. Reserve in liquor. Reheat, enrich with a little butter and check the seasoning.

To prepare the pine oil, blitz the pine needles, parsley, oil and salt together in a Vita-Prep until it reaches 64°C. Chill in an ice bath. Leave to steep for a day, then hang in a muslin cloth pouch, in the refrigerator, overnight.

To cook the venison fillet, wrap the venison fillet in layers of cling film to form a cylinder shape, then hang in the fridge for a day to firm up. Portion into 120g pieces, place on a tray and reserve until required. Season and sear the fillet portions in hot olive oil on all sides, then caramelise in foaming butter. This process must be done quickly to avoid overcooking and forming a grey layer on the venison pieces. Place the pieces of venison on grease proof paper in a fan oven and cook at 62°C for 14 minutes, or until the core temperature reaches 52°C. Remove from the oven and rest for half of the cooking time. Discard the fat from the pan and deglaze with a little water to collect the meat juices. Roll the venison pieces in the pan juices, slice and serve.

Serve as pictured, with a little cavolo nero, cooking half in a hot oven at 200°C until blackened for a garnish.

ANDREW GREEN

" Wood Street Mission has been working since the 19th century with children in poverty. This is a great local charity that The Lowry Hotel is thrilled to be able to support by being a part of this collection by ChariTable Bookings."

SLOW COOKED CHESHIRE BEEF FILLET with mustard crust, butternut squash purée, girolles and beef jus

SERVES 2 | PREPARATION TIME 20 MINUTES (PLUS 24 HOURS TO MARINATE) | COOKING TIME 2 HOURS 30 MINUTES

Equipment
sous vide
1 vacuum pack bag

For the Herb Crust
100g baked potato
100g brioche bread crumbs
1 tsp wholegrain mustard
10g parsley, chopped
10g Parmesan, grated
50g salted English butter, melted

For the Slow Cooked Beef Fillet
170g beef fillet, centre cut
1 clove of garlic
1 tbsp olive oil
3 sprigs of thyme

Beef Jus
100g beef trimmings
50g mirepoix
20g mushrooms
20ml port
20ml Cabernet Sauvignon
10ml Madeira
500ml beef stock
3 sprigs of thyme
2 sprigs of tarragon

For the Butternut Squash Purée
1 whole butternut squash
2 shallots, chopped
2 sprigs of thyme

For the herb crust, bind all ingredients together, roll out to about 1cm thick and allow to set in the fridge. Once set, cut a disc that matches the size of the fillet of beef and place in the fridge until needed.

Place the fillet of beef, garlic clove, thyme and olive oil in a vacuum pack bag and seal. Leave to marinate for 24 hours, then cook at 54°C in a water bath for 1 hour. Next, open the bag and sear the fillet on all sides in a hot pan, using the marinade in the bag. Top with the herb crust and grill until golden brown. Allow to rest for 5 minutes, then slice.

Brown the beef trimmings, then stir in the mirepoix and mushrooms. Add in the port, wine and Madeira and reduce. Pour in the beef stock and herbs and reduce to a sauce consistency. Season to taste.

Roast the butternut squash in the skin under some aluminium foil until soft, at 180°C for 60 minutes. Sweat the chopped shallots in a little butter until soft, then add the garlic and thyme and soften. Remove the skins from the squash and add the flesh to the shallots. Blend, pass through a fine mesh sieve and season to taste.

Pan fry some girolle mushrooms and cherry vine tomatoes, season to taste.

For the Butternut Squash Purée *continued*
    ½ clove of garlic, chopped
    salted English butter
To Serve
    400g girolles
    1 punnet of cherry vine tomatoes
    truffle potato, optional

MARTIN GREEN MCA

" I'm really happy to support Cancer Research through ChariTable Bookings' new initiative. A great way to promote the amazing work of this charity! On behalf of White's, I hope you enjoy our signature dish."

SUPREME OF CORN FED CHICKEN with creamed forest mushrooms, baby leeks and winter truffle

SERVES 4 | PREPARATION TIME 15 MINUTES | COOKING TIME 40 MINUTES

For the Chicken
- 4 corn fed chicken breasts
- 25ml rapeseed oil
- 25g butter
- 75ml Madeira
- 100ml chicken stock
- 150ml double cream
- salt and pepper, to taste

For the Mushrooms
- 150g seasonal wild woodland mushrooms
- 1 knob of butter
- 1 pinch of salt

For the Leeks
- 12 baby leeks
- 15g butter
- 1 pinch of salt

To Serve
- 20g black truffle

To make the chicken supreme, season the breasts and fry in oil and butter, sealing all sides of the meat. Place into a preheated oven at 180°C for 15 minutes or until cooked. Remove from the oven and rest in a warm area. In the same pan, remove the grease and oil, and deglaze with Madeira and chicken stock. Reduce the mixture to a syrup, pour in the double cream, and boil until the sauce coats the back of a spoon. Season well and pass through a fine sieve into a clean saucepan.

For the creamed forest mushrooms, clean, cut and wash the mushrooms so they are free from dirt and grit. Leave to dry on a cloth. Season and fry in a hot pan with a generous knob of butter until golden brown. Drain off the excess moisture and add to the reserved Madeira and stock sauce.

To prepare the leeks, clean and wash the baby leeks by trimming the root and dark green tops. Place into a small pan, just cover with water, add 15g of butter, a pinch of salt, and boil until tender, which should take approximately 5 minutes. Drain and put aside.

To serve, slice each chicken breast into three equal pieces, spoon over some mushroom sauce, drape the leeks on top and liberally shave black truffle on top of the dish.

MARK GREENAWAY

How great that ChariTable Bookings has provided a platform for chefs to shout about charities, especially those that focus on their industry. Hence why I present Restaurant Mark alpay's roasted salmon recipe in aid of Hospitality Action!"

ROASTED WILD SALMON and cucumber

SERVES 4 | PREPARATION TIME 30 MINUTES (PLUS 2 HOURS TO MARINATE) | COOKING TIME 15 MINUTES

Equipment
vegetable spiraliser

For the Cucumber
2 cucumbers, peeled

Saffron Mayonnaise
1 whole egg
1 egg yolk
1 tsp Dijon mustard
2 tbsp sherry vinegar
1 large pinch of saffron
30ml water
500ml rapeseed oil
sea salt

For the Salmon
4 x 140g salmon fillets
1 drizzle of rapeseed oil
1 pinch of sea salt
50g butter
½ lemon, juiced

To Garnish
dill
chives

To prepare the cucumbers, using a blowtorch, burn one of the cucumbers all over. Vacuum pack the blowtorched cucumber and refrigerate for 2 hours. Remove from the vacuum pack bag and cut the flesh of the cucumber into 4cm by 2cm rectangles.

Pass the other cucumber through a spiraliser and set aside.

To make the mayonnaise, combine the egg, egg yolk, mustard and vinegar in the container of a food processor. Bring the saffron to the boil in the water. Set the food processor on medium speed and gradually drizzle in the oil while blending, then add the saffron water. Once emulsified, taste and season with salt. Store in a small squeezy bottle or piping bag.

Cut each salmon portion into 4 equal size pieces. Heat a non-stick pan until almost smoking hot and drizzle with rapeseed oil. Place the salmon skin-side down in the pan, then turn down the heat. Once cooked halfway up, sprinkle with salt, then add the butter and lemon juice. Take the pan off the heat, turn the fish over and allow it to finish cooking in the residual heat of the pan, basting with the butter mixture. Remove the salmon from the pan and keep warm until plating up. It should be rare in the middle but warmed all the way through.

To serve, place 4 pieces of salmon down the centre of each plate. Spread 5 rectangles of cucumber around them, 3 at the back and 2 in the front. Drape the cucumber laces over and under the fish. Dot the saffron mayonnaise over and around the salmon and garnish the plates with dill and chives.

MATT GREENWOOD

It's just as important to me that we give back as much as we get out. In our industry, Switchback works to rehabilitate offenders by training them for careers in hospitality. On behalf of the team at The Balcon, I'm delighted to share our recipe with ChariTable Bookings to raise awareness for what they do."

SLOW COOKED LAMB SHOULDER with pearl barley and broad bean pesto

SERVES 8 | PREPARATION TIME 45 MINUTES | COOKING TIME 8 HOURS

For the Lamb
- 1 lamb shoulder, bone in
- 5l brown lamb or chicken stock
- 500g pearl barley
- 2 red onions
- 500g baby carrots
- 1 bunch of cavolo nero
- 250g broad beans, peeled
- 1 clove of garlic, chopped
- ¼ bunch of mint
- 100ml olive oil

To Season
- salt
- sugar

The day before the lamb is needed, heat a large heavy-based frying pan. Season the lamb well, brown nicely in the pan and transfer to a large casserole dish. Heat the brown stock and pour over the lamb. Seal well with foil and cook for 8 hours at 110°C. When cooked, the shoulder blade should come easily out of the shoulder. Remove from the tray and leave to cool. Strain the cooking liquor, put aside and chill once cool. When the lamb has cooled to room temperature, remove the remaining bones and refrigerate. Once chilled, remove from the fridge and roughly cut into portions, then put aside. Depending on the size, you may have excess which can be reserved for curries and stir fries. Remove the solid fat from the cooking stock, reserve 1 litre and pour the rest into a large pot. Reduce over a medium heat until it reaches sauce consistency.

For the pearl barley and trimmings, sauté the red onion then add the pearl barley and cook as a risotto with the reserved lamb stock. Once cooked, place to one side. Blanch the carrots and halve. Pick the cavolo nero from the stems and blanch. Set aside for later. Blend the broad beans, mint, garlic and olive oil until a rough pesto forms. Season well with sugar and salt.

To finish the dish, slowly heat the lamb pieces through in the sauce. In a pan, sauté the carrots until they have a little colour, add the pearl barley, cavolo nero and heat through, adding lamb sauce if needed. Finish with a knob of butter and check the seasoning.

Place a portion of pearl barley in the centre of each plate, top with a portion of lamb and some sauce. Spoon a good amount of broad bean pesto on the top and serve.

HYWEL GRIFFITH

It is great that ChariTable Bookings is able to support Ty Hafan, the leading children's hospice in wales. The Beach House actively supports this pivotal organisation that means so much to so many children and their families."

TANDOORI SPICED COD with leek, spring onions and capers

SERVES 4 | PREPARATION TIME 1 HOUR | COOKING TIME 2 HOURS 30 MINUTES

For the Tandoori Spiced Cod
- 1kg cod
- 50g salt
- tandoori powder, to dust
- 1 drizzle of vegetable oil

For the Leek Purée
- 1kg leeks
- 20ml vegetable oil
- 1 pinch of salt
- ¼ tsp xanthan gum

For the Tandoori Butter
- 10g tandoori powder
- 100g butter
- 1 lemon, juiced

For the Garnish
- 4 spring onions
- 1 handful capers
- vegetable oil to fry
- 200ml almond milk
- ½ tsp lecithin
- salt and pepper

To prepare the tandoori spiced cod, scale the fish, remove all the bones, salt the fish and leave for 1 hour. Wash thoroughly and pat dry. Cut the cod into 4 pieces and dust generously with the tandoori powder. Heat a little oil in a frying pan and cook the cod, skin-side down, for 3 minutes until crispy. Turn the cod over and allow to rest for 2 minutes off the heat.

Slice the leeks, wash thoroughly, then drain well. Place in a heavy-bottomed pan with the oil and a pinch of salt, then cook until the leeks are completely dry. The pan will catch and colour the leeks, this is perfectly fine. Blend with the xanthan gum to help smooth and stabilise the purée. Pass through a fine chinois.

Make the tandoori butter by dry frying the spices in a hot pan. Next add the butter, cook till nut brown and finish with the lemon juice.

For the garnish, thinly slice the spring onions, cover with cold water and refrigerate for 2 hours to make crisp. Fry the drained capers in hot oil until crispy. Place on a cloth to absorb any excess oil. Combine the lecithin with the warmed almond milk, season and use a hand blender to froth.

To serve, place the purée into the bowls, set the cod on top, then dress with the tandoori butter and garnishes.

MARCEL GRZYB

"With so many good causes supported by ChariTable Bookings, it seemed fitting that this dish from the Galley should support Cancer Research UK which is fighting something that affects so many people."

SEA BASS with gnocchi, wild mushrooms, peas and truffle

SERVES 2 | PREPARATION TIME 20 MINUTES | COOKING TIME 1 HOUR

For the Gnocchi
rock salt
1 large potato
100g plain flour
100g Parmesan cheese, finely grated
1 egg yolk
salt and pepper

For the Sea Bass
1 tbsp olive oil
2 sea bass fillets, skin on
salt

For the Sauce
50g butter
100g wild mushrooms, sliced
100g peas, fresh or frozen
2 cloves of garlic, finely chopped
1 shallot, finely chopped
50ml vegetable stock
2 tsp parsley, chopped
Parmesan, to serve
50ml truffle oil

For the Garnish
pea shoots

To prepare the gnocchi, preheat an oven to 170°C. Scatter salt onto a baking tray, place the potato on top and bake in the oven until fluffy in the middle, which should take approximately 1 hour. Allow to cool slightly and scoop out the flesh. Pass through a potato ricer or sieve whilst still warm. Add the flour, Parmesan and the egg yolk, season with salt and pepper and gently mix to combine into a dough. Divide into 2 and roll into sausage shapes around 2cm thick. Cut into 2cm pieces and store on a lightly floured tray until ready to cook.

To cook the sea bass, heat the olive oil in a non-stick frying pan over a medium-high heat. Season the fillets with salt and place in the pan skin-side down. Using a fish slice, press down on the fillets to prevent the fish from curling and to ensure even cooking of the skin. Cook for 3–4 minutes until golden and crisp, then turn over to cook for 1 minute. Remove the pan from the heat and keep the fish warm.

To make the sauce, heat a large sauté pan over a high heat. Add the butter, then sprinkle in the mushrooms. Let the mushrooms caramelise, without stirring, for 7–8 minutes. Add the peas, stir and season. Add the garlic and cook for 1 minute. Add the shallot and cook for another minute. Add the stock and simmer for 4–5 minutes until slightly reduced. Season to taste and sprinkle with half the parsley.

To cook the gnocchi, bring a pan of salted water to the boil. Add the gnocchi while stirring the water and cook for 2–3 minutes. Remove the gnocchi with a skimmer and transfer to the warm sauce. Grate the Parmesan over the top and drizzle with the truffle oil.

To serve, place the gnocchi and mushrooms on the plate, add the sea bass and finish with parsley and pea shoots

SIMON GUELLER

On behalf of all the staff at The Box Tree, I'm delighted to share our signature scallop recipe with ChariTable Bookings in support of the fantastic work done by The Haven for breast cancer patients. Enjoy!"

HAND-DIVED SCALLOPS with butternut squash, Parmesan and Pedro Ximénez jelly

SERVES 2 | PREPARATION TIME 25 MINUTES | COOKING TIME 2 HOURS 30 MINUTES

Equipment
- siphon and N₂O
- spiraliser
- sous vide and vacuum pack bags

For the Jelly
- 100ml Pedro Ximénez sherry
- 1 pinch of salt
- ¾ tsp sugar
- 5g vegetable gelatine

For the Parmesan Purée
- 150g Parmesan,
- 150ml crème fraîche
- 150g potato, peeled and diced

For the Butternut Squash Purée
- 1 butternut squash
- 175g butter
- 1 pinch of salt

For the Pickled Butternut Squash
- 1 butternut squash
- 150ml white wine
- 150ml white wine vinegar
- 150g sugar
- 1 star anise

For the Parmesan Foam
- 150ml water
- 2g salt
- 50g Parmesan, grated
- 5g lecithin

To make the jelly, place all of the ingredients in a pan, bring to the boil and pass through a fine sieve. Leave to set in the fridge until desired firmness is reached.

For the Parmesan purée, vacuum pack the potatoes and cook at 85°C for 90 minutes. Blend the Parmesan and crème fraîche with the cooked potatoes until smooth. Pass through a fine sieve and put into a piping bag for serving.

Peel, deseed and dice the butternut squash. Heat the butter in a large pan, add butternut squash and season with salt. Cover the pan and sweat for 20 minutes. Once soft, blend and pass through a sieve to create a purée.

Place all the ingredients for the Parmesan foam in a pan, bring to the boil, then take off the heat, making sure to mix thoroughly. Pass through a sieve and season to taste. Place the mixture into a siphon and leave to one side. To reheat for serving, boil a deep pan of water and remove from the heat, once slightly cooled, place the siphon inside to thoroughly warm the liquid without over heating the mixture.

To make the pickled butternut squash, using a spiraliser, make squash spaghetti. Boil the pickling liquids, pour over the squash and leave to cool in the liquid.

For the scallops, heat oil in a pan until hot. Season the scallops with salt then place into the hot pan. Cook the scallops for 30 seconds on each side. Add butter and lemon juice, then cook for a further 30 seconds on each side until they develop a golden brown colour. Take the scallops out of the pan and leave to rest for 2 minutes.

To serve, smear the butternut squash purée on the base of the plate, then dress the dish as pictured, leaving the foam until the last minute before serving.

For the Scallops
1 drizzle of oil
2 large hand-dived fresh scallops
1 pinch of salt
50g butter
1 tbsp lemon juice

For the Garnish
1 tbsp Parmesan foam
1 tbsp pumpkin seeds, toasted
rocket cress
1 tbsp Parmesan powder – finely
grated and dried Parmesan

WILLIAM HALSALL

A deliciously healthy dish from Le Caprice to help promote the work of the British Heart Foundation as part of this great collection of recipes by ChariTable Bookings."

THAI BAKED SEA BASS with fragrant rice

SERVES 8 | PREPARATION TIME 30 MINUTES | COOKING TIME 1 HOUR

For the Dipping Sauce

25ml sesame oil

1 small red chilli, deseeded and finely chopped

35g ginger, peeled and finely chopped

1 stick of lemongrass

3 lime leaves

2 cloves of garlic, crushed

125ml sweet soy sauce

100ml light soy sauce

For the Fragrant Rice

2 sticks of lemongrass, bulbous ends crushed

8 lime leaves

1.5l salted water

225g basmati rice, rinsed twice in cold water

For the Sea Bass

35ml sesame oil

3 medium chillies, deseeded and roughly chopped

3 sticks of lemongrass, peeled and bulbous ends roughly chopped

80g root ginger or galangal, peeled and roughly chopped

4 cloves of garlic, crushed

8 lime leaves, roughly chopped

15g coriander

8 x 200g sea bass fillets, descaled

1–2m banana leaf

To make the dipping sauce, heat the sesame oil in a pan and fry the chilli, ginger, lemongrass and lime leaves slowly with the garlic for 1 minute to soften and release the flavours. Add both soy sauces and bring the mixture to the boil. Leave to cool and pour into a bowl or individual dipping dishes.

For the fragrant rice, simmer the lemongrass with the lime leaves in 1.5l salted water for 10 minutes. Add the rice and simmer for 10–12 minutes until just cooked. Drain, return to the pan with a lid on and let it stand for 10 minutes before serving. This will help it to become nice and fluffy. Serve the rice in individual bowls or in a large bowl to pass around to guests.

Preheat the oven to 200°C

While the rice is cooking, heat the sesame oil in a pan and fry the chilli, lemongrass, ginger, garlic and lime leaves for a couple of minutes. Put the mixture into a food processor with the coriander and blitz to a fine texture.

Spread the paste on each sea bass fillet and wrap in a piece of banana leaf like a parcel. Fold the leaf so that the edges join underneath the fillet. Place in an oven tray and bake for 10–15 minutes.

Serve the fish on individual plates with the dipping sauce and rice.

Editor's Note: You can find banana leaves in good Asian supermarkets or greengrocers.

ADAM HANDLING

"The SSAFA is a great charity that supports not just the brave people in our armed forces but also their families. Proud to submit my signature dish from The Frog in this ChariTable Bookings recipe collection."

CHICKEN AND LOBSTER YELLOW CURRY

SERVES 6 | PREPARATION TIME 20 MINUTES | COOKING TIME 1 HOUR

For the Lobster, Claws and Chicken
2 female lobsters
salt
100ml white wine vinegar
3 lobster claws, cooked
200g boneless chicken thighs, skin on
3 cloves garlic, lightly crushed
7 sprigs of thyme, lightly crushed
4 sprigs of rosemary, lightly crushed
6 white peppercorns, lightly crushed
olive oil, to coat

For the Curry Paste
4 dried red chillies
120g shallots, chopped
100g garlic, minced
100g Thai ginger, chopped
80g lemon grass, chopped
80g Thai ginseng
50g shrimp paste
10g each kaffir lime peel, chopped,
fresh coriander root and turmeric
2½ tsp coriander seeds
1½ tsp cumin seeds
5 dried peppercorns

For the Yellow Curry
30ml oil
100ml palm sugar
6 tins coconut cream
1 tin of coconut milk
40ml fish sauce
salt and pepper, to season

To prepare the lobsters, fill a large pan with water, add salt and vinegar and bring to the boil. Put the lobsters in another large pan. Pour the boiling water over the lobsters, off the heat, and then boil for around 9 minutes until cooked. Remove from the water and place on a tray in the fridge. When cold, open the shell and carefully remove the meat. Cut into good sized pieces.

To prepare the lobster claws, dice the claw meat and place in the warm sauce, ready for serving.

To prepare the chicken thighs, remove the skin and reserve. Combine the meat with all the garlic, thyme, rosemary and peppercorns and add olive oil to coat. Place in a lined, metal oven tray and cook for 20 minutes at 180°C.

To prepare the reserved chicken skins, scrape the excess fat. Place in an oven in between 2 trays and cook at 170°C for 8 minutes or until crispy.

Put all the curry paste ingredients in a blender and blitz into a fine paste.

To make the yellow curry, add the oil, palm sugar and coconut cream to a wok on a low heat. Add the curry paste and bring to a simmer, stirring continuously for 1–2 minutes. Add some coconut milk to prevent the spices from burning and overcooking. Add in the fish sauce and season to taste, pass through a fine sieve and set aside.

To serve, assemble the dish as pictured.

ANNA HANSEN

Action Against Hunger tackles malnutrition and hunger amongst children the world over and so it feels poignant to me to support them in this ChariTable Bookings recipe book. I hope you enjoy The Modern Pantry's signature salmon as well!"

SALMON with a black garlic, liquorice and macadamia crust, and tomatillo salsa

SERVES 4 | PREPARATION TIME 30 MINUTES | COOKING TIME 15 MINUTES

For the Black Garlic, Liquorice and Macadamia-Crusted Salmon

4 x 160g salmon fillets,
⅛ of a liquorice juice stick
½ tsp flaky sea salt
170g of macadamia nuts
1 tsp water
25g black garlic, finely chopped

For the Tomatillo Salsa

500g tomatillo, washed and finely diced
90g lime, flesh only, diced
75g shallots, finely diced
150ml extra virgin olive oil
50ml moscatel vinegar
20g coriander, finely chopped
12g chervil, finely chopped
12g mint, finely chopped
salt and pepper, to taste

To Finish

2⅔ handfuls of baby watercress, picked and washed

To prepare the black garlic, liquorice and macadamia-crusted salmon, grind the liquorice and salt together until a fine powder forms. Toss this together with the macadamias and water and lightly toast in a pan over a medium heat. Cool the mix, coarsely grind in a food processor, then add the black garlic and mix thoroughly. Preheat the oven to 200°C. Meanwhile, place a large pan over a medium heat. Rub the salmon skin in oil and place into the hot pan, skin-side down. Cook for 3 minutes, or until the salmon fillets are cooked to halfway through. Remove the salmon from the pan and place onto a baking tray lined with baking paper, skin-side up. Firmly press the macadamia crust onto the skin and place on the bottom shelf of the oven to cook for 5–6 minutes. Remove the salmon from the oven and place onto plates.

To make the tomatillo salsa, mix all of the ingredients together, season and set aside until ready to serve.

To finish the dish and serve, decorate the plates with the tomatillo salsa and watercress. Serve immediately.

MARC HARDIMAN

" *What better way to raise money for charity than by cooking exquisite food! I hope you enjoy making one of my favourite lobster dishes from Great Fosters in this ChariTable Bookings collection, and that as many charities are helped as possible.*"

NATIVE LOBSTER RISOTTO with shellfish, plankton and dill

SERVES 2 | PREPARATION TIME 30 MINUTES (PLUS 12 HOURS TO REST) | COOKING TIME 45 MINUTES

For the Risotto

- 300g Arborio rice
- 2 shallots, finely diced
- 1 clove of garlic
- 75ml olive oil
- 50ml white wine
- 300ml mussel cooking liquor
- 700ml fish stock
- 5g dill
- 1 tbsp mascarpone
- 50g butter

For the Plankton Sphere and Bath

- 100ml mineral water
- 14g Plankton Marino Veta la Palma
- 2.5g salt
- 3g gluconolactate
- 0.4g xanthan gum
- 2.4g alginate, mixed with 500ml water

For the Lobster

- 1 each onion, stick of celery, leek, fennel, star anise, bay leaf
- 3 cloves of garlic
- 6 black peppercorns
- 200ml white wine
- 1 pinch of saffron
- 1 lemon
- 2l water
- lobster tail

For the Mussels

- 1 shallot
- 1 clove of garlic
- 1 sprig of thyme
- 145ml white wine
- 500g fresh mussels

For the Scallop

- 1 scallop
- lemon juice and salt

For the Garnish

- dill, picked
- squid cracker

First make the plankton sphere. Using a blender, mix all ingredients until well dissolved, cover the mixture and leave to rest for 12 hours. Prepare the plankton sphere bath by mixing the mineral water with the alginate, again using the blender, cover and rest for 12 hours. Using a teaspoon, place small spoonfuls of the plankton mixture into the alginate solution, move around gently with a perforated spoon and leave for 2–3 minutes depending on the size of the sphere. Plunge the spheres into a clean bowl of mineral water to rinse, ready for serving.

Wash the mussels, discarding any that are cracked or broken and those that do not shut upon agitation. Sweat the shallots and garlic in a pan with a little olive oil, add the thyme, wine and mussels. Cover and continue to steam until they have opened. Strain and chill, remembering to save the cooking liquor to use for the risotto. Pick the meat from the shells and remove the "beard."

To cook the lobster, first peel and wash the vegetables and cut into 1cm dice. In a large pot sweat down the vegetables, add all other ingredients and bring to the boil. Add the lobster tail, reduce to a minimal heat and cook for 6 minutes. Remove from the pan and chill. Crack and remove the flesh from the shell.

To prepare the scallop, dice into 5mm cubes and season (lightly cure) with a squeeze of lemon juice and a pinch of salt.

To make the risotto, heat the fish stock and mussel liquor but do not boil. In a heavy bottomed pan, gently sweat down the shallots in the olive oil, add the garlic and continue until soft and translucent. Add the risotto rice and fry until all grains are coated in the olive oil. Pour in the wine white and cook until almost dry. Add the stock, one ladle at a time, stirring intermittently until the liquid has been absorbed before adding more. Continue until the grains still have a little bite to them, adding more stock if necessary. Remove from the heat and add the butter and mascarpone, cover and leave for 2 minutes Finish with dill and season to taste.

To finish the dish and serve, warm the shellfish in a butter emulsion starting with the lobster followed by the mussels. Spoon the risotto into a bowl. Place the shellfish on top and garnish with the plankton sphere, squid cracker, and picked dill.

CHRIS HARROD

Rays of Sunshine makes amazing wishes come true for seriously ill children. Couldn't be more proud to support this amazing charity by sharing The Whitebrook's plaice dish with ChariTable Bookings."

CORNISH PLAICE with heritage carrots, buttermilk and estuary findings

SERVES 4 | PREPARATION TIME 1 HOUR (PLUS 12 HOURS TO DRY) | COOKING TIME 30 MINUTES

For the Plaice
4 x 130g plaice fillets
40g salt
400ml water
1 spritz of lemon juice

For the Heritage Carrots
500g plain flour
250g sea salt
250ml water
20 heritage carrots, cleaned

For the Buttermilk Emulsion
25ml milk
25ml double cream
200ml buttermilk
2.5g xanthan gum
1g lecithin powder
salt
1 tsp lemon juice

For the Buttermilk Powder
200ml buttermilk
50g butter

For the Estuary Findings
200ml water
100g unsalted butter
12g salt
sea spinach, picked and cleaned
sea blight, picked and cleaned
sea aster, picked and cleaned
rock samphire, picked and cleaned

To make the plaice fillets, make a brine by mixing the salt and water until dissolved. Submerge the plaice fillets and leave for 4 minutes. Remove and dry on absorbent cloth.

To make the carrots, place the flour and salt in a bowl and gradually incorporate the water until a smooth dough forms – you may not need all the water. Roll out the dough and completely encase the carrots, making sure there are no gaps. Bake at 190°C for 20 minutes. Allow to cool before cracking open the salt dough and remove the baked carrots.

To make the buttermilk emulsion, bring the milk and cream to the boil, remove from the heat and add the buttermilk, xanthan gum and lecithin. Blitz with a hand blender until all incorporated and frothy. Season lightly with salt and lift with lemon juice as required.

To make the buttermilk powder, put the buttermilk and butter in a saucepan and bring to a simmer. Allow to split and continue cooking out until you have a golden sand texture. Strain before spreading onto a tray with absorbent cloth and allow to dry overnight.

Make an emulsion for cooking the estuary herbs by bringing the water, butter and salt to the boil. Emulsify with a hand blender. Reserve until required.

To finish the dish and serve, gently warm the salt-baked carrots through in a low temperature oven. Meanwhile heat a non-stick frying pan until very hot. Add the fish and cook over a medium-high heat for 2–3 minutes, then carefully turn over and cook for 1–2 minutes longer. The fish should be golden but only just cooked through. Remove from the pan, lift with lemon juice and keep warm. Bring the emulsion for the estuary vegetable to the boil and cook the sea aster and rock samphire together for 1 minute. Add the sea blight and sea spinach for 10 seconds then drain the vegetables immediately. You want to keep them crisp and vibrant. Warm the buttermilk emulsion and froth with a hand blender. Spoon a bed of sauce onto each plate. Arrange the carrots around before adding the plaice fillet in the centre. Sprinkle the top of the plaice with the caramelised buttermilk powder. Finish the plate with the estuary herbs.

ANGELA HARTNETT

" Myself and everyone at Murano are delighted to share my popular dish with ChariTable Bookings in support of the wonderful work of The Terrence Higgins Trust with the ability to help raise much needed unrestricted funds - I hope you enjoy it!"

HAKE with romesco crust

SERVES 4 | PREPARATION TIME 20 MINUTES | COOKING TIME 2 HOURS

For the Dish

1 x 290g jar roasted red peppers, drained and quartered

1 tbsp fresh rosemary leaves, chopped

2 cloves of garlic, thinly sliced

3 tbsp olive oil

50g skinned, salted almonds

50g dry white breadcrumbs

2 medium courgettes

4 x 150g hake portions, skin on

salt and freshly ground black pepper

Preheat the oven to 100°C, lay the peppers on a baking sheet and sprinkle with the rosemary, garlic, 1 tablespoon of olive oil and some seasoning. Place in the oven and bake for 2 hours to dry out the peppers. Remove from the oven and allow to cool. Once cool, place the peppers in a food processor with the almonds and breadcrumbs and blend until they have a sandy texture.

Increase the oven temperature to 180°C.

Slice the courgettes into discs 5mm thick. Heat 1 tablespoon of olive oil in a non-stick frying pan, add the courgettes and season. Cook for 2–3 minutes on each side or until golden. Remove from the pan and set aside.

Heat the remaining 1 tablespoon of olive oil in the frying pan over a high heat. Add the hake portions, skin-side down, and cook for 2 minutes, or until the skin is golden brown.

Transfer to a baking sheet, skin-side up, and sprinkle the prepared topping over the fish. Bake in the oven for 5–7 minutes, or until the flesh offers no resistance when you pierce it with the tip of a knife.

To serve, place the courgettes on individual plates and top with a piece of hake. Finish by spooning over some of the cooking juices.

ANNA HAUGH

Age UK provides support for the fastest growing age group in the country, the over 60's. There are many lonely old people in the UK and that is why I am keen to support them by raising awareness through ChariTable Bookings."

BEEF WELLINGTON

SERVES 2 | PREPARATION TIME 2 HOURS | COOKING TIME 2 HOURS

For the Chicken Liver Parfait

2 shallots, sliced

3 cloves of garlic, crushed

1 bay leaf

1 sprig of thyme

200g butter, room temperature

50ml brandy

100ml Madeira

200g chicken livers

3 eggs

For the Pancake Batter

100g plain flour

1 pinch of salt

1 tsp chopped chives

2 eggs

300ml semi-skimmed milk

2 tbsp vegetable oil

For the Duxelle

3 shallots, peeled and chopped

200g mushrooms, finely chopped

50g butter

1 pinch of salt

For the Beef

400g beef fillet

1 tbsp English mustard

salt and pepper, to taste

1 sheet puff pastry, 26x29cm

1 egg , beaten for eggwash

To make the chicken liver parfait, sweat the shallots, herbs and garlic in 50g of butter then deglaze with the brandy and Madeira. Reduce by three quarters and purée in a blender. Add the liver and eggs and blend, slowly adding the butter bit by bit. Pass through a fine sieve and pour into moulds. Cook the mixtures in a bain-marie, covered with tin foil, for about 40–50 minutes. The centre should be at 66°C.

To make the pancake batter, place the flour, salt and chives in a bowl, making a well in the centre, and whisk in the eggs and milk until a smooth batter is formed. Add a little oil to a frying pan and allow to heat. Add a small ladle of batter and roll it around the pan. Once the sides have just turned brown, use a butter knife or spatula to lift it gently off the edge and flip over.

To make the duxelle, fry the mushrooms and shallots on a high heat in butter, adding salt to taste. A lot of liquid will initially come out, make sure to stir constantly until all of this has evaporated. Check seasoning and set to one side.

To assemble the dish, season the beef well and sear in a very hot pan until all sides are golden. Chill and rub the mustard over the beef. Lay the pancake on top of a sheet of cling film twice its size. Spread 2 tablespoons of parfait on top, with a further 2 tablespoons of duxelle on top of the parfait. Place the beef at the end closest to you and roll it away until it is completely wrapped in the pancake. Roll tightly in cling film and rest in the fridge for as long as you can, but for a minimum of 1 hour. Unwrap the beef from the cling film and place on the end of the pastry closest to you. Egg wash around and roll tightly, making sure to squeeze the edges. Egg wash the top and rest in the fridge for another hour, until you are ready to cook.

Preheat an oven to 180°C and insert a heavy–based tray. On a sheet of grease proof paper, place the Wellington in the oven for 30 minutes for medium rare. Take out of the oven and rest for 5–10 minutes. Carve, plate and serve with desired trimmings.

NIGEL HAWORTH

" I hope you enjoy making my signature pigeon dish that's so popular here at Northcote, and that through ChariTable Bookings I can further support Scotty's Little Soldiers, a charity very close to my heart."

TARLETON WOOD PIGEON with sweetheart cabbage, morels and Garstang blue cheese

SERVES 4 | PREPARATION TIME 40 MINUTES | COOKING TIME 2 HOURS

Equipment
- sous vide
- Paco Jet

For the Chicken Mousse
- 100g chicken breast, diced
- 125ml UHT cream
- ¼ tsp salt
- 1 egg yolk
- 4 tsp chives, chopped
- 4 tsp chervil, chopped

For the Pigeon
- 4 wood pigeons
- 4 sprigs of thyme
- 20g butter

For the Onion Caramel
- 1 onion
- 1 tsp sugar
- 1 knob of butter

For the Pigeon Sauce
- 1 drizzle of vegetable oil
- 50g banana shallots, finely sliced
- 4 pigeon carcasses, roasted and chopped
- 4 juniper berries, crushed
- 100ml port
- 150ml chicken stock
- 150ml veal stock

For the Sweetheart Cabbage
- 1 sweetheart cabbage
- salt, to taste

To prepare the chicken mousse, place the diced chicken, 50ml of cream, salt and egg yolk into a Paco Jet beaker and freeze to –20°C. Once frozen, blend 3 times. Transfer the chicken into a metal bowl over ice and beat in the remaining cream until smooth and shiny. Mix in the chives and chervil and check the seasoning. Place into a piping bag and set aside.

For the pigeon, remove the legs, wish bone and skin from the pigeons. Take each crown off the pigeon and place into a vacuum pack bag. Add the thyme and butter into each bag and seal tightly. Carefully remove the bone from each leg of pigeon. On a sheet of cling film, lay the leg meat flat in a line with no gaps. Season with salt. In the middle of the leg meat, pipe a line of chicken mousse. Roll the leg meat around the mousse, wrap tightly in cling film and tie a knot in each end. Place the pigeon crown and leg meat into a water bath at 68°C. Cook the legs for 15 minutes and the crowns for 20 minutes. Once cooked, remove from the water bath. Rest for 5 minutes and keep the leg meat warm. Remove the crowns from the bags and season with salt evenly. Sweat the onions in the butter until translucent. Stir in the sugar and allow to caramelise. Place the pigeon crowns into a hot non-stick pan and paint with onion caramel. Seal each side of the pigeon to caramelise with the caramel. Cut the leg meat into 8 even pieces and remove the breast from the bone.

To make the pigeon sauce, add a small amount of oil and the shallots to a hot pan and cook until lightly caramelised. Add the pigeon carcasses, juniper berries and port, then reduce by half. Pour in the chicken and veal stocks, bring back to the boil, turn down the heat to a simmer and reduce to a sauce coating consistency. Pass through a sieve lined with muslin, check seasoning.

Place the cabbage into the oven at 180°C. Cook for 30–40 minutes until the cabbage is crispy on the outside and soft in the middle. Remove from the oven. Remove the crispy leaves and reserve for the plate. Cut the cabbage into 4 quarters, remove the core on an angle and season with salt.

For the Morels

16 small morels
1 tsp roast garlic
1 drizzle of olive oil
1 pinch of salt
3 tsp pigeon sauce

To Serve

16 small chunks Garstang blue cheese
4 pieces crispy cabbage leaves

Wash the morels twice in lightly salted water to remove any grit. In a hot frying pan, add a drizzle of olive oil, the morels and garlic. Cook for 1 minute. Add 3 teaspoons of the pigeon sauce and cook until the morels are slightly soft.

To serve, just off centre of the plate place a sweetheart cabbage quarter and put some crispy cabbage over it. Arrange 2 pieces of leg meat on the plate and 4 chunks of blue cheese. Place the pigeon breast on top. Scatter the morels around the plate and finish with the sauce.

PRAHLAD HEGDE

Hope for Children helped over 37,000 children and their families last year in the UK, Africa and Asia by providing access to healthcare and education. I love that we can support children everywhere by donating a recipe from the Bombay Brasserie to ChariTable Bookings."

MASALA SEA BASS

SERVES 4 | PREPARATION TIME 20 MINUTES | COOKING TIME 20 MINUTES

For the Dish

2 tsp chilli powder

2 tsp turmeric

1 lime, juiced

salt

4 x 180g Chilean sea bass, deboned, skin on

2 tbsp vegetable oil

For the Base

1 tbsp vegetable oil

4 tsp cumin

1 clove of garlic, chopped

80g mushrooms, sliced

200g baby spinach, shredded

1 pinch of salt

For the Garnish

4 chilli flowers, made using fresh green or red chilli

4 chives

a few drops of chilli oil

4 lemon wedges

To make the dish, in a bowl, mix the chilli powder, turmeric and lime juice and season with salt. Spoon this over the sea bass. Set aside for 20 minutes to marinate. Preheat the oven to 180°C. Heat the vegetable oil in a pan and sear the marinated sea bass on both sides. Place on a tray and bake in the oven for 5 minutes.

To make the spinach and mushroom base, heat the oil in a pan, add the cumin and chopped garlic, and fry until the garlic turns golden brown. Add the mushrooms and shredded spinach and stir-fry until cooked. Season with salt.

To prepare the chilli flowers, snip off the tip of a fresh red or green chilli, leaving the stalk intact, and then make a few lengthways cuts at the snipped end. Place the chilli in ice water – after a while the ends will curl up like flowers.

To serve, divide the spinach and mushroom mixture among 4 large plates. On each base, place a sea bass fillet, skin-side up, and garnish with a chilli flower, a chive and a lemon wedge. Drizzle a few drops of chilli oil or a sprinkle of paprika powder on the plate.

MATT HIDE

" Support Macmillan with me and spread the word about this recipe collection by ChariTable Bookings. Celebrate the work of this great charity and enjoy the Turf Club's sea bass at the same time!"

PAN-FRIED SEA BASS with crushed Jersey Royals, asparagus, tomato and red onion salsa

SERVES 4 | PREPARATION TIME 1 HOUR | COOKING TIME 20 MINUTES

For the Basil Oil
150g basil leaves
270ml extra virgin olive oil

For the Tomato and Red Onion Salsa
1 large red onion, chopped into
small dice
4 plum tomatoes, blanched, peeled,
deseeded and diced
1 red chilli, finely chopped
1 lime, juiced
1 tsp olive oil
20g coriander, roughly chopped
salt and pepper, to taste

For the Crushed Jersey Royals
500g small Jersey Royal potatoes,
washed
25g butter
salt and pepper, to taste
1 handful of chives

For the Asparagus
8 asparagus
salt and pepper, to taste

For the Sea Bass
4 x 180g sea bass fillets, pin boned
oil, for cooking
30g butter

For the Garnish
micro coriander
purple amaranth

To prepare the basil oil, blanch the basil leaves in boiling water for 30 seconds then plunge into ice water to chill. Remove and pat dry with a paper towel. Place in a liquidiser and blitz slowly, adding the oil. Place into a small squeezy bottle and keep for later.

To make the tomato and red onion salsa, place all of the chopped ingredients in a bowl, add the lime juice, olive oil, coriander, seasoning and mix together. Cover and reserve for serving.

To make the crushed Jersey Royals, place the Jerseys in boiling, salted water. Bring back to the boil and simmer for 10–12 minutes or until tender. Drain the potatoes, add the butter and seasoning and crush with a fork or masher. Add the snipped chives and set aside.

To make the asparagus, place the asparagus in a pan of boiling, salted water. Boil for 2 minutes, remove from the water, cut down the centre and season.

To cook the sea bass, wash the fillets and pat dry. Using a knife, score across the skin and season well. Place a non-stick frying pan on a medium high heat, drizzle in some oil to coat the bottom of the pan. When hot, add the fillets skin-side down, press down on the fillets with a fish slice in order to cook evenly and prevent them from curling. Cook for 3–4 minutes until nice and crisp then turn over onto the flesh side, adding the butter and cook for another 1–2 minutes. Remove from the pan ready for serving.

To serve, place a metal ring in the centre of the plate and fill with the crushed potatoes. Arrange the asparagus around the potato, then place the sea bass skin-side up on the potato. Spoon the salsa along the length of the sea bass, drizzle the basil oil around the plate and finish with some micro coriander and purple amaranth.

MATT HILL

A great idea by ChariTable Bookings to support charities across the UK by sharing recipes. I hope you enjoy The Grill Room at Down Hall's beetroot dish and we all raise as much for charity as we can."

SALT-BAKED BEETROOT with Jersey curd and pickled walnuts

SERVES 4 | PREPARATION TIME 4 HOURS 30 MINUTES (PLUS OVERNIGHT TO SOAK) | COOKING TIME 3 HOURS

Equipment
Thermomix
mandoline

For the Salt-Baked Beetroot
2 each red, golden and candy beetroot
10 egg whites
450g salt

For the Pickled Walnuts
100g walnuts
400ml Cabernet Sauvignon vinegar
200g caster sugar
1 stick of cinnamon
2 star anise
1 pinch of yellow mustard seeds

For the Pickled Beetroot
2 red beetroot
500ml Chardonnay vinegar
200g caster sugar
1 tbsp clear honey
2 sprigs of thyme
lemon juice, to taste

For the Beetroot Dressing
3 red beetroot
500ml water
100ml rapeseed oil
2 tbsp beetroot pickle liquor

For the Walnut Milk
200g walnuts
400ml water
100ml walnut oil

To make the saltbaked beetroot, whisk the egg whites to soft peaks and slowly add the salt. Place the beetroots on a tray and completely cover with the meringue. Bake at 160°C for 3 hours. When cooked, allow to rest for 1 hour. Peel carefully and slice into wedges.

To make the pickled walnuts, place the caster sugar and vinegar in a pan and bring to the boil. Add the cinnamon, anise and mustard seeds then reduce the volume by a quarter. Fold in the walnuts and leave to cool.

To make the pickled beetroot, place the caster sugar and vinegar in a pan and bring to the boil. Add the honey, thyme and lemon juice to taste then allow to cool. Slice 2 of the red beetroots thinly with a mandoline, cut out discs with a 50ml cutter. Place the beetroot slices into the pickling liquid.

To make the beetroot dressing, peel and dice the beetroot, blitz with the water then pass through a sieve. In a pan, reduce to a syrup making sure to skim off the foam. Split with organic rapeseed oil. Add 2 tablespoons of beetroot pickle liquor, check seasoning.

To make the walnut milk, soak the walnuts in water overnight. Blitz in a Thermomix to a pulp-like consistency then hang in muslin cloth for 4 hours. Collect the milk and whisk in the walnut oil. Check seasoning.

To serve, dress the plate with the beetroot dressing. Place salt-baked beetroot, pickled beetroot, pieces of curd and pickled walnuts around the plate. Finish with the walnut milk dressing, red chard and mustard leaf.

For the Garnish
Jersey cow curd
red chard
mustard leaf

NATHAN HILL

" Rowcroft Hospice provides specialist care to people with life-limiting illnesses in South Devon. Orestone Manor is thrilled to be supporting them in this ChariTable Bookings recipe book."

NOISETTE OF LAMB with herb crust, navet purée, wild garlic, pomme fondant and rosemary juice

SERVES 4 | PREPARATION TIME 40 MINUTES | COOKING TIME 1 HOUR 30 MINUTES

For the Noisette of Lamb

2 prepared racks of lamb

8 tbsp olive oil

2 sprigs of rosemary, needles removed, chopped

4 cloves of garlic, roughly chopped

For the Rosemary Jus

3 tbsp fresh rosemary, chopped

2 tbsp shallots, chopped

1 tbsp garlic, crushed

½ tps salt

½ tsp ground black pepper

130ml each lamb stock, veal or beef stock and ruby port

For the Navet Purée

1kg turnips, peeled and roughly chopped

3 cloves of garlic, peeled

350ml double cream

50g butter

For the Fondant Potatoes

4 large potatoes, cut into rounds using a cookie cutter

1 knob of butter

75ml chicken or vegetable stock

2 cloves of garlic, crushed

3 sprigs of fresh thyme, to season

For the Heritage Carrots

500g heritage carrots, cut into

To prepare the noisette of lamb, mix together the olive oil, rosemary and garlic and smother the mixture over the lamb joints. Marinate overnight in the fridge.

To make the rosemary jus, add the dry ingredients to a pan on a high heat for 30 seconds. Add the stocks and port, and bring to the boil. Simmer until reduced by half, then pass through a chinois. Return to a clean pan and reduce further to adjust the consistency if needed.

To make the navet purée, boil the turnips in plenty of water until very tender. Drain, return to the pot, add the garlic and heat until dry for 2 minutes. Mix in the cream and butter and bring to the boil. Blend and pass the mixture through a chinois using a spoon to push it through. Season to taste and add extra cream if the consistency needs adjusting.

To make the fondant potatoes, fry the potato rounds on each side in butter until golden brown. Add the stock, garlic, herbs and seasoning. Simmer with a lid on until they become tender. Remove from the stock.

To make the heritage carrots, place the carrots in a pan with enough water to just cover them. Add the sugar, salt, thyme and butter. Bring to the boil, then simmer until the water has evaporated.

To make the wild garlic, gently wilt the wild garlic with a little water, butter and seasoning in a shallow frying pan for 1 minute.

To make the herb dust, blitz the panko breadcrumbs with mixed herbs in a blender until it becomes a green-coloured powder.

Preheat the oven to 200°C. Season and seal the lamb in a hot pan until golden. Transfer to the oven for 15 minutes, this will give you a pink lamb. Cook for longer if you prefer. Roll in the herb dust and leave to rest for at least 10 minutes. Return the lamb to a hot oven for another 2–3 minutes just before carving. Serve as pictured.

For the Heritage Carrots *continued*
  barrel shapes
  1 tsp sugar
  ½ tsp salt
  6 sprigs of thyme
  50g butter

For the Wild Garlic
  240g wild garlic leaves
  1 knob of butter

For the Herb Dust
  100g panko breadcrumbs
  3 tbsp mixed fresh herbs, chopped

For the Garnish
  wild garlic flowers

SHAUN HILL

Through this ChariTable Bookings tasty initiative, The Walnut Tree Inn team and I are excited and proud to support the amazing work of the Red Cross and we hope to raise as much for them as possible with your help."

SCALLOPS with lentil and coriander sauce

SERVES 4 | PREPARATION TIME 15 MINUTES | COOKING TIME 1 HOUR

For the Dish

12 medium scallops
1 shallot, peeled and chopped
1 small knob of ginger, peeled and chopped
1 clove of garlic, peeled and chopped
½ red pepper
½ tsp ground coriander
½ tsp ground cinnamon
½ tsp ground cumin
½ tsp ground cardamom
25g brown lentils, boiled until tender
50ml stock or water
1 tbsp butter
1 tbsp crème fraîche
1 tbsp fresh coriander leaves
lemon, salt and Tabasco, to taste

Fry the garlic, shallot, ginger and pepper until coloured. Add the spices and continue to cook for a moment before adding most of the cooked lentils, then the stock or water. Liquidise in a blender along with the butter and crème fraîche, then scrape into a saucepan with the remaining lentils. Adjust the consistency by adding more stock or more butter. Season with lemon, salt and Tabasco, then stir in the coriander leaves at the last moment.

Cut the scallops into coin sized discs, brush lightly with oil, then sear in a hot, dry frying pan.

Serve the scallops on top of a pool of sauce.

JAMES HOLDEN

Adopt a School is a wonderful charity that delivers food education in schools all over the country and many in deprived areas. As a Chef Lecturer for the North West, I am delighted to donate this dish to ChariTable Bookings to raise awareness for this worthy cause."

CRISP PAN-FRIED MACKEREL FILLET with niçoise vegetables, roasted baby peppers,
aubergine caviar and balsamic syrup

SERVES 4 | PREPARATION TIME 30 MINUTES | COOKING TIME 1 HOUR 30 MINUTES

For the Mackerel
2 x 500g large fresh mackerel, cut into 4 plump fillets and pin boned
olive oil, for cooking

For the Aubergine Caviar
2 whole aubergines
ground cumin, to sprinkle
salt and pepper
½ lemon, juiced

For the Niçoise
50g each onion, courgette, aubergine and yellow pepper
100g plum tomatoes
2 cloves of garlic
1 tbsp tomato purée
salt and pepper

For the Roasted Peppers
4 baby red peppers
4 baby yellow peppers
4 baby orange peppers
Maldon rock salt

To Garnish
extra virgin olive oil
balsamic syrup
a few sprigs of basil

To prepare the aubergine caviar, cut the aubergines in half lengthways, and score the flesh in a criss-cross fashion on each half. Heat a roasting tray on the stove with some olive oil in it, lightly fry the aubergines until golden and sprinkle with the cumin, salt and pepper. Place in the oven at 160°C, and roast until the flesh is soft, about 30 minutes. Remove from the oven, scrape out the flesh and blitz in a food processor. Adjust seasoning if needed and add the lemon juice.

To prepare the niçoise, cut the vegetables into 5mm cubes, making sure to square off edges to create the perfect dice. Remove all the skin and seeds from the tomatoes and dice the flesh to the same size. Crush the garlic cloves in a press, or pestle and mortar. Heat some olive oil in a pan, then add the chopped onion with the garlic and sauté, cooking for 2 minutes and making sure not to brown. Add the peppers, aubergine and courgette and cook for a further 2 minutes, ensuring they do not turn mushy. Add the tomato purée and diced tomato flesh, fold together and adjust the seasoning with salt and pepper. Leave to one side for serving.

To prepare the roasted peppers, de-seed, roll in a little olive oil and place on a tray in the oven at 180°C. Sprinkle with a little Maldon salt and cook for 20–25 minutes until tender and browned.

To prepare the fish for cooking, make slits across the skin along the entire length of the mackerel, without cutting through the flesh, leaving gaps of roughly 1cm. This is to stop the fish curling when cooked. Cut each fillet of fish in half across the middle, not lengthways.

To cook the fish, heat some olive oil in a heavy-bottomed frying pan, and when reasonably hot, place the fillets of mackerel skin-side down first. Press them down flat with a fish slice or spatula as they will try to curl up slightly. Cook with a medium heat to crisp and colour the skin, do not be tempted to turn over too soon as you will take the skin off. As the fish is cooking skin down, the flesh will begin to change colour from the side initially, and spread. Once appropriately coloured, turn over and cook for a final 2 minutes, being careful not to overcook.

Whilst the fish is cooking, reheat the niçoise, roasted peppers, and the aubergine caviar.

To serve, using a ring mould, spoon in the niçoise vegetables, lightly patting down to make a firm base for the fish to sit on. Shape the aubergine caviar into a quenelle, using 2 dessertspoons and place at the side of the niçoise, arrange 1 of each colour of the roasted peppers on the plate and finally, place 2 pieces of fish per portion across the niçoise mound. Drizzle the dish with extra virgin olive oil and balsamic syrup, then garnish with a nice sprig of fresh basil.

LUKE HOLDER

"It's really important for those of us that work in the food industry to remember those that don't have the basics we are used to. Action Against Hunger fights to prevent malnutrition and starvation in children around the world. Glad to share my polenta agnolotti from Hartnett Holder & Co restaurant at Lime Wood with ChariTable Bookings to support them."

POLENTA AGNOLOTTI with artichokes, tomatoes and truffle

SERVES 6 | PREPARATION TIME 20 MINUTES | COOKING TIME 2 HOURS

For the Pasta
200g 00 flour
9 egg yolks, free range, organic are best

For the Polenta Mix
2.5l water
300g polenta
300g aged Parmesan
100g butter
50ml of olive oil

For the Garnish
50g butter
cooked artichoke hearts, quartered
oven-dried tomatoes – cherry tomatoes cut in half, seasoned with salt, sugar, thyme and garlic, dried in 90°C oven for 90 minutes
a few leaves of oregano
1 truffle, about 3g, finely sliced

For the pasta dough, tip the flour onto your work surface, making a well in the centre. Add the eggs to the well, pop the yolks in and begin to gently incorporate the flour from the outside edges into the middle. The 200g flour is just a guide amount – you may not need to incorporate it all into the dough. Bring the flour and eggs together until it starts to form a loose dough then, combine enough of the flour so that the dough holds itself and is not dry and crumbly or soft and wet. The dough should be firm to squeeze with a slight tackiness and good elasticity. Roll out the dough into a large sheet. Remember, the amount of flour required will depend on the size of the egg yolks and how well they have been separated from the whites.

To prepare the polenta, bring the water to the boil and then sprinkle in the polenta, cook for 1 hour then blend with the Parmesan, butter and olive oil. Pass through a sieve and set in the fridge in piping bags.

To assemble the agnolotti, when chilled, pipe a straight line of polenta mix lengthwise on the pasta sheet, leaving enough pasta at the top to fold over the filling. Fold the pasta top over the filling. Press firmly to seal. Use a wheeled pasta cutter or a sharp knife to cut the filled tube of pasta away from the rest of the sheet, making sure to keep the sealed strip intact. Use the tips of your fingers to pinch the tube of pasta into equally-sized sections, creating a seal between pockets of filling. Use the wheeled pasta cutter or a sharp knife to separate the sections. Quickly cut through each, leaning the tube of pasta in the direction you're cutting. You should be left with small, individual pockets of filled pasta. Place the finished agnolotti in a tray of loose polenta.

To prepare the garnish and serve, place the agnolotti into salted boiling water and leave until just cooked, they should take about 2 minutes to become al dente. In a separate pan, slowly melt the butter, add the cooked artichoke hearts, oven dried tomatoes, a few leaves of oregano and the chopped truffle. Add the cooked pasta and a touch of water to make it into a silky emulsified sauce. Serve immediately.

WILL HOLLAND

Ty Hafan is an important charity to us and one we support across the whole business, so it's fantastic to extend this support through the ChariTable Bookings' initiative. We hope that you enjoy our recipe as well!"

GINGERBREAD CRUSTED JOHN DORY with braised white beans, chargrilled grelot onions and artichokes, and saffron emulsion

SERVES 4 | PREPARATION TIME 15 MINUTES (PLUS 24 HOURS TO SOAK) | COOKING TIME 2 HOURS 30 MINUTES

For the Gingerbread
25g candied stem ginger
100g golden syrup
60g soft, dark brown sugar
125g self-raising flour
10g ground ginger
2g bicarbonate of soda
1 large egg
70ml whole milk

For the Braised White Beans
150g dried white beans
1l fish stock

For the Saffron Emulsion
1 large Maris Piper potato, baked for 1 hour
45ml whole milk
1 pinch of saffron
¼ clove of garlic
2 egg yolks
50ml light olive oil
1 spritz of lemon juice
salt and cayenne pepper to taste

For the Grelot Onions and Artichokes
8 grelot onions
4 globe artichoke hearts, cooked

For the John Dory Fillets
4 x 150g John Dory fillets, skinless
50ml light olive oil

To make the braised white beans, start by soaking the beans in cold water for 24 hours. Drain from the water and place in a saucepan with the stock. Bring to the boil, reduce the heat and simmer gently for an hour or until tender.

To make the gingerbread, start by preheating a fan oven to 150°C. Finely grate the stem ginger and place in a saucepan with the syrup and sugar. Warm until the sugar has dissolved. Transfer to an electric mixer and add the remaining ingredients. Beat well before transferring to the prepared tin. Bake for 45 minutes. Allow to cool before roughly chopping and leaving to dry. Once completely dry, place in a food processor and blend to a crumb.

To make the saffron emulsion, warm the milk and saffron in a saucepan. Weigh out 60g of baked potato flesh and combine with the warmed milk, garlic and egg yolks in a liquidiser. Blend until smooth before gradually adding the oil. Season to taste with salt, cayenne pepper and lemon juice.

To make the grelot onions and artichokes, blanch the onions in boiling, salted water for 2 minutes. Refresh in ice water and reserve until required. When ready to serve, cut each artichoke heart in half and lightly chargrill with the grelot onions.

To cook the John Dory fillets, preheat a large, heavy-based frying pan until hot. Add the oil, followed by the fillets. Fry for 2–3 minutes on each side until caramelised. Remove from the pan, sprinkle generously with gingerbread crumb and keep warm.

To assemble the dish, flick the saffron emulsion over each plate. Scatter the white beans over, add 2 chargrilled onions, 2 half artichoke hearts, 1 gingerbread crusted John Dory fillet and a pinch of gingerbread crumb to each plate. Serve immediately.

SEBBY HOLMES

Dan Turner and I at Farang are passionate about food. The Bee Cause by Friends of the Earth is chamioning the UK bee population as their decline will directly impact food production globally. We hope you enjoy our recipe shared with you through ChariTable Bookings."

KHAO SOI – chiang mai curried egg noodles with barbecue butternut squash

SERVES 4 | PREPARATION TIME 20 MINUTES | COOKING TIME 40 MINUTES

For the Dish
- 2 medium butternut squash

For the Paste
- 4 long red chillies
- 5 bulbs of garlic
- 10 medium round shallots
- 6 stalks of lemongrass
- 1 piece of galangal, 1 inch long
- 2 pieces of fresh red turmeric
- 1 tbsp coriander seeds
- 1 black cardamom pod
- 4 coriander roots

For the Curry
- 500g flat egg noodles
- 75ml coconut oil, or vegetable oil
- 50ml fish sauce, or soy sauce
- 50g palm sugar
- 2 tbsp of dark soy sauce
- 1 tbsp mild curry powder
- 500ml coconut cream
- 150ml chicken or vegetable stock

To Serve
- deep fried egg noodles
- roasted chilli oil
- Thai shallots, or red onion
- coriander leaf
- lime wedge

To prepare the bbq squash, peel and cut into large chunks, then blanch in salted water on a low boil for 6–8 minutes until soft on the outside but still reasonably firm. Drain and allow to cool briefly before smearing with a little oil. Place on a hot BBQ grill and cover. Check after 4–5 minutes and turn the squash pieces once they start to char. They will be cooked once soft in the middle. Next, scorch the chillies over the coals until slightly blackened. Place the whole garlic bulbs and shallots on the grill and turn when the outsides start to blacken and burn, remove when soft to the touch. Grill the lemongrass, galangal and turmeric until coloured but not black. If using a BBQ, it's a good idea to place some wood smoking chips or use wood as the fuel to really impregnate the ingredients with a smoky flavour. Allow the grilled vegetables to cool.

Take a pan and place on a low flame or on the BBQ grill and gently toast the coriander and black cardamom seeds until fragrant. Grind to a fine powder in a pestle and mortar.

Using a knife slice off the very bottom and top parts of the lemongrass stalk and remove the outer sheath. Finely slice the lemongrass innards. Peel the galangal with a peeler or sharp paring knife, removing any stalk and also finely chop. Cutting off the bottom of the garlic bulb, squeeze out the now softened cloves, then peel the shallots and chop. Chop the chillies roughly. Remove the seeds with a spoon if you prefer a little less heat. Peel the turmeric. Wash the coriander root and finely slice. Using a pestle and mortar pound the roots to a paste using salt as an abrasive if necessary. Next add the lemongrass and continue to pound until a smooth paste is achieved. Then add the galangal, turmeric, chillies, shallots and garlic in that order. At each stage make sure a fine paste is achieved before adding the next ingredient. Stir in the pounded spices.

To make the curry, blanch the egg noodles in salted water until soft then remove and place to one side to cool and drain. Take a large flat bottomed pan and put on a medium high heat. Add the coconut oil. Once hot, add the curry paste and stir with a flat headed spoon, scraping the base of the pan so the paste does not stick and burn. Do this for about 6–8 minutes then add the fish sauce, curry powder, dark soy sauce and palm sugar. Turn the heat down and allow the palm sugar to melt and caramelise, then stir in the stock and coconut cream and simmer for 8–10 minutes. Add more stock and coconut cream if the curry starts to dry out.

Whilst the curry simmers, take a large pan and fill with enough oil to deep fry some of the noodles. Make sure the oil reaches around 190–200°C but be very careful when deep frying at home. Have a tray spread with kitchen roll or an old tea towel ready and place to one side. Using a large slotted spoon, or pair of tongs, place a small child's handful of cooked noodles into the hot oil. It will spit and splutter so stand back. Allow to fry for 40–50 seconds then turn them over and fry for another 30 seconds or so until golden. Remove from the oil and place on the kitchen towel to drain. They should be crispy and golden. Repeat until you have enough noodles to garnish with.

Place the boiled noodles and butternut squash in the simmering curry and serve piping hot in large deep bowls. Garnish with coriander leaf, a few sliced Thai shallots, torn pickled mustard greens and your deep-fried noodles. Drizzle a little roasted chilli oil. The curry should not be too thick, almost like a soup but with body and have a thin coconut oil slick on top. It should taste smoky, rich, salty and sweet with a spicy edge. Squeeze a wedge of lime to add a sour element.

KEN HOM

Spending as much time as I do around the world, cooking and sourcing new recipes, it is quite poignant for me to choose Action Against Hunger who work with children all across the globe. I am sharing my savoury beef recipe with ChariTable Bookings to remind those more fortunate of Action's good work."

SAVOURY BEEF with asparagus

SERVES 4 | PREPARATION TIME 15 MINUTES | COOKING TIME 30 MINUTES

For the Beef

450g lean beef steak
450g fresh asparagus
3 tbsp groundnut oil
100g onions, thinly sliced
2 tbsp black beans, coarsely chopped
1½ tbsp garlic, finely chopped
2 tsp ginger, finely chopped
3 tbsp home-made or good-quality bought chicken stock or water
1 tbsp Shaoxing rice wine or dry sherry
1 tsp sugar
1½ tsp salt
½ tsp pepper
2 tbsp oyster sauce

For the Marinade

2 tsp light soy sauce
2 tsp Shaoxing rice wine or dry sherry
2 tsp sesame oil
2 tsp cornflour
½ tsp salt
¼ tsp pepper

Put the beef in the freezer for 20 minutes. This will allow the meat to harden slightly for easier cutting. Cut it into thin slices, each 4cm long. Put the beef slices in a bowl and add all of the marinade ingredients. Mix well and let the slices steep in the marinade for 15 minutes. Meanwhile, slice the asparagus on the diagonal into 7.5cm pieces and set aside until needed.

Heat a wok or large frying pan over a high heat until it is very hot. Add the oil and when it is very hot and slightly smoking, add the beef from the marinade and stir-fry for about 2 minutes. Remove the meat and drain it in a colander. Pour off all but approximately 1 tablespoons of the oil and reheat it over a high heat. When it is very hot, add the onions, black beans, garlic and ginger and stir-fry for 1 minute then add the asparagus and stir-fry for 1 minute. Now add the stock or water, rice wine or sherry, sugar, salt and pepper. Continue to stir-fry for 3 minutes or until the asparagus is slightly tender. Add more water as necessary.

Quickly return the meat to the wok, add the oyster sauce and stir well. Turn the mixture onto a warm platter and serve at once.

PHILIP HOWARD

I have supported many charities over the years but none has demonstrated a combination of such a truly worthy cause and such operational accountability and professionalism as Ace Africa. Here is a charity which, as I have witnessed in Kenya, does exactly what is claims on the packet – the promotion of sustainable development to help alleviate poverty in rural African communities."

CAESAR SALAD

SERVES 4 | PREPARATION TIME 30 MINUTES

For the Salad

2 cos lettuce, trimmed of exterior leaves

4 boneless chicken thighs

40g salt

8 tarragon leaves

4 small organic eggs

4 radishes

16 smoked anchovy fillets, halved

4 tbsp coarse breadcrumbs

25g butter

8 tender runner beans

For the Dressing

2 egg yolks

4 good quality anchovy fillets, unsmoked

1 small clove of garlic, minced

1 tspn Dijon mustard

1 lemon, juiced

200ml grapeseed oil

1 dstp Parmesan, grated

To make the salad, dissolve the salt in 400ml cold water and sit the chicken thighs in the resulting brine for 20 minutes. Remove, pat dry, place 2 tarragon leaves in each thigh where the bone was, and roll tightly in cling film – securing each end with string. Poach at 75°C, using a thermometer in a pan of water, for an hour. Remove from the water, transfer to a bowl of ice water and chill. Set aside in the fridge.

To make the dressing, place the egg yolks, Parmesan, anchovy fillets, garlic, Dijon mustard and lemon juice into a blender. Switch on and gradually add the oil in a steady stream. This should result in a rich mayonnaise like emulsion. If it seems very thick add a splash of water – so it will drop off a spoon easily. Transfer to a plastic squeeze bottle if possible. Place the eggs into boiling water for 5.5 minutes. Refresh under running water, peel and chill. Fry the breadcrumbs in the butter until golden, drain onto absorbent paper and season with salt. Blanch the runner beans in salted boiling water until tender, remove, refresh in ice water briefly and cut into 3cm lengths on the diagonal. Finely slice the radishes.

To serve, trim the top off each of the Cos lettuce. Cut 2 3cm slices off each one and place each into a large bowl or plate. Loosen the leaves of each slice so they open out like a flower. Carve the chicken thighs into thin slices and tuck randomly throughout the Cos leaves. Similarly tuck the runner beans throughout the salad. Drizzle each plate generously with dressing – ensuring that the salads are thoroughly, but not over, dressed. Trim the base of each egg, cut the top third off to expose the yolk, season with salt and pepper and place one into the centre of each salad. Finish with the anchovies, radishes and breadcrumbs.

CLIVE HOWE

Dementia is one of the most fast-growing and common diseases in the UK which is why the restaurant team at The Garrick are pleased to be supporting the Alzheimer's Society through ChariTable Bookings' exciting new recipe book."

GARRICK GAME PIE with wild mushrooms

SERVES 4 | PREPARATION TIME 1 HOUR 40 MINUTES | COOKING TIME 2 HOURS

For the Game Pie

300g game, grouse, pheasant, partridge or venison

50g game or chicken liver

50g smoked pancetta, diced

1 shallot, finely chopped

1 small clove of garlic, finely chopped

25ml port

25ml Madeira

1 nutmeg and mace, freshly ground

1 tsp salt and milled pepper

400g butter puff pastry

1 egg yolk, for egg wash

15g parsley, rosemary and thyme, chopped

For the Sauce

100g game bones, chopped

25g bacon trimmings

25g butter

1 shallot, roughly chopped

1 clove of garlic, roughly chopped

2 juniper berries, crushed

1 bay leaf

1 sprig of thyme

50ml red wine

25ml port

400ml game or veal stock

salt and pepper

To Finish

100g wild mushrooms, trimmed

4 sprigs of thyme or rosemary

For the pie filling, place the chopped shallot, garlic, port and Madeira into a saucepan and reduce to a glaze. Allow to cool. Quickly fry the pancetta in a hot pan, then allow to cool. Mix the glaze with the game meat and livers. Preferably mince, or place in a Robot Coupe, and blend to make forcemeat. Mix in the cooled, diced pancetta, herbs, a little nutmeg and mace. Season with salt and milled pepper.

Thinly roll out the puff pastry, cut 8 discs, 10cm in diameter, 4mm thick and allow to rest in a refrigerator for a few minutes. Lay 4 of the discs onto a non-stick baking tray and egg wash the edges. Divide the forcemeat equally between the 4 discs. Place the remaining puff pastry discs over the top, sealing and crimping the edges. Brush with the egg wash and, with a small knife starting in the middle of the pies, score to make a spiralling effect. Allow to rest for 1 hour in a refrigerator. Bake in a preheated oven at 180°C for 20 minutes until golden brown.

To make the sauce, heat a saucepan with half of the butter and brown the game bones, bacon trimmings, shallot and garlic. Add the juniper berries, bay leaf, thyme, red wine and port, and reduce by half. Add the game or veal stock and bring to the boil. Skim off any fat that may have come to the surface and simmer for 30 minutes. Strain and reduce to the required sauce consistency. Season with salt and milled pepper and stir in the remaining butter to give the sauce a shine. Do not re-boil or the butter will separate from the sauce.

Quickly sauté the wild mushrooms and season. Place the pies onto 4 plates and spoon around the wild mushrooms and a little of the sauce.

Make an incision into each pie and push in a sprig of thyme or rosemary and serve.

DAN HOWES

"The originality of this project from ChariTable Bookings has allowed The Gilbert Scott to support the Aldingbourne Trust and to spread the word about this great cause."

GRILLED IBERICO PORK with romesco

SERVES 4 | PREPARATION TIME 30 MINUTES | COOKING TIME 1 HOUR 30 MINUTES

For the Dish
600g Iberico pork secreto

For the Romesco Sauce
100g piquillo peppers
6g garlic
10ml Cabernet Sauvignon vinegar
6g sugar
3g salt
2g smoked paprika
20g roasted almonds
20g roasted hazelnuts
100g crème fraîche, hung overnight
in muslin cloth

For the Fennel
1 bulb of fennel
1 drizzle of olive oil
1 spritz of lemon juice
1 pinch of salt

For the Nduja Onions
200g celeriac, peeled and cut into
thin strips
400g onions, thinly sliced
50g nduja
10g garlic, chopped
5g sage
30ml olive oil
1 bunch of grelot onions

To prepare the romesco sauce, blitz everything except the crème fraîche in a food processor until smooth then fold in the crème fraîche. Check the seasoning.

To prepare the fennel, thinly slice the fennel and dress with some olive oil, lemon juice and salt.

To prepare the nduja onions, lightly salt the celeriac and put to one side. Put the rest of the ingredients in a covered pan and cook on a low heat for around 1 hour, remove the lid and allow some of the moisture to evaporate. Mix the onions with the celeriac and check the seasoning, keep warm.

To prepare the grelot onions, cut the onions in half and pan fry in a little olive oil.

To prepare the pork, season and grill over coal for a few minutes turning often. Allow to rest for a few minutes and slice.

To serve, assemble per the image shown.

RICHARD HOWSON

" I'm supporting the fantastic work of Macmillan through ChariTable Bookings' new initiative of sharing recipes and promoting charity. The team at Annabel's and I hope you enjoy our signature miso cod!"

MISO GLAZED BLACK COD

SERVES 4 | PREPARATION TIME 10 MINUTES (PLUS OVERNIGHT TO MARINATE) | COOKING TIME 20 MINUTES

For the Cod
- 4 x 150g black cod fillets
- 3 tbsp mirin
- 3 tbsp sake
- 170g white miso paste
- 110g sugar

For the Stir Fry
- 2 large pak choi
- ½ each red and yellow pepper
- ½ red chilli
- 1 tbsp light soy sauce
- 1 tsp sesame oil

To Garnish
- coriander leaves

To prepare the marinade, in a small saucepan bring the mirin and sake to a boil. Whisk in the miso paste until dissolved. Add the sugar and cook over moderate heat, whisking until just dissolved. Transfer the marinade to a large baking dish and leave to cool. Add the fish and turn to coat in the marinade. Cover and refrigerate overnight.

To prepare the stir fry, cut the pak choi into quarters and blanch in boiling water for 30 seconds. Cool and dry. Slice the peppers into strips 3–4 mm thick and reserve.

To prepare the cod, preheat the oven to 200°C. Scrape the marinade off the fish. Place the fish onto a heavy rimmed baking sheet and roast for 10 minutes, until flaky. Transfer under a grill and colour.

To finish, while the cod is under the grill, stir fry the pak choi, chilli and peppers over a high heat, adding the soy sauce and sesame oil last. Transfer to a plate and place the black cod on top. Garnish with coriander leaves.

RICHARD HUGHES

6 people a day in the UK are diagnosed with MND but there still isn't a cure. This is why the Lavender House Restaurant supports the Motor Neurone Disease Association in this fantastic ChariTable Bookings collection of recipes for charity."

ROASTED COD with shellfish minestrone

SERVES 4 | PREPARATION TIME 30 MINUTES | COOKING TIME 45 MINUTES

For the Cod
- 4 thick cut cod escalopes, pin boned, skin on
- 1 drizzle of olive oil
- 1 lemon, chopped
- a few sprigs of parsley, chopped

For the Minestrone
- 1 drizzle of olive oil
- 1 small onion, finely chopped
- 1 small leek, finely chopped
- 1 clove of garlic, crushed
- 1 small carrot, finely diced
- 1 dsp olive oil
- 100ml white wine
- 150ml fish stock
- 250g fresh mussels, scrubbed and beards removed
- 125g cockles
- 175ml tomato passata
- salt and pepper
- 50g cooked peeled prawns

For the Tagliatelle
- 4 nests fresh tagliatelle
- 2 tbsp pesto

To Serve
- freshly shaved Parmesan
- extra virgin olive oil
- fresh parsley, chopped

To prepare the dish, marinate the cod fillet in a little olive oil, chopped fresh lemon and chopped parsley for at least 20 minutes. Place the cod fillet in a roasting dish and put in a preheated oven at 190°C for between 6–12 minutes, depending on the thickness of the cod fillet.

For the minestrone, heat the olive oil in a separate pan, add the onion, leek and garlic and cook until softened. Stir in the carrot and wine and bring to the boil, reducing the mixture by half. Add the fish stock and bring to the boil. Throw in the scrubbed, cleaned mussels. Place the lid on and cook until the mussel and cockle shells open, for approximately 3 minutes. Remove the mussel and cockle meat, keep to one side. Add the passata and bring to the boil. Season with salt and pepper. Add the cooked prawns, along with the cockles and the mussels, back to the pan.

Cook the tagliatelle in boiling, salted water, drain and toss in a little pesto dressing.

Ladle the minestrone into a deep bowl. Place the tagliatelle in the centre and top with the cod. If desired, add a little shaved Parmesan, a drizzle of extra virgin olive oil and garnish with chopped parsley.

JAMES HULME

" Quaglino's is wholeheartedly behind ES's Campaign 'Food for London' to help address the imbalance between London's food waste and the poverty line. We hope you enjoy our fantastic duck dish in this great ChariTable Bookings' recipe collection."

ROAST GOOSNARGH DUCK with salsify, pickled cherries and pistachio

SERVES 4 | PREPARATION TIME 40 MINUTES | COOKING TIME 2 HOURS

For the Dish
1 whole corn-fed duck, legs and breast removed

For the Brine
800ml water
80g each of salt and rosemary
50g each of garlic and thyme
8g bay leaves
16g black peppercorns

For the Sauce
200g chopped duck bones
2 shallots
2 cloves of garlic
2 sprigs of thyme
1 bay leaf
150ml white wine
500ml veal stock
500ml chicken stock

For the Pickled Cherries
50g sugar
50ml water
40ml red wine vinegar
1 vanilla pod, seeds scraped
1 bay leaf
10 cherries, pitted

For the Garnish
2 stalks of salsify
toasted pistachios
red chicory leaves

To make the brine, bring all of the ingredients to the boil and allow to cool. Add the duck breasts and legs for 20 minutes, remove and pat dry.

Cover the legs in duck fat in a tray and cover with foil, place in an oven at 140°C for 2 hours or until tender. Shred the meat off of the legs into nice pieces and reserve, you can keep the duck fat for other dishes.

To make the sauce, roast the bones in the oven until golden brown at 140°C. Sweat the vegetables and herbs with the bones, add the wine and reduce to a glaze. Add the stocks and simmer for 20 minutes, then pass through a fine sieve and reduce to a desired consistency.

To prepare the pickled cherries and garnishes, bring everything to the boil and pour over the cherries and leave to cool. Peel and cook the salsify stalks in boiling salted water and cut into small pieces ready to garnish.

To cook the breasts, fry in a pan on the skin-side until crisp, then place in a hot oven at 190°C for 5 minutes. Remove and allow to rest for 5 minutes.

Carve and serve with the salsify, some toasted pistachios, pickled cherries, pieces of the confit duck leg and red chicory leaves, serving the sauce on the side.

KIERAN HUNT

" Sparks is important. It funds medical research into cures for children's diseases. The Wood Norton and ChariTable Bookings understand that every penny counts so please support this hope giving charity."

STONE BASS WITH SEA VEGETABLES AND SCALLOP

SERVES 2 | PREPARATION TIME 15 MINUTES | COOKING TIME 40 MINUTES

For the Bass
2 x 150g stone bass fillets
2 knobs of butter
2 tsp rapeseed oil
2 fresh scallops, with the roe removed
sea salt

For the Purée
1 head of cauliflower
125g unsalted butter
salt

For the Garnish
50g samphire, stalks removed and blanched in boiling water for 30 seconds
olive oil
20g oyster leaf
20g ice lettuce
20g butterfly sorrel
salt and pepper

To make the purée, remove the core of the cauliflower and finely chop the florets. Place in a medium pan with the butter and tightly cling film the top of the pan to ensure it is airtight. Cook on a low heat and regularly shake to prevent the mixture from sticking or burning. When the cauliflower is completely cooked, which should take 15–20 minutes, remove from the heat and leave for 5–10 minutes. Place in a blender and purée, adding salt to taste.

To cook the stone bass and scallops, dry the skin of the stone bass with a j-cloth and score the surface 3 times. Dry the surface of the scallops in the same way. Heat 2 non-stick frying pans to flashpoint, so a small amount of smoke is produced from the surface of the pan. Add a teaspoon of rapeseed oil to each pan. Place the stone bass skin-side down in one pan and lightly press to ensure it remains flat. Cook for 3 minutes. Lightly season the white flesh of the stone bass and turn the fish over. The skin should be crispy but not burnt. Add a knob of butter, this will foam up quickly. Gently spoon the butter over the fish. Cook like this for a further 2 minutes. Remove the pan from the heat and allow to rest in the pan for a further minute. Rest the fish on a clean j-cloth and allow the fat to drain. Place the scallop in the other pan with the largest, flattest side first and leave to colour for 1 minute. Add a pinch of salt to the underside of each scallop and cook for a further 30 seconds. Turn over each scallop. Add a knob of butter and remove from the heat. Leave in the pan to allow the residual heat of the pan to finish cooking for a further minute.

To serve, lightly dress the sea vegetables in olive oil and plate with the fish and purée. Additional garnishes could be: asparagus, spinach, salty finger, spring greens or Romanesco, depending on your taste. Season and serve.

TOM HUNTER

"Surfers Against Sewage champions our coast and seas to keep them clean for generations to enjoy. All of us at The Scarlet endorse them by submitting our recipe in this amazing ChariTable Bookings collection."

OX CHEEK RAGU with saffron pasta, mushrooms and Parmesan

SERVES 4 | PREPARATION TIME 20 MINUTES | COOKING TIME 3 HOURS

For the Dish

3 ox cheeks, trimmed, sinew removed
1 white onion, finely diced
1 leek, finely sliced and washed
2 sticks of celery, peeled and finely diced
1 large carrot, peeled and finely diced
2 large cloves of garlic
1 bottle of good red wine
2 tins of chopped tomatoes
250ml good quality chicken stock
2 tbsp extra virgin olive oil
400g fresh saffron pappardelle, shop bought or good quality dried pasta is fine
150g wild mushrooms, such as chanterelles, wood blewits or ceps
butter
lemon, to taste
salt and pepper, to taste
Parmesan cheese, for grating

First, sear the ox cheeks in a very hot pan until well coloured and caramelised all over. In a saucepan big enough to hold all the ingredients, sweat the onion, leek, celery, carrot and garlic over a medium heat until well softened, which should take about 10 minutes. Add the wine and let it bubble away and reduce by half. Add the chopped tomatoes and chicken stock. Stir, bring to the boil and season. Reduce the heat to a very low simmer, then place the ox cheeks in the pan. The liquid should cover the cheeks.

Cook very gently for about 3 hours, until the cheeks are extremely tender and are almost providing no resistance. This cooking time will depend entirely on the cheeks themselves: it may take less time, and it may take more. Be patient and do not rush it. The mixture should now be much thicker and richer. Using a spoon, begin to break down the ox cheek in the pan into bite sized chunks or pieces. It really won't matter if it breaks down more. Taste and adjust the seasoning. At this stage, add a couple of tablespoons of extra virgin olive oil and stir it in. This will add some more richness to the ragu. Turn off the heat and set aside.

Cook the pasta in a large pan of salted water. While you're cooking the pasta, sauté your chosen mushrooms in a little oil and butter. Season with salt, pepper and a squeeze of lemon juice.

Now bring the dish together. We like to mix the ragu with the pasta in a pan. Be careful not to break up the pieces of pasta as you do this. It is worth having another taste at this stage to check the seasoning and adjust if needed.

To serve, divide out into bowls. Add a generous helping of mushrooms on top of each, and grate over fresh Parmesan. Enjoy.

WALTER ISHIZUKA

Hospitality Action is clearly a charity that sits closely with restaurateurs and hoteliers alike. Brasserie Joel is just as protective over our industry workers and are thrilled that we can support them through ChariTable Bookings' new recipe book."

HONEY AND SOY SAUCE GLAZED BLACK COD with verbena pea purée
and cider vinegar roasted peaches

SERVES 4 | PREPARATION TIME 20 MINUTES | COOKING TIME 40 MINUTES

For the Cod
4 x 160g black cod fillets, descaled and deboned
1 tsp olive oil
1 clove of garlic
1 sprig of thyme

For the Peaches
4 peaches
50g unsalted butter
50ml cider vinegar

For the Verbena Pea Purée
1kg fresh peas, blanched
200ml double cream
1 shallot, diced
25g unsalted butter
5 verbena leaves
salt and pepper, to taste

For the Honey and Soy Sauce Glaze
50g honey
200ml soy sauce
1 tbsp five spice

For the Garnish
1 lime, zested
peashoots

To make the honey and soy sauce glaze, put the honey and the five spice in a small saucepan to reduce and caramelise . Add the soy sauce and cook on a low heat until it forms a thick syrup. Place to one side and keep warm.

To make the verbena pea purée, in a small saucepan, cook the shallot with the butter until golden and translucent. Add the blanched peas, the double cream and the verbena leaves. Heat the mixture until it breaks down and forms a mash. Blend well until a purée is formed. Season to taste with salt and pepper.

For the peaches, begin by halving them and removing the seeds. Sauté the halves in butter. Once they have a roasted colour, deglaze the pan with cider vinegar and allow the peaches to poach for a minute or so.

To prepare the black cod, pan fry the fillets for 1 minute, skin-side down in olive oil. Add the garlic and thyme towards the end of cooking. Finally, pour over the glaze and place the fish in the oven at 160°C for a further 2 minutes. Make sure to baste often to give the fish a good coating and shine.

To serve, spread the verbena pea purée on the bottom of the plate and top with the glazed black cod fillet in the centre. Surround with roasted peach halves and finish with generous amounts of glaze, some peashoot tendrils and grated lime zest.

MARK JARVIS

Cancer is a terrifying disease that sadly many of us will experience. Macmillan provides the care and support that can ease that experience. Anglo is very happy to share our recipe with ChariTable Bookings to remind foodies of their amazing work."

WHOLE PLAICE with carrot purée and baby carrots
SERVES 2 | PREPARATION TIME 20 MINUTES | COOKING TIME 1 HOUR

For the Dish
1 whole plaice

For the Carrot Purée
500g large carrots
500g carrot juice
1 knob of butter
1 pinch of salt
1 pinch of sugar

For the Verbena Butter
1 bunch verbena leaves
1 knob of butter

For the Garnish
2 bunches of baby carrots
10 sea beet leaves – similar to sorrel but with a more woody flavour, large spinach can be used as substitute
1 packet of dried seaweed, optional

To prepare the plaice, begin by removing the plaice fillets from the bone and remove the skin.

To prepare the purée, slice the large carrots into 3mm slices and sweat them in a pan with a small knob of butter. Season with salt and sugar. When completely soft, add the carrot juice and reduce the mixture by half. Blend to a smooth purée.

To prepare the baby carrots, peel and wash. Add the baby carrots to the pan with a knob of butter, some verbena leaves, water and salt. Bring to the boil and cook until soft, yet still holding their shape.

To serve, begin by lightly seasoning the plaice fillets. Bake them in the oven at 150–170°C for around 8–10 minutes or until just cooked and still juicy. Warm the baby carrots in the verbena butter and the sea beet are cooked until soft. Warm the carrot purée and season to taste. Plate up, serve and enjoy.

ANDREW JONES

Chamberlain's is proud to support the work of the Royal British Legion by donating our signature dish to ChariTable Bookings recipe book and raise money for all our service men and women both serving and veterans."

TEA SMOKED MACKEREL with apple and crispy shallots

SERVES 4 | PREPARATION TIME 45 MINUTES (PLUS OVERNIGHT TO MARINATE) | COOKING TIME 45 MINUTES

For the Mackerel

4 fillets fresh mackerel, pin boned

2 tsp dark soy sauce

1 tsp runny honey

2 Darjeeling tea bags

salt

freshly ground black pepper

40ml sunflower oil

½ lemon, juiced

For the Apple Purée

1 Bramley apple, peeled and diced

2 tsp caster sugar

1 clove

2 tsp water

For the Apple Salad

100g green apple, finely diced

30g celery, peeled and finely diced

20g candied stem ginger, finely diced

10g chives, chopped

2 tsp stem ginger syrup

For the Crispy Shallots

1 shallot, finely sliced

1l vegetable oil

For the Garnish

micro cress or small salad leaves

spring onions, shredded

To prepare the fish, mix the soy sauce and honey together. Coat the mackerel with the mixture and leave overnight to marinate.

The next day, remove the fish from the marinade and pat dry with kitchen paper. Place on greaseproof paper, skin-side up, in a steamer basket. Put the loose tea leaves in the base of a dry pan and put the steamer basket on top. Put on a high heat until the tea begins to produce smoke, which visibly escapes. Remove from the heat and allow to stand for 15 minutes. Transfer the mackerel to a lightly oiled grill tray, skin-side up.

For the apple purée, place all the ingredients in a pan and cook on a medium heat until soft enough to blitz with a liquidiser or hand blender until smooth. Allow to cool and adjust the consistency with a little more water if too stiff.

To assemble the salad, mix the diced green apple, celery, chives, ginger and ginger syrup together. Season with salt and pepper to taste.

To make the crispy shallots, heat the oil in a pan to 150°C, add the sliced shallots and cook until golden and crisp. Remove with a slotted spoon and drain on some kitchen paper to remove any excess oil.

To finish and serve, mix the sunflower oil with the lemon juice and season to taste. Place the mackerel under a hot grill until the skin is crisp, slightly charred and cooked through. Put a spoonful of the purée on each plate and sit the mackerel on top. Spoon the apple salad down the back of the fish and add a little lemon dressing. Dress with the crispy shallots and salad leaves over the diced salad and serve.

MARK JORDAN

" The team at The Atlantic are all fully behind Scotty's Little Soldiers and pleased to be part of this recipe book by ChariTable Bookings, supporting charities throughout the UK."

TRANCHE OF JERSEY TURBOT with crispy potato scales and mussel cream

SERVES 1 | PREPARATION TIME 20 MINUTES | COOKING TIME 45 MINUTES

Equipment
mandoline

For the Turbot
1 large King Edward potato
200g clarified butter, hot
1 turbot fillet, trimmed to 140g
1 dash of vegetable oil
1 knob of butter

For the Leek Julienne
1 leek
100ml double cream
½ lemon, juiced
1 pinch of salt

For the Mussel Cream
250g large mussels
1 shallot, sliced
1 stick celery, sliced
1 clove of garlic, sliced
2 sprigs of thyme
150ml white wine
300ml double cream
1 spritz of lemon juice

For the Garnish
2 spears of asparagus, buttered
fresh English pea shoots

Peel and wash the potato and trim down the height to about 2.5cm thick. Using a small cutter the size of a one penny piece, cut out 4 cylinders from the potato. Slice thinly on a mandoline and place into hot clarified butter. Keep warm.

To make the leek julienne, using the white part from the leek, cut lengthways in half. Peel the layers from the leek and slice thinly into 1mm strips. Blanch in boiling, salted water for 1 minute to soften. Strain and place into a saucepan along with the double cream and reduce by two thirds. Finish with a squeeze of lemon and adjust the seasoning.

To make the mussel cream, wash the mussels and remove their beards. Brown the vegetables and herbs in a hot pan. Add the mussels and white wine and cook off the alcohol. Cover with a lid, shaking from time to time until the shells begin to open. Strain off the mussels, reserving the cooking liquor. Reduce the liquor down by two thirds, add the cream and lemon juice, then season to taste. Remove the mussels from their shells, place into the mussel velouté and keep warm.

To cook the turbot, remove the potatoes from the butter and arrange one by one, each slightly overlapping on the turbot, so you end up with a set of fish scales. Place into the fridge and chill for 10 minutes. Cut out a piece of baking paper to fit the turbot and place on top of the potato scales. Preheat a non-stick pan with a dash of vegetable oil. Place the turbot in the pan, potato-side down, and cook on a medium heat for 4–5 minutes. The trick here is to cook the turbot slowly so that you have a nice even, golden brown crisp exterior on the potatoes.

Add a knob of butter and remove from the heat. Using a fish slice, carefully flip over the turbot and baste. Leave to rest on the flesh side in the butter for 2 minutes.

To serve, place a spoon of the leek julienne in the centre of a bowl, and spoon the mussels around, along with some of the sauce. Place the turbot on top and garnish with a couple of spears of buttered asparagus and some fresh pea shoots.

PETER JOSEPH

"The team at Tamarind are proud to champion Born Free through ChariTable Bookings."

MALABAR PRAWN CURRY

SERVES 4 | PREPARATION TIME 20 MINUTES | COOKING TIME 45 MINUTES

For the Curry

12 prawns, peeled and deveined

3 tbsp coconut oil

¼ tsp fenugreek seeds

1 tbsp ginger, julienned

1 tbsp garlic, finely sliced

1 tbsp green chillies, julienned

20 curry leaves, sliced into strips, a
few extra to serve

50g shallots, sliced

½ tsp turmeric

½ tsp ground coriander

1 tsp degi mirch

200g tinned plum tomatoes

1 plum tomato, finely sliced

55g coconut powder

60ml water, plus extra if required

3 tbsp coconut milk

salt, to taste

To make the curry, heat the coconut oil in a wide, deep pan and add the fenugreek seeds, ginger, garlic, chilli and curry leaves. Sauté well over a medium heat, stirring regularly to ensure nothing catches on the pan. Add the shallots to the pan and cook for a further 10 minutes, then stir in the turmeric, coriander and degi mirch powders. Cook for 2–3 minutes.

Blitz the tinned tomatoes to form a purée and add this to the pan along with the fresh tomato slices. Mix well to combine, then allow the curry mixture to simmer until boiling. In a small dish, mix together the coconut powder and water to form a watery paste, adding more water if required. Gradually add this paste to the pan until fully incorporated, then reduce the heat a little and simmer for 5–10 minutes.

Once the sauce has a smooth and velvety texture, add the prawns to the pan, along with a little extra water to loosen the consistency if required. Place a lid on the pan and leave to cook for a further 2–3 minutes. Once the prawns are cooked through, stir in the coconut milk and bring the curry up to the boil. Boil for 1 minute, then remove from the heat and adjust the seasoning to taste.

To serve, divide the prawns between serving dishes and spoon any leftover sauce over the top. Garnish with curry leaves and serve immediately with steamed rice.

ADAM KÄLLMAN

"Delighted to share Smaka's signature cod dish in aid of Best Beginnings, a fantastic charity that focuses on giving children the best start in life from conception to adolescence. Love this concept by ChariTable Bookings of chefs sharing their recipes for charity."

PAN-FRIED COD with pickled swede, cauliflower purée, golden beetroot crudité and smoked butter sauce

SERVES 4 | PREPARATION TIME 1 HOUR | COOKING TIME 45 MINUTES

For the Dish

- 600g cod fillet, pin boned
- 15ml sunflower oil
- 15g butter
- 1 pinch of salt
- 800g new potatoes, cooked
- 4 dill sprigs

For the Pickled Swede

- ⅓ swede, cubed
- 20ml sugar
- 20ml water
- 20ml acetic vinegar

For the Golden Beetroot Crudité

- 1 golden beetroot
- 5ml lemon juice
- 5ml olive oil
- 5g shallots, finely chopped
- 5g chives, finely chopped
- 1 pinch of salt

For the cauliflower purée

- ½ head of cauliflower
- 13g butter
- 13ml double cream
- ¼ lemon, zest of
- 4ml lemon juice
- 4ml crème fraîche
- ¼ tsp salt
- 1 pinch of ground white pepper

For the smoked butter sauce:

- 135g butter
- 10g wood chips
- 20ml white wine vinegar
- 20ml white wine
- ¼ lemon
- 1 pinch of salt
- 1 juniper berry
- 1 tbsp water
- 30g flour

To make the pickled swede, peel the swede and cut into half centimetre cubes. Bring the sugar, water and acetic vinegar to the boil, then simmer until the sugar dissolves. Remove from the heat, add the swede cubes to the hot liquid and leave until totally cool.

To make the golden beetroot crudité, wash the beetroot in cold water and cut into 0.2cm thick slices. Place the slices in a bowl and cure with lemon juice for 1 minute. Incorporate the olive oil, shallots, chives and salt. Leave to marinate for 30 minutes.

To make the cauliflower purée, cut the cauliflower in even pieces. Place them in a saucepan and cover with cold water. Bring to the boil, reduce to a simmer and cook until soft. Drain in a colander and leave them to air-dry for 3 minutes. Transfer the cauliflower to a blender with everything except seasoning. Blend to a very fine purée, then season to taste.

To make the smoked butter sauce, cut the butter in small pieces and place in a small bowl. Place the wood chips in a pan big enough to hold the bowl. Cover the pan with tinfoil and place on a hot hob. When smoke comes out, remove the tinfoil, place the bowl with butter on the wood chips, then cover with the tinfoil again. Leave on the heat for 2 minutes, remove from the heat and cool. Cook the vinegar in a saucepan until reduced to a third. Add wine and continue to cook until reduced by half. Add everything, except the flour, to the simmering liquid and blitz with a stick blender. Finally, put the flour in and blend again until creamy. Strain through a chinois.

To cook the pan-fried cod, season the fish with salt and rest for 30 minutes. Preheat the oven to 100°C. Cut the fillet in 4 even pieces. Heat a little oil with a pinch of salt in a non-stick frying pan. Put the fillets in, skin-side down. Cook until the skin is golden, then add a knob of butter. Baste the fillets for 1 minute. Turn the fish and baste for another minute. Finish the fish in the oven for a further minute.

To serve, gently heat the butter sauce and cauliflower purée. Using a spoon, add some cauliflower purée to the middle of each plate. Carefully place the fish on top of the purée, using a spatula. Spoon over some of the sauce. Add a teaspoon of pickled swede and slices of golden beetroot on each side of the fish. Garnish with dill sprigs and serve with the potatoes and more sauce in a sauce boat on the side.

PAVEL KANJA

Guide Dogs for the blind provide invaluable mobility and freedom for those of us not lucky enough to have the gift of sight. The team at Flat Three are donating our signature sea bass dish to ChariTable Bookings in the hope of raising more awareness for this great charity."

SEA BASS with fermented cauliflower

SERVES 2 | PREPARATION TIME 45 MINUTES (PLUS 2 WEEKS FOR KIMCHEE) | COOKING TIME 1 HOUR 30 MINUTES

For the Sea Bass
1 large sea bass
10g sea salt

For the Cauliflower Kimchee
500g cauliflower leaves, inner leaves only
1l water
25g salt
40g fresh ginger, chopped
40g fresh garlic, chopped
1 sterilised jar with lid

For the Cauliflower Kimchee Liquor
bones from the bass, excluding the head and pinbones
1l cauliflower kimchee liquid
1 small piece kombu

To Serve
5g parsley, finely chopped
pickled cauliflower leaves

To prepare the cauliflower kimchee, wash and finely chop the leaves and place them in the sterilised jar. Add the water, salt, ginger and garlic and store the mixture at room temperature for 2 weeks. Allow the mixture to become pungent and sour. Strain the contents and keep the leaves for a stir fry or eat them with this dish as they are. Set the liquid aside and begin to prepare the fish.

Once your kimchee liquor is ready, begin preparing the sea bass. Remove the scales, gut and head of the fish and fillet it. Retain the bones for the fermented cauliflower liquor. Lightly season both fillets with the sea salt and wrap loosely in cling film for 10 minutes. After this time has passed, wash the salt off with cold running water and pat the fillets dry with a clean tea towel. With small fish tweezers, remove the small pin bones from both fillets, commonly around 5–6. Place the fillets to one side.

To make the cauliflower kimchee liquor, wash the bones of the bass and place them into a medium size saucepan, pouring over the cauliflower kimchee liquor and kombu. Heat the ingredients to 60°C, making sure to keep this temperature as constant as possible for around 1 hour. It's okay if it goes a little higher but be sure it doesn't go lower as you won't end up with such a flavourful stock. After 1 hour, strain and set aside.

To cook the sea bass, bring 500ml of cauliflower kimchee liquor back up to 60°C and poach the bass for 15 minutes. Carefully remove from the stock and place on the plate. Heat 300ml stock to 80°C and pour over the dish.

To serve, garnish with a little parsley and a few cauliflower leaves from the kimchee process if desired.

JUDE KAREAMA

It's really important for Kota to support the people that work in our industry and that is why I have chosen to support Hospitality Action in ChariTable Bookings' new recipe collection. I hope you enjoy the dish!"

NORI WRAPPED CORNISH HAKE with mussels, cockles, seaweed, crispy rock shrimp, crab ravioli and dashi

SERVES 4 | PREPARATION TIME 2 HOURS (PLUS OVERNIGHT TO SOAK) | COOKING TIME 30 MINUTES

Equipment
- sous vide
- Robot Coupe
- two tiered steamer

For the Dashi Stock
- 10cm square of kombu
- 2l spring water
- 75g bonito flakes
- 100ml sake
- 2 yuzu fruit, juiced
- 100ml white shoyu – Japanese white soy sauce

For the Crab Ravioli
- 1 whole large free range egg
- 14g squid ink
- ½ tsp salt
- 125g pasta flour
- 75g lemon sole fillet
- 150ml double cream
- 1 pinch of white pepper
- 50g picked white crab meat
- 25g brown crab meat

For the Seafood
- 4 fillets of hake, roughly 8x4cm
- 4 sheets of nori
- 20 mussels, washed and de-bearded
- 20 cockles, purged in water

For the Garnish
- 50g Cornish dried seagreens
- 50g Cornish dried red dulse
- 50g Wakame dried seaweed
- 4 shiitake mushrooms, sliced and warming in the dashi stock
- 1 tin wasabi caviar
- 20 small florets of Romanesco, steamed
- 60g rock shrimp, deep fried to crisp
- 80g samphire gently steamed
- a few leaves of crispy deep fried kale

To prepare the Dashi stock, soak the kombu in the spring water overnight and leave at room temperature. The next day, heat the water and kombu to 60°C. Hold the temperature for 1 hour, then remove the kombu. Increase the temperature to 80°C, add the bonito flakes and soak till the bonito sinks to the bottom, this will only take up to 30 seconds. Pass through a muslin cloth, then add the sake and season with the white soy sauce and yuzu juice. If you need additional seasoning, add salt to taste. Leave warm on the side.

To prepare the ravioli, mix the egg, squid ink, and salt in a Robot Coupe to combine. Add the flour and mix until it resembles a breadcrumb texture. Transfer the dough to a floured work top and knead until smooth, approximately 8 minutes. Cover with cling film and rest in a fridge for at least 30 minutes.

To prepare the filling, first chill the Robot Coupe bowl in a fridge, remove and add the lemon sole and salt, then blend quickly until smooth. Drizzle in the cream until it's all incorporated, then pass through a sieve. Season with the pepper, fold in the white and brown crab meat, place in a piping bag and chill. Roll out the pasta dough in a pasta machine, folding over and putting it back through while bringing the thickness setting down to number 2. Cut the pasta sheet in half, then on one side pipe 4 mounds of fish mousse on to it, leaving room between each mound. Brush the other side of the pasta sheet with water and place on top of the other sheet. Seal all around the mousse mounds, pushing out any excess air. Cut out with a round cutter. Cook the ravioli in a pot of salted simmering water until they float, refresh in ice water and then wait to reheat when needed.

To prepare the hake, place a piece of fish on each nori sheet. Cut off any excess length and width of nori, leaving enough to completely roll the hake into cylindrical shapes with a bamboo sheet. Seal with a brush of water on the edges. Heat up a two tiered steamer to a simmer. Keep the hake in the fridge until needed.

To serve, have the dashi stock warming but not boiling on the side and add the cockles and mussels. In a steamer, place the hake fillets wrapped in nori. The hake will take about 8 minutes. Warm the ravioli in a pan of salted water. Sprinkle a little of each kind of seaweed at the bottom of 4 large bowls, then place the ravioli on top. Place the mussels and cockles around the bowls and add the hot stock. The hot stock will rehydrate the seaweeds so do put a little extra. Spoon some shiitakes around each plate. Slice each hake fillet into 3 and place around the bowls. Dot each piece of hake with wasabi caviar and then arrange the Romanesque cauliflower around the bowl. Garnish with deep fried rock shrimp, samphire and crispy kale leaves.

JONAS KARLSSON

Comic Relief was originally started to tackle famine in Ethiopia so it's fitting that I choose them when giving 100 Wardour Street's duck dish to this great ChariTable Bookings fundraising book."

ROASTED DUCK BREAST with savoy cabbage and parsnip

SERVES 4 | PREPARATION TIME 20 MINUTES | COOKING TIME 30 MINUTES

For the Duck

4 duck breasts
fine sea salt
freshly ground black pepper

For the Parsnip Purée

275g parsnips, cut into thin slices
125ml full-fat milk
125g whipping cream
½ vanilla pod, seeds and pod
fine sea salt, to taste

For the Red Wine Glazed Shallots

2 large banana shallots, peeled
fine sea salt and freshly ground
pepper, to taste
10ml blended oil
2 sprigs of thyme
250ml red wine
1 tbsp honey
10g unsalted butter

For the Savoy Cabbage

1 savoy cabbage, thinly sliced
2 tbsp unsalted butter
salt and pepper

For the Duck Jus

200g sliced shallots
½ tsp pink peppercorns
300ml medium bodied red wine
500ml demi-glace
salt and pepper
25g unsalted butter, diced

Season the duck with fine sea salt and freshly ground black pepper. Place in a frying pan, skin-side down. Cook slowly over a medium heat for about 8–10 minutes or until the skin goes golden brown and crisp. Turn over and cook for another 30 seconds to 1 minute. Baste the breasts with the roasting juices a few times, then allow to rest for 8 minutes.

Bring the parsnips, milk, cream, vanilla and a pinch of salt to boil. Reduce the heat and cover with a lid, leave to simmer 12–15 minutes. Remove the lid and leave to reduce the liquid to half. Remove from the heat, discard the vanilla pod and purée the parsnips in a liquidiser. Check seasoning and set aside.

Cut the shallots in half lengthwise and season with salt and pepper. Heat the oil in an ovenproof pan, add the shallots with the cut side hitting the pan. Fry gently until golden brown then add the thyme, red wine, honey and butter. Bring to boil then simmer for 4–5 minutes. Cover with a lid then transfer into a preheated oven at 180°C. Bake for a further 10–15 minutes or until tender. Every now and then remove the lid and baste with the reduction.

Place the cabbage in a large pan of salted, boiling water and cook for 1 minute. Drain, then put into a pan with melted butter. Check seasoning and keep warm.

For the duck jus, brown the shallots and let them caramelise with pink peppercorns for a few minutes. Deglaze with the wine, leave to reduce until syrupy. Add the demi-glace, leave to simmer to your desired consistency. Check seasoning. Whisk in the unsalted butter, one cube at a time.

To serve, use the picture as a guide.

HANAN KATTAN

Tabun Kitchen has selected to support the Galilee Foundation, supporting the Palestinian minority in Israel, through ChariTable Bookings to help young people make the most of their academic opportunities."

LAMB THREE WAYS

SERVES 2 | PREPARATION TIME 30 MINUTES | COOKING TIME 30 MINUTES

For the Lamb Fillet

300g lamb fillet, sliced or cubed

1 lemon, juiced

20ml olive oil

1 tsp paprika

salt and pepper

For the Kofta Skewers

500g minced lamb

70g onion

150g tahini

50g chillies

100g parsley

5g salt

5g pepper

10g cinnamon

10g paprika

10g allspice

For the Kofta Balls

½ kofta mix, previously made

50g green chilli, finely chopped

45g parsley, finely chopped

100g tahini

15g pomegranate molasses

Marinate the lamb fillet slices or cubes in the oil, lemon, salt, pepper and paprika, and keep aside.

Mix all the kofta ingredients together. You can prepare this ahead of time and keep in the fridge for the flavours to absorb.

Divide the kofta mixture in half. One half can be formed around the skewers ready to grill.

To the other half of the kofta mix, add the chopped green chilli, parsley, tahini and pomegranate molasses. Form the mixture into 1.5cm round balls, and place them on a foil-covered tray. Place both the skewers and tahini balls under a very hot grill for 6–8 minutes, turning halfway through cooking.

To serve, pan fry the lamb for 2 minutes on each side, and plate as pictured.

SEAN KELLY

" Trees for Life is an award-winning charity working to restore Scotland's ancient Caledonian Forest. On behalf of The Lovat Hotel, I'm delighted to donate our Aberfeldy Wood Pigeon recipe to ChariTable Bookings' new book and raise awareness of this great charity."

ABERFELDY WOOD PIGEON with salt-baked celeriac and liquorice

SERVES 4 | PREPARATION TIME 40 MINUTES | COOKING TIME 2 HOURS

For the Pigeon
4 wood pigeons
80g sausage meat
1 knob of butter
1 clove of garlic, chopped
1 sprig of thyme
salt and pepper

For the Celeriac
1 whole celeriac
1 stick of liquorice
500g plain flour
200g coarse salt
450ml water
double cream, to cover
25g unsalted butter

For the Sauce
800ml brown chicken stock
bones from the pigeon
1 stick liquorice
cornflour, if required

To Finish
4 baby turnips with the tops
12 small chanterelles
100g unsalted butter
100ml water

To prepare the pigeon, remove the breasts and legs and remove the thigh bone from 4 of the legs. Chop the remaining legs and carcass into pieces and roast for 15 minutes at 180°C. Place 2 breasts on top of each other in opposite directions, roll very tightly in cling film to form a sausage shape and tie at both ends. Place around 20g of sausage meat into the space where the thigh bone was and wrap the whole leg in cling film tightly and tie at both ends. Simmer the legs in boiling water for 2 hours and the breasts for 12 minutes. Keep warm and remove the cling film when required.

For the salt pastry crust, chop the liquorice into small pieces, add the flour, salt and water and mix to form a soft dough.

Wrap the celeriac in the dough and cook at 180°C for 1 hour and 15 minutes. Allow to cool slightly, then remove from the crust. Cut the skin from the celeriac and cut into 6mm slices. Cut out 8 discs in varying sizes. Chop the remainder into small pieces and place in a saucepan with just enough cream to cover. Add in the butter, simmer for 10 minutes, then liquidise to create a soft purée.

To make the sauce, reduce the stock by three quarters then add the pigeon bones and chopped liquorice. Simmer for 10 minutes and then strain. If the sauce is not thick enough, either continue to reduce or thicken with a little cornflour. Season to taste with salt and pepper.

To finish, unwrap the legs and glaze in the pigeon sauce. Unwrap the breasts, season with salt and pepper and fry in a little butter with garlic and thyme until browned.

Boil the butter and water to create an emulsion. Cook the baby turnips and chanterelles in the emulsion, add the celeriac discs to heat through and serve all ingredients as in the picture.

Serve the sauce in a separate sauce jug and pour at the table.

DAVID KELMAN

I am proud to support Ty Hafan who offer comfort, care and support to life-limited children, young people and their families, so they can make the most of the time they have left together. What a great idea from ChariTable Bookings to raise money for charity. I hope you enjoy this classic dish from The Old Swan and Minster Mill."

PAN-FRIED DUCK BREAST with fondant potato, chicory and baby vegetables

SERVES 2 | PREPARATION TIME 15 MINUTES | COOKING TIME 25 MINUTES

For the Dish

- 4 large Maris Piper potatoes
- 2 cloves of garlic
- 2 sprigs of thyme
- 2 duck breast
- 150g butter
- 8 small leaves of chicory, blanched until soft
- 4 baby carrots, peeled and cooked
- 4 baby leeks, cooked
- 40g wild mushrooms, cleaned then pan-fried
- 2 tender stem broccoli, trimmed and blanched

To prepare the dish, peel and slice the potatoes, then cut into discs with a pastry cutter. Warm the butter in a heavy-bottomed pan and add the potato with the garlic and thyme. Cook until coloured on one side, then turn them over and colour the other side. Place into a medium oven at 160°C until cooked through, which should take roughly 10–15 minutes.

To cook the duck, trim the fat around the breast and season. In a hot pan, add a little oil and place the duck breast into the pan skin-side down. Colour the skin for about 1 minute, then turn the duck over and cook for 3–5 minutes. Turn the duck back onto the skin-side and place into a high temperature oven at 190°C for 4 minutes. Remove and leave the meat to one side to rest.

To serve, toss the chicory in the same pan used for the duck breast, then add the vegetables to warm through. Slice the duck into 4 pieces and place onto a cloth to dry any excess moisture. Arrange the duck and vegetables onto the plate and finish with a little of the duck's cooking liquor.

LOUIS KENJI HUANG

"The team at Oliver Maki know how important it is to think of others and are supporting the Cancer Fund For Children through this ChariTable Bookings' fundraising activity."

FOREST HAZE SALAD

SERVES 2 | PREPARATION TIME 10 MINUTES | COOKING TIME 20 MINUTES

For the Salad

170g quinoa

250ml vegetable stock

1 handful of assorted wild mushrooms

4 cherry tomatoes

1 carrot

salad leaves

1 handful of basil leaves

For the Dressing

1 small onion

1 small carrot

1 stick of celery

1 apple, chopped

1 dash of soy sauce

1 dash of olive oil

1 dash of vinegar

truffle oil or salt (optional)

For the Garnish

dried cranberries

pine nuts, lightly fried

truffle oil

fresh coriander

Wash the quinoa thoroughly, then place in a pot with 250ml of either water, broth or vegetable stock. Bring to the boil, then lower the heat. Taste and add salt or vegetable stock to season if necessary. Simmer for about 15 minutes or until the quinoa is cooked and fluffy.

Meanwhile, wash and clean the vegetables, chop them and keep to one side.

Place the quinoa in a bowl once cooled. Add the mushrooms, tomatoes and some greens.

For the dressing, blend the onion, carrot, celery and apple, then add a dash of soy sauce, olive oil, vinegar until it thickens. Add the optional truffle oil or truffle salt if desired.

Finally, garnish with pine nuts, dried cranberries, coriander, and truffle oil.

DANIEL KENT

"Wilton's and its sister restaurant Franco's have been great supporters of ChariTable Bookings from its inception and we are pleased to continue to support them and Cancer Research in this fantastic new book."

WILTONS' ROAST GROUSE

SERVES 1 | PREPARATION TIME 30 MINUTES | COOKING TIME 1 HOUR

For the Grouse
1 grouse
20ml sunflower oil
50g diced celeriac, carrot and shallots
1 sprig of fresh thyme
1 dstp brandy

For the Gravy
200g grouse trimmings
1 streaky bacon rasher
1 banana shallot, roughly diced
1 bulb of garlic, peeled and sliced
1 sprig of thyme
1 bay leaf
5 white peppercorns
salt, to taste
5 juniper berries
1 tsp sherry vinegar
1 tbsp port
1 tbsp red wine
500ml veal stock
500ml chicken stock

For the Garnish
2 streaky bacon slices

To make the roast gravy, colour off the grouse trimmings and bacon in a saucepan. Add the shallot, garlic, herbs and spices. Cook this on a medium heat for 5 minutes. Now add the sherry vinegar and let it reduce down to syrup. Keep stirring this to release any tasty morsels left on the pan. When it has become a syrup, add the port and reduce to a glaze. Add the red wine and reduce again to a thick syrup. Add the stocks and bring to the boil. Simmer, skim and cook out for about 40 minutes. Strain and place in the fridge until needed.

To cook the grouse, heat the oil in a heavy-duty pan that will just contain the grouse. Lay the bird on one side of its breast and begin searing it. Turn it over on to the other side. Add the mirepoix and thyme. Turn it onto its back and continue to fry. Hold up the grouse and sear the plump ends of the breast. Pour the brandy into the pan. Transfer the pan with the grouse to a preheated oven at 200°C. Allow 8 minutes for medium rare and 12 minutes for medium. Rest the grouse at least 10 minutes before carving it.

To plate, carve the grouse and cover generously with reheated gravy, serving with all the trimmings.

LAWRENCE KEOGH

"I'm supporting the important work being carried out by Kidney Research UK through this great initiative from ChariTable Bookings."

RISOTTO NERO with saffron chilli squid

SERVES 4 | PREPARATION TIME 20 MINUTES | COOKING TIME 45 MINUTES

For the Risotto
700ml chicken stock
8ml squid ink, from a sachet is fine
20g butter
2 shallots, finely chopped
½ leek, finely chopped
250g arborio rice
50ml white wine
1 tsp saffron
30g Parmesan
salt and pepper

For the Squid
2 whole squid
100ml extra virgin olive oil
1 whole red chilli, finely chopped
5g garlic, chopped
1 whole lemon, juiced and zested
10g parsley, chopped

For the Garnish
1 punnet of green basil cress or
coriander cress

For the risotto, place the chicken stock into a pan and bring to a gentle simmer and add ink so that it infuses. Meanwhile, heat another pan until hot and add the butter. Once the butter has melted, add the shallots and leek and cook for a few minutes until softened, but not coloured. Add the oil and rice to the pan and stir with a wooden spoon until the rice is translucent and coated with the oil. Add the wine and cook until the liquid has reduced by half. Pour in the squid ink stock, a ladle at a time, and keep stirring until each ladleful is absorbed. Add the saffron. Keep adding the stock, stirring as often as possible until the rice is tender, but still with a slight resistance to the bite – this should take about 15 minutes.

Meanwhile, clean the squid. Pull the tentacles away from the squid's body. Remove the quill from inside the body and discard. Clean the body by running it under a tap or cleaning it in a bowl of water. Remove the 'ears' from either side of the squid body and remove the skin with your fingers. Cut the tentacles just below the eyes, being sure not to cut the ink sac. Be sure to remove the 'beak' at the base of the tentacles. Remove the tentacles and slice the body of the squid in half lengthways. With a sharp knife, score the inside of the squid in a diagonal pattern and then sprinkle with saffron and rub through your fingers as if you were making crumble mix for a dessert; this is good to do a couple of hours in advance so that the squid has a chance to dye yellow. When the rice is just ready, add your Parmesan and season with salt and freshly ground black pepper keep the consistency similar to porridge.

For the marinated squid, preheat a pan until hot add olive oil and sear for 1–2 minutes or until the squid starts curling into tubes. Remove the squid from the heat and add the chopped chilli, garlic and lemon juice plus zest and chopped parsley. Season with a little salt and freshly ground black pepper.

To serve, spoon the risotto into the centre of each of individual plate and top with a pile of marinated squid and a drizzle of the marinade.

TOM KERRIDGE

"The MS Society does amazing work to help sufferers live as positively as possible. It's great that I can support them with my recipe from The Hand and Flowers in this ChariTable Bookings collection."

RUMP STEAK STEW

SERVES 4 | PREPARATION TIME 30 MINUTES | COOKING TIME 1 HOUR 30 MINUTES

For the Stew

30g dried mixed mushrooms
100ml boiling water, for soaking
4 x 250g rump steak pavés
1 drizzle of vegetable oil
50g butter
300g girolle mushrooms, cleaned
2 banana shallots, finely diced
2 cloves of garlic, grated
400ml beef stock
50ml brandy
50ml double cream
50ml ruby port
2 plum tomatoes, blanched, peeled, cored, deseeded and diced
1 tbsp tarragon, finely chopped
200g broad-leaf spinach, tough stems removed
½ lemon, juiced
salt and freshly ground black pepper

To Serve

mashed potatoes or chips

To prepare the stew, place the dried mushrooms into a bowl and pour over about 100ml of boiling water; leave them to steep and rehydrate for 20 minutes. During this time, take the rump steaks out of the fridge to come to room temperature.

Warm a large, heavy-bottomed frying pan over a medium heat and drizzle in a little oil. Add half of the butter and heat until foaming. Season the rump steaks and fry on both sides until nicely coloured all over. Keep cooking them until they're cooked to your liking; this should take 7–8 minutes for medium rare. Remove the steaks from the pan, put them on a plate and place them in a cool oven at 50°C to rest until needed.

Place a sieve over a bowl and drain the steeped mushrooms. Now line the sieve with muslin, place it over a clean bowl and pass the soaking liquid through it to remove any dirt. Roughly chop the mushrooms. Melt the remaining butter in the frying pan over a medium-high heat and when it foams, fry the girolles for 2–3 minutes. Add the shallots and garlic, then fry for 5 minutes or so, stirring from time to time until softened. Add the steeped mushrooms and stir. Pour in 50ml soaking water, the beef stock and brandy and bring to the boil. Simmer to reduce the liquid by a third, then add the cream and return to the boil. Add the port, then stir in the diced tomatoes and tarragon. Place the spinach on top and put a lid on the pan or cover tightly with tin foil. Turn the heat off and leave for 2 minutes.

To finish, remove the lid and stir the wilted spinach into the stew. Stir in the lemon juice and season to taste. Remove the steaks from the oven, slice into thick pieces and place in the stew, along with any resting juices.

To serve, place on warmed plates with creamy mashed potatoes or chips.

RACHEL KHOO

" FUN is a local, Bedfordshire charity supporting children and young people with disabilities. I love these crispy duck legs and I hope you enjoy making them. Honoured to be part of 365 great UK chefs in this ChariTable Bookings tome!"

CRISPY SPICY DUCK LEGS with plum sauce

SERVES 2 | PREPARATION TIME 30 MINUTES | COOKING TIME 2 HOURS

For the Crispy Duck Legs
2 duck legs

For the Plum Sauce
6 plums, ripe and destoned
4 tbsp plum conserve
2 knobs of soft butter
1 tsp ground cumin
1 tsp ground ginger
1 tsp white pepper
½ tsp ground cinnamon
salt

To Serve
steamed greens
smashed new potatoes

To make the plum sauce, preheat the oven to 160°C. Put the plum halves with the plum conserve into a baking dish or tray. Combine the soft butter with spices and salt, mix together with the plums and place in the oven.

For the crispy duck legs, rub the spice paste on the legs until well coated. Put them in a pan, skin-side down, then cover with aluminium foil and place them in the oven. Cook for 1.5 hours. Occasionally baste the duck legs with the juices from the pan. Remove from the oven and take off the aluminium foil. Turn the oven up to 200°C. Turn the legs over and baste again. Roast for a further 30 minutes. If the legs brown too quickly, turn the heat down or remove from the oven.

Serve with steamed greens and smashed new potatoes. Place a leg on top of the vegetables and pour over the sauce. If you prefer a smooth sauce you can blend the plums.

RONNIE KIMBUGWE

I'm sharing Bel & The Dragon's Salt-Baked Lamb dish in this original book by ChariTable Bookings. I have chosen to support the work of the Bone Cancer Research Trust to help continue the fight for a cure."

SALT-BAKED SADDLE OF LAMB

SERVES 4 | PREPARATION TIME 20 MINUTES | COOKING TIME 40 MINUTES

For the Lamb

1.4kg loin of lamb on the bone, trimmed and scored

4 sprigs of rosemary

2 sprigs of thyme

1 clove of garlic, sliced

For the Salt Crust Dough

250g plain flour

185g table salt

60g Maldon sea salt

½ egg

60ml water

To Serve

roasted seasonal vegetables

To prepare the lamb, trim any excess fat and score the skin diagonally – alternatively you can ask your butcher to do this for you.

To make the salt crust dough, mix the flour and salt together in a large bowl. Add the egg and water, then stir together with a wooden spoon to form a firm dough. Tip the dough onto a lightly floured surface and knead for 5 minutes or until smooth. Roll the pastry thinly until it is half a centimetre thick and large enough to encase the lamb.

Preheat the oven to 220°C. Place the lamb, skin-side down, on to the pastry and top with a few sprigs of rosemary, thyme and the sliced garlic. Tightly wrap the loin of lamb completely with the dough and press the pastry to the meat so there are no gaps. Turn it over and decorate with a few sprigs of rosemary. Place on a baking tray and bake for 20 minutes. Remove from the oven and leave to cool. Using a bread knife, slice open the top of the pastry and remove the lamb. Carve the lamb from both sides of the bone so you have two loins.

To finish, sear the lamb loins in a hot pan flesh-side down then turn the lamb onto the skin-side and sear until golden brown.

To serve, slice the lamb thinly then lay it back across the bone and return to the pastry case to bring to the table. Plate with roasted seasonal vegetables of your choice. The lamb is best accompanied with roasted seasonal vegetables.

RICHARD KIRKWOOD

Ellenor is a small charity that does fantastic work looking after terminally ill patients of all ages. On behalf of Wright Brothers Spitalfields, I'm proud to raise awareness of them by donating our Octopus recipe to this fantastic book by ChariTable Bookings."

GALLICIAN OCTOPUS with chorizo, broad beans and rocket

SERVES 4 | PREPARATION TIME 40 MINUTES | COOKING TIME 2 HOURS

For the Dish

1kg approx Galician double sucker octopus – you will need to go to a good fishmonger, and please ask for the 'double sucker' octopus. If you can't get this then you can buy frozen or cooked octopus.

300g raw chorizo

200g fresh (or frozen) broad beans

50g rocket

For the Garlic Butter

6 cloves of garlic

sea salt

150g butter, softened

1 bunch parsley, finely chopped

salt and pepper

To prepare the octopus, if raw, it is best steamed for about 1.5 hours. Although it looks like a lot of octopus, this will shrink down to about 400g. Once the octopus is cooked, allow to cool, cut into bitesize pieces, and leave aside in the fridge until needed.

To prepare the garlic butter, cook the garlic cloves in boiling water until soft and crush with some sea salt using the back of a knife. Mix this in with the softened butter and finish with chopped parsley. It is important to season the butter with salt and pepper to taste. Set aside until required.

To prepare the chorizo, it is best to buy uncooked chorizo. Preheat the oven to 200°C, peel the skin off the chorizo, and mould into small, uneven balls. Place on a baking tray and bake in the oven for 10–12 minutes. You want to see a little bit of colour on the outside of the chorizo. A lot of oil will be released from the chorizo, keep this for finishing the dish.

To prepare the broad beans, lightly blanch the beans in boiling water and plunge directly into ice water. When chilled, pop from their outer skins and reserve until needed. If in season, buy fresh broad beans but if unavailable, frozen is a good alternative.

To serve, place the garlic butter, the octopus pieces, chorizo, broad beans and rocket into a pan, and gently warm until hot. Do not sauté this dish on too high a temperature, it is all about warming the components together. Serve in a bowl and eat immediately.

TOM KITCHIN

The Mayhew Animal Home has been saving animal lives for over 130 years. ChariTable Bookings has created a great initiative to share both of my passions, food and charity. I hope you enjoy The Kitchin's Shellfish Rockpool!"

SHELLFISH ROCKPOOL

SERVES 4 | PREPARATION TIME 30 MINUTES | COOKING TIME 1 HOUR 25 MINUTES

For the Rockpool
olive oil
8 mussels
2 razor clams
8 surf clams
1 shallot, chopped
1 tbsp parsley, chopped
50ml white wine
50g squid
8 squat lobster tails
40g brown shrimps
50g fresh cooked crab
1 scallop
4 oysters
1 fillet mackerel
20g keta salmon eggs
60g samphire
200g seaweed

For the shellfish stock
1kg langoustine bodies
1kg lobster heads
500g crab shells
1 tbsp vegetable oil
6 carrots, thinly sliced
1 orange, peel and juice
5 cardamom pods
20g fennel seeds
100g ginger
3 star anise
½ onion, diced

Preheat the oven to 180°C. Roast the langoustine, lobster and crab shells in a roasting tray for 15 minutes.

In the meantime, heat a large, heavy-bottomed pan and add the vegetable oil. Sweat the carrots slowly, until the oil becomes orange in colour, then add the orange juice, cardamom pods, fennel seeds, ginger and star anise. Add the onion, fennel, leek, celery and garlic along with the shells. Then add the tomato purée and brandy, before reducing until dry. Once dry, cover with water and bring to the boil.

Reduce and leave to simmer for 1 hour, skimming when required. Remove from the heat and leave to cool. Once cooled, pass through a wet muslin cloth to remove all traces of shells. Season to taste.

Heat a heavy-bottomed pan and add some olive oil. Add the mussels, razor clams and surf clams. Add the shallot, parsley and white wine and place a lid on the pan. The razor clams should be the first to open, so as they do, take them out of the pan. Then add in the squid, squat lobster tails and brown shrimps and cook in the pan. Once the mussels and surf clams have opened, take them out of the pan. Take off the heat and remove from the shells.

Prepare the razor clams by removing the tender flesh from the intestine.

Start to build the dish by dividing the shellfish between 4 bowls. Next, divide the cooked crab between the bowls evenly. Add a quarter slice of raw scallop, an oyster, a quarter of the mackerel and some salmon caviar to each. Garnish with the blanched seaweed and samphire. Pour the shellfish consommé into a jug and serve.

> **Editor's Note:** *As per the chef's recommendation, you can use any combination of fish, shellfish and seaweed for the rockpool. The types listed in the ingredients are some suggestions for you to try.*

For the shellfish stock *continued*
    1 fennel, diced
    ½ leek, diced
    1 celery, diced
    ½ bulb garlic
    2 tbsp tomato purée
    100ml brandy
    salt and pepper

PAUL KITCHING

Marie Curie is an important organisation, supporting cancer sufferers and their families and the 21212 Restaurant is proud to stand shoulder to shoulder with ChariTable Bookings in support of this worthy cause."

TROUT AND SCALLOP with cabbage, broccoli and pea sauce

SERVES 1 | PREPARATION TIME 20 MINUTES | COOKING TIME 20 MINUTES

For the Dish

1 fillet of trout
olive oil
1 scallop
2 cherry tomatoes
6 florets of broccoli
400ml natural yoghurt
500g frozen peas
¼ savoy cabbage, trimmed, cored
and finely sliced
2 hazelnuts
70ml cream
70ml vegetable stock

To prepare the trout, remove the skin, cut the fillet in half depending on size and cook over a low heat with some olive oil until the fish becomes tender and soft. Bake the scallop in the oven for 10 minutes at 80°C and finish over a low heat with some olive oil.

To prepare the vegetables, confit the tomatoes in olive oil until they become soft but still hold their shape. Cook 2 of the broccoli florets in salted water so they're slightly soft all the way through. Blend the remaining broccoli with the yoghurt until it's smooth. Spread thinly on a piece of baking parchment and dry out in the oven at 50°C. Cook the peas in salted water, being careful not to discolour them. Place in a blender and blitz until smooth and pass through a fine sieve. Finely slice the cabbage, blanch in salted water and finish in olive oil or butter.

To serve, place a spoonful of the cabbage in the bottom of a bowl. Place the scallop and trout on top of the cabbage. Top the trout with the tomato, broccoli crisp and hazelnuts. Finish the sauce by heating the pea purée with cream and vegetable stock. Add to the plate and serve.

ATUL KOCHHAR

All of us at Benares are pleased to be able to support the British Asian Trust which tackles inequality in South Asia through this great project by ChariTable Bookings. We're donating our signature lamb rump recipe which I hope you enjoy!"

CHANA GOSHT LAMB RUMP with chickpeas

SERVES 4 | PREPARATION TIME 1 HOUR (PLUS OVERNIGHT TO SOAK AND 2 HOURS TO MARINATE) | COOKING TIME 1 HOUR

For the Lamb
4 x 180–200g lamb rumps
2 tbsp sunflower oil
150g masala chickpeas
sea salt

For the Marinade
100ml olive oil
10 cloves of garlic, crushed
2–3 sprigs of rosemary, chopped
1 tsp ground coriander
½ tsp each red chilli powder,
turmeric and freshly ground black
pepper
¼ tsp garam masala

For the Masala Chickpea Spice Powder
4cm stick of cinnamon
3 black cardamom pods
3 cloves
1 bay leaf
2 dried red chillies
1½ tsp coriander seeds
½ tsp cumin seeds

For the Masala Chickpeas
400g chickpeas, soaked overnight
2 tbsp sunflower oil
1 large green chilli, chopped
3 cloves of garlic, finely chopped
1½ tsp fresh ginger, finely chopped
1 tsp cumin seeds
1 large onion, finely chopped

To prepare, cover 450g of chickpeas with cold water and soak overnight.

The next day, mix all of the ingredients to marinate the lamb together in a large bowl, rub all over the meat, then place in the fridge for 2 hours. Preheat the oven to 180°C, heat an ovenproof frying pan until it is really hot, then add very thin layer of oil. Scrape the excess marinade off the rumps, add them to the pan and sear until browned, around 2 minutes on each side. Transfer to the oven and roast for 10–12 minutes for medium rare to medium, longer for more well done. Leave to rest for 5 minutes, covered with foil.

Toast all of the ingredients for the spice powder in a dry frying pan over a medium heat until aromatic. Immediately tip out of the pan and grind to a fine powder in a spice grinder.

To cook the chickpeas, drain and transfer them to a saucepan with fresh water to cover. Boil hard for 10 minutes, skimming the surface as necessary. Lower the heat, add salt to taste and simmer for 20 minutes, or until tender. Drain and set aside.

For the masala chickpeas, heat the oil in a saucepan, then add the chilli, garlic, ginger and cumin seeds. Sauté over a medium heat until the seeds crackle. Add the onion and continue sautéing for 8–10 minutes until soft and light brown. Pour in the water, tomato, 400g drained chickpeas, the ground coriander, mango powder, cumin, turmeric, garam masala and salt to taste. Continue stirring over a low heat, uncovered, for 12–15 minutes until the chickpeas are very soft. If necessary, stir in extra water to loosen the mixture. Sprinkle with the spice powder and keep warm.

For the masala hummus, remove the whole spices from 250g of the masala chickpeas. While still warm, blend with the remaining hummus ingredients to a fine paste. Keep warm.

For the green herb oil, put all the ingredients into a food processor and blitz until blended. Strain through a sieve lined with muslin cloth. Transfer to a suitable bottle for serving. Any oil not used with the dish can be decanted and stored in the fridge for up to 2 days.

For the Masala Chickpeas continued

150ml water
1 large tomato, chopped
1½ tsp ground coriander
1½ tsp dried mango powder
¾ tsp ground cumin
¾ tsp turmeric
½ tsp garam masala
sea salt

For the Masala Hummus

250g masala chickpeas
2 cloves of garlic
2 tbsp each plain yogurt, olive oil,
finely chopped coriander leaves,
and lemon juice
1 tbsp tahini
1 tsp cumin seeds, toasted
¼ tsp garam masala
¼ tsp freshly ground black pepper

Green Herb Oil

150ml sunflower oil
25g coriander sprigs
25g mint leaves
5mm piece of fresh ginger, peeled
and coarsely chopped
1 small pinch of sea salt

For the Chickpea and Feta Fritters

50g chickpeas, soaked overnight
30g feta cheese, drained
½ clove of garlic, finely chopped
4 tbsp finely chopped onion
1 tbsp chopped coriander leaves
1½ tsp lemon juice
¾ tsp gram flour, toasted, plus an
extra tsp for dusting
½ tsp each cumin seeds, toasted
and finely ground, grated lemon
zest, toasted white sesame seeds
and sweet paprika
¼ tsp coriander seeds, toasted and
finely ground
sunflower oil, for deep-frying

To Garnish

pea shoots
mint leaves

For the fritters, blend the remaining 50g of chickpeas into a coarse paste. Transfer to a large bowl and gently mix in the other fritter ingredients, except the oil and gram flour for dusting. Heat enough oil for deep-frying to 190°C. Put the gram flour on a dish, add level tablespoons of the chickpea mixture and roll around to coat, shaping the mixture into balls. Gently add them to the oil, frying for 1–2 minutes until they are golden brown and float to the surface. You should get at least 8 fritters. Drain well on kitchen paper to absorb excess oil.

To serve, cut the rumps into thick slices. Smear a portion of masala hummus on each plate, then add the rump slices, chickpea fritters and chickpea masala. Dot the green herb oil next to the chickpeas and sprinkle the lamb with sea salt. Garnish with the pea shoots and mint leaves. Serve immediately.

PIERRE KOFFMANN

I love this opportunity to raise awareness of Scotty's Little Soldiers by sharing Koffmann's sea bass recipe with ChariTable Bookings. Working with kids who have lost a parent through active service is so important to restore their confidence and give them their childhood back."

PAN-FRIED SEA BASS with broccoli purée and citrus sauce

SERVES 4 | PREPARATION TIME 30 MINUTES | COOKING TIME 6 HOURS

For the Bass
4 x 160g sea bass fillets, deboned
2 tbsp vegetable oil

For the Broccoli Purée
2 heads of broccoli
2 cloves of garlic
½ chilli, or, to taste
olive oil
salt and pepper

For the Citrus Sauce
2½l water
375ml white wine
450g fennel, finely chopped
300g onions, finely chopped
450g carrots, finely chopped
225g celery, finely chopped
250g leeks, finely chopped
37g garlic, finely chopped
1 bay leaf
1 sprig of thyme
1 orange, zested
17g sugar
19g chicken stock powder
salt and pepper
37g lemon segments, peeled,
reserve a few extra
125g orange segments, peeled,
reserve a few extra
25g ginger
chives, finely chopped

To make the broccoli purée, cook the broccoli until very tender. In a saucepan, heat some olive oil and infuse with the garlic and chilli. Strain the broccoli and add to the infused olive oil. Toss until the broccoli is well coated in the oil. Add everything to a blender and blitz until smooth, or until you reach a desired consistency. If needed, add more olive oil. Season to taste; chill as quickly as possible. Set aside in the fridge.

To make the citrus sauce, bring the water and wine to the boil; add all the ingredients except the lemon and orange segments. Allow to simmer for 3 hours, then add the segments and ginger. Allow the mixture to infuse for another 2 hours. Strain and reduce to a sauce consistency. When ready to use, warm gently with a little butter and some roughly chopped segments of lemon and orange. Finish with a dash of finely chopped chives.

To cook the sea bass and serve, score the skin and pan fry skin-side down in a hot pan in the vegetable oil for 5 minutes, then on the flesh side for another 2 minutes until the flesh becomes opaque. While you are cooking the bass, warm the broccoli purée and sauce. Add the broccoli purée to the plate, top with the sea bass and add the sauce around the plate.

NICOLAS LARIDAN

Mark's Club is honoured to support the Royal British Legion which provides lifelong support for members and veterans of the British armed forces, and ChariTable Bookings will help us continue to maximise our backing of this incredible organisation."

SCOTTISH STEAMED HALIBUT with baby leeks and grilled langoustines

SERVES 4 | PREPARATION TIME 30 MINUTES | COOKING TIME 1 HOUR 30 MINUTES

For the Langoustines
8 whole medium langoustines
4 baby plum tomatoes
Sea salt and pepper, to taste

For the Halibut and Vegetables
4 x 180g halibut fillets
8 baby leeks
a drizzle of olive oil

For the Sauce
1 tbsp olive oil
langoustine heads and carcasses
3 shallots, sliced
1 carrot, diced
½ clove of garlic, crushed
½ tps red chilli, chopped
½ tbsp tomato paste
2 sprigs of tarragon
2 sprigs of dill
100ml cognac
250ml fish stock
200ml double cream

For the Garnish
4 sprigs of dill

To prepare the langoustines, cook the langoustines in salted boiling water for 2 minutes, drain and when cool, remove the heads and shell the tails. Keep four heads aside for presentation and keep the others with shells for the sauce.

To make the sauce, in a saucepan, heat up the olive oil and roast the carcasses and heads until slightly golden. Crush them a little, add the shallots, carrot, garlic and chilli, cook for another 2 minutes, then add the tomato purée, herbs and Cognac. Reduce the alcohol by two thirds, then add the fish stock. Simmer gently for 30 minutes, then add the cream and a little salt and cook for a further 15 minutes, to a coating consistency. Pass through a sieve, pushing through with a spoon to extract the flavours. Check seasoning and reserve for serving.

To cook the fish and vegetables, bring a conventional home steamer to boiling temperature. Cut both ends of the baby leeks, wash and make sure no grit remains between the layers, steam them so they are still a little crisp. Place the halibut with a little sea salt in the steamer for 10 minutes on a piece of baking paper with a drizzle of olive oil. Meanwhile, heat up a grilling pan and roll the langoustine tails with the halved tomatoes in olive oil. Season with a little salt and pepper. Grill the tails for a minute on each side and add the tomatoes, flat side down at the end, just for a slight colour. Dress on plates as shown.

PRANEE LAURILLARD

Being Thai myself, it wasn't a hard decision to support the Thai Children's Trust who provide vital, nourishing meals to children living in abject poverty. Fitting then that I share Giggling Squid's red curry with ChariTable Bookings!"

THAI CHICKEN RED CURRY

SERVES 2 | PREPARATION TIME 5 MINUTES | COOKING TIME 15 MINUTES

For the Red Curry paste
3 tbsp vegetable oil
1 tbsp red curry paste, to taste
1 can of coconut cream

For the Vegetables
1 medium size courgette
½ red pepper, cut in half lengthways
12 fine green beans

For the Chicken Breasts
2 chicken breasts
150–200ml water
2 tsp salt
1 tsp sugar
1 small handful of fresh basil leaves

To prepare the curry sauce, put the red curry paste with the vegetable oil into a saucepan and stir on a gentle heat for 10 minutes, until the chillies start to release colour into the oil. Add a quarter of the coconut cream and keep stirring for a further 5 minutes. This will bring out the coconut oil, giving a shiny texture to the finished curry sauce. Finally, add the rest of the coconut cream.

To prepare the vegetables, halve and slice the courgette, 2cm thick. Chop the beans in 4cm pieces and chop the red pepper.

To cook the chicken breasts, slice them across, 2cm thick, and put them into boiling water. Simmer until the breast is cooked through, which should take 10–15 minutes. Turn the gas off and add the crunchy vegetables. Season with salt and sugar to your liking and then finish with basil or coriander leaves.

Combine the curry sauce, vegetables and chicken and serve with steamed rice.

GARY LEE

"With 7 young people being diagnosed with cancer every day, the team at The Ivy has chosen to donate our famous shepherd's pie recipe to this ChariTable Bookings' project to support the great work of the Teenage Cancer Trust."

THE IVY SHEPHERD'S PIE

SERVES 6 | PREPARATION TIME 30 MINUTES | COOKING TIME 1 HOUR 40 MINUTES

For the Filling
- 200g lean lamb mince
- 200g lean rib of beef mince
- sunflower oil for frying
- 2 shallots, peeled and finely chopped
- 3 sprigs of fresh thyme, leaves removed
- 100g button mushrooms, washed and finely chopped
- 1 medium sized carrot, finely chopped
- 1 tbsp tomato purée
- ½ tin chopped tomatoes
- 100ml red wine
- 1 tbsp plain flour
- 2 tbsp Worcestershire sauce
- 300ml veal stock
- 3 sprigs of fresh oregano, leaves removed and chopped
- salt and freshly ground black pepper

For the Topping
- 1kg King Edwards/Maris Piper potatoes, peeled
- 50g unsalted butter
- salt and white pepper

For the filling, lightly oil both the lamb and beef mince. Heat a frying pan until smoking and cook the meat, mixing continuously for about 5 minutes until light brown in colour. Pour the meat and juices into a dish and set to one side. In the same pan, heat a little oil and gently sweat the shallots, thyme, button mushrooms and carrots for about 8 minutes. Add the mince, mix in the tomato purée and cook for about 5 minutes. Add the chopped tomatoes, red wine and reduce for about 10 minutes. Add flour and mix thoroughly. Add the Worcestershire sauce, veal stock and reserved meat juices. Bring to the boil and simmer for 30 minutes. Season with salt, pepper, more Worcestershire sauce to taste and the oregano. Keep to one side.

Preheat the oven to 180°C.

To make the topping, peel and cut the potatoes into even-sized pieces. Cook in salted, boiling water for around 15 minutes until soft. Drain and return to the pan over a gentle heat to remove any excess moisture. Using an old-fashioned masher or potato ricer, mash the potatoes well, mix with butter and season to taste.

To serve, put the filling into an oven proof dish and pipe the mashed potato on top. Place in the oven and bake for around 30 minutes until golden in colour.

PAUL LEONARD

I hope you enjoy making my Isle of Eriska signature recipe. Please spread the word to all your friends to purchase The ChariTable Bookings Signature Dish recipe book and help raise vital funds for Chest Heart and Stroke Scotland."

CRISPY CALEDONIAN OYSTERS with pickled garden vegetables and oyster mayonnaise

SERVES 4 | PREPARATION TIME 40 MINUTES (PLUS 24 HOURS TO MARINATE) | COOKING TIME 3 MINUTES

Equipment
mandoline

For the Garden Vegetables
1 fennel bulb
2 banana shallots
2 carrots
6 baby turnips
3 golden beetroots
100g caster sugar
100ml each white wine vinegar,
white wine and water
1 pinch of Hebridean sea salt

For the Mayonnaise
2 egg yolks
15ml lemon juice
2 oysters, shucked, juices retained
300ml Cullisse rapeseed oil
1 pinch of Hebridean sea salt

For the Dish
50g plain flour
1 egg, beaten
75g panko breadcrumbs
12 large Caledonian oysters,
shucked, juices retained, shells
cleaned and retained for serving
oil, for frying
salt and pepper, to taste
lemon wedges, to serve
edible flowers, fennel fronds and a
bed of sea salt, to garnish

To prepare the pickled vegetables, wash and slice thinly on a mandoline. Place in a clean container that can be kept airtight. Put the wine, white wine vinegar, water and sugar in a pan and stir over a low heat until dissolved. Pour the vinegar mixture over the vegetables and season with Hebridean sea salt. Seal the container and leave for at least 24 hours before using.

To make the oyster mayonnaise, put the yolks, lemon juice and oysters into a food processor and blend for 30 seconds. With the processor still running, slowly pour in the oil until it has all emulsified. Add the reserved oyster juice from all the oysters in the recipe and season with Hebridean sea salt. Set aside for later.

For the crispy oysters, put the flour, beaten egg and panko breadcrumbs in separate bowls, making sure to season the flour with salt and pepper. Heat a deep-fryer to 180°C. Pat the shucked oysters dry with kitchen paper, then pass them through the flour, then the egg, and finally the breadcrumbs, making sure they are thoroughly coated. Deep fry the panko coated oysters in the hot oil for around a minute until golden.

To serve, set the cleaned oyster shells on a bed of salt on 4 plates. Drain the vegetables and place a nice pile in the shells. Top with a good spoonful of oyster mayonnaise, then finish with the oysters, taking care to share equally between the plates. Serve with a wedge of lemon.

TOM LEWIS

I am delighted to share this delicious venison dish with you, and I hope you enjoy cooking it as much as I do. Here at Monachyle we see the importance of supporting charities so we are delighted to take part in the ChariTable Bookings Signature Dish book so we may help those who are most in need."

MONACHYLE VENISON with garden chard and Balquhidder chanterelles

SERVES 4 | PREPARATION TIME 20 MINUTES | COOKING TIME 40 MINUTES

For the Venison
1–1.5kg venison haunch, seam trimmed
salt and pepper, to taste
1 knob of butter

For the Roast Shallot and Garlic Purée
3 cloves of garlic, unpeeled
1 sprig of thyme
12 whole shallots, unpeeled
2 tsp sea salt flakes
1 tsp freshly ground black pepper
2 tbsp olive oil
50ml double cream

For the Garden Vegetables
2–4 runner beans, washed, cut evenly
4–6 carrots, peeled, halved
4–6 turnips, peeled, halved
1 knob of butter
4–6 rainbow pink chard leaves, washed
salt and pepper, to taste

For the Balquhidder Chanterelles
150g chanterelle mushrooms
1 knob of butter
salt and pepper, to taste
1 tbsp parsley, chopped
3 leaves tarragon, chopped
1 sprig of parsley
½ lemon, juiced

To make the venison haunch, preheat the oven to 210°C. Season the venison well. Heat a frying pan, add the knob of butter and pan fry the venison quickly, until coloured on all sides. Place the venison in the oven for 4–7 minutes, depending on the size. Remove and transfer to a warm plate to rest for 5 minutes. Reduce the juices in the pan to make a jus.

To make the roast shallot and garlic purée, preheat an oven to 180°C. Place the garlic, thyme and shallots in a small baking dish. Sprinkle with salt, pepper and olive oil, cover with foil and bake until soft, for about 30 minutes. Leave to cool to room temperature. Peel the garlic and shallots, then purée in a food processor with the double cream. Keep hot.

To make the garden vegetables, blanch the carrots, runner beans and turnips in boiling, salted water until tender, but still crunchy. Place in ice water to refresh. Warm a pan, on a medium heat, and melt the butter. Add the blanched garden vegetables and chard leaves. Wilt for a minute, season well with salt and pepper. Serve immediately.

To make the Balquhidder chanterelles, clean the mushrooms with a pastry brush. Heat a pan on a medium to hot heat, add a knob of butter, then the chanterelles. Season with salt and pepper. Add the chopped parsley and tarragon. Dress with a squeeze of lemon juice.

To serve, plate as pictured.

LEE CHE LIANG

"The Park Chinois team proudly support Children with Cancer UK in this new fundraising effort by ChariTable Bookings. We hope that you enjoy our recipe!"

COBIA AND CHINESE CHIVE FLOWER STIR-FRY

SERVES 1 | PREPARATION TIME 20 MINUTES | COOKING TIME 40 MINUTES

For the Stir-Fry
- 100g Chinese chive flowers
- 180g cobia fillet
- 20g garlic, peeled and sliced
- 20g shallots, sliced
- 20g ginger, sliced

For the Seasoning
- 2 tbsp soy sauce
- 2 tsp rice wine
- 1 tsp black bean sauce
- 2 tsp sugar
- 1 tsp dark soy sauce
- 2 tsp olive oil
- 30g potato starch

To prepare the dish, clean the fish and dry with a paper towel. Slice the chive flowers into 2.5cm pieces and place to one side. In a pan on a low heat, fry the garlic, shallots and ginger until golden and crispy.

To cook the fish, heat a pan until searing hot. Sprinkle the fillet with potato starch and pan fry the cobia until almost cooked. Add the chive flowers, stirring gently in the pan. Add in all of the seasoning and cover with a lid for 10 seconds. Bring the pan up to a high heat and add the crispy ginger, shallots and garlic. Stir fry the mixture together until cooked through and plate.

JOSE LOPEZ

Best Beginnings does so much to help children and mothers, from conception to 3 months, get the best start in life. Paternoster Chop House's team and I couldn't be happier to support them with ChariTable Bookings and raise as much awareness for them as possible."

DUCK AND BEAN CASSEROLE

SERVES 6 | PREPARATION TIME 1 HOUR (PLUS OVERNIGHT TO MARINATE AND SOAK) | COOKING TIME 4 HOURS

For the Duck Casserole

500g haricot beans, soaked overnight

1l ham or chicken stock

500ml water

350g cooked or smoked gammon cubes

6 rashers of streaky bacon fat, cut into lardons

1 onion, sliced

1 carrot, sliced

2 cloves of garlic, sliced

2 sprigs of thyme

1 bay leaf

salt and pepper, to taste

For the Duck Legs

6 duck legs

6 cloves of garlic

500g rock salt

4 sprigs of rosemary

1 tbsp duck fat

To Serve

100g black pudding

oil

To prepare the casserole, soak the beans for at least 12 hours. Add the stock, water and gammon cubes and take to a boil. Skim well and cover with a cartouche. Let it simmer for approximately 2 hours or until the beans are cooked. Pour into a tray and chill. Cook the lardons in a large pan at a medium heat until they start to crisp up. Meanwhile, dice the onion, carrot and garlic. Add them to the pan with the thyme and bay leaf, season with salt and pepper and cook until soft.

To make the duck legs, blend together the rock salt, garlic and rosemary. Sprinkle over the duck legs and leave to marinate for 12 hours. After that, rinse them well, place them on a baking dish and cover with duck fat. Cover the dish with tin foil and bake at 120°C for 4 hours. Lift the duck legs from the duck fat and chill. You can reuse the duck fat a few times if it isn't too salty.

To serve the duck casserole, preheat the oven to 180°C. Place a sheet of parchment paper over a flat oven tray and lay the duck legs with the skin-side facing down. After 12 minutes, the leg should be soft so you can flatten it using a pallet knife. Put the duck back in the oven and bake for a further 5 minutes. Dice the black pudding into 1cm cubes and fry with a little oil in a saucepan until crispy. Add the bean mixture to the pan and bring to a gentle simmer. Place a couple of spoons of the bean casserole on a plate and sit the crispy duck leg on top.

BRUNO LOUBET

Really pleased to be supporting the work of Scotty's Little Soldiers, helping kids get over bereavement. Enjoy The Grain Store's watermelon and crab dish and support them too. Good idea by ChariTable Bookings!"

COMPRESSED SALTED WATERMELON and curried crab

SERVES 4 | PREPARATION TIME 30 MINUTES | COOKING TIME 30 MINUTES

For the Watermelon
600g thick watermelon slice, skin on
salt and pepper, to taste
½ tsp fennel seeds, crushed and toasted

For the Dressing
4 tbsp olive oil
1 tsp lime juice
1 tbsp lemon juice
1 tsp dijon mustard
salt and pepper, to taste

For the Curried Crab
200g white fresh crab meat
10g smoked paprika
150g coriander seeds
100g cumin
22g black pepper
25g ras el hanout
15g cinnamon
25g turmeric
30g fennel seeds
100ml corn oil
50ml olive oil
1 egg yolk
1 tsp dijon mustard
salt and lime juice, to taste

For the Garnish
borage flowers
fresh coriander

For the watermelon, remove the skin and the white part around the slice of watermelon. Season with salt on both sides and sprinkle the fennel seeds, also on both sides. At the restaurant, we vacuum pack the watermelon to extract the air, which gives the flesh of the melon a wonderfully meaty texture and deep colour. This result can be closely achieved by squeezing the slice of watermelon between 2 sheets of cling film with a plate on top and a weight over to push it down. Leave it for a minimum of 20 minutes.

To make the dressing, mix all of the ingredients in a small bowl with a little whisk and check the seasoning.

To prepare the curry oil and curried crab, toss the spices for the curry mix one by one in a frying pan, except the paprika, so that the spices release their scented oil. Do not colour. Cool all the spices on a flat tray then crush finely in a pestle and mortar or coffee grinder. In a small pan, place 1 heaped tablespoon of spices with 100ml of corn oil, then place on a very low heat, stirring from time to time for 15 minutes. Then take off the heat and leave it to cool down. When completely cool, add 50ml of olive oil and pass through a muslin cloth. With 1 egg yolk, a teaspoon of dijon mustard and 50ml of curry oil, make a mayonnaise. Season with salt and lime juice. Mix the crab with the mayonnaise and set aside.

To serve, slice the watermelon finely, then fold and drape to create a bed in the centre of each plate. Place a quenelle of the crab mixture onto the centre of the watermelon slices. Finish with the borage flowers, coriander and a drizzle of curry oil. The remaining curry oil can be stored in an airtight container for later use.

JASON LOY

The MS Society is a worthy cause very close to my heart, so I am honoured to present you with my signature dish in the ChariTable Bookings Signature Dish book in order to raise awareness for those who are most in need."

BRILL with mussels and brown shrimp beurre blanc

SERVES 2 | PREPARATION TIME 30 MINUTES | COOKING TIME 45 MINUTES

For the Beurre Blanc
100ml white wine
100ml white wine vinegar
1 small banana shallot, peeled
1 bay leaf
5 sprigs of thyme
1 clove of garlic
3 black peppercorns
300ml double cream
100g cold butter, chopped
½ lemon
20g hot English mustard
30g dill, chopped

For the Brill
2 x 180g brill portions
salt and pepper
200g fresh Cornish mussels
100ml good white wine
100g brown peeled shrimps
20g Lilliput capers

For the Garnish
parsley cress
olive oil

To make the beurre blanc, add the white wine, white wine vinegar, shallot, bay leaf, thyme, garlic and peppercorns to a pot and reduce until all the liquid has almost completely evaporated. Add the double cream and reduce on a slow heat. Reduce by half and strain, place back into a clean pot and gradually whisk in the butter. Add the lemon juice and hot English mustard. Once the sauce becomes shiny on the surface and looks velvety, season to taste.

To cook the brill, season well with salt and pepper. In a medium to hot pan, add the fish for 2–3 minutes or until golden brown, turn and place in a preheated oven at 180°C for around 6–8 minutes, depending on the thickness.

While the fish is cooking, steam open the mussels with the wine. Once cooked, pick the meat out. Add back to a pot with the brown shrimps, capers and finished beurre blanc.

To serve, remove the fish from the oven and place in the centre of the plate. Add the chopped dill to the sauce and drizzle over the fish. Finish with a little drizzle of good olive oil and the parsley cress.

JONATHAN MACHIN

"Supporting life savers by donating recipes - easy! I hope you enjoy Cloisters' Salmon Gremolata in this collection by ChariTable Bookings in aid of South Western Air Ambulance."

SALMON GREMOLATA

SERVES 2 | PREPARATION TIME 1 HOUR | COOKING TIME 3 HOURS

Equipment
sous vide and vacuum pack bags
Thermomix

For the Salmon and Gremolata
1 x 200g responsibly sourced
salmon fillet, trimmed of fat, skin on
1 generous handful of flat leaf
parsley, chopped
1 unwaxed lemon, zest of
1 clove of garlic, finely crushed

For the Horseradish Cream
1cm horseradish root
2 tbsp whipped cream
sea salt, to season

For the Spinach Purée
1 bag of spinach
1 tbsp of plain mashed potato

For the Pickled Carrot
1 large carrot
6 radishes
equal parts mix of sugar, water and
vinegar, to cover
1 star anise
a couple of cloves

For the Mini Fondant
2 large, waxy potatoes
1 knob of butter, to cook

For the Artichoke Crumb
1 Jerusalem artichoke
butter and rapeseed oil, to fry

Start by removing the skin from the salmon. Season the skin with salt only, cover with parchment paper top and bottom and place between 2 heavy trays. Roast in the oven for 7 minutes at 190°C. After 7 minutes check to see if fully crisp. If not, repeat the process for another 2 minutes.

To make the gremolata, mix a handful of chopped flat leaf parsley, the zest of an unwaxed lemon and a clove of garlic together. Halve your salmon into 2 portions and spread the gremolata on top. Wrap in cling film and poach in a water bath at 45°C for 1 hour. Refresh in ice water to reduce temperature for storage in the fridge until required. Prior to serving the salmon, reheat for 1 minute at 50°C, just to take the chill off the dish.

To make the horseradish cream, fold freshly grated horseradish root, seasoned with sea salt, into softly whipped cream. In the restaurant we use the rocher or one-handed method which gives a quenelle with 3 sides and no apparent edges. The ingredients must be the consistency of butter at room temperature, or firmer, so the rocher will form and hold its shape. The horseradish cream should be uniform, without large voids of trapped air, which would show up as craters in the rocher. Use a deep bowled rather than flat spoon, hot enough to release the rocher but not so hot that it melts the horseradish.

To make the spinach purée, blanch the spinach in boiling water for no more than 1 minute, then refresh in ice water to maintain the colour. Purée in a Thermomix with a little bit of plain mashed potato to create texture without adding flavour – you could try using a food processor to do this at home.

For the pickled carrot, create a pickling liquor with 3 equal amounts of sugar, water and vinegar, flavoured with star anise and cloves. Bring the liquor to a steady boil. Shave the carrot and radish, but keep in separate containers otherwise the radish will colour and taint the carrot. Cover with the liquor, seal, cool and then refrigerate until use. At home, this will keep for several weeks until opened, but use within 7 days of opening for best results.

To make the mini fondant, use an apple corer to create 2 equal sized potato cylinders. Seal the cylinders' tops in a buttered, heavy frying pan. Add boiling water until just under the height of the cylinders. Cook until tender. Cool and reheat in butter to bring to serving temperature.

To make the artichoke crumb, peel and finely grate a Jerusalem artichoke. Shallow fry in a mixture of butter and rapeseed oil until lightly golden brown. Drain on kitchen towel to remove the fat. Once dried, this can be crumbled and stored until use.

To finish and serve, swipe the spinach purée around half the plate. On the opposite half of the plate, place your salmon fillet, gremolata side up. Place the rocher of horseradish cream in the centre of the plate and the salmon skin shard on top to add height. Finish with the potato fondant and a sprinkling of the crumb across the salmon and spinach purée.

JAMES MACKENZIE

At The Pipe and Glass Inn, we pride ourselves on our standards of quality. I feel that Macmillan has the same approach to it's work and am proud to support them throughout the year, as one of our named charities, and through ChariTable Bookings by sharing one of our signature recipes with you. Enjoy!"

BAKED HALIBUT with cobnut crust, cauliflower and cockles

SERVES 4 | PREPARATION TIME 25 MINUTES | COOKING TIME 30 MINUTES

For the fish
4 x 200g chunky portions of halibut
or cod
400ml fish stock

For the Cobnut Crust
100g cobnuts, roughly chopped
100g breadcrumbs
40g Parmesan cheese, grated
50g butter, melted
1 tbsp chives, chopped

For the Cauliflower Champ
1 cauliflower
200ml whipping cream
100ml water
salt and white pepper
1 bunch spring onions

For the Cockle Sauce
1kg fresh cockles
1 shallot, sliced
200ml white wine
150ml double cream
1 bunch of dill, chopped

For the Garnish
150g cobnuts
Romanesco cauliflower, optional
yellow cauliflower, optional
purple cauliflower, optional

To prepare the cauliflower champ, thinly slice the white cauliflower florets and place in a saucepan with the whipping cream and water. Cover the pan with a lid and cook on a medium heat until the cauliflower is just cooked, about 20 minutes. Remove from the heat and place the cooked cauliflower and cream into a food processor and blend until a smooth purée. Season with white pepper and salt to taste. Reserve until needed. Finely slice the spring onions ready to add to the cauliflower purée.

To make the cobnut crust, mix all the ingredients together in a bowl with your hand until it forms a rough crumb.

To prepare the fish, place the halibut fillets into a deep baking tray and top each one with the cobnut crust. Pour the fish stock around the fish and place in the oven at 180°C to bake for about 8–12 minutes, dependent on the size and thickness of the fish. Try to use nice, thick pieces of fish. Remove from the oven, the crust should be golden brown.

To prepare the cockle sauce, heat a large saucepan. Add the cockles, sliced shallot and white wine. Put a lid on and cook over a high heat until the cockles open. Remove the cooked cockles, pick out the meat and reserve. Pour the cream into the cockle cooking stock and reduce to a sauce consistency. Transfer the cockle meat back to the sauce, warm through and finish with chopped dill.

If you are able to get hold of the optional coloured cauliflowers, boil the Romanesco in salted water until just tender and finish with a little butter. I like to cook the yellow one with some saffron in the water but you can leave this out. To give a contrast to the dish, simply thinly slice the purple cauliflower and place in some white wine vinegar to pickle for 2 minutes.

To serve, add the spring onion to the cauliflower purée and warm through. Place a large spoonful of the champ on each plate, place the coloured cauliflower around, if using, and place the fish on top. Garnish with some toasted chopped cobnuts and spoon around the cockle sauce.

MARTIN MAJOR

"Over 7 million people live with heart disease in the UK. The British Heart Foundation researches the causes and works to prevent premature death from heart failiure. Very pleased to support them by sharing this recipe that was first served at L'Autre Pied, with you in this new book by ChariTable Bookings."

FALLOW DEER baked in cocoa crumb with baked celeriac, onion and stout purée with cranberry and juniper

SERVES 2 | PREPARATION TIME 30 MINUTES | COOKING TIME 1 HOUR 30 MINUTES

For the Onion Stout Purée
3 onions, finely diced
1 tbsp olive oil
1 can of stout
20g risotto rice

For the Celeriac
1 celeriac, peeled
1 tbsp olive oil
1 cube of good chicken stock
1 knob of butter

For the Juniper Salt
1 tsp juniper berries
1 tbsp Maldon sea salt

For the Jus
100ml venison or beef stock
100g cranberries, fresh or canned

For the Cocoa Crumb
200g panko breadcrumbs
50g cocoa nibs
70g cocoa powder

For the Deer
2 x 140g fallow deer loins
100g egg whites
100g unsalted butter

For the Garnish
1 head of cavolo nero
olive oil
wild mushrooms

Start with the onion stout purée. Sauté the onions in a hot pan with a little olive oil until soft and golden brown. Add your can of stout and the risotto rice. Stir constantly for roughly 20 minutes or until all liquid has reduced. Blend to a smooth purée. Set aside.

Halve the celeriac, and chop one half into slim wedges. Preheat an oven to 180°C. Place a tray with a dash of olive oil into the preheated oven. When the oil is smoking hot, put your wedges onto the tray. Bake for approximately 20 minutes or until soft and golden brown. Meanwhile, dice the other half of celeriac into 2cm cubes. Make up the chicken stock and add a knob of butter. Place the diced celeriac in the stock and bring to the boil. Cook for approximately 15 minutes or until soft. Strain off all liquid and crush slightly with a fork creating a very rough mash.

To prepare your juniper salt, roast the juniper berries in a dry, hot pan until aromatic. Crush in a pestle and mortar and add half the Maldon sea salt. Set aside for serving.

To create the jus, pop some high quality ready made venison or beef stock into a pan with your cranberries and reduce until it becomes thick and glossy.

To create your cocoa crumb, simply combine the ingredients.

Preheat the oven to 160°C. Meanwhile melt the butter in a pan under a medium heat until foaming. Take your 2 fallow deer fillets and roll in egg whites, then in your cocoa crumb. Place into the hot pan and turn constantly for 1–2 minutes, coating in butter. Place in the oven for 4 minutes for rare, 6 minutes for medium and 8 minutes for well done. Take it out of the oven and allow it to rest for 5 minutes before serving.

Finally, prepare your cavalo nero by cutting all stems off. Blanch in boiling, salted water for 1 minute, strain. Sauté some wild mushrooms in olive oil and serve immediately.

ROB MALYON

"I'm supporting Macmillan in this fantastic new collection by ChariTable Bookings. Enjoy my Beef and Oyster Pie from Wright Brothers Borough and I hope you support them too!"

BEEF AND OYSTER PIE

SERVES 4 | PREPARATION TIME 1 HOUR 20 MINUTES | COOKING TIME 20 MINUTES

For the Beef Mixture
- 2kg diced beef chuck
- 40g large cut mirepoix, diced carrots, onions and celery
- 2 bay leaves
- 40g tomato purée
- 50g plain flour
- 500ml beef stock
- 455ml of Guinness

For Each Serving
- 100g cooked beef mix
- 100g puff pastry
- 2 rock oysters

To prepare the beef mixture, sweat the mirepoix, thyme and bay leaves without giving it colour for about 15–20 minutes. Add the tomato purée and cook for 5 minutes. Add the flour to form a roux-like paste and cook for a few minutes. Slowly add the stock and Guinness to form a thick sauce.

Season the beef and seal off in small batches in hot oil, so that it's nicely browned. Pour into a colander to drain away the oil. Add the meat to the thick sauce and slowly bring to the boil, skimming off any fats that form. Cook on a low heat for about 1 hour until the beef is tender, then take off the heat.

To serve, pour the mixture equally into 4 oven proof pots, alternatively you can use one larger one, and seal with puff pastry. Place in the oven until the puff pastry is golden brown and finish with 2 rock oysters per serving.

KEVIN MANGEOLLES

The Neptune team are happy to share our Monkfish dish with you in aid of supporting Alzheimer's UK in this ChariTable Bookings recipe collection."

MONKFISH with baby artichoke, broccoli flowers and pesto

SERVES 4 | PREPARATION TIME 15 MINUTES | COOKING TIME 15 MINUTES

For the Pesto
250g basil
100ml olive oil
50g spinach
2 cloves of garlic
100g Parmesan, grated
75g pine kernels, toasted

For the Artichoke
½ head of garlic
100ml white wine vinegar
200ml rapeseed oil
300ml water
salt
4 baby artichokes

For the Monkfish
4 x 200g monkfish portions
1 tsp oil
100g butter
1 sprig of basil
16 cherry tomatoes, halved and dried
400g pesto
16 broccoli flowers, blanched
4 baby artichokes, halved and fried

To prepare the pesto, blend all of the ingredients together well and pass through a fine sieve.

To prepare the artichoke, peel the outside leaves of the artichoke and trim off the tough outer parts. Pour all the liquid ingredients into a pan together with the garlic and salt. Peel the stalk and place in the cooking mixture. Bring to the boil and cook until soft. Once ready, halve and fry on the flat edge to caramelise.

To cook the monkfish, in a large saucepan on a high heat, add a little oil and the monkfish fillets. Once golden, add the butter and a sprig of basil. Place in a preheated oven at 170°C for approximately 6 minutes. Take out of the pan and let rest for 10 minutes before plating.

To serve, place 3 tablespoons of pesto on the right hand side of the plate, put the monkfish on the pesto and 2 artichoke halves next to the monkfish. Place the blanched broccoli flowers over the artichoke and garnish with the dried tomatoes.

GREGORY MARCHAND

" Being the biggest children's charity in the world, Save the Children doesn't need much more awareness. However, the team at Frenchie choose to support them in this ChariTable Bookings recipe book out of respect for the amazing work they do."

SKATE WING À LA GRENOBLOISE with seaweed

SERVES 4 | PREPARATION TIME 15 MINUTES | COOKING TIME 15 MINUTES

For the Skate
　4 skate wings, peeled and trimmed
　seasoned flour, for dredging
　salt and pepper, to taste
　2 tbsp butter
　1 tbsp vegetable oil, for frying

For the Seaweed Grenobloise
　50g butter
　2 tbsp capers, drained and rinsed
　½ cup croutons
　2 lemons, 1 juiced, 1 segmented
　1 cup mixed seaweeds, dulse, sweet
　tangle, sea green, nori

To prepare the skate, put the flour in a shallow tray and dredge the fish in the flour. Shake off the excess. Re-season the fish with salt and pepper.

To cook the skate, heat a sauté pan and melt 1 tablespoon of the butter and the vegetable oil over a medium-high heat. Once the butter is foaming, add the fish and cook for 2–3 minutes. Add the other tablespoon of butter, turn the fish and cook for a further 2–3 minutes. Transfer the fish to a warm platter.

To finish the dish, discard the butter from the pan and add the remaining 50g butter. Cook over a high heat until it gets foamy, then add the capers and croutons. Cook for 30 seconds, then add the lemon juice and seaweeds. Take off the heat and add the lemon segment. Season with salt and pepper, and spoon over the fish.

BEN MARKS

"*Perilla Dining are supporting White Helmets Syria and with endorsement from ChariTable Bookings, are looking to raise much needed funds and awareness.*"

FRIED DUCK EGG with mussels and lovage
SERVES 4 | PREPARATION TIME 30 MINUTES | COOKING TIME 30 MINUTES

For the Mussel Remoulade
- 400g mussels
- 75ml white wine
- 1 lemon, juiced
- 1 tbsp finely chopped shallots

For the Lovage Sauce
- 1 bunch of lovage

For the Duck Eggs
- 4 duck eggs
- 2 tbs grapeseed oil

For the Garnish
- sea purslane or sea rosemary
- freshly cracked black pepper
- (optional)

To prepare the mussel remoulade, steam the mussels in white wine until the shells begin to open. Remove from the pan and place in the fridge. Pass the mussel liquor through a fine sieve and keep to one side. Remove the mussels from the shell and finely chop. Mix through the lemon juice and the chopped shallots.

To prepare the lovage sauce, blanch the lovage and refresh in ice water. Place the mussel liquor and lovage in a blender and blend until the lovage is fully broken down. Strain through a fine sieve.

To serve, in 4 small pans heat a tablespoon of oil and fry the duck eggs on a medium heat so as not to crisp the outer edges. Lay small piles of chopped samphire and mussel remoulade on top of the egg. Garnish with sea purslane leaves and/or sea rosemary branch ends. Lightly heat the lovage sauce and serve on the side.

ANTHONY MARSHALL

Carney's Community does amazing work in getting disadvantaged and excluded young people off the street and away from a life of crime. The team at the Hilton on Park Lane are pleased to offer their signature dish to ChariTable Bookings to help raise vital funds for this London charity."

BEEF FILLET with celeriac purée, pickled onions, baby vegetables, ceps and thyme jus

SERVES 1 | PREPARATION TIME 30 MINUTES | COOKING TIME 45 MINUTES

For the Scotch Beef Fillet
170g Scotch beef fillet
1 baby carrot
1 asparagus spear
1 baby leek
60g potatoes
2 ceps
200g butter

For the Caramelised Baby Onions
2 baby onions
200ml water
200ml white wine vinegar
100g sugar

For the Celeriac Purée
90g celeriac
200ml whole milk
1 bay leaf
¼ tsp nutmeg
salt, to taste

For the Sauce
2 shallots
2g thyme
200ml beef jus
50ml red wine
20g leek, diced
1 small carrot

For the Garnish
1 tsp Marmite
pea shoots

To start, cut the shallots and sauté with thyme, carrots and leek. Add the red wine and reduce by half, then add the beef jus and reduce by half again. Bring the white wine vinegar, sugar and water to the boil and add the peeled baby onions. Leave to cool in the syrup and chargrill to add colour.

Peel and cut the celeriac into quarters. Add the celeriac, milk, bay leaf, nutmeg and salt into a saucepan and bring to the boil. Once the celeriac has softened, remove from the heat, purée the mixture and pass through a fine sieve.

For the sauce, cut the shallots and sauté with thyme, carrot and leek. Add the red wine and reduce by half, then add the beef jus and reduce by half again.

Clean the baby vegetables, then blanch until cooked. Cut the peeled potatoes into small cubes, then cook in butter on low heat until soft and golden in colour. Clean the ceps and sauté in a bit of butter until cooked.

Seal the meat in a hot pan. Season and cook as desired. Leave to rest for a couple of minutes and brush with Marmite.

Pour the sauce onto the beef fillet and finish with pea shoots.

MICHAEL MATHIESON

We love the idea that donating a recipe can raise money for charity. Maggie's provides drop-in centres across the UK offering free, practical, emotional and social support to people with cancer. Chez Roux Restaurants has included our famous widgeon recipe in the ChariTable Bookings' book to help raise funds for this great charity."

POACHED AND ROASTED BORDERS WIDGEON with leg and cep bolognese,
heritage carrot and purple cauliflower

SERVES 10 | PREPARATION TIME 45 MINUTES (PLUS 12 HOURS PICKLING AND OVERNIGHT RESTING) | COOKING TIME 2 HOURS

Equipment
sous vide and vacuum pack bags

For the Pickle
300ml champagne
100ml champagne vinegar
5g star anise
85g sugar
1 sprig of thyme

For the Cauliflower and Ceps
1 purple cauliflower
100g butter
150ml water
salt and pepper
10 ceps

For the Widgeon and Bolognese
5 widgeons
100g unsalted butter
20ml rapeseed oil
3 cloves of garlic, thinly sliced
3 sprigs of thyme
1 banana shallot, finely diced
8 large ceps, minced
1 stick celery, finely diced
1 small carrot, finely diced
100g tomato petals, quartered,
deskinned and deseeded
½ tsp sugar
250ml Shiraz red wine
sherry vinegar
250ml white chicken stock
150g minced female duck leg

For the Carrot Purée
4 small carrots, diced
1l carrot juice
50g butter
1 pinch each of salt and sugar

For the White Carrot Salad
10 white carrots
100g butter
500ml white chicken stock

To Garnish
sea rosemary, blanched
sea purslane

To make the pickling liquid, bring the ingredients to the boil for 1 minute, remove from the heat and allow to cool.

Cut the florets off the cauliflower and set aside. Thinly slice some stalks and place into the pickle for 12 hours. Place the cauliflower florets in a saucepan with 100g butter and 150ml water. Season and simmer until the water has gone, keep warm. Cook the ceps until golden brown. Set aside until ready to serve, to be assembled with the pickled cauliflower stalks when plating.

To prepare the widgeon, remove the skin, breasts and legs, the liver and heart. Mince the leg meat, liver and heart and set aside.

To make the bolognese, lightly foam the butter and oil and add the sliced garlic. Cook gently until golden brown, add the thyme and let pop for a few seconds. Add the shallot and cook for 1 minute. Season with a touch of salt and add the ceps, celery and carrot. Cook for 5 more minutes. Add the tomato petals, then season with salt and half a teaspoon of sugar. Cook until a thick sauce is achieved. Fry the minced legs and offal in a hot pan, moving continuously until fully incorporated. Add the tomato sauce and red wine, reduce almost completely then add the stock. Reduce until a nice bolognese is made. Season and add a splash of sherry vinegar.

For the widgeon, make an incision into the breasts and fill with bolognese. Vacuum pack and rest in the fridge overnight. Remove the widgeon breasts from their packets, season and seal in foaming butter and continue to cook, turning constantly until nice and pink. Rest for 10 minutes.

To make the carrot purée, place all the ingredients in a saucepan and place a cartouche on top. Cook until tender and little liquid is left. Blitz to a purée adding butter to loosen if needed.

For the white carrot salad, peel and cut the carrot into nice, even rectangles and place in a deep saucepan with 100g butter and stock, season and place a cartouche on top. Cook until all the water has evaporated and the butter has caramelised the carrot.

Use the photo as a guide to serve.

LUKE MATTHEWS

Very proud to share my venison dish from Chewton Glen with ChariTable Bookings in support of BBC Children in Need. I hope you enjoy it and keep raising key funds for this incredible charity."

NEW FOREST VENISON POIVRADE with polenta chips, roasted root vegetables and blueberry sauce

SERVES 4 | PREPARATION TIME 20 MINUTES | COOKING TIME 1 HOUR

For the Polenta Sticks
50g red onion, diced
500ml milk
125g polenta, plus a little extra
50g Parmesan, grated
1.5l vegetable oil, for frying

For the Venison Sauce
200g of diced onion, carrots, celery
and leek
5 juniper berries
1 sprig of thyme
200ml red wine vinegar
500ml red wine
2l veal stock
1kg assorted venison trimmings and
chopped bones
1 knob of butter

For the Garnish
4 baby carrots with the top, peeled
and halved lengthwise
2 purple beetroots, peeled and
sectioned
2 golden beetroots, peeled and
sectioned
½ celeriac, cut into batons
8 baby leeks, blanched
1 splash of olive oil
1 clove of garlic, crushed
1 sprig of rosemary

To make the polenta sticks, sweat the red onion in a pan. Add the milk and bring to the boil. Next, add the polenta and cook for about 6 minutes until the mixture detaches from the side of the pan and starts to form a ball – this is critical for the frying. Add the Parmesan and turn out onto a lightly oiled tray to set. Once set, cut into sticks and then roll in a little dry polenta. These can be made and frozen ahead of time. When ready to serve pre-heat a deep fryer to 180°C and fry the polenta until lightly golden; drain on kitchen paper and season to taste.

To make the venison sauce, pre-heat oven to 180°C. Roast the trimmings and bones until browned, then drain. Colour the assorted vegetables in the pan with the juniper and thyme. Deglaze the pan with the red wine vinegar and reduce until almost gone. Pour in the red wine and reduce by two-thirds. Add the stock bones and trimmings, bring to the boil and simmer for 3 hours, skimming regularly. Pass through a fine sieve, reduce to a sauce consistency and stir in a knob of butter. Season to taste.

To prepare the garnish, pre-heat an oven to 180°C and roast all the vegetables with olive oil, garlic and rosemary until golden. Keep warm.

To cook the venison, preheat an oven to 200°C. Roll the meat in the pepper, heat a frying pan with a little oil and seal off on all sides. Roast the venison in the oven for about 5 minutes, turn halfway through, remove and rest.

To make the vinaigrette, mix all the ingredients together and season to taste.

To finish and assemble the dish, arrange the polenta on plates with the vegetables. Warm the sauce and stir in a knob of butter. Carve the meat and arrange on top of the vegetables and polenta. Pour over the sauce and serve.

For the Venison

4 x 180g medallions of venison
saddle, save bones and trimmings
1 handful of black peppercorns,
crushed
curly kale, wilted and dressed with
vinaigrette
salt and pepper, to taste

For the Vinaigrette

500ml olive oil
1 tbsp dry mustard
1 splash of balsamic vinegar
1 clove of garlic, crushed
1 shallot, finely chopped
¼ cup of fresh herbs
1 egg yolk
salt and pepper, to taste

BRIAN MAULE

Cancer remains one of the major causes of premature death in Scotland. The team at Chardon d'Or are thrilled to offer their famous salmon dish to ChariTable Bookings to raise money to help beat this disease."

PAN-FRIED SCOTTISH SALMON with crushed turnip, baby girolles and light lamb jus

SERVES 4 | PREPARATION TIME 20 MINUTES | COOKING TIME 30 MINUTES

For the Salmon

4 salmon fillets, descaled and pin boned
1 large turnip
150g butter
150ml chicken stock
1 packet of spinach
80g baby girolles
100ml olive oil
2 bunches of spring onions
150ml lamb jus/demi glace
salt and pepper, to taste

Start by peeling the turnip and cutting it into sizeable chunks. Cook in boiling, salted water until tender. When cooked, remove from the pan and dry thoroughly. Place in a pot and crush with a fork, folding the butter through at the same time. If needed, add a little chicken stock to loosen the mixture and season to taste.

Pick and wash the spinach leaves, then fry quickly in a hot pan until wilted. Season and set to one side.

Clean the girolles, making sure to remove any grit or dirt. If they are big, trim them down slightly to a uniform size. Once washed and trimmed, fry lightly in olive oil.

Cut the spring onions into even sized batons and cook in boiling, salted water.

To cook the fish, season both sides generously and add a little olive oil to a hot pan. Place the fish into the pan skin-side down and fry until golden in colour. Turn the fish over and fry until nicely coloured, then return to the skin-side. Place in an oven preheated to 180°C. Leave to cook for 4–5 minutes, until the fish is slightly pink. While the salmon is cooking, warm the previously prepared garnishes.

To serve, place the crushed turnip in the centre of the plate, the salmon on top and decorate with the spring onions, girolles and spinach. Drizzle with a little lamb jus and serve immediately.

FRANCESCO MAZZEI

Leuka does amazing work in the research of leukaemia and other blood cancers and Sartoria is proud to be able to support that work by donating our signature stracciatella to ChariTable Bookings' fantastic new recipe book."

STRACCIATELLA RICOTTA TORTELLI

SERVES 4 | PREPARATION TIME 1 HOUR 30 MINUTES | COOKING TIME 15 MINUTES

For the Pasta Dough
200g 00 flour
200g hard durum wheat flour
4 fresh eggs

For the Filling
500g stracciatella di bufala
500g ricotta
150g Grana Padano Riserva
10g truffle butter
egg yolk, to bind the pasta
salt and black pepper, to taste

For the Garnish
10 sage leaves
16 hazelnuts
200g unsalted butter
a few drops of balsamic vinegar
microcress

To form the dough, mix the 2 flours together on the table, then make a hole in the middle. Put the eggs in the middle and mix slowly with the flour. The pasta needs to be kneaded by hand until it has a smooth surface. When the dough is ready, wrap it in cling film and store in the fridge for about an hour.

To prepare the filling, mix the stracciatella until the consistency is smooth. Add the ricotta cheese, 100g of Grana Padano and a pinch of salt and pepper. Melt the truffle butter in a pan and add gradually to the mixture.

To make the tortelli, with a rolling pin, stretch out the dough into 1mm thick sheets, and cut it into 6–7cm squares. Put a little filling at the centre of each square, brush some egg yolk around the edges and close into a rectangular shape, making sure that the borders adhere well and no air is left inside.

Cook the tortelli in boiling water for approximately 3–4 minutes. In the meantime, melt the unsalted butter. Once it browns, add the sage and hazelnuts.

To serve, plate the tortelli and season with the brown butter and remaining grated Grana Padano. Drizzle with a few drops of balsamic vinegar and sprinkle with microcress.

IAN MCANDREW

This is a great way to raise awareness for fantastic charities across the UK and get people cooking! I hope you enjoy Blackaddy's signature sea bass dish in aid of Cancer Research UK and try many of these recipes, all here to celebrate charity in ChariTable Bookings recipe book."

PAN ROAST SEA BASS with roast salsify, new potatoes, spinach, baby onions and puy lentil jus
SERVES 4 | PREPARATION TIME 20 MINUTES | COOKING TIME 1 HOUR

For the Sea Bass
- 4 x 150g sea bass fillets, descaled
- 40ml olive oil
- salt and freshly ground white pepper

For the Salsify
- 350g salsify, peeled
- 1l water
- 1 lemon
- 30g flour
- 12g salt
- 4g sugar
- 20ml vegetable oil
- 40g butter

For the Puy Lentils
- 40g puy lentils, rinsed
- 1 shallot, peeled
- 2 cloves of garlic
- ¼ stick celery
- 150ml veal jus

For the New Potatoes
- 320g new potatoes, peeled
- 50g butter

For the Baby Onions
- 20 baby onions, peeled
- 20ml olive oil
- 20g butter
- salt and pepper

For the Spinach
- 175g spinach leaves, stalks removed
- 20g butter

To make the salsify, cut the salsify into 10cm lengths, allowing for 4 lengths per portion. If the salsify is quite thick then, once cooked, halve the thick pieces lengthways. Squeeze the lemon juice into the water and whisk in the flour. Add the remaining lemon peel, the salt and the sugar. Plunge the salsify into this and bring to the boil, stirring often to prevent the flour from sitting on the bottom of the pan and burning. Simmer until the salsify is just cooked. Remove from the heat and cool. Wash the salsify and dry. When ready to serve, heat the oil in a frying pan and, when hot, add the butter. When sizzling, add the salsify, season and fry gently until lightly brown. Drain and keep warm.

To make the puy lentils, place the lentils in a pan with the shallot, garlic and celery. Cover well with water, bring to the boil and simmer until just cooked. Drain and cool. Discard the vegetables. Heat the veal jus with the drained lentils.

To make the new potatoes, cook the potatoes in boiling, salted water. Drain and roughly crush. Set aside. To serve, warm the potatoes with the butter and season as necessary.

To make the baby onions, blanch the baby onions in boiling, salted water until half cooked. Drain and cool. Heat the oil and butter in a frying pan, season and fry the onions until lightly browned. Drain and keep warm.

To make the sea bass, season the sea bass on both sides. Heat the olive oil in a frying pan, and when hot, place the fish in, skin-side down. Fry until golden, then turn over. Remove the pan from the heat, but leave the fish in the pan. Keep warm.

To serve, place a pile of the crushed potatoes in the centre of the plate. Arrange 4 pieces of salsify on the potato and a piece of fish on top of the salsify. Divide the spinach to allow 5 small piles per plate around the fish. Top each one of these with an onion and spoon the lentils around.

DAVE MCCARTHY

"Scott's happily lends its famous cod recipe to ChariTable Bookings in aid of The National Autistic Society. I hope this raises much needed funds for such a worthy charity, struggling to improve the lives of those with autism."

SCOTT'S ROASTED COD with arrocina beans, chorizo and Padrón peppers

SERVES 4 | PREPARATION TIME 30 MINUTES (PLUS OVERNIGHT SOAKING) | COOKING TIME 1 HOUR 30 MINUTES

For the Cod

4 x 180g cod fillets
80g chorizo, diced
50g Padrón peppers
100g arrocina beans, soaked overnight
25ml extra virgin olive oil
2 shallots, diced
1 medium sized mild red chilli, finely
25ml white wine
500ml chicken stock
½ small bunch of parsley, chopped
20g unsalted butter
1 clove of garlic, crushed
½ lemon
salt and freshly ground black pepper

Heat some olive oil in a pan, then add the shallots and chilli. Cook on a low heat to avoid burning the mixture. Drain the arrocina beans, add to the pan and sweat down for 5 minutes. Season with salt and pepper. Add the white wine and reduce by half. Add the chicken stock and simmer slowly for 45 minutes or until the beans are cooked. You may need to add extra chicken stock. Set aside in a warm place.

Season the cod with salt and pepper. Heat a non-stick frying pan, add olive oil and place skin-side down in the pan. Cook for around 5 minutes, until the skin is crispy. Turn over and cook for another 3 minutes. If the cod fillets are thin, reduce the cooking time accordingly. As soon as you turn the cod over, heat another non stick frying pan with olive oil until smoking. Add the Padrón peppers and cook until they start to wilt. Next, add the chorizo, chopped parsley, butter, garlic and a generous of squeeze of lemon juice, then cook for a further minute.

When ready to serve, spoon the cooked beans onto the middle of each warm plate. Sit the cod on top of the beans and pour over the Padrón peppers and chorizo.

Editor's Note: *If you prefer to use fresh beans, borlotti or broad beans work well too.*

RORY MCCLEAN

It is with much pleasure that I am involved with ChariTable Bookings to help raise funds for charities. I would like to champion the Matt Hampson Foundation who seriously inspire and support young people injured through sport. I hope you enjoy our recipe from the White Swan."

VENISON LOIN AND FAGGOT with roasted cauliflower, peat and blue cheese

SERVES 4 | PREPARATION TIME 30 MINUTES | COOKING TIME 1 HOUR

For the Venison
1 venison loin
knob of butter
½ clove of garlic
¼ sprig of rosemary
¼ sprig of thyme

For the Cauliflower and the Purée
2 cauliflowers
salt, to season
knob of butter
1 tbsp salt
150ml cream
100ml milk
20g white chocolate

For the Port and Pear
1 bottle port
1 stick of cinnamon
1 star anise
1 orange
100g demerara sugar
1 commis pear

For the Faggots
½ onion
1½ cloves of garlic
¾ sprig of rosemary
¾ sprig of thyme
100g venison mince
50g sausage meat
50g chicken livers, chopped
1 juniper berry

To prepare the cauliflower, break down the cauliflower into its natural large florets, reserving any trimmings for the purée. Blanch the florets in salted, boiling water for 3 minutes, then refresh in ice water.

To make the purée, chop down the remaining cauliflower, cook under a lid in foaming butter with 1 tablespoon of table salt without colouring. Once tender, add the cream, milk and white chocolate. Cook out until the liquid is reduced and blend until smooth.

Reduce the port by half with the cinnamon, star anise, orange zest and sugar. Peel and cut the pear into quarters, removing the core. Poach the pear gently in the reduced port until softened, and set aside.

To make the faggots, dice the onion and garlic, and sweat gently with chopped rosemary and picked thyme. Once cooked and chilled, mix with the venison mince, sausage meat and chopped chicken livers. Season with grated juniper, nutmeg, salt and pepper. Wrap the faggots into 50g sausages using cling film. Once wrapped, poach in hot water for 8 minutes and chill.

To cook the venison and assemble the dish, season the venison loin and roast in foaming butter, add any remaining rosemary, thyme and garlic to the pan. Transfer to the oven, along with the faggots at 180°C for 5 minutes, remove from the pan and rest the meat. Also roast the cauliflower florets in butter and transfer to the oven. To plate the dish, first add the cauliflower purée to the plate, followed by pieces of blue cheese and the poached pear slices. Add the roasted cauliflower and venison faggots. Carve the venison, plate as pictured and serve.

For the Faggots *continued*
  ½ nutmeg
  salt and pepper, to taste
To Serve
  10g Fourme D'Ambert (blue
  cheese)

PIP MCCORMAC

There are so many children in the world in need of a boost. ChariTable Bookings is helping me support Msizi Africa, giving so many kids a vital step up."

LEMON AND HERB SPAGHETTI

SERVES 2 | PREPARATION TIME 10 MINUTES | COOKING TIME 15 MINUTES

For the Dish
olive oil
100g spaghetti
2 cloves of garlic, chopped
1 tsp dried chilli flakes
1 courgette
1 lemon, juiced
2 stalks of lemon balm, or mint, leaves only
1 tbsp chopped parsley
grated Parmesan, for serving, optional

To cook the spaghetti, add a splash of olive oil to a large pan of water and bring to the boil. Once bubbling, add the spaghetti and cook according to the packet instructions.

To prepare the sauce, add a glug of oil to another saucepan with a lid, and set over a medium heat. Once warm, add the garlic and chilli and cover, letting them sweat for 2–3 minutes until the garlic is a golden brown. Trim the courgette, halve lengthways and cut into slices about 1cm thick. Add the courgette to the pan of garlic, stir, cover and cook for around 5 minutes, until the courgette is soft and beginning to brown. Remove the courgette pan from the heat and stir in the lemon juice, expect the mixture to splutter a little. Return to the heat to cook off some of the liquid. Once cooked, drain the pasta and add it to the courgette pan with the leaves from the lemon balm. Stir everything together, place the pan back on the heat for another minute to warm through if needed.

To serve, divide the spaghetti mixture between 2 bowls, sprinkle over the parsley and some Parmesan if you like. Eat immediately.

RYAN MCCUTCHEON

"I'm donating Greywalls Halibut recipe to ChariTable Bookings in aid of the great work that Child Health, the children's wing at York Teaching Hospital does on a daily basis. Enjoy and support!"

PAN-SEARED NORTH ATLANTIC HALIBUT with mussel and clam gratin with sweet
cider sauce and sauce rouille

SERVES 5 | PREPARATION TIME 1 HOUR 30 MINUTES | COOKING TIME 2 HOURS

For the Halibut

- 700g halibut, deskinned and pin boned

For the Herb Crust

- 200g bread crumbs
- 150g emmental cheese, grated
- 100g fresh parsley, chopped
- 160g butter

For the Rouille

- 1 medium Golden Wonder potato
- 1 pinch of saffron
- 1 clove of garlic
- 2 egg yolks
- 250ml olive oil
- 2 piquillo peppers
- salt, to taste

For the Mussel and Clam Gratin with Sweet Cider Sauce

- 200g shallots, diced
- 100g white leek, diced
- 400g mussels
- 400g clams
- 1g thyme
- 150ml white wine
- 50g butter
- 200ml sweet cider
- 300ml single cream
- 1 pinch of salt and pepper

To Serve

- 100g red bell pepper, diced
- 125g fresh corn
- 175g diced potato, blanched
- 30g mixed sea herbs, sea rosemary, sea purslane and samphire

To prepare the halibut, remove the skin and ensure no bones remain.

To make the herb crust, divide into 140g portions. Place the ingredients for the herb crust into a blender and blitz until the mixture comes together to a crumb consistency. It could also be worked together by hand. Once the desired texture is achieved, set aside.

For the rouille, cook the potato in a little water with the saffron and garlic. Once suitably soft, drain, leave to cool and reserve the garlic. Place the cooked potato in a blender, add the yolks and begin to blitz. Add the piquillo peppers and continue to mix. Slowly add the olive oil until a mayonnaise consistency forms and season to taste.

For the mussel and clam gratin, sauté half the shallots, half the diced leek and the reserved clove of garlic. Once everything is soft, add the mussels, clams, thyme and the white wine. Cover with a lid for 2–3 minutes and allow everything to sweat. Once the shells have opened, drain the shellfish, reserving the liquid, then chill.

Sauté the remaining shallots, leeks and a little garlic in the butter. Once soft, add the liquid from the shellfish pan and reduce by two thirds. Add the cider and reduce by half. Finally, add the single cream, bring the mixture to the boil and leave to simmer for no more than a minute. Season to taste and pass through a fine sieve.

To serve, begin by removing three quarters of the meat from the shells of the mussels and clams, leaving a quarter of the meat in the shells for garnish. Season and lightly oil the halibut and place in a preheated pan, frying for 2–3 minutes. Add a knob of butter to the pan and put in a preheated oven at 160°C for 1 minute. Remove from the oven and place on a dry cloth presentation side up.

To finish the dish, heat the potato, red pepper and sweet corn in the cider sauce. Two minutes prior to serving, add the shellfish and shells into the sauce to heat. Once done, incorporate the sea herbs and set to one side for serving.

To serve, place all the vegetables, sauce and shellfish into a bowl, top with the herb crust, gratin and place the fish on top. Sauce some of the shells with rouille and serve.

ENDA MCEVOY

I love being able to support local charities at Loam. Cope Galway does incredible work for homelessness, domestic violence and the elderly in our area. Proud to support them alongside ChariTable Bookings."

CARROTS with buttermilk and nasturtium

SERVES 4 | PREPARATION TIME 15 MINUTES | COOKING TIME 4 HOURS

Equipment
slide lock bags

For the Braised Carrots
14 assorted heritage carrots, tops removed and reserved
60g butter
1 sprig of tarragon
1 sprig of thyme
1 sprig of sage

For the Chewy Carrots
5 small carrots

For the Buttermilk Sauce
500ml carrot juice
150ml buttermilk
100g cold butter, diced

For the Garnish
chervil
reserved carrot tops
nasturtiums

To make the braised carrots, in a heavy, shallow saucepan add the butter, herbs and whole carrots. Cook on a low heat. Cover with a lid and ensure that all the carrots are in a single layer on the bottom of the pan. Keep moving the carrots and baste them regularly until the carrots are cooked. Change the butter or herbs if they burn.

To make the chewy carrots, cook the carrots in a ziplock bag in boiling water until just undercooked. Then dry the carrots in a low oven, 80–100°C, for 4 hours.

To prepare the buttermilk sauce, reduce the carrot juice to a glaze. In a separate saucepan, heat the buttermilk and whisk in the butter bit by bit. Next whisk in the glazed carrot juice and keep warm.

To assemble the dish, carve the larger braised carrots into more manageable sizes. Reheat the chewy carrots with the glaze and arrange amongst the braised carrots. Pour over some of the carrot buttermilk sauce and dress with the herbs.

ANDY MCFADDEN

" It is terrible when anyone finds out they have cancer but always worse when it is a child which is why all of us at Pied à Terre support Children with Cancer UK alongside ChariTable Bookings."

LAVINTON LAMB with ratatouillle, ricotta and anchovy

SERVES 4 | PREPARATION TIME 30 MINUTES | COOKING TIME 1 HOUR

For the Dish

1 x 300g lamb loin, from best end

1 egg white

oil and butter, for cooking

For the Green Crumb

100g panko breadcrumbs

50g parsley, chopped

1 sprig each of rosemary and thyme

1 clove of garlic

1 egg white

For the Red Pepper Ketchup

4 large red peppers

100g shallot

100g apple

500ml apple juice

125ml Cabernet Sauvignon vinegar

1 red bird's eye red chilli

1 star anise

1 clove

50g sugar

½ tsp salt

45ml pineapple juice

For the Aubergine Caviar

1 large aubergine

3 tbsp Greek yoghurt

1 tsp garlic, minced

¼ tsp piment d'Espelette

½ tsp sea salt

½ lime, juiced

2 tbsp extra virgin olive oil

To make the green crumb, place all of the green crumb ingredients in a blender, and pulse several times until completely combined. Pass through a drum sieve. Pour the mixture into a medium size bowl and set aside.

To make the red pepper ketchup, combine all of the ingredients and simmer until everything is tender, about 1 hour. Blend until smooth. Pass through a fine sieve and season to taste.

To make the aubergine caviar, roast the aubergine directly over an open medium flame until the skin is cracking and completely charred, about 10 minutes. Wrap the aubergine tightly in heavy-duty foil, as it rests it will continue to release steam and will soften and cook through while it cools. Once fully cooled, unwrap the aubergine and reserve the liquid that has collected at the bottom of the foil. Carefully peel away all the charred skin and discard it. Remove the stem, cut the aubergine from top to bottom and gently split it open. Remove the big packets of seeds, a few left behind is fine. Use a spoon to scrape out the seeds and cut out any sections you miss with a pairing knife. Once you have separated all the flesh from the skin and seeds, start to finely chop the flesh with a large, sharp chef's knife. Use a rocking motion and be sure to go over each and every section as you don't want to leave any stringy pieces behind. Place the chopped aubergine in a glass mixing bowl and pour in 2–3 tablespoons of the reserved smoky aubergine liquid. Gently stir in the yogurt, garlic, piment d'Espelette, salt, lime juice, and olive oil. Check for seasoning and adjust with more salt or lime if needed.

To make the confit tomatoes, preheat the oven to 90°C. Bring a large saucepan of salted water to a boil. Using a paring knife, mark a shallow cross on the bottom of each tomato. Add to the boiling water for 3–4 seconds. Immediately transfer to an ice bath and, once cool, remove the skins with a paring knife, being careful not to cut into the flesh. Toss the peeled tomatoes in the olive oil, salt, and sugar. Place on a baking tray lined with parchment paper and bake for 1.5 hours, until the tomatoes are slightly shriveled and about one quarter of their original size.

For the Confit Tomatoes
12 cherry tomatoes
1 tbsp olive oil
1 pinch of salt
1 pinch of sugar

For the Ricotta and Courgette Flowers
750ml whole milk
1 lemon, juiced
salt and pepper, to taste
4 courgette flowers

For the Basil Oil
150g basil, picked
250ml pomace oil

For the Anchovy Mayonnaise
350g marinated white anchovies
35g egg white
15g sushi vinegar
500ml pomace oil

To Serve
onion, baked in skins, separated into
petals and charred
courgette pureé
garlic pureé
marjoram, picked for sauce

For the ricotta, bring the milk to the boil and add the lemon juice. Allow to infuse for 30 minutes and then carefully pass through a muslin cloth. Season with salt and pepper and stuff the courgette flower. This will need to be steamed for 3–4 minutes.

To make the basil oil, place the basil into a pot of boiling water for 30–45 seconds, drain and refresh in ice cold water. Once the basil has completely cooled, squeeze the basil to remove as much water from the leaves as possible. Place in a blender with 100ml pomace oil. Blend on a high speed, slowly adding the remaining oil until smooth. Pour into a small bottle and refrigerate.

To make the anchovy mayonnaise, blend the anchovies with the egg white and vinegar for 1 minute until a smooth purée. Emulsify with the oil, check for seasoning and keep in piping bags.

To cook the lamb and serve, season the lamb loin with salt. Roll in egg white and then in the green crumb. Cook on a medium heat in oil and butter gently for 1 minute on each side for approximately 5–6 minutes. Allow to rest for as long as you cook it. Carve the lamb into long slices and arrange on the plate with the other elements as you like. Add the marjoram to the lamb cooking juices and spoon around. Add a few drops of basil oil and serve.

KEVIN MCFADDEN

"May the Fifteenth love the fact that Farm Africa educates their beneficiaries rather than just provides food. This is why we are happy to support them through ChariTable Bookings' recipe book in the hope they might raise even more funds."

GOAT MEATBALLS with dumplings

SERVES 4 | PREPARATION TIME 1 HOUR | COOKING TIME 1 HOUR 30 MINUTES

For the Meatballs

- 300g minced goat
- 200g minced beef
- 1 whole onion, finely diced
- 4 cloves garlic, crushed
- 1 thumb ginger, grated
- 1 tbsp each toasted and ground cumin seeds, fennel seeds, cinnamon and sweet paprika
- 2 tbsp each chopped mint, parsley, dill and coriander
- 100g breadcrumbs
- 1 egg, beaten
- salt and pepper
- olive oil to shallow fry

For the Sauce

- 4½ tbsp olive oil
- 6 spring onions, sliced
- 5 cloves of garlic, crushed and chopped
- 2 thumbs of ginger, grated
- 4 tomatoes, peeled and chopped
- 1 red pepper, roasted, peeled and chopped
- 3 sprigs of rosemary, picked and chopped
- 2 sprigs of thyme
- 600ml chicken stock
- 1 lemon, zested and juiced
- 200g kale or spinach
- 1 tbsp each chopped coriander, parsley and mint

For the Dumplings

- 300g fine white cornmeal
- 100g self raising flour
- 300ml tusker lager
- 6 spring onions, sliced
- ½ tbsp coriander seeds
- 1 tbsp cumin, toasted and ground
- 3 cloves of garlic, crushed to a paste
- 2 thumbs of ginger, grated
- 300g feta cheese
- 1 handful of coriander, chopped
- 1l sunflower oil, for deep frying
- lemon wedges

To prepare the meatballs, cook the onions, garlic, ginger and spices until soft and sweet; tip out onto a plate and leave to cool. Once cool, place with the rest of the ingredients in a mixing bowl, together with a teaspoon of salt and some ground black pepper. To test seasoning, make a small ball, cook through and taste, adding more salt and pepper if desired. Mix thoroughly with your hands and shape into golf ball sized portions. Use a bowl of warm water to wet your hands before moulding – this will make it easier. Place the meatballs in the fridge to rest for 30 minutes.

To cook the meatballs, use a heavy-based pan, wide enough to fit all the meatballs, and sear in 2 batches, with a tablespoon of olive oil for each batch. Remove from the pan and add the remaining oil, spring onions, garlic and ginger. Cook over a medium heat for 5 minutes. Keep it moving and add the tomatoes, red pepper, rosemary, thyme and 110ml of stock. Scrape around the bottom of the pan with a wooden spoon to incorporate any caramelized remnants into the sauce. Return the meatballs to the pan with the rest of the stock and the lemon zest. Cook on a gentle heat for around 20 minutes or until the meatballs are cooked through.

To prepare the dumplings, put the cornmeal flour and self-raising flour into a bowl. Add the lager and leave to sit for 10 minutes. Then add the spring onion, spices, garlic and ginger, and mix well. Gently fold in the feta cheese and herbs. The consistency of the batter should be thick enough to hold on a spoon but will slide off gently.

Pour vegetable oil into a large, sturdy pan on the back of the stove and heat to 170°C. If you don't have a thermometer, drop a small amount of batter in to test, if it turns crisp and golden and rises to the top, then it is ready to fry. Make sure the oil isn't too hot or the dumplings will burn on the outside and be raw in the middle. Drop spoonfuls of the mixture into the oil 6 at a time, being careful not to overcrowd. Transfer carefully to a plate lined with kitchen towel and keep warm while frying the other batches.

To finish the meatballs, check the stock. If too thin, remove the lid and reduce until you have a thick, glossy sauce. Now add the kale or spinach and fold through gently. Replace the lid to heat thoroughly.

To serve, finish with the herbs and a squeeze of lemon juice, wedges of lemon and sea salt.

COLIN MCGURRAN

Lindsey Lodge Hospice is very much a local charity to Lincolnshire, just as Winteringham Fields is a local restaurant. We believe in supporting good causes close to home which is why we are happy to donate our dish to this ChariTable Bookings collection."

DUCK AND PISTACHIO

SERVES 4 | PREPARATION TIME 10 MINUTES (PLUS 2 HOURS TO COOL THE RILLETTE AND 1 HOUR TO COOL THE DUCK) | COOKING TIME 3 HOURS 30 MINUTES

For the Duck

1 large whole duck, butchered into
legs and breasts
1l duck fat
3 cardamom pods
3 juniper berries
3 cloves
3 tsp thyme, finely chopped
3 cloves of garlic, crushed
3 bay leaves
1 tbsp lovage, finely chopped
salt and pepper, to season

For the Rillette

1kg potatoes
100g butter, cubed
100ml cream
100g Parmesan, grated
salt and pepper, to season
200g plain flour
3 eggs, beaten
200g breadcrumbs
fresh herbs for seasoning, if desired

For the Pistachio Purée

500g pistachios, peeled and
unsalted
salt
a little of the duck fat

For the Garnish

500g English black cherries

For the rillette, wash and bake the potatoes whole at 180°C for 90 minutes. Remove from the oven, halve the potatoes and leave to cool for 5 minutes. You want them to still be warm when you use them. Scoop out the potato flesh and pass through a fine sieve, alternatively you can mash. In a pan, place the sieved potatoes on a medium heat, adding the butter cubes in slowly. Beat it through the potato using a wooden spoon. Slowly add the cream whilst continually beating, then incorporate the Parmesan. Season to taste with salt and pepper. You could also mix in some fresh herbs like chives, lovage or parsley for an extra dimension. Roll in to sausage shapes and place in the fridge for 2 hours. When chilled, roll them in the flour, tap off any excess, then roll in the egg and the breadcrumbs. Place back in the fridge until 2 minutes before serving, then deep fry at 180°C until golden brown. Set aside on kitchen paper.

Place the duck fat in a saucepan with the cardamom, juniper berries, cloves, thyme, garlic and bay leaves and bring the fat up to 90°C. Remove the duck legs, season them with sea salt, place them in the duck fat and leave at 90°C for 2 hours to confit. Remove from the fat, take off the skin, then pick the meat from the bone and place in a bowl. Season with salt and pepper. Add 50ml cooled duck fat back into the meat, mix and gently fold in the chopped lovage. Lay out a strip of cling film, giving yourself a metre to play with. Place the confit duck leg meat in the middle of the cling film ready to roll into a sausage shape. Wrap the cling film and twist at the ends to make a solid and tight duck leg roll. Place in the fridge for 1 hour to cool. To serve slice into portions, remove the cling film and fry the ends.

Remove the breasts from the duck and season the skin with salt and pepper. Fry it in a saucepan at a low heat, skin-side down, so that the fat comes out of the skin. Place your pan in the oven at 120°C for 10–12 minutes. This is for very pink but stay calm, you will rest it for 15 minutes which will allow the blood to come out of the meat. It will not look raw, and the meat will be very tender.

Place the pistachios on an oven tray, season with a little salt, then bake for approximately 5 minutes until golden at 180°C. Blitz them in a blender until smooth, using a little duck fat to create a purée.

Dice up your cherries roughly, then use the picture as a guide to plate all the elements of the dish and serve.

PETER MCKENNA

With more than 1 in 3 people affected by cancer in the west of Scotland, which in fact is the highest in Europe, myself and the team at The Gannet want to get behind and support Beatson and the specialist services this internationally renowned charity provides."

SCOTCH BEEF DIAMOND MUSCLE with Ayrshire beets, artichoke, shallot, broccoli and Madeira sauce

SERVES 4–6 | PREPARATION TIME 1 HOUR 30 MINUTES | COOKING TIME 1 HOUR

For the Beef
1kg beef diamond muscle
4l water
320g salt
4 bay leaves
8 black peppercorns

For the Salt-Baked Beetroots
2 medium beetroots
200g salt
30g egg white
1 sprig of thyme
1 clove of garlic
a little water

For the Globe Artichoke
2 globe artichokes
vegetable stock, enough to cover

For the Shallots
1 large banana shallot
100g caster sugar
1 splash of sherry vinegar

For the Beef Dripping Potatoes
4 Maris Piper potatoes
beef dripping, to cover
10g salt
1 clove of garlic
1 sprig of thyme

For the Tender Stem Broccoli
200g tender stem broccoli

For the Madeira Sauce
Jacob's ladder bones
2 shallots, sliced
1 clove of garlic, peeled
5 button mushrooms, sliced
1 tbsp sherry vinegar
100ml Madeira
1l chicken stock
200ml veal stock or demi glaze
20g butter

Brine the beef cut in an 8% brine with the bay leaves and black peppercorns for 1 hour before cooking. Once brined, rinse off lightly and pat dry. Shallow fry the meat until browned on all sides. Place in the oven at 160°C for 10 minutes, turning regularly. You can cook the meat to your own preference, in the restaurant however, we prefer medium rare. It's important to leave the beef to rest for 10 minutes in a warm place after it comes out of the oven.

For the salt-baked beetroots, blend all the ingredients, apart from the beetroots, until you have a firm paste. It should not be too wet or too dry. Coat the beetroot in the paste, then bake at 170°C for 25–30 minutes. To check whether cooked, turn upside down and insert a knife. The flesh should be tender and the knife should slide out. Once cooked, leave to cool for 5 minutes. Crack and scrape off the salt crust and peel. Cut into rounds and purée the trimmed beetroot.

Peel the globe artichokes and cook in a light vegetable stock until tender, leaving to cool in the liquid. Once cold, cut each into 6 pieces.

Cut the shallot into 4 discs. Leave the skin on while you do this to help maintain the shape, then discard it. Salt the shallot discs for 5 minutes, then dry the excess moisture on kitchen paper. Fry in oil and a little butter until golden brown. Drain the fat from the pan and add the sugar. Make a caramel, then once the shallot is golden and cooking nicely, add a splash of vinegar. Cook until soft but not falling apart.

For the beef dripping potatoes, peel and cut each potato into 3 circles, it's best to slice each one into thirds, then cut out circles using a pastry cutter. Once the desired shape has been achieved, blend the salt, thyme and garlic together. Coat the potatoes in the salt mix, leave for 15 minutes, then rinse under a tap. Melt the dripping and cover the potatoes in the fat. Cook in the oven slowly, at 160°C, until tender. This should take around 45 minutes.

Cut the tender stem broccoli to the desired size. Cook quickly in boiling, salted water and refresh in ice water, to retain bite.

To make the Madeira sauce, roast the bones at 180°C for 45 minutes, until nice and golden. Sweat the shallots with the garlic in butter. Once they are soft and the natural sugars have been released, add the mushrooms. Cook until the juices having evaporated and the mushrooms have also softened. Deglaze the pan with the vinegar, then reduce once more, until the pan is almost dry. Pour in the Madeira and reduce by a fifth. Incorporate the chicken and veal stock, along with the bones. Bring to the boil, then skim and simmer for 45 minutes. Make sure to skim as much as possible. Strain the liquid into a clean pan and reduce until the mixture coats the back of a spoon. Season to taste.

To plate, assemble as pictured, trying not to be too rigid in your approach.

STEPHEN MCLAUGHLIN

For us at Andrew Fairlie Restaurant at Gleneagles, which charity to support wasn't a question for us. The Radiotherapy Research Project at the Beatson Centre has not only helped our chef patron but could be on the cutting edge of new treatment. We are proud to support awareness of it through ChariTable Bookings."

PERTHSHIRE ROE DEER with damson purée and toasted spices

SERVES 6 | PREPARATION TIME 30 MINUTES (PLUS OVERNIGHT TO SET) | COOKING TIME 2 HOURS 30 MINUTES

Equipment
vacuum pack bags

For the Venison
650g trimmed roe deer loin

For the Damson Purée
1kg damsons
50g butter
100g sugar
½ lemon, juiced

For the Carrot Purée
1kg carrots, peeled and sliced
1 block of butter, cold
½ orange, juiced
2 cardamom pods

For the Polenta Discs
500ml chicken stock
3 cloves of garlic, lightly crushed
1 sprig of rosemary
1 sprig of thyme
salt and pepper
340g fine polenta
250g unsalted butter
60g Parmesan, grated
700ml water

For the Spice Mix
1 tbsp coriander seeds
2 tbsp black peppercorns
¼ stick cinnamon
1½ tbsp cloves
2 tbsp four spice powder

Wash the damsons and remove their stones. Put them into a vacuum pouch with the remaining purée ingredients. Seal the bag and steam until the fruit is very soft, about 45 minutes. Remove the damsons and juices from the pouch and blitz.

For the carrot purée, put the carrots, butter, orange juice and cardamom pods in a sous vide bag. Steam for 1 hour. Remove the pods, place the contents of the bag in a blender and blitz until smooth.

For the polenta discs, infuse the chicken stock with the garlic, thyme, rosemary, salt and pepper. Bring to the boil and let sit for 5 minutes. Strain through a sieve to remove the garlic and herbs. Place the polenta in a large bowl, over a pan with 700ml of simmering water. Add the hot stock and whisk thoroughly. Cover the bowl in cling film and leave over the simmering water for 5 minutes. Remove and whisk the mixture. Re-cover with cling film and continue to cook for 25 minutes, whisking intermittently until the polenta is cooked. Pour the mix into the bowl of a food processor. Beat with the paddle attachment, adding the butter and Parmesan. Line a tray with cling film and pour the polenta into it, 1cm thick. Leave to set in the fridge overnight. Carefully tip the polenta out onto a clean table and cut into discs of 6cm in diameter. Cut out rounds 1.5cm in diameter from the centre of each disc. Store in the fridge until needed.

For the spice mix, gently toast the coriander seeds, peppercorns and cinnamon stick. Grind with the cloves, pass through a sieve, mix with four spice and keep covered.

For the venison jus, heat the oil until almost smoking. Add the venison and cook evenly until caramelised. Add the vegetables, aromats and continue to cook over a high heat until the vegetables are a light golden colour. Deglaze with the port and reduce to a syrup. Add the red wine and reduce by two thirds. Add the veal jus and simmer gently for 30 minutes. Pass through a fine sieve and muslin cloth. Check the seasoning and consistency.

To serve, arrange on the plate as pictured.

For the Venison Jus

   1 drizzle of light olive oil

   200g venison trimmings, diced

   20g shallots, finely diced

   20g carrots, finely diced

   20g celery, finely diced

   6 black peppercorns

   4 juniper berries

   75ml port

   150ml red wine

   200ml veal jus

ANDREW MCLAY

In support of the continued work of Cancer Research in tackling this terrible disease, J Sheekey are pleased to contribute their famous tempura oyster recipe to ChariTable Bookings' fantastic initiative to raise more funds for charity."

TEMPURA OYSTERS with wasabi dressing

SERVES 4 | PREPARATION TIME 20 MINUTES | COOKING TIME 45 MINUTES

For the Oysters
16 rock oysters, shucked and removed from the shells, clean the shells and keep to one side
sea salt and freshly ground black pepper

For the Wasabi Dressing Base
50ml light soy sauce
200ml mirin
5g ginger, peeled and finely chopped
2 limes, juiced

For the Wasabi Dressing
1 red pepper, roasted, peeled and finely chopped
½ cucumber, skin on, cubed with seeds removed
1 jalapeno, finely diced
1 medium red chilli, finely diced
2 spring onions, finely chopped
½ small bunch of coriander, finely chopped
1 tsp wasabi

For the Tempura Batter
150g tempura flour
ice water
vegetable oil

For the Garnish
micro coriander
chopped red chilli
sea salt

To prepare the wasabi dressing base, bring the soy, mirin and ginger to the boil in a small saucepan. Simmer for 10 minutes, remove from the heat, stir in the lime juice and allow to cool on one side.

To make the wasabi dressing, transfer the now cool base into a bowl and add the rest of the ingredients.

To prepare the tempura batter, slowly add ice water to the tempura flour in a large bowl. Whisk continuously until a pouring cream consistency is achieved.

To fry the oysters, pour 6cm of oil into a medium-sized, heavy-bottomed saucepan or a deep fat fryer and heat to 160°C. If using a saucepan, please be careful as the oil will be very hot. Season the oysters with the salt and pepper. Dip them into the batter and fry in small batches until golden brown. Remove with tongs and place onto kitchen paper to soak up any excess oil.

To serve, warm the oyster shells under the grill. Pour a spoonful of the dressing into each shell, place the oyster on top and sprinkle with some chopped red chilli and sea salt.

BRIAN MCLEISH

Maggie's Centres provide unrivalled support to cancer sufferers and their families across the UK. The Moonfish Cafe are proud to support our local centre in Aberdeen through this great recipe book by ChariTable Bookings. We hope you enjoy the halibut!"

POACHED HALIBUT with cauliflower, mussels, saffron and hazelnut

SERVES 4 | PREPARATION TIME 30 MINUTES | COOKING TIME 1 HOUR 30 MINUTES

Equipment
mandoline

For the Hazelnut Crumb
200g hazelnuts, blanched and peeled
50g chives, finely chopped

For the Poached Halibut
4 x 150g halibut fillets, centre cut
500ml chicken stock
1 bay leaf
10 white peppercorns
1 sprig of rosemary
1 slice of smoked pancetta
1 clove of garlic

For the Cauliflower Florets
300g cauliflower
olive oil, to fry
1 clove of garlic
1 sprig of thyme
100g unsalted butter
gratings of nutmeg
salt and pepper, to taste

For the Cauliflower Purée
250g cauliflower, sliced
80ml milk
80ml double cream
1 sprig of thyme
1 tsp icing sugar
white truffle oil
salt, to taste

To make the hazelnut crumb, roast the hazelnuts for 5 minutes at 180°C. Allow to cool, then pulse. Mix with the chives and set to one side.

To cook the halibut, simmer the stock with the aromatics for 15 minutes. Reduce the heat to 45°C. Gently cook the fillets until the core temperature is also 45°C. Drain on kitchen cloth. Carefully remove the skin, season the fish, and spoon the hazelnut crumb on top.

To make the cauliflower florets, cut into large florets and blanch. Cut each floret in half to leave a flat side. Gently fry, flat-side down, in a hot pan with oil until caramelised. Add the other ingredients and allow the butter to foam. Season and drain on kitchen paper.

To make the cauliflower purée, simmer the cauliflower with the milk, cream, sugar and thyme until tender. Strain the liquid into a clean pan and reduce to a creamy consistency. Remove the thyme and blitz the cauliflower in a blender, adding a little reduced liquid until thick and velvety. Season to taste. Pass through a sieve, keep warm in a squeezy bottle.

To make the pickled cauliflower, slice the cauliflower thinly on a mandoline, sprinkle with sea salt and leave for 20 minutes. Rinse and pat dry. Bring the other ingredients to the boil, allow to cool, then pour over the cauliflower. Leave for 1 hour.

To make the spring onions, blanch the onions in salted, boiling water, and refresh in ice water. Drain and pat dry. Brush the onions with the oil and season. Chargrill to get good markings and a bitter flavour. Drain on kitchen paper.

To prepare the mussels, boil the wine with the shallot, garlic and bay leaf. Add the mussels, cover and shake occasionally until the shells have opened, discarding any that don't. Drain into a colander lined with muslin over a bowl. Keep the cooking liquid for the sauce. Pick the meat from the shells and chill until needed. Gently warm the mussels in some stock before serving.

For the Pickled Cauliflower
- 150g cauliflower
- 30g sea salt
- 300ml rice wine vinegar
- 20g caster sugar
- 3g lemon zest
- 2g table salt

For the Spring Onions
- 12 spring onions, trimmed
- 10ml vegetable oil
- salt and pepper, to taste

For the Mussels
- 1kg mussels, scrubbed and beards removed
- 200ml dry white wine
- 1 clove of garlic, sliced
- 1 banana shallot, sliced
- 1 bay leaf

For the Saffron Sauce
- 200ml reserved mussel stock
- 4g saffron
- 2g orange zest
- 100ml milk

To make the saffron sauce, boil the stock and saffron until reduced by half. Add the milk and zest, bring to the boil, correct the seasoning and foam using a hand blender. Serve the froth from the top of the sauce.

To serve, plate as pictured, spooning on the foam just before serving.

NOEL MCMEEL

"The Northern Ireland Children's Hospice is the only service of it's kind in Northern Ireland that looks after children with life-threatening illnesses. The whole team at The Catalina Restaurant want to do all we can to support them and this great new book by ChariTable Bookings let's us do just that!"

PAN-SEARED IRISH HAKE FILLET with roast cauliflower purée, broad beans, bacon lardons and vanilla foam

SERVES 2 | PREPARATION TIME 25 MINUTES | COOKING TIME 30 MINUTES

For the Hake
2 large hake fillets

For the Cauliflower Purée
2 heads of cauliflower
250g unsalted butter
570ml single cream

For the Broad Beans
100g broad beans
salt and pepper, to taste
2 tbsp rapeseed oil

For the Bacon Lardons
1kg cured bacon

For the Vanilla Foam
10ml cider
1 vanilla pod
½ lemon, juiced
280ml milk
sugar and salt, to taste

To cook the hake, season the fillets and pan fry, skin-side down for 2–3 minutes. Place in an oven at 180°C and cook for approximately 7–8 minutes.

To make the cauliflower purée, break the heads into small pieces, place in a saucepan with butter and cook until tender and lightly coloured. When cooked, pass off the excess butter and liquidise for 2 minutes. Pour in the cream until the consistency is smooth, then season to taste.

To prepare the broad beans, remove from their husks and blanch in hot, boiling water for one minute. Dress in a bowl with oil and season.

To make the bacon lardons, slice the bacon into small strips and fry in a pan until light brown and crispy.

To make the vanilla foam, begin by placing the cider in a saucepan and reducing by half. Place the reduction, the vanilla, lemon juice and milk in a saucepan and leave for 10 minutes to infuse. Remove the vanilla pod, season to taste with sugar and salt, then foam with a small stick blender.

To finish, place a spoonful of purée in the middle of the plate. Rest the fish on top, then scatter the beans and lardons around. Dress with the foam and serve.

BEN MELLOR

" The NSPCC operates the famous Childline, helping hundreds of children every year who need somewhere to turn to. The Blandford Comptoir is proud to support them through ChariTable Bookings and hope you will do too."

HAKE AND ARTICHOKE BARIGOULE

SERVES 4 | PREPARATION TIME 15 MINUTES | COOKING TIME 30 MINUTES

For the Hake
- 4 x 150g hake fillets
- 50ml olive oil
- salt and pepper

For the Artichoke Barigoule
- 6 baby artichokes, halved lengthways
- 100ml extra virgin olive oil
- 1 large carrot, peeled and cut into 5mm dice
- 4 sticks of celery, peeled and cut into 5mm dice
- 1 pinch of salt
- 200ml white wine
- 2 cloves of garlic
- 3 sprigs of thyme
- 1 pinch of sugar
- 250ml chicken or vegetable stock
- ½ tbsp Chardonnay vinegar
- 3 plum tomatoes, peeled, de-seeded and diced into 5mm dice
- 100g broad beans, popped from skins
- 1¼ tsp each basil, tarragon and flat leaf parsley, chopped

To Serve
- a handful of pea shoots

To prepare the dish, heat 100ml of olive oil in a large pan over a medium heat. Add the carrot, celery and a pinch of salt. Sweat for 2–3 minutes until soft and without colour. Add the artichokes and cook for a further 2 minutes.

Turn up the heat and add the white wine, garlic and thyme. Cook until the pan is almost dry. Add a pinch of sugar and the stock, turn down the heat and simmer until the artichokes are cooked and the liquid has reduced. You should be able to put a sharp knife into the artichoke, feeling no resistance. Add the vinegar and check seasoning. Just before serving, bring back to the boil and add the diced tomato, broad beans and herbs.

Heat the remaining oil in a non stick pan over a medium heat, season the hake fillets and place in the pan skin-side down. Turn up the heat and cook for 2–3 minutes. Turn the fish on to the flesh side, then place in a preheated oven at 180°C for a further 2 minutes until cooked through.

To serve, divide the barigoule between 4 bowls, with a portion of hake on top and a few pea shoots for garnish.

VINCENT MENAGER

Scotty's Little Soldiers is a fantastic charity working with children who have lost a parent through active service. I'm happy to share Rhubarb's salt marsh lamb recipe with ChariTable Bookings to support them."

ROASTED SALT MARSH LAMB BEST END with girolles, carrot and coriander purée, and spring vegetables

SERVES 4 | PREPARATION TIME 35 MINUTES | COOKING TIME 15 MINUTES

For the Lamb
1 best end of Salt Marsh lamb
1 drizzle of vegetable oil

For the Girolles
100g fresh girolles
10g shallots, chopped
20g unsalted butter

For the Coriander Purée
200g carrots, peeled
10g coriander seeds
white chicken stock, to cover
60ml double cream
Maldon salt and cracked black pepper

For the Baby Vegetables
1 bunch of green asparagus
4 baby carrots
4 baby artichokes
10g unsalted butter

To Serve
100ml reduced meat jus
baby herbs
Maldon salt and cracked black pepper

To prepare the purée, cook the carrots and coriander in the chicken stock until tender. Drain the excess liquid, add the cream and bring to the boil. Place the mixture into a food processor and blitz to make a very thin purée. Season and reserve.

Clean the girolles and sauté in fresh butter with the diced shallots. Wait until the liquids have evaporated, drain, cool and reserve.

Clean all the baby vegetables and blanch in boiling salted water. Refresh them in ice water after a few minutes. Drain and reserve.

To cook the lamb and finish the dish, in a hot pan with oil, cook the lamb saddle and the lamb chops. Finish in a hot oven and let the meat rest for 5–6 minutes in a warm place before serving. Warm the vegetables through in seasoned water and finish in a pan with fresh butter and the girolles to colour.

To serve, slice the saddle as pictured and arrange on the plate. Display the vegetables and girolles around the meat, then reheat the carrot purée and drizzle over the dish. Finish the plate with the meat jus and some baby herbs, adding a pinch of Maldon salt and black pepper to taste.

KEITH MITCHELL

Springboard is a charity close to the heart of the hospitality industry, helping young people achieve their goals and the unemployed get back into work. The Grand is proud to offer ChariTable Bookings its signature dish to raise funds for our industry charity."

HOME CURED BEETROOT SALMON GRAVADLAX with poached duck egg,
hollandaise sauce and asparagus
SERVES 8 | PREPARATION TIME 30 MINUTES (PLUS 48 HOURS TO CURE) | COOKING TIME 1 HOUR 30 MINUTES

For the Gravadlax
- 800g salmon fillet, trimmed and pin boned
- 100g coarse sea salt
- 100g demerara sugar
- 2 large raw beetroot, peeled and coarsely grated
- 2 lemons, zest finely grated
- 1 orange, zest finely grated
- 1 bunch of fresh dill, chopped with stalks
- 50ml vodka
- 1 tsp white pepper

For the Hollandaise Sauce
- 400ml white wine vinegar, good quality
- 8 white peppercorns, crushed
- 1 sprig of tarragon
- 5 egg yolks
- 400g unsalted butter, clarified
- ½ lemon, juiced

For the Asparagus Tips
- 800g asparagus tips, about 24 pieces

For the Duck Eggs
- 8 very fresh duck eggs

For the Garnish
- purple radish shoots

To make the gravadlax, halve the salmon fillet. Mix all the ingredients, apart from the salmon, together to make the cure. Roll some cling film across a cutting board and spread a quarter of the cure onto it. Put one of the salmon pieces onto the cure, skin-side down. Place half of the cure onto the salmon flesh and spread evenly. Put the other piece of salmon on top, skin-side up. Add the final quarter of the cure and spread over the top skin. Wrap tightly, rolling in several layers of cling film. Leave the ends of the cling film open to allow liquid to drain away. Place in a stainless steel dish with another weighted dish on top to press and refrigerate. After 24 hours, drain away any excess liquid, turn and press, then refrigerate again. After a further 24 hours, unwrap the salmon and brush off the cure. Rinse very lightly with water and dry with a paper towel. Thinly slice the salmon at a 45° angle, ready to use.

To make the hollandaise sauce, simmer the vinegar with the peppercorns and tarragon in a stainless steel pan until almost dry. Remove from the heat, discard the tarragon and allow to cool. Add 25ml of water with the egg yolks and whisk continuously in a bain-marie of almost simmering water until moderately thickened. Do not pause whisking whilst over the heat. Remove from the heat and continue whisking until cooled to approximately 30–35°C. Very gradually add the room temperature butter whilst continuing to whisk vigorously. Add a little salt and the lemon juice to taste. Pass through a muslin cloth or fine strainer. Adjust the consistency if necessary with a little hot water. Keep lukewarm and cover with cling film.

To prepare the asparagus tips, leaving the top 7–8cm, lightly peel the remaining stalk of the asparagus and trim to 10–12cm in length. Simmer in salted water until just tender. Drain and plunge into ice water. Reheat in boiling, salted water for 1 minute as required.

To prepare the duck eggs, gently boil 10 parts water to 1 part white wine vinegar in an open pan. Break the eggs into the water and simmer for approximately 4 minutes until the white is firm but the yolk is still soft. Remove the eggs with a perforated spoon and lower into ice cold water. Trim the loose edges. Reheat in very hot, salted water for 1 minute as required. Drain on a clean cloth before serving.

To serve, arrange the sliced gravadlax on a plate and carefully place the hot poached egg on top. Coat the egg with the warm hollandaise sauce and garnish with the asparagus tips.

MAURIZIO MORELLI

As part of the ongoing enterprise from ChariTable Bookings, Margot Restaurant is pleased to endorse the selfless work carried out by the RSPCA."

STEWED FILLET OF COD with courgettes, tomato and fresh herbs

SERVES 4 | PREPARATION TIME 10 MINUTES | COOKING TIME 20 MINUTES

For the Courgette Base

2 large white onions, cut long and thin

1 pinch of dried red chilli flakes

1 clove of garlic, finely chopped

75ml extra virgin olive oil

2 courgettes, sliced into rounds 1cm thick

2 large vine tomatoes, finely chopped

50ml white wine

100ml water

parsley, basil, chives and dill, finely chopped

zest of 1 lemon

salt and black pepper

For the Cod

4 x 170g cod fillets

salt and pepper

parsley, basil, chives and dill, finely chopped

To prepare the courgette base, fry the onions, chilli and garlic in 50ml olive oil in a large shallow pan. Lay the courgettes to cover the bottom of the pan, then add the tomatoes, wine, water, chopped herbs, lemon zest, salt and pepper.

To prepare the cod, season the fillets with salt and pepper and place in the pan on top of the courgettes. Cover with a lid and let it gently cook for 10 minutes. When it is ready, add the rest of the olive oil and more fresh herbs.

To serve the cod, place on a shallow plate with the courgettes and the sauce.

ANTON MOSIMANN

I am very pleased to nominate The Prince's Trust as our chosen charity to support in this collection of recipes by ChariTable Bookings. Mosimann's prides itself on the quality of its restaurant service and is always impressed by the quality of work undertaken by this fantastic charity."

POT-AU-FEU

SERVES 4 | PREPARATION TIME 15 MINUTES | COOKING TIME 1 HOUR

For the Pot-Au-Feu
1 free range or organic chicken
2l white chicken stock
3 onions, peeled and each studded
with 2 cloves
1 bay leaf
2 cloves of garlic, peeled
a few white peppercorns
1 small bunch of mixed thyme,
rosemary and parsley
4 small carrots, peeled
4 pieces of celery, about 5cm in
length
4 pieces of leek, about 5cm in length
8 small onions, peeled
1 small celeriac, peeled and quartered
salt and freshly ground pepper

For the Garnish
flat leaf parsley, freshy chopped

To prepare the Pot-au-feu, bring a large saucepan of water to the boil. Add the chicken and bring back to the boil. Drain and allow to cook slightly.

In another large pan, boil the chicken stock with the onions, bay leaf, garlic, peppercorns and bunch of herbs. Simmer for 20 minutes. Add the chicken and poach for 20 minutes. Lift the chicken out of the pan. Strain the stock, absorb and remove the fat with strips of kitchen paper, then return the liquid to the cleaned out pan. Remove the skin from the chicken, then put it back in the pan with the stock. Add the vegetables. Bring to the boil and simmer for 10 minutes. Lift out the chicken and vegetables and keep warm. Boil the chicken stock rapidly to reduce by half. Adjust seasoning to taste.

To serve, carve the chicken and arrange in soup plates with the vegetables. Pour over some stock and garnish with parsley. Serve at once.

YOSHIHIRO MURATA

I'm proud to be involved with educating children in Japan about Japanese food. Through this ChariTable Bookings initiative, I am also pleased that Tokimeite can support Adopt A School in the UK."

BEEF TERIYAKI

SERVES 2 | PREPARATION TIME 10 MINUTES | COOKING TIME 15 MINUTES

For the Teriyaki
1½ tbsp sugar
3 tbsp soy sauce
6 tbsp sake

For the Beef
1 tbsp vegetable oil
2 x 100g sirloin steaks
English mustard, to taste
sesame seeds, to taste
2 sprigs of watercress

To make the teriyaki sauce, mix together the soy sauce, sugar and sake, bring to the boil and reduce to a loose syrup.

Heat a frying pan over a medium high heat, add the oil and sear the steaks on both sides until browned. Lower the heat to medium. Add the teriyaki sauce and simmer. Shake the pan from time to time, basting the steaks with a spoon until the sauce thickens slightly and glazes the steaks. This should take approximately 4 minutes.

To serve, transfer the steaks to a cutting board and cut into 1.5cm thick slices. Arrange the steak slices on a serving plate and pour the sauce from the pan over. Sprinkle with the sesame seeds. Brush the English mustard at the base of the plate. Garnish the top of the plate with watercress.

RONNIE MURRAY

Food is often seen as a leveller amongst people and Scope is the equivalent in the charity world, looking to ensure disabled people have the same opportunities as everyone else. I am delighted to share Peckham Manor's lamb dish with ChariTable Bookings to raise awareness for this wonderful charity."

CROWN OF SALT AGED GLENARM ESTATE LAMB

SERVES 6 | PREPARATION TIME 2 HOURS (PLUS 3 HOURS TO MARINATE) | COOKING TIME 4 HOURS

For the Roasted Curry Powder

5 tbsp each of fenugreek seeds and leaves, fennel seeds, cumin seeds, mustard seeds, ground cumin, ground coriander, turmeric

3 tbsp each of podded cardamom seeds, caraway seeds, nigella seeds

5 tsp ground cinnamon

15 cloves

For the Curry

800g lamb neck

500g natural yoghurt

5 medium red onions, finely chopped

8 cloves of garlic, peeled and crushed

60g ginger, scraped and finely grated

2 pinches of saffron

20 curry leaves

1 tbsp each of fenugreek, cumin and podded cardamom seeds

2 black cardamom pods

150g clarified butter

5 tbsp roasted curry powder

5 tbsp dried chillies

2 tbsp tomato purée

2l lamb or beef stock

2 sprigs of coriander and parsley

For the Green Apple Relish

2 green dessert apples, cored and roughly chopped

2 large green chillies, chopped

To prepare the roasted curry powder, grind the seeds and leaves in a spice grinder or with a mortar and pestle. Mix them with the already ground spices and sprinkle into a heavy-bottomed frying pan. Cook over a medium heat, stirring constantly and not letting the mixture burn, until it turns dark brown. Transfer to a plate and leave to cool, then store in a sealed jar.

For the lamb neck curry, marinate the necks in yoghurt for 2–3 hours before cooking. Gently cook the onion, garlic, ginger, saffron, curry leaves, fenugreek, cumin and cardamom seeds and black cardamom in 100g the clarified butter for 3–4 minutes until soft. Add the roasted curry powder and tomato purée, then stir well. Add the stock and dried chillies, bring to the boil and simmer gently for 40 minutes. Blend half of the sauce in a liquidiser until smooth, then add back to the remaining sauce in the pan. Return to a low heat and continue simmering until the sauce has reduced and thickened. Heat the remaining clarified butter in a frying pan, remove the excess yoghurt from the necks and season. Fry until lightly coloured. Add the necks to the sauce and pour into a roasting pan. Cook at 150°C for 2–3 hours until tender, stirring occasionally. Mix with the chopped coriander and parsley.

For the green apple relish, blend all the ingredients together in a food processor or smoothie maker until really smooth.

For the samphire pakora, preheat a deep fryer to 170°C. Mix the onion seed and both types of flour together, then whisk in enough water to make a light batter. Fold in the samphire. Using a tablespoon, drop a spoonful of the mixture in the fat as a tester. Move around in the pan with a slotted spoon for a minute or so until golden and then transfer on to kitchen paper. Taste and adjust the consistency with more water if stodgy. You can briefly cook these without colouring them too much first, so they will just need a reheat in the hot fat when you serve them.

To assemble the dish, season the lamb, render the fat side in a pan on medium heat for about 5 minutes, then cool. Preheat the oven to 200°C. Turn the racks over so the rendered side is away from you. Make a vertical cut about 1cm deep in between each bone, then make another horizontal cut, this time along the rack, just under the bones.

Repeat for the other rack, this will allow the racks to bend in on themselves. Bend the racks into a semi-circle with the bones sticking up so it looks like a crown. Tie with string around both racks in the long cut just under the bones. Tie a long piece of string around the outside of the bones where the meat starts. Using a trussing needle, sew together the ends of both racks to form a circle. Place on a roasting tray and cook for 15–20 minutes. Using a meat thermometer, check that the middle of the rack is about 60°C and medium rare. Rest for 6 minutes. Heat the lamb neck curry in a deep roasting tray in the oven, this will help to stop the lamb neck pieces falling apart.

Cook the kale for a few minutes in a large pan of boiling water, until just wilted. Drain well and arrange on the base of the serving dish. Put the lamb rack back in the oven for 5 minutes if needed, then place on top of the kale and carefully remove all the string. Fill the centre with the neck curry. Add the samphire pakoras around the edge. This is a sharing dish so should be carved at the table, 2 cutlets per person, with a spoonful of curry, kale and a pakora. The green apple relish goes in a serving dish on the side for guests to help themselves.

MARTYN NAIL

I feel privileged that I am able to create my dishes in the special setting of the kitchen at Claridge's and that through ChariTable Bookings this dish is able to support the Royal Academy of Culinary Arts."

LOBSTER RISOTTO

SERVES 2 | PREPARATION TIME 30 MINUTES | COOKING TIME 1 HOUR 45 MINUTES

For the Lobster Sauce

- 180g lobster shells, cracked
- 2 tbsp vegetable oil
- 60g unsalted butter, cubed
- 70ml brandy
- 90ml white wine
- 70g mirepoix
- 230ml chicken stock
- 470ml single cream

For the Truffle and Madeira Sauce

- 30g salted butter
- 50g shallots, chopped
- 50g mushroooms, sliced
- 350ml Malmsey Madeira
- 3 white peppercorns
- ½ bay leaf
- 1 sprig of thyme
- 500ml veal stock
- 25g unsalted butter
- 20g fresh truffle, finely chopped
- 50ml Malmsey Madeira wine
- 50ml port

For the Risotto

- 120g onion, finely diced
- 1 tbsp vegetable oil
- 400g arborio rice
- 1.6l double chicken stock
- 25g chives, finely chopped
- 140g butter
- salt, to taste
- 100g Parmesan
- 2 whole lobsters, cooked, halved
- butter emulsion – butter and water 1:1
- 8 tops of rock samphire

To make the lobster sauce, in a heavy based pan, roast the shells with the oil until lightly caramelised. Add the butter and roast again until the butter foams, approximately 5 minutes. Then add a third of the brandy, this will remove any sediment from the base of the pan. Reduce to syrup, this will take 2–3 minutes and the pan should have very little liquid in at this stage. Repeat with the other two thirds, a third at a time, reducing to a syrup. When all the brandy has reduced, add white wine and reduce to a syrup again. By this time the shells will be glossy from all the reduced alcohol and butter. Add the mirepoix and soften. Add the chicken stock and reduce by one half, for around 15 minutes. Finally, add cream and simmer gently. Skim any fat from the sauce and cook until a coating consistency is reached, which should take approximately 25 minutes. Pass through muslin and season to taste. As the listed quantities will make far more than needed for the dish, the sauce can be made ahead of time and can be kept in a refrigerator for up to 2 days and used with a variety of dishes.

To make the truffle and Madeira sauce, heat a medium-sized pan over medium heat. Once hot, add the butter, then the shallots and mushrooms. Sweat until the mushrooms have released their liquid and the shallots become soft, starting to lightly colour. Add the 350ml of Madeira, peppercorns, bay leaf and thyme and bring to a boil. Reduce by half over a medium-low heat, about 10 minutes. Stir in the veal jus and simmer for 40 minutes, or until the jus coats the back of a spoon. When you run a finger along the back of the sauced spoon, exposing the metal, the sauce should not re-cover your finger's trail. Check and adjust the seasoning to taste.

Chop the truffle finely. Over a low-medium heat, add 25g salted butter and the truffles to a small pan, then sweat for 4 minutes. Add the 50ml each of Port and Madeira. Gradually reduce by half. Pour the truffles over the Madeira sauce and bring back to a boil. Lower the heat and allow to simmer very gently, skimming occasionally for 20 minutes. Season to taste and remove from the heat.

To prepare the risotto, place a heavy-bottomed pan on the heat. Add the onions and sweat until translucent and soft. Add the rice and glaze to the onions and oil. Turn up the heat and pour in the stock slowly, in small amounts. Make sure the stock has been soaked up by the rice before adding any more. Keep stirring until the rice becomes slightly translucent. Finish with chives, finely chopped butter, salt to taste and Parmesan.

To finish, carefully place the lobsters in the warm water and butter. Mix for 2 minutes to warm through and infuse. Warm and foam the lobster sauce ready for serving. Blanch the rock samphire in boiling, salted water, then drain and reserve.

To serve, place a 100g risotto in each warm serving bowl. Drain the lobster and place half in the centre of each dish. Glaze the lobster with truffle jus and garnish with the rock samphire. Sit the lobster on top of the risotto and serve.

REX NEWMARK

"Thank you ChariTable Bookings for including Beach Blanket Babylon and my recipe for Cancer Research in this great collection."

SALMON TERIYAKI with burnt broccoli, sesame and miso sauce

SERVES 4 | PREPARATION TIME 20 MINUTES | COOKING TIME 20 MINUTES

For the Teriyaki Glaze
- 75g honey
- 150ml teriyaki sauce
- 4 tbsp rice wine vinegar
- 2 shallots, thinly sliced
- 2 cloves of garlic, puréed

For the Salmon
- 4 salmon fillets, skin on
- 1 pinch of chopped chilli
- sesame oil

For the Chargrilled Broccoli
- 1 packet of tender stem broccoli

For the Miso Sauce
- 50ml miso paste
- 100ml mayonnaise

For the Garnish
- 1 tsp sesame seeds
- 2 chillies, halved
- 2 sprigs of coriander

To prepare the teriyaki glaze, place all of the ingredients in the blender, blitz until smooth and reduce in a pan on the stove until thick and sticky.

To cook the salmon, pan fry, skin-side down, in a hot pan with sesame oil. When the skin has crisped up and half the fish has gone opaque, turn over and add the teriyaki glaze and chopped chilli. Cook until the fish is completely opaque, this should take roughly 2 minutes on each side. Season to taste. Reserve the pan juices to spoon over the broccoli.

To make the chargrilled broccoli, place on a baking tray, turn the grill up to full heat, spoon over the juices from the salmon and grill until blackened.

To make the miso sauce, mix the paste and mayonnaise together until smooth.

To assemble and finish the dish, toast the sesame seeds in a pan, ready to sprinkle over as a garnish. Spoon the miso sauce on the plate, then the broccoli. Sprinkle with the sesame seeds and place the salmon on top. Garnish with a little chilli and coriander.

CHANTELLE NICHOLSON

" *The kitchen at Tredwells is behind The Springboard Charity and is able to raise additional funds with the help of ChariTable Bookings.*"

DUCK with tamarind, cashew and fig

SERVES 4 | PREPARATION TIME 40 MINUTES (PLUS 12 HOURS TO SOAK) | COOKING TIME 1 HOUR 30 MINUTES

Equipment
sous vide and vacuum pack bags

For the Duck and Meat Brine
4 duck breasts
1l water
70g salt
¼ tsp each white peppercorns, coriander seeds and fennel seeds
4 sprigs of thyme
2 bay leaves

For the Tamarind Sauce
2 tbsp vegetable oil
2 carrots, peeled and sliced
4 shallots, peeled and sliced
1 bulb of garlic, halved horizontally
100g fresh ginger, peeled and sliced
3 star anise
200ml each red wine and Madeira
50ml soy sauce
200g tamarind concentrate
2l each chicken and veal stock

For the Cashew Butter
100g roasted cashew nuts
½ tsp table salt

For the Garnish
1 ripe fig
4 tbsp roasted cashew nuts, finely chopped
borage leaves

To prepare the brine, place all ingredients except for the meat in a saucepan and bring to the boil, to dissolve the salt. Set aside and allow to cool completely, then refrigerate.

To prepare the tamarind sauce, heat the vegetable oil in a large saucepan until smoking. Add the carrots, shallots, garlic, ginger and star anise. Brown well. Deglaze with the red wine and Madeira and simmer to reduce to a syrup. When syrup-like, add the remaining ingredients and simmer gently for 30 minutes. Pass and season as necessary.

Remove the skin and sinew from the duck breasts and place in the cold brine for 40 minutes. Remove and pat dry. Vacuum pack each duck breast individually with a knob of butter and 1 tbsp tamarind sauce.

To prepare the cashew butter, place the cashews into a small container, cover with cold water and the salt. Allow to soak for 12 hours. Strain off half of the water then blend until smooth, using more of the soaking water if required. Pass through a fine sieve. Season to taste.

To serve, cook the duck breasts at 65°C for 20 minutes. Remove from the bag, glaze with the sauce and sprinkle over the chopped cashew. Carve each breast in half vertically. Dress the plate with the duck, cashew butter, fig slices, tamarind sauce and borage flowers.

JEAN CHRISTOPHE NOVELLI

This is a great way by ChariTable Bookings to support local charities and share great recipes. I'm sharing my Couscous de mon voisin recipe with you to support Addenbrookes, the teaching hospital in Cambridge."

COUSCOUS DE MON VOISIN - couscous made my neighbour's way

SERVES 4–6 | PREPARATION TIME 30 MINUTES | COOKING TIME 1 HOUR 30 MINUTES

For the Dish

- 1kg lamb neck fillet, diced
- 2 chicken legs, cut through the joint to create 4 pieces
- 2 onions, quartered
- 4 baby carrots, whole
- 2 baby turnips, halved lengthways
- ½ celeriac, diced
- 50g ginger, peeled and thinly sliced
- 1 tsp each cumin and coriander seeds
- ½ tsp turmeric powder
- ½ bulb of garlic
- 400g tin chopped tomatoes
- 400g tin chickpeas
- 2 tbsp tomato purée
- 500ml hot lamb or vegetable stock
- 1 courgette, roughly cubed
- 1 aubergine, roughly cubed
- 1 sweet potato, sliced into thirds
- 1 bulb of fennel, diced
- 100g raisins
- 2 tbsp harissa paste

For the Couscous

- 450g couscous
- 4 tbsp extra virgin olive oil
- ½ tsp mild curry powder
- ½ tsp turmeric
- 400ml hot lamb or vegetable stock

For the Garnish

- fresh green herbs

Seal the lamb in a very hot, deep pan. Add the chicken pieces and seal altogether. Add the onions, carrots, turnips, celeriac and ginger. Place the lid onto the pan and shake the ingredients. Next, add the cumin and coriander seeds, turmeric, the half garlic bulb and the tinned tomatoes. Stir, then add the chickpeas and the tomato purée and stir again. Add the stock to cover everything in the pan, approximately 500ml. Cover with the lid. Bring to the boil and reduce to a simmer for 30 minutes. After 30 minutes of cooking, add the rest of the vegetables and bring back to a simmer. Cover and leave to simmer for 30 minutes. Taste the sauce and adjust the seasoning. At this point, add the harissa and dried raisins and continue to simmer for a further 30 minutes.

To prepare the couscous, using a stainless steel or large glass bowl, mix the couscous and the olive oil with your hands. Add the curry powder and turmeric, then the 400ml of stock. Stir using a fork and cover with cling film. After approximately 10 minutes, the couscous can be stirred lightly with the fork and served immediately.

To serve, place the couscous on a large serving plate or bowl. Spoon the meat and vegetables into the middle of the dish and decorate with green herbs. Serve immediately.

ANDREW NUTTER

Great to be able to support our local Springhill Hospice which does such great work with terminally ill patients. Support them too through ChariTable Bookings and enjoy Nutters' sea bass at the same time!"

PAN-SEARED WILD SEA BASS with Jersey Royal gratin and English asparagus with a chive and lemon hollandaise

SERVES 4 | PREPARATION TIME 30 MINUTES (PLUS 24 HOURS TO PRESS) | COOKING TIME 2 HOURS

For the Sea Bass
4 x 115g sea bass fillets, skin on and deboned
1 tbsp olive oil
2 cloves of garlic, cut into wafer thin slices
4 cloves of fermented black garlic, cut into wafer thin slices
2 lemons, zest and juice
3 tbsp extra virgin olive oil
1 tbsp chives, chopped

For the Jersey Royal Gratin
500ml whipping cream
1 clove of garlic, finely chopped
1 sprig of rosemary, chopped
500g baking potatoes, peeled
300g Jersey Royals, washed
3 carrots, peeled
50g Gruyere cheese, grated
50g Kirkham's Lancashire cheese, grated

For the Chive and Lemon Hollandaise
3 egg yolks
1 tbsp lemon juice
1 tbsp white wine vinegar
115g butter, bubbling hot
2 tsp fresh chives, chopped
salt and ground black pepper

To make the Jersey Royal gratin, preheat the oven to 130°C. Heat the whipping cream in a casserole pan. Add the garlic and rosemary and reduce by half. Season to taste. Slice the potatoes and carrots into 2mm thick slices. Line a deep 15x25cm oven tray with non-stick paper. Layer the vegetables into the prepared tray, interlayered with the cream and cheeses. Cover with foil and bake in the oven for 1.5 hours until cooked through. Remove from the oven. Place a tray on top and a weight on top of that. Leave overnight in the fridge. The next day, slice the gratin into 12x3cm rectangles. Place on a tray ready to be reheated. When you are ready to serve, heat the gratin through in a preheated oven, at 180°C for 8 minutes.

To make the chive and lemon hollandaise, place the egg yolks into a food processor, then add the lemon and vinegar. Pulse a few times, then slowly pour in the hot butter as you mix on a high speed for 30 seconds. Stir in the chives. Season to taste.

To cook the sea bass, heat the oil in a non-stick pan and seal the sea bass, skin-side down, for 3 minutes until lightly coloured. Turn over and cook for a further 2 minutes. In a small pan, warm the garlic and black garlic, lemon, oil and chives. Spoon on top of the fish.

To serve, warm through the blanched asparagus and lay on the plates. Place the gratin on top and spoon around the hollandaise. Finally, top with the sea bass, a scattering of the carrot balls, a sprig of fresh basil, the sautéed girolles and edible flowers.

To Finish

2 bunches of English asparagus, peeled
and blanched
heritage carrot balls, blanched
4 sprigs of fresh basil
girolles, sautéed
edible flowers

MALACHI O'GALLAGHER

The Delaunay team are proud to partner with ChariTable Bookings and the hundreds of other leading UK chefs in support of a charity close to your heart by simply buying this recipe book for yourself or as the perfect gift. It's as simple as that!"

FILLET OF BEEF STROGANOFF

SERVES 6 | PREPARATION TIME 20 MINUTES | COOKING TIME 45 MINUTES

For the Stroganoff Sauce
25g garlic, chopped
75g shallots, finely diced
30ml vegetable oil
500g chestnut mushrooms, washed and quartered
10g each sweet and hot paprika
60ml brandy
560ml double cream
100ml sour cream
100ml veal jus or equivalent
lemon juice and salt, to taste

For the Basmati Rice
400g basmati, washed and drained
1 bay leaf
50g shallots, finely diced
50g butter
40ml vegetable oil
750ml light chicken stock, simmered

For the Dish
600g beef fillet, cut into 2cm squares
1 tsp each sweet and hot paprika
20ml vegetable oil
800ml stroganoff sauce
1 whole pickled cucumber, finely sliced
20ml pickled cucumber juice
30ml double cream, if required
1 tbsp parsley, chopped
400g cooked basmati rice, see above

For the stroganoff sauce, sweat the garlic, shallots and mushrooms in the vegetable oil over a medium heat, until the mushrooms have let out their juices and the resulting liquid has evaporated. Add both kinds of paprika and stir together with the mushrooms and onions for 30 seconds. Turn up the heat and deglaze with the brandy, scraping the pan to remove the paprika before it burns. Add the cream and sour cream along with the veal jus, and bring to a simmer. Reduce the sauce until it thickens, stirring occasionally. Remove from the heat and add salt and lemon juice to taste.

To make the basmati rice, sweat the bay leaf and shallots in the butter and vegetable oil until the shallots clarify. Add the rice and coat well. Add the hot chicken stock and mix well. Cover the pan with foil and bake in an oven at 180°C for 12–15 minutes. Remove the foil and add salt to taste.

To assemble the dish, toss the beef in the paprika and coat with vegetable oil. In a medium pan, lightly brown the meat, remove and set aside. Warm the stroganoff sauce in a medium saucepan. If the sauce begins to split, add a little cream to bring back to desired consistency. Add the pickled cucumber juice. Once boiling, add the beef. Stir the sauce for about 2–3 minutes, or until the beef is rare. Mix in the chopped parsley.

Plate with warm basmati rice, top with the finely sliced pickled cucumber and a sprinkle of sweet paprika.

TOM OLDROYD

The NET Patient Foundation is the only charity in the UK and Ireland dedicated to providing support and information to people affected by neuroendocrine cancers. Being such a niche charity, I am very pleased to support it through ChariTable Bookings and share with you Oldroyd's grilled mackerel!"

GRILLED MACKEREL with beetroot, horseradish and salsa verde

SERVES 6 | PREPARATION TIME 30 MINUTES | COOKING TIME 1 HOUR

Equipment
mandoline

For the Mackerel and Beetroot
6 mackerel fillets, deboned
500g purple beetroot
100ml cider vinegar
25ml light olive oil
1 pinch of salt
2 tbsp caster sugar
2 golden beetroot, peeled and thinly sliced on a mandoline
2 candy striped beetroot, peeled and thinly sliced on a mandoline
½ red onion, thinly sliced on a mandoline

For the Salsa Verde
1 handful of capers, finely chopped
1 handful of cornichons, finely chopped
1 handful each of parsley, mint and basil, chopped
3 tbsp mustard vinaigrette
150ml olive oil
salt and pepper, to taste

For the Horseradish Cream
2cm piece of horseradish, grated
200g crème fraîche
1 tbsp Dijon mustard
1 pinch of caster sugar
salt and pepper, to taste

To prepare the beetroot, place the purple beetroot in enough water to just cover and add 25ml of cider vinegar. Boil until cooked, this should take roughly 40 minutes depending on the size of the beetroot. You should be able to easily pierce the beetroot with a knife. Drain and allow to cool a little before peeling. Chop into chunky wedges and dress with another 25ml of cider vinegar, most of the olive oil and a little salt and pepper. Decant 50ml cider vinegar and stir in the caster sugar until dissolved. Pour over the thinly sliced beetroot and red onion. Leave to pickle for 15 minutes, whilst the purple beetroot is cooking.

To make the salsa verde, simply combine all of the ingredients except the oil. Mix together and using a fork to stir, slowly pour in the olive oil until well combined and of a spoonable consistency.

To make the horseradish cream, combine all of the ingredients, stir together well and season to taste.

To prepare the mackerel, cook on either a barbecue or hot pan, skin-side down and seasoned for a few minutes. Once the skin is crisp, turn over onto the flesh for 10 seconds, before removing from the heat.

To assemble the dish, take a plate and spread a heaped tablespoon of the horseradish cream on the base. Scatter over the pickled slices of golden and candy-striped beetroot, followed by the wedges of cooked purple beetroot. Place the mackerel on top, drizzle with salsa verde and serve.

ROBERT ORTIZ

It is a delight to offer you this Lima signature dish in the ChariTable Bookings recipe book. What a perfect gift for all foodies who also wish to support their favourite charity, mine being StreetSmart."

STONE BASS CEVICHE

SERVES 2 | PREPARATION TIME 20 MINUTES

For the Ceviche
240g stone bass, cut into even-sized pieces
100ml leche de tigre
canchita
sweet potato glaze

For the Sweet Potato Glaze
2 large sweet potatoes, diced
50ml mandarin juice

For the Leche De Tigre
100ml fresh lime juice
2 cloves of garlic, smashed
1 tbsp fresh coriander leaves, chopped
20g rocoto chilli, diced
100g pink onions, sliced
salt, to taste

For the Garnish
micro amaranth, optional
reserved pink onion slices

To make the leche de tigre, blitz together the lime juice, garlic, coriander and rocoto chilli until smooth. Add the onions and blend again. Season to taste and chill.

To make the sweet potato glaze, cook the diced sweet potato in salted, boiling water and refresh in ice water. Blend to a purée with a little mandarin juice.

To assemble the ceviche, place the stone bass into a bowl. Season with a little salt and pour over the leche de tigre. Leave to marinate for approximately 2 minutes. Serve with the sweet potato glaze and canchita.

DALE OSBORNE

Aqua Shard are proud to support Make A Wish by donating this recipe to the ChariTable Bookings Signature Dish book."

LOCH ETIVE HOT AND COLD SMOKED TROUT

SERVES 4 | PREPARATION TIME 30 MINUTES | COOKING TIME 1 HOUR 30 MINUTES

For the Trout
½ side of fresh trout or salmon skin
200g cold smoked trout
200g hot smoked trout

For the Sea Greens
100g sea greens, samphire or sea aster
lemon juice, to taste
olive oil

To Serve
200ml crème fraîche
50g dill, chopped
1 jar of trout eggs

Scrape the trout skin clean of scales and any excess flesh. Lay on a tray with baking paper and dehydrate in a low oven at 100°C until crisp and dry, this should take around 1 hour.

Heat a pan of oil or a deep fryer to 180°C. Cut the skin into 4 pieces and fry in the hot oil. The skin will puff up like a prawn cracker. Drain on a cloth and set aside.

Mix the dill with the crème fraîche.

Pick the sea greens, blanch in boiling water for 30 seconds, then chill and refresh in ice water. Drain and set aside.

Slice the cold smoked trout into finger width pieces, allowing for 3 pieces per portion. Break the hot smoked trout into large flakes, again allowing 3 pieces per portion.

To finish and serve the dish, spoon the dill crème fraîche onto plates and spread to cover the base. Place your cold smoked trout on the plate, and top with flakes of hot smoked trout. Crack the crispy skin into shards, and stand up against the trout. Dress the sea greens with olive oil and a squeeze of lemon juice, then scatter them over the dish. Finish with a few spoons of trout eggs, and serve.

JEREMY PANG

Just like cookery, SeeAbility doesn't just focus on one area but disability in general. I hope you enjoy my School of Wok steamed wontons and enjoy using ChariTable Bookings to raise funds for charities all over the UK."

STEAMED WONTONS in chilli broth

SERVES 4 | PREPARATION TIME 1 HOUR | COOKING TIME 10 MINUTES

For the Wontons
1 clove of garlic
1 spring onion
1 large handful of coriander, plus extra to garnish
10–15 Chinese chives
3 dried shiitake mushrooms, drained and soaked
2 leaves Chinese leaf cabbage
150g raw tiger prawns, peeled and deveined, optional
1 tbsp light soy sauce
½ tsp granulated sugar
2 tsp sesame oil
20 wonton pastries

For the Chilli Broth
200ml chicken stock
½ tbsp oyster sauce
2 tsp Chiu Chow chilli oil

For the filling, finely chop the garlic, spring onion, coriander, Chinese chives, soaked shiitake mushrooms and Chinese leaves and place in a mixing bowl. Finely dice the prawns, if using, and add to the mixing bowl, along with the soy sauce, sugar and sesame oil. Mix together well.

To wrap the wontons, place 1 teaspoon of filling in the centre of each pastry. Using the tip of your finger, wet all sides with cold water. Fold the bottom corner over the filling to the top corner and press the pastry down to seal all sides, forming a triangle. Holding the base of the filling with your thumbs, pull the 2 corners of the triangle towards each other. Overlap the ends and press together to form a trough shape. Set aside and fold the rest of the wontons the same way.

To cook the wontons, place them all in a large, deep bowl. Bring the chicken stock to a simmer in a saucepan, then stir in the oyster sauce and chilli oil. Pour the broth ingredients over the wontons. Set the wok up with a steamer stand and fill with boiling water, a third of the way up the sides. Put the wonton bowl into the wok, cover with a lid and steam for 6–8 minutes, until the wontons have shrivelled slightly and are cooked through. Remove from the wok and serve garnished with a little chopped coriander.

Editor's Notes: You can find all these ingredients in any good Oriental supermarket. Dumplings like these can be kept in the freezer once made. They must be cooked from frozen for 2 minutes longer than the recommended cooking time when cooking fresh, rather than allowing them to thaw out and lose their shape.

ANTONIA PARKER

" I am pleased to be supporting Tusk and to know that organisations like ChariTable Bookings have the reach to make sure that what is needed to make a difference actually gets out to the public."

MOUNTAIN RISOTTO with roast butternut squash and sage

SERVES 2 | PREPARATION TIME 20 MINUTES | COOKING TIME 40 MINUTES

For the Dish

500g butternut squash, chopped
into equal-sized small cubes
6 tbsp extra virgin olive oil
sea salt and black pepper
½ banana shallot, diced
1 medium leek, roughly chopped
1 bunch of fresh sage
2 cloves of garlic, diced
150g risotto rice, arborio
125ml white wine
450–500ml hot chicken stock
100g Emmental cheese, grated, plus
extra for serving

Preheat the oven to 190°C and line 2 baking trays with baking parchment. Add the butternut squash pieces and season with 2 tablespoons of the olive oil, salt and pepper. Make sure that the squash is evenly coated and place into the oven for about 35–40 minutes until golden and soft. Remove from the oven and roughly mash up half the squash with a fork and leave to one side.

To prepare the risotto while the squash is cooking, set a large saucepan to a medium to high heat and, when hot, add 3 tablespoons of olive oil followed by the shallot and leek. Chop up the sage leaving 6 leaves to one side and stir the rest into the pan. Fry until the onions soften and then add the diced garlic. Stir for another minute before adding in the rice. Continue stirring and then pour in the white wine and let the alcohol burn off for a moment. Keep stirring until most of the wine has been absorbed and then pour in some chicken stock. Let this stock be absorbed by the rice before adding more and carry on until the rice becomes quite tender. This will take about 20–25 minutes and when the rice is nearly cooked scrape in the squash. Season generously with salt, pepper and the Emmental. Taste to double check the seasoning and serve hot.

To serve, minutes before the risotto is ready, set a small frying pan to a medium to high heat and add the remaining tablespoon of olive oil. When hot, add the last few sage leaves and fry for a couple of minutes until the leaves have crisped up. Drain on kitchen paper and use to garnish the risotto.

TOM PARKER BOWLES

" I love the idea behind ChariTable Bookings new book, promoting worthy causes and sharing recipes. Tommy's is my chosen charity for the work they do in pregnancy research."

TACOS AL CARBON

SERVES 4 | PREPARATION TIME 1 HOUR 30 MINUTES (PLUS 30 MINUTES TO HEAT BARBECUE) | COOKING TIME 15 MINUTES

For the Dish
2 x 300g large sirloin or skirt steaks
groundnut or sunflower oil, for cooking
sea salt and freshly ground black pepper, to taste
12 spring onions
12 corn tortillas

For the Pickled Red Onion
1 red onion, thinly sliced
1 habanero chilli, thinly sliced
1 tbsp white wine vinegar

For the Pico de Gallo
2 tomatoes
2 long green finger chillies
1 small onion, roughly chopped
lime juice and salt, to taste
1 handful of coriander leaves

For the Guacamole
3 avocados
1 red onion, finely chopped
1 jalapeño or finger chillies, finely chopped
2 tomatoes
1 lime, juiced
salt and pepper

To Serve
1 bottle of Tabasco sauce
1 small cabbage, shredded
lime wedges, for squeezing

For the pickled red onion, put the onion and habanero chilli in a small bowl with the vinegar, cover and marinate for 1 hour. Drain and serve.

To make the pico de gallo, peel, deseed and roughly chop the tomatoes. Deseed and finely chop the green chillies. Mix the tomatoes, green chillies, onion and lime juice in a bowl. Add salt to taste and leave for 1 hour. Roughly chop the coriander leaves, stir in and serve.

To prepare the guacamole, peel, deseed and mash the avocados roughly, using a large fork. Peel, deseed and finely chop the tomatoes. Add the red onion, jalapeño chillies, tomatoes and lime juice. Season to taste and serve.

Light your barbecue and wait until the coals are white-hot, or heat your griddle pan until it's smoking hot. Brush the steaks with oil, season well with salt, then grill for 2 minutes on each side. Leave to rest for 2 minutes. This will give rare steak. Slice very thinly. Brush the spring onions with oil, season and cook for 4–6 minutes, until charred. Cut them in half, slice into 2cm pieces, or leave whole. Heat the tortillas on the barbecue, or in a hot dry pan, then wrap them in a tea cloth to keep warm.

Serve the steak on one plate and the tortillas on another. Place the spring onions, pickled red onion, pico de gallo, guacamole, cabbage and lime wedges in small bowls alongside. Put the Tabasco on the table and let people pimp their tacos however they wish.

DEAN PARKER

Running a restaurant, you naturally believe in good, healthy nutrition. Action Against Hunger takes that belief and works with children the world over to prevent malnutrition and hunger. Great that ChariTable Bookings is helping The Manor promote them."

LADY HAMILTON SMOKED COD with potato sorrel

SERVES 4 | PREPARATION TIME 2 HOURS (PLUS 5 DAYS TO REST) | COOKING TIME 2 HOURS

Equipment
cold smoker

sous vide and vacuum pack bags

siphon gun and N$_2$O

For the Dish
4 x 80g cod portions

salt

apple wood chips, for smoking

1 scallion

3 small Maris Piper potatoes, skin
on, finely sliced

For the Sorrel Emulsion
2 bunches of fermented sorrel

salt, for fermentation, 20g per litre

4 sheets kombu

4l filtered water

100ml each dashi and virgin olive oil

2 bunches fresh sorrel

For the Nori Butter and Salt
3 blocks of butter

9 sheets nori

15g wakame

3 peppercorns

150g sea salt

For the Bonito Butter
500g butter

5g bonito flakes

1 eel skin, also used in the mousse

For the Mousse and Potatoes
100ml keffir or yoghurt

fish sauce, to taste

1 lemon, zested

10g wakame

1 sheet kombu

3g gelespressa

1l dashi

500g Maris Piper potatoes, 5cm dice

500g Cherie potatoes

50g smoked butter

1l cream

50g sour cream

200ml buttermilk

50g bonito butter

lemon zest and fish sauce, to taste

To prepare the cod, skin, salt well and allow to sit for 5 minutes. Rinse in a tray of ice water and dry in the fridge on a cloth. The cloth will become damp before the fish is dry, so change it for a fresh one once before smoking. Cold smoke the cod with apple wood chips for 5 minutes. Lay the fillets on the cloth in the fridge for 3 hours.

To make the sorrel emulsion, ferment 2 bunches of sorrel with 2% salt in vacuum pack bags, at around 15°C for 5 days. Soak 4 sheets of kombu in 4l filtered water for 2 hours, then simmer for 2 hours and bring up to 1% salinity. Cover the top of the pan in cling film and leave the kombu to cool in the liquid. Blend the fermented sorrel and the stalks of the fresh sorrel first, adding all of the olive oil and dashi liquid from the boiled kombu. Once smooth, pulse in the fresh sorrell leaves.

To make the nori butter, blend together the butter, 6 sheets of nori, 10g wakame and the peppercorns. To make the nori salt, toast 3 sheets of nori, 5g wakame and blend with 150g sea salt.

Make the bonito butter by melting together the butter, bonito flakes and the eel skin. Remove the eel skin and blend with the kombu, wakame and a little fish sauce. Add the gelespressa to the mixture, combine, pass through a fine sieve and chill. Fill a siphon gun, equipped with 2 cartridges, with the mixture.

To make the mousse, sweat the eel skin in 250g nori butter and add the yoghurt, fish sauce, lemon zest, wakame, the sheet of kombu used in the dashi and 2g gelespressa. Blend well, using a litre of dashi. Cook the diced Maris Piper potatoes in half of the blended mixture, boiling until soft. Do the same in a separate pan with the Cherie potatoes. Blend the Maris Pipers with enough of the liquid and smoked butter to make a tight purée. Place the cream, sour cream and buttermilk in a water bath at 37°C, leaving the liquid to heat gradually for 5 days until it has completely soured.

On a barbecue, char the spring onion or scallion and peel off the blackened outside level. Split down the middle before serving and reheat with nori butter. Make crisps by frying a few slices of Maris Piper potato at 160°C. Season with nori salt.

To serve, poach the cod portions in bonito butter at 42°C for 10 minutes. Warm the potato mousse in the siphon by placing it in a pot of boiling water, making sure to take the pan off the heat once the liquid has boiled. Shake well once warm. Warm your Cherie potatoes in kombu emulsion, drain and sprinkle with chopped chives. Warm the spring onions in the oven. Flake the cod and season with lemon. Spread sorrel emulsion on warmed plates. Place the potatoes, onions and cod around the plate and the foam mousse in the centre. Garnish with a few crisps and a sorrel leaf.

RAJESH PARMAR

Since 1869, Action for Children has been working to make sure every child has the love and support they need to reach their potential. Courthouse is thrilled to be able to carry on that support by donating their tiger prawn dish to ChariTable Bookings to raise money for this great cause."

GRILLED TIGER PRAWNS with quinoa salad and mango salsa

SERVES 1 | PREPARATION TIME 30 MINUTES | COOKING TIME 30 MINUTES

For the Tiger Prawns
4 tiger prawns

For the Marinade
2 fresh red chillies
1 clove of garlic
5cm Krachai, lesser galangal/
Chinese ginger
lemon juice
salt, to taste

For the Quinoa Salad
50g organic quinoa
20g fresh baby spinach leaves
6 cherry tomatoes
salt and lemon juice, to taste

For the Mango Salsa
1 raw green mango, diced
2 sprigs of coriander, chopped
6 cherry tomatoes, halved
lemon juice, salt and sugar, to taste

To prepare the tiger prawns, bring all the ingredients for the marinade together in a blender and blitz to a fine paste. Shell and de-vein the prawns and rub the marinade into the flesh. Let the prawns rest for 30 minutes.

While the prawns marinate, thoroughly wash and boil the quinoa. Allow to rest in preparation for the salad.

Gently combine all the salsa ingredients and leave to rest and infuse for 30 minutes.

Combine the cooked quinoa with the spinach and tomatoes, seasoning to taste with salt and lemon juice.

To finish and serve, grill the tiger prawns until tender. Use a food ring to plate the quinoa salad. Arrange the prawns next to it, covering generously with the mango salsa.

AARON PATTERSON

I needed a decadent recipe to stand out from 365 other chefs! What better than Hambleton Hall's truffle lasagne and I get to help Scotty's Little Soldiers to stand out too. A great charity helping children grieving from the loss of a parent in active duty. Great idea by ChariTable Bookings."

TRUFFLE LASAGNE
SERVES 2–4 | PREPARATION TIME 1 HOUR | COOKING TIME 1 HOUR 30 MINUTES

Equipment
  pasta machine
For the Chicken Mousse
  ¼ chicken breast
  4 egg yolks
  200ml whipping cream
  salt and pepper, to taste
For the Truffle Sauce
  ¼ bottle Madeira wine
  100ml chicken or veal stock
  1 whole truffle
  100ml cream
  50g butter
  1 spritz of lemon juice
  salt and pepper, to taste
For the Pasta
  1 saffron powder sachet
  1 tsp water or olive oil
  4 egg yolks
  1 whole egg
  200g 00 pasta flour
For the Garnish
  artichokes
  truffle shavings

To make the chicken mousse, place all the ingredients in a fridge for approximately 1 hour until cold. Place the chicken in a food processor and pulse until it looks minced, then add the egg yolks. Pour the cream in slowly, like a mayonnaise, until all cream is incorporated and the mixture is smooth. Season with salt and pepper. Roll in cling film and tie each end with string tightly to form a cylinder shape. Poach in boiling water for 15–20 minutes until firm.

To make the truffle sauce, add the Madeira and stock to a warm pan. Place half of the truffle in the stock and simmer for 10 minutes, then leave to steep for 30 minutes. Place back on the stove, add the cream and reduce the mixture by a third. Whisk in the butter and season with lemon juice, salt and pepper.

To make the pasta, add the saffron to the oil and water and warm slightly. Combine with the egg and yolks. Mix into the flour until it comes together. Place onto a work surface and knead until smooth and firm. Leave to relax in a cling film covered bowl for 15–20 minutes. Using a pasta machine, roll through the finest setting on a lightly floured bench. Cut to size and boil for 1–2 minutes.

To serve, wrap the poached chicken mousse in a sheet of pasta, cover generously with sauce, and garnish with artichokes and truffle shavings.

ANDREW PERN

"What a great way of getting something and giving to charity both at the same time. Glad that the Star Inn can support the MS Society by donating our signature dish to ChariTable Bookings."

WHITBY LOBSTER with cod roe paté, Lowna Dairy goat's curd, squid ink crackers and soft herbs

SERVES 2 | PREPARATION TIME 1 HOUR | COOKING TIME 1 HOUR

For the lobster
1 x 500g live native lobster
court bouillon
100g Lowna dairy goat's curd

For the paté
250g smoked cod's roe
100ml water
1 clove of garlic, peeled and crushed
1 lemon, juiced
6 drops of Tabasco
400ml rapeseed oil

For the lemon water vinaigrette
100g heritage tomatoes, preferably zebra tomatoes
50ml lemon oil
15ml reduced lime cordial
15ml lemon juice

For the crackers
100g brown rice
300ml water
50ml squid ink

For the soft herbs
chervil
nasturtium leaves
Jack-by-the-hedge
thyme and chive flowers
salt and pepper, to taste

To make the paté, start by removing the fine membrane from the roe. Blitz into a paste in a blender, then add the water, crushed garlic, lemon juice and Tabasco. Whilst still blending, slowly add the oil to create a mayonnaise consistency and pass through a coarse sieve. Refrigerate if preparing ahead, removing in time to return to room temperature.

Next, slice the tomatoes very finely and prepare the lemon water vinaigrette by combining the ingredients. Cover the tomatoes lightly with vinaigrette and allow the flavours to develop for around 30 minutes.

To make the crackers, first cook the rice in the water and ink until soft. Drain well and spread out on a tray. Place in the oven at the lowest heat until dried out. Form crackers, roughly 6cm in diameter, then deep-fry at 180°C until crisp for approximately 10 seconds each. Remove, drain and season.

Take your lobster and pierce with a knife between the head and the body. Remove the head, claws and tail. Snap the tail at the bottom and remove the dark intestinal thread. Place a spoon in the body to keep it straight whilst cooking. Bring a pan of court bouillon to the boil and drop in the claws. After 2 minutes, add the tail and the body, and cook for a further 4 minutes. Remove from the pan and refresh with cold water.

Slice the lobster and arrange on the serving plate or dish with the paté, dressed tomatoes, curd and herbs. The crackers can be served separately or as an integral part of the dish.

Editor's Note: *Jack-by-the-hedge is also known as garlic mustard and is generally a foraged herb but may be available at some farmer's markets.*

ANNE-SOPHIE PIC

"I'm really looking forward to serving this dish at the new Four Season's Trinity Square, even more happy to share the recipe with ChariTable Bookings in aid of the EU Solidarity Fund."

80-DAY MATURED HIGHLAND BEEF marinated in Zacapa rum, Phu Quoc pepper and Café Liberica de São Tomé, carrots and girolles from the garden

SERVES 10 | PREPARATION TIME 30 MINUTES | COOKING TIME 5 HOURS

Equipment
centrifugal juicer

For the Highland Beef
4kg 80-day matured Highland beef
100g grapeseed oil
200g unsalted butter
100g Café Liberica de São Tomé
100g Sobacha
200ml Zacapa rum
100g Phu Quoc pepper
200g half-salted butter

For the Carrot Purée
1kg carrots
2 combawa lemon leaves

For the Fine Salt Garnish
1kg girolles
vinegar water
1 deep purple carrot – black
1 yellow dubs carrot – yellow
1 white Kuttingen carrot – white
1 Nantaise carrot – orange
1 Meyer lemon
1 shallot
100g rocket
combawa leaves
100g butter
fine salt

To prepare the beef, roll it and tie with a string so that it will cook evenly, keeping all the trimmings aside to make the gravy. Roast the trimmings and bones in oil and when well-coloured, add the half-salted butter to create a gravy. Remove the bones and trimmings and store the excess fat and cook the remaining liquid over a low heat for 5 hours. Sieve and cool to let the fat set. Remove the excess fat again and reduce the gravy until it has reached the desired consistency. One hour before cooking, mix the São Tomé coffee, Phu Quoc, Sobacha, rum and pepper. Pass though a large mesh sieve, roll the beef fillets in some of the mixture and set aside.

To prepare the carrot purée, make a juice with two thirds of the carrots in a centrifugal juicer, finely trimming the rest. Cook the carrots in their juices until they are cooked through as quickly as possible. Drain the carrots, keeping the juice. Mix in the blender until they are finely chopped with a little of the cooking juice, then pass through a fine sieve. Reduce the remaining juice and stir into the purée. Spread a thin layer of carrot purée over a plate and dry at 65°C for about 30 minutes, then form into a triangle shape. Fry the leaves one by one, placing them onto a cone shaped mould to give the illusion of a core. Keep warm in an oven.

To prepare the garnish, wash the girolles several times in vinegar water and then dry them well. Julienne the carrots and lemon, keeping the 2 ingredients separate. Pass the dried rocket through a very fine sieve. Heat the carrot purée and add the combawa leaves. Leave them to infuse for a few minutes and then remove. Adjust the seasoning and fill a piping bag with the mixture.

To finish, brown the beef in butter until cooked evenly. Cut into 3 equal pieces for each serving, glaze with the fat of the beef and sprinkle with the remaining spice and coffee mixture. Sauté the girolles in butter, cook well and add the shallot.

To Finish

50g dried rocket
1 cressonnette tray

To finish, Sprinkle the powdered rocket on a plate. Using the piping bag filled with carrot purée, reproduce the shape of a small carrot on the plate, arranging the girolles on both sides. Place the julienne carrots and lemon pieces at the end of the purée, to look like the carrot top. Finish with the cressonnette. Add the thin slices of beef, the crispy carrot cone and serve the juice separately.

STEVE PIDGEON

All of us at Arundell Arms believe in supporting local causes which is why I have chosen to support Devon Air Ambulance Trust by donating our Venison and Chocolate Casserole recipe to ChariTable Bookings new book of 365 recipes."

VENISON AND CHOCOLATE CASSEROLE

SERVES 4 | PREPARATION TIME 20 MINUTES | COOKING TIME 2 HOURS 30 MINUTES

For the Dish

500g venison haunch, diced

bacon lardons

3 tsp olive oil

2 tsp flour

3 tsp olive oil

4 cloves of garlic, peeled and crushed

3 banana shallots, peeled and chopped

1 stick of celery, finely chopped

4 carrots, peeled and halved

3 flat mushrooms, roughly chopped

1 tbsp chopped thyme

1 tbsp chopped rosemary

700ml red wine

500ml beef stock

salt and pepper

2 tbsp red currant jelly

40g butter

30g dark chocolate buttons, good quality

Preheat the oven to 160°C.

Pour half the olive oil into an ovenproof dish and gently warm. Add the bacon lardons, cook for 4 minutes, then remove from the heat.

Put the diced venison and flour in a bowl and toss well. Once coated, shake off any excess flour. Place the ovenproof dish back on the heat and return the venison to it. Cook until browned all over.

Add the rest of the olive oil, garlic, shallots and celery, then cook for 1–2 minutes. Next, add the carrots, mushrooms and herbs. Cook for 15 minutes, pour in the red wine and bring to the boil. Add the beef stock and season with salt and pepper. Place a lid on top and cook for 1 hour 45 minutes to 2 hours, until the meat is tender.

Once tender remove from the oven. Strain the meat and vegetables in a sieve, keeping the liquid. Put the liquid back in the pan and re boil. Once boiling, whisk in the red currant jelly, butter and chocolate.

Pour over the venison and vegetables, stir well and serve.

ANTON PIOTROWSKI

"ChariTable Bookings have come up with a great way for The Treby Arms to support Muscular Dystrophy UK while showcasing our menu."

PIGEON WELLINGTON

SERVES 1 | PREPARATION TIME 20 MINUTES | COOKING TIME 40 MINUTES

For the Pigeon Wellington
30g spinach
salt and pepper
30g girolles, cleaned
1 knob of butter
1 spritz of lemon juice
1 pigeon breast
1 slice of Parma ham
1 sheet of filo pastry
1 egg yolk, beaten

For the Bubble and Squeak Croquette
25g potato
100ml water
15g salt
1 carrot, finely diced and sautéed
2 leaves of cabbage, cut chiffonade and sautéed
panko breadcrumbs
vegetable oil, for frying

For the Girolles
4 girolles, cleaned
½ lemon, juiced
5g butter
fresh dill, tarragon and parsley

For the Wellington, blanch the spinach in boiling, salted water, leave to cool and season well. Cook the 30g girolles, finishing with butter, salt, pepper and lemon juice. Leave to cool. Seal the pigeon breast on both sides in a smoking hot pan, this should take seconds. Put on a resting rack, leave to cool and season well.

Place the spinach on top of the pigeon breast and the mushroom on top of that. Roll the layered pigeon in the sheet of Parma ham. Fold the filo pastry to the size of the pigeon breast, just slightly longer. Egg wash lightly, place the wrap onto the filo and roll up. Season well and place into a hot pan for 4 minutes, colouring on the 2 shorter sides and the bottom. Place the un-coloured side onto the pan, then put the pan in the oven for 2 minutes at 180°C. Turn over and cook for another 2 minutes. Once cooked, allow to rest for 3 minutes.

To make the bubble and squeak croquette, bring the water to a boil, add the salt and cook the potatoes until soft. Drain away the water through a sieve, allowing the potato to steam. Pass it through a drum sieve twice, then combine with the cooked carrot and cabbage. Season the mixture well, panée in panko breadcrumbs and fry to order.

To cook the girolles, add them to a smoking hot pan and add a splash of water. Allow to steam for about 10 seconds. Add the butter, seasoning and finish with lemon juice and fresh herbs.

ALESSIO PIRAS

Cancer is sadly becoming more prevalent every year. 11 children and young people will hear the news that they have cancer today alone which is why Albert's is thrilled to support CLIC Sargent through ChariTable Bookings and supply one of the 365 recipes involved."

MONKFISH TAIL wrapped in Parma ham, sweet and sour peppers, and samphire and caper dressing

SERVES 1 | PREPARATION TIME 15 MINUTES | COOKING TIME 45 MINUTES

For the Monkfish
180g monkfish tail, cleaned, you can ask your fishmonger to do this
2 slices of Parma ham
vegetable oil, for frying

For the Pepper, Samphire and Caper Dressing
½ red bell pepper
½ yellow bell pepper
50g samphire
2 tbsp lemon juice
1 tbsp sugar
30g capers
1 pinch of cracked black pepper
1 tsp parsley, chopped

To Finish
2 tbsp olive oil
1 tsp red amaranth

To begin preparing the dish, preheat an oven to 180°C. Put the peppers on a baking tray and place in the centre of the oven. Cook until soft, this should take approximately 15–20 minutes.

While the peppers are roasting, take the cleaned monkfish tail and wrap with 2 slices of Parma ham. Once wrapped, place the monkfish tail in a hot frying pan with vegetable oil and cook until golden on all sides. Once coloured, place in the oven to finish cooking for 6 minutes.

After the peppers have roasted, remove from the oven and carefully peel off the skin before cutting them into small, even squares. Next, boil the samphire in salted water for 5 minutes. Immediately transfer to a bowl of ice water to chill and preserve its colour. Mix the lemon juice, sugar, capers, cracked black pepper and fresh parsley in a small bowl and delicately drizzle over the warm, chopped peppers and chilled samphire.

To serve, place the dressed peppers and samphire on a warm plate. Slice the monkfish and layer on top. To finish, add some red amaranth and a drizzle of olive oil.

MARK POYNTON

"LymeAid UK aims to provide the gap between someone with suspected Lyme Disease getting tested abroad and then getting treatment on the NHS. Alimentum is really pleased to promote their work by contributing to this new collection of recipes by ChariTable Bookings."

ROASTED HALIBUT with cauliflower, chicory salad and caviar sauce

SERVES 4 | PREPARATION TIME 20 MINUTES | COOKING TIME 1 HOUR 30 MINUTES

Equipment
sous vide and vacuum pack bags

For the Dish
4 x 150g pieces of halibut, deskinned and deboned, retain the bones
1 whole head of chicory, to garnish
6 slices of cauliflower, to garnish

For the Cauliflower Purée
100g butter
500g cauliflower, finely sliced
100ml water
salt and pepper

For the Pickled Cauliflower
40 small florets of cauliflower
100ml white wine vinegar
100g sugar
200ml water

For the Caviar Sauce
1 splash of rapeseed oil
1 shallot, sliced
1 clove of garlic, sliced
250ml white fish stock
750ml reduced chicken stock
1 halibut bone, roasted
caviar, to finish

For the Onion Confit
2 each red and white onions, peeled
1 head of garlic
5 bay leaves
300ml rapeseed oil

For the cauliflower purée, melt and brown the butter to make a beurre noisette. Sweat the cauliflower in the beurre noisette until lightly roasted, add the water and continue to cook until emulsified. Blend, pass through a fine mesh sieve and check for seasoning.

To pickle the cauliflower, bring the pickling liquor to the boil and chill. Vacuum pack the florets with enough liquor to cover and put on full pressure.

To make the caviar sauce, sweat the shallot and garlic in a little rapeseed oil. Add the fish stock and reduce by three quarters. Pour in the chicken stock, bring to the boil and skim. Add the roasted fish bone and simmer for 10 minutes. Pass through a chinois and muslin cloth, then add caviar to finish.

For the onion confit, make a tin foil packet, put all the ingredients inside and seal. Place in a preheated oven at 180°C and cook en papillote for 40 minutes. Once cooked, reserve all liquid and let the onions cool. Quarter the onions and char one side of each piece. This will be your presentation side and will face upwards on the plate.

Pan fry the halibut skin-side down in a hot pan. When the skin is golden brown, add a small knob of butter and place in the oven at 190°C for 2–3 minutes. Remove when the inside of the fish is opaque.

To serve, swipe the cauliflower purée on the plate, then add 10 pieces of pickled cauliflower and 14 of confit onion. Dress the chicory leaves in the onion cooking juices and arrange the salad as pictured. Add 6 pieces of raw sliced cauliflower and place the halibut next to the salad. Drizzle sauce over the fish and salad.

ALFRED PRASAD

No child should have to suffer grief through loss of a parent, no matter what the reason. Scotty's Little Soldiers helps to fill that gap when a child loses a parent through military service and I'm pleased to support them by donating Tamarind's dish to ChariTable Bookings."

LAMB SHANK CURRY

SERVES 4 | PREPARATION TIME 20 MINUTES | COOKING TIME 3 HOURS

For the Curry
4 lamb shanks
4 tbsp vegetable oil
4 sticks of cinnamon
4 cardamom pods
6 cloves
3 medium onions, sliced
3 tbsp ginger and garlic paste
1 tsp turmeric powder
1 tsp chilli powder
salt, to taste
4 tbsp yoghurt
3 ripe tomatoes, puréed

To Serve
½ tsp garam masala powder
½ bunch of mixed micro cress
crispy, golden fried onions
steamed rice or naan bread

Wash the lamb shanks and leave to drain in a colander.

Heat oil in a saucepan large enough to accommodate all the shanks. Add the cinnamon, cardamom and cloves, then sauté for half a minute. Add the sliced onions and sauté on medium-high heat, stirring occasionally, until golden brown. This could take about 30 minutes.

Put the lamb into the saucepan and sear over high heat for 5 minutes, stirring constantly. Add the ginger and garlic paste, stir well for a couple of minutes, then add the turmeric, chilli and salt. Lower the heat and sauté for a further 5 minutes. Next, pour in the yoghurt and sauté for 5 more minutes, over a high heat. Add the puréed tomato, stir well and simmer for 15 minutes. Pour in enough hot water to cover the shanks and bring to a boil. Cover with a lid, simmer and cook for about 1.5–2 hours, or until the lamb is tender.

Remove the shanks using a pair of tongs and leave to cool. Strain the sauce into a container, squeezing all of the juices out of the residue. Cook the strained sauce over a medium heat, stirring occasionally, for a further 30 minutes or until reduced to the desired consistency. Check seasoning and leave to cool.

To finish the dish and serve, transfer the sauce to a large saucepan and bring to a boil. Meanwhile, microwave the shanks for 4–6 minutes and add to the sauce. Cover and simmer for a further 20 minutes. Transfer to a serving platter, sprinkle with garam masala powder, then garnish with golden fried onions and mixed micro cress. Serve hot, accompanied with steamed rice or naan bread.

GLYNN PURNELL

On behalf of all of us at Purnell's - enjoy my recipe and the many others in this unique book and support Cure Leukaemia in partnership with the team at ChariTable Bookings."

MONKFISH MASALA with red lentils, pickled carrots and coconut

SERVES 4 | PREPARATION TIME 1 HOUR (PLUS 3 WEEKS TO PICKLE AND OVERNIGHT TO CHILL) | COOKING TIME 1 HOUR 30 MINUTES

Equipment
sous vide and vacuum pack bags

For the Pickled Carrots
3 carrots, washed, peeled and sliced
1 tbsp fenugreek seeds
1 tsp ajwain seeds
1 tsp mustard seeds
½ tsp onion seeds
1 tsp cumin seeds
⅓ tsp chilli flakes
1 tsp salt
vegetable oil, to cover carrots

For the Monkfish
300g rock salt
4 x 130g monkfish fillets
25g butter

Purnell's masala spice mix
38g fenugreek seeds
20g cinnamon stick
10g fennel seeds
33g black mustard seeds
1 tsp cloves
13g coriander seeds
28g cumin seeds

For the Red Lentils
½ onion, chopped
1 tsp vegetable oil
1 tbsp mild curry powder
225g red lentils
500ml chicken stock
½ red chilli, finely chopped
2 heaped tbsp fresh coriander, chopped
½ lime, juiced
salt, to taste

For the Coconut Garnish
400ml coconut milk
½ fresh coconut, flesh thinly sliced into strips on a mandoline
fresh coriander shoots
1 kaffir lime leaf
1 pinch of salt

To prepare the pickled carrots, dry carrot slices out in a warm oven overnight, then place them in a sterilised jar. Mix the spices with the oil and pour into the jar. Leave for a few weeks, longer if possible.

For the masala spice mix, snap the cinnamon stick into a few pieces, then whizz with all the spices in a food processor for about 1 minute, until nicely broken up. Using a coffee grinder, grind 2 tablespoons of the mixture at a time for 10 seconds, ensuring that the grinder doesn't get too hot. Pass the spice mix through a fine sieve with a ladle and store in an airtight jar.

To make the monkfish, sprinkle the salt over the monkfish fillets and leave for 5–6 minutes to remove moisture. Wash the salt off thoroughly under cold running water. Wrap the washed monkfish in a clean tea towel and leave overnight in the fridge. Put 4 tablespoons of masala spice mix on a plate and roll the monkfish fillets in the mixture. Seal each fillet in a vacuum pack bag and cook for 11 minutes in a water bath at 63°C. Melt the butter in a frying pan on a medium heat until foaming. Remove the fish from the bags, then sear each fillet on both sides for 2–3 minutes until golden-brown and crisp all over.

To make the red lentils, sweat the chopped onion in a pan for 4–5 minutes or until softened. Stir in the curry powder and add the red lentils. Stir well, then cover with chicken stock and simmer for 10–15 minutes or until the lentils are tender. When the lentils are cooked, stir in the chilli, coriander and lime juice. Season with salt to taste and set aside.

Pour the coconut milk into a pan with the lime leaf and add a pinch of salt. Simmer for 15–20 minutes or until reduced by half. Heat a frying pan and dry toast the thinly sliced coconut strips until golden-brown and fragrant.

To serve, spoon some lentils onto each plate. Carve the monkfish fillet in half and place one piece of monkfish on top of the lentils and the other piece next to them. Drizzle over a bit of the reduced coconut milk, then garnish with the toasted sliced coconut, pickled carrots and fresh coriander shoots.

Editor's Note: The masala spice mix makes 110g. You only need 4 tablespoons for this recipe. Store the remaining blend in an airtight jar for next time you make the dish.

THEO RANDALL

"Fighting to battle blood cancers with Leuka and donate the InterContinental's tagliatelle with squid to this great new book by ChariTable Bookings."

TAGLIATELLE with squid, zucchini, tomatoes and bottarga

SERVES 2 | PREPARATION TIME 20 MINUTES (PLUS 30 MINUTES TO CHILL) | COOKING TIME 30 MINUTES

Equipment

mandoline

pasta machine with tagliatelle cutter

For the Pasta

200g Italian 00 flour

1 whole free range egg

6 free range egg yolks

50g fine semolina flour, to dust
pasta

For the Sauce

2 courgettes, finely sliced using a
mandoline, cut to the same size as
the tagliatelle

200g fresh tagliatelle, made above

2 tbsp olive oil

8 Datterini tomatoes or other small
tomatoes, peeled

1 clove of garlic, finely chopped

200g fresh squid, cleaned, scored
and sliced as thick as the tagliatelle

1 tsp chopped parsley

1 pinch of dried chilli

salt and freshly ground black pepper

20g bottarga, shaved

To prepare the pasta, place the flour, egg and egg yolks into a food processor. Pulse until well combined and the mixture comes together as a dough. Place the dough into a bowl, cover with cling film and place into the fridge to rest for 30 minutes. Cut the pasta dough in half and feed one of the pieces through a pasta machine, following the machine instructions, ending on the thinnest setting. Add the tagliatelle cutter to the pasta machine and pass the pasta through the machine to make thin strips. Repeat the process with the remaining dough, then dust the pasta with semolina flour and place onto a plate. Refrigerate overnight or use immediately.

To cook the pasta and courgette ribbons, bring a large saucepan of salted water to the boil. Add the tagliatelle and sliced courgettes and return to the boil for 2 minutes.

For the sauce, heat a frying pan until medium hot. Add the olive oil, tomatoes, garlic, squid and parsley and cook gently for 2 minutes.

To finish, add the pasta and courgettes to the frying pan and stir together. Season with chilli, salt and freshly ground black pepper. Scatter the bottarga on top and serve

SHAUN RANKIN

I love the idea of combining good food and charity which is why I am supporting Caring Cooks of Jersey, a local charity that educates families on good nutrition and even caters for those most hard up. I'm sharing Ormer's sea trout recipe with ChariTable Bookings, which I hope you enjoy."

SEA TROUT with asparagus and pink grapefruit sabayon

SERVES 4 | PREPARATION TIME 15 MINUTES | COOKING TIME 1 HOUR

For the Sabayon
- 20g butter
- 400ml water
- 1 pink grapefruit
- 3 egg yolks
- sea salt and cracked black pepper
- 1 tbsp chopped chives

For the Trout
- 4 sea trout steaks
- salt and pepper
- 100g unsalted butter, softened
- 1 lemon, juiced
- olive oil, to drizzle
- 12 spears of asparagus

To prepare the dish, put the butter in a heavy saucepan and melt slowly over low heat. Remove the pan from the heat and leave to stand for 5 minutes. Skim the foam from the top, slowly pouring into a container. Discard the milky solids in the bottom of the pan.

To make the pink grapefruit sabayon, put the water in a saucepan and bring to the boil. Cut the skin and pith from the grapefruit. Next, using a sharp serrated knife, carefully cut down between the grapefruit segments to remove the segments of fruit. Squeeze the remaining pulp to get all the grapefruit juice and reserve separately. Meanwhile, in a bowl that can sit comfortably over the saucepan of boiling water, combine the egg yolks with 1 tablespoon of cold water. Once the water in the saucepan has reached boiling point, put the bowl of eggs and water on top of it. Using a hand whisk, continuously whisk the mixture until the eggs become very light and airy. Make sure that you take the bowl off the heat every 10 seconds or so to ensure the eggs don't scramble. When the mix is 4 times the size of its initial volume, taste to ensure it no longer tastes of egg. Add 1 tablespoon of the clarified butter and 2 tablespoons of the grapefruit juice to the sabayon. Season with salt and pepper, then finish with the chopped chives. Remove from the heat, cover with cling film and keep warm.

To cook the sea trout, preheat the grill to high heat. Place the sea trout steaks onto a grill tray and season with salt and pepper. Using a pastry brush, brush the soft butter over the top of each fillet. Pour over the lemon juice, followed by a drizzle of olive oil. Place the sea trout steaks under the grill and cook for 4–5 minutes. Use a tablespoon to baste any melted butter back onto the fish and stop the steaks from drying out. Meanwhile, bring a saucepan of water to the boil. Add the asparagus spears and simmer for 5 minutes or until cooked to your preference. Remove from the heat and drain. Remove the sea trout steaks from under the grill.

To serve, arrange the fish on plates with the asparagus spears on top. Garnish with pink grapefruit segments and spoon over the sabayon sauce.

JURI RAVAGLI

"Our chosen charity is Action Against Hunger who we work closely with. Thank you to ChariTable Bookings for helping to raise awareness alongside 1 Lombard Street."

CARAMELISED SABLEFISH with vegetable spaghetti

SERVES 4 | PREPARATION TIME 10 MINUTES | COOKING TIME 15 MINUTES

Equipment
  mandoline
For the Vegetable Spaghetti
  2 green courgettes
  2 yellow courgettes
  2 carrots
  4 pak choi
For the Caramelised Sablefish
  4 x 200g sablefish fillets – black cod, cleaned
  400ml soy sauce
  160g caster sugar
  100ml olive oil
For the Dish
  1 banana leaf

Preheat the oven to 180°C.

Cut the banana leaf into 4 flat diamond shapes. Put a damp cloth on top to retain moisture and place to one side for later.

To prepare the vegetable spaghetti, take the courgettes and carrots and slice them with a mandoline, lengthways. Then with a knife, cut spaghetti like long, thin strands. Cut the pak choi in half, then blanch in salted boiling water for 2 minutes. Strain them and place in cold water, then dry them off using a cloth.

To make the caramelised sablefish, marinate the cod fillets in the soy sauce for a few minutes and then roll them in sugar. Place them in a preheated frying pan with a tablespoon of extra virgin olive oil, skin-side up. Gently cook until the base is caramelised. Repeat on the other side, then remove the fish from the frying pan. Add the remaining sugar and soy from the marinade to the pan. Let it boil for approximately 2 minutes. Place the fish on a baking tray lined with greaseproof paper and a little olive oil. Add the pak choi and pop in the oven for 5–6 minutes. In a separate pan, fry the vegetable spaghetti with 1 tbsp of olive oil, salt and pepper for approximately 2 minutes.

To serve, place a banana leaf diamond in the centre of each plate. Put the vegetable spaghetti on top, then layer the sablefish and pak choi. Dress the dish with the sweet soy sauce you prepared earlier and finish with a drizzle of extra virgin olive oil.

ROBERTO REATINI

ChariTable Bookings advocates many good causes. None can be more vital in the world today than Save The Children and Frescobaldi is glad to be in a position to promote this awesome crusade."

VEAL CHOP with mashed potatoes and mushrooms

SERVES 4 | PREPARATION TIME 10 MINUTES | COOKING TIME 30 MINUTES

For the Veal
- 4 x 250g veal chops
- 4 tsp Laudemio olive oil
- salt and pepper
- oil, for frying

For the Mashed Potatoes
- 1.4kg floury potatoes, peeled and quartered
- 60g unsalted butter
- 50ml fresh milk
- salt and pepper

For the Sautéed Mushrooms
- 80g morel mushrooms
- 80g Pied-du-mouton mushrooms
- 80g whole ceps mushrooms
- 1 tbsp vegetable oil
- 1 clove of garlic, crushed
- 1 knob of butter
- 100ml white wine
- 3g parsley, chopped

To make the dish, rub the chops all over with the olive oil and season with salt and pepper. Set aside on a plate for 15 minutes.

Preheat the oven to 190°C.

Meanwhile cook the potatoes in lightly salted water until tender to the tip of a knife.

Heat a large frying pan over a medium high heat and add a slosh of oil. Add the chops to pan and cook until golden brown on one side, about 5 minutes. Turn over and cook for another 5 minutes. Remove the chops from the pan, transfer to a baking dish, lower the oven to 180°C and roast for 15 minutes. Leave to rest for 10 minutes.

Drain the potatoes, return to the pan and mash with the butter and milk. Add salt and pepper to taste.

Use a slightly damp paper towel to wipe the mushrooms clean. Never clean them directly under running water, they will absorb water and become soggy. Alternatively, use a pastry brush to dust the dirt from the mushrooms. Heat a large skillet to a high heat and add a glug of oil. Wait 1–2 minutes for it to come up to the smoking point. Add the garlic and toss furiously so that the garlic doesn't burn. Add the mushrooms with the knob of butter and toss until all mushrooms are golden brown and caramelised. Add the wine and reduce until the liquid disappears. Remove from the heat, season with salt and pepper to taste, toss in the parsley and serve.

To serve, spoon some mashed potato in the middle of each plate and top with a veal chop. Scatter the mushrooms around the plate and drizzle any mushroom juices over.

MICHAEL REID

Very pleased to be able to share one of M's recipes with ChariTable Bookings in honour of The School of Hard Knocks. This is a great and growing charity that uses rugby and boxing to change the behaviour of men in certain areas and situations.

BEEF SHORT RIBS

SERVES 4 | PREPARATION TIME 1 HOUR (PLUS OVERNIGHT TO PRESS) | COOKING TIME 48 HOURS

Equipment
mandoline
sous vide and a large vacuum pack bag

For the Spice Coating
1 tbsp smoked paprika
2 tbsp onion salt
1½ tsp Sri Lankan black curry powder
1½ tsp sea salt
½ tsp of each chilli powder, garlic powder and dried oregano
½ tsp of each ground ginger, turmeric and cumin

For the Short Ribs
80g soft light brown sugar
1 tbsp spice coating
1.4kg beef short ribs, in one piece on the bone
6 bay leaves
120ml red wine jus
salt and freshly ground black pepper, to taste

For the Compressed apple
1 apple, sliced wafer thin
100ml apple juice

For the Garnish
hazelnut purée
fresh horseradish, grated
blanched hazelnuts, toasted and grated

Begin preparing the short ribs 3 days before you plan to serve.

Mix the brown sugar and 1 tablespoon of spice coating together, then rub all over the short ribs. Place the ribs and bay leaves in a large vacuum seal bag and seal securely. Set a sous vide water bath to 58°C, add the sealed bag and leave the ribs to cook for 48 hours. Once cooked, remove the bag from the machine and very carefully pour off and discard the liquid. After 48 hours of cooking the meat will be so tender that only a few slices next to the bone will be required to free 4 large pieces of meat.

Taking care not to break up the meat, line a baking tray that will fit in the fridge with cling film. Add the pieces of meat in a single layer, topping with another sheet of cling film. Place another tray on top and weigh it down with cans. Chill for at least 6 hours, but ideally overnight.

To prepare the compressed apple, cut the apple into almost translucent slices and place in a bag with the apple juice, chilling until required.

To serve, heat the oven to 160°C and remove the pieces of meat from the fridge to return to room temperature. Transfer the rib meat to a baking tray, then reheat in the oven for 15 minutes, or until hot all the way through. Put the jus in a large sauté pan over a medium-high heat. Add the pieces of meat and leave the jus to reduce and glaze the meat. Adjust the seasoning with salt and pepper to taste if necessary. Meanwhile, remove the apple slices from the apple juice and pat dry. Divide the glazed ribs among 4 plates, top each rib with compressed apple slices and add a spoonful of hazelnut purée. Finely grate over the hazelnuts and horseradish to garnish, then serve immediately.

ROBERT REID

"Balthazar's Duck Shepherd's Pie had to be included in ChariTable Bookings' compendium of 365 recipes. We also wanted to support the incredible work of Children in Need. I hope you enjoy it!"

DUCK SHEPHERD'S PIE

SERVES 6 | PREPARATION TIME 30 MINUTES (PLUS OVERNIGHT TO MARINATE) | COOKING TIME 5 HOURS 30 MINUTES

For the Duck
8 large duck legs, skin on

For the Marinade
2 bottles good quality red wine

2 carrots, diced

3 celery stalks, diced

1 large onion, diced

3 sprigs of thyme

1 bay leaf

½ head of garlic, halved horizontally

For the Filling
the marinated duck legs

4 cloves of garlic, finely chopped

1.5 tsp salt

2 tbsp sunflower oil

2 tbsp tomato purée

3 tbsp plain flour

1l chicken stock

For the Topping
7 medium waxy potatoes, peeled and cut into 5cm pieces

3 parsnips, peeled and cut into 5cm pieces

2 heads of celeriac, peeled and cut into 5cm pieces

4 tbsp double cream

30g unsalted butter

salt and freshly ground black pepper

4 tbsp Parmesan cheese, grated

Prepare the marinade. In a large bowl, combine the duck legs, wine, carrots, celery, onion, thyme, bay leaf and the half head of garlic. Cover with cling film and marinate in the fridge overnight.

The next day, strain the duck and vegetables, reserving the liquid. Keep the vegetables to one side. Season the legs. In a large casserole dish, heat a tablespoon of oil until smoking. Brown the duck legs, starting skin-side down, for about 5 minutes on each side and reserve. Carefully discard the excess fat and wipe down the casserole dish with kitchen roll when cool enough. Add the remaining oil to the pan and cook the marinated carrots, celery, onion and chopped garlic over a medium heat until golden brown. Stir in the tomato purée and the flour. Turn the heat up and add the marinade. Bring to a boil and cook until the liquid reduces by half.

Preheat the oven to 190°C. Return the duck legs to the pot, add the stock and bring back to the boil. Cover the pot with a tight-fitting lid and cook in the oven, or on the stove at a low simmer, for about 3 hours. Remove the duck from the oven and reduce the heat to 180°C.

Meanwhile, to prepare the topping, put the diced potatoes, parsnips and celeriac into a large saucepan and cover with cold, salted water. Bring to the boil and cook until tender. Strain thoroughly and mash. Stir in the cream and butter. Season, cover with foil and set aside.

When the duck has finished cooking, remove from the pot and strain the cooking liquid into a large saucepan. Reserve the solids, but remove and discard the bay leaf, thyme sprigs and garlic remnants. Skim the fat from the surface of the sauce using a ladle. Set the pan over a high heat and boil until the liquid has reduced by about half, continuing to skim as necessary.

When the duck legs are cool enough to handle, remove the fatty skin and take the meat off the bones. Discard all excess fat and put the meat into a large bowl. Stir in the reserved diced carrots, celery and onion, then pour in just enough of the sauce to bind the meat and vegetables loosely. Spoon the duck mixture into the gratin dishes and spread the mashed root vegetables over the top, about 2cm high, leaving a 5mm border around the edges. Sprinkle with Parmesan and bake for 30 minutes. If not golden brown, put under a hot grill for 2 minutes before serving.

SIMON RIMMER

Very proud to be supporting the great work by Alison Baum and her team at Best Beginnings. I hope you enjoy Earle's Saffron Prawns in this incredible collection of 365 recipes by ChariTable Bookings."

SAFFRON PRAWNS with fennel

SERVES 4–6 | PREPARATION TIME 20 MINUTES | COOKING TIME 45 MINUTES

For the Fennel
50ml olive oil
3 red onions, cut into wedges
2 baby fennel bulbs, cut into wedges
8 strands of saffron, soaked in hot water for 30 minutes
20ml red wine vinegar
15g honey
6 plum tomatoes, each cut into 6 wedges
15g golden raisins

For the Prawns
1kg king prawns, deveined, tail intact
200g chickpea flour
15g ground cumin
15g ground coriander
5g chilli flakes
7g sea salt

For the Garnish
fresh mint, chopped
fresh coriander, chopped
fresh flat leaf parsley, chopped

To prepare the dish and cook the fennel, heat some oil in a large pan, cook the wedges of onion for 6 minutes, turning once a little charred. Add the fennel and cook for 4 minutes. Once coloured, add the saffron accompanied by the water it was soaked in, the honey, vinegar, plum tomato wedges and raisins. Cover and simmer for 20 minutes.

To cook the prawns, combine the flour, spices and salt. Toss the prawns in the mix, shake off any excess and deep fry for 2 minutes, preferably in 2 batches, until golden. Drain off any excess oil and set to one side ready for serving.

To serve, spoon some of the fennel mix into pasta bowls, top with the prawns and garnish with chopped mint, coriander and parsley.

MATT ROBINSON

Delivering delicious dishes at Dickie Fitz is like a dream come true - with ChariTable Bookings we can help fulfil the dreams of some very courageous children by supporting the Make A Wish Foundation."

LOBSTER SHORT SOUP

SERVES 4 | PREPARATION TIME 40 MINUTES | COOKING TIME 1 HOUR 30 MINUTES

For the Dumpling Mix

1 whole lobster

200g raw prawns, shell on

30g red chillies, diced

30g each kaffir lime leaf, ginger,

chives, finely chopped

5g salt

15 gyoza or wonton wrappers

For the Soup

1.5kg prawn or lobster shells

1 tbsp tomato purée

1 large carrot, diced

1 onion, diced

1 head of fennel, diced

1 head of garlic, diced

5 black peppercorns

1 star anise

50ml wine

3l chicken stock

500ml water

3 kaffir lime leaves

2 sticks of lemon grass

½ red chilli

1 large thumb of ginger

50ml soy sauce

2g salt

5g sugar

a few drops of sesame oil

To Clarify the Stock

150g raw prawn

150g raw chicken

20g carrot, diced

20g shallot, diced

2 sticks of lemon grass

2 lime leaves

1 red chilli, chopped

2 cloves of garlic

1 stalk of coriander

2 spring onions, finely sliced

2 heads of pak choi, quartered

10 egg whites

For the Garnish

2 spring onions, finely sliced

2 heads of pak choi, quartered

To prepare the dumpling mix, cook the lobster in salted boiling water for 6 minutes then set aside to cool. Peel and devein the prawns and the lobster, retaining the shells for the stock. Dice the meat, place into a bowl and mix with the remaining ingredients. Weigh the mix into 25g balls and set in the fridge for an hour.

To make the dumplings, place a ball of the mix into the centre of a wrapper, brushing the edges with water. Fold into a half moon shape, then bring the 2 pointed edges together to form a tortellini shape. Press the edges together with a little extra water to help stick.

To make the soup, in a large roasting tray, place the shells and the tomato purée and roast for 10 minutes in a 180°C oven. Stir the shells half way through. After 10 minutes, add the chopped vegetables, the peppercorns and the star anise, roasting for a further 10 minutes and stirring again half way through.

Once roasted, remove from the oven and place the tray on the stove on a medium heat; add the white wine. Once the wine has almost disappeared, add the remaining liquid and bring to a simmer for 30 minutes. For the last 10 minutes, add the lime leaf, lemon grass, chilli, ginger, soy sauce, salt, sugar and sesame oil. Then, once cool, strain the liquid through a fine sieve into a sauce pan.

To clarify the stock, blend all of the ingredients together in a food processor until smooth. Place the mixture gradually into the cooled soup to create a raft that will sit on top. Place on a medium heat, and stir the mix until the soup almost comes to a light simmer. Once this happens, do not stir again or the raft will break and spoil the soup. Create a hole in the centre or on the side of the raft for the soup to boil over and allow the raft to set.

Simmer the soup for 5–10 minutes until the raft has completely set and become solid. You should see crystal clear liquid below the raft. Carefully strain the liquid, making sure not to break the raft, otherwise the stock will become cloudy.

To serve, bring the soup stock to the boil, add the dumpling and poach for 3 minutes before adding a garnish of pak choi and the finely sliced spring onions.

SIMON ROGAN

If we didn't educate our next generation in good food and nutrition practices, the interest in culinary art would die out and health in general would suffer. That's why I'm supporting Adpot a School, the charity that chefs use to teach kids about food. On behalf of my restaurant L'Enclume, I am proud to share their recipe with ChariTable Bookings to support them."

GRILLED SALAD SMOKED OVER EMBERS with Isle Of Mull cheese, custard and cobnuts

SERVES 4 | PREPARATION TIME 30 MINUTES | COOKING TIME 1 HOUR 45 MINUTES

Equipment
sous vide and vacuum pack bags

For the Salad
2 baby spring cabbages

50g cavolo nero

50g curly kale

25g red Russian kale

1 large head each of cauliflower
broccoli and celeriac

For the Isle Of Mull Cheese Sauce
500g grated Isle Of Mull cheese

450g water

2g xantham gum

salt and pepper

For the Truffle Custard
200ml whole milk

200ml double cream

30g black English truffle, finely
chopped

3 egg yolks

1 whole egg

salt and pepper

For the Cobnut Crisp
50g T55 flour

260g rye flour

5g table salt

70g warm water

5g fresh yeast

25g cobnut oil

300g sourdough starter

150g cobnuts, peeled and chopped

For the Chilli Herb Oil
50g garlic, chopped

1 small chilli, chopped and ½ the seeds

200ml grapeseed oil

2g glice, monoglyceride, to emulsify

40g flat parsley, picked

3g table salt

For the Garnish
mustard frills and black mustard flowers

black English truffle, sliced julienne

For the Isle Of Mull cheese sauce, melt the cheese into the water at 80°C and leave to stand for 30 minutes. Then pass through a fine sieve, add xantham gum to lightly thicken the sauce and season with salt and pepper. When needed, heat and froth with a hand blender.

For the truffle custard, bring the milk and cream to the simmer and add the truffle. Take off the heat and infuse for 15 minutes. Add the yolks and whole egg into a bowl, whisk in the truffle cream and allow to cool. Pass through a fine sieve, check the seasoning and place in a ceramic dish, cover with cling film and steam until just set. Then keep in the fridge until cold and needed.

For the cobnut crisp, mix the fresh yeast with the water and combine with the flour, salt and sourdough starter in a mixer. Mix until a firm dough is achieved, remove, wrap in cling film and leave to rest in the fridge for 2 hours. Roll pieces of the dough through a pasta machine to the lowest setting possible, trying to keep them intact and in long sheets. Then place them onto a lined baking sheet, then rub with a little bit of the cobnut oil and sprinkle with the chopped cobnuts, next place a piece of silicone paper on top and cover and press with another tray. Cook in an oven at 180°C for 8 minutes, remove the sheet and cook for another 4 minutes. Then allow to cool, and break up into medium sized pieces.

For the chilli herb oil, bring up the garlic, chilli and grapeseed oil from cold and cook until golden. Then strain through a fine sieve and add more grapeseed oil to bring it back to 200ml. Add the glice to the oil at 65°C. Blanch the parsley in boiling water, refresh into ice water and squeeze dry. Then liquidise the oil with the parsley and 3g of salt until you have a bright green oil then strain through a fine sieve into a bowl over ice water, whisk until slightly thickened.

For the grilled leaves, peel and slice the celeriac thinly, place in a vacuum pack bag and seal on full pressure. Cook in a water bath at 85°C for 1 hour. Arrange the vegetables into nice small leaves and florets. Cook on a stone over the embers of a Big Green Egg at 200°C, constantly turning the vegetables and introducing cherry wood chips to the embers to create smoke. Season with salt and pepper.

To assemble the dish, place a spoon of truffle custard onto the plate and arrange the grilled vegetables around. Place over pieces of the cobnut crisp, the mustard frills, flowers and a drizzle of the chilli herb oil. Finish with sprinkling over fresh English truffle and spooning over some of the cheese froth.

ANDY ROSE

Boisdale Canary Wharf are proud supporters of Great Ormond Street Children's Hospital, and ChariTable Bookings have provided another way for them to continue their invaluable work."

PRESSED TERRINE OF WILD SALMON with horseradish and wild garlic

SERVES 12 | PREPARATION TIME 30 MINUTES | COOKING TIME 2 HOURS

For the Salmon
1 side of wild salmon
250g wild garlic
celery salt
ground black pepper

For the Terrine Sauce
1 onion, chopped
½ bulb of fennel, roughly chopped
10g butter
100ml white wine
50ml Noilly Prat sauce
1 sprig of thyme
1 pinch of black peppercorns
1.5l strong fish stock
600ml double cream
7 gelatine leaves
200g horseradish, freshly grated

To Serve
micro herbs
crusty bread

To make the sauce, sweat the peeled and chopped onions and the roughly chopped fennel bulb with the butter, without colouring. Pour in the white wine and Noilly Prat, add the thyme and peppercorns and reduce to a syrup. Add the fish stock and reduce by half. Add the double cream and reduce until you are left with 1 litre, after which remove from the heat. Soak the gelatine leaves in cold water, squeeze and add to the sauce. Stir until it is dissolved. Pass the sauce through a fine sieve and leave to cool. Place the terrine mould into the freezer. Once cooled, pour the sauce into the frozen terrine mould, wait 45 seconds and pour out – this will leave a thin layer around the mould. Dip the garlic leaves in the sauce and line the terrine mould over the set outer-layer.

To make the wild salmon, trim its side to the width and length of the terrine mould. Remove the skin and slice lengthways so you are left with 2 pieces. Poach for 4 minutes until pink, remove and leave to stand until cool. Season the salmon fillets, place 1 inside the mould and pour over a ladle of sauce, just covering the fish. Place another layer of wild garlic leaves on the top of the fish, then place the other side of salmon on top sandwiching the 2 pieces of fish together. Pour another ladle of sauce over the top. Place a layer of cling film over the top and press down using another terrine as a weight and put in the fridge. Once cold, remove the terrine and cling film. Dip the remainder of the garlic leaves and place across the top, leave to cool. Finally ladle a final layer of sauce over the top. Leave for 2 hours in the fridge until set.

To serve, slice into 12 slices and serve with a little sea salt sprinkled over the top and some crusty bread.

GERALD ROSER

The team and I from Mirabelle would like to support Springboard in their amazing work getting young people into employment in the hospitality industry. This is a perfect collaboration with ChariTable Bookings, combining food and charity!"

RED MULLET roasted on fennel grass with vine tomato concasse, balsamic and olive oil

SERVES 2 | PREPARATION TIME 30 MINUTES | COOKING TIME 2 HOURS

For the Red Mullet
4 x 100g red mullet fillets
salt and pepper
fennel grass

For the Salt-Baked Potatoes
500g Maldon sea salt
6 new potatoes

For the Tomato Concasse
2 vine tomatoes

For the Wilted baby Spinach
200g baby spinach
1 knob of garlic butter
1 grating of nutmeg, to season

To Serve
olive oil
balsamic vinegar

To make the salt-baked new potatoes, cover the bottom of a small, ovenproof dish with sea salt. Lay the potatoes on top and cover with more salt. It will take about 2 hours to bake at a medium temperature.

For the tomato concasse, use ripe, full-flavoured vine tomatoes. With a small, sharp knife, cut the core from the stalk end of each tomato, then slash the top of the opposite end to pierce the skin. Place the tomatoes in boiling water for 1 minute 30 seconds until the skins start to curl. Run them under cold water and remove the skins. Cut the tomatoes in half, remove the seeds and inner flesh, chop into a fine dice and season to taste.

Score the red mullet fillets diagonally, making 3–4 slashes on each one. Season with salt. Heat the olive oil in a heavy-based frying pan, add half the fennel grass and then place the fillets on top. Sauté for 2 minutes, skin-side down and 30 seconds on the flesh side. Remove from the pan and drain.

Wash the baby spinach well, then heat a little olive oil in a large frying pan. Add the spinach and cook for about 30 seconds, turning frequently. Add some garlic butter and nutmeg.

To serve, divide the wilted baby spinach between each warmed plate. Place some in a mound in the centre and scatter the rest around. Stack the fillets on top of the mound. Arrange the salt-baked potatoes and seasoned tomato concasse around the mullet. Use the fennel grass as garnish. Finish by trickling over the olive oil and balsamic vinegar dressing.

ALBERT ROUX

Adopt A School is a great charity which allows chefs to directly influence the next generation with the importance of quality ingredients and healthy eating. With the participation of so many fine chefs and restaurants, ChariTable Bookings is the platform that could help fast-track this fantastic nationwide activity."

ROAST BRESSE PIGEON with fresh peas
SERVES 6 | PREPARATION TIME 40 MINUTES | COOKING TIME 2 HOURS

For the Pigeon
6 Bresse pigeons
salt and pepper, to season
1 drizzle of olive oil
18 baby onions
1 large carrot
400g shelled fresh peas
120g butter, cubed
275g smoked bacon
225ml chicken stock
1 round lettuce, shredded

For the White Chicken Stock
2kg chicken bones
1 calf's foot, split
5l water
1 onion
1 small leek
2 sticks of celery
2 sprigs of thyme
6 stalks of parsley

To cook the pigeon, heat an oven to 230°C. Season inside the pigeons, then smear the pigeons with olive oil and sprinkle with salt. Place in a hot roasting pan over high heat and brown the birds all over. Turn them onto their backs and roast in the oven for 12 minutes; the meat should be rosy pink. Remove from the oven, turn them breast-side down so the juices permeate the breast meat, cover with kitchen foil and leave to rest in a warm place for 15 minutes before serving.

To make the trimmings, peel and trim the baby onions. Peel and cut the carrot into 3cm long batons. Cook the onions, carrot batons and peas separately in boiling, salted water until just tender. Refresh in ice-cold water and drain well. Cut the bacon into thin batons and blanch for 1 minute in boiling water; drain well.

To make the peas, melt 1 tablespoon of butter in a wide saucepan. When it foams, add the bacon and cook until beginning to brown. Add the onions to cook for a further 3 minutes, rolling them around the pan from time to time. Then add the peas, carrots and chicken stock and simmer for 10 minutes. Season well, then add the butter, a little at a time, shaking the pan so the butter emulsifies and thickens the sauce. Just before serving, fold in the shredded lettuce leaves. Serve with the pigeons.

To make the chicken stock, place the bones and calf's foot in a large saucepan, cover with the water and bring to the boil. Skim off the scum and fat that comes to the surface. Turn the heat down, add the remaining ingredients and simmer for 1.5 hours, skimming occasionally. Pass through a fine sieve and leave to cool. This can be kept in the refrigerator for up to 5 days, or frozen.

RUPERT ROWLEY

Everyday brings new choices and new possibilities. Please support the Bluebell Wood Hospice from all of us at Fischer's at Baslow Hall through this ChariTable Bookings recipe book initiative and raise vital funds for this well deserving charity."

GOOSNARGH DUCK BREAST with fondant potato, garden vegetables and poached cherries
SERVES 2 | PREPARATION TIME 30 MINUTES | COOKING TIME 1 HOUR 30 MINUTES

For the Goosnargh Duck
1 Goosnargh duck crown
1 Goosnargh duck heart

For the Fondant Potatoes
1 white or Désirée potato
1 tsp oil
125g butter

For the Garden Vegetables
2 baby beetroots
4 baby turnips
10 baby chard leaves
2 baby carrots
1 grelot onion
1 handful of peas and broad beans

For the Poached Cherries
10 cherries
100ml red wine
50ml port
1 star anise
½ stick of cinnamon

To prepare the duck, remove the breasts from the crown. Score the fat in a crisscross motion and season. Slowly render the duck, skin-side down, in a dry pan and continually remove any excess fat. After 8–10 minutes the skin will tighten, appearing golden and crispy. Turn the breasts over and leave flesh-side down for 2–3 minutes. Remove the duck from the pan and leave to rest.

Remove the stones from the cherries. Add the red wine, port and spices to a pan and bring to the boil. Once boiled, remove from the heat, add the cherries, and leave to soak.

Remove the ends from the potato, cut into two, and stamp with a ring to form 2 round cylinders. Place a splash of oil and the butter in a pan and heat until the butter foams. Place the potatoes in the pan and reduce the heat to keep the butter foaming and avoid burning. Cook until tender and evenly coloured.

Place all the vegetables in a pan of salted, boiling water and cook as required, cooking the beetroots last. Remove the skins and warm back through in a little butter and water. Use a separate pan for the beetroots when re-heating.

To serve, gently warm the duck breast in a pan. Turn up the heat and sear the duck heart quickly, for approximately 30 seconds to a minute. Arrange the vegetables on the plate. Slice the duck breast and place on top. Finally, scatter the cherries around the dish and finish with a little jus.

PASQUALE RUSSO

Action For Hunger is a great organisation and it's a pleasure to know that ChariTable Bookings are spreading their message with this dish from Cotswold House."

HERB CRUSTED HAKE FILLET with pickled girolles, seaweed and coco beans

SERVES 4 | PREPARATION TIME 15 MINUTES (PLUS OVERNIGHT TO SOAK) | COOKING TIME 45 MINUTES

For the Hake
1 fillet of fresh hake
200g dry coco beans, soaked overnight in water
100ml olive oil
200g panko breadcrumbs
1 sheet of nori seaweed, optional
salt and pepper
lemon juice
fresh herbs, chopped (parsley, chervil, tarragon, chives, thyme, and marjoram)
8 tenderstem broccoli

For the Pickle
100ml cider vinegar
25ml white wine vinegar
100g sugar
1 star anise
1 stick of cinnamon
3 cloves
1 tsp yellow mustard seeds
200g baby girolle mushrooms, cleaned

Prepare the pickle by mixing all the ingredients and bringing to the boil for 2 minutes. Pass the liquid through a sieve and pour onto the mushrooms. Add a pinch of salt. Leave to cool.

Cook the beans in water until soft. Purée them in a food processor, reserving some for garnish. Portion the fish, slicing the fillet in 4 parts. In a hot pan, pour 2 tablespoons of olive oil and toss the breadcrumbs until golden brown. Away from the heat, add the herbs and some sea salt. Fry the fish skin-side down on a medium heat, turn it over, remove the skin and cover with breadcrumbs. Leave it to rest. Add some seaweed to the bean purée and blitz with a stick blender. Season to taste with salt, pepper, and lemon juice. Boil the broccoli in salted water. Place the bean purée in the centre of the plate; finish the fish in the oven for 1 minute at 180°C. Put the broccoli on the side of the purée, place the fish on top.

Garnish with beans, girolles, some flowers and herbs of your choice.

ARMAND SABLON

I love that a cookbook is shouting about multiple charities and not just one, or none! For me, however, I am supporting Leuka in this ChariTable Bookings project to hopefully help them to find a cure for this terrible disease. Enjoy my chicken dish!"

CHICKEN AND BOUDIN BLANC

SERVES 6–8 | PREPARATION TIME 2 HOURS | COOKING TIME 4 HOURS

Equipment
sausage machine
red hot poker

For the Chicken
1.6kg chicken
salt and pepper, to taste
50g butter
duck fat, for confit
1 sage leaf
1 sprig of thyme
2 cloves of garlic
25g foie gras, optional

For the Chicken Roasting Jus
1 carrot, roughly diced
1 celery, roughly diced
2 banana shallots, roughly diced
1 small glass white wine
500ml veal stock
500ml chicken stock
1 sprig of thyme
1 clove of garlic
1 small knob of butter

For the Boudin Blanc
200g chicken purée
100g pork fat purée
ice
2 whole eggs
150ml double cream
2 shallots, chopped
25g dried brioche crumbs

To prepare and cook the chicken, ask the butcher to take off the legs and cut the legs in half. Remove the bone from the thigh and keep the drum stick for the sauce. With the crown, French trim the wing, roast the winglet in the oven at 180°C for 10 minutes or until golden brown, leave to cool. When cooled, trim the top and bottom and push the two bones out. Season the thigh and then roll and tie with string, then confit in duck fat for 2 hours at 120°C. Take out and leave to cool. When cooled, colour in a pan until golden brown and place in the oven for 5 minutes to heat up. Take the crown and slide butter in between the skin and the breast meat, then place one sage leaf on top of the butter. Season the chicken breast, then seal in a hot pan with thyme and garlic. Once sealed golden brown all over, place in the oven at cook at 180°C for 20 minutes, turning half way through cooking. Then take out and leave to rest for 10 minutes before carving. Once carved, place a little seared foie gras on top as an added luxury.

To make the chicken roasting jus, using the pan from the chicken, drain off the excess fat. Brown the vegetables over a medium heat, then deglaze with white wine to release all of the sediment. Add the stocks, thyme and garlic, and bring to the boil. Reduce by half, pass through a fine sieve and add a small knob of butter.

For the boudin blanc, make sure all of the ingredients are cold. Mix the purée of chicken and pork fat together, and place over ice. Slowly incorporate the beaten eggs and cream, add the finely chopped shallots and brioche crumbs. Soak the crustless bread in the milk and liquidise, mix with the other ingredients. Blend the potato starch with the port and mix in, last of all, the salt. Using a sausage machine, make the boudin 12cm long. Poach in a seasoned mixture of water and milk for about 40 minutes at 70°C. Take off the heat and leave to cool in the liquid, when ready to serve, cut in half and score the top with a red hot poker, then warm in the oven for 3–4 minutes.

To serve, plate as pictured, alternating between boudin blanc and any good quality black pudding, lightly pan-fried and cooked in an 180°C oven for 3 minutes.

For the Boudin Blanc *continued*

  2 slices white bread, crusts removed
  150ml milk, for soaking the bread
  4g potato starch
  2 tbsp port
  5g salt
  2l water
  500ml milk

For the Garnish

  seasonal vegetables
  black pudding

LAURA SANTINI

Young Minds is a vital charity supporting the mental health of children and young people throughout the UK. Myself and the team at Santini are donating our signature dish to ChariTable Bookings in support of them and hope they raise more funds for their incredible work."

TRUFFLED MAC 'N' CHEESE

SERVES 2–4 | PREPARATION TIME 20 MINUTES | COOKING TIME 40 MINUTES

For the Mac n Cheese

950ml double cream
¼ tsp nutmeg, freshly grated
¼ tsp cayenne pepper
1 bay leaf
2 tbsp butter
4 shallots, finely chopped
3 cloves of garlic, crushed
1 salted anchovy fillet
500ml dry white wine
130g cheddar cheese, grated
130g gruyere cheese, grated
45g Parmesan cheese, grated
2 tbsp black truffle oil
sea salt
freshly ground black pepper
500g macaroni pasta

For the Garnish

75g panko breadcrumbs, toasted
1 tbsp flat-leaf parsley, finely chopped
25g Parmesan cheese

To make the sauce, heat the cream in a large, heavy-based saucepan until almost boiling, then turn down the heat. Add the nutmeg, cayenne pepper and the bay leaf and allow to simmer slowly until reduced by half and set aside. In a medium saucepan, heat the butter until melted, then sauté the shallots, garlic and anchovy until the shallots are soft and translucent but not browned. Pour in the wine and simmer until the majority has evaporated. Pour the cream mixture into the shallots. Add the cheeses, truffle oil and season to taste and set aside.

Meanwhile, fill a large saucepan with salted, boiling water and bring to the boil. Add the pasta and cook until al dente. Transfer the macaroni to a colander and drain, reserving a small amount of the pasta cooking water. Return the pasta to its cooking pot and add just enough sauce to coat the pasta, along with 3–4 tablespoons of the pasta cooking water. Return to the heat for a minute, and give everything a good mix to make it extra creamy. Pour into a suitable serving dish.

To serve, mix the breadcrumbs, parsley and the Parmesan cheese together and sprinkle over the dish. Serve immediately.

STEFANO SAVIO

We at Quirinale are sending one of our classics, baked red mullet, in order to support the great work of Action for Children through this innovative new venture by ChariTable Bookings. We hope it raises them lots of extra funds!"

BAKED RED MULLET with Taggiasche olives and tomato

SERVES 2 | PREPARATION TIME 15 MINUTES | COOKING TIME 35 MINUTES

For the Mullet
2 x 400g red mullets, filleted and head removed
6 chive stems, blanched

For the Tapenade
100g Taggiasche olives, pitted
15g capers, Pantellerian if possible
10g anchovies
½ clove of garlic
50g breadcrumbs

For the Tomato Sauce
50g shallots
½ clove of garlic
200g cherry tomatoes
1 tbsp extra virgin olive oil
salt and pepper
1 small bunch fresh basil

To Serve
micro organic sprouts
basil leaves

To make the tapenade, blend together the olives, capers, anchovies and half of the garlic clove in a food processor. Squeeze the paste through a muslin cloth and get rid of the excess liquid. Add the breadcrumbs to the paste and mix together.

Next make the tomato sauce. Sauté the shallots, the other half of the garlic and cherry tomatoes in a pan with some extra virgin olive oil, salt and pepper for about 20 minutes. Add the basil, then blend and pass through a sieve to obtain a smooth sauce.

Spread the tapenade between the two red mullet fillets. Tie the fillets together with the blanched chive, cut the fish in half and bake for about 7–8 minutes at 200°C.

To serve, spread the tomato sauce on a plate, lay the cooked mullet over it, and top with some basil leaves and micro organic sprouts.

ANDREW SCOTT

Helen & Douglas House is a fantastic charity looking after young people with life shortening conditions. They need all the help they can get which is why I am sharing 56's Cornish crab recipe in this ChariTable Bookings encyclopedia of recipes!"

CORONATION CORNISH CRAB, crab biscuit and panna cotta, apricot and almond

SERVES 4 PREPARATION TIME 45 MINUTES | COOKING TIME 1 HOUR 30 MINUTES

Equipment
Thermomix or standard liquidizer
fine mesh sieve

For the Crab Biscuit
200g strong white flour
80g oats, blitzed
1 tsp each of celery salt and sugar
1 pinch of cayenne
1 lime, zested
100g butter, soft, diced
100g brown crab

For the Almond and Curry Emulsion
300g whole almonds
20g butter
¼ tsp curry powder
2 pinches of celery salt
2 pinches of garam masala
75ml sherry vinegar
250ml water
salt, pepper and lime juice, to taste

For the Dressed White Crab
1 whole cock crab
1 pinch of salt
1 stick of celery, finely chopped
20 dried apricots, chopped
100g golden raisins, chopped
100g whole almonds, finely chopped
almond emulsion
1 pinch of ground coriander
1 spritz of lime juice

To make the crab biscuit, place all the dry ingredients into a mixing bowl with the soft diced butter. Using the paddle attachment on the food processor, combine. Finish by adding the crab and allow the mixture to rest for 20 minutes. Roll the mixture out and cut into rings, bake at 160°C for 8–10 minutes until hardened.

For the almond and curry emulsion, roast the almonds until golden. Melt the butter in a pan, add the spices and cook for 2 minutes. Deglaze with water and sherry vinegar. Blitz the almonds with the spiced liquid in a Thermomix until smooth. Season with salt, pepper and lime juice to taste.

To cook the dressed white crab, cover the crab in cold water. Add salt and bring to the boil, refreshing in ice after 10–15 minutes. Break down and pick out the white meat, reserving the brown meat for the panna cotta. Dress the crab with the chopped fruit and almond emulsion. Season with lime and coriander.

For the crab panna cotta, boil the milk and cream, mix in the agar and boil again. Pour over the brown crab in a Thermomix, season with salt, pepper and a little lemon juice and blitz until smooth. Pass the mixture through a fine mesh sieve onto a greased tray and refrigerate.

To make the apricot gel, boil the purée and syrup together. Leave to cool, then taste. Cook for longer if the flavour needs to develop further. When satisfied with the results, measure the liquid and add 1g of agar agar to 100ml of liquid. Boil again, cool and leave to set in the fridge. Blitz once chilled and transfer into a sauce bottle for serving.

For the soaked apricots and raisins, boil the ginger wine and apple juice together and bring the fruit up to the boil in separate pans. Cool, cover in cling film and refrigerate.

To assemble and serve, plate as pictured and garnish with coriander cress, celery cress, whole almonds and the soaked apricots and raisins.

For the Crab Panna Cotta
    200ml milk
    800ml double cream
    8g agar agar
    400g brown crab
    1 lemon, juiced

For the Apricot Gel
    500g apricot boiron
    200ml stock syrup
    10g agar agar

For the Soaked Apricots and Raisins
    300ml apple juice
    200ml Stone's ginger wine
    100g dried apricots
    100g golden raisins

For the Garnish
    whole almonds
    coriander cress
    celery cress

RYAN SHILTON

Animals native to the British Isles form as much a part of our heritage as anything else and are essential to the recipes in this ChariTable Bookings collection. The Rare Breeds Survival trust helps protect our natural heritage and fully has the support of the Four Seasons Restaurant and our team!"

WILD SEA BASS with bacon emulsion, butternut squash, curried granola and sprouts

SERVES 8 | PREPARATION TIME 3 HOURS | COOKING TIME 3 HOURS

For the Dish
8 x 140g sea bass fillets
10 rashers of smoked back bacon
20 brussels sprouts
vegetable oil, to drizzle

For the Bacon Emulsion
10 rashers smoked bacon
300ml olive or vegetable oil
5 egg yolks

For the Butternut Squash Purée
2½ butternut squash, deseeded
200g butter, plus a little extra for roasting
curry powder and salt, to season

For the Curry Granola
6 tbsp sunflower seeds
6 tbsp pumpkin seeds
1 tsp curry powder
1 tsp garam masala
1 egg white

To make the bacon emulsion, roast the bacon at 180°C for 10 minutes, or until very crispy. Place in olive oil to infuse for 2 hours. Once infused, blitz together, pass through a fine sieve and place in the fridge. Whisk 5 egg yolks in a blender, then slowly add the bacon oil until emulsified.

To make the butternut squash, take a butternut squash half, drizzle with oil, season and roast at 180°C for 45 minutes. Scoop the flesh out with a spoon and set to one side.

To make the butternut squash purée, peel and dice the remaining 2 butternut squash, cook in a pan with the butter until soft. Blitz with a touch of salt and curry powder.

To prepare the bacon pieces, grill the smoked back bacon for 15 minutes, dry on a cloth, then pulse to form a crumb.

To make the curry granola, mix all of the ingredients together and place on a flat tray. Roast at 160°C for 7 minutes.

To prepare the brussels sprouts, peel the sprouts and blanch in boiling water for 4 minutes. Refresh in ice water, then roast in foaming butter until golden brown.

To cook the sea bass, pan roast skin-side down in a non-stick pan over a medium heat for approximately 4 minutes. Turn over and allow to rest in the brown butter for a minute.

Assemble the dish as pictured and serve.

DAN SHOTTON

Yorebridge House is pleased to introduce ChariTable Bookings to the vital work that North Yorkshire Fire and Rescue do."

BELLY PORK with pan-fried squid and carrots

SERVES 4 | PREPARATION TIME 20 MINUTES | COOKING TIME 2 HOURS 5 MINUTES

For the Belly Pork and Squid
500g trim belly pork, skin on
4 squid portions
2 carrots, chopped
1 onion, sliced
1 star anise
1 sprig each of thyme and lemon grass
1 clove of garlic
1 knob of butter
1 drizzle of honey

For the Pickled Carrots
2 bunches of baby carrots
50ml water
50ml white wine vinegar
50g caster sugar
1 star anise
1 sprig of coriander
1 pinch of chilli flakes

For the Carrot Purée
400g carrots
25g butter
salt

For the Sauce
100ml chicken stock, good quality
200ml veal stock
25ml squeezy honey
10ml sherry vinegar

For the Garnish
micro coriander
spring onions, optional

To prepare the pork, place the chopped carrots and sliced onions with the pork, star anise, lemon grass, thyme and garlic in an oven tray and cover with water. Cover the tray with tin foil and cook in the oven at 170°C for 2 hours. When cooked, remove the pork from the tray and place in the fridge to cool. Once cool, cut into portions. To reheat, cook in the oven for 5 minutes at 180°C on a medium heat or until the skin is crispy. Finish with butter and honey.

Slice the raw squid into 2cm thick rings, sear in a hot pan with a small amount of olive oil for 90 seconds or until golden brown.

To prepare the pickled carrots, bring the water, white wine vinegar, caster sugar, star anise, coriander and chilli flakes to the boil. Add 2 bunches of cleaned baby carrots. Boil for 1 minute, remove from the heat and leave to cool in the pickling liquor.

To make the carrot purée, boil 400g carrots until soft, remove from the water and blend with the butter until smooth. Add salt to taste.

To make the sauce, bring the chicken and veal stock to the boil together with the squeezy honey and sherry vinegar.

To serve, garnish with coriander and spring onions.

JOGINDER SINGH DHAM

Thank you ChariTable Bookings for letting me shout about Great Ormond Street Hospital while sharing The Butlers Wharf Chop House signature lamb shanks in this fantastic collection of recipes."

BRAISED LAMB SHANK

SERVES 4 | PREPARATION TIME 10 MINUTES | COOKING TIME 2 HOURS 30 MINUTES

For the Lamb
4 lamb shanks
salt and pepper
2 tbsp vegetable oil
1 onion, roughly chopped
1 carrot, roughly chopped
1 stick of celery, roughly chopped
1 sprig of rosemary, picked
2 cloves of garlic, crushed
250ml red wine
750ml chicken or lamb stock

For the Bashed Neeps
150g swedes, peeled and roughly chopped
150g turnips, peeled and roughly chopped
50g carrots, peeled and roughly chopped
80g butter
Salt and freshly ground black pepper

Heat a large, heavy-bottomed saucepan over high heat, season the lamb shanks and fry in the oil until evenly browned all over. Remove from the pan and set aside.

Add the vegetables, rosemary and garlic to the pan and caramelise to a golden brown. Put the shanks back into the pan and deglaze with the red wine. Pour in the stock and bring to the boil.

Skim any impurities that rise to the surface and reduce the heat. Simmer for 2 hours, until the meat comes away from the bone easily. Allow to cool a little in the liquid before removing the shanks. Set aside and keep warm.

Strain the braising liquid, reduce to a sauce consistency and reserve.

To make the bashed neeps, cover the vegetables with water, then season with salt and pepper. Bring to the boil and simmer gently for 10–15 minutes until they are soft enough to mash. Drain in a colander, then coarsely mash with a potato masher. Adjust the seasoning if necessary and stir in the butter.

Divide the bashed neeps between 4 warm serving bowls, placing slightly to one side within each dish. On the other side, nestle a shank against the neeps. Pour the sauce into a jug and serve on the side.

HARJEET SINGH

Giving back is part of the culture of the team at Bombay Palace and supporting Great Ormond Street Children's Hospital with our friends at ChariTable Bookings is another way we can help others."

NALLI GOSHT

SERVES 4 | PREPARATION TIME 15 MINUTES (PLUS OVERNIGHT TO MARINATE) | COOKING TIME 1 HOUR 30 MINUTES

For the Dish

4 lamb shanks

6 cloves of garlic

2.5cm ginger

2 tsp kashmiri chilli powder, or mild paprika

1 tsp coriander powder

For the Curry

3 tbsp vegetable oil

1 tbsp butter

2.5cm stick of cinnamon, broken in half

6 green cardamom pods

5 cloves

12 black peppercorns

2 medium white onions, thinly sliced

2 green chillies, slit lengthways

½ tsp kashmiri chilli powder, or mild paprika

1 tsp turmeric powder

2 tsp coriander powder

1 heaped tbsp tomato purée

4 tbsp Greek yoghurt

400ml water

salt, to taste

½ tsp nutmeg

fresh coriander, chopped for garnish

1 tbsp lemon juice

To prepare the lamb shanks, place them in a bowl. Blend the garlic and ginger with a little water to a fine purée to form a paste. Mix the chilli powder and coriander powder with the paste. Marinate the lamb shank in the spice paste for a few hours or even overnight.

To prepare the curry, in a heavy-bottomed, large saucepan, heat the oil along with the butter. Add the cinnamon stick, green cardamom, cloves and peppercorns. Sizzle for a few seconds as they infuse the oil. Now add the onions and cook on a medium flame for 10–12 minutes stirring often. Add the slit chillies and stir. The onions will start to soften and go light brown; at this stage add the chilli, turmeric and coriander powder. Stir well to cook the spices. If it gets too dry, add a splash of water. Add the tomato purée and fry for a minute making sure the spice mix does not stick to the bottom of the pan.

To finish, seal the marinated lamb shanks by just tossing in a hot pan with some oil, cooking for 7–10 minutes, then add to the cooking tomato purée. Add the Greek yoghurt along with the water and stir well to make a creamy gravy. Season to taste. Bring the curry to a boil and simmer for an hour stirring halfway through the cooking process. Make sure to turn the lamb shanks over to coat them in the curry. Now add the nutmeg powder. Stir well and simmer with the lid slightly open for 20–25 minutes. The lamb at this stage will be tender and the curry will thicken. Garnish with coriander and some lemon juice. Serve with roti or naan and your choice of salad.

VIVEK SINGH

Action Against Hunger fights against malnutrition globally. The Cinnamon Club are proud to be able to support this worthy charity via ChariTable Bookings' recipe book by providing the recipe to our signature Rajasthani roast rump of lamb."

RAJASTHANI ROAST RUMP OF LAMB with corn sauce

SERVES 4 | PREPARATION TIME 45 MINUTES | COOKING TIME 1 HOUR 30 MINUTES

For the Lamb
4 x 175–200g lamb chump chops or
saddle steaks, fat trimmed
1 tbsp vegetable or corn oil

For the Marinade
½ tsp red chilli powder
½ tsp salt
1 tbsp vegetable or corn oil

For the Corn Sauce
100g ghee or clarified butter
8 cloves
2 black cardamom pods
1 bay leaf
2 onions, finely chopped
3 green chillies, chopped
½ tsp tumeric
1 tsp salt
1 tbsp garlic paste
110g lamb, finely diced
200g sweetcorn
4 tbsp plain yoghurt
150ml lamb stock
6cm fresh ginger, finely chopped
50g fresh coriander, chopped
1 lemon, juiced

To prepare the lamb, mix together all the ingredients for the marinade and rub over the lamb chops or steaks. Set aside to marinate for 20–30 minutes.

For the corn sauce, heat the ghee or clarified butter in a heavy-based pan and add the cloves, cardamom and bay leaf. As soon as they start to crackle, add the onions and cook on a medium heat until golden. Add the chillies and cook for 1–2 minutes. Next add the turmeric and salt, sauté briskly for a minute, taking care that the dry spices do not start to burn. Add the garlic paste and cook, stirring for a couple of minutes. As soon as the fat starts to separate out at the sides of the mixture, stir in the finely diced lamb. Cook for 4–5 minutes, until browned. Add three-quarters of the corn and all the yoghurt. Cook gently for about 30 minutes, stirring occasionally, until the corn is nearly mashed and the sauce thickens. Add the lamb stock, bring back to the boil, then add the ginger, coriander and the remaining corn. Reduce the heat to medium and simmer for 10 minutes. Check the seasoning and add the lemon juice.

Heat the oil in a large ovenproof frying pan over a medium heat, add the marinated lamb chops or steaks and sear for 4 minutes on each side. Transfer to an oven preheated to 180°C and roast for 6–7 minutes. Leave the meat to rest for 3–4 minutes, then cut into slices.

To serve, divide the sauce between 4 serving plates, place the lamb on top and serve with star anise pilau rice.

LEE SKEET

" I have contributed my recipe on behalf of the St Ives RNLI who are our preferred charity to support with sales of this ChariTable Bookings book. I hope you enjoy the turbot!"

BARBECUED TURBOT with cauliflower, shiitake and beef roasting juices

SERVES 4 | PREPARATION TIME 30 MINUTES (PLUS 48 HOURS TO PREPARE STOCK) | COOKING TIME 25 MINUTES

Equipment
  mandoline
For the Turbot
  1 whole turbot, around 2kg
  3l cold water
  150g sea salt
  olive oil
For the Cauliflower and Shiitake
  2 cauliflower heads
  1l milk
  250g salted butter
  300g shiitake mushrooms
For the Sauce
  3kg beef bones
  1kg beef mince
  10l water

For the sauce, place the beef bones on a roasting tray and cook at 200°C, turning regularly until evenly and deeply roasted. Place in a large saucepan, ensuring you scrape everything from the roasting tray into the pan, including the fat. Cover with water and leave on the stove, just below boiling point, overnight. Skim the floating beef fat from the pan every now and then and keep to one side. The following day, repeat the roasting process, this time with the mince, and add to the stock. Leave again overnight. On the third day, carefully drain the stock through a colander, and then again through a fine sieve into another pan. Bring to the boil, and allow the stock to reduce down until it thickens to slowly pour from a spoon, but is not too sticky. Strain through a fine sieve, and reserve.

To prepare the fish, fillet the turbot and reserve the bones for a stock. Make a brine by mixing the water and salt until dissolved. Lay the 4 fillets flat in a shallow tray and cover with the brine. After 30 minutes remove the fillets, pat dry and place in the fridge. When ready to cook, cut the turbot into about 2cm thick slices and place skin-side down on a tray drizzled with plenty of olive oil. Ensure the barbecue is extremely hot – alternatively you could use a griddle plate on the stove, on full heat. Place the turbot pieces skin-side down on the barbecue and cook at full heat until the fish flesh is cooked about half the way up. Take the fish off the barbecue and place skin-side up on a metal tray to rest for 2 minutes.

To prepare the cauliflower, finely chop 1 of the cauliflowers and place in a saucepan with the milk and butter. Bring to a simmer and cook until the cauliflower is very tender. Pass through a sieve, keeping the milk, and blend the cauliflower in a food processor until silky. Add as much of the milk as you need to achieve the correct consistency. With the second cauliflower, carefully separate into florets and slice thinly on a mandoline or with a sharp knife to create thin strips. Do the same with the shiitake mushrooms.

To serve, gently warm the cauliflower purée and beef sauces, adding a couple of spoonfuls of the reserved beef fat into the sauce, but not stirring too much. Place the cauliflower purée on the plate, creating a thick base. Place 3–4 pieces of the turbot on the purée and scatter the cauliflower and mushroom slices on top. Spoon over the beef sauce, trying to include some fat on each spoonful.

GEOFFREY SMEDDLE

"The team at The Peat Inn is proud to back Macmillan in this fantastic recipe book by ChariTable Bookings. Our pappardelle with shaved asparagus is one of our most popular dishes which I hope you enjoy as much as our diners."

PAPPARDELLE with shaved asparagus, broad beans, marjoram and pea purée

SERVES 4 | PREPARATION TIME 15 MINUTES | COOKING TIME 40 MINUTES

For the Pappardelle

500g fresh peas in the pod
salt
1 pinch of sugar
150ml double cream
500g fresh broad beans, still in the large outer pod
2 bunches of asparagus
320g pappardelle
10g fresh marjoram
black pepper, freshly ground
olive oil

Boil the peas for 1 minute, then drain, reserving 1 cup of the cooking water, and place into ice water. Place the peas in a blender with some of the cooking water, add a pinch of salt and sugar then process to a purée. Add just enough double cream to help it process, then set aside.

Shell the broad beans from the outer pod then cook in boiling, salted water for 1 minute before draining and refreshing in ice-cold water. Once cold, drain and pop off the outer pod from each bean then set aside. Set aside 6 spears of asparagus per person. Cut off the tips and keep them to use as a garnish. Add the remainder of those spears to the others, which will be used to make ribbons. Trim the woody base from the asparagus – this will be about 2.5cm or so at the base of each spear, which can be reserved for soup. Using a swivel-head peeler and working from the head of the spear to the base, shave ribbons of asparagus and place them in a bowl.

Bring a large pan of water and a second smaller one to the boil and salt both well. Gently reheat the pea purée in a small pan, taste for seasoning and set aside in a warm place. Place the pasta in the large pan of boiling water and cook until al dente. Boil the reserved asparagus tips in the smaller pan for 4 minutes. Drain the pasta when done, reserving a few tablespoons of the cooking water. Return the pasta to the pan, along with the cooking liquid, broad beans, a dash of olive oil, half the asparagus ribbons and half the fresh marjoram. Season with salt and add half the asparagus spear tips.

To serve, divide the pea purée between 4 plates, making a round bed in the centre of each. Pile the pasta in the centre of each then finish with the rest of the shaved asparagus and the asparagus tips. Add one last dash of salt and pepper and scatter the rest of the marjoram over the top.

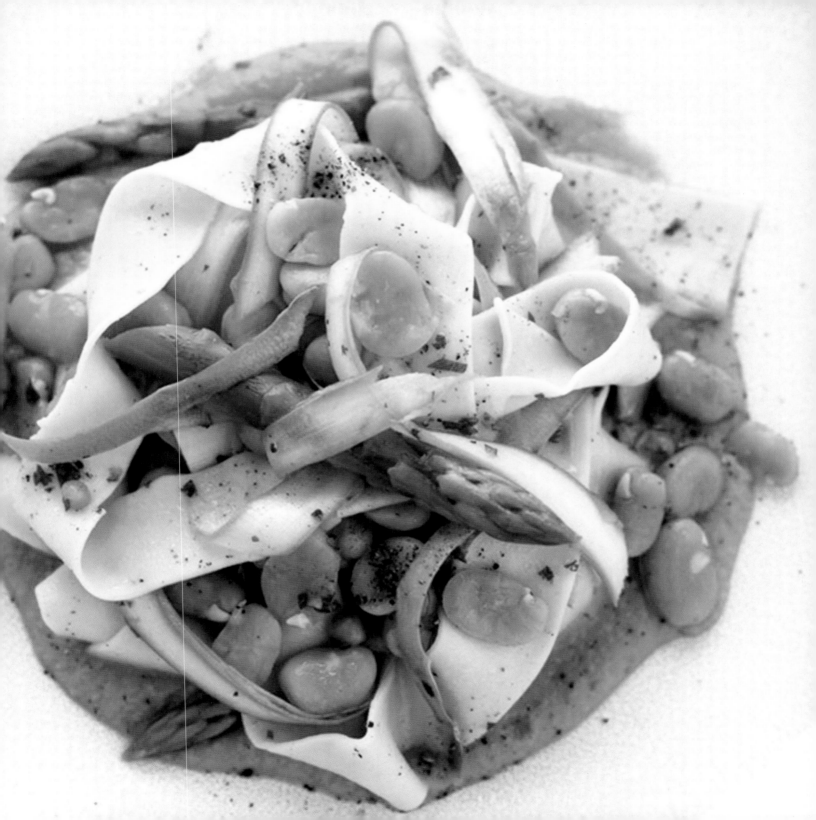

ADAM SMITH

Small, local charities are often overlooked in favour of the larger, well-known organisations and so I'm pleased to be able to help raise awareness for the Ascot District Day Centre by sharing Coworth Park's salt-baked cod with ChariTable Bookings."

SALT-BAKED CARROT with goat's curd, hazelnuts and truffle

SERVES 6 | PREPARATION TIME 45 MINUTES | COOKING TIME 1 HOUR

For the Salt-Baked Carrots
12 medium carrots, reserve the tops
50g of each thyme and rosemary
500g salt
1.5kg strong flour
10 egg whites
400ml water

For the Truffle Mayonnaise
100g egg yolk
1 tsp Dijon mustard
1 tsp sea salt
½ tsp sugar
1 tsp Cabernet Sauvignon vinegar
1 tsp aged balsamic vinegar
25g chopped truffle
325ml grapeseed oil
2 tsp Madeira
1 tsp truffle oil

For the Carrot Glaze
1 star anise
1 tsp each cumin and coriander seeds
8 cardamom pods
300ml carrot juice
20g ginger
100g butter

For the Pickled Carrots
1 large purple carrot
20ml white wine vinegar
½ tsp grapeseed oil
½ tsp sea salt
19g sugar

For the salt-baked carrots, blitz the herbs with the salt in the food processor then add the flour to the herb salt and mix together. Add the egg whites and bring together in the bowl. Slowly add the water and beat the mix well in the bowl for 8–10 minutes until smooth and dry to the touch. Roll the pastry to the thickness of a £1 coin, then wrap the pastry around the carrots individually. Cook the carrots for 12 minutes at 200°C and then allow to rest for a further 10 minutes before removing from the pastry.

To prepare the truffle mayonnaise, place the egg yolks, Dijon mustard, sea salt, sugar, vinegars and chopped truffle in a food processer and start to blend. Slowly add the grapeseed oil until thick and glossy. Finish with the madeira and truffle oil.

To glaze the carrots, toast all of the spices in a dry pan and crush. Add the spices back to the pan with the carrot juice and ginger. Reduce the liquid by half, remove from the heat and whisk in the cold butter to create a beurre monté.

For the pickled carrot, peel the purple carrot and slice into 2mm thick slices. Cut out identical rounds with a small round cutter to make 18 discs. Mix the vinegar, oil, salt and sugar. Put the carrot discs and pickle mix into a container with a tight fitting lid. Shake the container well and then reserve for 1.5 hours before using.

To prepare the quail eggs, boil the quail egg for 2.5 minutes and refresh in ice water. Peel the egg. Coat the eggs, by rolling them first through the flour then in the whisked eggs and then into the breadcrumbs.

To serve, reheat the carrots in the glaze and reduce until the carrots are thickly coated. Spread the truffle mayonnaise onto the plate, and alongside it spread the goats curd in equal quantity onto the plate. Place the carrot on top. Deep fry the quail egg at 180°C until golden and crispy, cut in half and add to the plate. Place 6–8 halves of the roasted hazelnuts alongside the carrot. Wash the carrot tops, and garnish the dish with the carrot tops and the sliced truffle.

For the Quail Eggs
  6 quail eggs
  100g flour
  1 egg, whisked
  100g breadcrumbs
For the Garnish
  180g goat's curd
  8–10 hazelnuts, roasted
  carrot tops
  sliced truffle

DANIEL SMITH

Leuka not only works with patients suffering from blood cancer but also funds vital research at the highest level to try to beat this disease. Please support them with me and enjoy The Ingham Swan's recipe with ChariTable Bookings!"

DESTRUCTED CROMER CRAB SALAD with blowtorched mackerel

SERVES 2 | PREPARATION TIME 20 MINUTES | COOKING TIME 45 MINUTES

Equipment
Thermomix
blowtorch

For the Salmon Salsa
50g Keta caviar
100g whole piece cold smoked salmon, skin and membrane removed
1 red pepper, roasted, deskinned, deseeded and finely diced
¼ cucumber, peeled and finely diced
½ lemon, juice only

For the Avocado Purée
1 avocado, skin and seed removed
1 lime
1 green chilli, small, deseeded
25ml olive oil
25ml milk

For the Lemon Purée
1 lemon
stock syrup

For the Crab Salad
1 large dressed Cromer crab or 2 small dressed Cromer crabs
1 lemon, zest and juice
1 pinch of chives, finely chopped
1 tbsp mayonnaise
50g baked mash potato
100g panko breadcrumbs
50g flour
egg wash

For the salmon salsa, combine the caviar, salmon, roasted pepper and cucumber. Pour in the lemon juice and season to taste.

Combine the avocado, lime, green chilli, olive oil and milk in a Thermomix and blend for 40 seconds on full power. Pass through a fine chinois.

To make the lemon purée, blanch the lemon whole and cool under running water. Repeat this process 4 times. Blitz in a Thermomix, then add the stock syrup. Continue to blend until a gel-like consistency is achieved. Pass the mixture through fine chinois.

For the crab salad, zest the lemon and set the shavings aside. Remove the white crab meat and mix with the chives and juice of the lemon. Season to taste, combine with the mayonnaise and reserve. Remove the brown meat and mix with the mashed potato, lemon zest and seasoning. Form into walnut sized crab cakes, roll in the flour, then dip in the egg wash and finally the breadcrumbs. Deep fry them until golden.

Season both sides of each fillet and add lemon juice. Rest for 10 minutes. Remove any excess seasoning and lay the fillets on a tray, skin-side up. Char the skins with a blowtorch until crisp.

Dress the plate with a swipe and quenelle of avocado purée. Make a line of the salmon salsa and pipe small dots of lemon purée around the plate. Quenelle the white crab meat and position with the crab cake and blowtorched mackerel.

For the Blowtorched Mackerel
2 mackerel fillets
½ lemon, juice only

STEVE SMITH

The team at Bohemia and I are thrilled to support the work of Macmillan Jersey. Give back in style by buying this ChariTable Bookings recipe book and raise vital funds for this great charity. Enjoy the dish too!"

POACHED JERSEY OYSTERS with oyster velouté

SERVES 8 | PREPARATION TIME 1 HOUR | COOKING TIME 2 HOURS

Equipment
vacuum pack bags

For the Oyster Velouté
60g shallots, finely diced
100ml Noilly Prat
100ml oyster juices
120g fresh oysters
200ml double cream
200ml crème fraîche
40ml Chardonnay vinegar
lemon juice and salt, to taste

For the Oyster Emulsion
20g seaweed butter
60g shallots, finely sliced
100ml Noilly Prat
100ml oyster juice
120g fresh oysters
40ml Champagne vinegar
200ml double cream
200ml crème fraîche
1 pinch of salt
lemon juice

For the Oyster Poaching Liquid
100ml Champagne
100ml oyster juice
25g seaweed butter

For the Oyster Tapioca
50g cooked tapioca
50ml oyster velouté
2 tbsp cucumber, finely chopped
1 tbsp fennel, finely chopped
10ml yuzu juice
salt

For the Cucumber Pickle
¼ cucumber, finely diced
2 shallots, finely chopped
1 tbsp dill or fennel, chopped
3 tbsp white balsamic vinegar

Begin by preparing the oysters. Shuck, taking care to empty the juices into a bowl. Expect about 200ml of juice from 10 large oysters. You will need about 350ml in all for the recipe, so approximately 17–20 oysters in total. Pass the juice through a fine sieve and reserve. Rinse the oysters in their juice to remove any grit or traces of shell. Take them out and reserve. Sieve the juice again and reserve for the velouté, emulsion and poaching liquid.

To make the oyster velouté, put the shallots and Noilly Pratt into a medium-sized pan. Reduce the liquid by half over a gentle heat so that the shallots become transparent. Add 50ml oyster juice and 60g oysters. Bring back to the boil and reduce by a quarter. Add the double cream and crème fraîche, then bring back to the boil. Take off the heat and blend. Return to the pan and add the remaining 50ml juices and 60g oysters. Bring to the boil and take off the heat. Add the Chardonnay vinegar and blend. Pass the sauce through a fine sieve, then add lemon and salt as necessary.

To make the oyster emulsion, combine the shallots and Noilly Prat in a saucepan. Reduce by half over a medium heat. Again, add 60g oysters and 50ml oyster juice and reduce by a quarter. Add the cream and crème fraîche, cover in cling film and leave to steep for 20 minutes. Add the remaining 60g oysters, 50ml juices and the seaweed butter. Place in a blender and blend until smooth. Pass through a fine sieve and add the vinegar. Season with salt and a little lemon juice to taste.

To prepare the oyster poaching liquid, combine the Champagne, 100ml oyster juices and seaweed butter and warm the mixture to 62°C.

For the oyster tapioca, warm the velouté and tapioca, mixing thoroughly. Allow to cool and add all the other ingredients. Season to taste.

Place the cucumber into a vacuum pack bag with the vinegar, and seal on the highest setting. Open straight away and drain the vinegar. Lay on a blue cloth to drain for a few minutes. Place in a small bowl and mix in the shallot and fennel fronds. Keep at room temperature.

To serve, poach the remaining oysters in the poaching liquid. Assemble the dish as pictured, making sure to place a little pickle on each oyster.

CLARE SMYTH

My team at Restaurant Gordon Ramsay are delighted to share our sea bass dish with ChariTable Bookings in order to raise awareness for Hemihelp, a much unknown illness yet one that affects 1 in 1000 people in the UK. We hope you enjoy it and raise lots for charity too!"

SEA BASS with shellfish and sea vegetable minestrone

SERVES 4 | PREPARATION TIME 2 HOURS (PLUS 12 HOURS TO HANG THE LOVAGE) | COOKING TIME 3 HOURS

Equipment
Thermomix
pasta machine
sous vide and vacuum pack bags

For the Lovage Oil
2 bunches of lovage
250ml olive oil
salt, to taste
sugar, to taste

For the Sea Bass
4 x 125g sea bass portions, skin removed

For the Brine
50g each smoked salt and sugar
6g kombu seaweed
1l water

For the Bass Braising Liquor
4 long shallots, finely sliced
10 button mushrooms, finely sliced
250g unsalted butter
1 clove of garlic
1 sprig of thyme
¼ bay leaf
400ml Noilly Prat
1.5l fish stock

For the Garganelli
250g 00 flour
1 pinch of sea salt
3 egg yolks
2 whole eggs
10ml olive oil

To make the lovage oil, wash and pick the lovage. Place all the ingredients into a Thermomix and blend on full speed for 3 minutes at 70°C. Season and cool down over an ice bath. Once cool, hang in muslin cloth for 12 hours in the fridge.

To prepare the sea bass, blend together the ingredients for the brine and mix with the water. Place the fish portions in the brine for 7 minutes. Remove, pat dry, wrap in cling film to shape, vacuum pack and cook for 14 minutes in a 54°C water bath.

For the braising liquor, sweat the shallots and mushrooms in the butter until tender; do not colour. Add the garlic, thyme and bay leaf, along with the Noilly Prat, reduce by half, add the stock and bring to the boil. Reduce by half again, pass through a fine chinois and emulsify.

To make the garganelli, place the flour and salt into a food processor. Gradually add the eggs and olive oil until a fine crumb is achieved. Turn the dough out on to a work surface and knead for 5 minutes. Tightly wrap the dough in cling film and rest in the fridge for one hour. Once rested, roll and work the pasta using a pasta machine to a finished thickness of 2mm. Cut into 2x2cm squares. Take each square and roll around a 2mm dowel from one point to the other and secure with a little water. Remove the dowel and place on a pasta drying rack. Cook the pasta in seasoned boiling water for 3 minutes until tender. Refresh and store for serving.

To prepare the shellfish, wash thoroughly under cold, running water for 20 minutes. Place three small lidded pans on the stove and heat. Divide the mirepoix between the pans. One at a time, add the shellfish to the pans with the mirepoix and 50ml of white wine in each; quickly replacing the lids. Cook on a high heat until the shellfish open. Once open, strain off the liquid and reserve. Remove the shellfish from the shells, and clean and trim them. The razor clams need to be cut on the diagonal, usually 5 slices per clam. Set aside in the fridge.

To prepare the sea vegetables, wash, trim and pick the sea leaves. Blanch the leaves in boiling water for 30 seconds and refresh.

For the Shellfish

200g each razor clams, large
mussels and clams
200g small diced mirepoix
150ml white wine

For the Sea Vegetables

50g rock samphire
50g marsh samphire
30g sea beet
30g sea purslane

For the Shellfish Broth

2l vegetable stock
100ml white wine
1 carrot
1 stick celery
6 button mushrooms
2 spring onions
2 long shallots
1 sprig of thyme
1 clove of garlic
shellfish cooking juices

For the Coco Beans

100g fresh coco beans
250ml vegetable stock
250ml water
1 bouquet garni – garlic, thyme, bay
leaves and black peppercorns

To Finish

12 nasturtium leaves
12 sea purslane
12 borage shoots
12 land seaweed shoots
12 pennywort
lemon, zest and juice

To make the shellfish broth, wash and finely slice the vegetables. Place all the ingredients, except the reserved shellfish juices, into a pot and bring to the boil. Turn down the heat and simmer until reduced by a third. To finish the broth, use the shellfish cooking juices. Season to taste.

For the coco beans, place all of the ingredients in a cocotte and bring to a simmer. Season and cook gently until the beans are tender. Once ready, cool the beans in the liquor and store in the fridge.

To finish the dish and serve, place the sea bass portions into the braising liquor for three to 4 minutes. Mix together the coco beans, shellfish, sea vegetables and garganelli to make the minestrone. Lightly warm through. Season and finish with a little lemon juice and fresh zest. Arrange the minestrone in the centre of each bowl and place the sea bass on top with the herbs and shoots. Bring the broth to the boil and, right at the end, add two tablespoons of lovage oil. Divide the broth equally between the bowls and serve.

Editor's Note: To approximate the results of a Thermomix you could try using a high powered blender and then heat the resulting mixture in a saucepan together with a cook's thermometer. A cocotte is otherwise known as a cast iron casserole dish.

ERIC SNAITH

The team at Titchwell Manor and I are sharing our BBQ Onion recipe in support of the fantastic work of the Teenage Cancer Trust who provide both treatment and support to young people under 24 suffering from the disease. I wish ChariTable Bookings the very best in raising more funds for them and all UK charities."

BBQ ONION with potato gnocchi, avocado, brazil nuts and burnt onion crème fraîche

SERVES 4 | PREPARATION TIME 20 MINUTES | COOKING TIME 1 HOUR

For the Onions
- 2 large white onions
- 100g butter
- 1 tsp Maldon salt
- 150g crème fraîche

For the Gnocchi
- 500g King Edward potatoes
- 2 medium eggs, beaten
- 150g 00 pasta flour
- 1 tbsp olive oil
- 1 pinch of salt

For the Avocado
- 1 ripe avocado
- 50g crème fraîche
- lemon juice, to taste
- salt, to taste

To Finish
- 1 handful of brazil nuts, roughly chopped
- olive oil
- 1 knob of butter

Barbecue the onions with their skins on until black, allow to cool, then halve. Separate the flesh from the skins and retain both. Top the onion flesh with a knob of butter and the Maldon salt, then return with the skins to the barbecue. When the onion is soft, remove from the barbecue and keep aside until later. When the skins are black and crispy remove them also and allow them to cool. Blitz the skins to a powder in a food processor and combine with the crème fraîche.

To prepare the gnocchi, boil the potatoes in salted water until just cooked, strain and pass through a potato ricer. Pass them through the ricer again onto a floured surface so that there are no lumps. Make a well in the middle, add the oil, eggs and flour and gently bring together into a dough but be careful not to overwork. Roll into finger size pieces and poach in salted water at just below boiling. When they float they are done. Drop them into ice water, then pat dry.

For the avocado, blitz it together with the crème fraîche until smooth. Mix with lemon juice and salt to taste.

To finish, place the onion in an oven at 180°C until warmed through. Pan fry the gnocchi in a little olive oil on medium heat. When golden brown, add a knob of butter and allow to foam. Assemble as pictured.

JAMES SOMMERIN

"*Huggard has been tackling homelessness in Cardiff for over 20 years. They need the generosity of the public to keep their day centres and hostels open all year round. By sharing Restaurant James Sommerin's recipe with ChariTable Bookings, I am delighted to keep awareness raised for the vital services they provide in Cardiff.*"

LAMB with broad beans, asparagus and tarragon

SERVES 4 | PREPARATION TIME 30 MINUTES | COOKING TIME 1 HOUR

For the Lamb
500g lamb loin, deskinned, fat removed

For the Jus
2 shallots, thinly sliced
1 drizzle of oil
1 tsp cumin seeds
100ml Madeira
500ml lamb stock
20g butter

For the Tarragon Crème fraîche
1 bunch of tarragon, finely chopped
250g crème fraîche
1 lemon, juiced

For the Turnip Purée and Slices
4 turnips, preferably pink, peeled
whole milk, to cover
50g butter
salt, to taste

For the Asparagus
100g butter
50ml water
1 bunch of asparagus

To Serve
500g broad beans
1 punnet of nasturtium leaves

To cook the lamb, seal the loin of lamb for 3 minutes on each side and allow to rest. For added flavour, marinate the lamb loin in olive oil and rosemary 1 hour before cooking.

To make the jus, lightly sauté the shallots in a little oil in a pan. Add the cumin seeds and deglaze the pan with Madeira. Pour in the lamb stock and reduce by half, then blend in the butter.

To make the tarragon crème fraîche, mix the finely chopped tarragon with the crème fraîche and lemon juice.

To make the turnip purée and the turnip slices, chop 3 of the turnips and place them in a pan. Cover with milk, add the butter and bring to the boil. Cook until soft. Once cooked, drain and keep the liquid to one side. Place the turnips into a blender and gradually add the liquid to form a purée. Thinly slice the remaining uncooked turnip and sprinkle with salt.

To make the asparagus, place the butter and water in a pan and bring to the boil to melt and emulsify the butter. Trim the bottom of the asparagus, place into the pan and cook until the asparagus is just cooked.

To make the broad beans, pod the beans and blanch in boiling water for 2 minutes. Remove and cool in ice water. Pod again to remove the grey skin.

To assemble the dish, preheat the oven to 180°C. Warm the loin in the oven for approximately 4 minutes. Warm the broad beans and asparagus through the emulsion. Place a swirl of tarragon crème fraîche onto the plate followed by a spoonful of turnip purée. Cut the loin, serving 2 pieces per person, and place on the plate. Arrange the broad beans and asparagus, followed by the sliced turnip on top and nasturtium leaves to make the dish look pretty. Finish with a little jus.

TIM STAMP

"A worthwhile cause like Basset Law Hospice needs to raise funds and awareness, and Ye Olde Bell is delighted that ChariTable Bookings allows us to do this at no cost to the charity."

DEXTER BEEF FILLET with maple glazed cured ham, grilled goat's cheese and baby root vegetables

SERVES 2 | PREPARATION TIME 40 MINUTES | COOKING TIME 3 HOURS

For the Dish

2 x 225g Dexter beef fillets
4 slices of British cured ham
50ml maple syrup
150g goat's cheese
100g butter
20g caster sugar
6 baby beetroots
6 baby turnips
6 baby purple carrots
6 baby yellow carrots
6 edible viola flowers, optional
4 sprigs of fresh thyme
1 tbsp vegetable oil

Place the slices of cured ham on a tray with greaseproof paper, brush the ham with maple syrup until evenly glazed. Pre-heat the oven to 80°C and cook the ham for 3 hours until crisp – do this a few hours before preparing the rest of the meal.

To prepare the grilled goat's cheese and steak, break the goat's cheese down using your hands until it is lump-free and smooth, then roll into 2cm spheres. Make sure they are even. Set to one side until the vegetables and beef fillet are ready to serve. Season the beef fillet on both sides with sea salt and black pepper. Heat a tablespoon of oil in a frying pan. When the oil is hot add the steaks to the pan. After one side is browned turn the steaks then add 20g butter, basting while cooking. Cook for 7 minutes on each side until medium rare. Leave to rest.

To prepare the vegetables, peel all the vegetables. In 4 separate pans, add 400ml water and 20g butter, 5g caster sugar and 1 sprig of thyme to each pan. Add each vegetable to a different pan, even the carrots so the vegetables do not bleed and discolour each other. Cook the beetroot for 15 minutes, the turnips for 12 minutes and both varieties of carrots for 8 minutes. When all the vegetables are cooked, drain and season. Put the goat's cheese balls, prepared earlier, under a hot grill until the top has a nice golden glaze.

To serve, add the vegetables to the plate so that they overlap each other. Carve the beef by squaring off the sides, add to the plate leaning over the vegetables. Lay the grilled goat's cheese between the vegetables. Finally add the shards of glazed ham and violas to finish.

JACK STEIN

" I hope you enjoy cooking my braised hake signature dish that's much loved in Rick's Café in aid of the RNLI Lifeboats! What a great idea from ChariTable Bookings to raise money for thousands of charities across the UK by cooking and discovering delicious food."

BRAISED HAKE

SERVES 6 | PREPARATION TIME 20 MINUTES | COOKING TIME 1 HOUR

For the Dish

7 medium-sized beetroot, peeled
1 pinch of caster sugar
salt
1 pared strip of lime zest
1 pared strip of lemon zest
2 cloves
2.5cm stick of cinnamon
100g red cabbage, finely shredded
100g green winter cabbage, such as hipsi, finely shredded
100g white cabbage, finely shredded
50g kale or cavolo nero, finely shredded
1 tbsp sea purslane leaves, optional
1 small bunch of sea beet leaves, finely shredded, optional
1 small bunch of chives, chopped
1 small handful of fennel fronds
4 x 100g hake fillets, skin on
25g butter
50ml dry white wine
100ml fish stock
sea salt flakes

For the Dressing

1 tbsp cider vinegar
1 tbsp rapeseed oil
salt
½ pomegranate, seeds only, to serve

Place 2 of the beetroot into a small pan with the sugar, a good pinch of salt, the lime and lemon zest, cloves and cinnamon. Cover with cold water, bring to the boil, lower the heat and leave to simmer very gently for 1 hour or until tender when pierced through to the centre with a fine skewer. Remove the cooked beetroot and set aside to cool.

Meanwhile, roughly chop 4 of the remaining beetroot and blend in a food processor to a smooth purée. Tip the purée into a sieve, set over a bowl and press out all the liquid with the back of a spoon or spatula. You should yield about 75ml of liquid. Set this aside for the dressing.

Cut the remaining beetroot into thin slices, then slice into fine matchsticks. Mix the shredded cabbages, sea purslane, sea beet, chives, fennel fronds and beetroot matchsticks together in a large bowl. Set aside. Season the hake on both sides with salt and set aside for 10 minutes.

Meanwhile, for the dressing, whisk the beetroot juice with the vinegar, oil and some salt, to taste. Set aside. To cook the hake, melt the butter in a non-stick frying pan large enough to sit the fish comfortably side by side. Pat the hake dry with kitchen paper, add to the pan skin-side down and cook for 1–2 minutes over a medium-high heat, or until pale goldenbrown. Turn the pieces over, add the white wine and fish stock to the pan, cover and cook for 2–3 minutes, or until cooked through. Keep warm. Whisk 2 tablespoons of the cooking liquid from the fish pan into the beetroot dressing and season, to taste, with salt. Add four tablespoons of the dressing to the cabbage salad and mix until well combined. Season, to taste, with sea salt flakes. To serve, thinly slice the cooked beetroot and overlap the slices to create a disc in the centre of each of four serving plates.

Place a 10–12cm cooking ring into the centre of the beetroot slices and fill with the salad mixture. Carefully lift off and repeat for each of the remaining plates. Stir the pomegranate seeds into the remaining dressing. Place a piece of fish on top of the salad and spoon the dressing and pomegranate seeds around the outside of the plate.

RICK STEIN

The Dyslexia Trust recognises that children's talents don't just lie in reading and writing but have to be found in other areas, possibly cooking! Very pleased to support them in this ChariTable Bookings initiative by sharing The Seafood Restaurant's steamed mussels recipe with you."

STEAMED MUSSELS with tomato and tarragon

SERVES 4 | PREPARATION TIME 15 MINUTES | COOKING TIME 10 MINUTES

For the Dish
- 30ml extra virgin olive oil
- 2 cloves of garlic, finely chopped
- 1kg mussels
- 30ml dry white wine
- 30g unsalted butter
- 60g tomatoes, peeled, deseeded and finely chopped
- 5g French tarragon, finely chopped
- salt and pepper, to taste

For the Garnish
- fresh bread or linguine

To prepare the dish, make sure the mussels are tightly closed. If they are fresh-farmed ones there is no need to wash them, but if they are showing any signs of grit or sand wash them in copious amounts of cold water.

Take a large saucepan, add the olive oil and garlic and soften over a medium heat for about a minute. Add the mussels, turn up the heat and add the white wine. Put a lid on the pan and cook for a few minutes until all the shells have opened, but only just. Stir the shells once or twice during the cooking to distribute them evenly. Remove and pour through a colander set over a bowl.

Keep the mussels warm while you transfer the liquor to a pan, heat until boiling, whisk in the butter then add the tomato and tarragon. Check the seasoning; it's always a good idea to leave seasoning to the end with shellfish as you never know how salty they are going to be, then add salt if necessary and freshly ground black pepper.

To serve, add the mussels back into the pan and plate with plenty of crusty bread or alternatively with a mound of al dente linguine pasta.

ARNAUD STEVENS

Sixty One is proud to support Leuka in their great work researching a cure for blood cancer by contributing to ChariTable Bookings new publication. I hope we help raise lots of money and awareness for them."

SQUAB PIGEON with snails, cauliflower and parsley risotto

SERVES 4 | PREPARATION TIME 20 MINUTES | COOKING TIME 5 HOURS

For the Pigeon Sauce
- 5kg pigeon bones
- 50g tomato paste
- 5l chicken stock
- 500ml veal stock
- 100g Paris mushrooms
- 200g banana shallots, finely sliced
- 5 juniper berries
- 10 black peppercorns
- 100ml red wine vinegar
- 100ml brandy
- 1.5l red wine
- 1 bay leaf
- 1 sprig of thyme

Pot-Au-Feu Garnish
- 150g pancetta
- 100g carrots
- 100g shallots
- 30g garlic
- 50g thyme
- 50g tarragon
- 20g parsley
- 400ml nage
- 50ml Pernod

For the Risotto
- 250g Vialone Nano rice
- 100g white onion
- 2 cloves of garlic
- 2 bay leaves
- 75ml white wine

To prepare the pigeon sauce, roast the pigeon bones until golden in a roasting tin, strain, then roast the garnish adding the tomato paste at the end. Put everything in a tall stockpot and add the chicken stock. Cook for at least 5 hours then pass through a fine chinois. Reduce to a proper consistency.

Slice the Paris mushrooms, shallots, and add to the crushed juniper berries and black peppercorns. In a small rondelle pot caramelise the mushrooms and shallots deglaze with the red wine vinegar, brandy, and the red wine. Put in the rest of the aromatic garnish. Reduce by one third before adding into the pigeon stock. When the sauce is reaching the proper consistency, pass through a muslin cloth twice and check seasoning.

To prepare the risotto, in a large sauté pan cook the chopped onions with the garlic and the bay leaves until clear, add in the rice and cook until clear as well. Pour in the white wine and cook until the liquid has evaporated, then add the warm stock, without stopping and making sure to beat the risotto on the side of the pan. This will ensure the risotto becomes creamy. When the rice is almost transparent with a little white point in the middle taste it and check that it is still al dente.

To prepare the cauliflower purée, blitz all the ingredients at 80°C for 8 minutes. Refresh in a blast chiller.

Blanch the parsley in boiling salty water cook until the leaves break in between your fingers, blend at 80°C with a little of the blanching water for 8 minutes, pass through a sieve and chill. Remove the risotto from the heat and add in the parsley purée, Parmesan cheese the butter and a little bit of cream. Check the seasoning and the fluidity of the risotto, to finish put in the olive oil and a little more parsley purée to taste.

To prepare the snails in garlic wine, first rinse the snails a few times with some fresh water. Then cook them with some of the pot-au-feu garnish until they become tender. Strain them. Pan fry with some butter and deglaze with the garlic infused white wine.

For the Risotto *continued*
- 3l vegetable stock
- 250g Parmesan
- 100g butter
- 50ml double cream
- 150ml olive oil
- salt
- black pepper

For the Cauliflower Purée
- 150g blanched cauliflower
- 150ml cream
- 50g almond powder

For the Parsley Purée
- 300g flat leaf parsley
- 300g curly parsley

For the Snails and Garlic Wine
- 1 tin of snails
- 100ml white wine
- 10g garlic
- 50g butter

For the Pigeon
- 4 squab pigeons
- 80g unsalted butter

For the Garnish
- 2 pieces of orange zest, dried

To cook the pigeon, remove the breasts and legs from the carcass and trim any sinew. Sear in melted butter for 2–3 minutes on the skin-side and 1 minute on the flesh, then place in an oven at 180°C for 5 minutes. Serve on top of a bed of purée and serve immediately with all the trimmings.

MARK STINCHCOMBE

" Eckington Manor supports the essential service provided by the Air Ambulance and raises a glass to ChariTable Bookings for helping us to do this."

CONFIT PORK BELLY with granola, Earl Grey soaked prunes and spiced fritter

SERVES 6 | PREPARATION TIME 4 HOURS | COOKING TIME 4 HOURS

For the Pork Belly

½ pork belly, deboned and deskinned

1 head of garlic

1 sprig of fresh thyme

1 sprig of fresh rosemary

100g rock salt

2l duck fat

For the Granola

35g honey

35g maple syrup

40g butter

75g sugar

10g salt

6g mixed spices

200g porridge oats

For the Prunes

200g pitted prunes

2 Earl Grey tea bags

100g sugar

400ml water

1 star anise

For the Spiced Fritter

1 cooking onion, finely diced

2 celery sticks, finely diced

2 carrots, peeled and finely diced

small splash of vegetable oil

1 tbsp mixed spice

1 tsp ginger powder

3cm piece fresh ginger, chopped

2 cloves of garlic, chopped

To cook the pork belly, place in a roasting tin. Cut up the garlic, thyme and rosemary, then mix all together with the rock salt and sprinkle over the pork belly. Massage the seasoning into the meat and cover with cling film, place in the fridge to marinate for 4 hours. Once marinated, wash the salt mix off the pork belly by holding under cold running water, pat dry the meat in a clean tea towel. Place the duck fat in an ovenproof, large saucepan, melt the fat over a medium heat, do not boil. Once melted, add the pork belly. Make sure the meat is fully submerged in the duck fat and then cover with tin foil. Cook in preheated oven 120°C for 1.5 hours. Once cooked, remove the pork belly from the duck fat. Allow to cool before portioning into 6 pieces, then colour in a frying pan until golden. Reserve for plating.

To make the granola, bring the honey, maple syrup, butter, sugar, salt and mixed spice to the boil. Add the porridge oats and stir. Once incorporated, place into preheated oven 180°C for 12 minutes or until golden. The granola will keep for several months in an airtight container.

To prepare the prunes, bring all the ingredients to a gentle boil, then remove from the heat. Steep the prunes in the liquid and reserve for plating. The prunes can be kept in the fridge if you don't use them all.

To make the spiced fritter, in a large, ovenproof saucepan over a medium heat, sweat the onion, celery and carrots in oil until soft. Add the spices and tomato purée, place in the pork shoulder and top with cold water. Bring the saucepan up to the boil, then cover with tin foil and braise in preheated oven at 120°C for 4 hours. Once cooked, remove the shoulder from the liquid and shred into small pieces. Pass the liquid through a sieve and add 4 tablespoons of liquid to the meat, season to taste. Roll into balls and set in the fridge. Dip and coat the balls firstly in the flour, then beaten egg mixture, finally coat in breadcrumbs. Deep fry before serving. Reduce the remaining liquid until it begins to thicken, this will be about three quarters. This is the sauce to go onto the plate.

For the Spiced Fritter *continued*
200ml tomato purée
800g pork shoulder
flour for coating fritter
3 free range medium eggs. beaten
200g bread crumbs
oil, for deep frying

To Serve
greens

To serve, place the pork on the plate next to the spiced fritter. Serve 3 prunes per plate. Sprinkle the spiced granola around. Cover with greens and the spiced fritter stock.

ADAM STOKES

"I really hope you enjoy our signature dish from Adam's and, by buying this ChariTable Bookings recipe book, support the amazing work of StreetSmart at the same time."

CHARRED RAINBOW TROUT with potato salad

SERVES 4 | PREPARATION TIME 2 HOURS | COOKING TIME 1 HOUR

For the Rainbow Trout
  4 rainbow trout fillets, descaled and
  pin boned
  100g salt
  100g sugar
  10g coriander seed
  40g lemon zest
  20g lime zest

For the Potato Salad
  500g Jersey Royal new potatoes
  salt and pepper
  1 drizzle of olive oil
  1 large banana shallot, finely diced
  1 bunch of chives, finely chopped
  100g crème fraîche

To Serve
  sweet pickled gherkins, sliced
  radishes, sliced
  100g chives
  1 drizzle of olive oil
  cucumber flowers

To prepare the fish, begin by making the cure. Blend together the salt, sugar, coriander, lemon and lime zest until coarsely chopped.

Lay the cure mostly on the flesh side of the trout fillet with a little on the skin-side. Leave for 1.5 hours. Wash the cure off the trout well, place onto kitchen towel and transfer to the fridge until ready to use.

Place the potatoes in a small pan and cover with water. Add a good pinch of salt, black pepper and a drizzle of olive oil. Bring the pan up to the boil, then gently simmer for approximately 20 minutes, depending on the size of the potatoes. When almost cooked, remove the pan from the heat and allow the potatoes to cool in their cooking liquor. When cold, strain and discard the liquid. Cut the potatoes into 2cm pieces and stir though the crème fraîche, shallot and finely chopped chives. Season with salt and a little cracked black pepper.

Finely slice the gherkins and radishes and set aside. Boil a pan of water and put the chives in, simmering for 5 seconds. Strain the liquid and cool the chives in ice water. Remove the chives and pat dry. Place into a small food processor with just enough olive oil to allow the machine to blend.

Place a little potato salad in a bowl and have the radishes, gherkin and chive oil ready. Lightly oil the skin of the trout fillet and place skin-side down onto a preheated, very hot griddle pan. Allow the skin to char and crisp. Remove from the pan and slice into neat strips.

Arrange the fish on the plate with the radish, gherkins and chive oil. Garnish with the cucumber flowers and serve immediately.

FERNANDO STOVELL

" Newlife is the UK's largest charity funder of children's specialist disability equipment. Without them, thousands of disabled children would go without essential equipment for their basic needs. Very happy to be sharing Stovell's foie gras with ChariTable Bookings to support them."

FOIE GRAS with barbecue silverskin onions, toasted Kentish cobnuts, hay dressing and nasturtium

SERVES 4 | PREPARATION TIME 45 MINUTES | COOKING TIME 45 MINUTES

Equipment
blowtorch

For the Dish
300g foie gras
500g dry fragrant wood
250g hay
500ml water
100ml grapeseed oil
12 shallots
2 star anise
250ml sherry vinegar
250g sugar
salt and black pepper
1 brioche loaf, cut into thick batons
100ml chicken glaze
100ml xerex vinegar, for deglazing
peanut butter, for spreading
100g cobnuts, peeled and toasted
nasturtium leaves and petals

To make the foie gras, prepare and separate 5 portions of approximately 60g. Spread the wood over a grill tray and dry in the oven, using a blowtorch to help the wood ignite. When the wood starts smoking, add the foie gras pieces, cover with a lid and allow to smoke for 5 minutes. Then put back into the fridge for 10 minutes before serving.

To make the hay dressing, just cover the hay in a large pan with water. Boil until reaching a strong hay taste, which should take approximately 30 minutes. Strain the hay and, keeping the juices hot, add a portion of foie gras, blending to a smooth purée. Slowly add oil until a mayonnaise like consistency is reached. Season to taste with salt and pepper.

To make the pickled silverskins, blanch the shallots in boiling, salted water. Bring the water, anise, vinegar and sugar to the boil, add the cooked shallots and season with salt and pepper. Allow to cool in the liquid, strain and slice in half.

To finish, lightly grill the brioche batons. Warm the chicken glaze. Season the slices of foie gras and put them in a very hot, non-stick pan or plancha for 1 minute on each side. Colour the shallots flat side down. Deglaze the pan with xerex vinegar.

Serve warm with the chicken glaze, hay dressing and brioche, covered with a little peanut butter. Garnish with toasted cobnuts, and the nasturtium leaves and petals.

THOMAS STRAKER

MIND works tirelessly to promote awareness and understanding of mental health issues and it is with great pleasure that I can support it by sharing Casa Cruz's gnocchi with you. Great idea by ChariTable Bookings to promote charity through food!"

POTATO GNOCCHI, GORGONZOLA, SPINACH

SERVES 2 | PREPARATION TIME 25 MINUTES | COOKING TIME 1 HOUR 10 MINUTES

For the Gnocchi
6 medium potatoes
350g dry mash potato
5g cornflour
salt
1 egg yolk
50g 00 flour
olive oil

For the Spinach Pesto
25g picked basil
75g picked spinach
100ml olive oil
40g toasted hazelnuts
salt and pepper

To Serve
100g sweet gorgonzola
50g crushed roasted hazelnuts
lemon juice
olive oil

To make the gnocchi, place the potatoes in a baking tray with salt. Bake at 200°C for 1 hour or until soft. Halve the potatoes whilst still piping hot and mince in a food processor twice. Allow the potatoes to cool, then gently mix the dry mash, cornflour, egg yolk and salt together by hand, being careful not to over work them. Add 00 flour where necessary so that the dough is quite dry. Place the gnocchi dough in a piping bag, cut the end to the desired size. Pipe long tubes of gnocchi on to a floured chopping board. Cut and shape. Bring a large pan of salted water to the boil. Place the gnocchi in the water and cook until they float to the top. Chill in ice water, drain on a j-cloth and store in the fridge until needed.

To make the spinach pesto, place the basil and spinach in the blender, slowly adding olive oil until the right consistency is achieved. Add the hazelnuts, salt and black pepper and blitz. The pesto should not be completely smooth. Leave the hazelnuts slightly chunky.

To serve, fill a large saucepan with lightly salted water, bring to the boil and have a slotted spoon ready. Add the spinach pesto to a large saucepan, together with the gorgonzola and some water. Place on a medium heat, allowing the cheese to melt. Stir together to make a homogeneous sauce. Now add the gnocchi to the boiling water and cook for 90 seconds. Remove and place in the sauce. Toss over a medium heat for another 2 minutes, ensuring the gnocchi are well coated.

Garnish with toasted hazelnuts, lemon juice and olive oil.

AGNAR SVERRISSON

It's an honour to be part of The ChariTable Bookings Signature Dish recipe book and to share Texture's signature Icelandic Fish Pie in support of the incredible work of Cancer Research."

ICELANDIC FISH PIE

SERVES 2 | PREPARATION TIME 30 MINUTES | COOKING TIME 1 HOUR

For the Fish Pie
- 200g cod fillets
- 8 new potatoes
- 15g cheddar, grated
- 10g Parmesan, grated

For the Sauce
- 25g butter
- 250ml milk
- 1 onion, sliced
- ½ tsp salt
- 15g plain flour
- ¼ tsp madras curry powder

To Serve
- 1¼ tsp chives, chopped
- 4 slices of rye bread
- lemon wedges

For the sauce, place the butter in a pan and melt on a low heat. In a separate pan, warm the milk and set to one side. Add the sliced onion and salt to the butter, and cover with a lid. Cook on a low heat for around 3–5 minutes until soft and tender. Add the curry powder to the onions and cook for 3–4 minutes until they're almost dry in the pan. Add the flour to the onion curry base to make a roux, and cook for 3–4 minutes on a low heat. Using a ladle and wooden spoon, slowly incorporate the milk to the roux until all the milk is in the sauce. Cook the sauce for 10 minutes until thickened and set to one side.

To assemble the fish pie, preheat the oven to 180°C. Put the potatoes in a pan of salted water and boil until cooked. Lightly season the cod fillet with a little salt and black pepper and place in a cast iron baking pan. Arrange the potatoes around the cod, add the sauce and spread well, making sure to cover everything. Sprinkle cheddar and Parmesan over the top and place the dish in the oven for 15–20 minutes to cook. Just before taking out your fish pie, warm the rye bread in the oven for 1–2 minutes.

To serve, remove from the oven, sprinkle with chives and garnish with rye bread and lemon wedges.

JUN TANAKA

"The team at The Ninth is proud to support Action Against Hunger and help fight hunger in children across the world by sharing our recipe with you and ChariTable Bookings."

IBERICO PORK PLUMA with herb vinaigrette and piquillo peppers
SERVES 4 | PREPARATION TIME 2 HOURS | COOKING TIME 20 MINUTES

For the Dish
4 x 180g Iberico pluma
50g chickpeas, cooked

For the Brine
1l water
80g sea salt
40g caster sugar
1 sprig of thyme

For the Herb Vinaigrette
½ bunch of parsley, finely chopped
¼ bunch of oregano, finely chopped
1 clove of garlic, crushed
1 green chilli, deseeded and finely chopped
½ tsp cumin seeds, crushed, keep half for chickpeas
½ tsp sweet paprika, keep half for chickpeas
1 tsp salt
½ shallot, finely chopped
50ml red wine vinegar
100ml extra virgin olive oil

For the Piquillo Pepper Purée
1 shallot, finely sliced
1 clove of garlic, sliced
1 tbsp olive oil
200g piquillo peppers
1 red pepper, diced
25ml sherry vinegar
50ml white wine

To make the brine, place all of the ingredients in a saucepan and heat until the salt and sugar dissolves. Allow to cool, then place the pork in the brine and leave for 2 hours. Take out of the brine, rinse well in fresh, cold water and pat dry.

From the herb vinaigrette ingredients, mix half the paprika and cumin with a teaspoon of salt and keep to one side. Combine all the other ingredients to make the vinaigrette, mix well and set aside.

To make the purée, sweat the shallot and garlic in olive oil for 5 minutes, then add the peppers followed by the vinegar and white wine. Cook for 10 minutes, then blitz and pass through a fine sieve. Season to taste.

To prepare the pork and chickpeas, lightly oil the pork on both sides and place on a hot griddle. Cook for 3 minutes, then flip over and cook for a further 2–3 minutes. Deep fry the chickpeas for 2 minutes, then drain and season with the spiced salt.

To serve, slice the pork and place on a plate, spoon the vinaigrette over the top, then add a spoon of the purée to the side. Scatter the chickpeas over the pork and serve.

CHRIS TANNER
JAMES TANNER

"It's really important that we continue to fund research into finding a cure for Leukaemia. On behalf of the team at Kentish Hare, we hope you enjoy our pork plate and join ChariTable Bookings in supporting Cure Leukaemia and all the other amazing charities."

KENTISH HARE PORK PLATE

SERVES 6 | PREPARATION TIME 2 HOURS (PLUS 12 HOURS TO SOAK) | COOKING TIME 24 HOURS

Equipment
sous vide and vacuum pack bags
Thermomix

For the Pig's Head, Belly and Cheeks
1 split pig's head
1 bulb of garlic
2 shallots
1 bunch of chives
4 tbsp sherry vinegar
seasoning
flour, egg and breadcrumbs, for pané
oil, for frying
½ pork belly
6 pig cheeks

For the Vegetables
1 each savoy cabbage, head of
celery, leek and carrot
1kg yukon gold potatoes
2 bulbs of garlic
200ml cream
1 tbsp salt
1 block of butter
500ml water
200ml white wine
100ml white wine vinegar
100ml rape seed oil

For the Black Pudding Purée
400g black pudding
100ml apple juice
reduced red wine

Soak the pig's head for 12 hours, then cover with water and cook at 150°C in the oven for a further 12 hours. Once this is done, flake the flesh. Reduce the cooking liquor by two thirds and add the garlic, shallots and chives. Finish with seasoning and sherry vinegar. To create the fritters, roll the meat into equal sized balls, panée, and set to one side for frying.

Remove the rib bones from the belly and any sinew from the cheeks, then vacuum pack them separately and sous vide simultaneously for 12 hours at 82.2°C. Afterwards, press the belly meat between two trays until set.

Roast the garlic at 150°C until soft and cut 1 bulb in half to infuse the cream. Cut the other and brown in a pan for garnishing. Peel the yukon gold potatoes and cut into even pieces. Boil the potatoes in a pan of water with 1 tablespoon of salt. Once cooked, pass through a ricer, then a drum sieve. Incorporate the butter and infused garlic cream to finish.

Cut the celery into sticks, then cover with 500ml of water, white wine, white wine vinegar and rapeseed oil. Cook at 160°C for 30 minutes until soft, then cut into half centimetre dice.

Remove the stems from the savoy cabbage, chiffonade, then blanche. Cut a macedoine of leek and carrot and blanch.

Blend the black pudding with apple juice in a Thermomix until smooth, then reheat the purée when needed.

To finish the dish and serve, crisp the belly in a pan, glaze the cheek in the reduced red wine, deep fry the pig head fritter, then heat the black pudding purée and other garnish. Finish with fennel cress.

ROBIN TARVER

I hope you enjoy Madison's halibut recipe in this ChariTable Bookings collection in support of The Woodland Trust, protecting forests across the UK."

ROAST WILD HALIBUT with smoked eel and leek fondue and Avruga caviar

SERVES 4 | PREPARATION TIME 20 MINUTES | COOKING TIME 30 MINUTES

For the Halibut

4 x 200g halibut fillets

olive oil

salt and pepper

1 squeeze of lemon

For the Leek and Smoked Eel Fondue

50g unsalted butter

1 pinch of salt

2 leeks, finely chopped

2 tbsp crème fraîche

1 tbsp chives, chopped

150g smoked eel, cut into ½cm pieces

For the Garnish

1 tbsp cucumber, finely diced

1 tbsp Avruga caviar

black truffle, sliced

To cook the fish, place the fillets skin-side down on a baking tray, rub them with a little olive oil and season with salt and pepper. Roast in the oven at 180°C for about 15 minutes or until you can easily pierce a cocktail stick through the flesh. Finish with a squeeze of lemon.

To make the leek and smoked eel fondue, melt the butter in a pot and add a pinch or 2 of salt, add the chopped leeks and cook slowly on a low heat for about 5 minutes until soft. Add the smoked eel, crème fraîche and chives. Cook for a further few minutes until most of the liquid has evaporated.

For the garnish, mix the diced cucumber with the caviar.

To serve, place the leek fondue in the middle of the plate and place the halibut on top. Add a teaspoon of the cucumber and caviar mix and finish with the sliced truffle.

STEPHEN TERRY

" Ty Hafan tackles the hardest job to give dying children and their families the best support possible in their final few months. I'm very proud to support them by sharing The Hardwick's chargrilled pepper recipe with ChariTable Bookings."

CHARGRILLED PEPPER with mozzarella and pesto

SERVES 4 | PREPARATION TIME 15 MINUTES | COOKING TIME 10 MINUTES

For the Vegetables and Mozzarella
2 large Italian yellow or red peppers
8 large leaves radicchio lettuce
4 x 100g balls buffalo mozzarella
1 shallot, peeled

For the Pickled Kohlrabi
vinegar, to cover
1 chilli, halved
1 small kohlrabi, peeled and diced

To Serve
4 tbsp good quality pesto
12 radishes, finely sliced
2 tbsp extra virgin olive oil
lemon juice and sea salt, to taste

To prepare the dish, chargrill the peppers, then peel them. Remove the seeds and cut the flesh into 4 equal pieces. Lightly chargrill the radicchio lettuce leaves. Slice each mozzarella ball into quarters. Finely slice the shallot and deep fry until crispy. You can put the peppers under the grill or use a blowtorch, both methods work equally well.

To make the pickled kholrabi, bring the vinegar to the boil in a pan with the chilli, pour it over the kohlrabi and leave to pickle until the liquid has cooled.

To plate, layer the mozzarella and grilled pepper with pesto. Dress the radicchio and radish with olive oil and lemon juice. Season with salt. Finish by garnishing the radicchio with the diced kohlrabi and fried shallots and serve as pictured.

ALEX THAIN

"The Crossbasket Castle supports the excellent work of Glasgow children's hospital charity and ChariTable Bookings' initiative will help them reach more people."

ROAST BREAST AND CRISPY LEG OF WILD MALLARD with salt-baked
beetroot and blackberry jus

SERVES 4 | PREPARATION TIME 1 HOUR 30 MINUTES | COOKING TIME 4 HOURS

Equipment
sous vide and vacuum pack bags

For the Mallard Legs
2 whole mallards, gutted

100g Maldon salt

100g sugar

3 sprigs of thyme

4 juniper berries, crushed

500g duck fat

1 sheet of spring roll pastry

10g cornflour

50ml water

For the Mallard Breasts
2 mallard crowns

2l brown chicken stock

3 sprigs of thyme

salt and pepper, to taste

For the Salt-Baked Beetroots
1 bunch of baby golden beetroot

1 bunch of baby candy beetroot

1 bunch of baby ruby beetroot

Maldon salt

4 cloves of garlic, crushed

3 sprigs of thyme

drizzle of rapeseed oil

For the Blackberry Ketchup
1kg blackberry purée

200ml red wine vinegar

200ml beetroot juice

To prepare the mallard legs, remove the legs from the mallard, reserving the crowns for roasting later. Season the legs with salt, sugar, thyme and juniper, and marinate for an hour. After an hour, rinse off the excess marinade and pat dry. Place in a pan and cover with duck fat, confit on a very low heat for 1–2 hours, until the meat can be removed easily from the bone. Mix the confit leg meat with a little reduced brown chicken stock, checking for seasoning. Mix the cornflour and water together to make a light paste. Cut one sheet of spring roll pastry into 4 long strips. Place 30g of leg meat at the bottom of the pastry. Brush with the cornflour mix and roll up into a samosa. Repeat with the remaining mix.

To make the mallard breasts, place the chicken stock and thyme in a tall saucepan and bring to a simmer. Season the mallard crowns with salt and pepper and submerge in the simmering stock, cooking for 4 minutes. Remove the crowns and chill rapidly. Remove the breasts from the bone and trim. Place in vacuum pouches and seal on high. Set aside until ready to cook. Keep the carcasses and stock for the sauce.

To make the salt-baked beetroot, place the beetroot in a roasting tray on a bed of Maldon salt, thyme and garlic. Drizzle over a little rapeseed oil. Wrap tightly with tin foil and bake in the oven at 170°C for 45–50 minutes. Peel the beets while hot and cut into quarters.

To make the blackberry ketchup, in a saucepan combine the blackberry purée with red wine vinegar, beetroot juice, sugar and agar agar. Place on the heat and bring the mixture to the boil, whisking continuously. When it reaches the boil, keep on the heat for 1 minute and then pour into a bowl. Place the mixture in the fridge to set completely. Once set, transfer to a blender and blend until smooth, adding a touch of water to achieve the correct consistency. Place the blackberry ketchup in a plastic container and vacuum package with no lid, 3 times to remove air bubbles and achieve a glossy finish. Place in a plastic squeezy bottle until needed.

For the Blackberry Ketchup *continued*

    sugar, to taste

    14g agar agar

    1 splash of water

For the Blackberry Jus

    1 drizzle of oil

    1 knob of butter

    carcasses from mallards, chopped

    3 banana shallots, finely sliced

    2 cloves of garlic

    50ml sherry vinegar

    400ml Madeira

    2 large dates

    4 sprigs of thyme

    2l brown chicken stock

    500ml veal stock

    50g cold butter, diced

    75g blackberry purée

To Finish

    50ml pomace oil

    savoy cabbage, sliced and blanched

    50g butter

    red vein sorrel, to garnish

    12 fresh blackberries, halved

To make the blackberry jus, heat the oil and butter in a large saucepan over a high heat. Add the chopped carcasses and pan roast until golden brown and caramelised. Drain into a colander. Add the shallots and garlic to the pan and cook until nicely caramelised. Drain into the same colander. Deglaze the pan with sherry vinegar and reduce until almost evaporated. Add Madeira to the pan and reduce by half. Add the bones and shallots back into the pan along with the dates, thyme, chicken and veal stocks. Bring to a simmer and cook for about 45–60 minutes, skimming constantly. Pass the sauce through a muslin-lined sieve into another saucepan. Place back onto the heat and reduce to a nice glossy sauce consistency. Finish by whisking in cold diced butter and blackberry purée until emulsified.

To finish the dish and serve, place the vacuum packed mallard breasts in the water bath set at 56°C for 15 minutes. Drizzle the quartered beets with rapeseed oil and warm under the grill. Warm the cabbage in a pan with a little butter and seasoning. Deep fry the samosas until golden and crispy, place in the oven at 180°C for 3 minutes. Remove the mallard breasts from the sous vide bags and sear in oil in a hot pan. Add butter and baste the breasts for a couple of minutes. Remove from the pan and leave to rest for a few minutes. Plate as pictured and serve.

LUKE THOMAS

Best Beginnings works to support children between conception and 3 years to ensure they have the best start in life possible. Luke's Eating House is delighted to share their signature sweet and sour pork broth with ChariTable Bookings to support them further in their great work."

SWEET AND SOUR PORK BROTH

SERVES 4 | PREPARATION TIME 20 MINUTES | COOKING TIME 3 HOURS 30 MINUTES

For the Pork Broth

80g fresh root ginger

8 spring onions, cut into 2.5cm lengths

70g palm sugar, chopped, or soft brown sugar

2 star anise

1 stick of cinnamon

60ml dry sherry

120ml soy sauce

1.5l chicken stock

2.2kg pork shoulder, cut into 2cm dice

300g fresh pineapple, diced

4 small heads of bok choi

2 tbsp fresh coriander leaves, chopped

To prepare the broth, put the ginger, half the spring onions, the sugar, star anise, cinnamon stick, sherry, soy sauce and chicken stock into a deep wok. Bring to the boil and simmer for 5–10 minutes so that the sugar dissolves and the flavours infuse. Add the pork pieces and leave to simmer gently for about 3 hours. The pork should be lovely and tender.

Once it is cooked, strain the broth through a sieve into a clean saucepan set over a medium heat. Skim off any fat from the surface. Transfer the cooked pork to a bowl and cover loosely with foil to keep warm. Add the pineapple chunks and the remaining pieces of spring onion to the broth and simmer for 10 minutes. The broth will reduce and have an even more intense flavour.

While the broth is reducing, bring a saucepan of water to the boil and cook the bok choi for about 5 minutes. It should be tender, but still with a bit of bite.

To serve, place some warm bok choy in each serving bowl and top with some of the pork. Spoon over the hot broth and finish with a sprinkle of chopped coriander leaves.

PHIL THOMPSON

Leuka needs to raise over £1m a year to carry out the great work it does in fighting blood cancer and supporting those that suffer from it. Great to see that ChariTable Bookings can help with that and I'm very pleased to be part of this."

POACHED AND ROASTED WOOD PIGEON with confit leg pastilla, red cabbage and pear

SERVES 4 | PREPARATION TIME 40 MINUTES (PLUS 24 HOURS TO DRAIN CABBAGE JUICE) | COOKING TIME 4 HOURS

Equipment
sous vide and vacuum pack bags
Thermomix

For the Wood Pigeon Breast and Pastilla
2 wood pigeons
2 sprigs of thyme
1 tbsp olive oil
salt and pepper, to taste
1 clove of garlic, crushed
1 tbsp duck fat
1 shallot
1 handful of parsley
2 sheets of spring roll pastry
1 egg
10g butter

For the Red Cabbage Ketchup
1 small red cabbage
1 pinch of salt
agar agar, 1g for each 100ml of juice
1 dash of Chardonnay vinegar

To Serve
50g crosnes
1 pear, diced
½ lemon, juiced
10g hazelnuts

To prepare the wood pigeon, blowtorch to remove any excess feathers. Take off the breasts and legs, place the breasts into a vacuum packed bag with 1 teaspoon of olive oil, a pinch salt and a sprig of thyme. Cook at 54°C for 15 minutes, remove from heat and chill. Marinate the legs with a pinch of salt, crushed garlic clove and the sprig of thyme for 6 hours. Wash the legs and place into a vacuum bag with duck fat and cook at 80°C, until soft approximately 3–4 hours. When the legs are cooked, pick off the meat, finely chop the shallot and handful of parsley and mix. Season and roll 4 spring rolls sealing the pastry with egg white.

To make the red cabbage ketchup, roughly cut the red cabbage and blend in a Thermomix until fine, with a little pinch of salt. Hang in muslin cloth for one day to drain. Bring the liquid up to the boil and mix with agar agar. Use a ratio of 1 gram of agar agar to every 100ml of cabbage liquid. Leave to cool and set, then blend until smooth, adding a touch of Chardonnay vinegar to taste.

To prepare the garnish, dice half the pear into cubes and vacuum pack with a little lemon juice for 20 minutes. Baton the other half into matchstick sizes and put to one side in lemon water. Roast off the crosnes in a little butter for 2–3 minutes, and drain.

To serve, roast off the pigeon breast in butter until coloured, fry the pastilla. Smear the red cabbage ketchup onto the plate, sprinkle the crosnes and diced pear on top, cut the breasts in half and place in the centre of the plate with the pastilla. Sprinkle the pear batons on top, grate over the hazelnuts and finish with a tablespoon of roasting juices.

KEVIN TICKLE

Air ambulances all over the country are a critical service for saving lives. The Great North saves lives near us at The Forest Side all year round and so we are very pleased to support them by sharing our recipe with ChariTable Bookings."

LINE-CAUGHT HALIBUT with oyster dressing, caviar, charred lettuce and dittander

SERVES 2 | PREPARATION TIME 15 MINUTES | COOKING TIME 30 MINUTES

For the Dish

250g halibut loin

4 oysters

40g egg white, approx. 2 egg whites

1 pinch of salt

½ lemon, juiced

50g dittander, rocket will do as a replacement

200ml sunflower oil

1 little gem lettuce, or similar

10 sandwort tips

75ml water

75g butter

2 tsp caviar

salad shoots, to garnish, spicy ones if possible

To prepare the dish, skin, trim and portion the halibut. Shuck the oysters, remove all of the shell and grit, reserve the juices. Emulsify the oyster meat with the egg white with a hand blender until thick. Pass and add the reserved juices until saucing consistency is achieved. Finish with a little salt and lemon juice.

To make the dittander, blend the dittander with the oil in a food processor until it reaches 60°C, pass through muslin and cool instantly in the fridge.

To cook the halibut, season and cook the halibut in a non-stick frying pan with oil, start off quite hot then pull to the side and gently finish with foaming butter. Char the lettuce in a hot pan with a little oil until the edges start to crisp up, the stalk should remain juicy and crunchy. Cook the sandwort in a mix of butter and water for 10 seconds to gently heat through.

To serve, spoon the oyster dressing onto a warm plate, add the charred lettuce, halibut and sandwort. Next, spoon over the caviar – use sparingly as it is quite salty. Sprinkle the salad shoots over the top and drizzle the dittander dressing over everything.

STEVE TITMAN

" Leuka is the leading UK charity focused on research into finding a cure for blood cancer. All of us at The Summer Lodge support Leuka and are donating our slow cooked beef short rib dish to ChariTable Bookings to raise awareness for this great charity."

SLOW COOKED BEEF SHORT RIB with watercress, beer pickled onions and cheddar fritter

SERVES 4 | PREPARATION TIME 1 HOUR | COOKING TIME 12 HOURS

Equipment
sous vide and vacuum pack bags

For the Beef Ribs and Marinade
500g beef ribs, deboned
1 bottle of stout
1 sprig of thyme
2 cloves of garlic
35ml soy sauce
50g honey

For the Braising Sauce
2 shallots
5 button mushrooms
1 bottle of stout
100ml Madeira
200ml chicken stock

For the Pickled Onions
12 baby onions, peeled
100ml stout
125ml water
80ml white wine vinegar
35g sugar

For the Watercress Purée
2 bunches of watercress
salt

For the Cheddar Fritters
100g potato, mashed
50g mature cheddar
1 pinch of chopped chives
salt, to taste
flour, egg and breadcrumbs to panée

Combine all the marinade ingredients together and cover the beef. Leave for 24 hours, then remove the beef from the marinade and sear in a hot pan. Leave to cool.

To prepare the braising sauce, sweat the shallots and mushrooms, then add the 300ml of the previously made marinade, stout and Madeira and reduce until almost evaporated. Add the chicken stock and bring to a boil. Place the beef with the sauce in a vacuum bag and when cool, seal on full power and place in a water bath for 12 hours at 82°C, alternatively braise for 6–7 hours at 140°C.

To prepare the pickled onions, reduce the stout by half then add the remaining ingredients and bring to a boil. Pour over the baby onions and leave to cool. This can be done well in advance as the onions will improve over time.

To make the watercress purée, blanch the watercress in plenty of boiling, salted water for 3 minutes, then strain and refresh in ice water. Blend the watercress on high speed until a fine purée is achieved.

To prepare the fritters, combine the mashed potato with the cheese and chives and season to taste. Panée in breadcrumbs. These must then be deep fried just before serving.

To serve, place a spoonful of watercress purée in the middle of the plate. Place the beef rib in the centre of the plate and arrange the cheese fritters and pickled onions around. Finish with a spoonful or two of the beef sauce and a few watercress leaves to garnish.

CYRUS TODIWALA

As a chef, sourcing sustainable and well-cared for livestock is very important to me. The ethos of the RBST, and their commitment to the protection of our native species, is one that I personally share. I am happy to provide Café Spice Namasté's signature dish to ChariTable Bookings to help raise money for their great work."

CHICKEN CURRY with butternut squash, potato and rum

SERVES 6–8 | PREPARATION TIME 3 HOURS 30 MINUTES | COOKING TIME 1 HOUR

For the Marinade

¼ tsp ground turmeric

2 tsp ground coriander

1 tsp black mustard seeds

4 cloves of garlic, roughly chopped

2 fresh green chillies, coarsely chopped

1 tsp sea salt

ground pepper

For the Curry

6–8 chicken legs, with skin, chopped in half through the bone

4 tbsp vegetable oil

2 red onions, chopped

500g butternut squash, deseeded and cubed

2–3 large waxy potatoes, cut into 4cm pieces

400ml coconut milk, well shaken

500ml chicken stock

1 tbsp tamarind paste

3 bay leaves

2 tbsp dark rum

½ lime, juiced

1 tsp salt

½ tsp black pepper, freshly ground

To Serve

steamed rice

1 tbsp fresh coriander, chopped

To prepare the marinade, combine the ground turmeric and coriander, mustard seeds, garlic cloves, chillies and sea salt in a blender with a little water. Blitz to a smooth paste. Put the chicken in a bowl, rub in the salt and pepper, and stir in the marinade. Cover and refrigerate for at least 2–3 hours.

For the curry, heat half the oil in a large, heavy-based saucepan or flameproof casserole dish over a medium heat. Scrape the excess marinade off the chicken pieces and reserve for later. Sauté the meat for 3–4 minutes on each side, turning regularly until browned all over. Transfer to a plate and keep warm. Heat the remaining oil in the empty pan, then add the onions and sauté for about 6–8 minutes, or until soft.

Add the squash and potatoes and sauté for 5–7 minutes, stirring regularly, until just soft and pale golden brown in colour. Add the reserved marinade to the pan and stir well to coat the vegetables. Cook for another 3–4 minutes, stirring often, until the spices are fragrant.

Return the browned chicken to the pan and pour in the coconut milk and chicken stock. Add the tamarind paste a bit at a time, tasting as you go, then the bay leaves. Stir well and bring the mixture to the boil. Lower the heat and simmer until reasonably thick, then pour in the rum. Cover the pan and simmer for 20–30 minutes, or until the chicken is tender and the sauce has thickened. At that point, gently stir in the lime juice. Taste and adjust the seasoning as necessary.

Sprinkle with the chopped coriander. Serve with steamed or boiled rice.

STEPHEN TOMAN

While all charities are great, I believe in supporting those close to home which is why Ox Belfast is championing Children's Heartbeat Trust, the Northern Irish charity looking after kids with heart disease. Great book by ChariTable Bookings raising awareness for so many charities."

HALIBUT with curry, Romanesco, bergamot and oyster leaf

SERVES 4 | PREPARATION TIME 15 MINUTES | COOKING TIME 45 MINUTES

For the Halibut
4 x 120g pieces of halibut, skin on

For the Sauce
450g halibut bones
250ml vin jaune
2l filtered water
300ml cream
salt
lemon
30g butter

For the Curry
50g butter
1 bulb of fennel
½ medium onion
1 tbsp good quality curry powder
1 unwaxed lemon, zest only
200ml water

For the Bergamot Oil
200ml rapeseed oil
bergamot rind from 1–2 bergamots

To Serve
1 Romanesco, cut into small florets
12 oyster leaves

To prepare the sauce, cover the bones in water and bring to a simmer for 30–40 minutes. Sieve the liquid and reduce to a quarter. Add the wine and return to the boil. Add cream and reduce by half again. Season with salt and lemon juice. Add the butter and keep hot.

To prepare the curry, finely slice the fennel and onion. Melt the butter in a pan on medium heat. Add the fennel and onion to the pan and sweat until soft. Add the curry powder, then stir for a few minutes on the heat to release its aroma. Add the water, bring to the boil, then stir in the lemon zest. Simmer for 15 minutes, then remove from the heat. Purée in a blender and add salt to taste. Keep in a warm place until needed.

To prepare the bergamot oil, heat the rapeseed oil to 80°C in a pan over a gentle heat, then add the bergamot rind. Remove from the heat, cover with cling film and allow to infuse for 30 minutes. Sieve the oil into a squeezy bottle.

To finish and serve, cook the Romanesco in salted, boiling water until tender, for 3–4 minutes. Cook the fish in a hot pan, skin-side down. Turn over and finish in a hot oven at 160°C for 3–4 minutes. Rest in a warm place for another 3–4 minutes. Peel off the skin and sprinkle with salt. Place on a hot plate. Spoon curry on to the plate. Garnish with hot Romanesco and oyster leaves. Drizzle with bergamot oil. Foam the sauce using a hand blender and spoon on to the fish.

BARRY TONKS

I'm supporting the continuous great work that Cancer Research does in fighting this horrible illness by sharing Searcy's recipe with ChariTable Bookings. Enjoy, and I hope you think of others while doing so!"

ROAST LOIN OF DENHAM ESTATE VENISON with pumpkin purée, confit cabbage, braised chestnuts, blackberries and chocolate

SERVES 4 | PREPARATION TIME 45 MINUTES | COOKING TIME 2 HOURS

For the Venison
- 4 x 150g venison loin portions
- 1 tbsp olive oil
- 50g unsalted butter
- garlic, thyme, bay leaves, to season
- salt and pepper, to taste

For the Venison Sauce
- 5kg venison bones, chopped small
- 100ml olive oil
- 500g mirepoix
- 500g button mushrooms, sliced
- thyme, bay leaves, to season
- 1 stick of cinnamon
- 5 juniper berries
- 3 oranges, zested
- ½ bottle of Armagnac
- 1 bottle of port
- ½ jar of redcurrant jelly
- 5l chicken stock
- 250ml glace de viande

For the Confit Cabbage
- 1 savoy cabbage
- 1 onion
- 1 carrot
- 50ml duck fat
- 1 clove of garlic, crushed
- thyme, bay leaves, to season
- salt and pepper, to taste

To make the venison sauce, roast the venison bones in a hot pan with olive oil. When the venison bones are caramelised and roasted all over, remove from the pan. In the same pan, add the vegetable mirepoix, the button mushrooms, aromatics, cinnamon stick, juniper berries and orange zest, and begin to caramelise the mixture. Once caramelised, add the venison bones back in the pan. De-glaze the pan with Armagnac and port, then add the redcurrant jelly, chicken stock and glace de viande. Bring to the boil and simmer for 2 hours, skimming constantly. After 2 hours, pass through muslin cloth into a clean pan and reduce on a high heat until a desired consistency is reached.

To make the confit cabbage, peel and cut the onion and carrot into a small dice. Cut the cabbage into four, removing the outer leaves and coarse inner stalk, then finely shred the leaves. Blanch and refresh the shredded leaves in ice water. In a pan, sweat the onion, carrot and 1 crushed garlic clove in duck fat with the aromatics. Add the cabbage and season to taste. Once the cabbage is cooked, check the seasoning again and adjust to taste.

To make the pumpkin purée, quarter the butternut squash and remove the seeds. Wrap in tin foil and roast in an oven for an hour at 200°C. Remove the tin foil, scoop out the flesh of the butternut squash and discard the skin. Place the mixture into a blender and purée until silky smooth, gradually adding diced butter until a purée consistency is reached.

To make the braised chestnuts, in a pan, sweat the shallots, garlic, thyme and bay leaf with the olive oil. Add the chicken stock and celery and simmer gently for 30 minutes. Pass the celery stock through a fine chinois into a clean pan. Add the chestnuts and butter and reduce the stock so it glazes the chestnuts.

To make the poached blackberries, mix the stock syrup and crème de mûre in a pan. Bring to the boil, then remove from the heat. Add the blackberries and leave to poach until service.

For the Pumpkin Purée

1 butternut squash
50g unsalted butter, diced

For the Braised Chestnuts

100g shallots, peeled and sliced
garlic, thyme, 1 bay leaf, to season
50ml olive oil
500ml chicken stock
1 celery head, small dice
12 chestnuts
50g unsalted butter

For the Poached Blackberries

12 blackberries
200ml stock syrup
100ml crème de mûre

To Serve

1 tbsp pumpkin seed oil
2 tbsp roasted pumpkin seeds
Maldon sea salt, to taste

To cook the venison and serve, season the loin with salt and pepper. Heat a sauté pan, add olive oil and brown the venison, turning it until evenly caramelised. Add butter gradually, allowing it to foam, then add the aromatics. Spoon the butter and aromatics mixture over the venison, gradually basting the meat. This should take 5 minutes. Transfer the venison to a warm plate and allow to rest. Reheat all the other ingredients. Spoon and swipe the pumpkin purée on each serving plate. Scatter the braised chestnuts and poached blackberries, spoon the confit cabbage into a round pastry cutter, carefully removing the cutter once done. Place the venison atop the confit cabbage. Reheat the venison sauce, pass through a small strainer and sauce over and around the venison. Sprinkle with some Maldon salt, garnish with pumpkin oil and roasted pumpkin seeds, and serve.

JOHN TOPHAM

"Where else can you find 365 chefs together for great causes? This is a great idea by ChariTable Bookings and I am championing Leuka, the leading blood cancer charity, for their incredible work."

RACK OF LAMB with haggis and confit shoulder

SERVES 4 | PREPARATION TIME 20 MINUTES (PLUS OVERNIGHT TO CONFIT AND OVERNIGHT TO PRESS) | COOKING TIME 40 MINUTES

For the Lamb
1 lamb shoulder, deboned
1.1l duck fat
5g parsley
salt and pepper, to taste
8 bones rack of lamb, French trimmed

For the Herb Crumb
20g thyme
20g rosemary
15g parsley
100g panko breadcrumbs

For the Pea Purée
½ block of butter
50ml water
300g peas

For the Haggis
4 x 30g haggis
4 courgettes

To prepare the dish, confit the lamb shoulder overnight in duck fat at 90°C. Remove from the fat, pick off the meat, mix with some of the parsley and season to taste. Place the mix into a tray, add 100ml of duck fat and press overnight.

Make a herb crumb by blending together the remaining parsley, thyme and rosemary together with the panko breadcrumbs.

Bring the butter and 50ml water to the boil, add the peas and blend. Pass through a fine sieve and season to taste.

Wrap each portion of the haggis in courgette ribbons, portion the leftover courgettes and set aside.

To cook the lamb, roast the rack of lamb, 2 bones per person, for 10 minutes at 180°C. Once cooked, coat in the herb crumb. Roast the shoulder and haggis for 5 minutes.

To serve, plate as pictured.

KENTARO TORII

" This dish from Bella Cosa is lovingly provided to ChariTable Bookings in support of the Children With Cancer charity."

WAGYU with mushroom, cauliflower, carrot, and black garlic bagna cauda
SERVES 2 | PREPARATION TIME 30 MINUTES (PLUS OVERNIGHT TO MARINATE) | COOKING TIME 30 MINUTES

Equipment
  food processor
For the Dish
  2 x 120g pieces Wagyu Beef
  4 pieces of cauliflower, blanched
  4 slices of fresh cauliflower
  4 pieces of baby carrots, blanched
  4 porcini mushrooms
  10 pieces of girolle mushrooms
  fennel flowers
  8 pieces of butterfly sorrel
  Maldon salt
  extra virgin olive oil
For the Glaze
  50ml red wine
  40ml balsamic vinegar
  40ml veal jus
  20g honey
  1 sprig of rosemary
  5 black peppercorns
For the Black Garlic Bagna Cauda
  25g garlic
  25g black garlic
  25g brown anchovy
  50ml grapeseed oil
  5ml Saba, grape must
  45ml water
For the Pickled Carrots
  50g orange or yellow carrots
  25ml white balsamic vinegar
  salt

To make the glaze, put the red wine, balsamic vinegar, veal jus in a pot together with the honey, rosemary and black peppercorn. Bring it to boil and reduce by half.

For the bagna cauda, peel and cut the garlic and black garlic in half. Put in a pot with cold water. Cover and cook on a high heat. Strain the garlic once the water has boiled. Repeat this method 4–5 times until the garlic is completely cooked. Blend the cooked garlic and the anchovy, grapeseed oil and saba with a high speed blender, making a smooth purée.

To prepare the pickled carrots, slice them with a peeler, sprinkle with salt and dry up the excess water with kitchen paper. Vacuum pack with white balsamic vinegar, marinate for at least 3 hours or overnight if possible.

To prepare the beef, season the wagyu with salt and olive oil. Cook it over a high heat on a grill or iron pan. Heat up the glaze in a separate pan. Glaze the grilled wagyu for 2–3 minutes until the sauce is thickened and the beef is cooked to the desired temperature. Rest it for 3–4 minutes in a warm place.

To serve, grill the blanched baby carrot, blanched cauliflower and mushrooms. Season with salt and extra virgin olive oil. Plate the pickled carrot, grilled cauliflower, baby carrot and mushrooms. Garnish with fennel flower, butterfly sorrel, sliced fresh cauliflower and black bagna cauda. Cut the beef in half and plate, sprinkle with Maldon salt.

DAVE TREWIN

Children's Hospice South West does incredible work for life-limited children and their families and I'm very happy to support them on behalf of the team at Samphire Bistro in this ChariTable Bookings recipe book."

TRIO OF CORNISH FISH with chorizo, tomato and butterbean stew, and potato griddle cake

SERVES 4 | PREPARATION TIME 30 MINUTES | COOKING TIME 1 HOUR

For the Tomato and Butterbean Stew

200g chorizo, diced

½ tbsp olive oil

1 red onion, finely chopped

2 cloves of garlic, chopped

2 sprigs of rosemary, leaves picked

400g tin butterbeans, drained

1kg tomatoes, cut into 8, cores removed

300ml chicken stock

200g spinach

2 tbsp flat leaf parsley, chopped

seasoning, to taste

For the Potato Griddle Cakes

250g mashed potatoes

1 tsp baking powder

100g plain flour

salt and freshly ground black pepper

1 tbsp fresh thyme

2 tbsp vegetable oil

For the Fish

2 monkfish tails, fillted, trimmed and halved

2 small haddock, filleted, descaled and pin boned

2 sole, filleted and split down the middle

salt and pepper

oil, for frying

To Serve

200g French beans, trimmed

1 tbsp butter

200g spring greens, sliced

1 spritz of lemon

parsley, chopped

To make the tomato and butterbean stew, fry the chorizo in olive oil over a medium heat in a large saucepan for 2–3 minutes. Add the onion and cook for 10 minutes, adding the garlic and rosemary for the final 2 minutes. Stir in the butterbeans, tomatoes and stock. Bring to a gentle simmer, then cover and cook for 10 minutes until thickened. Stir in the spinach and parsley until the spinach is just wilted. Season to taste.

To make the potato and griddle cakes, mix all the ingredients together in a bowl until well combined, then shape the potato mixture into 8 patties. Heat the oil in a frying pan and fry the patties for 3 to 4 minutes on each side, or until crisp and golden brown on both sides.

To cook the fish, heat 3 frying pans with a little oil. Season the fish with salt and pepper. Place the 4 pieces of monkfish into the first pan, followed by the haddock skin-side down into the second, and cook for about 3–4 minutes. Turn over the monkfish, now add the sole skin-side down in the third pan and cook for a further 3–5 minutes. Turn over the sole and haddock, then remove all 3 pans from the heat.

To serve, cook the French beans in a pan with a little water and butter for 3 minutes adding the spring greens halfway through. Arrange the stew, vegetables and potato cakes onto the plates. Stack the fish on top and finish with a squeeze of lemon and a sprinkle of parsley.

MARCELLO TULLY

Very happy to donate this dish from Kinloch Lodge to ChariTable Bookings in aid of the NSPCC. I hope this great book raises lots of funds for this great charity!"

DUCK BREAST AND WILTED SPINACH with orange, tomato and chilli dressing

SERVES 2 | PREPARATION TIME 30 MINUTES | COOKING TIME 45 MINUTES

For the Duck

1 duck breast, with skin on

salt and pepper

For the Orange, Tomato and Chilli Dressing

20g fresh ginger, finely chopped

2 cloves of garlic, finely chopped

10g red chilli, finely chopped

10g green chilli, finely chopped

2 oranges, juice and zest

2 tbsp cornflour, diluted with a little cold water

10g caster sugar

1 pinch of salt

1 dash of Tabasco

50g tomato concasse

For the Wilted Spinach

20ml sunflower oil

200g baby leaf spinach

salt and black pepper

To prepare the duck breast, remove any fatty sinews and score the skin. Heat a heavy-based frying pan, without any oil, and put the duck breast in, skin-side down. Fry until the skin renders and turns to a golden brown. Turn the breast over and place in a preheated oven at 180°C for 2 minutes. Take out and turn over, then return to the oven for a further 1 minute. Allow the duck breast to rest for 3 minutes in a warm place, then carve into thin slices.

For the dressing, sweat the ginger, garlic and chillies for 2–3 minutes. Add the orange juice and zest, and bring to the boil. Whilst the liquid is boiling, add the cornflour and whisk in thoroughly. Add the caster sugar, salt and Tabasco, and mix. Remove from the stove. Add the tomato concasse, stir and serve.

To make the wilted spinach, heat the oil in a heavy based pan, add the spinach and turn with a large spoon. Remove from the pan as soon as the spinach starts to wilt, this should take approximately 30 seconds to 1 minute.

Serve the duck slices on a bed of wilted spinach and drizzle with the sauce.

STEFANO TURCONI

We love this idea! What better way to give back to Cancer Research than by simply buying this unique ChariTable Bookings' recipe book. I very much hope you enjoy making our Franco's Italian speciality for many years to come."

PORCINI MUSHROOM RISOTTO

SERVES 1 | PREPARATION TIME 15 MINUTES | COOKING TIME 30 MINUTES

For the Risotto

80g carnaroli rice

10g dried porcini mushrooms

30g butter

30g Parmesan

½ onion, finely chopped

½ glass of white wine

1l vegetable stock

10 parsley leaves

1 pinch of salt

To make the risotto, soak the dried porcini mushrooms in cold water for 10 minutes. While the mushrooms soak, finely chop the onion. Lightly toast the rice in a pan for 3 minutes on a medium heat, with half the butter and the chopped onion. Add the white wine and stir together.

When the wine has evaporated, add the porcini mushrooms and slowly ladle in the vegetable stock, continue to do so for 15 minutes. Once the rice is cooked through, add the remaining butter along with the parsley and Parmesan and mix together.

Season with salt and leave to rest for 1 minute to allow the dish to thicken, then serve.

ANDREW TURNBULL

Cancer doesn't differentiate and at Inverlochy Castle we are pleased to help ChariTable Bookings and Macmillan to take the battle straight to the source."

STUFFED SADDLE OF RABBIT with rabbit pie, carrots and garden turnips

SERVES 4 | PREPARATION TIME 45 MINUTES | COOKING TIME 30 MINUTES

For the Stuffed Rabbit Saddle
2 rabbit loins with the belly attached
100g chicken mousse
50g mushroom duxelle
10g chives, chopped
5g tarragon, chopped
5g shallots, brunoise
3 slices of Parma ham
1 drizzle of oil
1 knob of butter

For the Rabbit Pie
100g puff pastry
120g rabbit leg and kidney, braised
egg wash

For the Date Purée
250g dates, pitted and dried
orange juice, to cover
hot water, for blitzing

For the Carrot Cooking Liquor
2 large carrots, peeled and quartered
500ml water
375g caster sugar
10 star anise
125g butter

For the Turnip Cooking Liquor
2 turnips, sliced
250ml white chicken stock
25ml extra virgin olive oil
25g caster sugar

To make the stuffed rabbit saddle, mix the chicken mousse, duxelle, chives, tarragon and shallots together. Lay out the rabbit with the belly flat and the loin on top. Pipe the mousse mix along the belly next to the loin and roll tightly. Lay the Parma ham down next to each other and wrap around the rabbit. Roll in cling film and tie off the ends, place in a pan of boiling water for 20 minutes. Remove from the water, remove the cling film and dry off on a cloth. Place into a hot pan with oil and butter, and baste until golden brown all over.

To make the rabbit pie, cut out eight 5cm discs of puff pastry, place 30g of braised rabbit mix on the bottom of four. Lightly wet the edges, then place the lids on top, sealing all sides. Egg wash and bake in a preheated oven at 180°C for 12 minutes.

To make the date purée, place all of the ingredients into a pan and boil until cooked. Once cooked, blend until smooth and pass through a fine sieve.

To make the carrot cooking liquor, cook the carrots in the water, sugar, star anise and butter. Once the carrots are cooked, reduce the liquid to a glaze and use to reheat the carrots.

To make the turnip cooking liquor, cook the sliced turnips in the stock, oil, sugar, salt and lemon juice for 5 minutes until tender.

To make the carrot reduction, reduce the carrot juice by two thirds and whisk in the butter to thicken.

To serve, place a swipe of date purée across the plate. Cut the rabbit into pieces and place along the purée with the carrots, pie and turnips. Finish with the turnip tops, carrot reduction and a little jus.

For the Turnip Cooking Liquor *continued*
    8g salt
    ½ lemon, juiced
For the Carrot Reduction
    125ml carrot juice
    25g butter
For the Garnish
    turnip tops
    rabbit sauce or jus

ANDREW TURNER

"What a great opportunity to share Alfred's signature sea bass dish in memory of a fellow chef and his charity, the John King Brain Tumour Foundation. ChariTable Bookings has come up with a fantastic solution to combine great food and charity awareness."

LINE-CAUGHT SEA BASS FILLET with red pepper purée, young fennel and smoked olive oil

SERVES 10 | PREPARATION TIME 15 MINUTES (PLUS 27 HOURS SMOKING AND CONFIT) | COOKING TIME 25 MINUTES

Special Equipment
sous vide and vacuum pack bags
smoker

For the Sea Bass
5 x 1kg (approx) whole line-caught
Atlantic sea bass, filleted and pin
boned to yield 10 x 140g fillets
olive oil
1 pinch of rock salt
fennel pollen, to dust

For the Smoked Olive Oil and Fennel
1l premier quality olive oil
200g hickory saw dust
1kg fennel trimmings

For the Piquillo Pepper Purée
700g piquillo pepper, finely chopped
200g white onion, finely chopped
80ml virgin olive oil
50ml tomato purée
500ml white wine
2 cloves of garlic, finely chopped
½ tsp thyme
1l chicken stock
salt and pepper, to taste

For the Garnish
300g fennel confit, diced
100g black olive cheeks – thinly
sliced outer curves of olives
½ bunch of dill, picked
1 handful of picked basil cress, picked

To prepare the oil and fennel confit, trim and discard the leaves from the fennel, vacuum pack and cook sous vide on a low heat for 24 hours. Remove from the bag and place the olive oil and fennel into a suitable airtight container. Make a small hole the size of the smoking nozzle and using the hickory, smoke the mixture three times until the wood is fully burnt. Cover the hole and leave to infuse for 3–4 hours. Once done, pass the oil off and reserve for serving.

To make the piquillo pepper dressing, sweat the chopped red pepper, onion and garlic until soft, without colour. Add the tomato purée and cook out. Add the wine and stock, then cook on a high heat until all the liquid has almost evaporated. Add the thyme and blend the mixture in a liquidiser until smooth. Adjust seasoning to taste. .

To prepare the fish, vacuum seal it with a touch of olive oil and cook sous vide for 10–12 minutes at 50°C. Remove the fish, pat dry and flash fry until golden. Finish with rock salt and fennel pollen.

To prepare the garnish, carefully mix the diced fennel with the olive cheeks, picked dill and basil, diced tomatoes, salt and pepper.

To serve, place the garnish on a bed of red pepper purée, set the fish on top, and sprinkle with the smoked olive oil.

For the Garnish *continued*
300g plum vine tomatoes, diced and
blanched
1 pinch of salt and pepper
1 tsp olive oil pearls, per plate

BRIAN TURNER CBE

With my recipe in the ChariTable Bookings' Signature Dish book, I am delighted to champion the great work carried out by Anthony Nolan, who match incredible individuals willing to donate their blood, stem cells, or bone marrow to those desperately needing transplants. As a supporter I have seen how a simple act or gesture can make such a difference to so many people."

ROAST SPICED FILLET OF VEAL with Provençal vegetables and Madeira sauce
SERVES 4 | PREPARATION TIME 30 MINUTES | COOKING TIME 30 MINUTES

For the Veal
800g centre cut veal fillet
2 tbsp rapeseed oil

For the Rub
2 tbsp fennel seeds
1 tbsp black peppercorns
1 tbsp sea salt
1 tsp garlic powder
½ tsp ground cumin
1 tsp smoked paprika

For the Provençal Vegetables
1 tbsp oil
2 tbsp each courgette, carrot, shallot and red pepper, finely diced
1 tbsp parsley, chopped
1 tbsp garlic, finely chopped
salt and pepper, to taste

For the Madeira Sauce
1 shallot, chopped
4 tbsp Madeira
1 tbsp dry white wine
300ml chicken stock
100g cold butter, plus a knob of butter
salt and pepper

To prepare the rub, heat the fennel seeds in a dry pan for 2 minutes and grind in a mortar with a pestle together with the peppercorns and salt until fine. Add the garlic powder, cumin and paprika, and mix well.

To prepare the veal, heat the rapeseed oil in a pan. Colour and sear the outside of the veal. Once nicely coloured, allow to rest and cool. Once well rested, sprinkle over the aromatics and rub into the meat. Allow to rest and heat an oven to 180°C. Place the veal on a roasting tray and cook until pink, approximately 10–15 minutes. Remove and rest again.

To prepare the Provençal vegetables, heat the oil and gently cook the finely diced vegetables to keep colour and crispness. Season and allow to drain.

To make the Madeira sauce, heat a knob of butter and gently cook the chopped shallot. Add the Madeira and reduce by half, then add the white wine. Simmer for a few minutes and add the chicken stock. Reduce by half again and beat in the cold butter with a little seasoning.

To serve, cut a medallion of veal, spoon a little sauce around and top with the vegetables.

JEFF TYLER

"ChariTable Bookings have provided an incredible resource that has created another opportunity for Novikov to support Parkinson's UK."

KING CRAB LEG with wasabi gratin

SERVES 1 | PREPARATION TIME 20 MINUTES (PLUS DEFROSTING TIME) | COOKING TIME 15 MINUTES

For the Crab
1 pre-steamed frozen king crab leg, defrosted

For the Wasabi Gratin
90ml mayonnaise
25ml Greek style yoghurt
10g wasabi paste
1 squeeze of lemon juice
salt, to taste

For the Garnish
grated daikon
lime wedges

Preheat the oven grill to 200°C.

To prepare the king crab leg, starting at the base of the leg where the flesh is exposed, take a pair of scissors and carefully cut the white part of the shell lengthways, all along right up to the tip. Do this on both sides. Next peel off the white shell, so that you are left with the flesh exposed. This is where you will put the gratin.

To prepare the gratin, mix everything together and adjust the salt to your taste. Remember that the king crab is quite salty so you will not need to add too much extra.

Spoon your wasabi gratin mix generously onto the leg, taking care not to spill over the sides of the shell. Place under the grill and cook until golden brown and bubbling.

Place on the plate and garnish with the grated daikon and lime. Serve hot.

IGOR TYMCHYSHYN

" I love the idea of sharing recipes while raising awareness for Cancer Research at the same time. The team at Orrery want to share our Tournedos Rossini with ChariTable Bookings and support the fight against cancer."

TOURNEDOS ROSSINI with sauce Périgourdine

SERVES 4 | PREPARATION TIME 45 MINUTES | COOKING TIME 2 HOURS 30 MINUTES

For the Beef
4 x 200g beef fillet
salt and pepper
50g butter

For the Celeriac Purée
1 celeriac
200ml full-fat milk
200ml double cream
1 pinch of salt

For the Shallots
6 banana shallots, peeled
20g butter
1 bay leaf
1 sprig of thyme
150ml chicken stock
salt and pepper
5g icing sugar

For the Sauce Périgourdine
6 chicken legs
½ bottle of Madeira
850ml chicken stock
1l veal stock
100g butter
20g Perigourd truffles, chopped

For the Ceps
2 large ceps, halved
30g butter

To Serve
4 x 50g foie gras
4 thin brioche slices

Season the fillet with salt and pepper and sear with 50g of butter all the way around, place it in the oven to cook at 220°C for 10 minutes. Remove and leave to rest for 5–8 minutes before serving.

Remove the outer skin of the celeriac and chop in to small pieces. Place in a pan, add milk, cream and salt and cook slowly until the celeriac is very soft. Drain in a colander, put in a blender and blitz for around 2 minutes or until smooth.

Add the shallots, 10g of butter, herbs, stock and seasoning to a saucepan and cook very slowly for 15 minutes. Take the shallots out of the chicken stock and cut them in halves, lengthways. Dust them with icing sugar, add the remaining butter and caramelise in a pan until golden.

To make the sauce Périgourdine, sear the chicken legs in a pan, colouring well on both sides. Deglaze the pan with the Madeira, reduce by half and add the chicken and veal stock. Cook for 1 hour, then pass the cooking liquid through a muslin cloth. Whisk in the butter, add the chopped truffles and cook the liquid for a further 10 minutes.

Brown the cep halves in a knob of butter and set aside.

For the brioche toast, preheat the oven to 150°C. Cook the brioche between two flat trays for around 20 minutes, or until crispy.

On each plate, add 2 tablespoons of celeriac purée, slightly off centre. Put the beef tournedos in the middle and cap each with a cep half. Place a shallot half next to the fillet and top with a piece of foie gras. Pour hot sauce over the fillet and lean one crispy brioche against its side.

ALEX TYNDALL

Wheeler's of St James' are proud to stand along side ChariTable Bookings in support of Great Ormond Street Children's Hospital."

RAGU OF VEGETABLES AND PULSES with a smoked oyster dressing

SERVES 4 | PREPARATION TIME 30 MINUTES | COOKING TIME 3+ HOURS

For the Ragu
2 medium onions, finely chopped
½ bulb of garlic, or a few wild garlic
leaves if in season
1 tbsp rosemary and thyme, finely
chopped
1 small swede, diced
1 small celeriac, diced
500ml vegetable stock
1l passata
2 romano peppers, diced
300g pinto and borlotti beans
1 handful of roasted chestnuts,
chopped
50ml olive oil
½ bunch each of parsley, tarragon,
coriander and basil
salt and pepper, to taste

For the Smoked Oyster Dressing
3 banana shallots, brunoise
2 cloves of garlic, brunoise
50g smoked oysters, chopped
50g roast chestnuts, chopped
15ml merlot vinegar
30ml olive oil
lemon, few drops to taste

To Serve
8 slices of good quality rustic loaf

To make the ragu, sweat the onions and garlic together. Add the hard herbs and diced vegetables. Cook together until the moisture has totally gone and then add the vegetable stock. Bring to a simmer, then add the passata and chopped peppers. At this point, put the mixture into a slow cooker with the beans and leave to cook out for at least 3 hours, stirring occasionally. Thirty minutes before serving, stir in the roasted chestnuts, half of the olive oil and some of the herbs, reserving a little for the dressing.

To make the dressing, in a little oil, soften the shallots and garlic on a low heat. Stir in the oysters, chestnuts and remaining herbs. Mix in the oil and vinegar, and season to taste. Just before serving, add a few drops of lemon juice to give it freshness.

Serve the ragu with toasted slices of a good quality rustic loaf, such as bread made with cheddar and beer. The oyster dressing gives a wonderful smokiness if added just before serving, or can be left in a small dish on the side.

JAMES TYRRELL

Scope works incredibly hard to give people in the UK with disability the same opportunities as the rest of us. Thank you ChariTable Bookings for letting me and the team at L'Escargot support them in your book."

CHILLI CRAB ON TOAST
SERVES 4 | PREPARATION TIME 45 MINUTES | COOKING TIME 20 MINUTES

For the Crab On Toast
1 whole cooked crab
100g crème fraîche
1½ limes, juiced
¼ bunch of flat parsley
¼ bunch of dill
¼ bunch of chives
1 large red chilli, medium heat
1 pinch of salt
1 piece of baby fennel, shaved
1 spring onion, sliced
¼ bunch of breakfast radish, sliced
4 slices of good quality sourdough bread
olive oil

For the Pickled Cucumber
1 cucumber
100ml white wine vinegar
10 whole peppercorns
100ml water
50g sugar

For the Garnish
2 limes, halved
fresh parsley and dill, to taste

To make the pickled cucumber, create a pickling liquor by combining white wine vinegar, peppercorns, water and sugar. Bring to simmer and remove from the heat. Peel the cucumber into long ribbons removing the dark green skin. Once the pickling liquor is cool, add the cucumber and leave for 20 minutes.

To prepare the crab, crack open the crab and separate the white and brown meat, ensuring there is no shell in the meat. Mix brown crab meat with crème fraîche, juice of 1 lime, half the chopped parsley, dill and chives, and chopped chilli. Season the white crab meat with a pinch of salt and pepper and the juice of half a lime. Add the rest of the parsley, dill, and chives, add the shaved baby fennel, sliced spring onion and sliced breakfast radish.

To assemble the dish, toast four slices of sourdough bread until golden brown with a little olive oil. Take the brown crab meat and place on the sour dough, then add the white crab meat and shaved fennel. Garnish with some torn parsley, dill, pickled cucumber ribbons and half a lime each.

BARRY VERA

Cancer is the biggest child killer in the UK. Children with Cancer is a wonderful charity that raises awareness, funds, research and supports families throughout the UK. STK London is thrilled to be able to take part in ChariTable Bookings' latest venture and support them."

PARMESAN BAKED SCALLOPS

SERVES 6 | PREPARATION TIME 10 MINUTES | COOKING TIME 12 MINUTES

For the Scallops

24 scallops, cleaned

24 scallop shells, fishmongers will be able to get these for you easily and you can wash them and use again

200g herb butter

300g Parmesan, finely grated

1 handful of Italian parsley leaves, finely chopped

100-120ml soy sauce

3 limes, halved

For the Herb Butter

500g soft butter

20g shallots, finely chopped

7 cloves of garlic, minced

½ bunch of flat leaf parsley, finely chopped

½ bunch of tarragon, finely chopped

1 tbsp cornichons, finely chopped

2 tbsp capers, finely chopped

2 tsp fine salt

½ tsp freshly ground black pepper

1 lemon, juiced and zested

75ml Pernod

Preheat the oven to 220°C.

To make the herb butter, place the butter in a mixer with a paddle or whisk attachment and whip until the butter is almost white. Remove, put in a mixing bowl and fold in all remaining ingredients until thoroughly and evenly mixed. Place to one side.

Take each scallop, wash well and place on a cloth to absorb excess water. Make sure the shells are washed and dry. Place about a teaspoon of the soft herb butter in the centre of each shell. Then place the scallop meat over the butter and push down so the butter forms around each scallop. Mix the Parmesan and parsley together and cover the scallop meat evenly. Drizzle about 1 teaspoon of soy sauce over each scallop. Place in the oven and cook until they are golden brown, 10–12 minutes. The scallops must be tender and not overcooked.

To serve, place 4 scallops per plate, with half a lime each. Accompany with a glass of white wine, great artisan bread and a simple dressed salad.

Editor's Note: *The quantities for the herb butter will make more than the 200g required for this recipe. You can keep the remaining amount in the fridge for another dish.*

JÁNOS VERES

A great opportunity to raise awareness in many charities while learning about great food at the same time. I have chosen Project Aware, a global network of divers trying to protect our oceans and the wildlife within them. Naturally I've donated a fish recipe to ChariTable Bookings for you to enjoy!"

WHOLE FILLETED PLAICE with girolles, brown shrimps, cucumber and lemon sorrel

SERVES 4 | PREPARATION TIME 30 MINUTES (PLUS 48 HOURS TO PICKLE AND 4 HOURS TO GLUE) | COOKING TIME 1 HOUR

For the Whole Plaice

1 whole plaice, filleted into
4 x 130–150g loin and belly fillets
Activa meat glue
1¼ tsp garlic butter
¾ tsp lemon juice
Maldon salt and ground black pepper
¼ tsp kombu, chopped

For the Pickled Dulse

1.8l water
360ml Chardonnay vinegar
180ml white soy
100g dried dulse
24g each white caster sugar and salt

For the Pickled Lemon

450ml water
300ml white wine vinegar
150g white caster sugar
3 unwaxed lemons

For the Pickled Cucumber

50g white caster sugar
100ml white wine vinegar
150ml water
400g cucumber, peeled and thinly
sliced lengthways

For the Wholegrain Mustard Cream

50g unsalted butter
10ml olive oil
200g shallots, peeled and finely chopped
40g fennel, thinly sliced
1l white wine
2l fish stock
500ml double cream
1 tbsp Pommery mustard, or to taste

For the Girolles

200g girolles
1¼ tsp clarified butter
10g pickled dulse
½ tsp pickled lemon
30g brown shrimp
1¼ tsp pickled cucumber
¼ tsp chopped dill

To Garnish

¼ tsp chopped lemon sorrel

With a sharp, thin-bladed knife, remove all 4 fillets from the plaice, or ask your fishmonger to do this for you. Discard the bones. Using Activa meat glue, attach each of the loin fillets to the bone side each of the belly fillets, being careful not to apply too much Activa. Gently wrap each fillet in cling film and place onto a metal tray. Put into the fridge for a minimum of 4 hours to allow the Activa to fully set.

In a pan, heat the water, Chardonnay vinegar and white soy. Add the sugar and salt, then stir until dissolved. Remove from the heat and place it into a shallow container, allow to cool completely. Thoroughly wash the dried dulse in cold running water to remove any sand. Leave the dulse to stand for 10 minutes in the cold water. Using a fine sieve, strain the dulse and leave to drain. Add the dulse to the cooled pickling liquid. The ratio should be 1 part dulse to half a part of pickling liquid. Place in an airtight container in the fridge for 48 hours.

Heat the water and vinegar in a pan, then add the sugar and stir until dissolved. Remove from the heat, place in a shallow container and allow to cool. Using a slicer or mandoline, slice the lemons into 1.5mm thick slices. Place the lemons in an airtight container. Add the pickling liquid and place in the fridge until needed.

Place all the ingredients, except the cucumber, into a small pan over a medium heat. Whisk until the sugar has dissolved and remove from the heat. Pour the warm liquid into a shallow container and allow to cool completely. Place the cucumber into an air tight container, add the pickling liquid, seal and place in the fridge.

Melt the butter and olive oil in a saucepan over medium heat. Add the shallots and fennel and sweat without colouring. Pour in the white wine and gently reduce the liquid by half. Once reduced, add the fish stock and reduce by half again. Pass the sauce through a fine sieve then blitz in a blender until the sauce has fully emulsified. Pour in the double cream, simmer until it thickens, then add the wholegrain mustard to taste.

Clean the girolles by submerging in cold water and draining twice. Place the mushrooms on a tray lined with kitchen paper and leave to dry. Once the mushrooms are dry, cut into quarters. Weigh out 50g of mushroom per fillet of plaice.

To finish, put the plaice on a hot-plate and cook until golden in colour, approximately 5–6 minutes. Use a food thermometer to check the internal temperature of the fish is around 38–42°C. Finish with garlic butter, lemon juice, Maldon salt, freshly ground black pepper and kombu. Cook the girolles in the clarified butter. Add the pickled dulse, pickled lemon and the brown shrimps, allow to warm through. Finish it by adding the pickled cucumber and the chopped dill.

To serve, pour the mustard sauce in the bottom of a bowl. Add the mixture of girolles, pickled dulse, pickled lemon, brown shrimps, pickled cucumber and dill in the middle of the plate. Gently set the plaice on top of the mixture and finish it with lemon sorrel.

SIMON WADHAM

ChariTable Bookings' new signature dish initiative is a fantastic way to raise vital funds for charity while sharing the UK's great recipes. Rivington Greenwich is encouraging readers to back the great work of Cancer Research UK and enjoy our Newlyn cod!"

RIVINGTON GRILL'S NEWLYN COD with crispy bacon, lovage and peas

SERVES 4 | PREPARATION TIME 15 MINUTES | COOKING TIME 40 MINUTES

For the Cod

4 x 180g cod fillets, skin on
200g fresh peas, podded
extra virgin olive oil, for cooking
1 shallot, finely diced
120g streaky bacon or pancetta, cut into 1cm strips
50ml white wine
1 head little gem lettuce, finely shredded
10 lovage leaves, roughly chopped
70g unsalted butter, chilled and diced
salt and freshly ground black pepper
½ lemon, juiced

To prepare the dish, bring a saucepan of water to the boil, add the peas and cook until tender. Drain and keep to one side. Heat the olive oil in a heavy-bottomed saucepan. Add the shallot and bacon and cook for 2 minutes, allowing them to colour lightly. Add the wine, reduce by a third and add the peas, lettuce, lovage and butter. Stir well, season and cook for a further 2 minutes. Take off the heat and keep warm.

To cook the cod, heat a non stick frying pan, brush the cod with oil, place in a pan flesh side down and cook for 7 minutes. Turn over and cook for a further 4 minutes, or until the cod is just cooked through.

Place on a plate and spoon some of the peas, lettuce and lovage mixture over and around the fish. Spritz with lemon juice and serve immediately.

IAN WAGHORN

Based in West London, local causes are very important to us at Kensington Place and the Children's Services at Chelsea and Westminster Hospital are a prime example. I hope our signature dish for ChariTable Bookings will raise even more funds for the great work they do."

CONFIT CORNISH COD with glazed pumpkin, kale, chilli and lime

SERVES 1 | PREPARATION TIME 30 MINUTES | COOKING TIME 1 HOUR

For the Cod
- 1 x 160g cod fillet
- sea salt
- 200g unsalted butter, for browning

For the Maple Glazed Pumpkin
- 100g pumpkin, cubed. Reserve and toast the seeds
- 20ml maple syrup
- 1 tsp salt
- ½ tsp chilli flakes

For the Kale
- 50g curly kale

For the Lime and Chilli Butter
- 30g butter
- 15g banana shallot, finely diced
- ½ tsp salt
- 3g red chilli, finely diced
- ¼ lime, zested and juiced

To prepare the cod, cover with sea salt and allow to sit for 5 minutes. This will firm the fish up and season the flesh. Next, wash the salt crust off and set the portion to one side.

For the browned butter, melt 200g unsalted butter on a low heat. Once the butter has taken on a hazelnut colour remove from the heat, set aside and leave to cool.

For the maple glazed pumpkin, season the pumpkin cubes with around 15ml maple syrup, the salt and chilli flakes. Bake in an oven at 170°C, until tender and without colour. Meanwhile, blanch the kale in salted water for approximately 2 minutes and refresh in ice water. Once chilled, squeeze the kale to remove any excess water.

To prepare the lime and chilli butter, slowly cook the shallot and salt in the butter until tender, with no bite. Once soft, add the chilli, lime zest and juice. Cool over ice. Be sure to stir the butter whilst over ice to ensure the chilli and shallots are evenly incorporated.

Heat the beurre noisette to 55°C. Submerge the cod in the butter and confit for approximately 10 minutes. Take half the chilli butter and warm with the kale.

Reheat the pumpkin, adding some more maple syrup and a little beurre noisette to achieve a nutty, sweet flavour. Remove the cod from the butter and remove any excess butter.

Heat the remaining chilli butter, add a little beurre noisette and some toasted, chopped pumpkin seeds to create a sauce.

To serve, create a bed of glazed pumpkin, capped with the chilli buttered kale. Place the cod fillet on top and drizzle with the butter and pumpkin seed sauce.

STEVE WALKER

Restaurant Sirocco at the Royal Yacht are helping support and raise money for the Teenage Cancer Trust, every year we hold various events to raise awareness for this magnificent charity on Jersey."

FILLET OF JERSEY BEEF with morels, asparagus and beef cheek

SERVES 6 | PREPARATION TIME 30 MINUTES (PLUS 24 HOURS TO MARINATE) | COOKING TIME 4 HOURS

For the Jersey Beef

1 Jersey fillet of beef
3 beef cheeks
300ml red wine
2 bulbs of garlic, chopped
4 carrots, chopped
2 leeks, chopped
2 sprigs of thyme
1 sprig of rosemary
1 bay leaf
1l beef stock
500g mixed wild mushrooms
300ml Madeira
1l chicken stock
200ml double cream
1 bunch of white asparagus
1 bunch of green asparagus
200g girolles
200g morels
1 onion, chopped

To marinate the beef cheeks, place the beef cheeks in a pot with red wine, most of the chopped garlic, leaving 4 chopped cloves aside for later, chopped carrots, leaving one aside for later, chopped leeks, leaving one aside for later, 1 sprig of thyme, the sprig of rosemary and bay leaf and marinate for 24 hours.

To cook the beef cheeks, drain the liquid from the cheeks and keep the liquid in a jug on the side. Pan fry the beef cheeks to caramelise and place in an ovenproof dish, pour in the marinade – with carrots, leeks, garlic, thyme etc – add the beef stock and place in an oven covered with tin foil or a lid. Slow cook at 120°C for 4 hours.

To make the wild mushroom purée, sauté the mixed wild mushrooms, 2 cloves of chopped garlic and add 150ml of Madeira and reduce by half. Add 200ml of chicken stock and reduce by half, followed by the 200ml of double cream and reduce by half. Season and put in a blender and purée until smooth.

To cook the asparagus, peel each asparagus from the tip to the base and place into boiling, salted water for 45 seconds, take out and refresh in ice water.

To prepare the girolle and morel mushrooms, peel the girolles on the stalk using a pairing knife and scrape away from the cap until clean and peeled in appearance. The morels need to be brushed of all dirt but not washed and cut in half.

To make the sauce, sauté 1 chopped carrot, 1 chopped onion, 1 chopped leek, 2 cloves of garlic and the remaining sprig of thyme and deglaze with the rest of the Madeira and reduce by half. Add the chicken stock and half of the cooking liquor from the beef cheek and reduce by half or until sauce is the consistency of pouring honey.

To cook the steak, cook the steaks to your personal choice and plate as shown in the picture using a butter and water emulsion to reheat the asparagus, and butter, salt and pepper to cook the mushrooms.

KEN WANG

"Under the motto of 'Charity By All' The Chinese Cricket Club is pleased to promote the disaster relief carried out by Habitat For Humanity, one of the many excellent organisations supported by ChariTable Bookings."

STEAMED SEA BASS with chopped chilli sauce

SERVES 2 | PREPARATION TIME 15 MINUTES (PLUS 2 HOURS PICKLING) | COOKING TIME 10 MINUTES

For the Pickled Chilli
150g fresh red chilli, chopped
15g garlic, chopped
10g ginger, chopped
2 tbsp rice wine
2 tbsp rice wine vinegar
1 tbsp sugar
1 tbsp salt
10g Yang-jiang black beans
20ml chilli oil

For the Sea Bass
500g sea bass fillet

To Garnish
fresh coriander leaves
spring onions, chopped

To make the pickled chilli dressing, mix together the red chillies, garlic, ginger, rice wine, rice wine vinegar, sugar, salt and the black beans in a bowl and allow to pickle for 2 hours. Heat the chilli oil in a wok until smoking, and add the pickled chilli and black bean mix. Stir-fry for about 30 seconds until fragrant.

To prepare and cook the fish, on a plate, pick the bones from the fish fillet and cover with the stir-fried pickled chilli and juices. Place the plate in a steamer, and steam for 5 minutes, checking the fish is well done and juicy.

To serve, garnish with coriander and finely chopped spring onions.

GARETH WARD

" This Ynyshir recipe is a typical welsh dish with a Japanese twist! Very happy that I can share this with you and raise awareness of Bronglais Hospital to ChariTable Bookings followers."

SALT WELSH WAGYU RIB - SHIITAKE

SERVES 4 | PREPARATION TIME 20 MINUTES (PLUS 5 DAYS FOR BRINING) | COOKING TIME 15 MINUTES (PLUS 48 HOURS FOR CONFIT)

For the Ribs
1 medium-sized short-rib rack
1l duck or beef fat

For the Brine
200g sugar
200g salt
1l water

For the Shiitake Ketchup
200ml rice vinegar
100g sugar
500g fresh shiitake mushrooms
agar agar, 2g to each 100g
soy sauce, to taste

For the Shiitake Soy
200g fresh shiitake mushrooms
75ml sunflower oil
250ml soy sauce
mirin, to taste

To Serve
puffed wild rice, either bought from an Asian food shop or deep fry wild rice for about 2 seconds
dehydrated shiitake mushrooms
10g of washed sea lettuce, pickled in vinegar

To prepare the brine, dissolve the salt and sugar in the water.

To prepare the ribs, trim and brine beef ribs for 5 days in brine. Wash and dry. Confit in the fat at 72°C for 48 hours in a tray at the bottom of the oven or until the meat falls off the bone. Take out and leave to rest at room temperature in the fat, then chill in fat, which will help to preserve the meat for longer. Cut the Wagyu rib into desired portion sizes, then barbecue on all sides until nice and crispy. Leave to rest.

To prepare the shiitake ketchup – prepare when putting the beef in the oven – whisk together the rice vinegar with the sugar to make a pickle. Juice 500g fresh shiitake. Weigh the juice, add 2g of agar agar for each 100g, boil and set in the fridge. Blend the mixture, adding soy and pickle to taste. Pass through muslin cloth to remove bits.

To prepare the shiitake soy, in a pan, roast 200g shiitake mushrooms in the sunflower oil until golden and crispy, making sure not to burn. Add the soy sauce and leave to cool. Pass through muslin cloth and add mirin to taste.

To serve, place the Wagyu rib on the plate. Coat the top with shiitake ketchup. Place sea lettuce on top, shaking off excess vinegar. Crush dehydrated shiitake mushrooms over the top. Sprinkle on some puffed wild rice and spoon over the roast shiitake soy.

MARCUS WAREING

Streetsmart remembers the homeless in our city at the time of the year when we should be thinking about them most. I'm delighted to support them through this ChariTable Bookings recipe collection and hope you enjoy our signature dish from Marcus."

HERDWICK LAMB with beetroot and girolles

SERVES 2 | PREPARATION TIME 30 MINUTES (PLUS OVERNIGHT MARINATE) | COOKING TIME 4 HOURS

For the Lamb
1 best end of lamb, trimmed of sinew
50ml olive oil
4 sprigs of thyme
2 sprigs of rosemary
1 clove of garlic, crushed
2 tbsp vegetable oil
½ tsp table salt
25g unsalted butter, cubed

For the Beetroot Aioli
2 egg yolks
½ tsp Dijon mustard
1 tsp Cabernet Sauvignon vinegar
125ml olive oil
250ml beetroot juice, reduced to 25ml and chilled
½ tsp table salt

For the Cooked Beetroot
1 long beetroot
2 tbsp rock salt
olive oil, to dress

For the Girolles
10 girolle mushrooms
20g unsalted butter
½ tsp table salt

For the Garnish
1 globe artichoke, peeled, cooked and quartered
borage flowers

To prepare the lamb, marinate overnight with the olive oil, herbs and garlic.

To make the aioli, whisk the eggs with the mustard and vinegar until pale and fluffy. Slowly drizzle in the oil whilst whisking continually. Finish with the beetroot juice and season to taste. Place into a piping bag in the fridge until needed.

To make the cooked beetroot, preheat the oven to 160°C. Wrap the beetroot with the salt in foil and bake for 3 hours, or until soft. Remove from the oven and allow to cool slightly. Peel whilst still warm, then refrigerate. Cut into neat wedges. When ready to serve, remove from the fridge 1 hour before and dress with olive oil and Maldon salt.

To cook the lamb, heat the vegetable oil in a medium frying pan. Season the lamb all over, then place in the hot oil. Brown all over then add the butter. When foaming, baste the lamb all over until well caramelised and cooked through to your preferred liking. Remove and set aside somewhere warm to rest. Place the girolles in the pan with the lamb butter and cook through, add the artichoke quarters and warm through.

To serve, place the beetroot aioli on the plate. Carve the lamb into four, placing two pieces on each plate. Garnish with the beetroot, artichokes and girolles. Finish with the borage flowers.

BJOERN WASSMUTH

"Dogs truly are a man's best friend and cruelty towards them is intolerable. I love this opportunity to share German Gymnasium's signature goose dish with ChariTable Bookings and raise awareness for the work of Dogs Trust in the UK at the same time. Bon Appetit!"

ROASTED FREE RANGE GOOSE with braised red cabbage, dumplings and orange sauce

SERVES 8 | PREPARATION TIME 30 MINUTES (PLUS 24–48 HOURS TO MARINATE) | COOKING TIME 3 HOURS 30 MINUTES

For the Goose

1 goose, approximately 5.5kg

apple, orange, 2 onions, for stuffing

1 tbsp dried marjoram

For the Braised Red Cabbage

1kg red cabbage, very thinly sliced

110ml port wine

220ml red wine

1 tbsp sugar

150ml red wine vinegar

2 Granny Smith apples, sliced

3 tbsp butter

2 large onions, very thinly sliced

100ml duck broth

4 juniper berries

10 black peppercorns

3 cloves

2 sticks of cinnamon

4 tsp cranberry jam or redcurrant jam

1 orange, juiced

salt, pepper, 1 bay leaf, to season

For the Potato Dumplings

800g russet potatoes, about 2 large

1 large egg

30g potato starch, or corn starch

125g plain flour, more if needed

salt, pepper, nutmeg

For the Bread Dumplings

500g bread, diced

2 shallots, finely chopped

1 knob of butter

3 eggs, beaten with 150ml milk

1 handful of parsley, finely chopped

1 clove of garlic

salt, pepper, nutmeg

For the Orange Sauce

goose trimmings

1 each of carrot, onion and celery

1 tbsp tomato paste

50ml port, mixed with 75ml red wine

500ml duck stock

150ml orange juice, freshly squeezed

salt, bay leaves, black pepper

4 tbsp orange liqueur

Remove the giblets from inside the goose and season with salt and pepper, inside and out. Wash the apple and orange, peel the onions and cut into a dice of approximately 1cm. Season with salt, pepper and marjoram, and stuff the goose. Tie up and close the goose. Put the goose in a roasting pan and fill with water until the legs are just about submerged. Roast in the oven at 120°C for 3 hours. Set aside. To serve, place the goose back in the oven at 240°C for 20 minutes to crisp up the skin.

Put the cabbage in a mixing bowl together with wine, sugar, vinegar, orange juice and the apples and let it marinate for 24–48 hours.

Melt the butter in a braising pot over medium-high heat. Cook the onions until caramelised and just beginning to brown. Add the marinated cabbage and duck broth. Season with salt and pepper and stir thoroughly. Add the spices, bring to boil and reduce the heat to low. Cover and simmer for 2 hours, stirring occasionally. Add more broth if needed. At the end, finish with the jam and add more salt, sugar and vinegar to taste.

Cook the unpeeled potatoes in large pot of boiling water until tender, drain, cool slightly and peel. Mash the potatoes with a fork or run through a ricer. Add the egg, season with salt and nutmeg and add the potato starch and half the flour. Knead the mixture with your hands until a smooth dough forms, adding more flour by the tablespoonful if the dough is sticky. Form the dough into 60g balls. Cook the dumplings in a large pot of almost boiling salted water for 10–15 minutes, or until the dumplings rise to the top.

Roast the bread in the oven until a light golden brown. Sauté the shallots and garlic clove in butter and combine with the eggs, bread, and milk in a bowl. Season to taste, add the parsley and leave to rest for 15 minutes. Form a 5–6 cm and wrap in heat resistant cling film, then in tin foil and put in a pot with simmering water. Leave to simmer for about 20 minutes. Remove from the water and set aside to cool down. Unwrap and cut in 2.5cm thick slices. Melt some butter in a frying pan over medium heat, add the dumplings and cook until golden and slightly crisp.

Roast the goose trimmings, add the chopped carrot, onion and celery, and roast together until dark brown. Add tomato paste and deglaze with port and red wine. Reduce, add the duck stock and orange juice and slowly simmer. Reduce by half, strain and season to taste. Finish with the orange liqueur.

ANDY WATERS

Birmingham Children's Hospital is a leading UK specialist paediatric centre, offering expert care to 90, 000 children every year. Supporting local charities like this means a lot to Waters Restaurant, especially as my wife Beverley and I have needed to visit the children's hospital regularly with our son Lewis. Therefore we hope you will like the Spicy Salmon dish we have donated to ChariTable Bookings new recipe book."

SALMON IN SPICY COCONUT CREAM

SERVES 4 | PREPARATION TIME 15 MINUTES | COOKING TIME 30 MINUTES

For the Salmon
- 4 salmon fillets
- 2 tsp peanut oil
- 2 cloves of garlic, crushed
- 5g fresh ginger, grated
- 20g turmeric, fresh, finely grated
- 2 small red chillies, thinly sliced
- 355ml fish stock
- 400ml coconut cream
- 20g fresh lemongrass
- 2 tbsp fish sauce
- 2 green onions, thinly sliced
- 1 pak choi, 8 small leaves

For the Garnish
- 4 cherry tomatoes
- 1 red chilli, sliced
- edible flowers
- 4 dried bay leaves
- 1 tbsp sesame seeds

To begin, place a frying pan over a high heat and add the peanut oil. Once hot, stir-fry the garlic, ginger, turmeric and chilli until fragrant, then add the stock, coconut cream and lemongrass and bring to the boil.

Once boiling, add the salmon fillets so they are immersed in the sauce and flat. Lower the heat, cover the pan and simmer for approximately 8 minutes, or until the fish is just cooked through.

Using a slotted spoon, carefully remove the fillets from the sauce and place in a serving bowl, covering to keep warm. Remove the lemongrass from the sauce and discard. Bring the sauce back to the boil and cook for 5 minutes to reduce and thicken slightly.

Remove the sauce from the heat and stir in the fish sauce, sliced green onions and pak choi.

Place the salmon fillets into bowls and pour the sauce on top. Decorate with dried bay leaves, edible flowers, sliced red chilli and cherry tomatoes. Sprinkle with sesame seeds and serve immediately with steamed rice.

EMILY WATKINS

Thank you ChariTable Bookings for the opportunity for all of us at The Kingham Plough to support one of our favourite, local charities, Helen and Douglas House, in their work to help young people with tragically life-shortening illnesses."

VENISON LOIN AND BLACK PUDDING with heritage beetroots and millet risotto

SERVES 10 | PREPARATION TIME 1 HOUR 30 MINUTES (PLUS OVERNIGHT TO REST) | COOKING TIME 2 HOURS 30 MINUTES

Equipment
sous vide and vacuum pack bags
sausage machine

For the Venison Loin
500g venison loin, trimmed
10 juniper berries
1 sprig of rosemary
oil, for frying

For the Venison Pudding Sausage
500g venison liver, minced
50g milk powder
50g oats
125g cooked pearl barley
100g beef suet
25g breadcrumbs
5g black peppercorns
5g juniper
2g paprika
10g salt
250ml pig's blood
1 sprig of rosemary, to finish

For the Prunes in Sloe Gin
20 pitted prunes
250ml venison stock
125ml sloe gin

For the Roasted Beetroots
12 baby red beetroots
1 drizzle of oil
1 bunch of thyme
½ head of garlic

To prepare the venison, bruise the juniper berries a little to release flavours, and place the loin in a vacuum pack bag with the now bruised juniper berries, rosemary and oil.

To make the venison pudding sausage, mince the venison liver over an ice bath. Mix in the milk powder quite vigorously with the liver. Soak the oats, barley, suet, breadcrumbs, spices and seasoning in the pig's blood. Leave for an hour until absorbed. Mix the spiced blood mix with the liver mix. Again, keep over an ice bath all the time. It is best left overnight. Load the sausage machine with the mix. Carefully put the hog skins on the filler. Tie the sausages every 6cm with string. Poach sous vide at 85°C for 20 minutes in a vacuum packed bag. Refresh in ice water.

To prepare the prunes in sloe gin, simmer together all the ingredients until the prunes are sticky.

To make the roasted beetroots, place the beetroots in a pan of water and bring to a simmer. Simmer gently until only partly cooked. Peel while still warm. Place on a roasting tray with a little oil, thyme and the garlic cut in half. Bake at 180°C until tender.

To make the beetroot ketchup, bring the sugar and vinegar to the boil and reduce to a syrup. Add to the beetroot juice. Season to taste. Whisk in the agar agar and then bring to the boil. Pass through a chinois into a container and chill to set. Break up and blitz to a smooth purée in a blender.

To make the millet risotto, sweat the shallots, add the millet and season to taste. Stir well and have the stock ready in a pan. Slowly add the hot stock bit by bit, stirring all the time. When it has absorbed all of the stock spread on a gastro tray. To finish the risotto, heat a litre of venison stock in a pan. Heat the millet base in a saucepan. Slowly add the stock, stirring all the time. When it is thick and creamy add 100g cold, diced butter. Finish with chopped parsley, salt and pepper and a squeeze of lemon juice.

For the Beetroot Ketchup

15g sugar

50ml cabernet sauvignon vinegar

500ml beetroot juice

salt

5.5g agar agar

For the Millet Risotto

50g shallots

250g pinhead millet

500ml venison stock, for initial mix

1l venison stock, to finish

100g butter, cold and diced

chopped parsley, salt, pepper and a

squeeze of lemon juice, to finish

To Serve

cavolo nero or red Russian kale

To finish the dish and serve, place the venison in a water bath set at 64°C for 14 minutes. Heat a non-stick pan with some oil on a medium heat. Take the venison loin from the bag and pat dry. Place in the frying pan and start to colour, add the venison pudding sausages into the pan at the same time. When beginning to colour, add a large knob of butter and a sprig of rosemary. Baste the sausages and loin until ready. Take the loin out of the pan and leave to rest for a moment. Add the beetroots into the pan with the sausages and place the pan in the oven for 5 minutes. Take out of the oven and serve with some seasonal greens such as cavolo nero or red Russian kale. Warm some venison sauce with the prunes to finish.

JAKE WATKINS

Happy to put my name and JSW's signature dish to the ChariTable Bookings recipe book, especially in support of Cancer Research."

BUTTER POACHED PHEASANT with sticky ham hock, pickled chestnuts and lentils

SERVES 4 | PREPARATION TIME 20 MINUTES | COOKING TIME 1 HOUR 30 MINUTES

Equipment
    sous vide and vacuum pack bags

For the Butter Poached Pheasant
    2 pheasant crowns
    100g butter
    400g mirepoix
    400ml chicken stock

For the Ham Hock
    1 ham hock, cooked

For the Lentils
    100g puy lentils
    100g sprouts

For the Pickled Chestnuts
    16 fresh chestnuts

For the Pickling Liquid
    200ml water
    200ml white wine vinegar
    75g caster sugar
    ½ tsp salt

To prepare the pheasant, remove the breast from the crowns, chop the bones and set to one side. Sauté the bones and mirepoix in butter until golden. Drain and reserve the butter, and return to the pan with chicken stock and mirepoix. Simmer for 45 minutes, strain and reduce until syrupy. Vacuum pack the pheasant breasts with the now reduced pheasant butter and cook at 57°C for 30 minutes.

While the breasts cook, boil the lentils until tender and allow to cool. Blanch the sprouts and cut in half.

Peel and slice the raw chestnuts and set aside. Place the ingredients for the pickling liquid together in a pan and boil. Once boiled, simmer the sliced chestnuts in the liquid for 15 seconds, remove, pat dry and set to one side.

Once the pheasant breasts are done, caramelise them in a pan with the ham hock and sprouts. To serve, spoon some lentils into the centre of each plate and place a breast on top. Put a few sprouts, chestnuts and some ham hock around, adding sauce.

DAMIAN WAWRZYNIAK

Some disabilities make mastering simple cooking tasks a true challenge. SeeAbility supports individuals to gain greater independence in the kitchen and in all areas of life. You can support them by reserving your next table through ChariTable Bookings."

PIEROGIES with cabbage and wild mushrooms

SERVES 6–8 | PREPARATION TIME 45 MINUTES (PLUS 2 HOURS TO SOAK) | COOKING TIME 1 HOUR

For the Pierogi Filling
150g dried porcini mushrooms
450g sauerkraut
500ml vegetable stock
rapeseed oil
salt and pepper

For the Dough
500g wheat flour
1 pinch of salt
1 organic egg yolk
1 tsp cold unsalted butter, cubed
250ml warm water (36.6°C)

To Finish
1 medium sweet onion, finely chopped
1 splash of rapeseed oil
1 knob of butter
400g girolles, cleaned
flat leaf parsley, chopped

To make the filling, begin by soaking the dried mushrooms in cold water for at least 2 hours. Squeeze the excess liquid from the sauerkraut. Bring the sauerkraut to the boil in the stock for 10–12 minutes on a medium heat. This will help to reduce unwanted acidity. Drain the mushrooms and pan fry on medium heat to evaporate the water. Chop the boiled sauerkraut together with mushrooms, squeeze it again, add a touch rapeseed oil and season to taste.

To make the dough, combine the flour, salt, egg yolk and butter in a bowl and mix together well, turning by hand. Gradually keep adding water and mixing to keep the dough smooth.

For the pierogi, roll the dough onto a floured surface to a thickness of 3mm and cut into discs with a round cutter. Put a generous tablespoon of stuffing into the centre of the discs. Using your fingertips, pinch the edges of the dough together to close each pierogi. Gently place them in the boiling water, one by one and cook for 2 minutes.

Heat a pan with a touch of rapeseed oil and butter and sauté the onion on a medium heat. Once the onion begins to colour, increase the heat and put the pierogi in the pan. Fry until golden.

To serve, arrange the pierogi on a plate, pan fry some girolles with the onions and spoon the desired amount over the dish. Sprinkle with the parsley.

BRYAN WEBB

The gift that gives twice! What a great way to give to charity and get 365 fantastic recipes too. Myself and the team at Tyddyn Llan are thrilled to support the Motor Neurone Disease Association through ChariTable Bookings."

ROAST WILD BASS with laverbread butter sauce

SERVES 4 | PREPARATION TIME 30 MINUTES | COOKING TIME 30 MINUTES

For the Sauce
175ml Muscadet wine
1 tbsp white wine vinegar
4 shallots, finely chopped
250g unsalted butter
salt and cayenne pepper
½ lemon, juice only
2 tbsp laverbread
2 tbsp double cream

For the Wild Bass
4 x 150g wild bass fillets, skin on
and pin boned
olive oil
salt and pepper

To Serve
300g spinach
50g butter

For the sauce, put the Muscadet wine, vinegar and shallots into a saucepan and slowly reduce to a syrup. On a low heat, slowly add the butter a little at a time until it forms a slightly thick sauce. Season with salt and cayenne pepper, and add the lemon juice. Strain the sauce into a clean saucepan. In a separate saucepan, add the laverbread and cream, bring to the boil and add half the beurre blanc.

Season the fish and coat lightly with olive oil. Place onto a hot griddle pan, skin-side down, until the skin is crisp. Transfer to an oiled tray and bake in the oven at 200°C for 5 minutes. Meanwhile, in a large pan, melt the remaining 50g of butter and cook the spinach until wilted.

To serve, place the bass on a bed of spinach and pour the laverbread sauce around one side and the remaining beurre blanc around the other.

PAUL WEDGWOOD

Edinburgh Sick Kids does amazing work ensuring that children are children first and patients second. Help me support them with ChariTable Bookings and enjoy Wedgwood The Restaurant's dish at the same time!"

SESAME ROASTED SEA TROUT with braised pak choi, lobster and black bean nori roll and lobster mayonnaise

SERVES 4 | PREPARATION TIME 1 HOUR 30 MINUTES (PLUS OVERNIGHT TO SOAK) | COOKING TIME 3 HOURS 45 MINUTES

Equipment
blowtorch

For the Sesame Roasted Sea Trout
1kg side sea trout
1 tbsp sesame oil
1 sprinkling of black sesame seed
1 sprinkling of white sesame seeds
ground white pepper, to season
2 pak choi, shredded, reserve centre leaves to garnish
1 tbsp soy sauce

For the Black Beans
50g black beans, soaked overnight

For the Sushi Rice and Roll
200g sushi rice
400ml water
35ml sushi vinegar
10g sugar
5g salt
2 sheets of nori seaweed
500g cooked lobster, shell reserved

For the Lobster Mayonnaise
reserved lobster shells, crushed
250ml vegetable oil
2 egg yolks
20ml sherry vinegar

For the Garnish
12 slices of pickled ginger
reserved pak choi leaves

To prepare the black beans, place the soaked beans in a saucepan, cover with water and cook over a medium heat until tender, topping up the water as necessary. Allow to cool.

To make the sushi rice and roll, rinse the rice quickly in a bowl 3–4 times until the water is clear. Place in a heavy-bottomed pan with the water and bring to the boil. Once boiling, reduce to lowest heat and cover. Cook for 15 minutes. Remove from the heat and let the rice stand covered for 10 minutes. Whilst the rice is standing, add the sushi vinegar to a small pan with the salt and sugar and dissolve over a low heat. Allow to cool slightly. Fold through the rice and allow to cool to room temperature. Spread the rice evenly over the nori sheets, add a line of black beans and chopped lobster meat across the rice and roll with a bamboo mat to form the lobster roll. Toast the outside with a blowtorch.

To make the lobster mayonnaise, add the crushed shells to a pan with the oil and cook gently for 5 minutes until you get a lobster flavoured oil. Allow to cool. Blend the yolks and vinegar in a processor. Slowly add the lobster oil until it forms an emulsion. Add enough oil to reach your desired consistency.

To make the sesame roasted sea trout, preheat the oven to 190°C. Trim the belly and tail from the fish, remove the skin and dice the flesh into 0.5cm cubes. Set aside. Cut the remaining fish into four even portions. Add the sesame oil to a hot pan, place the fish in, skin-side down, and cook for 1 minute. Sprinkle sesame seeds on the top of the fish and place in the oven for around 5 minutes or until cooked to your specification. Remove from the oven, season with white pepper and allow to rest. Add the pak choi to the pan, adding soy sauce to soften.

To serve, place the pak choi on the plate and top with the fish. Carve each lobster roll into 6 pieces and place 3 on each plate. Add the chopped belly and tail flesh, garnish with lobster mayonnaise and pickled ginger.

PAUL WELBURN

" *Meningitis kills nearly 1,000 people every day. That is why The Leconfield is proud to support Meningitis UK's invaluable work by donating our signature recipe to ChariTable Bookings' exciting initiative.*"

HAY SMOKED MEREWORTH FARM DEER with red fruits, vegetables and leaves

SERVES 4 | PREPARATION TIME 2 HOURS | COOKING TIME 1 HOUR

Equipment
sous vide and vacuum pack bags

For the Smoked Roe Deer
1 roe deer loin, quartered
2 handfuls of dried hay
2 sprigs of thyme
1 bay leaf
50g butter
1 tbsp olive oil

For the Red Cabbage Gel and Powder
1 red cabbage, juiced to yield 500ml
50ml red wine vinegar
50ml apple juice
6g gellan gum powder
1 tsp mixed spice
50g red cabbage pulp, from juicing

For the Sauce
8 shallots, sliced
8 black peppercorns, crushed
5 juniper berries, crushed
2 sprigs of thyme
1 bay leaf
50ml red wine vinegar
250ml port
500ml red wine
1.5l brown chicken stock
1 tbsp oil

For the Baby Beetroots
500g baby beetroot
1 tsp sea salt

To make the red cabbage gel, bring all of the ingredients to the boil in a medium-sized saucepan and allow to set on a tray in the fridge. Once set, blend the jelly into a liquid gel, season and set aside.

To make the smoked roe deer, begin by trimming the deer loin of any sinew. Place the hay in a deep tray and light with a match. Once thoroughly burnt out, place the loin on top and cover with cling film to leave in the fridge for a minimum of 2 hours. In the meantime, heat a sous vide cooker to 57°C. Remove the deer from the fridge and roll the loin in the burnt hay powder. Roll tightly in cling film and cook for 20 minutes. Once cooked, remove from the water bath, take off the cling film and place to one side to rest.

To prepare the sauce, start by caramelising the shallots in the oil in a medium-sized saucepan. When golden, add the pepper, juniper and herbs, then deglaze with the vinegar. Reduce until the pan is almost dry, then add the port and reduce by a third. Add the wine, reduce by half, then add the chicken stock and simmer for 20 minutes. Remove from the heat, cover with cling film and leave to infuse for a further 20 minutes. Once infused, pass through a fine sieve into a clean saucepan, return to the heat and reduce until a sauce consistency is achieved. Season and set aside.

To make the baby beetroot, start by preheating the oven to 180°C. Wash and trim, then season and wrap in a single layer of foil. Bake for 30–45 minutes until tender. Leave to cool slightly and peel.

To make the pickled beetroot, peel the beetroot and slice to a thickness of 2mm. Bring the pickling ingredients to the boil, then remove from the heat and chill. Pour the liquid over the beetroot and place in the fridge to pickle.

To prepare the salsify, add the port, red wine and chicken stock to a saucepan and place over a medium heat with half the thyme. Peel the salsify and poach in the liquid until tender. Remove the salsify and reduce the liquor by half to create the glaze. When ready to serve, pour the glaze over the salsify.

To make the macerated blackberries, bring the water, sugar, port and thyme to the boil in a saucepan, pour over the blackberries and reserve.

For the Macerated Blackberries

250g blackberries

100ml water

100g sugar

25ml port

2 sprigs of thyme

For the Pickled Beetroots

500g Cheltenham beetroot

100ml each of white wine, port and
raspberry vinegar

100g brown sugar

2 sprigs of thyme

3 bay leaves

For the Salsify

50g salsify root

125ml red wine

100ml chicken stock

2 sprigs of thyme

100ml port

To serve, spread the pulp reserved from juicing the red cabbage onto an oven tray and place under the grill on a low heat until suitably dehydrated and crisp. Blitz into a powder. Just before serving, heat a frying pan over a high heat with the butter and a dash of oil. Once hot, add the 2 sprigs of thyme and 1 bay leaf, then sear the loin on all sides until caramelised. Finish the sauce with a teaspoon of liquor from the blackberries and heat. Slice the deer and allocate 3 slices per plate. Arrange the beetroot, salsify and pickled beetroot around the deer. Pipe dots of the cabbage gel and arrange pickled blackberries around the plate. Sprinkle the cabbage powder over the top and garnish with the beetroot leaves and puffed barley. Serve the warmed sauce on the side.

LEE WESTCOTT

" I really hope you enjoy my creation of this recipe and I am honoured to be able to share it in this ChariTable Bookings collection in aid of raising awareness for Autism Together."

SHORT RIB OF BEEF with carrot, salsify and parsley

SERVES 4 | PREPARATION TIME 25 MINUTES (PLUS 3 DAY TO BRINE) | COOKING TIME 8 HOURS

Equipment
mandoline

For the Brine
1l apple juice
4l water
100g coarse salt
75g caster sugar
25g garlic
1 bunch of thyme
9 bay leaves
20g juniper berries
15g fennel seeds
7.5g cloves
15g coriander seeds
5g black peppercorns

For the Pickled Salsify
4 sticks of salsify
1 lemon, juiced
500ml water
180g sugar
20g salt
4 sprigs of thyme
1 bay leaf
250ml white wine vinegar

For the Confit Shallot
2 banana shallots, finely diced
300ml duck fat
4 sprigs of thyme
2 bay leaves

To prepare the beef, place all of the ingredients for the brine into a large saucepan and bring to the boil. Simmer for 10 minutes. Allow to cool at room temperature. Place the meat in and brine for 3 days in the fridge.

To make the pickled salsify, wash the salsify. Peel and place into a bowl with water and the lemon juice to stop any discolouring. Cut off the ends of the salsify, then cut into thirds and slice thinly using a mandoline. Bring the remaining ingredients to the boil in a saucepan. Simmer for 3 minutes. Remove from the stove and add the sliced salsify.

To make the confit shallot, warm the duck fat with the herbs. Season with salt. Once the fat is infused, add the diced shallot and very gently and slowly cook on a low heat until they are tender. Drain well and chill.

To make the carrot purée, heat a medium saucepan and add the diced butter. Once melted, add the carrots. Sweat down with a lid on until tender and cooked. Remove the lid and add the carrot juice. Reduce it by two thirds. Season with salt and sugar. Blend until smooth. Pass through a fine sieve and chill.

To make the pickled chantenay carrots, reduce the orange juice to 150ml. Place all ingredients except the carrots in a saucepan with the reduced orange juice and bring to a simmer. Simmer for 2 minutes, then add the sliced carrots. Simmer until the carrots are cooked, but still have a slight bite to them. Remove from the heat and leave in the liquor to cool.

To prepare the breadcrumbs, chop the bread pieces into small chunks, discarding the crust. Heat the butter in a saucepan until brown and foamy. Add the breadcrumbs and cook in the butter until golden brown. Drain and dry on kitchen paper.

To cook the beef, remove from the brine and drain well. Sear the meat until golden brown all over. Preheat the oven to 120°C. Roast the vegetables in a large saucepan with vegetable oil until they are a nice, golden brown colour. Add the thyme and bay leaves. Drain the

For the Carrot Purée

- 500g carrots, thinly sliced
- 280ml carrot juice
- 100g unsalted butter, diced
- 1 pinch of salt
- 1 pinch of sugar

For the Pickled Chantenay Carrots

- 250g chantenay carrot, washed and sliced thinly
- 400ml orange juice
- 2 sprigs of thyme
- 50ml Champagne vinegar
- 60ml water
- 30ml rapeseed oil

For the Breadcrumbs

- 1 small sourdough loaf
- 150g unsalted butter, diced

For the Beef Shortrib

- 2kg shortrib on the bone
- 2 onions, peeled and chopped
- 3 carrots, peeled and chopped
- 1 head of garlic, halved
- 4 sticks of celery, chopped
- 1 leek, chopped
- ½ bunch of thyme
- 2 bay leaves
- 500ml red wine
- 4l brown chicken stock

vegetables in a colander to remove all the fat, then place all back into the saucepan. Deglaze with the red wine. Reduce by half, then add the brown chicken stock and bring to a simmer. Simmer for 30 minutes. Place the seared beef into a deep oven tray and pour over the above stock and vegetables. Cover with tin foil over the tray and bake in the oven for around 6–8 hours, or until tender. Once cooked, pop out the bones and carefully portion into 4 nice pieces. Strain the cooking liquor off and skim well. Reduce by half. Place the beef back into the sauce and remove from the heat.

To serve, place a spoonful of the warm purée onto the plate along with a pile of pickled carrots, warmed through. Drain the salsify strips from the pickling liquor, season and add chopped parsley. Arrange them on top of the pickled carrots. Place the beef onto the plate, adding a spoonful of the breadcrumbs on top. Add the confit shallot and more chopped parsley to the sauce, bring to the boil, spoon onto the plate.

CHRIS WHEELER

Great to be part of ChariTable Bookings' new publication, combining recipes and worthy causes. On behalf of the team at Stoke Park, I'm sharing our signature Pea Shell Farm lamb dish and promoting Addenbrooke's Charitable Trust, supporting innovation in patient care across Cambridge University Hospitals."

PAN-FRIED LOIN OF PEA SHELL FARM LAMB with a mini shepherd's pie, rosemary and garlic roasted root vegetables and redcurrant jus

SERVES 4 | PREPARATION TIME 20 MINUTES | COOKING TIME 40 MINUTES

For the Lamb
- 2 x 300g lamb loins
- 4 sprigs of red currants
- 200ml lamb sauce

For the Shepherd's Pie
- 1 medium onion
- 1 carrot
- 1 splash of olive oil
- 200g minced lamb
- 100ml lamb stock
- 50g peas
- 2 jacket potatoes, mashed
- 4 sprigs of thyme

For the Roasted Vegetables
- 1 medium sized turnip
- 1 small swede
- 1 large carrot
- 2 sticks of celery
- 1 small celeriac
- 1 parsnip
- 8 cloves of garlic, skin on
- 4 sprigs of rosemary

To prepare the shepherd's pie, finely dice the onion and carrot, sweat in a little olive oil, add the minced lamb and season with salt and pepper. Add the lamb stock and peas and cook for 10 minutes. Grease a small Tian ring, half fill each ring with your lamb mixture then pipe the mash potato on top and garnish with a sprig of thyme. Place in a medium hot oven for 10 minutes until the mashed potato is a golden brown.

To prepare the roasted root vegetables, peel and cut each vegetable into different shapes. Blanch separately in boiling water. Roast all of the vegetables in a little olive oil and butter with garlic cloves and sprigs of rosemary.

To prepare the lamb, season and seal in a hot pan with a little olive oil. Place in a warm oven for approximately 5 minutes or until the lamb is cooked to your required taste.

To serve, place the shepherd's pie at the top of the plate, carefully removing the Tian ring. Place a selection of the roasted vegetables at the bottom of the plate. Slice each lamb loin into 12 pieces. Place 6 pieces of lamb loin on top of the root vegetables. Warm the red currants up in the lamb sauce. Once warm, place on top of the lamb loin. Pour a little sauce around the lamb and shepherd's pie and serve.

ZAC WHITTLE

Charities of all sizes can be supported by ChariTable Bookings. The Fenchurch at Sky Garden is backing the St. Andrews Youth Club in Westminster, helping create a positive environment and a strong future."

PAN-FRIED MONKFISH with roast cauliflower, Romanesco and cauliflower purée

SERVES 1 | PREPARATION TIME 30 MINUTES | COOKING TIME 30 MINUTES

For the Dish
- 140g monkfish, cleaned
- 1 Romanesco
- ½ head of cauliflower
- 1 small handfull of kale
- butter, to cook

For the Cauliflower Purée
- 100g cauliflower
- ½ tsp English mustard
- ½ tsp turmeric
- 10g unsalted butter
- 50ml milk

To Serve
- 1 handful of almonds
- radicchio leaves
- olive oil
- lemon juice
- salt and pepper

To prepare the vegetables, cut both the Romanesco and cauliflower into walnut-sized florets. Wash and leave to drain in a colander. Heat a wide pan with enough butter to evenly cover the bottom. Add the vegetables, cooking one then the other. Season, cover with a lid, checking with a sharp, pointed knife every 15 seconds or so. Add splashes of water when there is none so as not to burn them. When cooked, remove from the pan and set aside to serve.

To cook the fish, bring to room temperature first. Heat another pan with olive oil to just below smoking point. Dry the fish and add to the pan. Roll it continuously until it is golden brown all over. Remove the fish and let the pan cool slightly off the heat. Add a knob of butter and return the fish to the pan. Baste until cooked, controlling the heat so as not to burn the butter. Add another knob of butter if needed. Check the fish is cooked with a temperature probe. It should be just hot to touch, about 40°C. Finish with lemon juice and sea salt.

Wash the kale well and rip into bite sized pieces. Heat a pan with olive oil until smoking hot. Add the kale, salt and a splash of water, then cover with a lid and cook until tender.

To prepare the cauliflower purée, melt the butter in a pan, chop the cauliflower and add it to the butter, cover with a lid. Cook on a low heat until tender. Remove the lid, add the mustard and turmeric, then cook until all of the liquid has evaporated. Add the milk, bring to the boil. Season and pass through a fine sieve.

To serve, toast almonds in an oven at 160°C until golden brown. Leave to cool. Rip the radicchio into bite-sized pieces, dress with olive oil, lemon juice, salt and pepper. Plate as pictured.

MICHAEL WIGNALL

Adoption UK is the leading charity supporting parents providing homes and families for children who cannot live with their birth parents. I'm delighted to share Gidleigh Park's Lamb dish with ChariTable Bookings to support their fantastic work."

LAMB with creamed kale and roasted pumpkin
SERVES 4 | PREPARATION TIME 30 MINUTES | COOKING TIME 45 MINUTES

For the Lamb
1 rack of lamb
20ml vegetable oil
30g unsalted butter

For the Creamed Kale
500ml double cream
1 sprig of thyme
3 bay leaves
1 clove of garlic
1 head of kale

For the Roasted Pumpkin
1 small crown prince pumpkin
25g butter

To cook the lamb, heat the oil in a large pan. Add the lamb and turn continuously until all the sides are golden brown. Add the butter to the pan and transfer the mixture into a roasting dish. Cook in a preheated oven at 180°C for around 2–3 minutes. Turn the lamb and cook for a further 1–2 minutes, depending on the size. Once cooked, allow to rest for 10 minutes.

To make the creamed kale, place the cream in a pan with the thyme, bay leaves and garlic, and bring to the boil; reduce the mixture by half. In the meantime, blanch the kale and refresh in cold water. Place the kale on a dry tea towel and squeeze out any excess water. Now, finely slice the kale. Pass the cream mix through a fine sieve onto the kale and season to taste.

To make the roast pumpkin, remove the skin and cut into 2cm deep slabs. Colour both sides of the slab in a pan of foaming butter. Place in an oven at 180°C and roast for 5 minutes. Once roasted, cut into 2cm cubes.

To serve, plate as pictured and drizzle with the roasting juices.

JOHN WILLIAMS MBE CMA

Through ChariTable Bookings' latest initiative, the team at The Ritz and I are thrilled to support Adopt a School, a wonderful charity that delivers food education in schools all over the country and many in deprived areas. We hope you enjoy the grouse!"

ROAST GROUSE with celeriac, salted grapes and walnuts

SERVES 10 | PREPARATION TIME 45 MINUTES (PLUS 24 HOURS TO CURE) | COOKING TIME 2 HOURS

Equipment
sous vide and vacuum pack bags
Thermomix

For the Grouse
10 grouse
200g celeriac purée
200g salsify
80g candied walnuts

For the Celeriac Purée
1 celeriac
250g butter
100ml double cream
salt, to taste

For the Candied Walnuts
1 bag of walnuts
1l water
1kg sugar
2 tbsp vegetable oil

For the Salsify
200g salsify
1 lemon
25g olive oil
salt, to taste

To Serve
350g white grapes
150g girolles
½ punnet of baby watercress
80g Alsace bacon lardons
20g chopped parsley
200ml roast juices

To make the candied walnuts, bring the water and sugar to the boil so the sugar dissolves. Place the walnuts in a large bowl and pour over the liquid. Soak in the fridge for 24 hours. Once soaked, strain off all of the liquid. Fry in a pan of oil, making sure to not have the oil too hot. Remove from the oil and dry on a j-cloth. Reserve in a sealed container.

To make the celeriac purée, peel and cut into small pieces that will cook quickly. Place in a vacuum pack bag with 50g of butter. Seal completely and steam until well cooked. Place into a Thermomix and blitz. Add the remaining butter in small amounts with the cream and salt and blitz until smooth. Do not process for too long as it will turn brown. Check for seasoning and chill immediately in a blast chiller.

To prepare the salsify, wash, peel and place in a vacuum pack bag with the lemon juice, olive oil and salt. Seal completely and steam until cooked. Chill and cut into batons.

To prepare the grouse, quickly seal the bird in foaming butter on all sides. Finish in an oven preheated to 180°C, 10–12 minutes to serve pink, or until the required cooking degree is reached. Sauté the bacon lardons in foaming butter then drain. Peel the grapes and lightly salt them. Cut the salsify into small batons then caramelise in oil and glaze with a small amount of sauce. Finally, finish with chopped parsley. Sauté the girolles.

To serve, dress the plate with celeriac purée swiped on one side, with the garnishes neatly arranged on top. Remove the breast from the crown and put both breasts together, skin-side facing out. Deglaze the roasting pan with the roasting juices, pass and serve on the side.

Editor's Note: *If you prefer not to do it yourself, you can ask your butcher to remove any lead shot from the flesh and bones. They can also remove any feathers that may have been pushed into the body via the bullet. It's advisable to get young birds for this dish. Older, tougher birds will require slow cooking, ideally braising, for about 45 minutes.*

PETER WILTON

" I am very proud to champion Cancer Research's vital work in their fight against cancer and support of those suffering from it. Leconfield is pleased to be part of this great ChariTable Bookings recipe collection supporting very worthy causes."

SEA BASS with seaweed potato dumplings, clementines and chestnuts

SERVES 6 | PREPARATION TIME 45 MINUTES | COOKING TIME 1 HOUR 45 MINUTES

For the Sea Bass
3 x 600–800g sea bass
vegetable oil
3 knobs of butter
salt and pepper

For the Brine
1l water
170g salt

For the Seaweed Potato Dumpling
1kg dry mashed potato, Maris Piper
1 egg
1 egg yolk
100g 00 pasta flour
1 big pinch of dried seaweed powder
50g butter

For the Clementine Purée
5 clementines
1 vanilla pod, split
175g sugar
salt and pepper, to taste

For the Chestnut and Clementine Glaze
250ml orange juice
50ml Chardonnay vinegar
50g butter
1 pinch of thyme
salt and pepper, to taste
100g chestnuts
2 clementines, segmented

For the Lemon Foam
5 lemons, juiced
125g sugar
100ml fish stock
20ml double cream
1 tsp lecithin

For the Garnish
20g sea purslane
20g sea beets

To prepare the sea bass, make sure the fish is descaled, pin boned and trimmed. Make the brine, place the fillets inside and leave for 10 minutes. Wash the fillets in fresh cold water and dry with paper towels. Cook the fish skin-side down, in a medium hot frying pan with a little oil. After 5–6 minutes, when the skin is golden and the fish is 3 quarters cooked, add a knob of butter and turn the fish for 30 seconds. Remove and serve.

Bake the potatoes in a hot oven until cooked, around 40–50 minutes at 180°C. Remove the flesh, which should be dry, from the skins. Pass through a drum sieve and weigh out 1kg. While still warm, add the eggs and flour. Mix well and season. If the mixture is still wet, it may need a little more flour. Roll the mixture into long cylinders and cut into 3cm pieces. Cook the dumplings in boiling salted water until they float, refresh in ice water, remove and keep on an oiled tray. Before serving, roast in a non-stick pan in butter until golden and finish with generous pinch of dried seaweed powder if desired. You can make this from fresh seaweed, dried overnight and blended, or blend any dried seaweed of your choice, purchased from a good Asian supermarket.

Cover the clementines with water in a large pan and add the split vanilla pods. Bring to the boil and cook until the clementines are soft. You may need to top up the water if the pan dries out before they're done, which should take approximately an hour. Once soft, remove the fruit and place whole, including skins, into a blender. Purée until smooth, add the sugar and seasoning, then blend again. Pass through a fine sieve and place in a bottle.

For the glaze, place the orange juice, vinegar and thyme in a pan, then cook until reduced by half. Sprinkle with salt and pepper to season and reserve until needed. Foam some butter in another pan, add the chestnuts and cook for 2–3 minutes. Put the clementine segments and glaze in with the chestnuts, then toss the pan to coat everything.

Make a syrup from the lemon juice and sugar. Add the stock, cream and lecithin. Blend with a hand blender to froth the liquid. Pick the leaves of the sea purslane and beets from the stalks, blanch them in salted boiling water for 10 seconds and set aside to garnish.

Assemble using the picture as a guide.

KUBA WINKOWSKI

"Preparing food at The Feathered Nest Country Inn is a pleasure and it feels good to work with ChariTable Bookings in supporting Cancer Research UK as they strive to bring hope and happiness to so many."

ROASTED YOUNG GROUSE with braised chicory, elderberry, 'bread sauce' polenta and gravy

SERVES 2 | PREPARATION TIME 20 MINUTES | COOKING TIME 40 MINUTES

For the Roasted Grouse and Gravy
- 2 young grouse
- 4 rashers of streaky bacon
- 250ml red wine
- 1 shallot, sliced
- 4 sprigs of thyme
- 250ml chicken stock

For the Elderberries
- 200g picked elderberries
- 200ml ruby port
- 80g sugar

For the 'Bread Sauce' Polenta
- 350ml milk
- 100ml whipping cream
- 6 sage leaves
- 3 sprigs of thyme
- 1 clove of garlic, halved
- 1 bay leaf
- 4 cloves
- ¼ nutmeg, finely grated
- 1 small onion, sliced
- 50g white polenta
- 1 tsp salt
- 40g Parmesan, grated
- 50g smoked bacon lardons

For the Glazed Chicory
- yellow or red chicories
- 50g butter
- ½ tbsp sugar
- 10ml maple syrup
- 1 tbsp orange juice

To prepare the grouse, season inside and outside of the birds and stuff with a few sprigs of thyme. Wrap each in a couple of streaky bacon rashers and roast at 200°C for 12 minutes for medium rare and 18 minutes for medium. Once out of the oven, rest for 10 minutes, remove the breast and legs and keep warm.

To make the gravy, roughly chop the carcasses and put back into the roasting tin with the red wine, shallots, thyme and chicken stock. Reduce for 10 minutes and then strain.

To prepare the elderberries, boil the port with sugar, add the elderberries and take off the heat. Chill.

To make the polenta, bring the milk, cream, herbs, onion and spices to the boil and infuse for 15 minutes. Put the polenta in the saucepan with the milk, which was passed through the sieve and season. Whisking constantly, bring the milk to the boil, cook for 5 minutes. Add the Parmesan and bacon lardons and cook for 3 minutes. Adjust the consistency with extra milk if necessary.

To prepare the chicory, cut them in half lengthways. Heat the butter in a frying pan and add the sugar to melt it. Place the chicories in, flat-side down and cook for 2 minutes. Add the maple syrup and orange juice, bring to the boil and gently simmer until syrupy.

MARTIN WISHART

" Eating well and giving to charity both make you feel good! I and the team at Restaurant Martin Wishart are supporting Kiran's Trust to help young people feel good. Thank you ChariTable Bookings for helping us help them."

LANGOUSTINE RAVIOLI with braised orange endive and langoustine jus

SERVES 4 | PREPARATION TIME 1 HOUR | COOKING TIME 1 HOUR 30 MINUTES

Equipment
pasta machine

For the Pasta Dough
½ egg, beaten
2 egg yolks
240g 00 flour
1 pinch of salt
50ml water
1 tbsp olive oil

For the Langoustine Filling
1.5kg langoustine, heads removed
and reserved for stock

For the Langoustine Jus
1kg langoustine heads
1 onion, peeled and diced
2 carrots, peeled and diced
3 celery sticks, diced
1 tsp fennel seeds
1 tsp coriander seeds
3 star anise
200ml white wine
2l fish stock
1 bulb of garlic, halved
2 tomatoes
50g unsalted butter
100ml olive oil

For the Braised Endive
60g unsalted butter
300g endive, finely sliced
35g caster sugar
1 tbsp sherry vinegar
1 orange, juiced

To prepare the pasta dough, add the beaten egg and egg yolks to a bowl and whisk together, then set aside. Add the flour and salt to an electric mixer, and mix on a very slow speed. Gradually add the egg until a smooth dough forms. Add the oil and water, slightly increase the speed and mix for 2–3 minutes, until smooth and even. Cut the dough into 4 equal balls, wrap in cling film and leave to rest in the fridge for at least 1 hour.

For the jus, place a heavy-based pan over a high heat and add oil. Once the oil is almost smoking, add the langoustine heads and sauté for 4–5 minutes until the heads begin to turn golden brown and caramelise. Tip the langoustine heads into a colander and set aside. Return the pan to the heat, then add the butter and the onion, carrot and celery. Sauté for 3–4 minutes. Add the fennel seeds, coriander seeds and star anise to the pan, then pour in the white wine and reduce to a glaze. Return the langoustine heads to the pan and crush with the end of a rolling pin. Pour in the stock, garlic and tomatoes and allow to boil until the liquid has reduced by two thirds, approximately 30–45 minutes. Once reduced, remove from the heat and leave to rest and infuse for 1 hour. Pass through a fine sieve, discard the heads and chill the liquid. Alternatively, freeze until ready to use.

To prepare the langoustines, remove the intestinal tracts and carefully pull away the central tail fins. Add the tails to a pan of heavily salted, boiling water for 10 seconds, then remove and place on a tray to cool. Remove and discard the shells from the tails, then coarsely chop the tail meat. Set aside until ready to use.

Roll out the dough for the ravioli, pass it through a pasta machine and lay each sheet out on a floured surface. Use an 8–10cm round pastry cutter to cut out 12 discs. Add a spoonful of the langoustine tail filling to the middle of each disc, use a pastry brush to dab a little water round the edges of the discs and fold in half around the filling, delicately smoothing out the pasta with your fingers to remove air pockets. Repeat to make the rest of the ravioli.

To make the braised endive, place a pan over a medium heat and add the butter. Once melted, add the endive and sauté for 2–3 minutes, then add the sugar. Once it begins to caramelise, add the vinegar and orange juice and continue to cook until reduced by two thirds, for approximately 2 minutes.

To cook the ravioli, bring a large pan of salted water to the boil and cook the ravioli for 90 seconds. Drain and serve with the langoustine jus and braised endive.

MIKE WOMERSLEY

Not many people realise that cancer is the UK's biggest killer of children. The Three Lions team have donated their signature galette to ChariTable Bookings to help raise funds for Children with Cancer UK, the biggest charity fighting for all children suffering from this terrible disease."

GALETTE OF SMOKED HADDOCK

SERVES 6 | PREPARATION TIME 30 MINUTES (PLUS OVERNIGHT TO SOAK) | COOKING TIME 45 MINUTES

For the Batter
- 250ml double cream
- 200g sweetcorn
- 35g soft flour
- 1 egg yolk
- 1 whole egg
- 1 pinch of nutmeg
- salt and pepper, to taste

For the Galette
- 1 large haddock fillet, deboned and deskinned
- 1 large knob of butter
- 1 medium shallot, finely diced
- 1 sprig of thyme
- 1 bay leaf
- 1 tbsp horseradish sauce
- 1 tbsp dill, chopped
- clarified butter or sunflower oil

For the Saffron Beurre Blanc
- 1 banana shallot, chopped
- 125g butter
- 1 sprig of thyme
- 1 bay leaf
- 30ml white wine vinegar
- 150ml white wine
- 50ml double cream
- 1 pinch of saffron, about 5–6 threads
- salt

For the Garnish
- 4 tiger prawns
- 1 tsp butter
- 1 clove of garlic, chopped
- chives, chopped

To prepare the batter, boil the cream and leave to cool a little. Put all the ingredients in a blender and pour in the warm cream. Blend for 2–3 minutes, the batter should have a smooth texture but with tiny little bits of sweetcorn visible. Place in the fridge until needed.

For the galette, melt the butter in a pan. Sweat the shallot, thyme and bay leaf for 2 minutes until translucent. Portion the haddock in 2 pieces and place on top with a tightly fitting lid and simmer until cooked, around 5–7 minutes. Remove the fish from the pan and transfer to a bowl. Reduce the liquor until a thick creamy texture is reached. Add the reduced liquor, horseradish sauce and chopped dill to the fish and flake the mixture together. Add a little clarified butter or sunflower oil to mini plain pie moulds, 10x3cm, and heat until it starts to smoke. Fill the moulds two thirds with batter and continue cooking for 30 seconds. Remove and rest for 5 minutes. Gently press in small pinches of the fish mixture. Bake in the oven at 200°C for around 15 minutes. Remove and rest for 5 minutes. Run a knife around the edge and turn out onto a plate.

To make the saffron beurre blanc, soak the saffron in a spoonful of water the night before to release its flavour. Sweat the chopped shallots in a knob of butter with a sprig of thyme and the bay leaf. Add vinegar and reduce by two-thirds. Add the white wine and reduce by half. Add 50ml double cream and reduce by half. Add the ice cold cubes of butter a little at a time, on a medium heat whisking continually. The sauce should be constantly bubbling to facilitate the emulsion. Remove from heat and add the saffron. Spoon around the galette to serve.

To finish and assemble the dish, sauté 4 tiger prawns in butter and garlic. Spoon some of the saffron beurre blanc on to the centre of the plate, place the galette in the middle and top with the prawns. Finish with chopped chives and a sprig of dill.

CRAIG WOOD

Diabetes UK is the leading charity focused on research, care and education into and around diabetes in the UK. The direct link between diet and diabetes makes it a logical charity for a chef to support and the Wee Restaurant is proud to share it's recipe with ChariTable Bookings for them."

PRESSED GAME TERRINE with pickled wild mushrooms

SERVES 12–14 | PREPARATION TIME 1 HOUR (PLUS 24 HOURS TO SET IN THE REFRIGERATOR) | COOKING TIME 45 MINUTES

For the dish

4 duck breasts
8 pigeon breasts
4 pheasant breasts
6 rabbit loins
salt and pepper
500g mixed wild mushrooms
vegetable oil, for cooking
1 knob of butter
1l game stock
4 gelatine leaves, soaked in cold water
1 packet of sliced Parma ham
1 bunch of flat leaf parsley, shredded
1 splash of white wine vinegar
1 pinch of sugar

Start by trimming all the meat so there is no skin or sinew. Season and seal it off in a little oil in a hot pan, then transfer to an oven tray and cook in a preheated oven at 190°C until medium rare. Cooking time will depend on the size of the pieces of game you are using, but approximately 6–8 minutes should do for medium sized pieces. Leave aside to cool down.

Sauté the mushrooms in a little oil and butter and season, allow to cool. Keep half aside for the pickle.

Reduce the game stock by half then add in the juice from the game. Melt the gelatine leaves gently into the liquid, whisking to ensure no lumps. Line a terrine mould with cling film then layer with Parma ham. The terrine is best assembled while everything is still warm. Carefully build up layers of meat, mushrooms and parsley spooning over some of the liquid at each layer and pressing down. Try to fill in gaps with different sizes of meat, mushrooms and parsley. Press firmly on the terrine and fold over the Parma ham to cover when the mould is full. Press down with a weight in the fridge. A heavy tray or something on top to make sure it is compact as this will ensure it doesn't fall apart when you cut it. Allow the terrine 24 hours in the fridge to set properly.

To pickle the mushrooms, add a few drops of white wine vinegar and a pinch of sugar to the remaining cooked mushrooms and taste.

To serve, carefully cut a slice of the terrine with a hot, sharp knife and place in the centre of a plate with the pickled mushrooms dotted around.

SIMON WOODROW

"Like our sister restaurants, Paradise Garage passionately believes in the global work of Action Against Hunger to give kids the best chance in life through nutrition. We're pleased to be able to share our recipe with ChariTable Bookings and hopefully raise more awareness for what they do."

WHOLE RABBIT with chicory, radish, capers and Jerusalem artichoke piccalilli

SERVES 4 | PREPARATION TIME 3 HOURS | COOKING TIME 3 HOURS

Equipment
butcher's string

For the Dish
1 whole rabbit
10 slices streaky bacon
2 sprigs of tarragon
250g crepinette

For the Piccalilli
25g salt
450ml water
150g Jerusalem artichokes
1 red pepper
1 banana shallot
1 red chilli
220ml cider vinegar
110g sugar
25g English mustard powder
5g plain flour
1 pinch of black pepper
1 pinch of turmeric

For the Sauce
250g chicken wings
200ml vegetable oil
2 onions
2 carrots
4 cloves of garlic
2 bay leaves
4 sprigs of thyme
250ml white wine
1½l chicken stock

To make the piccalilli, bring the salt and water to the boil together until the salt has dissolved, then chill. Dice the artichokes, red pepper and shallots, then finely chop the chilli. Pour the cold brine over the vegetables and leave overnight. The next day, strain the vegetables from the brine. Pour 150ml vinegar into a pan, add the sugar and bring to the boil. Mix the remaining vinegar with the mustard powder, flour, black pepper and turmeric. Combine the liquids until fully incorporated, return to the pan and cook until the mixture thickens slightly. Place the vegetables into a sterilised jar and pour in the boiling liquid. Stir, ensuring no air pockets remain, then close the lid. The pickle can be eaten once cold but ideally should be matured for a couple of weeks.

To prepare the rabbit, remove the legs and shoulder and lightly salt them. Set aside for 2 hours. Remove the liver, kidney and heart from the rabbit and soak in milk for at least 2 hours to remove the bitterness. Debone the rabbit saddle. Once the offal has soaked, drain off the milk. Rinse it all under cold water, dry and set the heart and kidneys aside until later. Cut the sinews from the liver, slice and season. Sear the sliced liver in a very hot pan, then chill. Stuff the rabbit saddle with the seared liver and tarragon. Roll the saddle and wrap in the bacon, then the crepinette. Tie with butcher's string and set aside.

To make the sauce, chop all the rabbit bones and chicken wings. Fry the bones in the vegetable oil until golden brown. Strain, reserving the oil, then set aside. Chop all the vegetables, then sweat with the herbs in some of the oil from frying the bones. Cook until soft, pour in the wine and reduce. Return the bones and add the stock. Bring to the boil, cook until the sauce begins to thicken, then strain through a sieve.

For the turnover, slowly confit the rabbit shoulders in duck fat. Dice the vegetables and add to the pan when the shoulders are nearly cooked. Once everything is cooked, strain off the fat and pick the meat from the shoulders. Take a quarter of the sauce and reduce until really thick. Incorporate the mustard, cooked shoulder meat, vegetables and parsley. Season to taste with salt, pepper and lemon juice. Allow to cool, then roll out the puff pastry and place the cooled filling in the centre. Fold the pastry over to create a triangle and crimp the edges to seal them. Brush with the beaten egg.

For the Turnover

- 500g duck fat
- 1 carrot, 1 small potato, 1 shallot
- 1 tsp Dijon mustard
- 1 tbsp chopped parsley
- salt, pepper and lemon juice, to season
- 1 sheet of puff pastry
- 1 beaten egg

For the Garnish

- 1 large head white chicory
- olive oil
- 25g butter
- 2 sprigs of thyme
- 15g Demerara sugar
- 15ml sherry vinegar
- 100ml chicken stock
- 1 orange
- 25ml olive oil
- 1 head of gem lettuce
- 1 head of red chicory
- 16 radishes
- 1 tbsp fine capers
- 1 tbsp chopped parsley

In a hot pan, colour the rabbit saddle on all sides, then put in the oven at 200°C. Cook for 4 minutes, turn and cook for 4 more minutes. Rest in a warm place for at least 15 minutes. The resting is the most important part of this cooking process, without it the saddle will not be cooked through. When you put the saddle in the oven, put the turnover in another oven at 180°C. If you only have one oven, put it in the same oven as the saddle and turn the heat down to 180°C when the saddle comes out. Cook for 20–25 minutes until the pastry is cooked and golden brown. Colour the rabbit legs in a hot pan and cook in the oven at 180°C until cooked through, approximately 10–12 minutes.

To prepare the garnish, quarter the white chicory and colour in a hot pan with some oil. Add the butter and thyme, then cook until the butter is golden brown. Add the demerara sugar, then deglaze with the vinegar and add the chicken stock. Cover and cook in the oven until the chicory starts to soften, approximately 5 minutes. Break down the gem lettuce and red chicory. Sauté in olive oil in a hot pan, together with the radishes, kidney and heart from the rabbit. Once the offal colours and leaves start to soften, add the capers, parsley and braising liquor from the white chicory. Sauté the rabbit kidneys and heart in a hot frying pan, approximately 2–3 minutes.

To serve, remove the string from the saddle and carve into 8 slices. Cut the legs in half through the bone, then cut the kidney and heart into uniform pieces. Serve 2 slices of saddle, half a leg and a piece of each type of offal per person. To every plate, add 1 piece of white chicory and some of the radishes, lettuce and offal, dressed with the braising liquor. Serve the turnover on the side to share, along with the piccalilli and remaining sauce.

MARK WOOLGAR

As a chef, the idea that recipes can help raise money for charity is fantastic. On behalf of the Ampersand Hotel, I am donating the recipe to our signature stone bass ceviche to ChariTable Bookings to raise money for Cancer Research UK."

STONE BASS CEVICHE

SERVES 4 | PREPARATION TIME 15 MINUTES | COOKING TIME 30 MINUTES

For the Stone Bass

1 side of stone bass, descaled and pin boned

For the Dressing

1 pink grapefruit

1 yellow grapefruit

250ml orange juice, smooth

5ml sherry vinegar

10g honey

25ml olive oil

For the Garnish

¼ cantaloupe melon

10 broad beans, blanched

15g samphire

1 banana shallot

50ml milk

25g flour

50ml vegetable oil

olive oil, to taste

red amaranth cress

baby nasturtium leaves

To make the dressing, segment both grapefruits and slice each segment into three. Juice the remaining grapefruit cores and add to a pan with the orange juice, honey and sherry vinegar. Place the liquid on the stove and reduce to approximately 150ml. Remove, pass through a fine sieve and cool, adding the olive oil. Store in the fridge until ready to serve.

To prepare the fish, slice into portions approximately 3–4mm thick, making sure to check for any remaining pinbones and loose scales. Wrap in cling film and place in a bowl in the fridge.

To make the garnish, scoop out the cantaloupe melon using a small parisienne scoop. Blanch the samphire in boiling, salted water for 5 seconds and refresh in ice water for 1 minute. Drain on a dry cloth and store in the fridge for serving. Peel and thinly slice the banana shallot. Separate the rings and store in milk. After 5–10 minutes drain, dust with flour and gently fry in vegetable oil at 140°C. Remove once cooked and lightly season with salt. Place to one side on a dry cloth to drain any excess oil.

To serve, put the sliced fish in a bowl with the dressing and a pinch of salt. Gently mix and leave for 1 minute. Place a round ring cutter in the centre of the plate, arrange marinated slices of fish inside and pour a little of the dressing over the top. Mix the broad beans, samphire, cantaloupe melon and grapefruit segments in a bowl, season with a pinch of salt and dash of olive oil, then arrange on top of the dressed fish. Top with the shallot rings, nasturtium leaves and red amaranth cress. Serve immediately.

ABDUL YASEEN

Action Against Hunger saves the lives of malnourished children the world over. When we work in a food filled world, it is important to me that I address this balance in my charity work which is why Darbaar is donating this fantastic prawn recipe to ChariTable Bookings."

ROYAL BENGAL STYLE WILD MADAGASCAR PRAWNS

SERVES 1 | PREPARATION TIME 15 MINUTES (PLUS 15 MINUTES TO MARINATE) | COOKING TIME 12 MINUTES

For the Dish
2 giant Madagascar prawns or similar

For the 1st Marinade
1 tbsp vegetable oil
1 tsp salt
½ tsp turmeric
1 tsp ginger, chopped
1 tsp garlic, chopped
2 green chillies, finely chopped
1 tsp fennel seeds, toasted and crushed

For the 2nd Marinade
100ml coconut cream
1½ tsp Bengali mustard paste, (kasundi), or wholegrain mustard
½ tsp salt
½ tsp sugar

For the Salsa
1 vine ripe tomato, roasted, peeled and chopped
1 banana shallot, finely chopped
½ tsp green chilli, chopped
1 tsp ginger, chopped
½ tsp red chilli powder
1 tsp salt
1 tsp sugar
¼ lime, juiced

To Finish
fresh coriander, finely chopped
1 lemon, juiced

Wash the prawns, then remove and discard the legs. Devein them and slit down the middle of the belly, keeping the heads and shells on. Wash them again in running water and pat dry.

Mix all the ingredients for the 1st marinade in a bowl, fold in the prawns and set aside for 15 minutes.

Bring the grill up to high heat and sear the prawns by placing the flesh flat on the grill. After 3 minutes, turn them over and repeat the process. Remove and place on a tray.

Preheat the oven to 175°C.

In another mixing bowl, prepare the 2nd marinade and pour over the prawns. Place on a tray in the preheated oven and cook the prawns for another 5 minutes.

To make the salsa, carefully fold all the ingredients together in a mixing bowl. Serve cold.

To finish, remove the prawns from the oven and serve hot, with a sprinkle of coriander and squeeze of lemon juice.

SIMON YOUNG

The restaurant team at Jumeirah Carlton Tower is very proud to support the work of the Nicholls Spinal Injury Foundation through ChariTable Bookings' latest initiative. NSIF fund essential research into finding a cure for Spinal Cord Injury."

LINE-CAUGHT COD with cockles, wild garlic and new season English asparagus

SERVES 4 | PREPARATION TIME 15 MINUTES | COOKING TIME 15 MINUTES

For the Cod
4 x 150g fresh line caught cod supremes, deskinned and pin boned
50g unsalted butter
¼ lemon, juiced
salt and pepper, to taste

For the Cockles
500g rinsed cockles, run under cold water for an hour
30ml virgin olive oil
1 fresh red chilli, finely chopped and seeds removed
2 cloves of fresh garlic, crushed
100ml white wine

For the Garnish
20g wild garlic
12 medium-sized spears of English asparagus
1 punnet of baby red-veined sorrel
1 head of broccoli
4 heads of bok choi

To prepare the vegetables, break down the broccoli into florets. Blanch them in salted, boiling water and refresh in ice water. Repeat the process for both the bok choi and the asparagus, making sure to peel and trim before hand.

To cook the cockles, put a pan on the stove and heat. When hot, add the olive oil, chilli and garlic. After 30 seconds, add the cockles and white wine. Once the shells have opened, strain and reserve the liquid.

To prepare the cod, season with salt and pepper. Cook the cod skin-side down for up to 5 minutes until the skin is crispy and golden brown. Towards the end of cooking, add a knob of butter and a squeeze of lemon juice.

Reheat the vegetables in boiling water and butter and add the wild garlic. Once the vegetables are hot and wild garlic is wilted, divide across four plates.

To serve, warm the cockles in the cooking liquor and arrange on the plates with some stock. Finish by placing pieces of cod on each plate and garnish with the red-veined sorrel.

VICTOR YU

"I'm proud to help raise awareness for Dementia UK, a charity that supports families of dementia sufferers. By sharing Yu Alderley Edge's black cod recipe, I hope we can raise more vital funds for them through ChariTable Bookings."

MARINATED BLACK COD with Champagne and miso

SERVES 2 | PREPARATION TIME 6 HOURS | COOKING TIME 15 MINUTES

For the Marinade
- 25ml mirin
- 65ml Shaoshing rice wine
- 25g caster sugar
- 25ml Champagne
- 75g miso paste

For the Cod
- 2 x 125g black cod fillets

For the Garnish
- selection of herbs and edible flowers
- 1 tbsp olive oil

For the marinade, pour the mirin, Shaoshing rice wine and caster sugar into a saucepan and bring to the boil. Once the sugar has dissolved and the liquid is at a rolling boil, remove from the heat and allow to cool for a minute. Add the Champagne and miso paste into the pan and whisk until smooth. Set aside until cooled down completely.

To prepare the cod, check the fish over to make sure all the skin and bones have been removed. Place into a sealable sandwich bag and pour in the cooled mixture. Extract as much air from the bag as possible, seal and give the fish a gentle rub so that it is well covered. Leave to marinate in the fridge for a minimum of 6 hours.

To cook the cod, preheat a fan oven to 220°C, and line a shallow baking tray with parchment paper. Remove the fish from the bag and wipe away the majority of the marinade. Place the fish onto the prepared baking tray and bake in the oven for 12 minutes.

To serve, place the herbs in a small bowl and drizzle with the olive oil. Carefully place a portion of fish in the centre of a small warmed serving bowl and arrange a salad next to the fish. Serve immediately.

Editor's Note: *When buying for the dish, remember that Shaoxing, Shaohsing and Shaoshing rice wine are variant spellings for the same product from the city of Shaoxing in the province of Zhejiang, eastern China.*

CHRIS ZACHWIEJA

"Boisdale Belgravia stands by the important work of the Rainbow Trust and will continue to support them through the ChariTable Bookings team."

RAVIOLI OF CORNISH MONKFISH with Hebridean langoustine, shellfish bisque, confit tomatoes and wild sea greens

SERVES 5 | PREPARATION TIME 1 HOUR | COOKING TIME 1 HOUR

Equipment
pasta machine

For the Pasta
340g 00 flour

160g semolina

4 eggs

1 pinch of salt

egg wash, to seal edges

For the Monkfish Mousse
400g monkfish meat

1 slice of white bread, crust removed

20ml milk

2 eggs

10g salt

2 sprigs of tarragon

380ml double cream

2 lemons, zested

For the Langoustine
500g whole langoustines

1 tbsp butter

For the Shellfish Bisque
1kg crab, shell on

20ml rapeseed oil

1 large onion, chopped

50g carrots

4 cloves of garlic, chopped

1 funnel bulb, chopped

20ml tomato purée

10g unsalted butter

20ml Noilly Prat

40ml white wine

100g tinned plum tomatoes

1l fish stock

¼ tsp saffron powder

50g galangal

20g ginger

10 kaffir lime leaves

2 sprigs of tarragon

500ml double cream

salt, white pepper, cayenne pepper
and lemon juice, to taste

To Garnish
wild herbs and sea greens

To make the pasta, place the flour and semolina in a bowl. Using your hands, shape the flour into a circular mound making a well in the centre. Place the eggs in the well with a pinch of salt and use a fork to lightly whisk. Knead until a good dough is formed. Place the mixture on a flat surface and knead together until smooth, silky and elastic. If the dough is crumbly, add a teaspoon of olive oil, and if it is too wet, add a little flour. Cover with cling film and rest for 30 minutes. Once rested, take a tennis ball sized amount of dough and, using a pasta roller, squash it flat with your fingers and push it through on the widest setting. Fold into thirds and repeat 3 times. Once you have a rough square shape, start working it through the machine, taking it down one setting at a time, adding a little flour to each side to prevent sticking. Cut 10 discs, 10cm in diameter, with a pastry cutter and reserve.

For the monkfish mousse, put all the ingredients into a food processor apart from the lemon zest and double cream. Blitz together until smooth, ensuring it is kept cold at all times. With the processor on full speed, slowly drizzle in the double cream. Pass through a drum sieve to remove any lumps, then fold in the lemon zest. Pipe 80g mousse onto a disc of pasta and brush its edges with a little beaten egg. Position the remaining pasta disc over the top, pinching the edges together to seal. Repeat the process with the remaining discs until you have 5 ravioli.

To prepare the langoustines, plunge them into a large pot of boiling water and simmer for 30 seconds. Remove with a slotted spoon and submerge immediately in ice water to prevent them from overcooking.

To make the shellfish bisque, sweat the crab shells with the rapeseed oil, then add the vegetables. Add the tomato purée, butter and combine. Deglaze with the Noilly Prat and white wine, then reduce the mixture by half. Add the tinned tomatoes and fish stock, bring everything to boil, then skim. Mix in the herbs and spices, cook for 30 minutes, then pass the stock through a sieve and reduce. Add the cream and reduce further until a desired consistency is achieved. Season to taste with salt, white pepper, lemon juice and cayenne pepper. Keep warm.

Poach the ravioli in salted, simmering water for 3 minutes until the mousse and pasta have set and cooked through. Using a slotted spoon, place them on absorbent paper and allow to rest.

In a pan, melt a tablespoon of butter and add the whole langoustines. Fry for about 1 minute, then add the ravioli and coat in butter.

To serve, divide the ravioli between 5 warm plates, spoon over the langoustines and pour the bisque over the top. Garnish with wild herbs and sea greens.

ALEXEI ZIMIN

Being a Russian in London, it's great that I can support Russian youngsters suffering from cancer in the UK. Cancer treatment in Russia is only part covered by the state so thank you ChariTable Bookings for helping Zima raise awareness of Gift of Life."

BEEF STROGANOFF

SERVES 4 | PREPARATION TIME 45 MINUTES | COOKING TIME 3 HOURS

For the Beef Stroganoff
2kg beef short rib
1 tbsp vegetable oil
20g dried ceps
4 sprigs of thyme
2 bay leaves
12 black peppercorns
1 onion, chopped
1 celery stalk, chopped
1 medium carrot, chopped
water, to cover
300ml double cream
20g English mustard
200g sour cream
salt and pepper, to taste

To Serve
600g new potatoes, roasted

For the Garnish
1 handful fresh enoki mushrooms
10g parsley, chopped
10g dill, chopped
pea shoots
red amaranth

To cook the beef, add the vegetable oil into a preheated pan and sear the ribs, forming a caramelised crust. Add the ceps, thyme, bay leaves, peppercorns, onion, celery and carrot to the pan. Sweat everything together on a low heat. After a few minutes, add water so that it just covers the contents of the pan. Cover with a lid and cook on a low heat for at least 2 hours, or until the meat is suitably tender.

Remove the beef from the pan and set aside to rest. Strain and reserve the cooking juices, retaining the ceps. Finely chop them and return to the pan together with the strained liquid. Add the double cream and reduce the sauce over a medium heat. Once a desired consistency is reached, add the mustard, sour cream and season to taste.

Remove the meat from the bone, taking care to remove any sinew, and return it to the pan with the sauce. Warm through on a low heat for at least 15 minutes.

To serve, cover generously in parsley and dill, and plate with roasted new potatoes and fresh enoki mushrooms.

SASHA ZIVERTS

Every year, the Battersea Dogs & Cats Home looks after over 8,000 animals waiting to be re-homed. As a London-based charity, Wright Brothers Soho are really happy to support them in this ChariTable Bookings book and hope it raises lots of money for all UK charities."

BLACK PEPPER CRAB

SERVES 2 | PREPARATION TIME 30 MINUTES | COOKING TIME 30 MINUTES

For the Crab
1 x 800g–1kg whole, live cock crab
1 tbsp vegetable oil

For the Sauce
250g salted butter
200g shallots, finely chopped
50g garlic, finely chopped
50g ginger, finely chopped
100ml Japanese soy sauce
80ml mirin
30g black pepper, freshly cracked
sugar, to taste

For the Garnish
almond slivers, toasted
curry leaves, deep fried
natural yoghurt

To prepare the crab, first despatch it humanely. Next, turn upside down and cut in half, removing the legs and dead man's fingers. Cut the crab into segments, cracking the larger pieces with the back of your knife and set aside.

To make the sauce, melt half the butter in a pan and add in the shallots, garlic and ginger. Cook on a low heat. When soft, add the soy sauce and mirin. When the mixture is reduced by half, add the black pepper and the rest of the butter. Season with a little sugar and set aside.

Heat a saucepan and add the vegetable oil. When smoking, add the crab pieces and a small amount of sauce to start the cooking process. Once evaporated, stir the crab well and add the rest of the sauce. Cook for 8–10 minutes.

To serve, arrange the plate as pictured and spoon over the remaining sauce. Garnish with toasted almonds, deep fried curry leaves and fresh natural yoghurt.

Editor's Note: *Live, sustainable English cock/male crabs, with their high white meat content, are recommended for this dish. They are in season from April to November, should feel heavy for their size and not have liquid moving around inside. To despatch them humanely it is recommended they be quickly placed in a large freezer, at -18°C, for at least 2 hours before intended use.*

Index

MEAT

BEEF

Fillet of huss with cauliflower purée and pork mince	239
Pappardelle with wild boar ragu, herb breadcrumbs and Tuscan Pecorino	247
Pork belly, carrot and apple	257
Braised saddleback pork cheeks in porter beer with creamed carrots	287
Grilled Iberico pork with romesco	347
Gallician octopus with chorizo, broad beans and rocket	395
Scott's roasted cod with arrocina beans, chorizo and Padrón peppers	449
Monkfish tail wrapped in Parma ham, sweet and sour peppers, samphire and caper dressing	527
Belly pork with pan-fried squid and carrots	573
Dexter beef fillet with maple glazed cured ham, grilled goat's cheese and baby root vegetables	597
Confit pork belly with granola, Earl Grey soaked prunes and spiced fritter	605
Iberico pork pluma with herb vinaigrette and piquillo peppers	615
Kentish Hare pork plate	617
Sweet and sour pork broth	625
Butter poached pheasant with sticky ham hock, pickled chestnuts and lentils	685

VEAL

Slow cooked veal shank	15
Lacquered English veal with lobster, strawberry and cabbage cake	25
Wiener schnitzel	41
La Genovese con pennette - slow-cooked onion sauce with pasta, followed by veal	161
Jerusalem artichoke panna cotta with veal sweetbreads, Wiltshire truffle and cep biscuit	215
Veal chop with mashed potatoes and mushrooms	541
Roast spiced fillet of veal with Provençal vegetables and Madeira sauce	653

POULTRY

CHICKEN

Pot roast chicken with fondant potatoes and watercress	33
Chicken Supremes in lovage butter en papillote	59
Chicken alla Milanese with gremolata	93
Obsiblue prawn and chicken wing	113
Scallops with crisp chicken wing and pea cream	139
Autumnal chicken tagine with a casserole of pumpkin, chestnuts, apples and prunes	171
Hickory smoked spring chicken jambonette with sweetcorn purée, pickled girolle mushrooms and piquillo pepper dressing	207
Chicken and chorizo lasagne	229
Partridge and truffle pie	235
Poached and confit baby chicken	267
Supreme of corn fed chicken, creamed forest mushrooms, baby leeks and winter truffle	295
Chicken and lobster yellow curry	309
Caesar salad	343
Thai chicken red curry	407
Pot-au-feu	483
Couscous de mon voisin - couscous made my neighbour's way	495
Truffle lasagne	517
Chicken and boudin blanc	563
Chicken curry with butternut squash, potato and rum	633

DUCK

Duck with beetroot and gooseberry	17
Crispy duck salad	35
Duck, chard and star anise	87

Crispy duck breast with sage and thyme
glazed butternut squash, shallots, cured
bacon and star anise jus   145

Duck biryani with onion, tomato and cucumber relish   189

Roast Gressingham duck with caramelised
carrot purée, roast carrots and fig jus   221

Roast Goosnargh duck with salsify,
pickled cherries and pistachio   353

Roasted duck breast with savoy cabbage and parsnip   375

Pan-fried duck breast with fondant potato,
chicory and baby vegetables   381

Crispy spicy duck legs with plum sauce   391

Duck and bean casserole   417

Poached and roasted Borders widgeon
with leg and cep bolognese, heritage
carrot and purple cauliflower   439

Duck and pistachio   463

Duck with tamarind, cashew and fig   493

Duck shepherd's pie   545

Goosnargh duck breast with fondant potato,
garden vegetables and poached cherries   559

Foie gras with barbecue silverskin onions, toasted
Kentish cobnuts, hay dressing and nasturtium   609

Roast breast and crispy leg of wild mallard with
salt-baked beetroot and blackberry jus   623

Duck breast and wilted spinach with
orange, tomato and chilli dressing   645

GOOSE

Foie gras with barbecue silverskin onions, toasted
Kentish cobnuts, hay dressing and nasturtium   609

Roasted free range goose with braised red
cabbage, dumplings and orange sauce   679

GUINEA FOWL

Guinea fowl with fresh truffle and ceps   125

Guinea hen with sage and onion,
bourguignon and roast parsnip sauce   243

QUAIL

Roast quail with hazelnut pesto, remoulade and foie gras   83

Quail   149

GAME

HARE

Roasted hare loin with sausage, caramelised
bacon and smoked shallot purée   107

Jugged hare   237

GROUSE

Grouse pie   47

Roast grouse with white polenta, cobnuts and blackberry   111

Wiltons' roast grouse   385

Roast grouse with celeriac, salted grapes and walnuts   703

Roasted young grouse with braised chicory,
elderberry, 'bread sauce' polenta and gravy   707

PARTRIDGE

Partridge and truffle pie   235

PHEASANT

Roast pheasant and winter vegetables   71

Honey roast pheasant with black pudding and celeriac   177

Butter poached pheasant with sticky ham
hock, pickled chestnuts and lentils   685

PIGEON

Pigeon with boudin blanc, croquette, red cabbage ketchup,
white asparagus, flower sprouts and caramelised apple   179

Tarleton wood pigeon with sweetheart cabbage,
morels and Garstang blue cheese   321

Aberfeldy wood pigeon with salt-
baked turnip and liquorice   379

Pigeon Wellington	525
Roast bresse pigeon with fresh peas	557
Squab pigeon with snails, cauliflower and parsley risotto	603
Poached and roasted wood pigeon with confit leg pastilla, red cabbage and pear	627

RABBIT

Miso glazed rabbit with cauliflower purée and pie crust	129
Stuffed saddle of rabbit with rabbit pie, carrots and garden turnips	649
Whole rabbit with chicory, radish, capers and Jerusalem artichoke piccalilli	715

VENISON

Roast venison and beetroot with poached pears	23
Venison with chesnut, quince, hispi cabbage and cranberry	65
Highland venison with pear, chicory and chocolate	119
Venison with chervil, elderberry and cavolo nero	153
Rosettes of venison with blueberries and spiced pear	165
Hedley roe deer loin baked in pastry with chicken liver pâté, field mushrooms and spring vegetables	175
Venison with salsify purée with roasted salsify and pine gnocchi	191
Loin of Highland venison in onion ash with charred beetroot, salt-baked celeriac and reindeer moss	195
Venison	197
Loin of venison with poached pear and blue cheese gratin	201
Venison and ale pie – Reindeer pie	219
Roasted venison loin with celeriac mousseline and cranberry marmalade	253
Saddle of Chiltern venison with caramelised shallots, salt-baked celeriac, hawthorn berry and rosehip emulsion, and venison sauce	275
Venison loin with pumpkin, cranberry, chestnut, maple and Douglas fir	291

Monachyle venison with garden chard and Balquhidder chanterelles	413
Fallow deer baked in cocoa crumb with baked celeriac, onion and stout purée with cranberry and juniper	427
New Forest venison poivrade with polenta chips, roasted root vegetables and blueberry sauce	441
Venison loin and faggot with roasted cauliflower, peat and blue cheese	451
Perthshire roe deer with damson purée and toasted spices	467
Venison and chocolate casserole	523
Roast loin of Denham Estate venison with pumpkin purée, confit cabbage, braised chestnuts, blackberries and chocolate	637
Venison loin and black pudding with heritage beetroots and millet risotto	683
Hay smoked Mereworth Farm deer with red fruits, vegetables and leaves	693

MEDLEY OF GAME

Garrick game pie with wild mushrooms	345
Pressed game terrine with pickled wild mushrooms	713

FISH

ANCHOVY

Truffled mac 'n' cheese	565

BASS

Bass with octopus, avocado and verjus	97
Roast wild bass with laverbread butter sauce	689

BREAM

Black bream ceviche	89

BRILL

Brill with mussels and brown shrimp beurre blanc	421

COBIA

Cobia and Chinese chive flower stir-fry	*415*

COD

Line-caught cod with black garlic, crosnes, samphire, brown shrimps, lemon verbena scented jus	*51*
Cod with fresh white beans, chorizo, peppers and basil	*63*
Cornish cod à la Grenobloise	*85*
Line-caught cod with cabbage, lovage, buttermilk and new potatoes	*157*
Cod, lardo, fennel	*281*
Tandoori spiced cod with leek, spring onions and capers	*301*
Miso glazed black cod	*349*
Roasted cod with shellfish minestrone	*351*
Honey and soy sauce glazed black cod with verbena pea purée and cider vinegar roasted peaches	*359*
Pan-fried cod with pickled swede, cauliflower purée, golden beetroot crudité and smoked butter sauce	*369*
Scott's roasted cod with arrocina beans, chorizo and Padrón peppers	*449*
Stewed fillet of cod with courgettes, tomato and fresh herbs	*481*
Lady Hamilton smoked cod with potato sorrel	*513*
Caramelised sablefish with vegetable spaghetti	*539*
Icelandic fish pie	*613*
Rivington Grill's Newlyn cod with crispy bacon, lovage and peas	*667*
Confit Cornish cod with glazed pumpkin, kale, chilli and lime	*669*
Line-caught cod with cockles, wild garlic and new season English asparagus	*721*
Marinated black cod with Champagne and miso	*723*

DOVER SOLE

Dover sole Veronique	*273*

EEL

Pain au unagi	*155*
Roast wild halibut with smoked eel and leek fondue, and Avruga caviar	*619*

HADDOCK

Royal fish pie	*167*
Cullen Skink	*205*
Trio of Cornish fish with chorizo, tomato and butterbean stew, and potato griddle cake	*643*
Galette of smoked haddock	*711*

HAKE

Hake with curried cauliflower, almond and kohlrabi bhaji	*143*
Pan-fried fillet of hake with roast garlic mash and peas served French style	*211*
Hake with romesco crust	*317*
Nori wrapped Cornish hake with mussels, cockles, seaweed, crispy rock shrimp, crab ravioli and dashi	*373*
Pan-seared Irish hake fillet with roast cauliflower purée, broad beans, bacon lardons and vanilla foam	*473*
Hake and artichoke barigoule	*475*
Herb crusted hake fillet with pickled girolles, seaweed and coco beans	*561*
Braised hake	*599*

HALIBUT

Peterhead halibut fillet with saffron potato risotto, steamed oyster and charred leeks	*19*
Halibut steak with new season peas à la Française	*39*
Gigha farmed halibut with bacon, onion, mushrooms and mustard sauce	*67*
Roasted halibut fillet with Scottish mussels, white asparagus and Grenobloise sauce	*265*
Pan-Roasted wild halibut with tomato confit, feta, rosemary crisps and aioli	*269*

Scottish steamed halibut with baby
leeks and grilled langoustines — 405

Baked halibut with cobnut crust, cauliflower and cockles — 425

Pan-seared North Atlantic halibut with mussel and
clam gratin with sweet cider sauce and sauce rouille — 455

Poached halibut with cauliflower,
mussels, saffron and hazelnut — 471

Roasted halibut with cauliflower,
chicory salad and caviar sauce — 529

Roast wild halibut with smoked eel and
leek fondue, and Avruga caviar — 619

Line-caught halibut with oyster dressing,
caviar, charred lettuce and dittander — 629

Halibut with curry, Romanesco, bergamot and oyster leaf — 635

HUSS

Fillet of huss with cauliflower purée and pork mince — 239

JOHN DORY

Fillet of John Dory with orange glazed endive — 271

Gingerbread crusted John Dory with braised
white beans, chargrilled grelot onions and
artichokes, and saffron emulsion — 337

MACKEREL

Josper grilled mackerel — 137

Crisp pan-fried mackerel fillet with niçoise vegetables,
roasted baby peppers, aubergine caviar and balsamic syrup — 333

Tea smoked mackerel with apple and crispy shallots — 363

Shellfish rockpool — 397

Grilled mackerel with beetroot, horseradish and salsa verde — 501

Destructed Cromer crab salad with blowtorched mackerel — 587

MONKFISH

Curried monkfish with soba noodle rolls,
sprout tops and tempura nori — 13

Red monkfish Thai curry with steamed
rice, broccoli and daikon — 255

Monkfish with baby artichoke, broccoli flowers and pesto — 431

Monkfish tail wrapped in Parma ham, sweet and
sour peppers, samphire and caper dressing — 527

Monkfish masala with red lentils, pickled carrots and coconut — 533

Trio of Cornish fish with chorizo, tomato and
butterbean stew, and potato griddle cake — 643

Pan-fried monkfish with roast cauliflower,
Romanesco and cauliflower purée — 699

Ravioli of Cornish monkfish with Hebridean langoustine,
shellfish bisque, confit tomatoes and wild sea greens — 725

PLAICE

Pan-fried plaice with capers, toasted hazelnuts,
golden raisins and brown butter — 7

Whole plaice in brown butter with brown shrimps — 159

Plaice fillet with gem lettuce, cucumber
and potted shrimp butter — 163

Cornish plaice with heritage carrots,
buttermilk and estuary findings — 315

Whole plaice with carrot purée and baby carrots — 361

Whole filleted plaice with girolles, brown
shrimps, cucumber and lemon sorrel — 665

RED MULLET

Red mullet roasted on fennel grass with vine
tomato concasse, balsamic and olive oil — 555

Baked red mullet with Taggiasche olives and tomato — 567

SALMON

Smoked salmon and cauliflower — 117

Royal fish pie — 167

Roasted wild salmon and cucumber — 297

Salmon with a black garlic, liquorice and
macadamia crust, and tomatillo salsa — 311

Salmon gremolata — 423

Pan-fried Scottish salmon with crushed
turnip, baby girolles and light lamb jus — 443

Home cured beetroot salmon gravadlax with poached duck egg, hollandaise sauce and asparagus — 479

Salmon teriyaki with burnt broccoli, sesame and miso sauce — 491

Pressed terrine of wild salmon with horseradish and wild garlic — 553

Salmon in spicy coconut cream — 681

SEA BASS

North Atlantic stone bass with fennel, langoustines, coastal herbs and bisque — 21

Chilean sea bass with truffle miso — 127

Sea bass baked with potato and fennel — 147

Pan-fried wild sea bass fillet with Coco de Paimpol beans, bacon and butter sauce — 181

Sea bass with miso glaze, baby spinach, fennel, pomodori secchi — 185

Griddled sea bass with stuffed courgettes, tomatoes, olives and basil — 213

Sea bass ceviche — 225

Sea bass with gnocchi, wild mushrooms, peas and truffle — 303

Thai baked sea bass with fragrant rice — 307

Masala sea bass — 323

Pan-fried sea bass with crushed Jersey Royals, asparagus, tomato and red onion salsa — 325

Stone bass with sea vegetables and scallop — 355

Sea bass with fermented cauliflower — 371

Pan-fried sea bass with broccoli purée and citrus sauce — 403

Pan roast sea bass with roast salsify, new potatoes, spinach, baby onions and puy lentil jus — 447

Pan-seared wild sea bass with Jersey Royal gratin and English asparagus with a chive and lemon hollandaise — 497

Stone bass ceviche — 503

Wild sea bass, bacon emulsion, butternut squash, curried granola and sprouts — 571

Sea bass with shellfish and sea vegetable minestrone — 591

Line-caught sea bass fillet with red pepper purée, young fennel and smoked olive oil — 651

Steam sea bass with chopped chilli sauce — 673

Sea bass with seaweed potato dumplings, clementines and chestnuts — 705

Stone bass ceviche — 717

SKATE

Skate wing à la Grenobloise with seaweed — 433

TROUT

Trout cured with chase rhubarb vodka, rhubarb gazpacho and yoghurt — 245

Trout and scallop with cabbage, broccoli and pea sauce — 399

Loch Etive hot and cold smoked trout — 505

Sea trout with asparagus and pink grapefruit sabayon — 537

Charred rainbow trout with potato salad — 607

Sesame roasted sea trout with braised pak choi, lobster and black bean nori roll and lobster mayonnaise — 691

TURBOT

Soy poached turbot with girolles and mushroom dashi — 135

Mousseline of wild turbot with lobster and langoustine — 183

Steamed Cornish turbot with line-caught squid and dashi — 263

Lobster and turbot with new potatoes, caviar, sea vegetables and beurre blanc — 289

Tranche of Jersey turbot with crispy potato scales and mussel cream — 365

Barbecued turbot with cauliflower, shiitake and beef roasting juices — 581

SHELLFISH

CLAMS

Clams and ham	109
Shellfish rockpool	397
Pan-seared North Atlantic halibut with mussel and clam gratin with sweet cider sauce and sauce rouille	455
Sea bass with shellfish and sea vegetable minestrone	591

CRAB

Lasagne of crab with beurre nantais	11
Crispy soft shell crab sliders	81
Crab	151
Nori wrapped Cornish hake with mussels, cockles, seaweed, crispy rock shrimp, crab ravioli and dashi	373
Shellfish rockpool	397
Compressed salted watermelon and curried crab	419
Coronation Cornish crab, crab biscuit and panna cotta, apricot and almond	569
Destructed Cromer crab salad with blowtorched mackerel	587
King crab leg with wasabi gratin	655
Chilli crab on toast	661
Black pepper crab	729

LANGOUSTINE

North Atlantic stone bass with fennel, langoustines, coastal herbs and bisque	21
Slow cooked pork belly with Scottish langoustine and cider pressed apples	79
Mousseline of wild turbot with lobster and langoustine	183
Scottish steamed halibut with baby leeks and grilled langoustines	405
Langoustine ravioli with braised orange endive and langoustine jus	709

Ravioli of Cornish monkfish with Hebridean langoustine, shellfish bisque, confit tomatoes and wild sea greens — 725

LOBSTER

Lacquered English veal with lobster, strawberry and cabbage cake	25
34 Mayfair's lobster mac	29
Mousseline of wild turbot with lobster and langoustine	183
Lobster thermidor	261
Lobster and turbot with new potatoes, caviar, sea vegetables and beurre blanc	289
Chicken and lobster yellow curry	309
Native lobster risotto with shellfish, plankton and dill	313
Shellfish rockpool	397
Lobster risotto	489
Whitby lobster with cod roe pâté, Lowna Dairy goat's curd, squid ink crackers and soft herbs	519
Lobster short soup	549
Sesame roasted sea trout with braised pak choi, lobster and black bean nori roll and lobster mayonnaise	691

MUSSELS

Mussels steamed with lemongrass, basil chilli and coconut juice	169
Roasted halibut fillet with Scottish mussels, white asparagus and Grenobloise sauce	265
Native lobster risotto with shellfish, plankton and dill	313
Roasted cod with shellfish minestrone	351
Nori wrapped Cornish hake with mussels, cockles, seaweed, crispy rock shrimp, crab ravioli and dashi	373
Shellfish rockpool	397
Brill with mussels and brown shrimp beurre blanc	421
Fried duck egg with mussels and lovage	435
Pan-seared North Atlantic halibut with mussel and clam gratin with sweet cider sauce and sauce rouille	455

Poached halibut with cauliflower,
mussels, saffron and hazelnut | 471

Sea bass with shellfish and sea vegetable minestrone | 591

Steamed mussels with tomato and tarragon | 601

OYSTERS

Crispy Porthilly oysters | 3

Crisp Loch Creran oysters with sauce gribiche | 259

Crispy Caledonian oysters with pickled garden
vegetables and oyster mayonnaise | 411

Beef and oyster pie | 429

Tempura oysters with wasabi dressing | 469

Poached Jersey oysters with oyster velouté | 589

Line-caught halibut with oyster dressing,
caviar, charred lettuce and dittander | 629

Ragu of vegetables and pulses with
a smoked oyster dressing | 659

PRAWNS AND SHRIMP

Line-caught cod with black garlic, crosnes, samphire,
brown shrimps, lemon verbena scented jus | 51

Obsiblue prawn and chicken wing | 113

Prawn malai curry | 131

Wasabi prawns | 141

Whole plaice in brown butter with brown shrimps | 159

Hand-made malloreddus with Mazara
prawns and bottarga | 251

Roasted cod with shellfish minestrone | 351

Malabar prawn curry | 367

Nori wrapped Cornish hake with mussels, cockles,
seaweed, crispy rock shrimp, crab ravioli and dashi | 373

Shellfish rockpool | 397

Brill with mussels and brown shrimp beurre blanc | 421

Steamed wontons in chilli broth | 507

Grilled tiger prawns with quinoa salad and mango salsa | 515

Saffron prawns with fennel | 547

Lobster short soup | 549

Whole filleted plaice with girolles, brown
shrimps, cucumber and lemon sorrel | 665

Royal Bengal style wild Madagascar prawns | 719

SCALLOPS

Roast scallops with polenta and squid ink sauce | 27

Baked scallops with citrus and fennel | 45

White onion risotto with white chocolate,
scallops and white truffle | 91

Scallops with crisp chicken wing and pea cream | 139

Hand-dived scallops with butternut squash,
Parmesan and Pedro Ximénez jelly | 305

Scallops with lentil and coriander sauce | 331

Stone bass with sea vegetables and scallop | 355

Trout and scallop with cabbage, broccoli and pea sauce | 399

Parmesan baked scallops | 663

SQUID AND OCTOPUS

Bass with octopus, avocado and verjus | 97

Risotto nero with saffron chilli squid | 387

Gallician octopus with chorizo, broad beans and rocket | 395

Shellfish rockpool | 397

Tagliatelle with squid, zucchini, tomatoes and bottarga | 535

Belly pork with pan-fried squid and carrots | 573

VEGETARIAN

VEGETARIAN

Mango curry	31
Butternut squash and old Winchester agnolotti with sage butter	95
Charred and mixed tomatoes with tofu mayonnaise, basil and jalapeño dressing	101
Roasted butternut squash with buckwheat grains, chickpeas, pomegranate and feta, harissa yoghurt and coriander dressing	105
Samba salad	121
Buffalo hot dog with Horny Devils	133
Coddled egg with smoked butter and mushrooms	187
Firepit beetroot with ewe's curd	233
Baked whole head of cauliflower, drenched in a creamy Mughlai gravy	277
Salt-baked beetroot with Jersey curd and pickled walnuts	327
Khao Soi – Chiang Mai curried egg noodles with barbecue butternut squash	339
Forest haze salad	383
Lemon and herb spaghetti	453
Carrots with buttermilk and nasturtium	457
Mountain risotto with roast butternut squash and sage	509
Pappardelle with shaved asparagus, broad beans, marjoram and pea purée	583
Salt-baked carrot with goat's curd, hazelnuts and truffle	585
Bbq onion with potato gnocchi, avocado, brazil nuts and burnt onion crème fraîche	593
Potato gnocchi, gorgonzola, spinach	611
Chargrilled pepper with mozzarella and pesto	621
Pierogies with cabbage and wild mushrooms	687

NON-VEGETARIAN CHEESE DISHES

Ravioli di porcini al burro e salvia, purea di sedano rapa	5
Beetroot risotto with feta, Parmesan and aged balsamic	9
Roasted cauliflower with lemon curry infused oil and aged Parmesan	249
Polenta agnolotti with artichokes, tomatoes and truffle	335
Stracciatella ricotta tortelli	445
Grilled salad smoked over embers with Isle of Mull cheese, custard and cobnuts	551
Porcini mushroom risotto	647

Acknowledgements

FH Publishing would like to thank the following for their invaluable assistance and encouragement in taking this concept and turning it into this beautiful book:

Lord Fink and David Johnstone, the founders at ChariTable Bookings,

Alon Shulman, Francesca di Belmonte, Toby FitzGerald, Gabriella Efthimiou, Laragh Chambers, Lina Benfarhat, Matteo Pozzuto, Susanna Jennens, Sophie Orde, Lucie Quilbeuf, Natalia Sánchez-Bell, Helen Mason-Belshaw, Kasia Szelagowska, Veronique Cabrol, Camille Percheron, Alberto Perlini, Polina Kudinova, Sultan Malik, Angelo Palmieri, Freida Paissidou, Diana Ometlic, Kamila Katanowska, Marzena Drewniak, Alexandra Preda Ralev, Will Simonds, Hoi-Ken Fung, Mantas Siurkus, Helen Stelmaconoka, Will Rockall, Alp Ozen and Lucy Self.

We gratefully acknowledge the chefs, restaurants and their teams, agents and PRs in supplying the recipes and images of the dishes and in helping us to support so many good causes.

Thanks to our many supporters who have embraced ChariTable Bookings including Free Holdings, Gravity Integrated Solutions, Pearl DME, Palladium PR, Duncan Peters and the team at Relish, Valerie McLeod, Andy Richardson, Glenn Ratcliffe and Joshua Ratcliffe at Seasoned by Chefs, Lee Fildes at LF Book Services, Helen Smith at The Dorchester Collection, Tahir Chowdry at Vizability, Louise Leftwich, Roland Fussel, Danny Rampling, Lee MacGregor at Mitchell Macgregor, Pepper & Spice, Julien James Davis, Andrew Munro at PSAV, Eddy Temple Morris, Jo Stevenson at The Dorchester, Naomi Hancock, Jori White and her team, Polly Dowson and Laura Hammond at Sauce Communications, and Sara Jayne Stanes OBE at the Royal Society of Culinary Arts.

With thanks to the many photographers who have supported the chefs and restaurants by providing them with images including: Avery Cunliffe, Gretel Ensignia, David Griffen, Palida Boonyarungsrit, Martin Poole, John Blackwell, John Carey, Thomas Alexander, Jean Cazals, Lara Messer, Great British Chefs, Jacqui Small, Tim Green, Chris Tubbs, Jo Woodhouse, Amy Murrell, Paul Johnston, Photo of Paul Ainsworth by David Williams, Marcus Bean's recipe photo ©Watkins Media Ltd, Cyrus Todiwala's recipe photo by Yuki Sugiura, Tom Parker Bowles recipe photo by Jenny Zarins, Jarvis Cocker photo by Tom Oldham. Every effort has been made to acknowledge all the photographers. If you have provided a photo and not been credited, please let us know so we can add you to the next edition.

With respect and admiration for the great work undertaken by the thousands of charities supported by ChariTable Bookings.

Find out more at charitablebookings.org.